A
Guide
to the
Historic
Architecture
of
Western
North
Carolina

The

Richard Hampton

Jenrette *Series*

in Architecture and

the Decorative Arts

A Guide to the Historic Architecture of

Western North Carolina

Catherine W. Bishir, Michael T. Southern, &

Jennifer F. Martin

The

University of

North Carolina

Press

Chapel Hill

& London

Publication of

this work has

been made possible

by a generous

grant from the

North Carolina

Department of

Cultural Resources.

© 1999 The University of North Carolina Press

Set in Adobe Garamond and Franklin Gothic
by Eric M. Brooks

Manufactured in the United States of America

The paper in this book meets the guidelines for permanence
and durability of the Committee on Production Guidelines for
Book Longevity of the Council on Library Resources.

Library of Congress Cataloging-in-Publication Data

Bishir, Catherine W.

    A guide to the historic architecture of western North Carolina /
Catherine W. Bishir, Michael T. Southern, and Jennifer F. Martin.

    p.   cm. — (The Richard Hampton Jenrette series in architecture
and the decorative arts)

    Includes bibliographical references and index.

    ISBN 0-8078-2465-8 (cloth: alk. paper). — ISBN 0-8078-4767-4
(pbk.: alk. paper)

    1. Architecture — North Carolina — Guidebooks.   I. Southern,
Michael T.   II. Martin, Jennifer F.   III. Title.   IV. Series.

NA730.N8B493   1999

720'.9756 — dc21   98-29626

            CIP

03 02 01 00 99   5 4 3 2 1

P. i: *Downtown Asheville, mid-twentieth century*
Pp. iv–v: *Big Sandy Methodist Church and Sandy Mush;
photograph by Catherine W. Bishir*

Contents

Historical and Geographical Maps

Regional and Site Maps

Preface

This book, a guide to historic architecture in Western North Carolina, is the second in a three-volume series that includes a volume on Eastern North Carolina (1996) and a forthcoming volume on Piedmont North Carolina. The series is part of the educational and outreach program of the State Historic Preservation Office, North Carolina Division of Archives and History. Each book is intended as a field guide and reference for the traveler, resident, student, and preservationist with an interest in North Carolina's historic architecture. Although too large for a coat pocket, it is meant to fit in a knapsack, glove compartment, or bike basket, for it is intended to accompany the traveler and visitor in the field as well as to rest on a bookshelf.

Originally the guide was envisioned as a single volume to cover the entire state, but at the suggestion of the University of North Carolina Press, the three-volume format was adopted as offering a more convenient and portable size for region-by-region use. This approach has also proved to offer a greater opportunity for focusing on the regions that delineate the state's varied landscape and shape its architectural, cultural, economic, and social history. For it is not so much the grandeur or fame of its individual landmarks that defines North Carolina's architectural heritage, but its intensely regional and local character, the sense of place, which captivates the traveler and sustains the residents in this old state. And it is that same sense of localism and regionalism that seems most at risk in the late twentieth century, as strip developments and megastores and endless suburbs reach out into the landscape, and traditional landscapes of farming and small-town life vanish almost overnight.

NORTH CAROLINA REGIONS

The three regional guides follow a familiar division of the state that reflects differences in topography, history, and architectural patterns. North Carolina is a large state—some 500 miles wide. Its three principal regions run roughly parallel to the diagonal line of the coast. The eastern 40 percent of the state is a gently rising, level land of tidewater and coastal plain dominated by sandy or loam soils and predominantly pine forests. This section was the first to be settled by immigrants. Beginning in the late seventeenth century, people of mainly British and African stock developed a maritime commercial agriculture and small port towns. The piedmont—"foot of the mountain"—is a rolling country across the central portion with chiefly clay soils and mixed hardwood and pine forests. In the mid-eighteenth century a tide of settlers came from the mid-

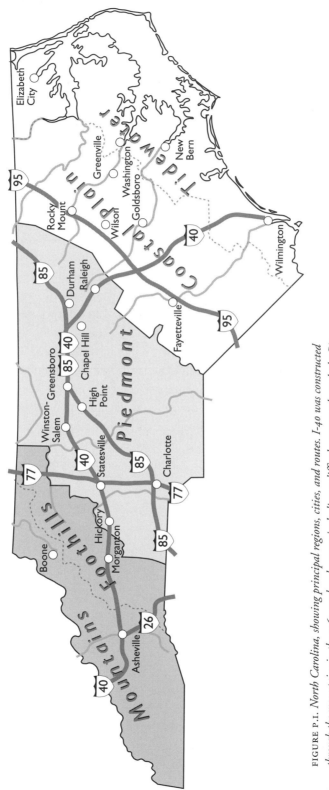

FIGURE P.I. *North Carolina, showing principal regions, cities, and routes. I-40 was constructed through the mountains in the 1960s and early 1970s, including a difficult segment through the Pigeon River Gorge in Haywood Co. and the steep climb of the Blue Ridge west of Old Fort, and the last links between Greensboro, N.C. and the Tennessee line were completed in 1974. I-26 was finished from Asheville to the South Carolina line in 1977. In the 1990s, construction began on the Madison Co. section of I-26 from Asheville north to the Tennessee line.*

Atlantic area and Virginia and created a society of smaller farms distant from markets, where in the nineteenth century waterpower and railroad networks supported industrial and urban development. In the west the mountains rise against and beyond the Blue Ridge, which is the Eastern Continental Divide; the ancient, timeworn slopes are cloaked in hardwood and evergreen forests. Much of this zone remained the domain of the Cherokees until after the American Revolution. Difficulties of transportation kept the region one of isolated rural communities and small towns until the railroad and highways spurred industrial and resort development in the late nineteenth and early twentieth centuries.

North Carolina's topography intensified the economic and cultural differences among the regions. The coastline is a treacherous one, and where the long barrier islands known as the Outer Banks hampered oceangoing trade and prevented the development of a port metropolis. Without a principal city, and with the rivers and other natural arteries of trade leading from the backcountry into neighboring states rather than into a North Carolina port, the sections of the state remained distinct and isolated from one another. By 1810 a Raleigh journalist found that "between the Eastern and Western parts of this State is as great dissimilarity in the face of the country, productions, and means of subsistence as usually exists between different and widely separated nations."

Even after rail networks developed and industrialization worked its changes, the population remained predominantly rural and dispersed, and regional differences persisted. Amid the urban growth of the late nineteenth and early twentieth centuries, little towns and cities of roughly equal size combined intense localism with spirited competition for growth. The makeup of the population also strengthened the sense of localism, for the state received scant inmigration after the eighteenth century. While thousands of people left the state, few came in, so that for many years the proportion of native-born residents was among the highest in the nation. The late twentieth-century sunbelt boom brought the first infusion of immigration from other states and countries. Today North Carolina ranks tenth among the states in population, but it is still one of the least urbanized states in the nation. Only toward the end of the twentieth century has there been an urban majority in population. This rapid urbanization has continued the old dispersed pattern among many small towns and cities rather than coalescing into a dominant metropolis. Although changes are blurring some boundaries, the long-standing sense of localism and regional identity survives.

We imagine this guide serving as a friend might do when introducing a visitor to the region and its communities—sketching a brief history of the place and outlining the human saga the architecture depicts, then pointing out and relating a story or two about the famous landmarks, strolling through the oldest neighborhoods, and discovering some of the special places that make each community itself. Our purpose is to present selected examples of common and uncommon architectural traditions, styles, and forms that define the particular character of each place and that compose broader regional and state patterns. This field guide is meant to complement existing studies. For fuller treatment of localities, the reader is encouraged to refer to the several published local surveys; for analysis of architectural practice and the state's architectural development, the reader may turn to *Architects and Builders in North Carolina, North Carolina Architecture*, and other works cited in the bibliography.

No guidebook can include every important landmark in each community and county. Selection and presentation of entries have followed several rules of thumb. Because the guide is aimed at the traveling public, the entries are generally restricted to those that may be seen reasonably well from a public thoroughfare. In a few rare instances, descriptions but no locational information are provided for exceptionally important properties that are not visible or accessible to the public. These are cited only in cases where the understanding of the region's architecture would be incomplete without acknowledging these places.

In choosing selections from many representative local building types, particularly farmhouses and farmsteads, we have focused on those that are located on readily accessible rather than remote roads and on those that are convenient to other properties mentioned in the text. (The selections are *not* intended to represent a list of properties worthy of preservation, which are far more numerous than can be included here.) Preference is also given to places that are occupied and in reasonably good condition. Many important properties have been omitted because they are in ruinous or vulnerable condition, drastic alterations have taken place, or vegetation or distance shields them from public view. Over the period of this project, conditions have changed for many properties. Some originally included have fallen into disuse or decay, while others that were in dire straits ten years ago have been rescued for new life. In this respect, we have tried to make the book as up to date as possible; however, circumstances are always changing, and we welcome updated information.

Several other factors affected the choice of properties. Different levels of architectural survey fieldwork and research from town to town and county to county are reflected by more or less complete representation and information for various towns and counties. So, too, some individual properties were selected over others when a strong history was available that illustrated trends in the region, or where a good story captured the mood of the time or place. We have also focused attention on those communities and areas with unusually rewarding concentrations of historic architecture accessible to public view.

On the other hand, it has not been feasible to treat some kinds of buildings as fully as they deserve within the entries. The state's architectural history has been defined by the prevalence of very simple, often rudimentary and short-lived buildings that have stood by the thousands, from the log and earthfast frame houses and barns of the eighteenth and nineteenth centuries to the log and frame tobacco barns, sheds and outbuildings, and modest workers' and tenant houses of the late nineteenth and early twentieth centuries. Today, because of the late twentieth-century revolution in agriculture, these are rapidly vanishing; particular examples are too fragile to cite reliably. Hence we have discussed these as important types in the introduction and mentioned their previous or continued presence in the landscape in counties where they are especially important. Travelers who keep an eye open for them will see scores of small farmhouses, barns, and other outbuildings along the back roads—and even in view of interstate highways.

PRIVATE AND PUBLIC PLACES

In using this guide, especially in rural areas, the reader is urged to remember that unless otherwise specified, the properties presented are *private and not open to the public.* Where private properties are easily visible from a public thoroughfare, attention is called to them as parts of the architectural landscape. This does not constitute an invitation to visit or trespass! Users of this book are strictly enjoined to respect the privacy of residents and owners—to remain on the public right-of-way, not to set foot or wheel upon private property uninvited, and to admire and learn from afar.

Where places are open to the public, this status is indicated. For the most part, detailed descriptions of interior features are restricted to properties that are open to the public in some fashion. As opening hours may vary markedly, visitors are advised to call the local chamber of commerce for information on local sites open to the public, bed and breakfast inns, and other businesses operating in historic buildings. The North Carolina Department of Travel and Tourism as well as state visitors' centers on principal highways offer flyers and other information about places open to the public. The nonprofit statewide preservation organization Preservation North Carolina has published the *Complete Guide to North Carolina's Historic Sites*, listing hours and telephone numbers for selected historic properties open to the public. Several local and regional guides are also available.

ORGANIZATION OF THE GUIDE

The guidebook is organized by regional clusters of counties, an arrangement that is meant to assist in organizing a visit and in understanding regional architectural patterns. As in most southern states, North Carolina's principal geographical and political unit traditionally has been the county, which encompasses rural as well as urban places. The county unit is the building block for this guide. Map and entry codes (such as BN 1, MD 2, etc.) employ the county code system used for the statewide architectural survey program.

The guide begins with the Blue Ridge Parkway, a scenic route created in the twentieth century that extends southwest through seventeen of the twenty-five counties in this regional volume. County sections, generally organized around river basins, begin in the northern foothills and move south through the foothills, then return to the northern counties of the mountains and run south and west through the ranges and valleys.

Each county unit begins with the county seat. Following the section on the county seat, entries are arranged in geographical order—typically clockwise from the north around to the east, south, and west—around the county. In several cases the shape of the county, the direction of ridgelines and river valleys, or the distribution of entries requires a different treatment. Within the county seat and other towns, the presentation usually begins with the courthouse or at the town center, then proceeds around the town core and then to outlying properties. Town properties are generally presented in clockwise, linear, or radiating order, depending on the layout of the community. Properties are treated either as individual entries or as components of group entries, depending on the density of the area and relationships among buildings in a community or neighborhood. Cross-references to properties treated elsewhere in the volume are denoted with an asterisk (*).

MAPS

Simplified county maps are grouped following the introduction; selected town maps appear within the text. These are necessarily much-reduced depictions of complex places, showing only a few of the many roads and streets that weave through the landscape. Four-digit SR (secondary road) numbers indicate secondary roads, which are part of the state-maintained highway system along with North Carolina (NC) and U.S. (US) highways. These roads have designated names as well as numbers, but for rural roads only the numbers are employed in this guide, for purposes of brevity and correlation with standard maps.

Serious travelers in the countryside are encouraged to acquire county-by-county road maps. These are available in commercially published atlases and individually from the Department of Transportation. These detailed maps complement the official state transportation map, available free from the Department of Transportation. Currently in North Carolina many changes are under way in the road system, including new construction and widespread renumbering, rendering even the most current maps outdated. In many communities, street numbers are being changed to conform to the 911 system. We have striven to make the locations clear and accurate, but we expect that readers, like the authors, will sometimes get lost and find something even more interesting down a winding back road.

ACKNOWLEDGMENTS

In the early 1980s the North Carolina State Historic Preservation Office (Division of Archives and History, Department of Cultural Resources) began the project to produce a guide to the historic architecture of the state, based primarily on the existing fieldwork and research in the Survey and Planning Branch of the Historic Preservation Office. The first phase of the project was completed in 1984–85 by the Historic Preservation Office with assistance from a 1983 grant from the National Endowment for the Humanities (RS-20386-83) to the Federation of North Carolina Historical Societies, a nonprofit affiliate of the Division of Archives and History. During subsequent years additional fieldwork has been conducted, the format has been modified, and much new information gained from recent county and town surveys and National Register of Historic Places nominations has been incorporated.

The principal source of historical, architectural, and locational information is the extensive collection of survey site files and National Register of Historic Places nomination files, located in the Survey and Planning Branch and in the Western Office of Archives and History in Asheville. These files reflect fieldwork and research conducted since the late 1960s as part of the ongoing statewide architectural survey and National Register of Historic Places programs in North Carolina. Many individuals—too numerous to list in full—have contributed to this growing body of information as staff members and consultants, and their contributions are gratefully acknowledged.

For this volume we have depended upon the fieldwork, research, and photographs from many town and county surveys conducted by a variety of architectural historians over the years as part of the statewide survey program. Some of these individuals have also assisted by recommending properties for inclusion and reviewing the text. These include the following:

Ted Alexander—regional reconnaissance surveys in Avery, McDowell, Mitchell, and Polk counties;
Rachel Barber—Jackson County;
Taylor Barnhill—Madison County;
David Black—downtown Asheville;
Sybil Bowers—Marion and several individual properties;
Claudia Brown—Linville and Tryon;
J. Randall Cotton—Burke and Haywood counties;
Barbara Jean Gilbert—Watauga County sites;
Davyd Foard Hood—New River valley, Blowing Rock, and several individual properties;
Carolyn Humphries—Jackson County and several individual properties;
Diane Lea—Tryon;
Jennifer Martin—Macon County;
Vicki Mason—Alexander and Caldwell counties;
Kimberly Merkel—Rutherford County;
Margaret Owen and Roger Manley—Western North Carolina Associated Communities regional reconnaissance survey in Madison, Henderson, Haywood, Transylvania, Jackson, Macon, Swain, Graham, Clay, and Cherokee counties;
Carol Perrin—Highlands;
Laura Phillips—Surry County, Transylvania County, Blowing Rock, Wilkesboro, and North Wilkesboro;
Mitzi Presnell—Yancey County;
Jean Sizemore—Alleghany County;
Doug Swaim—Buncombe County and several individual properties;
Deborah Thompson—Transylvania County;
Michael Ann Williams—Cherokee, Graham, Henderson, and Swain counties;
Suzanne Pickens Wylie—Morganton.

The surveys that have been published are cited in the bibliography.

Most of the photographs in this volume come from the photographic collection of Archives and History. The majority of these were made over the years by field surveyors and Archives and History staff members, including staff photographers. The excellent work of these staff photographers, including Tony Vaughan, JoAnn Sieburg-Baker, Randall Page, Bill Garrett, and Nick Lanier, is acknowledged with special thanks. Photographs by Mary Jo Brezny, Diane

Davis, and Roger Manley are also included. Assistance in locating photographs was provided by Steve Massengill, iconographic archivist. Additional photographs (see photo credits) were obtained from the Division of Travel and Tourism, the North Carolina Collection, Special Collections at Duke University, the Pack Library, Biltmore Estate, Special Collections at the Library of the University of North Carolina at Asheville, Special Collections at the Library of Western Carolina University, and the Great Smoky Mountains National Park Library. Thanks go to Jerry Cotten at the North Carolina Collection, Janie Morris and William Erwin at Duke, Ann Wright at the Pack Library, Hal Keiner at Biltmore, Tim Daniels at Special Collections at the University of North Carolina at Asheville, George Frizzell at Western Carolina, Annette Hartigan at the Great Smoky Mountains National Park Library, and Sarah Pope for their generous and knowledgeable assistance.

The preparation of this guide has also relied on the help of innumerable other individuals, organizations, and institutions. The late Robert M. Kelly of Greensboro gave important and timely assistance through his solicitation and coordination of several generous private donations to the Federation of North Carolina Historical Societies on behalf of the project. These gifts permitted the purchase of a computer, printer, and software compatible with the system used by the publisher. Contributors were Mr. and Mrs. Robert M. Kelly of Greensboro, Boren Clay Products Company of Pleasant Garden (Dean L. Spangler), the Dillard Fund of Greensboro (John H. Dillard), W. L. Burns of Durham, and Mr. and Mrs. A. P. Hubbard of Greensboro, whose gift was made in memory of Thomas Turner. These gifts are acknowledged with thanks.

In the initial stages of the project, Christi Dennis served as field and research assistant. She also prepared the original draft county maps that became the basis for the county maps used in this guide. Mark Mathis helped convert the text from one computer operating system to another, and Virginia Oswald assisted with word processing.

The county, municipal, and regional maps were prepared with computer graphics software by Michael Southern, with advice and assistance from Heidi Perov.

Throughout the project, staff at Archives and History in Raleigh and at the Western Office of Archives and History in Asheville have provided essential assistance, including technical help, architectural and historical expertise, and moral support and encouragement. Without their aid this project would not have been possible. Key among these are David Brook, Jeffrey Crow, and Michael Hill, as well as Heather Barrett, Debra Bevin, Jerry Cashion, Lloyd Childers, Jerry Cross, Linda Edmisten, Martha Fullington, Brent Glass, Renee Gledhill-Earley, Dolores Hall, Al Honeycutt, Davyd Foard Hood, Bill McCrea, Linda McRae, Greer Suttlemyre, Edward Turberg, Ellen Turco, Sondra Ward, and Mitch Wilds. We thank Chandrea Burch and Bill Garrett for their patience and skill in production of photographs. Susan Myers generously assisted with the index.

We are particularly grateful for the help of Western Office staff members Ron Holland, John Horton, Diane Jones, Nick Lanier, and David Moore for sharing their knowledge of the region, to Ron for reviewing the manuscript, to Nick for taking and printing photographs, and to David for contributing and reviewing material on Native American archaeology and history.

Special thanks go to Secretary Betty Ray McCain and Assistant Secretary Betsy Buford of the Department of Cultural Resources for their enthusiastic and effective support of this series.

For this volume we have also relied on the knowledge and invaluable assistance of Joan Baity, Millie Barbee, Robert Brunk, Cindy Neal Carpenter, Judy Dillingham, Richard Dillingham, Jim Dodson, Margie Douthit, Kevan Frazier, Andrew Glasgow, Jim Gray, Robert Griffin, Clay Griffith, Elizabeth Grossman, Lance Holland, David Jackson, Bruce Johnson, Hal Keiner, Rick King, Betty Lawrence, Frances Manderson, Richard Mathews, Marian Moffett, Jim Myers, Maggie O'Connor, Duane Oliver, Langdon Oppermann, Jim Priesmeyer, Tom Robbins, Betty Sherrill, Alan Smith, Charles Tichy, Marion Venable, John E. Wells, Alice White, and many others who provided key information or reviewed various sections. John Inscoe and Michael Ann Williams gave helpful readings of the entire manuscript; Kate Hutchins and John Bishir helped improve the introduction; and Michael Hill reviewed and offered guidance on the introduction and many county sections. Throughout the endeavor, Claudia Brown supplied unflagging moral support and leadership.

Among the many other friends and colleagues who have given guidance, help, and support in this endeavor over the years are John Bishir, Charlotte Brown, Robert Burns, Al Chambers, Ed Chappell, Dan Chartier, Betsy Cromley, Bernard Herman, Myrick Howard, John Larson, Carl Lounsbury, Gray Read, Orlando Ridout, Margaret Supplee Smith, Kathleen Southern, Dell Upton, and Camille Wells. We are especially grateful for the consistent encouragement and expertise of the staff of the University of North Carolina Press, particularly David Perry, Heidi Perov, Pamela Upton, and Rich Hendel.

In assembling this guide we have sought to make it as accurate as possible, but inevitably errors will have crept in undetected. Readers are encouraged to provide any corrections, particularly on property locations and factual information, to the authors at the Survey and Planning Branch, Archives and History, Department of Cultural Resources, 109 E. Jones St., Raleigh, NC 27601-2807, or at the Western Office of Archives and History, 1 Village Lane, Suite 3, Biltmore Village, Asheville, NC 28803-2677. Inevitably, too, we know we have left out some wonderful places, some of everyone's—including our own—favorite spots. For this we ask readers' forgiveness. We hope that for every place that does appear in the book, you will visit and delight in many, many more.

Catherine W. Bishir
Michael T. Southern
Jennifer F. Martin
Raleigh and Asheville, August 1998

Introduction

WESTERN NORTH CAROLINA

LAND & ARCHITECTURE

FIGURE 2. *The Great Smoky Mountains in N.C., photographed by Hugh Morton*

FIGURE I. *(overleaf) View of Mount Pisgah and the Rat from Loggia, Biltmore*

The mountainous wilderness . . . appearing regularly undulated as the great ocean after a tempest . . . the nearest ground to me of a perfect full green; next more glaucous; and lastly almost blue as the ether with which the most distant curve of the horizon seems to be blended. My imagination thus wholly engaged in the contemplation of this magnificent landscape, infinitely varied, and without bound, I was almost insensible of the charming objects more within my reach.
— *William Bartram,* Travels *(1791)*

LAND OF THE SKY

As the road leads westward in North Carolina, the land rises gradually into foothills where gentle slopes flank riverbottom meadowlands. The rolling foothills yield abruptly to the precipitous eastern slope of the Blue Ridge, which looms 2,000 feet and more above the level of the piedmont plateau. Beyond the Blue Ridge extends a rippling land of seemingly endless mountains, with peaks rising to more than 6,000 feet, and the whole veiled in blue haze.

The beauty of this section of the Southern Appalachians has captured the human imagination for centuries. The Cherokees called these mountains Shaconage, place of blue smoke, and white settlers called the long eastern edge the Blue Ridge and the western range the Great Smokies. As early as 1670 an explorer coming from Virginia heard of a westward land of great waves and thought he was approaching the Indian Ocean, only to learn it was a sea of mountain peaks. Late nineteenth-century poets and promoters coined countless phrases to capture the appeal of the region, of which Land of the Sky proved the most popular and longlasting.

This magnificent sea of mountains lies toward the southern end of the Appalachian chain. In contrast to many sections of the Appalachians where nature formed long, parallel ranges flanking linear stream valleys, here the land forms a scramble of crisscrossing ranges. Small bowls and plateaus lie between processions of forested peaks that recede in graduated shades of blue into the hazy distance.

For well over a century residents and outsiders have made the Southern Appalachians one of the most consciously defined regions in America. Tourists and tourism boosters, naturalists and industrialists, social improvers and students of folklore, and sociologists and historians have all focused attention on the glories and troubles of the region. The natural beauty of the land and the benefits of the cool mountain air have attracted millions of visitors since the colonial era. Be-

FIGURE 3. *Log house near Tryon, Polk Co. The log dwelling with its small cornfield in a mountain clearing was photographed by Margaret W. Morley for her* Carolina Mountains *(1913).*

ginning in the late nineteenth century, American local-color writers, educators, and missionaries developed a stereotype that portrayed Appalachia as a backward, isolated place at odds with modern America. This image, however widely believed, ignores a more complex picture.

Western North Carolina has a powerful sense of regional identity. It has shared the broader story of the Appalachians: a long Native American heritage, frontier settlements, railroad building and industrialized forestry, establishment of vast national forests and parks, and emergence of the modern tourist industry. An important difference, the absence of major coal deposits, permitted western North Carolina to escape the severest despoliation suffered by mountain states to the north. Its cultural and architectural traditions, however, place it firmly within the Appalachian region. Speech patterns and storytelling, conservative religious and family identity, basketry and other crafts, and dance and music have persisted with remarkable vitality, as carriers of British, African, and Cherokee traditions have responded to changing times.

The popular image of the architecture focuses on two extremes: the log cabin and the baronial mountain castle. But western North Carolina's architectural landscape is far richer. From the foothills into the deep mountain precincts,

FIGURE 4. *Biltmore Estate, early 20th-c. view from the vista* (BN 72)

agrarian valleys shelter a quiet history of farm life that continues in many places. Frame farmhouses—some containing an old log dwelling within—overlook the bottomlands, accompanied by barns, springhouses, and corncribs. Long-standing family ties link one farm to another and to a white frame church on a knoll above the valley. In the broadest river valleys, large farms and other enterprises created the wealth to build large and stylish houses from the early nineteenth century onward.

The slopes, plateaus, and valleys also hold a long history of tourism and summer retreats. These range from the fashionable summer houses of antebellum years to generations of hotels and inns, from rambling frame hostelries with capacious and breezy porches to sophisticated rustic lodges rendered in native chestnut bark and stone.

Dotting the region are towns that arose first as agricultural trading points, then blossomed as the railroads and highways brought tourism and industrial growth. Most center on a courthouse and a small commercial district, with residential sections reaching up the hillsides. Although much of the region's industrial architecture was short lived, especially the lumber mills and tanneries that came and went around the turn of the century, a few old factories and many new ones stand beside the streams, rails, and highways. Trade, industry, and

FIGURE 5. *Robert Livesay Farm, Grassy Creek, Ashe Co.* (AH 11)

FIGURE 6. *Porch of Grove Park Inn, Asheville, early 20th-c. view* (BN 53)

tourism created the region's only city, Asheville, with its stunning boom-era architecture, railroad-days Queen Anne concoctions, domed and towered churches, and sparkling Art Deco work of the Roaring Twenties.

Less obvious than the architecture but equally important are the hard-won roads that made all these settlements possible: the ancient trading paths, the early turnpikes, the rail network that opened up the region in the late nine-

FIGURE 7. *Basilica of St. Lawrence, from Battery Park Hotel, Asheville* (BN 32 and BN 33)

teenth century, and the paved highways of the twentieth century. During the Great Depression and World War II great public undertakings created immense hydroelectric dams and the artful ribbon of road that is the Blue Ridge Parkway.

From the humblest to the grandest architecture, one constant reigns: the power of the landscape. English naturalist William Bartram was so enthralled by its magnificence that he was "almost insensible of the charming objects more within my reach." Even today the landscape commands the imagination, deflecting it from the recent sprawl along the highways and offering respite from immediate cares. This same landscape gives a unique quality to the architecture built within it. The farmsteads nestled in hillsides or spread beside the bottomland, each country church on its knoll, the opulent resort on its mountainside, the small towns in valleys or on plateaus, and the towering dams in their ravines—each is at once dwarfed and dignified by its setting, its place among the ancient hills and mountains.

GEOLOGY OF THE APPALACHIAN LANDSCAPE

The landscape that shaped western North Carolina's settlement and culture and frames its architecture is very old and complex. The mountains are part of the Appalachian Mountain system, which stretches 1,500 miles in a southwest-northeast diagonal from Alabama to eastern Canada. In North Carolina and Tennessee the chain attains its greatest width of more than 100 miles. Its highest elevations are in North Carolina, with 43 peaks over 6,000 feet and another 82 over 5,000 feet. Mount Mitchell, at 6,684 feet, is America's highest mountain east of the Mississippi.

The chain is bounded in North Carolina by roughly parallel ranges. Along its western edge are the Great Smoky and Unaka ranges that mark the North Carolina–Tennessee border. On the east is the Blue Ridge, which rises sharply above the piedmont, presenting an undulating blue line across the horizon to travelers approaching from the east. The Blue Ridge forms the Eastern Continental Divide between the watersheds of the Atlantic Ocean and the Gulf of Mexico. From its eastern slopes the Yadkin, Catawba, and Broad rivers begin their journeys that lead through South Carolina to the Atlantic; from its western side the New River runs northward into the Ohio River basin, while the Watauga, Toe-Nolichucky, French Broad, Pigeon, Little Tennessee, and Hiwassee rivers flow into the Tennessee and eventually the Mississippi.

Between the two flanking ranges are many cross ridges and valleys—the Black, Pisgah, Balsam, Cowee, Nantahala, Snowbird, Newfound, and Valley River mountains—which separate the river basins and often provide natural boundaries between counties. Along some rivers the valley floors broaden sufficiently to support row-crop agriculture, and settlement concentrated in these plains before fanning up lesser streams and into the coves and hollows.

The present form of the mountains is only the most recent chapter in a geological saga that has unfolded through millions of years. The first great Appalachian chain rose about 350 million years ago, borne up by the collision of the continental plates of what are now North America and Africa. Through subsequent eons the conflict between uplift and erosion shaped the mountains. At their time of greatest elevation, the Appalachians may have reached 15,000 feet, more than twice their present height. For the past 300 million years, erosion has been the dominant force, sending sediments from 9,000 feet of eroded Blue Ridge rocks to accumulate in the Atlantic and Gulf coastal plains.

The Appalachians are now in their old age. Though many sheer cliffs and rocky formations remain, the elements have generally eroded the ancient heights into soft rounded forms and gentle folds, covered with soil that supports a rich plant and animal life. No peak rises above the timberline, and the region is heavily forested, though some mountains have treeless areas of uncertain origin known as balds. The environment encourages an astonishing variety of flora and fauna, with spruce and other plants common to Canada—migrants from the last ice age—thriving at the cool higher elevations, and plants more typical of the state's subtropical latitude in the lower areas. Both hardwoods and

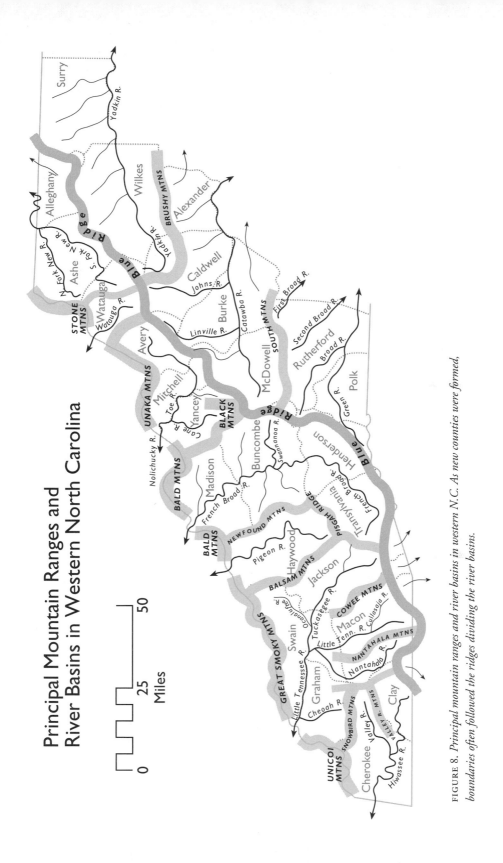

Principal Mountain Ranges and River Basins in Western North Carolina

FIGURE 8. *Principal mountain ranges and river basins in western N.C. As new counties were formed, boundaries often followed the ridges dividing the river basins.*

conifers abound. Great stands of oaks and chestnuts once blanketed the slopes, though the chestnuts were wiped out by the blight of the twentieth century. More than a thousand varieties of flowering plants, including azalea and rhodo-dendron, color the hillsides with bloom in spring and early summer. Animal life flourishes, though except for the black bear and deer, big animals such as buf-falo and elk have long since vanished.

Unlike sections of the Appalachians in states to the north, the North Carolina mountains do not harbor coal in commercial quantities. However, diverse other minerals appear in various deposits. Gold was once mined com-mercially in the South Mountains and other areas, and copper and iron have been extracted in places. The land also holds mica, feldspar, and some concen-trations of emeralds and other gems, as well as marble, slate, limestone, and granite.

SETTLEMENT AND DEVELOPMENT FROM
ANCIENT TIMES TO THE RAILROAD ERA

Native American Settlements

For more than ten thousand years the mountain slopes, foothills, and river valleys have been home to peoples who hunted in the forests and meadows, fished in the streams, and eventually farmed the bottomlands. It is generally be-lieved that nomadic hunters arrived in the Southern Appalachians ca. 10,000–8000 B.C., during what archaeologists call the Paleo-Indian period, and left traces of their hunting practices in the fluted (Clovis-type) stone spear points they used to kill big game animals. In the Archaic period (ca. 8000–1000 B.C.) people in the region began to hunt with spear throwers (atlatls) and to fashion soapstone vessels for storage of wild plants and nuts. During the Woodland pe-riod (ca. 1000 B.C.–ca. A.D. 1000) hunters shifted from the spear to the bow and arrow, settlements grew more stationary as families began to raise crops, and artisans developed skills in pottery making.

By the Mississippian period (ca. A.D. 1000–1550) the people of the region were part of a highly developed culture that extended through many tribes from the Southern Appalachians to the Mississippi River valley. In fertile streamside valleys, families lived in villages and towns and tended their crops of corn, squash, and beans. They continued to tap the natural bounty of forests and streams, hunting deer, bear, squirrel, and turkey; collecting shellfish; and catch-ing fish—often aided by V-shaped rock weirs they constructed in streambeds. In their compact, often palisaded villages they built small dwellings, circular or rectangular in plan, with wattle-and-daub walls and thatched or bark roofs over frame structures. In the larger towns the houses often clustered around a

FIGURE 9. *Nequassee Mound* (MA 2). *The most accessible of the townhouse mounds, *Nequassee, beside the Little Tennessee River in Franklin, is seen here in a 19th-c. photograph. Of the mounds he saw still in use in 1775, William Bartram reported, "The council or town-house is a large rotunda, capable of accommodating several hundred people: it stands on the top of an ancient artificial mount of earth, about twenty feet perpendicular, and the rotunda on the top of it being above thirty feet more, gives the whole fabrick an elevation of about sixty feet from the common surface of the ground. But it may be proper to observe, that this mount on which the rotunda stands, is of a much ancienter date than the building, and perhaps was raised for another purpose. The Cherokees themselves are as ignorant as we are, by what people or for what purpose these artificial hills were raised, they have various stories concerning them . . . but they have a tradition common with the other nations of Indians, that they found them in much the same condition as they now appear, when their forefathers arrived from the West and possessed themselves of the country, after vanquishing the nations of red men who then inhabited it, who themselves found these mounds when they took possession of the country."*

central townhouse, a ceremonial or civic building, which stood atop an earthen platform.

Townhouse mounds are the principal architectural landmarks of prehistoric culture in western North Carolina. Although by the eighteenth century memory of their origins had evidently faded, archaeological evidence suggests they were built by ancestors of the Cherokees in the Mississippian period. While construction details vary, the mounds share certain elements. Their builders piled up basketloads of earth to form a flat-topped platform upon which they erected the temple or townhouse. Over time the size of the mound grew as buildings burned or were replaced and soil was added. Standing 10 to 20 feet high—small in comparison with the great mounds elsewhere in the Mississippian region—these mounds represented the social and cultural focal points for their communities. By the seventeenth century the Cherokees were no longer building mounds, but they continued to use the old ones for a chief's house or a town or council house.

Europeans who entered the Southern Appalachians from the sixteenth century onward found that the mountains were the domain of the Cherokees. East of the Blue Ridge the Catawbas, who were Siouxan-speaking farmers and pottery makers, dominated the foothills and western piedmont. Hit especially hard by diseases introduced by Hernando de Soto's 1540 expedition to the region and subsequent European ventures, the surviving Catawbas coalesced into South Carolina by the mid-eighteenth century.

When the ancestors of the Cherokees came to the Southern Appalachians is uncertain. They were part of an Iroquoian language group that apparently separated from the northern Iroquois about 3,500 years ago; continuity in archaeological remains indicates that they have occupied the Southern Appalachians for 1,000 to 2,000 years. At the time of de Soto's arrival some 25,000 to 30,000 Cherokees lived and farmed on both sides of the Southern Appalachians and claimed a hunting range of 40,000 square miles in present-day North and South Carolina, Georgia, Tennessee, Alabama, and Virginia. They had three town groupings, each with its own dialect: the Lower Towns on the Savannah River in present-day South Carolina; the Upper (Overhill and Valley) Towns in far western North Carolina and eastern Tennessee on the Little Tennessee and Hiwassee rivers; and the Middle Towns in North Carolina on the headwaters and tributaries of the Little Tennessee River, with *Nequassee at present-day Franklin the principal town. The Middle Towns also encompassed a remote area called the Out Towns, including *Kituwah near present-day Bryson City, considered the ancient "mother town" of all the towns.

The Cherokees in all the towns shared religious and social traditions. Their

FIGURE 10. *(Opposite) Cherokee lands and sites in western N.C. This map of far western N.C. shows major surviving townhouse mounds, boundaries of the Cherokee Nation (1819–38), the present-day Qualla Boundary, and other lands of the Eastern Band of Cherokees. At least 15 townhouse mounds have been identified in western N.C. Five of these, located in towns inhabited by the Cherokees into the 18th c., are relatively well preserved: *Kituwah (SW 4), on the Tuckasegee River, considered the "mother town" of the Cherokees; *Nununyi (SW 15), on the Oconaluftee River at Cherokee; *Cowee (MA 6), on the Little Tennessee River; *Spikebuck Town (CY 2), on the Hiwassee River; and most accessible to the public, *Nequassee (MA 2), beside the Little Tennessee River in Franklin. A series of treaties and boundary changes from the early 18th c. to 1819 reduced Cherokee lands to the area known as the Cherokee Nation. In 1838 the Cherokees within that boundary were forced to move to Oklahoma. Others, however, owned holdings east of that boundary, near present-day Cherokee, and were able to retain their lands and remain. They and others who evaded removal or returned home formed the group that became the Eastern Band of Cherokee Indians; their largest tract is known as Qualla Boundary, and there are additional smaller holdings in the region. Map adapted from John R. Finger,* The Eastern Band of Cherokees, 1819–1900 *(1984).*

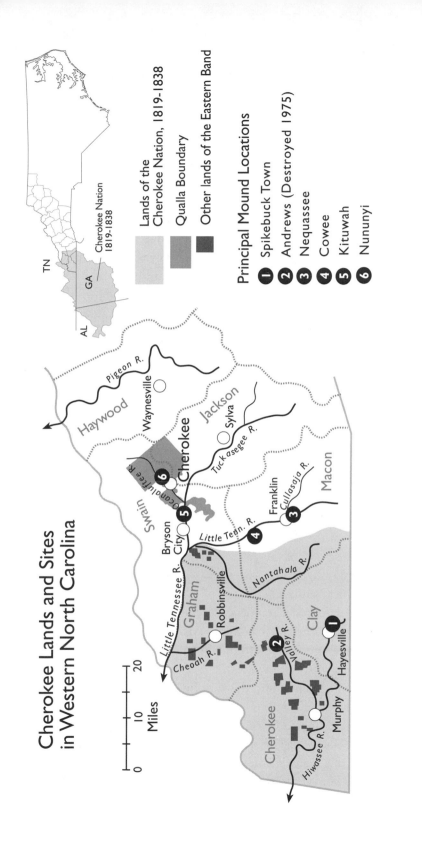

Cherokee Lands and Sites
in Western North Carolina

Lands of the
Cherokee Nation, 1819-1838

Qualla Boundary

Other lands of the Eastern Band

Principal Mound Locations

1 Spikebuck Town
2 Andrews (Destroyed 1975)
3 Nequassee
4 Cowee
5 Kituwah
6 Nununyi

TN

GA

AL

Cherokee Nation
1819-1838

Haywood

Swain

Jackson

Cherokee

Macon

Graham

Clay

Cherokee

Waynesville

Sylva

Bryson City

Franklin

Robbinsville

Murphy

Hayesville

Pigeon R.

Tuckasegee R.

Oconaluftee R.

Little Tenn. R.

Cullasaja R.

Little Tennessee R.

Nantahala R.

Cheoah R.

Valley R.

Hiwassee R.

Miles

0   10   20

religion, which included myths handed down through oral tradition to explain the origins and nature of the world, emphasized the concept of natural balance and the necessity for humans to maintain that relationship with nature. Their social system was organized according to clans, a matrilineal pattern that defined kinship, status, and loyalty. Marriage within a clan was forbidden. Ownership of land and house also descended through the mother, and women's roles included agriculture as well as household work. Each Cherokee town was an autonomous unit, governed by a local council; although linked by affiliation, the towns had no supralocal sovereign of the type the Europeans expected to meet.

As European settlement increased in the coastal plain and piedmont during the seventeenth and eighteenth centuries, the Indians of the Appalachians established trade relations with the newcomers. Many of the old Indian paths directed the routes of trade. In exchange for deerskins, furs, and baskets, they acquired iron tools and utensils, copper pots, glass beads and bottles, blankets, and guns. Trade contact also brought unfamiliar diseases that killed native people with catastrophic speed, including a smallpox epidemic in 1697. By 1715 the total number of Cherokees diminished to 11,000, and subsequent epidemics reduced their numbers further and led them to abandon old settlements. By the early eighteenth century, traders from the east, especially from coastal South Carolina, established Indian trading posts in the mountains, and many of them took Indian wives and were adopted by their kinspeople. In building their trading posts these men evidently introduced horizontal log construction, a method the Cherokees soon adopted for their own dwellings.

During the French and Indian War (1754–63), as British and French fought over competing claims to lands from the Appalachians westward, violence erupted in the Southern Appalachians in the Cherokee War of 1760–61. After initially siding with the British, late in the war the Cherokees, encouraged by the French and resentful of the growing white presence, attacked white settlements. British troops retaliated with large-scale destruction of towns, breaking the strength of the Cherokees.

To prevent further border conflicts, George III proclaimed a boundary along the Blue Ridge that pushed the Cherokees west of the line and prohibited white colonists from moving across it into Indian lands. White settlement had already begun in the foothills east of the boundary, the old Catawba territory. As thousands of immigrants poured into the Carolina "backcountry," pressure on the boundary grew, and a few settlers ventured into Cherokee lands. But while the boundary was often flouted, it nevertheless prevented substantial white settlement west of the Blue Ridge until after the American Revolution.

It was during this interwar era, in the spring of 1775, that the observant English naturalist William Bartram traversed the region. He found the native people depleted by disease and the recent war and saw ruins of villages of "the an-

FIGURE II. *Cherokee log house representing late 18th-c. examples, reconstruction, 1952, Oconaluftee Indian Village, Cherokee* (sw 11). *Adapting forms learned from traders, by the late 18th c. the Cherokees were living in log dwellings. William Bartram described houses he saw at *Cowee in 1775: "The Cherokees construct . . . one oblong four square building, of one story high; the materials consisting of logs or trunks of trees, stripped of their bark, notched at their ends, fixed upon one another, and afterwards plaistered well, both inside and out, with clay well tempered with dry grass, and the whole covered or roofed with the bark of the chestnut tree or long broad shingles. . . . Each house or habitation has besides a little conical house, covered with dirt, which is called the winter or hot-house; this stands a few yards distance from the mansion-house, opposite the front door."*

cients." But he also described a culture still vital in its blend of old traditions and new elements. Among their peach and plum orchards and tidy corn and bean fields, the Cherokees continued to live in compact villages, sited on the feet of the hills overlooking the "level rich vale and meadows in front, their planting grounds." The principal villages still centered on townhouses, but the individual dwellings showed the Cherokees' adaptation of European log construction techniques.[1]

The American Revolution transformed life in western North Carolina. In 1776 the Cherokees, siding with the British and again hoping to drive colonists

1. Bartram, *Travels and Other Writings*, 270–304, quote 283. Bartram visited the area in 1775 but published his account in 1791.

from their domain, attacked frontier settlements. The colonists quickly retaliated. Led in North Carolina by Gen. Griffith Rutherford, in September 1776 troops systematically burned Cherokee villages—*Cowee and *Kituwah among them—killing men, women, and children and destroying buildings, crops, and grain stores. The surviving Cherokees faced near-starvation as winter approached. In the wake of this destruction, in 1777 they ceded much of their land to the state.

After the American Revolution, treaties from 1783 to 1819 further reduced Cherokee holdings. The last of these compressed the tribe into an area west of the Little Tennessee River in North Carolina, Georgia, Alabama, and Tennessee. Encompassing primarily the old Upper Towns, this became the Cherokee Nation. In addition, nearly 600 Cherokee families remained east of that boundary on separate holdings in the remote Middle and Out Towns on the headwaters of the Little Tennessee.

Along with merchants who set up trading posts, Christian missionaries founded schools and churches and sought to convert the Indians and educate them in white ways. Though the Cherokees retained their language and aspects of their religion and social structure, by the early nineteenth century pressures from whites had weakened the matrilineal ownership system and shifted settlement patterns from compact farming villages to dispersed farmsteads. There Cherokee families built small farmhouses and agricultural buildings of log construction, essentially identical to those erected by the white settlers who came to the mountains in growing numbers.[2]

Colonial Settlements

From the mid-eighteenth century onward, a tide of white settlement pressed westward toward the Blue Ridge. As the piedmont filled with Scotch-Irish, German, and English settlers arriving from Pennsylvania, Virginia, South Carolina, and eastern North Carolina, land-hungry pioneers looked west for new territory. In the 1740s and 1750s the usual sequence of hunters and trappers, traders and cattlemen, followed by merchants and farmers, moved into the rolling foothill lands on the upper stretches of the Green, Broad, Catawba, and Yadkin rivers.

The French and Indian War interrupted settlement, but immigration surged after the Treaty of Paris in 1763. Because much of the western territory of the colony lay within the Granville District—the proprietary tract above 35°34' retained by Lord Granville when the other Carolina proprietors sold out to the crown in 1729—there were problems with land titles through the colonial pe-

---

2. This discussion of Cherokee history draws mainly on Finger, *Eastern Band of Cherokees,* and Sarah H. Hill, *Weaving New Worlds.* On traders' introduction of log construction, see Cooper, "Cabins and Deerskins."

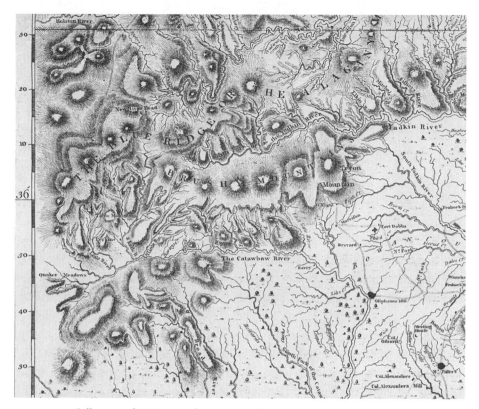

FIGURE 12. *Collet map of N.C., 1770, showing part of the western region, when European settlement was increasing rapidly toward the foot of the Blue Ridge Mountains. A French traveler in the colony in 1765 learned that "the lands back of the first of mountains, what they commonly call the blue ridge, are very rich, they are Inhabited by the Scotch Irish, Germans, and Dutch, which were sent thither to Serve as a bariere betwixt the lower setlers and the Indians; this however, turned out otherwise, luckily for the poor wretches that were sent there to be butcherd; necessity, and the great Distance from any seaport, or town, obliged them to be industrious in riseing all their necessaries within themselves, and at the same time to be watchful of the Indians and secure their little habitations with palisadoes and out works; the Soil answered beyond their Expectations, in So much that it is at present the plentifulest part of America, they have all sorts of Catle, grain, roots, and fruits, butter, Chees, and beer of their own brewing, they manufacture their own aparel and have Everything In short, Except salt and Iron: they Drive great Droves of Catle to the lower setlements, also butter, Chees and hemp which they Dispose of to advantage and a Considerable quantity of Flower"* ("Journal of a French Traveller in the Colonies, 1765," American Historical Review 26, no. 4 [1920–21]).

riod. Nevertheless, by the early 1770s settlers had claimed tracts and begun farmsteads up to the foot of the Blue Ridge. Beyond that boundary, colonists ventured southwest from Virginia to establish the Watauga settlement in a section of North Carolina that later became part of Tennessee.

Salisbury, located on the Great Wagon Road at the Yadkin River, served as the principal town for the western settlements. Smaller communities emerged at trading posts, fords, and crossroads. Forts were built for protection against the Indians and as bases for military expeditions, including Fort Davidson, namesake of Old Fort at the base of the Blue Ridge, and *Fort Defiance in present-day Caldwell County.

By the onset of the American Revolution, settlement at the foot of the Blue Ridge was sufficiently populous that the new state of North Carolina authorized new western counties—Burke in 1777, Wilkes in 1777, and Rutherford in 1779—and named them for British or local heroes of the patriot cause. These were huge "mother" counties whose initial territory reached far westward and eventually were divided into several offspring counties.

Men from these settlements took prominent roles during the American Revolution. Several fought in Griffith Rutherford's 1776 campaign against the Cherokees. At the 1780 Battle of Kings Mountain (just across the South Carolina line), western North Carolinians figured in the patriot militia who unexpectedly triumphed over British and Loyalist troops—a strategically vital victory that gained a heroic place in the annals of the region.

Western North Carolina in the New State

After the war white settlers poured into the North Carolina mountains. To reward Revolutionary soldiers with land, in 1783 the cash-poor North Carolina General Assembly revoked the 1777 agreement with the Cherokees and opened for settlement the area from the Blue Ridge to the Pigeon River. The broad and fertile valleys and forested slopes promised a good life, and many were attracted by "the salubrity of the air, the excellence of the water, and more especially the pasturage of these wild peas for the cattle." Although a federal treaty of 1785 returned a portion of the new territory to the Cherokees, thus intensifying inevitable conflicts, the tide was turned, and further treaties continued to open lands to white settlement. Meanwhile, settlement across the mountains grew rapidly as thousands headed west. Territory that had lain within North Carolina eventually became part of Tennessee when that state entered the Union in 1796.[3]

As white settlers crossed the Blue Ridge into North Carolina's mountain country, the presence of the Indians remained strong. Many white families took as their first homes log dwellings vacated by the Cherokees. For a time Cherokees continued to resist those who claimed their lands. Local lore recounts that one of the first white settlers west of the Blue Ridge was Samuel Davidson, who

3. This discussion of colonial and antebellum society and economy in the region is drawn chiefly from Blackmun, *Western North Carolina*; Inscoe, *Mountain Masters*; and Eller, *Miners, Millhands, and Mountaineers.* Quote from François André Michaux, 1802, quoted in Inscoe, *Mountain Masters*, 12.

was killed by Cherokees soon after he and his family claimed a tract near the Swannanoa River in 1784.

Within a few years, however, Indian resistance dwindled as the white presence grew stronger. In 1791 Samuel Davidson's brother William was among those petitioning for formation of Buncombe County from the western portions of Burke and Rutherford, creating a county itself so large it was known as the "state of Buncombe" and in turn spawned ten more counties. By the early nineteenth century, whites had moved deep into the old Cherokee country, along the Little Tennessee River and its tributaries among the old Middle and Upper Towns of the Cherokees, and in some sections white families lived and farmed alongside Cherokee families, learning Indian lore and skills.

While most of the new county names had British-American associations, the new settlers retained Cherokee place names for rivers and other natural features: Watauga (beautiful water), Hiwassee (meadow), and Tuckasegee (crawling turtle) capture the nature of the watercourses, and Nantahala (land of noonday sun) describes the shadowed gorge through which the river runs.

County seats were established to serve the new counties. In the foothills, Morganton was the oldest, founded in Burke County in 1777; Rutherfordton in Rutherford County came in 1787; and Wilkesboro was laid out around an existing courthouse in Wilkes County by 1801. West of the Blue Ridge, Asheville, seat of Buncombe County, was incorporated in 1797. Other county seats were founded as new counties were carved from old ones, usually with boundaries following ridgelines that separated river basins. County seats were typically platted with a grid plan adjusted to accommodate existing trading path routes, streams, and terrain. At the center of most stood an expedient wooden courthouse and jail, plus a few log houses and ordinaries to accommodate people attending court and trading in town.

Although urban growth was modest—Asheville and Morganton, the principal towns in the early nineteenth century, had but a few hundred people each—the leading merchants in the towns played an important regional role as links between local farmers and outside market networks. In Asheville and Morganton, Wilkesboro and eventually Lenoir, Marion, and Hendersonville, merchants maintained contact with their counterparts in Charleston and other markets down the river valley roads into the low country, and sometimes with Philadelphia and New York. Yet most western North Carolina towns remained essentially local villages. They, like the region as a whole, were shaped by the topography that surrounded them.

The terrain made travel and trade difficult. No rivers in the region were sufficiently navigable to serve as outlets. Old Indian trails and trading paths traversed the foothills and mountains, to be sure, but these were rough roads at best and, where they crossed mountains, perilously steep. Braving hardships to preach throughout the region for many years, Methodist minister Francis Asbury described a typical rural trek in 1806, through Mills Gap between Buncombe and Rutherford counties: "One of the descents is like the roof of a house, for nearly a mile: I rode, I walked, I sweated, I trembled, and my old knees failed: here are gullies, and rocks, and precipices; nevertheless, the way is as good as the path over the Table mountain—bad is the best." Well into the nineteenth century, even the main east-west route, which mounted the Blue Ridge through the Swannanoa Gap from Old Fort and led to Asheville, was a jolting, stony trail "almost perpendicular, and so narrow there [was] barely room for the coach." Some stories report that the principal business in Old Fort was supplying oxen to pull wagons up the trail. Even as better roads emerged as the norm elsewhere, the difficulties of transportation limited mountain residents' capacity to expand trade and profit from large-scale agriculture.[4]

Settlement followed the lay of the land. During the first years of white occupation, in nearly every section of the region a pattern was repeated. The earliest settlers were often ambitious individuals who took up the best land among the level bottomlands and gentle hillsides. The broad river valleys offered fine and fertile land, much of it long cultivated by the Indians, rejuvenated by occasional flooding, and hospitable to productive row crop agriculture. These locations also had the best connections to trade centers. In these valleys it was not long before a prosperous farming class emerged; some were descendants of those successful elsewhere, while others achieved new wealth.

By the 1790s and early 1800s many of the wealthiest valley farmers owned slaves; most had 10 or fewer slaves, but some owned as many as 70 to 100. The foothill counties such as Burke, Caldwell, and Wilkes, which had generous river valleys and good access to southerly trade routes, developed the most extensive plantation and merchant classes. Even west of the Blue Ridge, in the widest valleys, local elites emerged using slave workers to farm their lands and operate other industries and enterprises. Some of these early gentry families continued as local and regional leaders for generations to come.

Meanwhile, other settlers claimed smaller tracts and ventured into the higher lands, carving out farmsteads along the creek valleys and up the hillsides. A remarkably diversified agriculture combined self-sufficiency with various products grown for market. Farm families raised vegetables and grains—especially corn, which could feed the family and animals or be distilled into profitable and easily transported whiskey—fruits from apple and peach orchards, and livestock including sheep, cattle, and pigs. High meadows and grassy mountain balds provided seasonal grazing land for herds of cattle, including some sent upcountry by foothills and valley farmers. The cool climate and good pastures sup-

4. Asbury, *Francis Asbury in North Carolina*, 230; Reid, *"Land of the Sky,"* 8, 10.

FIGURE 13. *Quaker Meadows, Burke Co.* (BK 20). *The house was built in 1812 for the McDowell family, who settled in the broad valley of the Catawba River in the mid-18th c. and continued as a strong presence in the region. It is one of a group of 2-story brick houses in the foothills and western piedmont, which typically follow a 3-room plan that may have roots in Pennsylvania traditions. Several have two front doors. They are handsomely finished with Federal style woodwork, including mantels with reeded decoration.*

ported a major business in meat on the hoof—sheep, cattle, and pigs—to be herded to urban markets and low-country plantations, where the hot weather was considered unhealthy for livestock.

The forested slopes were also essential to the rural economy. Home to still-abundant game, the woods supported hunting and trapping for years, providing meat for the table and deerskins and furs for trade. Nutritious chestnuts, walnuts, and hickory nuts supplied an important winter staple food. The forests also nourished the thousands of pigs that fed on the rich mast of oak and chestnut trees. By the early nineteenth century the gathering of mountain plants was a profitable business, including ginseng collected for the Chinese market and shiny, evergreen galax leaves sent as seasonal decorations to northern American cities.

Whether their farms were large or small, western North Carolina families garnered from fields and forests most of the essentials of life. Their diversified farming also yielded some surpluses, which they usually sold through local merchants to markets in Charleston, New York, or beyond. A rough egalitarianism and self-reliance, grounded in strong family and local identity and leavened with varying degrees of contact with the outside world, came to characterize many mountain communities.

FIGURE 14. *Robert Cleveland House, Wilkesboro* (WK 3). *Although log structures once dominated the building stock of western N.C., few remain unchanged and in public view on their original locations. Some of the most intact log buildings stand in remote locations, and many are being lost to decay or removal. Several, like this one, have been moved to new locations and restored as local landmarks. The earliest log houses were often incorporated into larger structures. The *Carson House (MC 6) in Mc-Dowell Co. is a prominent and accessible house with a log dwelling at its core.*

During their first years on the land most families used log construction for their dwellings, barns, and other structures. Most of the first churches, too, were built of logs, as were many civic buildings. Log structures could be completed with relatively few tools and did not require sawed lumber or large quantities of manufactured materials. The expertise to build a log structure was held by many members of the community. Once the logs were hewed and the notches cut at their ends, raising the building was often a community event that drew on the strength and cooperation of neighbors.

There was considerable difference in the quality of construction in log buildings. As one early nineteenth-century account put it, "The temporary buildings of the first settlers in the wilds are called Cabins. They are built with unhewn logs, the interstices between which are stopped with rails, calked with moss or straw, and daubed with mud. The roof is covered with a sort of thin staves split out of oak or ash, about four feet long and five inches wide, fastened on by heavy poles being laid upon them." But, "If the logs be hewed; if the interstices be

Log House Form and Plan Types

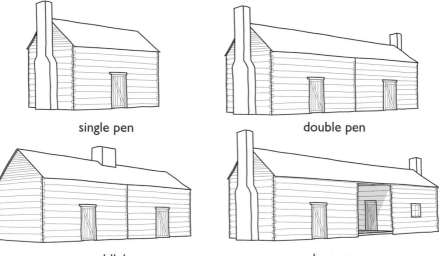

single pen

double pen

saddlebag

dogtrot

FIGURE 15. *Log house form and plan types (adapted from Doug Swaim, ed.,* Carolina Dwelling *[1978]). Like other residents of the upland South, western North Carolinians employed a few basic types in building log houses. Most common was the single-pen log house, typically with 1 room but occasionally subdivided by a board or log wall. (A "pen" is the rectangular structural unit formed by four linked log walls.) Typically a pen did not exceed 18 or 20 feet in length, and 14- to 16-foot wall lengths were common; both square and rectangular pens were built.*

Three main plans incorporate two pens, which might be built all at once or in stages as needed. Double-pen log houses have two pens adjoining, with chimneys at the gable ends. Saddlebag-plan houses consist of two pens flanking a central chimney, like saddlebags on a horse. Both of these types are seen in a number of western N.C. examples. Dogtrot houses have two pens separated by a roofed, open breezeway, with chimneys at the ends; this form is relatively rare in the region. Each house type might be built with logs exposed or covered with weatherboards, and most gained shed porches and rear shed rooms, features that could be included initially or added later.

stopped with stone and neatly plastered; and the roof composed of shingles nicely laid on, it is called a log-house."[5]

Log construction continued in the region for more than a century. Expedient "cabins" of unhewn logs and slab roofs were built for various purposes, particularly in more remote sections. The more substantial log "houses," with hewn logs joined at the corners with half-dovetailed or other notching methods, and roofed with split shingles, were erected from the eighteenth century through the nineteenth century and well into the twentieth century. Many of these had fine

5. Thaddeus Mason Harris, *Journal of a Tour into the Northwest Territory of the Alleghany Mountains* (Boston: Manning and Loring, 1805), 15, quoted in Carl R. Lounsbury, "The Building Process in Antebellum North Carolina," *North Carolina Historical Review* 60, no. 4 (Oct. 1983): 435.

Log Notching Types

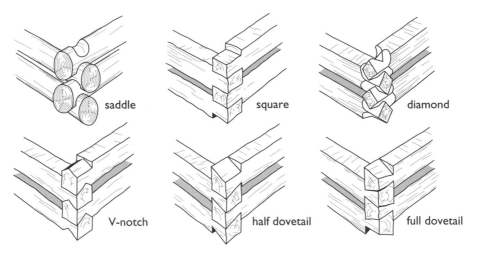

FIGURE 16. *Log notching types: saddle; square; half-dovetail; full-dovetail; V-notch; diamond (adapted from Doug Swaim, ed.,* Carolina Dwelling *[1978]). Although all of these notching types were used in western N.C., by far the most common is the half-dovetailed notch. The diamond notch is rarely seen. A variety of notching types appears in the piedmont region, but the half-dovetail becomes increasingly predominant farther west.*

stone chimneys. Log building persisted in the region long after it was relegated to rudimentary houses and farm buildings in other sections of the state, and it was employed for respectable farmhouses as well as for farm buildings. Only after the proliferation of sawmills in the late nineteenth century did widespread frame and boxed construction begin to supplant log buildings on small and middling farmsteads.

While most families relied on log construction, a few invested in frame and even brick construction within a few years or decades after settlement. These were exceptionally ambitious and successful individuals who lived in towns on the main roads and, especially, the emerging river valley gentry who developed a way of life akin to the planter culture eastward, complete with family connections and political dominance, slave ownership, and material goods. In each area erecting the "first frame house" or "first brick house" was a signal accomplishment. A few frame houses were built in the foothills as early as the 1790s, and brick dwellings began to appear by the 1810s and 1820s. West of the Blue Ridge a few frame houses—such as the *Shook House in Haywood County and the *Allison-Deaver House in Transylvania County—were constructed by the early nineteenth century, and brick houses appeared a decade or two later.

FIGURE 17. *Edwards-Franklin House, Surry Co.* (SY 27). *One of the oldest houses in the region, it typifies the first generation of substantial frame dwellings built for leading farmers. It has a 3-room plan with doorways entering both front rooms, and heavy brick chimneys at the ends. The interior is neatly finished with wainscoting and mantels similar to those employed in the piedmont and east. Other early frame houses open to the public include* *Fort Defiance (CW 16) and the* *Allison-Deaver House (TV 16).*

The Turnpike Era

During the early nineteenth century, western North Carolinians mounted the first of many campaigns to strengthen the region's links with the larger world. The state as a whole suffered from inadequate land and water routes, and the problem was especially intense in the rough western country. Business leaders worked persistently for internal improvements to make their promising land prosper. As early as 1828 reformers urged a railroad stretching from the coastal ports of Beaufort and New Bern across western North Carolina to Tennessee — a vision that took more than fifty years to fulfill. Of greater immediate benefit was the Buncombe Turnpike, constructed in 1824–28. Promoted by western legislators as a link between their constituents and eastern markets, the state-supported route, which some considered the finest road in the state, ran north and west from Greenville, South Carolina, to Greeneville, Tennessee, by way of Asheville.

FIGURE 18. *Sherrill's Inn, Buncombe Co.* (BN 115). *The inn and farmhouse served travelers on the road through Hickory Nut Gap throughout the 19th c. The house incorporates a saddlebag-plan log house and has been expanded over the years.*

The Buncombe Turnpike promptly became an artery of trade and change. Much traffic came in the form of drovers herding horses and mules, cattle and hogs, geese, ducks, and turkeys from North Carolina, Tennessee, and Kentucky down the trail to markets southward. As many as 160,000 hogs were herded through Asheville in a single season. Wagonloads of deerskins and farm products also traveled down the road. Settlements sprang up to house the drovers and feed the animals en route, providing a ready market for farmers and boosting corn production along the way.

Another kind of traffic came up the turnpike from the low country: summer people. Previously a few South Carolinians had made the onerous journey to the cool North Carolina mountains, but the Buncombe Turnpike sped the transformation of the mountains into a summer resort. With visitors arriving in the relative comfort of a carriage instead of a wagon, various points along the road developed into popular destinations. These included the summer colony of South Carolinians at Flat Rock—"Little Charleston of the Mountains"—near the South Carolina border; the newly flourishing town of Asheville, where businessmen James M. Smith and James W. Patton operated popular hotels; and the village of Warm Springs (present-day Hot Springs) near the Tennessee line,

FIGURE 19. *Patton's Hotel, Warm Springs (Hot Springs), Madison Co.* (MD 18). *The mineral springs hotel with its towering portico of thirteen pillars (said to represent the thirteen original colonies) was among the prime resorts in the southern Appalachians. Built beside the Buncombe Turnpike that led up the French Broad River, the hotel was begun in 1831, but the date of construction is uncertain; the left-hand wing was added after the Civil War. The hotel burned in 1884.*

site of a healing thermal springs long known to the Cherokees, where Patton opened a fancy hotel in 1831.

Another massive change came in the 1830s with the Cherokee Removal. North Carolina's Cherokees had been living quietly in the mountains, their way of life among the most traditional and remote in the Cherokee Nation. During the 1820s, efforts mounted to remove the Cherokees from the eastern states. The campaign spiked after discovery of gold in the heart of the Cherokee Nation in Georgia. In 1830 President Andrew Jackson led in passing a general removal act for Indian resettlement west. In the Treaty of New Echota in 1835, some Cherokee leaders gave up the Cherokee Nation lands in the Southeast in exchange for $5 million and land in the West. Despite the objections of other Cherokee leaders and widespread resistance, in 1838 federal troops rounded up the people of the Cherokee Nation and marched them on the "Trail of Tears" to Oklahoma.

In North Carolina most of the Cherokees living west of the Little Tennessee River were taken from their homes, though a few eluded removal. Fort Butler, site of the present-day town of Murphy, was the main military collecting point for the area. A small number of Cherokees living east of the Little Tennessee near Quallatown at present-day Cherokee, assisted by merchant and adopted tribesman William Holland Thomas, used their previous land claims to avoid removal. The Cherokees who remained in the mountains—about 1,000 people

FIGURE 20. *Walker's Inn, Cherokee Co.* (CE 17). *William and Margaret Walker married and moved here in 1844, not long after the Cherokee Removal. In a typical sequence, they began with a log dwelling, either newly built or a former Cherokee home. As the family grew, they expanded the house, covered it with weatherboards, and built a capacious 2-tier, full-width porch. This type of porch, often engaged under an extension of the main roof, is seen frequently in the coastal Carolinas. Its appearance in the western region is probably due to trade routes from the low country. For many years the house served as a popular inn, hosting the traveling journalist Frederick Law Olmsted in 1857.*

initially—eventually became known as the Eastern Band of Cherokee Indians. Many stayed in or moved to the Quallatown area, but some returned to homes in the Snowbird Mountains and other parts of the southwestern counties.

The last section of Cherokee territory in western North Carolina was quickly opened to white settlers. This land west of the Little Tennessee River embraced broad river valley farmland as well as some of the most rugged terrain in the region. Although by this time land westward, in Tennessee and beyond, had been occupied by European and African settlers for decades, in far western Carolina the process began anew. White families came from many parts of western North Carolina and occupied former Cherokee houses, built and expanded log dwellings, and established churches and villages, new counties, and county seats.

From the 1830s onward several intertwined developments brought much of western North Carolina into closer contact with the rest of the state and the nation. A new state constitution in 1835 gave more political power to the long underrepresented western counties and increased state investment in the region.

FIGURE 21. *Creekside, Morganton* (BK 16). *The broad and symmetrical form of the house, together with the simplified classical moldings and heavy portico, make this one of the region's prime examples of the Greek Revival style. In western N.C. as elsewhere, leading planters and merchants adopted the nationally popular Greek Revival mode, beginning in the 1830s and continuing until the Civil War. The advent of the style coincided with the widespread adoption of center-passage plans, often with two rooms on each side of the hallway. Creekside, said to have been built in 1837, was among the earliest examples. It was erected for Thomas Walton, of a prosperous river valley family. A rare example west of the Blue Ridge in N.C. appears in the *Smith-McDowell House (BN 66) in Asheville.*

Gold mining in Burke and Rutherford counties and extraction of other minerals such as iron ore and mica boosted local economies. Commercial agriculture in the river valleys reaped profits from abundant corn and other crops. Towns were growing, with the largest, Asheville, increasing from 350 people in 1830 to 1,100 in 1860. As population thickened, a bumper crop of new counties was established. Several western counties and county seats were named for eastern political leaders, a strategy to garner eastern legislators' support for the formation of western counties and to honor easterners sympathetic to western causes.

Roads were improved or built, including the long-awaited Western Turnpike completed in the 1850s. Paid for by state sales of Cherokee lands, the route ran from Salisbury through Morganton to Asheville and Waynesville, and thence through the old Cherokee country to Murphy—generally following an old trading path and presaging the routes of today's main highways. But the longer-awaited railroad construction only approached the region. With the state-supported North Carolina Railroad completed to Salisbury in the early 1850s, the Western North Carolina Railroad (WNCRR) was chartered in 1854. After

FIGURE 22. *St. John-in-the-Wilderness Episcopal Church, Flat Rock* (HN 13). *By the 1840s and 1850s, latticed and dormered summer "cottages" of Flat Rock and steep-gabled cottages and bracketed villas at various other points along the Buncombe Turnpike embodied the national taste for the "modern picturesque" popularized by the books of A. J. Downing and others, a style that was deemed appropriate to the mountain setting. Built as a summer church for Charlestonians, St. John-in-the-Wilderness was designed in Italianate style by Charleston architect Edward C. Jones and built by Ephraim Clayton, who also worked in Asheville. Only a few antebellum churches in the region displayed the Gothic Revival style, such as *St. Paul's Episcopal Church (WK 12) in Wilkesboro, where the design was influenced by the Ecclesiological movement. (Trinity Church in Asheville had a building designed by Ecclesiologist architect Frank Wills, but it no longer stands.)*

heated debate over its route, the first division of the line headed west from Salisbury and by 1861 was completed almost to Morganton.

In the most populous valleys and towns, the turnpike era brought extensive building, as the region shared in a "spirit of improvement" that ran through much of the state. Unprecedented numbers of town and country churches were built; while most congregations still worshiped in simple log buildings, some erected substantial and even stylish frame or brick structures. County leaders invested in their communities' first brick courthouses. More families than before had the resources to replace log houses with frame or brick ones, and a good number of the river valley and town gentry built quite handsomely.

The most substantial public buildings and private houses displayed the widely popular Greek Revival style, featuring broad, simplified classical forms including columned porticoes. An exception appeared in communities along the Buncombe Turnpike. In a pattern that would continue over the years, the wealth and taste of the resort people created islands and archipelagoes of fashionable architecture. Their picturesque Italianate and Gothic revival "cottages" and churches were cast into high relief by contrast with the generally simple and pragmatic buildings that dominated the region.

Civil War

The Civil War brought bitter conflict to western North Carolina. Within the region, attitudes toward slavery and secession differed greatly. Some counties, chiefly the foothill counties and Buncombe, which included Asheville, had substantial investment in slavery—with slaves constituting more than 15 percent of the population—and many political leaders were slave owners. In most other counties beyond the Blue Ridge, slave ownership was lower, 5 to 10 percent or less. Nevertheless, as was true in much of the state, in nearly every county both sides had strong advocates. When war began, loyalties were sharply divided, not only between one section and another but, more wrenchingly, between members of a community and even members of a family. Old friends and brothers took up arms on opposite sides. Early in the war, local leaders organized volunteer units to serve the Confederacy, such as Zebulon Vance's "Rough and Ready Guard" from Buncombe County and the Cherokee companies led by William Holland Thomas, but many individuals left to join Union forces, either initially or as the war continued.

As the conflict wore on and took its toll on civilians through shortages and onerous Confederate taxes in kind, tensions increased. Desertions mounted, and resistance to conscription sometimes took a violent turn. The state's Civil War governor, Zebulon Vance, sympathized with the plight of the people and sought to alleviate their troubles, but with little success. To make matters worse, the region suffered from raids from both Confederate and Union troops, the latter coming across the mountains from Unionist strongholds in eastern Tennessee. Lawless bands ("bushwhackers") living off the land continually threatened civilians. Although no major battles were fought in the region, the internal war was intense and destructive. Courthouses and dwellings were burned, citizens were taken from their homes and never seen again, and farm animals and family possessions were carried off in guerrilla raids.

The most notorious military action was Stoneman's Raid, a cavalry campaign organized in the last weeks of the war by Union general George Stoneman. His war-toughened horsemen swept from Knoxville across western North Carolina through Boone and Wilkesboro to Salisbury, where they burned the Confederate prison, then turned west in contingents to Morganton, Rutherfordton, Lenoir, Marion, and Asheville, burning strategic facilities and destroying bridges and railroads as they went.[6]

6. Nineteen North Carolina highway historical markers commemorate Stoneman's raids. See Michael Hill, *Guide to North Carolina Highway Historical Markers.*

After the war ended, the people of western North Carolina confronted the immense task of rebuilding. Four years of strife had devastated farms and towns, destroyed bridges and roads, and left families and institutions broken and impoverished. The internal conflict intensified political enmities in many communities. Some wartime outlaw gangs continued their depredations, especially in more remote sections. Although blacks were relatively few in the region, racial politics grew bitter in some sections, with Ku Klux Klan activities surfacing in several counties.

Black citizens constituted a significant if not large part of both rural and urban areas in the counties where slavery had been strongest. Gradually, however, the number of rural black residents dwindled, as many African American families moved into growing towns in the region or to distant cities.

Western North Carolinians took leading roles in the state political arena, including Reconstruction-era governor Tod Caldwell of Burke County and Buncombe County's Zebulon Vance, who in 1876 was once again elected governor, marking the end of Reconstruction in the state.

THE RAILROAD ERA TO WORLD WAR II

The most compelling task was to reclaim the region's hope of economic prosperity: to repair the existing railroads and build new ones, to rebuild farms, and to encourage industry, trade, tourism, and town development. High hopes hung on the completion of the WNCRR envisioned before the war, an endeavor that took more than two decades. At tremendous cost and with persistence born of the era's faith in the power of the railroad and the steam engine, western North Carolina slowly gained its railroad connections to the nation and the world.

The railroad made possible the exploitation of the seemingly limitless natural resources and brought diverse new influences into the region. Boosters predicted that the region with its untapped natural wealth "needs but the magic wand of the capitalist waved over it to become one of the richest sections of this Union." Developers concurrently promoted both tourism and industrial growth—mining, manufacturing, hydroelectric power production, and large-scale logging—which all had dramatic effects on the region's landscape, economy, culture, and architecture.[7]

Buoyed by the railroad and energetic boosterism, once-remote villages began to grow into towns, and Asheville emerged almost overnight as a boom city. Al-

7. Harriet Adams Sawyer, *Asheville, or the Sky-Land* (St. Louis: Nixon-Jones, 1892), 21, quoting "Lindsey's Guide-Book." This discussion of the post–Civil War era draws largely on Van Noppen and Van Noppen, *Western North Carolina*; Eller, *Miners, Millhands, and Mountaineers*; Williams, *Great Smoky Mountains Folklife*; and Finger, *Cherokee Americans*.

though the majority of citizens continued to live on the land as small farmers, the railroad and industrial age affected them as well. Farmers gained better access to markets, and manufactured goods became easier and cheaper to get. Industrial logging soon depleted the forests and transformed the use of the rural landscape, eroding the traditional way of life as well as the hillsides and spurring conservation and forestry efforts. Where it survived, the traditional rural culture attracted the attention of reformers, crafts revivalists, folklorists, and tourists.

All these changes emerged in the late nineteenth century at what then seemed a startling pace and scale. Yet in the early twentieth century those same trends expanded so rapidly as to dwarf the events of previous years. Moreover, by the 1920s railroads were augmented by paved roads for motor trucks and automobiles that hastened the pace of change and opened up long-remote areas. By 1930 the landscape and culture of the region had been forever altered. Into that landscape came sweeping programs of the Great Depression era and preparations for World War II, transforming the region in ways previously unimagined.

Building the Railroad

Rails had approached western North Carolina on the eve of the Civil War as the state-built WNCRR neared Morganton in 1861. In 1865 Stoneman's raiders destroyed much of that section, and repairs took until 1869. In 1868 a plan was adopted for completing the WNCRR, with two routes diverging at Asheville, one to follow the Buncombe Turnpike north along the French Broad River to Paint Rock, the other to run southwest to Murphy.

By 1873 the road was completed from Morganton to Old Fort, but work stopped when political corruption diverted millions of dollars into private pockets. Finally in 1879 work crews scaled the Blue Ridge between Old Fort and the Continental Divide at Ridgecrest. The same year, the Asheville & Spartanburg Railroad arrived at Hendersonville after breaching the Blue Ridge with the famous Saluda grade, the steepest standard-gauge mainline railroad grade in the United States, and a new era was upon the region.

The state sold the WNCRR in 1880 after it reached Asheville. From there private interests completed the line along the French Broad River to Tennessee in 1881, but the Murphy branch through the rugged Smoky Mountains took another decade to build. With connections reaching from the East Coast into the Deep South and Midwest, the former WNCRR and the Asheville & Spartanburg lines became part of the newly organized Southern Railway system in 1894. The only major competition to the Southern in this region was the Carolina, Clinchfield & Ohio (later known simply as Clinchfield), which was completed in 1908 from Kentucky to South Carolina by way of Spruce Pine and Marion, providing an alternate route through the mountains.

Once the major lines were in place, between the 1890s and the 1920s numer-

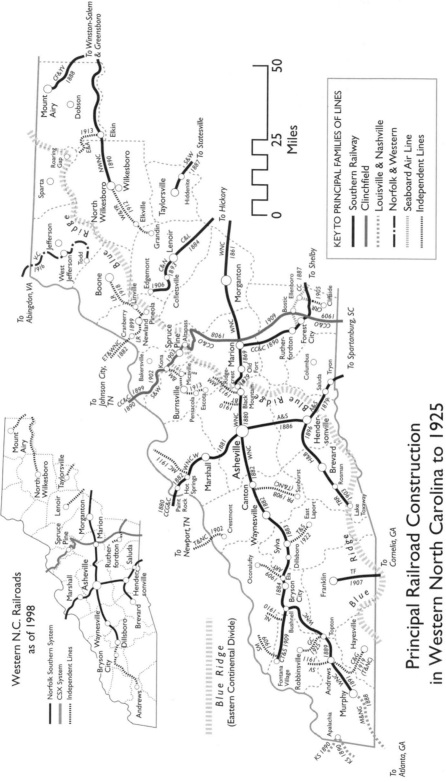

Principal Railroad Construction in Western North Carolina to 1925

KEY TO PRINCIPAL FAMILIES OF LINES

- Southern Railway
- Clinchfield
- Louisville & Nashville
- Norfolk & Western
- Seaboard Air Line
- Independent Lines

Miles
0   25   50

Western N.C. Railroads as of 1998

- Norfolk Southern System
- CSX System
- Independent Lines

Blue Ridge
(Eastern Continental Divide)

ous minor railroads sprouted along the way. Several were narrow-gauge lines, with rails 3 feet apart instead of the standard 5 feet, 8½ inches, which permitted lower construction and equipment costs in mountainous terrain. Many were built to serve private logging or mining operations, though some also provided limited common carrier service to remote sections. Even on Mount Mitchell, the tallest peak in eastern America, a private logging line carried tourist excursions nearly to the summit. Several of the small lines, both standard and narrow gauge, employed specially geared steam locomotives—the Shay and the Climax—designed to handle steep grades.

Every county except Alleghany eventually received some sort of rail service, though Ashe, Avery, Watauga, and Macon counties were reached only by lines from Virginia, Tennessee, or Georgia. Best remembered of the short lines is the "Tweetsie," a nickname for the East Tennessee & Western North Carolina Railroad and the Linville River Railway, which served Avery and Watauga counties by way of Johnson City, Tennessee. A locomotive from these lines operates at *Tweetsie Railroad, a tourist park that celebrates steam railroading in the mountains.

From these many new branches grew temporary tendrils of rail up into the coves and hollows, transforming logging and mining into huge, landscape-altering operations. Some of these operated only a few years until the timber was depleted; others carried on for decades. Floods (intensified by the clear-cut logging operations), the Great Depression, and motor trucks and automobiles eliminated the smaller lines one by one in the second quarter of the twentieth century, so that the region's railroad map resembled a vine pruned of its luxuriant overgrowth.[8]

8. See Poole, *History of Railroading in Western North Carolina*, and George, *Southern Railway's Murphy Branch*.

FIGURE 23. *(Opposite) Principal railroad construction in western N.C. to 1925 and western N.C. railroads as of 1998. Mainline rails breached the Blue Ridge at three locations in N.C.: Saluda on the A&SRR (1879), Ridgecrest on the WNCRR (1879), and Altapass on the Clinchfield Railroad (1908). A fourth line, the Tallulah Falls Railway in Macon Co., crossed a less daunting section of the Blue Ridge at Mountain City, Ga. The WNCRR and the A&SRR became part of the Southern Railway in 1894. As of 1998 the main lines of the Southern (now part of Norfolk Southern) and Clinchfield (now part of CSX) remain active for freight service. There is no passenger service in the region, but plans call for renewing passenger service as far west as Asheville. When the Norfolk Southern proposed to abandon the Murphy Branch from Dillsboro to Murphy in 1987, the state purchased the line and leased, then sold it, to the *Great Smoky Mountains Railway (JK 4), which carries tourist excursions along the route. Elsewhere, independent companies have taken over lines to Mount Airy, North Wilkesboro, Taylorsville, Lenoir, and Rutherfordton as the Southern divested itself of those branches. Sources: Interstate Commerce Commission Valuation and Abandonment Reports; Cary Franklin Poole,* A History of Railroading in Western North Carolina *(1995); Michael George,* Southern Railway's Murphy Branch *(1996); James A. Goforth,* Building the Clinchfield *(1989); S. David Carriker,* The North Carolina Railroad Map *(1993); N.C. Department of Transportation.*

FIGURE 24. *Western N.C. Railroad and Fountain (Andrews Geyser), near Old Fort* (MC 13). *Construction of the WNCRR from Old Fort over the Blue Ridge was a heroic and brutal engineering feat of tunnels and hairpin loops that cost the lives of at least 120 convict laborers. At the top of the climb was the 1,832-foot *Swannanoa Tunnel* (BN 109), *which crews bored from both ends toward the middle. On Mar. 11, 1879, chief engineer James W. Wilson telegraphed former governor Zebulon Vance: "Daylight entered Buncombe County today through the Swannanoa Tunnel. Grades and center met exactly." The resulting route above Old Fort was spectacular: "Here the railroad climbs by a tortuous path, winding over trestles, through tunnels and along shelving rocks in its panting journey to the summit, where the waters part which flow to the Atlantic shore and to the Gulf. The line winds and doubles upon itself in such a manner than in places a series of four tracks may be seen one above another"* (H. P. Gatchell, Western North Carolina: Its Resources, Climate, Scenery, and Salubrity *[1870, 1885]). Part of the attraction was the fountain called Andrews Geyser, a manmade fountain.*

Tourism

With railroad connections completed, tourism boomed, as thousands of visitors boarded trains in distant cities north and south for an invigorating and restful stay in the cool of the mountains. Some still came to spend the season and built ever more elaborate summer residences. But thousands more could now come by train to enjoy a few days or weeks in a boardinghouse or hotel. While many stayed in communities beside the railroad, carriages from railroad stops and, by the early twentieth century, automobiles carried others to more remote and picturesque resorts, and hikers and horseback riders ventured up the most challenging paths.

Entrepreneurs eagerly promoted the many attractions of the region. The beauty of the hazy blue mountain ranges, the rugged peaks and the spectacular waterfalls, and the diversity of plant species captivated the growing interest in healthful outdoor recreation and relief from urban life. Chambers of commerce and other promoters strove to coin the most enticing mottoes. Author Christian

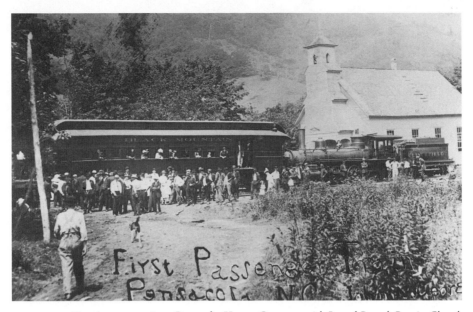

FIGURE 25. *First passenger train to Pensacola, Yancey Co., 1917, with Laurel Branch Baptist Church* (YC 4). *After the main lines were in place, many independent branch lines such as the Black Mountain (later Yancey) Railroad, which connected to the Clinchfield Railroad at Kona* (ML 8) *, reached into remote sections of the mountains to haul out timber and minerals. Some provided passenger service as well. These lines lasted at most a few decades until the depletion of timber, competition from motor traffic, or flood damage forced their abandonment.*

Reid dubbed the region "The Land of the Sky" in her travel book of 1876, and promoters have employed it regularly ever since.

Although the region had long been a popular resort for wealthy southerners, after the war pragmatic Asheville leaders saw the need to expand their market beyond the impoverished South. They published a brochure, *Western North Carolina: Its Resources, Climate, Scenery, and Salubrity* (1870, 1885), aimed specifically at northerners and designed to attract winter as well as summer visitors to "The Switzerland of America." Several communities soon capitalized on the benefits of mild winters as well as cool summers to create a year-round season.

To an industrializing and urbanizing state and nation, the mountains promised respite: "While health is borne upon the breeze, beauty and grandeur fill the eye and soul." A principal attraction was the pure mountain air believed to heal those suffering from tuberculosis and other respiratory ailments. Asheville became a center for tubercular treatment, drawing as many as 3,000 patients a year by 1917, and the nearby *Oteen Veterans' Administration Hospital was a national treatment center for tuberculosis.

Benefits were variously ascribed to the salubrious aura of the balsam spruce, the abundance of ozone, and the effects of barometric pressure. "Nature's Trundle Bed of Recuperation for Tourist and Health Seeker" was one Asheville pro-

FIGURE 26. *Old Fort Depot* (MC 10). *Early 20th-c. depots survive throughout the region, including a few places where the tracks have disappeared, such as Todd* (AH 4) *in Ashe Co. and Edgemont* (CW 22) *in Caldwell Co.*

FIGURE 27. *The first Battery Park Hotel, Asheville. Turn-of-the-century resort hotels displayed fashionable domestic styles of architecture, such as the ebullient Queen Anne or the more restrained Colonial Revival, built on an enlarged scale and lavishly endowed with porches to catch the breezes and frame the view. The grandest of these have been lost: this and the Kenilworth in Asheville, the Toxaway Hotel at Lake Toxaway, and the Fairfield Inn at Sapphire on Lake Fairfield. Among the many still standing are the *Balsam Mountain Inn* (JK 7) *at Balsam, the *Green Park Hotel* (WT 6) *in Blowing Rock, and the *Jarrett House* (JK 3) *in Dillsboro. This hotel was replaced by a second *Battery Park Hotel* (BN 33).*

FIGURE 28. *Old Kentucky Home (Thomas Wolfe Memorial), Asheville* (BN 16). *Julia Wolfe's boardinghouse, "Old Kentucky Home," was memorialized as "Dixieland" in her son Thomas's novel* Look Homeward, Angel. *Many families expanded their homes or built especially spacious dwellings to accommodate summer boarders, as seen in the *Palmer and Caldwell houses (HW 26) at Cataloochee in Haywood Co., the *Mast Farm Inn (WT 12) at Valle Crucis, and others. The family at the *Moss-Johnson Farm (HN 32) in Henderson Co. added a kitchen-dining wing for boarders, then built a summer boardinghouse beside their farmhouse. Such enterprises were usually run by women, who extended their domestic skills into the new marketplace. The tradition continues in the bed and breakfast inns of the late 20th c.*

moter's claim. Another assured readers that the long season for outdoor exercise would cure those "suffering from nervous debility, brain fag, or too close application to business." Healing springs blessed some resorts, including Hot Springs (the name changed from Warm Springs in 1886), *Thompson's Bromine Arsenic Springs, and others. In the 1920s, however, with new treatment methods and establishment of sanitariums, promoters shifted the emphasis from health resorts to tourism and recreation, and indeed Asheville developer E. W. Grove and others sought to avoid attracting consumptives to "America's beauty spot and all year playground."

The impact of tourism was immense. Town after town blossomed with tourist trade. Many who visited to regain health or enjoy outdoor pursuits came back to settle—and to shape the future of the region. Industrialist Joseph Silversteen of Pennsylvania returned to establish tanneries and timber companies at Rosman and Brevard; miner Charles Jenks stayed to develop Highlands with Samuel T. Kelsey; Michigan lumberman George Pack came to Asheville for its

FIGURE 29. *Highlands Inn, Highlands* (MA 18). *Certain resort communities drew regulars from specific cities and regions: South Carolinians continued at Flat Rock and Cashiers; Wilmingtonians enjoyed one another's company at Linville; Winston-Salem and Elkin industrialists built up Roaring Gap; Greensboro and Lenoir residents favored Blowing Rock; Charlotte business leaders flocked to Little Switzerland; and residents of Atlanta, Birmingham, and New Orleans came up to Highlands. Because of the long-standing desire of the vacationing elite for privacy, many of their mountain estates are far removed from public view.*

health benefits and stayed to become a major philanthropist; and pharmaceutical entrepreneur E. W. Grove sojourned in Asheville, then moved there to become its leading early twentieth-century developer.

The most famous vacationer who established a mountain retreat was George Washington Vanderbilt. He visited Asheville with his mother in 1888, fell in love with the view of Mount Pisgah, and soon acquired thousands of acres for his estate, *Biltmore. He commissioned leading American architect Richard Morris Hunt to design his buildings and Frederick Law Olmsted to plan the landscape. Creation of Biltmore had lasting effects: Vanderbilt's private forest and forestry school became the birthplace of scientific forestry in the United States; Biltmore architects and artisans established practices in the area; and the glamour attached to Biltmore instantly gave luster and sophistication to Asheville's national image and the reputation of the region as a tourist center.

The growing fame of western North Carolina as a scenic and healthful retreat had various spinoffs. The summer camp movement, which had begun in New England, found a home in the southern mountains. In the years after World War I, dozens of camps for girls and boys were established, making Brevard and

FIGURE 30. *Gatehouse, Montreat* (BN 108). *Montreat, established in 1907, was one of several religious retreat centers begun in the early 20th c. Its buildings exhibit the emphasis on natural stonework that developed in the early 20th c. The entrance gate is made of smooth river rock from the locale, while some other buildings feature stone cut from nearby quarries.*

Hendersonville nationally known camping centers and drawing campers from many states for a season of swimming, hiking, and campfire fellowship. Religious organizations also founded assembly and retreat centers in the mountains, with *Montreat for Presbyterians (1907) and *Lake Junaluska for Methodists (1909) among the first.

The presence of a well-developed and economically vital tourist business did much to define the course of the region. For a time the natural resources seemed limitless, allowing both industrial exploitation and tourism to expand endlessly. But by the early twentieth century, with industrial-scale logging stripping away much of the old forests, the picture had begun to change, and the future of the region hung in the balance. The coal-laden sections of the Southern Appalachians headed in one direction; for western North Carolina, the absence of coal and the strength of the tourist business pointed in another.

Industrial Development

Once the railroad entered the region, late nineteenth- and early twentieth-century developers emphasized the industrial potential of its natural bounty as enthusiastically as they promoted tourism. In mining, manufacturing, hydro-electric power production, and logging, small-scale operations begun by local or newly resident entrepreneurs were succeeded by much larger enterprises and outside firms.

FIGURE 31. *Granite capital carved at North Carolina Granite Corporation Quarry near Mount Airy (SY 10). Of the many mining and quarrying operations that exploited western N.C.'s minerals, the quarry of superb quality granite near Mount Airy has been among the largest and longest lasting. It is the world's largest open-face granite quarry, and its stone has been used in many important buildings and monuments in the state and the nation.*

Mineral deposits had been worked for many years, but production expanded rapidly with the advent of rails. The nation's leading mica producing mines operated in Mitchell and Yancey counties. Visiting the region in the 1880s, Charles Dudley Warner found that "mica was the rage," and many residents had "more or less the mineral fever. The impression was general that the mountain region was entering upon a career of wonderful mineral development, and the most extravagant expectations were entertained." Copper was mined in Ashe and Graham Counties, and emeralds and other gems in Alexander. A large iron-mining enterprise made Cranberry in Avery County an industrial town, and in the 1880s iron mines were operating in six other counties as well. Kaolin (used in ceramics) was dug for many years from sites in Jackson and other counties. Located near the WNCRR, the quarries of beautiful marble in Cherokee County gave the town of Marble its name. After the arrival of the railroad in Surry County in 1888, a 200-acre surface deposit of granite that had made the land useless for farming was transformed into a major quarry.

The waterpower of the region's swift and abundant streams had long supported manufacturing. From the first years after settlement into the twentieth century, millers ran waterpowered gristmills and sawmills, of which only a few now survive, such as *Kapp's Mill in Surry County and *Mingus Mill in Swain.

FIGURE 32. *Cheoah Dam and Powerhouse, Graham Co.* (GH 9). *During the 1910s and 1920s, Alcoa and its affiliate Tapoco developed several hydroelectric sites in western N.C. Cheoah, built 1916–19, was the first on the Little Tennessee River in N.C.*

Although textile mill development in North Carolina concentrated in the piedmont region, a good number of cotton mills were established in the foothills and a few beyond the Blue Ridge. Some of the state's first cotton mills were built on the upper reaches of the Yadkin River. The Elkin Manufacturing Co. was established at Elkin in 1848 by the Gwyn family, who also founded the *Chatham Manufacturing Co. The Patterson Cotton Mill, begun by Caldwell County men before the war as the first of several mills in the county, was burned by Stoneman's troops and rebuilt after the war.

As the state's postwar cotton mill building campaign gained strength, several entrepreneurs founded mills in the region, a few by the 1880s and many more from the 1890s into the 1910s. Waterpowered mills were established on the Catawba River, and an important cluster developed on the Second Broad River in Rutherford County, including *Cliffside and *Henrietta. West of the Blue Ridge, mills were built at Asheville and Marshall, alongside the railroad and the French Broad River. By the turn of the century, as steam and electric power came into use, mills were constructed away from the streams on sites convenient to the railroad at Spindale, Marion, and elsewhere.

Important to the whole region was the harnessing of the vast hydroelectric potential of its streams. Sections of the southern mountains receive as much as 80 to 100 inches of rain per year, rivaling the rain forests of the Pacific Northwest. The retentive quality of the long-forested land provided relatively steady

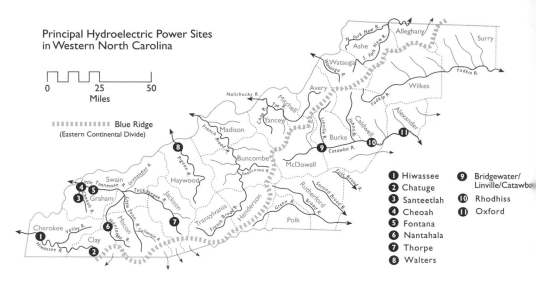

Principal Hydroelectric Power Sites in Western North Carolina

0   25   50
Miles

|||||||||||| Blue Ridge
(Eastern Continental Divide)

1. Hiwassee
2. Chatuge
3. Santeetlah
4. Cheoah
5. Fontana
6. Nantahala
7. Thorpe
8. Walters

9. Bridgewater/Linville/Catawba
10. Rhodhiss
11. Oxford

FIGURE 33. *Principal hydroelectric power sites in western N.C.*

stream levels in many areas. The first hydroelectric plants were small ones built for local purposes. Towns founded municipal power plants such as that at Franklin, and entrepreneurs built dams for local industries and municipal users such as *Cascade Power Co. near Brevard and Capitola at Marshall. Colleges built their own little power plants at Cullowhee and Boone; mission schools at Crossnore and Valle Crucis generated their own power; and some resorts produced their electric power from the dams that formed their recreational lakes.

Corporations headquartered outside the region entered the picture early in the twentieth century, absorbing small firms and building large dams to meet demands mounting elsewhere. The piedmont-based Southern (later Duke) Power Co. and Carolina Power and Light Co. established hydroelectric plants on the Catawba and the Pigeon rivers. From Tennessee the Aluminum Co. of America (Alcoa) ventured into North Carolina seeking sites on the Little Tennessee River to supply power for its growing aluminum production in Tennessee. By 1930 dams on every major river were producing hydroelectric power, and sites had been selected for more.

Logging

The most dramatic exploitation of the region came in the logging of the vast and ancient forests that blanketed the slopes. Logging had long operated on a small scale. Many communities had small waterpowered sawmills, often attached to gristmills, where the miller custom-cut logs for farmers and supplied lumber to local markets. Buncombe County had fourteen such mills in the 1880s, and Alleghany County had nine. Beginning in the 1880s with the completion of rail-

FIGURE 34. *Ritter Sawmill, Proctor. Around the turn of the century, the region's largest logging firm was the W. M. Ritter Co., a multistate corporation formed in West Virginia, which acquired several hundred thousand acres in N.C. Ritter's lumber town of Proctor on Hazel Creek in Swain Co. was one of many logging camps and towns that employed thousands of workers at the industry's early 20th-c. peak. The area is now part of the *Great Smoky Mountains National Park.*

road lines, northern companies inaugurated massive logging in the Appalachians, part of a nationwide sweep that had already depleted the forests of the Northeast and Great Lakes regions and would eventually move to the Pacific Northwest.

The first phase involved only selective cutting in areas near railroads and good streams. Northern firms set up big sawmills on the railroad lines, where they cut lumber from trees selected by their agents and supplied by local landowners. The old-growth forests yielded mammoth trees of superb quality. Some farmers hauled their logs to the mill, but most floated them along the streams, often using "splash dams" to build up and release enough water to carry logs pell-mell downstream. Cash from selling trees and occasional jobs in sawmills supplemented many mountain farmers' incomes but did not bring radical change.[9]

These erratic and inefficient methods gave way in the 1890s to a second phase in which northern timber companies—headquartered in New York, Pennsylva-

9. Eller, *Miners, Millhands, and Mountaineers*, 89; this discussion of logging and industrialization draws primarily on Eller's analysis.

nia, West Virginia, Michigan, and Ohio—bought up tracts of as much as 100,000 acres and laid narrow-gauge railroads deep into the woods and far up the slopes. Sawmills at camps in the woods allowed lumbermen to clear-cut thousands of acres of prime timberland in short order. Splash dams grew larger, and immense flumes were built to carry timber for miles in water-filled channels. At one site after another, companies built band sawmills, each capable of churning out 50,000 or more board feet a day.

"Machine logging" methods sped the pace and boosted profits. Hundreds of mountain farm families sold their land or their timber rights to agents, and thousands found lucrative jobs in lumber camps and sawmills. During the first decade of the twentieth century the southern Appalachians yielded as much as 4 billion board feet of timber per year, almost 40 percent of national production. By 1911 the loggers were cutting virgin spruce from Mount Mitchell, the highest peak in the eastern United States. It was this assault that spurred the creation of North Carolina's first state park, at Mount Mitchell in 1915.

Hand in hand with logging went other forest industries. Tanneries were usually built on good transportation routes near sources of tannin-rich tanbark—from chestnut and oak trees—and beside pure and abundant streams, the necessary ingredients for tanning hides into leather. The *Hans Rees Tannery on the French Broad River at Asheville is among the few whose buildings still stand. Others operated at Sylva, Old Fort, Andrews, Rosman, and North Wilkesboro. The tanneries were short lived, however, employing about 1,200 people in 1916 but fewer than 400 ten years later. Furniture and other woodworking industries established factories in Morganton, Marion, and other towns on railroads near sources of high-quality lumber. Other firms, including a Dutch rayon manufacturer at Enka (1928), located plants in the region because of its pure and abundant water as well as the timber. Having the greatest and most lasting impact on the region was the arrival of the paper industry in the form of the *Champion Fibre Co. in 1905. With vast holdings in timberlands Champion became the principal logging business, and its pulp and paper manufacturing plant at Canton was the world's largest.

By the 1920s industrialized logging had greatly depleted the forests of western North Carolina. Timber output from the Southern Appalachians dropped to 2.4 billion board feet in 1919 and to 2 billion by 1929. By the onset of the Great Depression some timber companies had already terminated business in western North Carolina, and others soon followed suit. For some areas the departure of the timber companies spelled an end to large-scale industry. The mineral sites and textile mills remained essentially local enterprises. With the collapse of the timber industry many people who had sold their timberlands or gone to work in lumber towns found themselves uprooted and unemployed. Some returned to farming, for better or for worse, while others left for factory

FIGURE 35. *Champion Fibre Co., Canton* (HW 13). *Needing a source of spruce wood pulp for his Ohio paper mill, in 1905 industrialist Peter Thomson acquired prime spruce forests in the Smoky and Balsam mountains and founded a pulp mill at Canton, where the WNCRR crossed the Pigeon River. Champion acquired some 400,000 acres of timberlands and built logging railroads far into the woods, creating lumber towns at Sunburst, Crestmont, and Smokemont. Expanded greatly since this early 20th-c. photograph was taken, the Canton plant has continued to be a major economic presence in the region and the state's largest private employer west of Asheville.*

jobs in the nearby foothills and piedmont cotton mills or in distant northern cities. Still others pursued work in coal mines elsewhere in the Southern Appalachians or followed the timber industry to the Pacific Northwest.

Forestry and National Forests

The late nineteenth- and early twentieth-century destruction of the forests catalyzed the development of scientific forestry management and the national forest movement. In western North Carolina many observers castigated the loss of natural beauty and economic potential. Floods worsened as the resilient sponge of the forest diminished, splash dams ravaged stream beds, and water coursed unhindered down the slopes to swell rivers at alarming speeds. Pioneers in the forestry movement emerged from the region in the 1890s as proponents of conservation and tourism confronted growing pressure on the forests. While some advocated protection of the natural landscape in its entirety, the more prevalent view favored managed forestry for long-term yield.

The first major step came in the mid-1890s when George Vanderbilt estab-

FIGURE 36. *Cutover farmland and hillsides, early 20th c.*

lished a forestry program to renew the land at Biltmore Estate and at Pisgah Forest, an expanse of old forest he had acquired nearby. Guided by European-trained foresters Gifford Pinchot and Carl Alvin Schenck, Vanderbilt's forestry program and school became known as the *Cradle of Forestry in America. In 1899 several Asheville business leaders concerned for the future of mountain tourism organized the Appalachian National Park Association and pressed Congress to protect the region's great forests. Although their idea of a natural forest park did not prevail at that time, there was national support for scientifically managed national forest reserves.

Aided by conservationist president Theodore Roosevelt; shaped by Gifford Pinchot, who had become chief forester for the U.S. Department of Agriculture; and supported by the more progressive timber interests, establishment of national forests was authorized by the Weeks Act of 1911. The new involvement of the federal government in forest conservation was justified under Congress's authority to regulate interstate commerce. Coming after disruptive floods on the Monongahela and other rivers in the Appalachians, the Weeks Act authorized purchase and conservation of "forested, cut-over, or denuded lands" to control floods and thus protect interstate commerce on navigable streams. In 1916 Pisgah National Forest, including Vanderbilt's tract, became the first national forest in the East. The National Forest Service soon acquired other forests in the East, and by 1920 national forests comprised more than 250,000 acres in western North Carolina alone.

FIGURE 37. *Flood of 1916, French Broad River at Asheville. Ironically, in the same year that Pisgah Forest became the first national forest in the east, western N.C. suffered from the most destructive flood in its history, demonstrating the intensity of the problems the Weeks Act of 1911 was meant to address through the creation of national forests. Caused by the coincidence of two hurricanes that drenched the "forested, cut-over, denuded lands," the flood of 1916 caused millions of dollars worth of damage to railroads, bridges, roads, and other property throughout the region. From* The Floods of 1916: How the Southern Railway Organization Met an Emergency *(1917).*

Roads

By the turn of the twentieth century, western North Carolina leaders involved in promoting tourism, conservation, and industrial growth were pressing for better highways to improve trade and agriculture and to boost access to tourist destinations. In 1890–91 the developers of Linville built the sixteen-mile *Yonahlossee Road from their town to Blowing Rock, a winding and scenic carriage route praised as "the most beautiful and best constructed mountain road in the State."[10] In 1899 Asheville formed the state's first Good Roads Association, with some of the same leaders who urged protection of forests. The Good Roads movement gained momentum statewide as the motor truck and automobile came into wider use. In 1908 state geologist Joseph Hyde Pratt proposed a "Crest of the Blue Ridge Highway." A route was surveyed and a few sections were begun by the Appalachian Highway Commission, but construction halted with the onset of World War I.

A state-supported highway system was established in 1921. The state's "Cen-

10. Arthur, *Western North Carolina*, 500.

FIGURE 38. *Log Cabin Motor Court* (BN 91), *Weaverville vic. Construction of roads for automobile travel transformed the region's economy and settlement patterns, and motels sprang up by the roads to accommodate motorists. Some, like this one and *Mac's Indian Village* (JK 22), featured log cabin or tepee motifs, and a few had both.*

FIGURE 39. *Broughton Hospital (Western N.C. Insane Asylum), Morganton* (BK 14). *Morganton's position at the railhead of the WNCRR made it a suitable site for one of the first major state institutions built after the Civil War, an insane asylum for the western region. The building was designed by Samuel Sloan, a Philadelphia architect who had long specialized in asylum designs; on the strength of his work at the asylum, he gained the commission to design the state's Executive Mansion in Raleigh.*

tral Highway" (later US 70), authorized in 1911, was completed in 1921. It stretched from Morehead City to Tennessee along the old roads and railroad routes and passed through Morganton, Marion, Old Fort, Asheville, and Marshall. Another east-west route, present-day US 64, stretched southwest from Morganton and brought automobiles into scenic tourist spots, including Lake Lure and Chimney Rock in Rutherford County and Highlands in Macon County. Other roads reached into areas hitherto little served by thoroughfares. The terrain presented immense challenges in grading and construction, such as the section of *US 64 from Franklin to Highlands on a scenic and perilous route beside the Cullasaja River. But despite the difficulties, many new roads were completed in the 1920s, bringing nearly every section within a few hours' drive of trading and government centers.

Town Growth

Railroads and highways combined with tourism and industry to stimulate the growth of towns throughout the region. Although only Asheville emerged as a city, many county seats and trading villages developed as local business centers. Morganton, Marion, and Lenoir were among the antebellum county seats that became manufacturing towns, and in Morganton, the railroad plus political connections also drew two major state institutions, the Western North Carolina Insane Asylum (*Broughton Hospital) and the *North Carolina School for the Deaf. New industrial towns also sprang up, such as the railroad towns of North Wilkesboro and West Jefferson, which soon outstripped neighboring county seats. Small settlements such as Mount Airy, Elkin, Spruce Pine, and Andrews grew into manufacturing centers after railroads reached them. And Canton, Sylva, and Bryson City emerged as railheads as the Murphy branch of the WNCRR inched westward.

Tourism gave birth to several towns and boosted the fortunes of many others. Highlands was laid out in 1875 by Kansas entrepreneur Samuel T. Kelsey and others as a summer resort literally capitalizing on its 3,838-foot elevation — the highest town in the state. In 1888 Kelsey initiated development of another resort community, Linville. At Blowing Rock a hotel was built by 1885, and a small resort village soon developed. Roaring Gap was created in the 1890s as a retreat for piedmont industrialists and their families.

Other towns grew up around colleges and normal schools. These small, hard-won institutions established in the 19th and early 20th centuries played important roles in the region's development. The schools that became *Appalachian State University at Boone, *Western Carolina University at Cullowhee, *Mars Hill College at Mars Hill, and *Lees-McRae College in Banner Elk were among the educational institutions that became the centerpieces of their communities.

The town of Valdese was founded by a colony of Waldenses, a Protestant

FIGURE 40. *All Saints Episcopal Church, Linville* (AV 2); *Henry Bacon, architect. Late 19th-c. entre-preneurs saw in the mountains opportunities both for industrial logging and mining and for tourist re-sorts. Linville was conceived as an industrial town but was soon reconstituted as a resort community. It is distinguished by its elegantly rustic chestnut-bark-covered architecture, including buildings designed by nationally prominent architect Henry Bacon, childhood friend of the MacRaes of Wilmington, who were among the developers.*

group who came from their homeland in northwestern Italy at the encourage-ment of Burke County business leaders in the 1890s. The Waldenses established hillside farms where they built traditional stone dwellings and outbuildings. In town they founded a bakery and textile mill and erected a handsome stuccoed stone church, stone and stuccoed houses, and in the 1910s and 1920s, stone bun-galows and a distinctive stone school.

Still other communities maintained their familiar roles as small county seats and local trading towns, with growth ebbing and flowing with the larger econ-omy and access to railroads and highways. Wilkesboro and Jefferson maintained their status as county seats despite economic competition from the nearby rail-road towns of North Wilkesboro and West Jefferson. In Jackson County, how-ever, after the railroad bypassed the county seat of Webster, the railroad town of Sylva launched a "removalist" campaign and became county seat in 1913. New courthouses rose in almost every county seat, part of a statewide courthouse building campaign.

Most towns continued to employ grid plans, modified to the terrain. Roads curved with the land as they approached the town center but usually straight-

FIGURE 41. *Jackson County Courthouse, Sylva* (JK 1). *The courthouse was designed by Smith & Carrier, the firm founded by Richard Sharp Smith, supervising architect at *Biltmore; the firm's other courthouses include those in *Swain, *Madison, and *Henderson counties. Many counties erected courthouses in the early 20th c., typically in a Neoclassical style with dome and central portico or a long front colonnade. Several were designed by Charlotte architect Oliver Wheeler and various associates, including those in *Wilkes, *Avery, and *Ashe counties.*

ened out when they met the grid. Main Street was the pride and joy of these growing little towns, most of which were essentially rebuilt in this era. Municipal leaders took satisfaction in the brick and stone-faced commercial buildings that lined the main business streets. Often replacing frame structures, they offered clear evidence that these long-remote villages had taken their place in the economic mainstream. The typically two- and three-story brick buildings were trimmed with corbeled brickwork or stone or pressed metal. Banks often presented a reassuring classical vault image. Hotels presented especially vivid and stylish appearances, from the porch-draped Queen Anne style inns of the late nineteenth century to the dwarf skyscrapers of the 1920s. Adjoining the business sector, big, functional brick, frame, or metal factories and warehouses reached to the railroad or river and beyond. Workers' housing usually lay near the factories, though some industrialists placed their housing in healthful situations up

FIGURE 42. *Trade St., Tryon* (PL 7), *typifies the 2- and 3-story commercial buildings that constitute the business districts of many downtowns that developed in the early 20th c., nourished by rail and automobile routes.*

FIGURE 43. *Alexander Martin Smith House, Elkin* (SY 21). *One of many eclectic late 19th-c. houses in western N.C. towns, the Queen Anne style frame house displays the lavish millwork that proliferated with the establishment of sawmills and sash and blind factories in the late 19th c. It was designed by Knoxville mail-order architect George F. Barber.*

FIGURE 44. *"Summer Daze" Bungalow, Lake Junaluska* (HW 10). *The bungalow, often incorporating local stonework, was a popular form throughout the region in the early 20th c. Typical bungalows have low profiles, deep porches with hefty, often tapered posts, and informal, natural materials.*

the hill. The principal churches and the prime residential section ranged up the gentler hills and along the ridges leading from the downtown.

The towns' architecture reflected popular national trends, but in a conservative way. Among commercial and public buildings, Italianate and Romanesque styles were succeeded by Neoclassical ones in the early twentieth century. For churches Gothic Revival and Neoclassical styles predominated. The finest residences shifted from the late Italianate and Queen Anne of the 1880–1910 era to the Colonial Revival and Tudor Revival styles of the early twentieth century. The Neoclassical and Colonial Revival styles were popular, but they did not dominate as strongly as in eastern North Carolina. Especially widespread were myriad renditions of the Craftsman bungalow and other Craftsman-detailed houses, large and small. Many of these were rendered in local stonework in keeping with the Arts and Crafts movement's emphasis on natural materials.

By the early twentieth century, clients in the region were commissioning key buildings from myriad professional architects. Although most of the architects in the region were headquartered in Asheville, a few, such as Erle Stillwell of Hendersonville, had offices in smaller towns. Commissions also went to architects from more distant cities. Charles C. Benton of Wilson and C. C. Hook, William Peeps, Oliver Wheeler, J. M. McMichael, and Louis Asbury of Charlotte were among those active in the foothills. Tennessee architects, including Donald R.

FIGURE 45. *Pack Square, Asheville, ca. 1900. Embodying the rapid and ambitious development of Asheville, its civic square was repeatedly expanded and transformed with taller and more elaborate civic and commercial buildings. Left to right are the Vance Monument (R. S. Smith, architect) (BN 3), the 1876 Buncombe County Courthouse, the City Hall, the Daily Citizen building, and the first Pack Library. The old Court Square was enlarged before the turn of the century and subsequently named for lumberman George W. Pack, who donated money for the Vance Monument and the public library and gave land for the expansion of the square.*

Beeson of Johnson City and Reuben H. Hunt of Knoxville, took commissions west of the Blue Ridge. A few clients commissioned designs from distant urban firms. Wilmingtonians persuaded Henry Bacon of New York to design buildings at Linville; Atlanta architect Neel Reid planned residences for clients in Lake Toxaway and Asheville; and Winston-Salem clients had a hotel in Roaring Gap designed by their favored Philadelphia architect Charles Barton Keen.

Asheville, the Mountain Boomtown

Topography and climate, tourism and industries, county seat and trading center, and river, rail, and highway connections all came together to make Asheville the metropolis of the mountains. The 1880 arrival of the WNCRR followed by other rail connections, and the early twentieth-century construction of the Central Highway and other roads made Asheville a boomtown. Its population grew from 1,500 in 1880 to 10,000 in 1890. By 1920 its 28,000 residents made it the fourth largest city in the state (after Winston-Salem, Charlotte, and Wilmington), and it grew to 50,000 by 1930. In contrast to the rest of the state,

FIGURE 46. *Pack Square, Asheville, ca. 1928 (BN 1–8). Seen here (left to right) are the present Buncombe County Courthouse (Frank Milburn, architect), the short-lived Buncombe County Courthouse of 1903, the City Building (Douglas Ellington, architect), the Vance Monument, the Jackson Building (Ronald Greene, architect), the Legal Building (Richard Sharp Smith, architect), and the Pack Library (Edward Tilton, architect). John Nolen's 1922 plan for Asheville had called for further expansion of the public square to the east.*

where no single city dominated urban growth, in western North Carolina Asheville emerged as the only real city.

Tourism gave Asheville its special energy and quality, attracting visitors and permanent residents of extraordinary diversity and ambition, who brought the town vitality and a cosmopolitan flavor unrivaled in the region and seldom in the state. The presence of Biltmore enhanced the city's pride and promise with a new air of sophistication and wealth. The downtown saw repeated rebuilding that produced increasingly large and elegant buildings. Residential suburbs and resort estates grew apace, as developers laid out fashionable suburbs with stylishly curving streets hugging the slopes. The city's development became linked to the Florida land boom of the 1910s and 1920s, and land speculation and prices spiraled upward. In the 1920s Asheville commissioned a city plan from nationally renowned planner John Nolen, embarked on an ambitious "Program of Progress," and undertook construction of grand civic buildings.

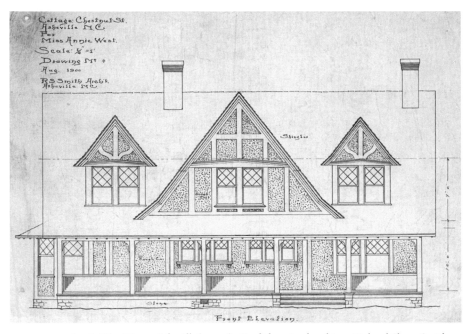

FIGURE 47. *Annie West House, Asheville* (BN 47). *English-trained architect Richard Sharp Smith repeated motifs from *Biltmore Village in many houses in Asheville and beyond. He often combined rough-textured stuccoed walls with shingles and various Tudor Revival, Neoclassical, and Craftsman elements. He typically specified "Rough Cast" for the mortared surface containing stone aggregates, chiefly pebbles. Locally, this treatment is popularly called "pebbledash."*

Asheville's boom eras created a trove of late nineteenth- and especially early twentieth-century architecture. The city was the center of the region's emerging architectural profession. A. L. Melton and J. A. Tennent designed the eclectic public buildings and residences of the 1880s and 1890s. Part of the Biltmore legacy were Spanish architect Rafael Guastavino, who came to work on Biltmore and established a residence and kiln near Black Mountain, and English architect Richard Sharp Smith, supervising architect at Biltmore, who founded a prolific regional practice. Ronald Greene designed buildings that ranged from the Gothic to the classical to the moderne. Beaux Arts–trained Douglas Ellington capped off the boom era with an extraordinary collection of Art Deco buildings of the late 1920s. Asheville clients also commissioned works by architects from eastern cities: hotels by Philadelphia architects Edward Hazlehurst and Francis and William Price and New Yorkers Bradford Gilbert and William Stoddart, a library by New Yorker Edward Tilton, and a church from Bertram Goodhue of the New York and Boston firm of Cram, Goodhue & Ferguson.

Residences and resorts took every imaginable guise. They ranged from ornate Queen Anne houses by diverse architects and builders to Richard Sharp Smith's sophisticated Craftsman and English cottage styles rendered in brick, roughcast stucco, and timber. Much of the city's character comes from its lively variations on the romantic and naturalistic motifs deemed suitable to the mountain setting: more or less craggy English baronial castles, Tudor Revival cottages, Swiss chalet Craftsman dwellings, and rustic boulder-clad lodges.

Regional Architecture

Although western North Carolinians built in a range of nationally popular styles, in Asheville and elsewhere some sense of a regional architectural character emerged by the early twentieth century. It was expressed in a preference for picturesque, romantic, and rustic designs and natural materials, most often displayed in resorts and residences and occasionally in schools and churches.

A variety of styles seemed suitably picturesque complements to the mountain setting. Fashion-conscious residents in the nineteenth century favored the peaked or bracketed cottage style, in keeping with A. J. Downing's recommendation of steep-gabled compositions for mountainous landscapes. Late in the century the cottage mode gave way to the still more picturesque Queen Anne, sometimes with Swiss chalet or Tudor Revival touches. Such landmarks as Biltmore and the *Grove Park Inn modeled images of the romantic chateau and the robust naturalistic retreat, and each of these ideals was repeated in smaller versions. Around the turn of the century, taste turned to a variety of English-inspired cottages and Elizabethan manor houses rendered in combinations of half-timbering, pebbledash, and stone, as well as rustic Adirondack-style houses featuring log and native stone. Influenced directly or indirectly by the national and international Arts and Crafts movement with its emphasis on direct expression of local natural materials, these themes blended with the equally popular Craftsman style seen in innumerable bungalows as well as in larger houses.

Conventional associative architectural ideas such as the Early English Gothic Revival church and the Tudor Revival school took on a different character when rendered in smooth, round river rocks, irregular fieldstone, or rough-cut quarried blocks. Local stonework in a variety of colors and textures gave individuality to otherwise standard building forms in such diverse examples as the dark stonework at Brevard, the bright orange rock in Robbinsville, the rounded river rock in Canton and Dillingham, the pale granite blocks in Mount Airy, and the rough formations featured at architect-designed buildings at *Lees-McRae College and *Mars Hill College.

The natural character of the materials was often the principal focus of the design. At Linville and at *High Hampton, architects working in a consciously simple Arts and Crafts mode used chestnut-bark shingles to define the architecture. In and around Highlands, builder Joe Webb developed a distinctive rustic style rendered with intricately wrought logs and laurel branches. Many camps were built with pole log structures and natural stonework, as were private

FIGURE 48. *Grove Park Inn, Asheville* (BN 53). *Influenced by the Arts and Crafts movement, early 20th-c. resort builders turned to natural materials and simple forms to complement the mountain setting. National models in the Adirondacks and the American West offered inspiration. At the Grove Park Inn, developer E. W. Grove wanted a naturalistic and informal luxury resort hotel in the spirit of the lodge at Yellowstone Park. After consulting with New York and Boston architect Henry Ives Cobb, Grove's son-in-law Fred Seely completed the project, using boulders rolled down the nearby mountainside. The inn was fitted out in full Arts and Crafts fashion, including work by the Roycrofters of East Aurora, N.Y. At *High Hampton Inn (JK 18), Hendersonville architect Erle Stillwell covered the walls with native chestnut bark. At the *Snowbird Mountain Lodge (GH 11) near Robbinsville, Asheville architect Ronald Greene used logs and local stone for a Chicago tourist agent's rustic mountaintop inn.*

houses, crafts schools, and community recreation facilities. The intentional rusticism of the Arts and Crafts movement often intersected with the continuity of indigenous building traditions. These materials and construction techniques repeated elements of the familiar log structures and fieldstone chimneys that local residents were still building, and that by the early twentieth century had begun to capture the attention of regionalists.

Rural Life of the Industrial Age

Beyond the growing towns and tourist resorts, the transformations wrought by new transportation networks and industries had profound effects on rural life. Late nineteenth-century descriptions of the region's farms convey a way of life little changed from the first part of the century. Small landowning predominated, as did reliance on diverse agriculture that yielded a modest surplus for trade. Many farmers continued to range their livestock in the woods and high

FIGURE 49. *St. Andrews Episcopal Church, Canton* (HW 16). *Like many churches in the region, a conventional Gothic Revival design gains distinction from the local stonework. As for many of the region's stone buildings, tradition relates the specific source of the rocks. For this 1922 church, congregation members and friends journeyed in 1921 to the East Fork of the Pigeon River to select smooth, round river rocks, which were carried to Canton on narrow-gauge railroad cars by the Champion Fibre Co., then delivered to the site by wagon.*

FIGURE 50. *Paint Gap community, Yancey Co.* (YC 5)

FIGURE 51. *Barn with burley tobacco, Alleghany Co.*

mountain meadows, while others restricted them to pastures on the smooth and rounded hills. Into the early twentieth century, farmers still drove herds of animals to market down old trails and roads.

To this familiar diversity was added tobacco cultivation. For a time during the late nineteenth century, mountain farmers raised flue-cured bright-leaf tobacco, the type also prevalent in the piedmont and, later, in eastern North Carolina. With shifts in the market, by the early twentieth century they had all but abandoned it. During the 1920s and 1930s, however, mountain farmers turned to growing small crops of burley tobacco, a heavier leaf air-cured in open barns.

As in earlier times farmers maintained a strong sense of community and family interdependence. Exchange of work—to raise a barn, bring in a crop, build a church, make a quilt, or tend the sick and dying—remained vital to community, family, and individual survival and identity. Rural communities typically evolved in response to topography, with farmsteads stretching along a winding valley or encircling a cove. A store, the storekeeper's house, and a church or two stood at the center, at the opening to a valley, or at a crossroads. Particularly in areas where settlements were rimmed by steep slopes and high ridges, communities operated in relative isolation from those across the ridge.

Differences between highland and valley farmers were never hard and fast. The terrain often wove alternating patterns within short distances. Some farms encompassed both level bottomland and steep slopes; large valley farms lay just below hillier tracts in some coves; and family connections tied together farmers up and down the land. In many a rural neighborhood by the turn of the century, painted frame houses and large barns prevailed in the lower section of a valley, interspersed with log houses and barns that continued in use, while a short distance up the cove or hollow the road narrowed into a settlement of sparsely placed log or boxed houses and narrow fields carved into steep hillsides. As the elevation rose, so did the prevalence of log buildings and woodland agriculture.

But as rails and roads increased access to market and contact with the outside world, old differences between valley settlements and highland coves intensified. In the lower, gentler lands, better transportation encouraged farmers to trade with distant as well as local markets. Further, emphasis on scientific farming and the work of agricultural extension agents boosted production among some farmers. Apple orchards continued their importance, and truck farming developed in some sections. Western counties topped the list of meat-producing and dairy farms in the state.

With greater access to market and more cash available, and with sawmills operating within reach of a wagon, more prosperous families replaced traditional log dwellings with frame houses and sometimes brick ones. Some of these were finished with a clear awareness of current style. Especially popular from the 1880s onward were two-story houses with a rear kitchen ell. Many houses displayed ornate porches lavished with the era's newly available sawn and turned millwork. Like townspeople, a few farmers built simplified Queen Anne style residences with a high roof, wraparound porch, and even a turret or porch gazebo. In the early twentieth century these were joined by simply finished foursquare houses with hip roofs and by large and small versions of the popular Craftsman bungalow, often enriched by foundations, porch piers, and chimneys in local stone.

Farmers also invested in outbuildings. Many followed traditional practices, building single- or multicribbed log barns, sometimes with big overhanging roofs to shelter work and equipment. Others built large frame barns, often with slatted eaves in decorative patterns or open cupolas to ventilate the haylofts. Dairy farmers, especially, built large gambrel-roofed barns. First frame, then masonry and concrete silos were raised to hold feed. Corncribs continued to be built of log, with ventilating space between the logs, and also in frame with slatted sides. Cribs often had sheds extending on one or both sides to shelter a wagon.

In the area around the dwelling, in a domestic work zone usually the purview of farm women, purpose-built structures served household needs. Freestanding kitchens with wood-burning fireplaces continued in use, but as stoves grew more available, more families attached their kitchens to the house or included the kitchen as a room within the dwelling. Snugly built log or frame smokehouses continued their important role for curing and storing pork. Spring-

FIGURE 52. *Donnelly Farm, Sutherland, Ashe Co.* (AH 6)

FIGURE 53. *J. H. Hardin House, Sutherland, Ashe Co.* (AH 6)

FIGURE 54. *Baird Farm, Watauga Co.* (WT 13). *Many barns had decorative vents beneath the eaves to ventilate the hayloft.*

FIGURE 55. *Corncrib, Thomas Divide, Swain Co., Charles S. Grossman, photographer, 1937*

FIGURE 56. *Springhouse and blacksmith shop, Palmer Farm, Cataloochee, Haywood Co.* (HW 26)

houses built into the land over or near a spring offered a cool spot for milk, cheese, and butter. Specialized can houses (for the fruits and vegetables women canned during the harvest for winter use) and apple houses and other storage buildings were set in a hillside or bank for semi-subterranean cool storage.

The positioning of the farm complex was a matter of careful thought and often considerable labor. Many farmers seated their farmhouse and its out-buildings on the lower slope of a hill, above the floodplain but short of the steeper slopes, the same pattern William Bartram had observed among the Cherokees in the eighteenth century. Some farmers located their buildings in a cove or valley, sheltered from the wind. Others placed them on gentle knolls. Some even carved out terraces or constructed promontories in the slope above the floodplain to form a level site for their house and immediate farm buildings.

Rural residents also built and rebuilt community facilities. They replaced many dark and drafty log schoolhouses with heated and well-lit frame struc-tures. Crossroads merchants, whose stores provided social centers as well as store-bought goods and credit, built frame or brick country stores, usually with wide porches and deep-shelved interiors centering on a woodstove. By the 1920s many also had a gas pump in front. Plain, often unpainted frame gristmills and sawmills provided essential local services, grinding farmers' corn or sawing their timber and often accepting a portion as payment for resale in the local market.

The principal landmarks of country and village life were the churches built

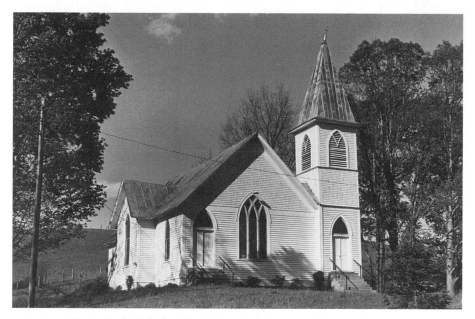

FIGURE 57. *Grassy Creek Methodist Church* (AH II). *The universal form in the region was a simple, gable-fronted frame church with one or two entrances opening into a vestibule or directly into the sanctuary, a large rectangular room with rows of pews and one or two aisles. Some churches after the turn of the century, such as Grassy Creek Methodist, had sloped, curved, or angled auditorium-plan sanctuaries. Plain, weatherboarded churches with clear-paned rectangular windows served many rural congregations. Many had "church-like" fittings such as pointed or triangular-headed windows, polygonal entrance vestibules or apses, and belfries in many different forms.*

in the late nineteenth and early twentieth centuries. Church building proliferated as new access to sawmills encouraged congregations to erect neatly finished frame structures. In a pattern formed in antebellum years, there were few Presbyterians, even fewer Episcopalians, and a very small number of Catholics. Baptists of various persuasions were the most numerous, with Methodists a close second. Membership in these two evangelical denominations had been nurtured by the missionaries and camp meetings of the earlier nineteenth century. Fundamentalism was a strong tradition, especially among rural congregations. Every village or rural community of any consequence had one denomination or the other, and most had both.

Particularly distinctive is the placement of many mountain churches, on knolls, promontories, or steep hillsides, which were often graded or terraced to ease access. The churchyard stretches out beside the church and often far up the slope above. On such carefully chosen sites many a small country church occupies a prominent position above the valley floor, giving churchgoers a prime view of the landscape beyond and making the church a beacon from a distance.

While improving the economic situation of some rural areas, at the same time the combined effects of railroads, lumbering, and tourism drastically altered the traditional landscape and livelihood of the highland farmers. From the early nineteenth century the upper coves and hollows had nurtured an independent life focused on family and neighborhood. Families raised small crops of corn and vegetables but relied on the customary use of the forests for their sustenance—gathering chestnuts and berries, hunting game, fishing, and allowing their livestock to range in the woods and feed on acorns and chestnut mast. In the early 1890s forester Gifford Pinchot explored George Vanderbilt's forests and reported that the mountain farmers

> regarded this country as their country, their common. And that was not surprising, for they needed everything usable in it—pasture, fish, game—to supplement the very meager living they were able to scratch from the soil of their little clearings, which often were no clearings at all, but merely "deadenings," filled with the whitened skeletons of trees killed by girdling. By immemorial custom and by law, the cattle and the long-legged hogs ran free over ridge and slope and bottom. You had to fence them out, not to fence them in. These people dwelt and slept mostly in one-room cabins.[11]

At the turn of the century the typical upland farmstead was a modest complex with a simple dwelling and a few outbuildings. Still the norm were log dwellings that repeated forms and notching patterns established a century earlier. Their construction reflected the traditions of mutual assistance and relative independence of the market that lay at the heart of the old social economy. Where sawmills were convenient, farmers as well as town dwellers built "boxed" houses, which followed floor plans akin to log dwellings but were constructed with vertical sawed boards instead of hand-hewn logs. Around their modest houses farmers continued to cut trees to clear land, leaving the stumps in the field and planting corn around them and cultivating their small crops with hand tools.

By the late nineteenth century, outsiders who saw the small highland farmstead no longer thought it a normal rural scene but considered it an archaic survival. Travelers told colorful tales of crude cabins and a "backward" way of life. At the same time industrial logging, by removing large swaths of forest and by purchasing land or timber rights, was changing the landscape on which the mountain farmer had thrived. For those who remained on the land the old balance between crops and the bounty of the forest was fading. The legislature enacted fence laws that reversed the custom of free range and required that animals, not crops, must be fenced in. Although many flouted the new laws and continued to hunt in the woodlands, many who had managed a sufficient living in the old system found it increasingly difficult to make ends meet.

---

11. Pinchot quoted in Van Noppen and Van Noppen, *Western North Carolina*, 305.

FIGURE 58. *Davis Log House, ca. 1900* (sw 16), *Thomas Divide, Swain Co., Charles S. Grossman, photographer, 1937. In most rural areas of the mountains and much of the foothills, log construction prevailed long after it had been substantially replaced elsewhere in the state. Even in the valleys beside the highways, log construction persisted, and it dominated in remote sections into the 20th c. Half-dovetailed notching continued its prevalence. Single-pen dwellings were most numerous, though 2-unit forms continued—saddlebag, double-pen, and dogtrot plans.*

Reformers and Revivalists

The traditional way of life associated with rural people in the Southern Appalachians attracted growing national attention. From the late 1860s onward, local-color writers, travel writers, missionaries, and educators constructed a popular and homogeneous image of Appalachia as an exceptional cultural island. Seen as a bastion of unchanged Anglo-Saxon culture—primitive and violent to some, quaintly antiquated and pure to others—the region came to be perceived chiefly through a stereotype that ignored much of its reality and focused on a narrow segment of its people.

The region did possess strong cultural traditions that were expressed in speech patterns, old ballads and fiddle tunes, and conservative religious and social beliefs as well as customs of hunting, farming, and building. The old ways were more evident in rural and mountainous sections than in the main towns and wealthiest valleys. It was this survival of preindustrial ways that captured popular interest. A seminal local-color travelogue of 1873 was titled *A Strange Land and Peculiar People*, and a subsequent account called the people of the Appalachians "our contemporary ancestors." From the 1880s into the 1920s one writer after another left behind the trappings of "civilization"—the region's rail-

FIGURE 59. *Boxed house. With the proliferation of sawmills, boxed house construction entered the vocabulary of modest building. Such houses were frequently built for lumber camps and sawmill towns, but they also found use among farmers with access to a sawmill. In some cases they reflected the breakdown of the old cooperative building traditions that produced log houses. A boxed house resembles superficially a board-and-batten building, but there is no independent frame as in the latter case. Rather, the builder nails vertical boards to a sill at the bottom and a plate above to form the walls, which are stabilized by narrow corner posts. Such houses were numerous in the late 19th and early 20th centuries, but relatively few still stand. See Michael Ann Williams, "Pride and Prejudice: The Appalachian Boxed House in Southwestern North Carolina." This "Cabin on Buck Creek Rd." was one of several photographed by Bayard Wootten in western N.C. and published in Muriel Sheppard's* Cabins in the Laurel *(1935). The house was located in Mitchell Co.*

road routes and its busy downtowns and modern factories, the fashionable suburb and the comfortable resort hotel, and even the prosperous farmstead with its substantial house and barns—to head up the narrow roads and rough paths in search of "genuine" mountain folk, the characters suited to the local-color movement's interest in the "olden days" that differed from modern America.[12]

This emerging notion of the region attracted people with diverse motives: tourists in search of a place "progress had passed by," folklorists and anthropologists who hoped to record its traditions before they vanished, social uplift educators and missionaries who wanted to improve the lot of its residents, and outdoors enthusiasts who hoped to benefit from or, eventually, preserve what remained of the wilderness landscape.

Horace Kephart was one who came to the region to escape the pressures of

12. See Shapiro, *Appalachia on Our Mind*; Whisnant, *All That Is Native and Fine*; and Williams, *Great Smoky Mountains Folklife*.

"civilized" urban life and stayed to learn from its people. For him it was the "great multitude of little farmers living up the branches and on the steep hillsides, back from the main highways, and generally far from the railroads," not the "relatively few townsmen and prosperous valley farmers," who constituted "the real mountaineers."[13] In *Our Southern Highlanders* (1913) he depicted the mountain character based chiefly on his sojourn on Hazel Creek in Swain County, where an old settlement was even then being transformed by timbering.

John and Olive Dame Campbell traveled in the Southern Appalachians to record folk traditions and to survey economic and social conditions, purposes that combined in *The Southern Highlander and His Homeland* (1921) and the founding of the *John C. Campbell Folk School (1925) along Scandinavian folk school lines to revitalize craft and agricultural methods. Several other schools were founded by individuals who sought to preserve the region's cultural traditions while improving its way of life. Presbyterian missionaries established schools and hospitals at Hot Springs, Banner Elk, and Crossnore, and Episcopalians revived an old mission school in Valle Crucis.

Growing tourism intersected with the schools intended for social uplift by creating a market for mountain crafts. The leaders were part of a national pattern that brought together settlement schools and the Arts and Crafts movement's emphasis on handicrafts and design standards. Frances Goodrich, a Presbyterian missionary and educator trained in art, began *Allanstand in 1897 as a school and crafts center to encourage local women in traditional weaving and other skills; she soon opened an outlet for their work in Asheville. At *Penland, Lucy Morgan, a native of Macon County, developed at an Episcopal agricultural school a crafts center that grew into an important crafts school attracting students from far and near. Whether repeating old forms or adopting new ones encouraged by teachers and the market, mountain residents gained a new source of income in the regionwide craft revival, making baskets, pottery, coverlets, rugs, and woodcarvings for a national market that grew rapidly in the early twentieth century.[14]

Appalachian music and dance traditions saw an even wider revival and transformation. English musicologist Cecil Sharp visited the region with Olive Campbell in 1916 and collected songs that appeared in his *English Folk-Songs from the Southern Appalachians*. Buncombe County resident Bascom Lamar Lunsford led in encouraging the collection and performance of traditional tunes and dances from the 1920s onward. In the late 1920s he helped organize the

13. Horace Kephart quoted in George Elliott, "Introduction," in Kephart, *Our Southern Highlanders*, xxxvii.

14. See Whisnant, *All That Is Native and Fine*; Becker, *Selling Tradition*; Cooke, "Talking or Working" and "The Aesthetics of Craftsmanship and the Prestige of the Past"; and various articles in Brunk, ed., *May We All Remember Well* (1997).

FIGURE 60. *Edward F. Worst Craft House, Penland School of Crafts* (ML 3). *Sharing a rustic aesthetic promoted by the Arts and Crafts movement and Adirondack architecture, a number of early 20th-c. buildings used log construction and rough stonework as an intentionally regional form. Reused local log houses and newly built log buildings offered an appealing setting for the presentation and production of local crafts, which were likewise influenced by the Arts and Crafts ideal. This 1935 building, designed by Tennessee architect D. R. Beeson for the crafts school at Penland, is said to be the largest log building in the state; it and other campus buildings were erected by local men familiar with traditional log construction, guided by director Lucy Morgan. It was at a 1928 meeting at the school's Weaving Cabin (1926) at the school that the Southern Highland Handicraft Guild had its beginnings, an organization that included Penland, *John C. Campbell Folk School (CE 20), *Allanstand (MD 16), the *Crossnore School (AV 7), the *Spinning Wheel (BN 77), and others throughout the region.*

Mountain Dance and Folk Festival in Asheville, among others, and he collected more than 300 songs as well as writing some new ones, including "Good Old Mountain Dew" in 1920. Folk music and dance festivals soon presented residents as well as tourists with a display of vibrant and dynamic indigenous culture that, while changing over time, affirmed a sense of regional and local identity.

Among the Cherokees, too, the forces of change had complex effects. The group that had remained in the region to become the Eastern Band of Cherokee Indians occupied land in the heart of the timber industry. Its governance operated in a sometimes difficult relationship between tribal leaders and officials of the Bureau of Indian Affairs (BIA). Several large tracts of timber were sold to lumber companies, and lumber camps provided employment to Cherokee workers. In the first decades of the twentieth century, rails were extended to Cherokee, and lumber spurs were constructed far up the river valleys. Here, too, wage labor and reduction of forests depleted traditional agriculture while temporarily boosting the economy.

Economic forces coupled with federal educational policies that discouraged use of the Cherokee language eroded the traditional Cherokee way of life. There was tension within the tribe between progressive and traditional thinkers, who favored different levels of engagement in mainstream American business and culture, as well as with the BIA over the legal and social status of the Cherokees. A controversial element was the stickball game, an ancient tradition sometimes called the "Little War"; it was continued by the Cherokees despite BIA discouragement early in the century. In 1914 Cherokees began the autumn Cherokee Indian Fair, which offered an opportunity to sell basketry and other goods. These events were open to both whites and Indians, in contrast to other dances and rituals still held in private.

For several years outsiders had taken a growing interest in traditional Cherokee culture. The first among these was James Mooney, who, beginning in 1887 under the Smithsonian's Bureau of American Ethnology, conducted fieldwork among the Eastern Band and learned from the old storyteller Swimmer and other elders the stories he published in *Myths of the Cherokee* in 1900. Trips to Cherokee communities became frequent expeditions for mountain tourists, and Indian crafts became popular souvenirs. Basketmakers, who did a small business at the turn of the century, found almost unlimited markets at the newly opened *Grove Park Inn (Fig. 48) in Asheville by 1913, and soon Cherokee residents opened the first of many local crafts stores to the tourist trade.

The Park and the Parkway, the Great Depression, and the War

The campaign to create a national park to conserve the forests of the Southern Appalachians, begun in the 1890s with support from western North Carolina leaders, had little success in the years before World War I. In the 1920s, however, the Appalachian National Park committee, with leadership from Tennesseans and North Carolinians, renewed the crusade. "Shall the Smoky Mountains be made into a national park or a desert?" inveighed Horace Kephart. Growing tourism, the existence of national parks in the American West, the decline of the timber industry, and the denuding of much of the forests gave the movement new strength.

In 1925 Congress authorized study of three eastern parks—Shenandoah, Mammoth Cave, and Great Smoky Mountains—and in 1926 passed the bill creating the *Great Smoky Mountains National Park, envisioned as covering 400,000 acres in North Carolina and Tennessee. State fund-raising for land acquisition was slow. There was resistance from some timber companies and from local constituents. In contrast to the western parks, the eastern parks covered land long inhabited and farmed; as the scale of removal of families and com-

FIGURE 61. *Enloe Barn, Mountain Farm Museum, Great Smoky Mountains National Park* (SW 16). *The intent for the *Great Smoky Mountains National Park was to create a natural forest preserve, a policy that entailed removal of thousands of longtime residents. Most buildings were eliminated when the park was developed, though in the park as along the *Blue Ridge Parkway, the policy was to keep a few structures—picturesque log cabins, farm buildings, and gristmills—that conformed with and thus intensified the popular image of the Appalachians as a primitive and rustic place. "Modern" frame houses, stores, and the remains of the lumber industry were razed. In the late 1930s, CCC employee Charles S. Grossman photographed the surviving buildings in the park (see Figs. 55 and 58), and with Hiram C. Wilburn encouraged the retention of some as part of the park program. This large barn has been preserved at the *Mountain Farm Museum (SW 16). Other farm and community buildings were preserved at *Cataloochee (HW 26) in Haywood Co., and some from that section were moved to the Mountain Farm Museum.*

munities from proposed parklands became evident, local opposition mounted. Nevertheless, aided by a $5 million Rockefeller donation, the states acquired the first 158,799 acres and deeded the land to the federal government in 1930. After long negotiation, Champion sold its 93,000 for the park in 1931, and by 1935 the initial goal of 400,000 acres was met. Eventually over 520,000 acres were encompassed by the park, a little more than half of that in North Carolina in Swain and Haywood counties. Development of the park began with the federal programs to create jobs during the Great Depression.

The stock market crash of 1929 and the ensuing Great Depression had widespread and lasting effects in the region. Asheville, like other towns tied to speculation, tourism, and land booms, plummeted into bankruptcy after its principal bank failed in 1930. The city government was forced to default on the bonds issued to support its ambitious municipal improvements. The boom city ground

FIGURE 62. *Micaville School, Yancey Co.* (YC 2). *A wide range of construction programs aided in the creation of much-needed civic facilities in rural as well as urban communities. Especially numerous are the consolidated and local schools built with WPA assistance, many of which display local stonework and whose construction provided employment for local men. Many towns gained handsome little brick or stone U.S. post offices in the conservative Colonial style favored by the supervising architect of the Treasury. Other construction projects employed round logs and rough-hewn stonework for small civic buildings from museums to recreational centers. Photograph, late 1930s.*

to a halt and did not recover fully until late in the twentieth century. Banks throughout the region, which had deposits in the Asheville bank, closed as a result—eleven within two days of its closing. Other banks and businesses and factories closed in town after town. Some major industries, including textile mills and hydroelectric power companies, were forced to retrench, while others survived and even expanded with the aid of government contracts.

In rural areas—already troubled by agricultural depressions, dislocation of farm families, and the collapse of the timber industry—the Great Depression brought more hardship. Some farm families with unencumbered land made it through the hard times through resilient skills of self-reliant rural life. As unemployment mounted nationwide, many natives who had left home for distant jobs came back to eke out a living on the land.

The federal work programs of the Great Depression brought new initiatives and talents to the region. The Civilian Conservation Corps (CCC), a federal program to train unemployed young men in work skills, had a strong presence. Working in national forests, CCC men built stone bridges along the road through Pisgah National Forest and erected picnic shelters and other outdoor facilities (cf. *Cliffside Lake), using the massive logs and hefty timbers typical of the CCC style developed nationally. Other CCC workers helped build the national Appalachian Trail through the region. In the Great Smoky Mountains National Park, CCC workers—as many as 4,300 in the 1930s—graded trails, built roads, erected visitor and administrative facilities, and undertook reforesting of cutover lands.

The most spectacular public works accomplishment of the era was the creation of the *Blue Ridge Parkway. Like the idea of the national park, the vision of a scenic highway along the Blue Ridge had originated years earlier. And like the national park, the idea had strong opponents as well as supporters, and its translation into reality was slow to come. In 1933 the first $4 million was directed to the building of the parkway as part of the national program to put men to work. Construction of the 469-mile scenic highway began in North Carolina in 1935, a longtime dream made possible by the need for public works projects; the last section was opened in 1987.

The Great Smoky Mountains National Park and the Blue Ridge Parkway stimulated tourism. By August 1939 nearly 170,000 people had visited the park, which was formally dedicated in 1940. The town of Cherokee, at a principal gateway to the park and a terminus of the parkway, successfully pursued tourist trade by appealing to national interest in Indian culture and crafts, and Cherokee leaders developed plans for a major tourist complex. Asheville, Waynesville, and other communities in the vicinity immediately added the park and the parkway to their campaigns to lure visitors and investors back to the Land of the Sky.

As the Great Depression eased, the threat of war in Europe worsened. Preparations for war engaged industrialists and political leaders. The demand for hydroelectric power to make aluminum for warplanes brought yet another overwhelming change to western North Carolina. Hydroelectric power dams had impounded rivers and flooded old riverbottom farmlands in several locations earlier in the century. The demands anticipated for the war, however, far exceeded what had come before. For several years Alcoa (the Aluminum Co. of America) had explored power sites on the Little Tennessee River. When war came, arrangements made between the federal Tennessee Valley Authority (TVA) and Alcoa quickly put prime power sites at *Hiwassee and *Fontana in TVA hands. Both dams were built in record time.

To create Fontana Dam and its lake, a bargain was struck among the state, TVA, and the National Park Service. A stretch of land along the north shore of the lake planned for the park—including the old lumbering town of Proctor and older farms along Hazel Creek—was finally acquired, and what was not flooded was brought into the park. After Fontana Dam was completed in 1944, the rising waters of the lake slowly covered the remains of farmsteads, railroads,

FIGURE 63. *Studies Building, Black Mountain College* (BN 105). *By the late 1930s and early 1940s, the Great Depression had begun to lift. As construction began again, a number of buildings reflected a modernist impulse emanating from Europe. At Black Mountain College, founded in 1933 in Buncombe Co., the modernist influence of the Bauhaus was especially strong. Through faculty member Josef Albers, Bauhaus architects Walter Gropius and Marcel Breuer, recent émigrés from Nazi Germany, were asked to design a main building. When it proved too costly, architect Lawrence Kocher was invited to design this simpler structure, which he and other faculty and students built in 1940–41.*

FIGURE 64. *Fontana Dam and Lake, Graham and Swain counties* (GH 6). *Thousands of workers laboring around the clock completed the huge concrete dam between Jan. 1, 1942, and Nov. 7, 1944. The dam is the highest in the eastern United States. The lake covers some 10,000 acres.*

FIGURE 65. *Linn Cove Viaduct, Blue Ridge Parkway, 1978–83; opened 1987, Avery Co.* (AV 4). *Completion of the Blue Ridge Parkway in 1987 and the often difficult construction of interstate highways (I-40 and I-26) and other thoroughfares through the region brought far-reaching changes in economic and settlement patterns.*

and lumber towns. When the war was over, Fontana's construction village was made into tourist accommodations.

THE LATE TWENTIETH CENTURY

In the last half of the twentieth century, western North Carolina has experienced great change, yet paradoxically its people have maintained and even heightened the sense of regional identity. Many of the patterns set in motion in the nineteenth century have persisted and expanded. The quest for prosperity, the emphasis on individual autonomy, the nurturance of community traditions, and the desire to protect natural beauty are sometimes in harmony, sometimes in conflict with one another.

In the years after World War II, western North Carolina leaders strove to generate economic growth. Much of the region suffered from unemployment, lack of educational and work opportunities, and out-migration. Economic and social problems that traced back to the nineteenth century were exacerbated by the Great Depression, and they were further compounded by mechanization of agriculture and manufacturing after World War II. Many western North Carolinians, like their fellow citizens in the east, believed that their region was neglected while the cities of the piedmont flourished, and some felt that national stereotypes of Appalachian culture hindered investment. Gradually, however, and with mixed results, much of the region has witnessed construction of highways and other public facilities, expansion of private and public colleges and schools, and new housing and businesses that have altered the landscape in nearly every section.

The monumental public works projects of the Great Depression and the succeeding preparation for World War II had a lasting impact. The electric power facilities created for wartime production provided abundant energy for urban and industrial development. The national forests, recreational lakes formed by the hydroelectric dams, the Great Smoky Mountains National Park, and the Blue Ridge Parkway added to the region's tourism potential. Local and regional promoters seized the opportunity to make the region a vacation destination for a nation of newly prosperous, automobile-owning families.

Promotion of tourism took many forms. Western North Carolina Associated Communities organized in 1946 to promote the economy in far western counties. Seeing the success of *The Lost Colony* at the coast, that group and the Cherokee Historical Association sponsored creation of *Unto These Hills*, an outdoor drama at Cherokee that traces the saga of the Cherokees and culminates in the heroic legend of Tsali, whose death permitted many to escape removal and remain at home. Drawing more than 5 million people since its first production in 1950, the drama appeals to residents as well as visitors, capturing the deep sense of the mountains as a place of sanctuary and escape. This was soon followed by re-creation of traditional Cherokee architecture at *Oconaluftee Indian Village and establishment of the *Museum of the Cherokee Indian and the *Boundary Tree Lodge and Tourist Motor Court. In the same period, *Horn in the West*, an outdoor drama of the pioneer experience, sponsored by the Southern Appalachian Historical Association, began its long run at Boone. Along the Blue Ridge Parkway and in the Great Smoky Mountains National Park, selected buildings were preserved and interpreted, and at various localities throughout the region, old houses and outbuildings were restored and interpreted as vestiges of the pioneer and small farmers' rapidly vanishing way of life.

These and other attractions vie for visitors' attention, from the lusty thrills of *Tweetsie Railroad's theme park celebration of steam railroading days to the dignified opulence of Biltmore Estate. The diversity of scenery has also attracted the filmmaking industry. Producers shot movies in the area from the 1920s onward, but the business has burgeoned in the later twentieth century, with the classic *Thunder Road* shot around Asheville, *The Swan* and *Being There* filmed at Biltmore, *The Last of the Mohicans* and *Dirty Dancing* shot around Chimney Rock, and *The Fugitive* featuring settings at Dillsboro and Bryson City.

FIGURE 66. *Clogging Dance Team, Smoky Mountain Folk Festival, at Haywood County Courthouse, Waynesville* (HW 1). *Folk festivals, including the Asheville-based Mountain Dance and Folk Festival begun in the late 1920s by Bascom Lamar Lunsford, offer a popular forum for old and new techniques and the transfer and development of traditions. Influenced by Lunsford and the festivals, dance traditions developed in new directions in the mid-20th c., including growing focus on team clogging.*

The preservation and promotion of folk traditions, begun around the turn of the century, have likewise expanded, and the traditions themselves have continued to evolve. The *John C. Campbell Folk School and *Penland School are nationally known arts and crafts centers. Numerous other centers and organizations focus on the heritage and the promotion of the region. Museums and galleries present a spectrum from traditional handicrafts to contemporary work by artists and craftspeople of every stripe. Music and dance traditions display great vitality. Music springing from British, African, and Native American roots has borne many branches, from the continuation of old tunes at festivals and among friends and families to the ebullient expression of contemporary life in country music and bluegrass music popularized on radio and television.[15]

Outdoor recreation is a booming business. Familiar pursuits such as hiking and fishing or quiet times in mountain retreats, along with the newly popular rafting and white-water canoeing, have attracted growing numbers to parks and private recreational sites. In the late twentieth century, development of snow-making technology spawned a new business in winter ski resorts, and by the 1980s as many as seven ski slopes were in regular operation.

Tourist accommodations have sprouted from long-established roots. To attract the automobile-driving public, motels along the highways have all but sup-

15. See Williams, *Great Smoky Mountains Folklife*, 33–90.

FIGURE 67. *Richmond Hill, Asheville* (BN 82). *The endangered residence was rescued from demolition in 1984 through combined efforts of the Preservation Society of Asheville and Buncombe Co., Preservation North Carolina, and the National Trust for Historic Preservation. Historic buildings in the region, including private residences, local museums, public buildings, and a great many renewed as inns, such as Richmond Hill, have been preserved through private and public efforts.*

planted the downtown hotels. Succeeding the boardinghouse tradition is the widely popular bed and breakfast inn. Building on traditions of healing from mineral springs and salubrious mountain air, scores of new health and renewal enterprises call the region home. Confirming late nineteenth-century promoters' claim of the region's all-season charms, many resort communities have been transformed from primarily summer retreats to year-round homes. The most pleasant areas of the region have drawn thousands of retirees, as well as Floridians and others building second homes, sometimes in isolated enclaves, sometimes in large new subdivisions. After a long period of relative stagnation in the mid-twentieth century, Asheville has blossomed from the combined effects of tourism, recreation, and arts, with its population approaching 70,000—the size its early twentieth-century boosters envisioned it would reach by 1950.

In industry and agriculture, the story is somewhat different. Some long-established industries continue their importance, including the granite quarry at Mount Airy and the paper plant at Canton, though the latter was announced for sale in 1997 and its future is uncertain. Furniture manufacturing and some of the textile mills still operate in the foothills. Other industries have all but vanished; iron and copper mines have shut down, and tanneries and sawmills are

FIGURE 68. *Museum of the Cherokee Indian, Cherokee* (SW 9); *Six Associates, 1976. The award-winning design is one of several examples of regional modernism built in western N.C. in the later 20th c. Six Associates, an Asheville practice formed by six local architects to qualify for wartime projects, developed into an important modernist design firm in the region, as did the office of J. Bertram King, a graduate of the School of Design at present-day North Carolina State University. (See *Warren Wilson College Chapel* [BN 103].*)*

long gone. The often unpredictable opening and closing of manufacturing plants brings wrenching local booms and busts. New operations have sprung up along the highways and in the old floodplains, with Lowe's Companies, which began as a hardware business in North Wilkesboro, mushrooming into the nation's largest retail building supplier in the mid-twentieth century.

As in most of the state and the nation, agriculture has been transformed by changing markets and methods. The labor-intensive family farm is no longer the vital economic unit it once was, and forest has reclaimed many of the slopes once tilled as marginal farmland. Yet the family farm remains a beloved social unit, as thousands of families continue to live on farms while holding outside jobs that allow them to raise a small crop and maintain ties to the land and community. More than in many areas, relatively small farms persist, with tobacco growing, dairying, poultry production, and apple orchards prime sources of income. In the late twentieth century, western North Carolina has developed into the nation's second highest producer of Christmas trees, specializing in the Fraser fir that grows on the cool slopes.

The architecture of the region embodies both the growing standardization of building nationwide and some sense of regional expression. Dozens of new schools, public facilities, office buildings, and manufacturing plants have generally adhered to standard, modernist models. Most of the small log, boxed, or frame dwellings of the early twentieth century have been enlarged for continued use or succeeded by modest new dwellings or, in many sections, the ubiquitous mobile home. Suburban growth and, in the late twentieth century, construction of a new breed of immense, eclectic residences have repeated trends seen throughout the state.

The regionalist architectural impulse that emerged early in the century has gained new dimensions. The idea of the mountains as a wilderness retreat and the appeal of its log building traditions have inspired various handcrafted building forms, environmentally adapted projects, and back-to-the earth, do-it-yourself architecture. Indeed, in 1974 *Mother Earth News* located its headquarters in Hendersonville and built several experimental houses in the area as research models for the alternative journal's 1.2 million national circulation.[16]

Conscious regionalism informs more substantial architecture as well. Several architectural firms rendered late twentieth-century designs in native materials, chiefly natural woods and roughly textured stonework, often in buildings whose forms emphasize their dramatic sites. While some of the finest works are private retreats, others, such as the *Museum of the Cherokee Indian and *Warren Wilson College, have a strong public presence.

At the turn of the twenty-first century, western North Carolina faces ever greater pressures of change, coupled with lasting devotion to old identities. Highway construction—including I-40 in the 1960s and early 1970s and I-26 from Asheville to South Carolina in 1977—has opened nearly every section to travel and development. More is on the way, including I-26 from Asheville northward to Tennessee. Roads, factories, and businesses fill the river valleys, and farmland and meadows are transformed overnight. Tourism, recreation, and retirement homes spread subdivisions around old resort villages and county seats. The tide of out-migration has turned. Yet the pursuit of the tourist dollar is countered by those who question its proliferation of low-paying service jobs and the disparity between well-heeled newcomers and economically struggling natives. Old conflicts between economic growth and preservation of the environment persist. Some fear that pollution and unregulated development will kill the golden goose of the region's natural beauty. Others resist any perceived infringement on individual property rights; only two counties in the region, for example, have countywide zoning.

In many arenas the vitality and complexity of the region's culture gains vibrant expression, strengthened by the very pressures of change. Music and dance, art and literature, and religion, politics, and family life cover a spectrum from experimental to deeply conservative, with a broad and resilient stretch in between of those who continue to balance old ways and new. The literature of the region has gained national attention, including the novels of Wilma Dykeman and John Ehle and, most recently, the poetry and novels of state poet laureate Fred Chappell and Charles Frazier's bestselling novel, *Cold Mountain*.

16. Bishir, Brown, Lounsbury, and Wood, *Architects and Builders in North Carolina*, 372–73.

For residents and visitors, western North Carolina has changed in ways that make it a place far different from what it was a few decades ago. The old ways of life observed by the social improvers and anthropologists of the early twentieth century have all but disappeared, though problems of poverty and unemployment persist. The forest has reclaimed many mountainside farms and left little evidence of the immense but short-lived logging operations. Multilane highways bring long-remote areas into easy reach. Yet beneath the changes, deeper continuities persist in the powerful, complex attachment of the people to old identities and traditions, and above all to the place itself—a land at once challenging and protecting, resilient and fragile, and overwhelmingly beautiful.

The Blue Ridge Parkway

Extending through or touching the borders of seventeen western North Carolina counties, the Blue Ridge Parkway is one of America's greatest public works achievements and most popular scenic attractions. For many visitors to the region, the parkway shapes their initial impression of the landscape and culture of the place. Construction of the 469-mile mountain highway connecting Shenandoah National Park in Virginia and the Great Smoky Mountains National Park in North Carolina commenced in 1935 and was not fully completed until the Linn Cove Viaduct opened at Grandfather Mountain, N.C., in 1987. The long construction history of the road and the consistently high quality of its landscape and engineering design reflect the enduring vision of its early promoters and planners and an unbroken commitment to a long-range public objective rarely seen in American political life.

The Blue Ridge is the long diagonal crest of the mountains through North Carolina and Virginia that forms part of the Eastern Continental Divide. Views from the highest points along the rim of this great natural barrier are often breathtaking, with long vistas down into the piedmont to the east, and panoramas over seemingly endless waves of ridges to the west. The idea of a highway along part of the Blue Ridge was promoted without success as early as 1909 and again in 1930, but it finally took root within New Deal programs in the midst of the Great Depression. Key political figures in Virginia, North Carolina, and Tennessee teamed with officials of the Roosevelt administration to promote the concept, and the National Industrial Recovery Act of June 18, 1933, authorized the project. Key to its early support was the national mandate to put the unemployed to work in public projects. Construction began in North Carolina around Cumberland Knob near the Virginia border on September 11, 1935.

The undertaking was not without controversy. Tennessee vied with North Carolina over the route to be followed south of Virginia until Secretary of the Interior Harold L. Ickes ruled in favor of North Carolina. The federal and state governments debated who should pay for the road, finally reaching a compromise whereby the states would acquire the right-of-way and the federal government would build the road. Some landowners objected, and for a time Cherokee leaders resisted construction through the reservation in Swain County. There was also criticism among those who stood in general opposition to New Deal programs. In 1937 a congressman from Ohio called the project "the most gigantic and stupendously extravagant and unreasonable expenditure made by the most extravagantly expensive administration in the history of the world." Despite such political antagonism and skirmishes over right-of-way, work proceeded.

The character of the road owes much to combined efforts of the Bureau of

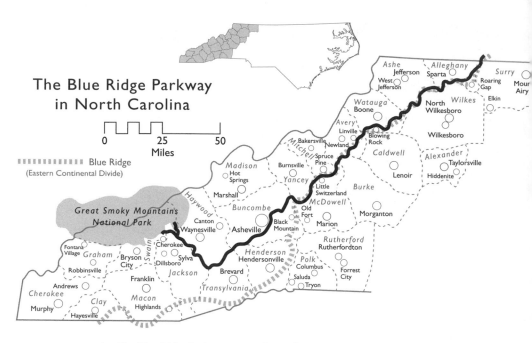

FIGURE 69. *The Blue Ridge Parkway in North Carolina*

Public Roads, the National Park Service, and the state's chief locating engineer, R. Getty Browning. The Park Service team was led by Stanley W. Abbott, landscape architect associated with the parkway from 1934 to 1948. Abbott, who had apprenticed with the Westchester County, N.Y., parks program in the design of a successful parkway and landscape along the previously despoiled Bronx River, articulated the parkway's purpose "to please by revealing the charm and interest of the native American countryside." He worked as an artist in a medium of "fields and fences, lakes and streams, and hills and valleys" and compared the task of designing and building the parkway to painting with "a ten-league canvas and a brush of a comet's tail."

Abbott recognized that too little variation, even in majestic scenery, could be monotonous, and thus he sought and achieved modulation and contrast in roadway placement. The route is one of constantly changing settings, scales, and visual experiences. The traveler passes along a rocky ridgetop with heartstopping vistas, through a cool dark tunnel, down a shady glen to open bottomland, and across rolling pasture. Abbott and his associates took a sculptural approach to the design, drawing on "insight into what is the main contour" of a particular landform, and the engineering is often so gently done as to be scarcely noticeable. Much of the right-of-way had been scarred by decades of clear-cut logging and heavy erosion, and conservation measures and new plantings helped reclaim natural beauty along the roadside. The planners extended

FIGURE 70. *The Parkway crossing NC 80 at Buck Creek Gap, Yancey County, with Mount Mitchell on the horizon*

their control beyond the 100-foot right-of-way through a combination of outright purchases and scenic easements, in some cases leasing the land back to farmers to bring fences, crops, and livestock right up to the roadway and creating a seamless blend of features in the landscape. In addition, strategically placed wayside parks and scenic overlooks provided what Abbott called "the rare gems in the necklace."

Though the region offered great natural beauty, it had long been settled and was not a wilderness. Unlike earlier scenic parkway projects that obliterated signs of previous habitation, the Blue Ridge Parkway incorporated at least selected aspects of regional culture into the traveler's experience. Sites such as the *Brinegar House in Alleghany County and several in Virginia were restored as principal attractions along the drive. However, buildings that did not fit a theme of rustic mountain culture were usually either removed or screened. Consequently the once prevalent late-nineteenth- and early twentieth-century weatherboarded wood frame houses with simple Victorian ornament, such as the *John Jackson Miller House in Alleghany County, are rare sights along the parkway. After *Flat Top Manor, the mountain estate of Greensboro industrialist Moses Cone, was transferred to the Park Service in 1949, the Colonial Revival manor house was adapted as a pioneer museum and crafts center, and all but a few outbuildings were removed.

An extraordinary sense of composition unifies the parkway, from the greatest panoramas to the smallest details. The rock masonry work is especially notable.

Italian and Spanish masons, including a contingent of 150 Spanish workers supervised by Joe Troitino, and many local men, including several Waldensian stonemasons from Valdese, worked locally quarried stone into handsome facings for the great arched concrete bridges, tunnel portals, and retaining walls.

Construction was initiated at unconnected locations along the route, both as a strategy for ensuring eventual completion and to provide jobs where they were most needed. Five Civilian Conservation Corps (CCC) camps were assigned to the project, and other work relief programs participated as well. Workers with the CCC did not do the heavy construction, which was let out on contract, but followed behind the rough engineering with the painstaking landscape work. About half of the route through the two states was open by 1942, when funds and labor were diverted to the war effort. Work resumed slowly after the war, with Abbott's successors, including Edward H. Abbuehl, Arthur H. Beyer, and Robert A. Hope, continuing in the spirit of his formative vision.

By 1967 all of the road was completed except a 7.5-mile section around *Grandfather Mountain in Avery Co., where work was held up for several years over disagreements with the landowner about the route and its effect on the fragile mountainside. The eventual solution was the *Linn Cove Viaduct, a 1,243-foot, double-s-shaped concrete ribbon composed of 153 precast segments and mounted on concrete pylons to minimize cuts into the hillside (see Introduction, Fig. 65). Inspired by similar roadways in postwar Alpine Europe, it was the first of its kind in the United States. Opened in 1987, the viaduct provided a graceful conclusion to a half-century of dedication to a grand idea. See Harley Jolley, *Painting with a Comet's Tail: The Touch of the Landscape Architect on the Blue Ridge Parkway* (1987) and *The Blue Ridge Parkway* (1969, 1977).

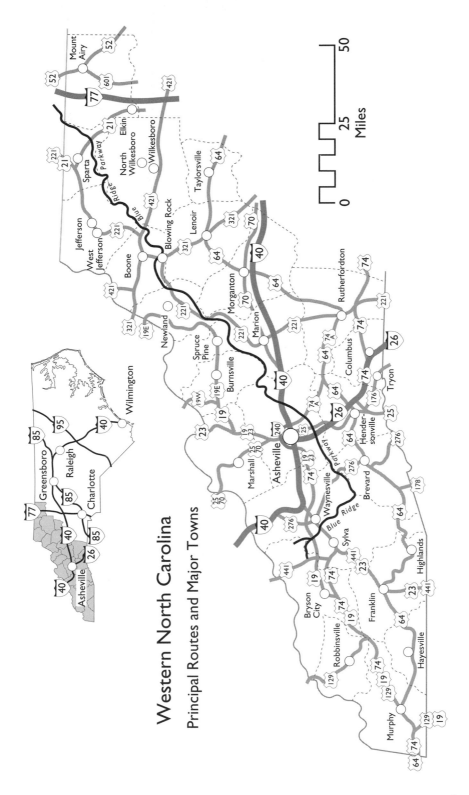

Western North Carolina
Principal Routes and Major Towns

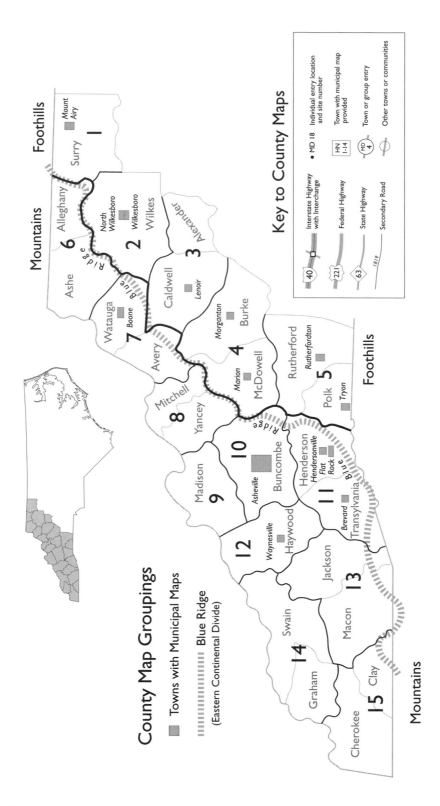

County Map Groupings

■ Towns with Municipal Maps

▨ Blue Ridge
(Eastern Continental Divide)

Key to County Maps

● MD 18   Individual entry location and site number

[HN 1-14]   Town with municipal map provided

(MD 4)   Town or group entry

◯   Other towns or communities

🛣 40   Interstate Highway with Interchange

221   Federal Highway

63   State Highway

1819   Secondary Road

Foothills

Mountains

Surry — 1 — *Mount Airy*

Alleghany

Ashe

6 — North Wilkesboro / *Wilkesboro*
Wilkes — 2

Alexander — 3

Watauga — 7 — *Boone*
Blue Ridge

Caldwell — *Lenoir*

Burke — *Morganton*

Avery

Mitchell — 8

Yancey

McDowell — 4 — *Marion*

Rutherford — *Rutherfordton*

Polk — 5 — *Tryon*

Foothills

Madison — 9

Buncombe — 10 — *Asheville*

Blue Ridge

Henderson — 11 — *Hendersonville / Flat Rock*

Transylvania — *Brevard*

Haywood — 12 — *Waynesville*

Jackson

Swain — 14

Graham

Macon — 13

Clay

Cherokee — 15

Mountains

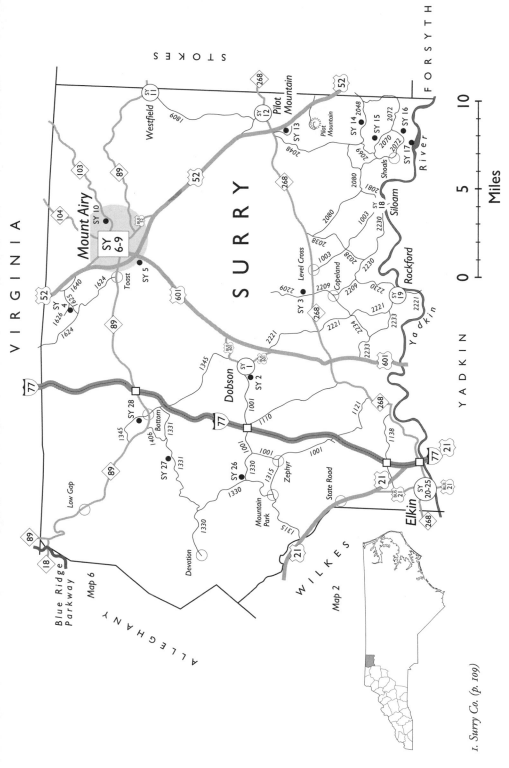

1. *Surry Co. (p. 109)*

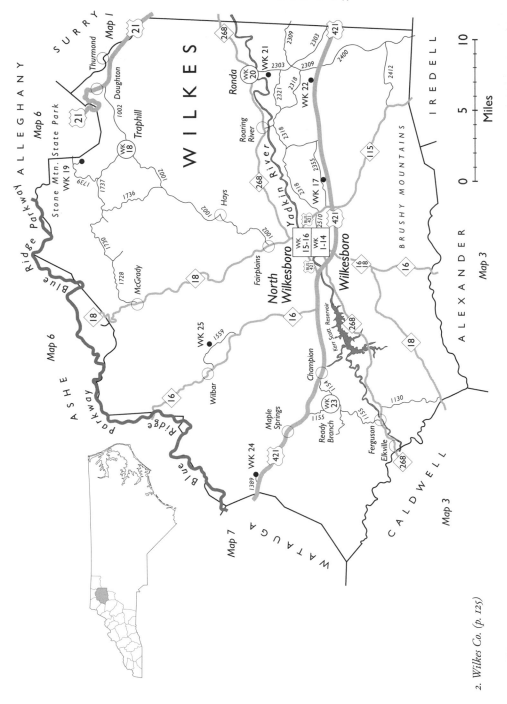

2. *Wilkes Co. (p. 125)*

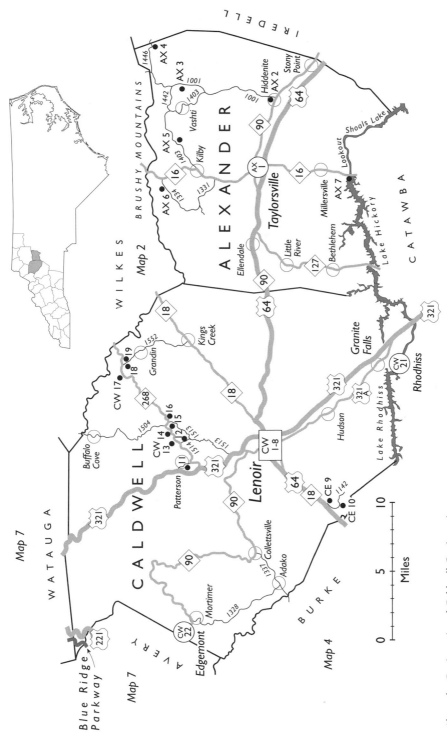

3. Alexander Co. (p. 136) and Caldwell Co. (p. 139)

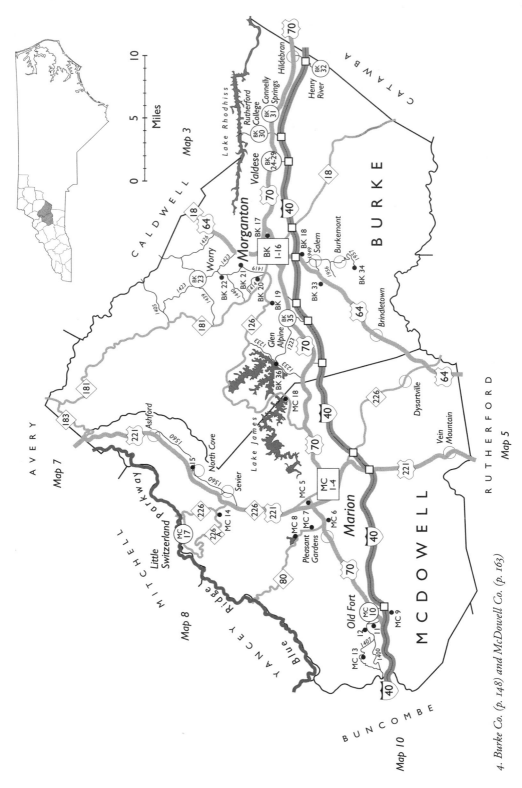

4. *Burke Co. (p. 148) and McDowell Co. (p. 163)*

Map 3

Miles

0   5   10

CALDWELL

BURKE

CATAWBA

Lake Rhodhiss

Hildebran

Connelly Springs   BK 32
Henry River

Rutherford College   BK 30
BK 31

Valdese   BK 24-29

Morganton

70

40

18

BK 17

BK 1-16   BK 18
Salem   Burkemont
1949   1951
1956   BK 34
BK 33

Worry   BK 21
BK 22   1419
1474
BK 20

BK 23   1423
1474

1426   1423   1639

64
18

181

126

Glen Alpine   BK 35
1233   70
1223
BK 36   1233

64   Brindletown

Brindletown

226   Dysartville   64

RUTHERFORD

Map 5

Vein Mountain

MC 18

181

AVERY

Map 7

183

221   Ashford

North Cove   1560
1551   Sevier   15
1551

MITCHELL   Little Switzerland   PARKWAY

MC 17   226
226 A   MC 14   226   221
80

YANCEY   Ridge

Blue   Ridge

Map 8

Lake James

MC 5
MC 8   MC 7   MC 6
Pleasant Gardens

MC 1-4

Marion

40   221
70

40

Old Fort   MC 10   MC 9
12
MC 13   11
1407   1400
70

40

MCDOWELL

BUNCOMBE

Map 10

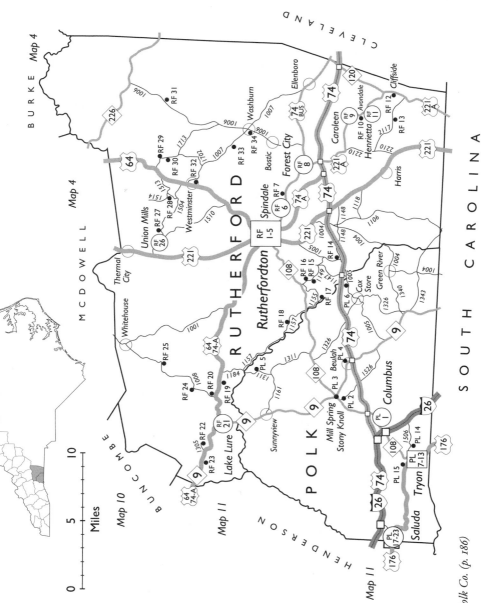

BURKE Map 4

CLEVELAND

BURKE Map 4

9001

RF 31

226

Washburn

9001

1007

Ellenboro

74 BUS

74

120

Cliffside

Caroleen

RF 9

Avondale

RF 10

RF 12

221

9001

RF 34

Henrietta

RF 11

RF 13

Map 4

64

RF 29

RF 30

713

RF 33

1702

1007

Bostic

Forest City

2117

RF 32

1707

RF 28

1504

1514

1510

RF 27

Westminster

RF 8

221 A

2210

Harris

2210

221

M
C
D
O
W
E
L
L

Map 4

Union Mills

RF 26

221

RF 7

74 A

6

74

148

1118

9011

Thermal City

Spindale

Rutherfordton

RF 1-5

221

1004

1148

Whitehouse

108

RF 16

RF 15

RF 14

1005

1148

1004

RF 25

RF 17

1155

1117

1005

Green River

1004

RF 18

PL 6

Cox Store

1340

1343

64 74-A

1001

1157

1326

1326

9

RF 24

1008

RF 19

RF 20

1184

1157

PL 5

1311

108

PL 4

Beulah

74

1526

1005

RF 23

RF 22

1305

RF 21

9

9

1161

PL 3

PL 2

Columbus

26

Lake Lure

Sunnyview

Mill Spring

Stony Knoll

PL 1

108

PL 14

176

64 74-A

9

PL 15

1506

PL 7-13

Tryon

26

74

Saluda

PL 17-23

176

Map 11

Map 11

B
U
N
C
O
M
B
E

H
E
N
D
E
R
S
O
N

S
O
U
T
H

C
A
R
O
L
I
N
A

Miles

0   5   10

R U T H E R F O R D

P O L K

Map 10

5. *Rutherford Co. (p. 173) and Polk Co. (p. 186)*

95

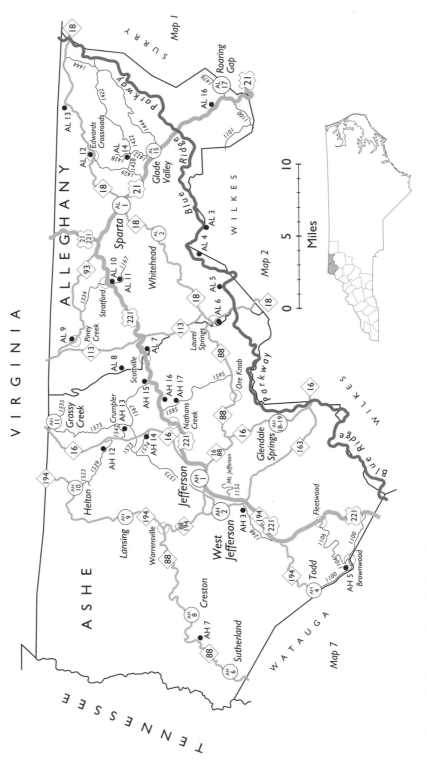

6. *Allegheny Co. (p. 197) and Ashe Co. (p. 202)*

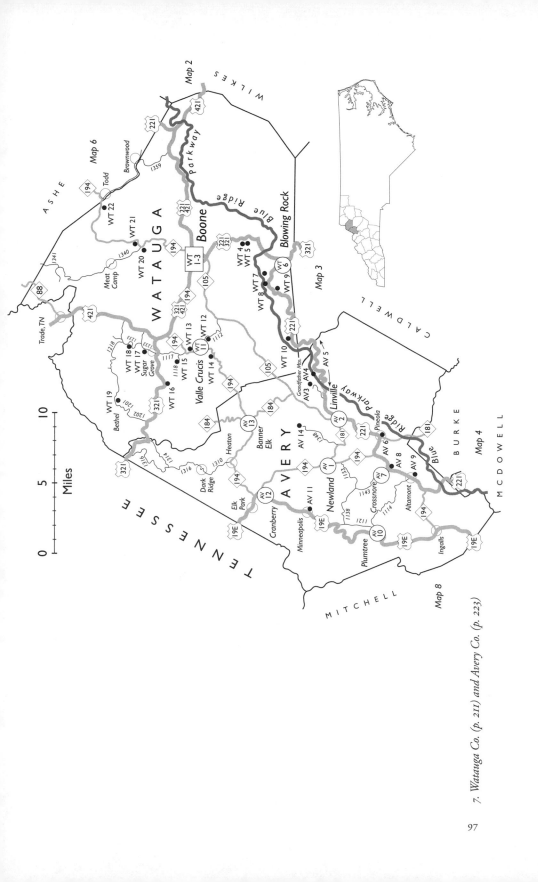

7. *Watauga Co. (p. 211) and Avery Co. (p. 223)*

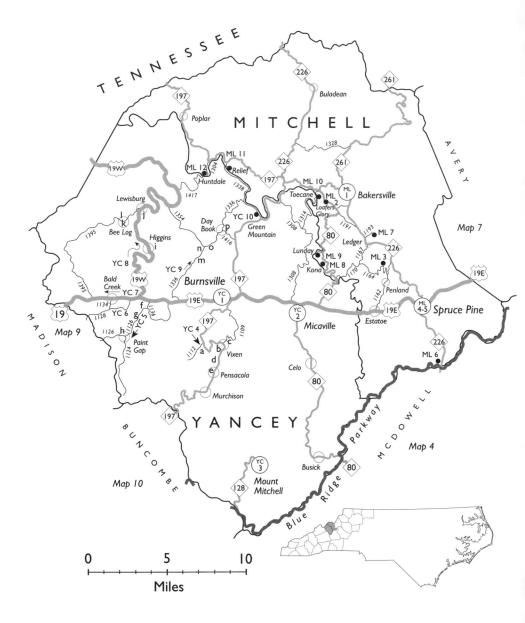

8. Mitchell Co. (p. 232) and Yancey Co. (p. 239)

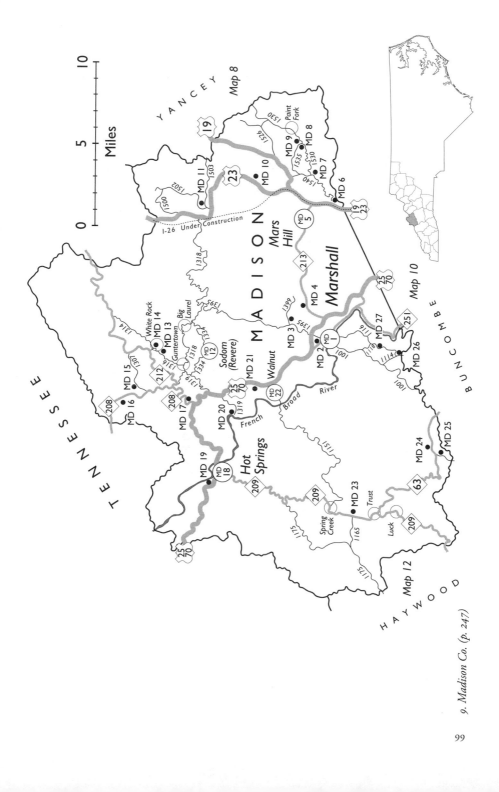

9. Madison Co. (p. 247)

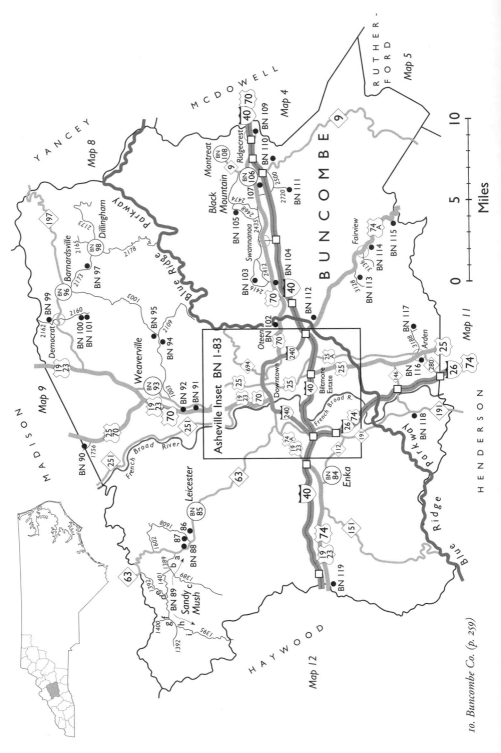

10. Buncombe Co. (p. 259)

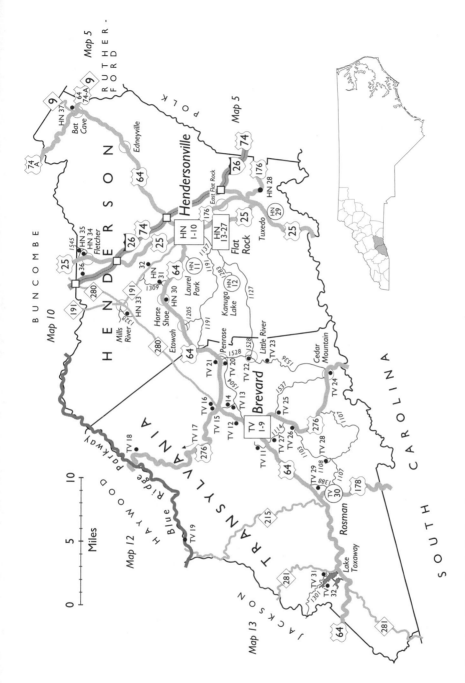

11. Henderson Co. (p. 310) and Transylvania Co. (p. 325)

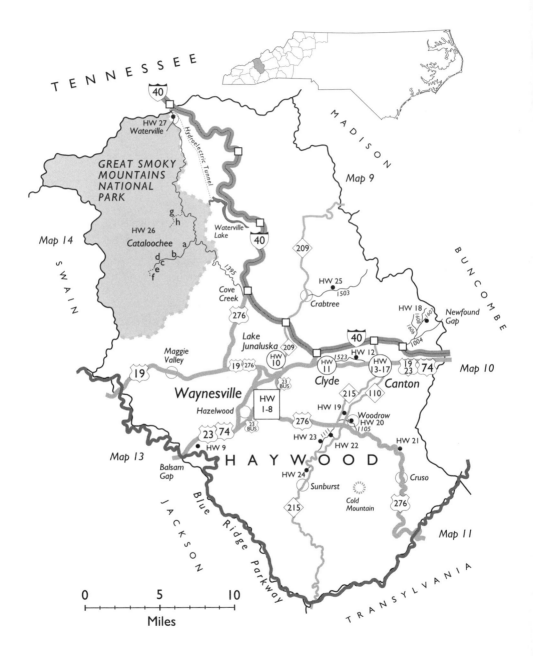

12. *Haywood Co. (p. 339)*

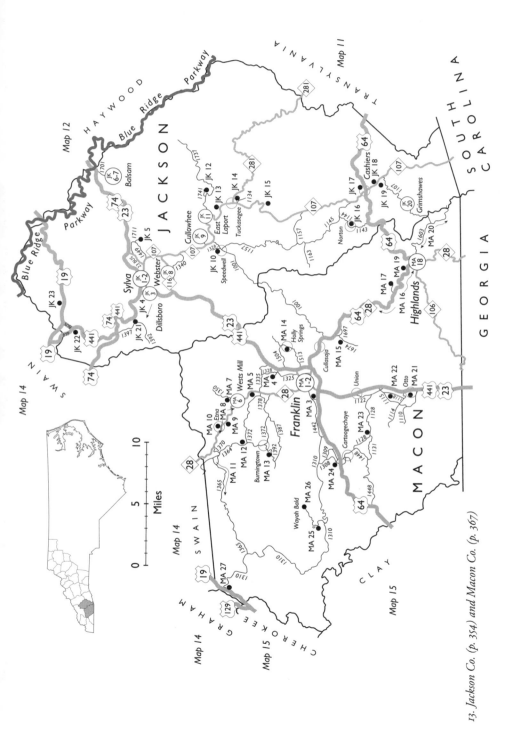

13. *Jackson Co. (p. 354) and Macon Co. (p. 367)*

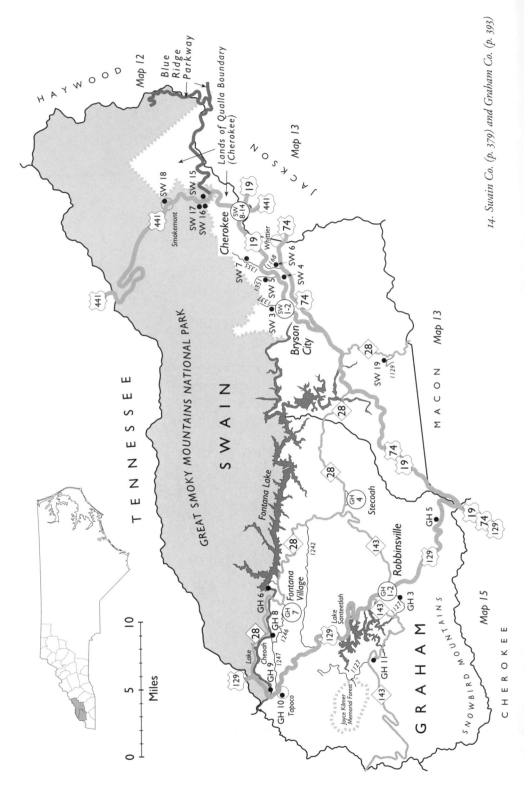

14. Swain Co. (p. 379) and Graham Co. (p. 393)

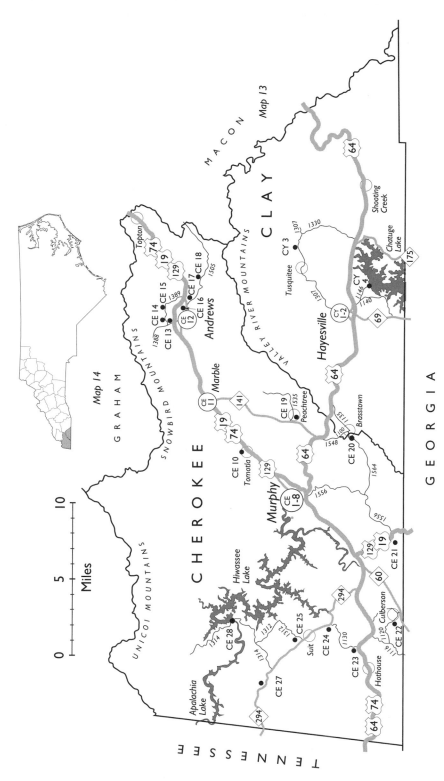

15. *Clay Co. (p. 401) and Cherokee Co. (p. 403)*

Foothills

Surry County (SY)

All across Surry County the Blue Ridge presides over the western and northern horizons. To the southeast the monadnock-like form of Pilot Mountain, an isolated remnant of an ancient and eroded mountain range, stands like a sentinel, visible across much of the county (18th-c. maps called it Mount Ararat, for the biblical mountain where Noah's ark came to rest after the flood). Between these eminences the rolling land is drained by the south-flowing Mitchell, Fisher, and Ararat rivers into the Yadkin River, which meanders along Surry's southern boundary. The county was settled from the mid-18th c. by settlers of mostly English and German descent who established small farms that characterized the economy for much of the county's history. By the late 18th and early 19th centuries a few planters were sufficiently prosperous to build substantial frame or brick houses, some of which display fine examples of an interior decorative painting tradition seen across the county and region. Log tobacco barns are still common, and a distinctive collection of double-crib log livestock barns is found in the southeastern quadrant of the county.

Early efforts to improve navigation along the upper Yadkin River were not successful; but the arrival of railroads in the late 19th c. opened the county to commerce, and manufacturing enterprises soon flourished at Mount Airy and Elkin. Both towns feature exceptionally good late 19th- and early 20th-c. domestic and commercial architecture, with a distinctive collection of stone buildings in Mount Airy fashioned from granite quarried nearby.

SY 1 Dobson

The centrally located county seat was established when Surry Co. was divided in 1850 to create Yadkin Co. (see Rockford) and named for a family long prominent in the county's public affairs. It flourished briefly as a local government and trading center but was bypassed by railroads at the end of the century and remained a village. Modern commercial development obliterated most of the 19th-c. buildings that once stood near the courthouse square. The **Surry County Court-house** (1916; Harry Barton [Greensboro] and R. James Hughes, architects) is a tan brick Neoclassical Revival building employing elements found in architect Barton's later Guilford, Johnston, and Cumberland county courthouses. Built to replace a simple Greek Revival courthouse of the 1850s, the 3-story building has front and rear entrances framed by massive pilasters; it was enlarged in 1971 with matching 2-story wings.

The best-preserved 19th-c. house in town is the **Alexander Hamilton Freeman House** (ca. 1870; 321 S. Main St.), a 2-story frame dwelling with a triplet of Gothic Revival-inspired gables across the facade, otherwise finished with Greek Revival details; it was built for farmer and longtime clerk of court Freeman and his wife Elizabeth.

SY 2 Cave Family Farm Tobacco Barns
Early 20th c.; S side SR 1001 (Kapp St.), 1.0 mi. W of the courthouse square, Dobson

Surry Co. marks the southwestern corner of the Old Tobacco Belt, a region extending

SY 1 *Surry Co. Courthouse*

SY 2 *Cave Family Farm Tobacco Barns*

across the northern piedmont of N.C. and Virginia where tobacco has been cultivated since the 18th c. Log and frame flue-cure tobacco barns are still a familiar sight across much of the county (tobacco grown elsewhere in western N.C. is burley tobacco, an air-cured leaf). Modern bulk curing systems have rendered the barns obsolete, and few, if any, are still used in production. Located only a mile from the courthouse square in Dobson, the complex of log and frame barns on the Cave Farm is one of the largest assemblages of traditional tobacco barns remaining in the Old Belt. The 15 barns, each with a deep lean-to shed, are laid out in two staggered rows alongside a farm road adjacent to the dark clay field, creating a strong rhythm across the landscape.

SY 3 Isaac and Satney Copeland House

Late 18th c.; E side SR 2209, 0.8 mi. N of NC 268, Copeland vic.; private, visible from road

The 2-story timber-framed house is one of the oldest in the county, built as the seat of the 800-acre farm of Isaac Copeland, namesake of the nearby Copeland community. Though modified over the generations, the house retains the distinctive vertical massing and big double-shouldered gable-end chimneys that characterize the most substantial houses of the period (cf. *Edwards-Franklin House). Outbuildings include a double-crib log barn, a form common across the south-

east quadrant of the county, and a stone springhouse.

SY 4 William Carter House

1834; S side SR 1626, 0.3 mi. W of SR 1625, Mount Airy vic.; private, visible from road

The oldest surviving brick house in the county is a compact, 2-story house of common-bond brick with late Federal style finish and a 1-story 20th-c. frame kitchen ell. Though the exterior door centered on the second story of the front wall suggests that there was once a 2-story porch, there is no physical evidence that such a porch existed. The house enjoys a commanding view above the bottomlands of Pauls Creek, where William Carter (d. 1840) farmed 800 acres. Later owned by four generations of the Miller family, it has been restored by the current owners.

SY 4 *William Carter House*

SY 5 Chang and Adelaide Bunker House (Hollyview Farm)

Ca. 1857; NW side US 601, 0.75 mi. SW of US 52 BYP, Mount Airy vic.; private, visible at a distance from road

Chang and Eng Bunker were "the original Siamese twins," whose nationality became the name for twins joined at birth. The two were physically normal except for a band of pliable flesh that connected them at the chest but allowed relative freedom of movement. Born in 1811 in Siam (now Thailand), they were brought to America in 1829 by a New England sea captain. They embarked on a successful touring career in the U.S. and Europe, working for a time with P. T. Barnum but later managing their own road show and becoming comfortably wealthy. In 1837 the twins appeared in Wilkesboro and, finding the region to their liking, retired to the section about 1840 and opened a store at *Traphill. There they met and married two Yates sisters; Chang and his wife, Adelaide, eventually had twelve children, and Eng and Sarah had ten. In 1846 they bought a tract near Mount Airy and built separate houses less than a mile apart. The twins alternated visits with their wives and families at three-day intervals. The Civil War ruined them financially, and they resumed touring after the war. The twins died in 1874. Their families prospered and multiplied, and they have as many as 1,000 descendants across the U.S.

Chang and Adelaide's house is a 2-story, 5-bay, frame farmhouse with a low-pitched gable roof, brick end chimneys, an original 2-story rear ell, and simple Greek Revival finish. The 1-story porch with an enclosed sun room on the second floor replaced the original pedimented entrance porch. The well-tended house occupies a shady knoll above the broad bottomlands of Stewarts Creek, with a complement of later barns and other outbuildings.

Eng and Sarah Bunker's house burned in 1956, but the **Eng Bunker Corncrib** (SE side US 601, 1.3 mi. S of US 52 BYP), a half-dovetailed log building with a cantilevered front gable, remains visible across the highway just south of Chang's place.

Mount Airy (SY 6–9)

Mount Airy is a lively small city with diverse industrial, commercial, residential, and institutional architecture. It is known as "Granite City" for its many buildings fashioned from the pale and beautiful granite from the nearby *North Carolina Granite Corporation quarry. Although Mount Airy lays claim to being the model for the fictional "Mayberry" in the classic television series *The Andy Griffith Show*—whose star was born and raised in the town—the TV image of a quiet southern village does not do full justice to its more dynamic history and character.

Settlement began by the mid-18th c. in the area known as "the Hollows" at the foot of the Blue Ridge. The community that grew up between Lovills Creek and the Ararat River on the road from Salem to Virginia apparently took the name of Mount Airy from an early plantation on the site. With about 500 people in 1880, it was described as "long a thriving village and the trade centre of a large and prosperous agricultural community."

The town blossomed through the mid-1880s as the Cape Fear & Yadkin Valley Railway made its approach from the distant port of Wilmington via Fayetteville and Greensboro. A railroad publication of 1889 claimed that as rails neared the town, "mercantile business straightway received a forward impetus; building lots were in eager demand . . . ; the tools of the architect and artisan were plied without ceasing; hotel accommodations were enlarged and improved." At "the railway celebration of June 20th, 1888, assembled thousands of visitors to behold a goodly flourishing town, with regular thoroughfares, handsome residences and blocks of commodious stores." Tobacco, textile, and furniture manufacturing thrived, and rail access to markets encouraged the opening of the quarry at the nearby granite deposit.

The town follows an irregular grid plan laid out over the rise between the river and the creek, with the commercial district centered on Main St., residential areas to the south and north, and industrial facilities concentrated on the west side of town near the railroad and Lovills Creek.

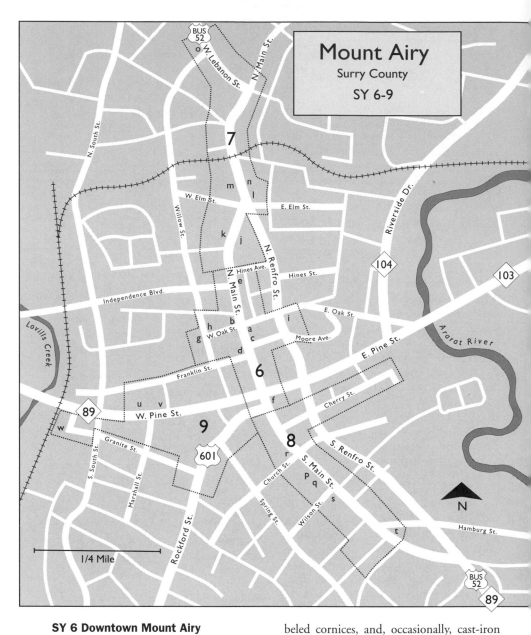

Mount Airy
Surry County
SY 6-9

SY 6 Downtown Mount Airy

In an era when strip malls have siphoned off business from many small-town centers, Mount Airy's downtown maintains an unusual degree of commercial vigor. The architecture dates primarily from the 1892–1920 period, with intact rows of 2- and 3-story buildings of brick or granite, their upper stories largely unaltered. Many feature round or segmental-arched windows, cor-

beled cornices, and, occasionally, cast-iron or pressed-metal details, such as the former **Midkiff Hardware Store** (ca. 1910; SE corner Main and Oak Sts.) (**a**) and the **Merritt Building** (ca. 1910; NW corner N. Main and Oak Sts.) (**b**).

Impressive commercial buildings in granite include the former **First National Bank** (1893, ca. 1915; NE corner N. Main St. and Moore Ave.) (**c**), with exceptionally rich texture in the rusticated granite veneer, and the

SY 6 *Bank of Mount Airy and N. Main St.*

SY 6 *William Alfred Moore House and Gazebo*

former **Bank of Mount Airy** (1923; NW corner N. Main and Franklin Sts.) (**d**), with a recessed entrance framed by monumental Tuscan columns.

At the northern edge of the district the Gothic Revival **Trinity Episcopal Church** (1896; J. A. Tesh, builder; E side N. Main St.) (**e**) was the first building in Mount Airy to be constructed primarily of the native granite. According to tradition, it was designed by Frank Woodruff, son of the founder of the *North Carolina Granite Corporation; builder Tesh worked at the quarry and in time erected several other

SY 6 *Sparger Brothers Tobacco Co.*

granite buildings in town. On the southern end of the district one of the last uses of the locally quarried material is seen in the **U.S. Post Office** (1932; George R. Berryman, architect; SE corner S. Main and Pine Sts.) (**f**), a streamlined version of Neoclassicism typical of public works projects of the 1930s.

In the industrial district west of Main St. stand brick buildings associated with the turn-of-the-century tobacco industry. Though the original firms were soon forced out of business by the powerful Duke and Reynolds tobacco companies, the buildings have remained in use by other industries. Two on the west side of Willow St. built for the **Sparger Brothers Tobacco Co.** (1891; W side Willow St. at Oak St.) (**g**) are 3- and 4-story brick structures with stepped parapet gables and segmental-arched doors and windows with hood molds. The **R. Roberts Leaf Tobacco House** (1891; NE corner Willow and Oak Sts.) (**h**) is of similar parapeted form, standing 4 stories, and the only one of the group that remains unpainted.

On the eastern side of the district is the **William Alfred Moore House** (ca. 1862, early 20th c.; 200 Moore Ave.; open by appointment) (**i**), a 2-story frame house with center facade gable and 1-story, hip-roofed porch maintained as a local house museum. In the yard stands a remarkable survival of 19th-c. romanticism, a hexagonal rustic summerhouse or gazebo covered with intertwining laurel roots. The form was probably inspired by a sketch published by A. J. Downing. An early 20th-c. postcard of a nearby mineral springs resort shows a similar gazebo, suggesting this one was copied from it or even rebuilt from it after the resort closed.

SY 7 North Main Street

The principal residential section lies north of the downtown along N. Main St. and connecting side streets. Frame, brick, and granite structures provide a rich visual texture in variations of the Queen Anne, Colonial Revival, Shingle, Romanesque Revival, Tudor, and later styles. The **William Edward Merritt House** (1901; J. A. Tesh, builder; 618 N. Main St.) (**j**), home of a

brickyard owner, is a 2-story, late Victorian brick structure with corner tower, granite trim, and wraparound porch. Across the street and equally expressive of its ownership, the **John D. Sargent House** (1919; 619 N. Main St.) (**k**) is a remarkable 1½-story bungalow with Tudor detailing, built of granite suitable to the owner's role as head of the *North Carolina Granite Corporation for a quarter of a century.

A block north is the **Gertrude Smith House** (1907; 708 N. Main St.; open by appointment, Mount Airy Visitors' Center) (**l**), a large frame house combining late Victorian and Colonial Revival detail, now operated as a local museum. The asymmetrical, Italianate-style **Thomas Woodruff House** (l. 19th c.; 715 N Main St.) (**m**) was built for the first developer of the granite quarry; its paneled pilasters and picturesque window hoods are features that recur elsewhere in the area. The monumental **First Baptist Church** (1906–12; W. C. Stepp, contractor; 714 N. Main St.) (**n**), a Romanesque Revival style building, is the largest of several churches in town built of locally quarried granite. The wide range of domestic forms and styles across the neighborhood includes the **Guy Bondurant House** (1939; 203 W. Lebanon St.) (**o**), a rare small-town example of the International style, with flat roof, stuccoed walls, and horizontal banding and railings giving a streamlined appearance.

SY 7 *John D. Sargent House*

SY 8 South Main Street

Along S. Main St. from Cherry St. to Welch St., various late 19th- and early 20th-c. houses, churches, and commercial buildings also combine frame, brick, and granite. The

W. F. Carter House (ca. 1908; 418 S. Main St.) (**p**), a monumental Southern Colonial Revival mansion with tetrastyle Ionic portico, is one of the finest examples of the style in the county. Next door the late Victorian **Thomas Benton Ashby House** (early 20th c.; 500 S. Main St.) (**q**) features contrasting granite, brick, and shaped wood shingles. The **First Presbyterian Church** (1910–14; J. A. Tesh, builder; NW corner S. Main and Church Sts.) (**r**) and the **Mount Airy Friends Church** (1907–14; Lee Jones, builder; SW corner S. Main and Wilson Sts.) (**s**) are handsome Gothic Revival structures in the local granite. The **G. C. Welch Store** (1890; SW corner S. Main and Hamburg Sts.) (**t**), a 2-story brick, flatiron-shaped building, is among the best preserved of Mount Airy's late 19th-c. commercial structures.

SY 8 *First Presbyterian Church*

SY 9 West Pine Street

Once the prestigious address of furniture and tobacco industrialists, W. Pine St. and parts of Franklin, Granite, and Rockford Sts. retain 2-story dwellings and cottages from the late 19th and early 20th centuries. Chiefly frame houses display a variety of styles: Queen Anne, Colonial Revival, Shingle, Italianate, Mediterranean, Tudor Revival, and Bungalow. One of the two prime examples of the Queen Anne style in the county is the **James A. Hadley House** (1890s; 400 W. Pine St.) (**u**), with granite featured in the basement, first story, and second-story trim, but with a brick second story. It is enriched with wood-shingled gables, a central tower, wraparound porch, elaborate brackets, and stained glass. Hadley was surrounded by the houses of his chil-

dren. One of these, the **James F. and Sallie Yokley House** (1920s; 350 W. Pine St.) (**v**), is an unusual stuccoed dwelling of Mediterranean influence with tile roof, arcaded porch with twisted columns, and turret. At the west end of Granite St. stands the **Mount Airy Passenger Depot** (ca. 1915; J. A. Tesh, builder) (**w**), a station of typical bracketed, hip-roofed form, here executed in material appropriate for Granite City.

SY 9 *James A. Hadley House*

SY 10 North Carolina Granite Corporation Quarry Complex

1889 to present; N side NC 103, 0.6 mi. E of Mount Airy city limits, Flat Rock; private, visible from road

Now the largest open-face granite quarry in the world, the tract east of town called "Flat Rock" contains a 200-acre surface deposit of granite that made it useless for farming. Stone was quarried on a very limited scale until the arrival of the railroad in 1888, which brought English-born contractor Thomas Woodruff (cf. *Thomas Woodruff House), whose Greensboro firm was building depots for the line. Woodruff and a consortium of Greensboro businessmen purchased the property and began quarry operations in 1889, with an annual production of 135 railroad carloads by 1900. The industry provided an important source of employment for local people and brought skilled quarrymen and stonecutters from New England and around the world, including John D. Sargent of Vermont, who arrived in 1910 and led the company as its president from 1918 to 1945 (cf. *John D. Sargent House, Mount Airy). (See also Introduction, Fig. 31.)

SY 10 *N.C. Granite Corporation Office Building*

The focus of the complex is the handsome **Office Building** (1928), constructed of precisely laid ashlar blocks cut from the quarry. The 3-story, 6-bay building has a recessed porch with a pedimented frontispiece inscribed "1928" flanked by carved scrollwork. The building conveys a sense of strength and permanence that served as an advertisement for the company's product. Emphatic stonework includes alternating thicknesses of stone in the block courses, a string course between the second and third stories, and modillions beneath the low hip roof.

Other buildings include a large 2-story frame cutting shed measuring 660 by 85 feet (1927), a granite blacksmith shop, and other more recent structures.

The quarry has produced the granite used in the construction of many nationally known structures, including the Bullion Depository at Fort Knox, the Arlington Memorial Bridge and the Albert Einstein Memorial in Washington, D.C., and the Wright Brothers Memorial at Kitty Hawk.

SY 11 Westfield

Quaker settlers branching off from the New Garden Meeting in Guilford Co. established this farming community before the American Revolution, and the meeting they initiated here in 1772 is the oldest religious congregation in Surry Co. First called Tom's Creek Meeting, as a western outpost of New Garden it was referred to as "the Western Field," which became "Westfield" by 1786. The present **Westfield Friends Meetinghouse** (ca. 1885, 1939, 1959; NW side SR 1809, 0.5 mi. SW of NC 89) stands across

the road from the site of the original building. It began as a big plain frame structure but was remodeled in 1939 and enlarged and brick veneered in 1959. **Westfield Baptist Church** (1927; N side NC 89, opp. SR 1809), a porticoed Colonial Revival church, was built for a congregation founded in 1879. Across the road from the Baptist church stands the former **Westfield Academy** (1883; ca. 1900; SW side NC 89, just N of SR 1809; private), a 2-story frame house erected as a private academy in 1883 and expanded with Queen Anne style projecting bays and a wraparound porch when converted to a residence. Along the rural roads fanning out from the intersection at Westfield are several frame farmhouses built between the 1880s and 1910s, many with simplified Queen Anne details and sharing a distinctive sawtooth shingle ornament in the gables.

SY 12 Pilot Mountain

Named for the nearby geological landmark, the town of Pilot Mountain owes its growth to the arrival of the Cape Fear & Yadkin Valley Railway in 1888, which connected Surry Co. via Greensboro and Fayetteville to the port at Wilmington and also stimulated the growth of Mount Airy. The town rose up quickly as a small mercantile and tobacco manufacturing center, and the nearby mountain and local mineral springs attracted tourists from piedmont industrial towns. With the decline of the tobacco businesses and the waning of tourism by rail, there was little growth after 1920.

Among the simple 1- and 2-story brick storefronts along the Main St. commercial district, an anomaly is the former **Bank of Pilot Mountain** (1900; SE corner E. Main and Depot Sts.), which, despite late 20th-c. remodelings, retains its bold curvilinear parapets, round-arched windows, and domed corner turret.

The town retains well-kept houses from its growth period along W. Main St. and side streets. Most are conservative, frame versions of late Victorian, Colonial Revival, and Bungalow styles. Especially prominent is the **Dr. Robert E. Lee Flippin House** (ca. 1900; 203 W. Main St.; B&B), a rambling 2-story house with wraparound porch, built for popular physician "Dr. Big Bob" Flippin, whose small, gable-fronted medical office remains in the side yard.

Key institutional buildings include **Pilot Mountain Primitive Baptist Church** (1896; SE side Key St. between W. Main and School Sts.), a plain gable-fronted building with paired front entrances in keeping with the conservative tenets of the faith, and **First Baptist Church of Pilot Mountain** (1927; SW side W. Main St. between Marion and Key Sts.), a Colonial Revival brick church with Doric entrance portico and octagonal belfry. **Pilot Mountain School** (1924; School St.) is a 2-story brick school typical of the era of public school consolidation, with an Ionic portico over the central entrance.

SY 13 John Zebulon Vaughn Log House

Mid-19th c.; in fork of SR 2097 and SR 2117, 0.5 mi. S of NC 268 near jct. w/US 52; Pilot Mountain vic.; private, visible from road

The small log house and its assortment of log and frame outbuildings under the shade of big trees at the foot of Pilot Mountain form an unusually complete example of a modest 19th-c. farmstead. The 1-story log house has half-dovetailed notching and a gable-end stuccoed stone chimney; the smaller, detached kitchen to its side is similarly constructed. Outbuildings include a V-notched corncrib, a saddle-notched barn, a privy, and other frame storage buildings. John Zeb Vaughn was a Confederate veteran who was captured at Gettysburg. After the war he and his wife Betty Key raised ten children at the place.

SY 14 Frank A. Butner House

1880; ca. 1900; N side SR 2048 opp. SR 2067, Shoals vic.; private, visible from road

The big 2-story brick house is one of the grandest 19th-c. rural houses in northwestern N.C., and one of only three 19th-c. brick houses in the county. Frank A. Butner, a merchant and gunsmith of German Moravian descent from Bethania in Forsyth Co., came to the Shoals area in 1850 to operate

William Wolff's store. Butner married Wolff's daughter Sarah and is said to have commenced construction of a new brick house to honor their fourth child and first daughter, Eliza Mae, born in 1880. The well-proportioned house is of traditional 3-bay form with gable-end chimneys and a center-passage plan; a pedimented porch with slender posts shelters the entrance. The frame rear ell with engaged 2-tier porch was added about 1900. Outbuildings include a double-crib log barn that predates the house. The Butners' second son was Gen. Henry Wolff Butner, a decorated World War I veteran and military leader between the two world wars, for whom Camp Butner near Durham (later Butner Hospital) was named.

SY 15 Billy Cundiff House

Late 1860s; N side SR 2070, off-road in Pilot Mountain State Park corridor to Yadkin River; permission and directions from park staff required

The log house is said to stand on land given to the former slave Billy Cundiff by his master, C. C. Cundiff (cf. *Siloam), at the close of the Civil War, and was erected by the freedman soon thereafter. The neatly built and little-altered 1-story, half-dovetail-notched house has a center-passage plan, with an enclosed corner stair rising to the loft. A V-notched kitchen addition is attached to the rear by a breezeway.

SY 15 *Billy Cundiff House*

SY 16 Horne Creek Living History Farm State Historic Site (Hauser Farm)

Mid-19th to early 20th c.; entrance S side SR 2072, 0.4 mi. W of SR 2070, Shoals vic.; open regular hours

The Hauser (pronounced "Hoozer") Farm on Horne Creek near the Yadkin River began in 1830 as a 100-acre tract obtained by John Hauser, grandson of German-speaking Alsatian immigrants. The operation was expanded by Hauser's son Thomas and his wife Charlotte in the late 19th c. and was worked by Thomas's son Hubert and his wife Ella until 1953. Since the 1980s the site has been under development by the state as a living history farm.

The centerpiece is the **Hauser House**, a frame, center-passage I-house built for Thomas and Charlotte Hauser soon after their marriage in 1875. It is typical of thousands built across the state in the late 19th c. A 2-tier front porch with turned posts and balusters shelters the entrance, and the 1-story rear ell of weatherboarded logs contains the kitchen and dining rooms. A well house is connected to the ell with a breezeway. The interior retains its flush-board sheathing, stylized Neoclassical mantels, and other woodwork, all now repainted in original hues of dark greens and browns.

Below the house is a fine double-crib log barn (1846) from the tenure of John Hauser. This barn form is often found in German-settled areas of the western piedmont and foothills. Other outbuildings include a log smokehouse, a log tobacco barn, a corncrib, and a fruit house. A fruit-drying house has been reconstructed. Staff and volunteers maintain a period garden and orchard and are working to re-create the facilities and activities of the farm to depict agricultural life around the turn of the 20th c.

SY 17 Bean Shoals Canal

1820–25; John Hixon, Hiram Jennings, and Hamilton Fulton, engineers; N bank of Yadkin River in Pilot Mountain State Park, Yadkin River Section; entrance S side SR 2072, 0.9 mi. W of SR 2070. Follow park road 1.3 mi. (fording three creeks) to dead-end loop above river, then take footpath to river and right path along riverbank.

The stone structures at Bean Shoals are among the state's principal vestiges of its early 19th-c. canal-building campaigns. Before the railroad era several canal projects were undertaken across N.C.—with varying degrees of success—to improve river navigation between the western sections of the

SY 17 *Bean Shoals Canal*

state and eastern ports. In 1817 the state legislature commissioned John Hixon and Hiram Jennings to survey the Yadkin River. The partners proposed construction of a canal around Bean Shoals, a place of rapids and shallow water, and formed the Yadkin Navigation Co. to build the canal. Beginning in 1820 their crews dug a channel nearly 2 miles long, lined on one side with a rock wall up to 20 feet high and 1,200 feet long. The cost of the work bankrupted the company, and though the talented British-trained state engineer Hamilton Fulton assumed supervision of the project for a while, it was never completed. Construction of a railroad in the 1880s beside the river obliterated some of the work. Two sections of dry-laid stone wall of coursed rubble are easily accessible beside the path along the riverbank, ranging in height from 5 to 12 feet. Two other wall sections, part of the original dam and canal channel, several culverts, and a spillway also survive.

SY 18 Siloam

The broad and fertile bottomlands along this section of the Yadkin River supported prosperous farms for generations. A community grew up around Old Siloam Methodist Church that was organized ca. 1800, and a post office was established with the name in 1837. Siloam's heyday began in 1890 with the arrival of the Northwestern N.C. Railroad on its run along the Yadkin between Winston and North Wilkesboro and continued until about 1930, when highways for motor traffic followed other routes. During the era of rail service, several tobacco factories, stores, and an academy were established and flourished. A lone but impressive commercial survivor and the center of the community is the former **Marion Brothers Store** (ca. 1905; SW corner SR 1003 and SR 2230), an intact 2-story brick structure with segmental-arched windows and shop fronts with recessed entrances. The **Aaron Whitaker House** (1891; N side SR 2081, 0.3 mi. E of SR 1003) overlooking the river exemplifies the quality of houses built in the area at the end of the 19th c., a 2-story frame dwelling with an ornate 2-story center porch and a bracketed cornice. Other late 19th-c. 2-story frame houses include the **Daniel Scott House** (w side SR 1003, opp. SR 2082; B&B), which retains a 2-tier porch at the rear ell with delicate millwork, and the **Samuel J. Atkinson House** (w side SR 2082, 0.5 mi. NE of SR 1003), where a big transverse crib frame barn, a well house, a corncrib, and other outbuildings remain.

The community's early 20th-c. prosperity is especially evident in the **Richard Nathaniel Marion House** (ca. 1914; Willard C. Northup [Winston-Salem], architect; N side SR 2230, 0.1 mi. W of SR 1003), a monumental Southern Colonial remodeling by a prominent regional architect of an 1860s 1-story cottage built by a previous generation of Marions. On the Yadkin River just west of Siloam is the **C. C. Cundiff House** (ca. 1865; S side SR 2230, 1.3 mi. W of SR 1003), one of three 19th-c. rural brick houses extant in the county. The seat of a 948-acre farm, it was apparently built soon after the Civil War to replace a house that burned. Possibly reusing parts of the older house, the 2-story structure has two distinct brick sections, one with 4 rooms and the other 2, joined by a frame stair passage.

SY 18 *Richard Nathaniel Marion House*

SY 19 Rockford

Rockford was the seat of Surry Co. from 1790 to 1853 and flourished as a governmental and trade community overlooking the Yadkin River. When Yadkin Co. was partitioned from the southern half of Surry in 1853 and the court moved to Dobson, the town declined until the 1890 arrival of the Northwestern N.C. Railroad, which followed the north bank of the Yadkin River between Winston and North Wilkesboro. Rockford reemerged as a shipping point for communities and farms on both sides of the river until motor highways bypassed the town in the 1930s. Today a few survivors of its two periods of prosperity line High St. (SR 2221) north of the river.

SY 19 *Rockford Methodist Church*

An important early landmark was the **Grant-Burrus Hotel**, a rambling frame building with 18th-c. origins; it burned in 1974, but its chimney and foundation ruins have been stabilized at the village center. The chief survivor of Rockford's early development is **Masonic Lodge** (ca. 1800; E side SR 2221), a 2-story frame building on a raised stone foundation, with gable end facing the street and simple Federal style finish. Across the street, the 2-story frame **York Tavern** (ca. 1830) was modified ca. 1900 with a new porch, windows, and roof treatment but otherwise retains Federal period detail. Near the top of the hill above the town, the **Old Surry County Courthouse** (1830; W side SR 2221) survives in part; used as a school after the court moved to Dobson, it burned in 1925, and a flat-roofed residence was constructed within the walls. Sections of Flemish-bond brickwork and four engaged, stuccoed brick pilasters across the front suggest the original Greek Revival character.

During the railroad era a few stores and hotels prospered, and new residences were built, including the 2-story, frame **J. F. Bland House** (ca. 1900; W side SR 2221), with an ornamented 1-story wraparound porch. **Rockford Methodist Church** (1914; W side SR 2221), north of the old courthouse, is a vernacular Gothic Revival frame building with a prominent corner entrance tower. Other buildings of the railroad era include a row of 1-story frame commercial structures (W side SR 2221), a railroad section foreman's house, and modest late Victorian cottages.

Elkin (SY 20–25)

Elkin retains an exceptionally good collection of 19th- and early 20th-c. architecture for a town of its size. Located at the confluence of the Yadkin and Elkin rivers, it traces its origins to the enterprises of founder Richard Gwyn, who moved to a 1,000-acre tract on the north side of the Yadkin around 1840 and soon established a cotton mill, gristmill, blacksmith shop, sawmill, store, and a combination school and chapel. The community grew steadily, and in 1889 the town was incorporated and formally platted. The following year the Northwestern N.C. Railroad reached Elkin on its route up the Yadkin from Winston to North Wilkesboro. With the railroad in place, the town experienced rapid growth, both in population—which more than doubled between 1890 and 1896—and in commerce and industry. In 1893 the *Chatham Manufacturing Co. was formed from an earlier woolen manufacturing interest and became the principal industry. Community leaders chartered a second railroad, the Elkin & Alleghany, and construction began in 1913 with hopes to scale the Blue Ridge at Roaring Gap and continue to connections in Virginia, but the line only extended 10 miles to the foot of the mountains and was abandoned in 1931. Elkin remains a small but lively town. The business district lies close to the river, while handsome residential neighborhoods spread westward and northward and include several residences of exceptional sophistication.

SY 20 Downtown Elkin

The commercial district, rebuilt after a fire swept Main St. in 1898, remains largely intact, especially on the south side of Main St. between Bridge and Church Sts. Brick or granite-faced buildings feature round-arched windows, decorative recessed panels, and corbeled cornices. Of particular note are the **Harris Building** (1902; 123 W. Main St.), whose second story is sheathed in ornamental cast iron and pressed metal, and the **Elk Twin Theatre** (1930s; W. Main St. opp. Church St.), whose streamlined design is typical of the small Art Deco theaters built

across America during the 1930s and 1940s. The **U.S. Post Office** (1937; Louis A. Simon, supervising architect of the Treasury, s side W. Main St.) typifies the modest, red brick Colonial Revival architecture of public works post offices in small towns and retains its original function. Across the street a tiny former **Pure Oil Station** (1930s; N side W. Main St.), with trademark steep gables and English cottage styling, has been adapted as a drive-in branch bank. The Northwestern N.C. Railroad Depot was demolished, but the former **Elkin & Alleghany Railroad Ticket Office** (1870s?, ca. 1913; s side W. Main St.) still stands, a tiny frame building with a pedimented central gable; local tradition claims it predates the railroad and was originally an office of Elkin Manufacturing Co. in the 1870s.

SY 21 Gwyn Avenue

Climbing the hill north of the business district, Gwyn Ave. retains several notable residences from Elkin's early years. Outstanding is the **Alexander Martin Smith House** (1893–97; George Franklin Barber [Knoxville], architect; T. A. Dean [Salem], builder; 131 Gwyn Ave.), one of the grandest Queen Anne style houses in N.C. Knoxville architect Barber, who specialized in mail-order designs, supplied shoe manufacturer Smith with the plans. (Barber also provided house designs for other leading N.C. industrialists, including tobacconist Richard J. Reynolds of Winston.) Characteristic of Barber's work are the complex massing with high hip roof, corner towers, front-facing gable, inset balcony, and wraparound porch, all finished with a combination of textures, including half-timbering, pebbledash, fish-scale shingles, sawnwork, spindles, stained glass, and iron cresting. (See Introduction, Fig. 43.)

Next door is the **Gwyn-Chatham House** (1873, 1912; 121 Gwyn Ave.), home to various members of the town's two leading families. The house began as a traditional 2-story frame structure on Market St. and was moved and expanded in 1912 in the Southern Colonial manner with a central portico flanked by 1-story porches. The **Horton House** (ca. 1895; 140 Gwyn Ave.) is a 2-story frame, late Victorian house with a triplet of steep gables across the front and an ornamented hip-roofed porch; it was home of Angie Smith Horton, sister of Alexander Martin Smith who lived across the street. The **Richard Gwyn Smith House** (1918; 151 Gwyn Ave.), home of A. M. Smith's son, is a Tudor Revival style house with stuccoed walls, half-timbered gables, and a big granite chimney on the facade. Several fine bungalows stand at the north end of the street.

SY 22 Gwyn School–Elkin Chapel

Ca. 1850; Old Virginia Rd.; open by appointment

Elkin's founder Richard Gwyn built this simple, 1-story frame structure as a combination school and chapel for the young community. As a chapel it served several denominations until they could build their own churches. The little building has a low hip roof, double-leaf entrance, and pairs of large shuttered windows on each side. It was rescued from demolition in 1953 by the local chapter of the Daughters of the American Revolution and is now a museum.

SY 23 Gwyn-Foard House

Ca. 1855; 115 Circle Ct.

First occupied by Richard Ransome Gwyn, son of Elkin's founder, Richard Gwyn, and later owned by R. W. Foard, superintendent of Gwyn's Elkin Manufacturing Co. plant, the 2-story frame, hip-roofed house occupies an elevated site on a spacious lot and has unusually academic Greek Revival details, such as the crossetted and slightly pedimented

SY 23 *Gwynn-Foard House*

door and window casings. But the dominant feature is the fanciful 2-tier front porch with latticework posts, spandrels, and sheaf-of-wheat balustrades. While such picturesque motifs are not unknown in the antebellum period, the porch details are similar to those of a later 19th-c. house built for R. R. Gwyn's brother, and may date from that era.

SY 24 West Main Street Area

A varied and well-preserved collection of residential architecture of the late 19th and early 20th centuries is found west of the commercial district and across the Elkin River along W. Main St., Surry Ave., and Terrace Ave. The neatly kept 1- and 2-story houses in their landscaped yards reflect the prosperity of Elkin's early development. The oldest house is that of Elkin's founder, Richard Gwyn, called **Cedar Point** (1840 and later; 350 W. Main St.). The 2-story frame house was modified by Gwyn's son in the 1870s or 1880s with a central gable on the facade and delicate front and rear porches. The **Ed Harris House** (ca. 1900; 332 W. Main St.) is one of the town's most striking late Victorian houses, with a mansard roof tower over the entrance in the elbow between the two wings of the 2-story frame house. The **Harry H. Barker House** (1916; 418 W. Main St.) is a fine Southern Colonial style dwelling of Flemish-bond brick with a 2-story Ionic central portico and a 1-story wraparound Doric porch. On Terrace Ave. stands the **A. B. Galloway House** (late 19th c.; 122 Terrace Ave.), an unusual Italianate townhouse with parapeted roof. Two Queen Anne style houses are found on Surry Ave. beside the river: the **John S. Roth House** (ca. 1900; 101 Surry Ave.) has dual facades facing Surry Ave. and the Yadkin River, and the **Weir-Bryan House** (ca. 1895; 218 Surry Ave.) features elaborate decorative gable inserts and a gazebo-like pavilion at one corner of the wraparound porch. On the east side of the district stands **Galloway Memorial Episcopal Church** (1897; NW corner W. Main St. and Terrace Ave.), a Gothic Revival frame chapel with pointed-arch doors and windows, bracketed eaves, and a corner entrance tower.

SY 25 Chatham Manufacturing Company

1918 and later; N side US 268 (E. Main St.)

The town's largest industry began as a small woolen mill established on the Elkin River in 1877 by Alexander Chatham and his brother-in-law Thomas L. Gwyn. By 1893 Chatham and his sons Hugh and Richard bought out Gwyn's interest and moved to a new plant by the railroad on the Yadkin River. After the flood of 1916 damaged the mill, work began on the present 3-story brick mill building on higher ground. The operation expanded over the years and grew from the manufacture primarily of woolen blankets to a wide variety of textile products. Hugh Chatham promoted several business and philanthropic ventures in the region and led in the establishment of the nearby Roaring Gap resort in Alleghany Co.

SY 25 *Chatham Manufacturing Co.*

SY 26 Kapp's Mill and House

Mid-19th c. to early 20th c.; N side SR 1330 at SR 1322, Mountain Park vic.; private, visible from road

A handsome 19th-c. house, intact gristmill, mill dam and pond, and other structures alongside the Mitchell River compose one of the best-preserved rural industrial complexes in the region. A mill was established here by the 1820s and was operated from the 1840s to the mid-20th c. by John M. Kapp and his descendants. The 2-story, weatherboarded mill building reflects several stages of construction and remodeling between the mid-19th c. and about 1930; it was converted from an overshot wheel power system to a turbine system in the early 20th c. For a time a general store, post office, and blacksmith shop accompanied the mill, providing a commercial and social center for the surrounding countryside. Though no longer in use, the mill stands in good condition with some of its machinery intact. A nearby 19th-c. store building has been remodeled as a dwelling. East of the mill stands the **Kapp House**, a late 19th-c. reworking by John C. Kapp of his father's mid-19th-c. house. The 2-story frame dwelling with center gable and decorative 1-story, wraparound porch occupies a picturesque setting with terraced lawn and picket fences.

SY 26 *Kapp's Mill and House*

SY 27 Edwards-Franklin House

1790s; 1820s; N side SR 1331, 0.1 mi. E of SR 1338, Blevins Store; open by appointment

The well-crafted 2-story frame dwelling is one of the finest early houses in northwestern N.C. Planter and longtime state senator Gideon Edwards built the house in the late 18th c., and it was remodeled in the Federal style by his son-in-law, Meshack Franklin, a wealthy landowner who held numerous political offices in N.C. and served in Congress. Of special distinction are the massive, double-shouldered chimneys of Flemish-bond brick, the 3-room plan served by two front doors, and the Federal style woodwork that is everywhere grained and marbled in one of the state's most remarkable exhibitions of decorative interior painting. It has been restored by the Surry Co. Historical Society. (See Introduction, Fig. 17.)

SY 28 Beulah Methodist Church

Ca. 1900; W side SR 1345, 10 mi. N of NC 89, Bottom vic.

The well-preserved frame church of starkly simple form and detail has a steeply pitched gable roof, paired entrances on the front, banks of windows along the sides, and a plain interior.

SY 29 Haystack Farm

1885; private, no public visibility or access

Haystack Farm typifies the larger and more successful farms in northwestern N.C. during the late 19th and early 20th centuries. At the height of its diverse enterprises, Christopher Wrenn Bunker's 1,000-acre farm complex included a flour mill, a molasses mill, a sawmill, an apple orchard for vinegar production, a government distillery, and a livestock business as well as cultivated acreage of wheat, corn, and tobacco. The 2-story frame farmhouse features Italianate-inspired detailing with a bracketed cornice, paneled corner posts, and latticework porch. Unique to the house was a gravity-flow running water system fed by a spring in the hills above the house. Outbuildings include a big gambrel-roofed barn, a board-and-batten packhouse, and a half-dovetailed plank apple-drying house. Bunker was the oldest son of Chang Bunker, one of the Siamese twins who adopted northwestern N.C. as their home in the mid-19th c. (see *Chang and Adelaide Bunker House).

Wilkes County (WK)

Wilkes Co. was established in 1778 as settlement pushed up the Yadkin River toward the Blue Ridge. It was named for John Wilkes, member of Parliament, who supported American rights. The county is framed by the Blue Ridge on the north and the Brushy Mountains on the south, with the Yadkin flowing east across the center and draining a deeply rolling landscape. The land has long supported an economy of mostly small farms; today poultry farming dominates, with signs on every farm lane proclaiming the family's contractual tie to one of the two leading chicken-processing companies. Home to independent rural people of largely Scotch-Irish ancestry, the county once had the reputation as a center for moonshine whiskey distilling. There are relatively few architectural survivors of 19th-c. agricultural life, but Wilkesboro retains its character as an old county seat, and North Wilkesboro is a regional railhead of the Yadkin Valley Railroad as well as a manufacturing center with turn-of-the-century commercial and residential architecture.

Wilkesboro (WK 1–14)

The small courthouse town grew up around the site of Mulberry Fields Meeting House, an 18th-c. Baptist meetinghouse on the south side of the Yadkin River. Though court was held at this central location from the creation of the county in 1778, the town was not laid out until about 1801 and was not incorporated until 1847. Gradually houses, law offices, and commercial buildings were erected around the courthouse square. A few houses and a jail, and two churches from the late antebellum period, along with later 19th- and early 20th-c. buildings near the courthouse give the town the quiet ambience of an old western N.C. county seat.

WK 1 Wilkes County Courthouse
1902; Wheeler & Runge (Charlotte), architects; E. Main St. at N. Bridge St.

The third courthouse on this site, following wooden buildings of 1799 and ca. 1830, the building is one of six surviving similar Neoclassical Revival courthouses designed by Charlotte architect Oliver Wheeler in association with various partners (cf. Ashe Co. and Avery Co.). Typical features of this distinctive group are the mansard-like cupola and Ionic portico.

WK 2 Old Wilkes County Jail
1858–59; Michael Shipwash, builder; 203 N. Bridge St.; open regular hours

One of the state's best-preserved antebellum jails, the rectangular 2-story brick structure has a combination of Flemish-bond and common-bond brickwork and a low-pitched hip roof with interior end chimneys. Inside are jailer's quarters and several cells that retain metal doors and grilles. Local tradition cites a Mr. Shipwash as builder, probably Michael Shipwash Sr. (of Virginia) or Jr. (of Surry Co., N.C.), the only brickmasons in the county in the 1850 census. In 1866 Confederate veteran Tom Dula was held here for murdering his pregnant lover, Laura Foster. Although Dula's attorney, former governor Zebulon Vance, obtained a change of venue for the trial to Statesville, Dula was convicted and hanged in 1868. Songs about the murder were being sung even before Dula's execution, and multiple versions circulated in the regional folk repertory. The best-known variant of the "Tom Dooley" ballad is that popularized by the Kingston Trio with their 1958 hit recording; it was based on a version collected from Frank Proffitt of Watauga Co. and later published by Alan Lomax. After serving as the county jail until 1917, the building has been restored as a museum and headquarters of Old Wilkes, Inc.

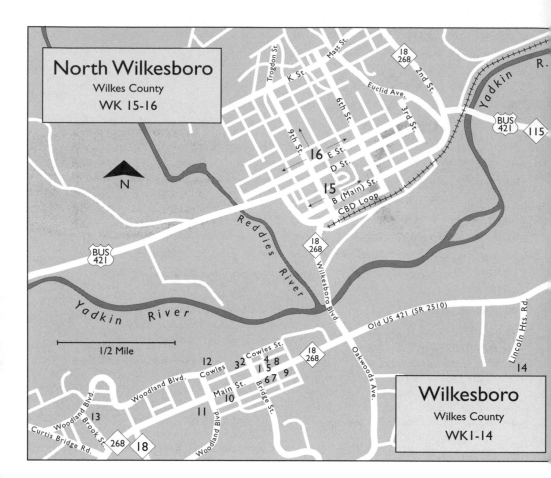

WK 3 Robert Cleveland House

Late 18th c.; N. Bridge St. behind
Old Wilkes Jail; open regular hours

The county's oldest building is among the finest of the few early log buildings surviving in the region, and one of few open to the public. It consists of two log pens, each with its own front and rear entrances and exterior stone chimney. The hewn logs are joined with diamond notches, a type of notching rarely seen in western N.C. The exposed logs of the interior are whitewashed. Robert Cleveland fought in the Battle of Kings Mountain and, with his brother Benjamin (cf. Ronda), conducted reprisals against local Tories. Neglected and ruinous at its rural site in western Wilkes Co., the house was disassembled in 1986 and rebuilt behind the *Old Wilkes Jail. (See Introduction, Fig. 14.)

WK 4 Thomas B. Finley Law Office
(Finley-Jordan Law Office)

1880; SE corner Broad and North Sts.

An excellent example of a once-common component of county seats across the state, the tiny freestanding law office stands adjacent to the courthouse square. The stylish 2-room structure features Gothic Revival style bargeboards and finials at the gable ends. It served as the office of attorneys Thomas B. Finley and, later, J. Floyd Jordan, the latter occupying the building for six decades. It was long shaded by the fabled "Tory Oak"—from whose boughs, legend has it, Col. Benjamin Cleveland hanged Tories during the Revolution. After time finished the ancient tree in 1992, a young oak took its place in 1997.

WK 5 Wilkesboro-Smithey Hotel

1891; NE corner E. Main and Broad Sts.

Dominating the small commercial district, the 3-story brick hotel and shop building features corbeled cornices, segmental-arched windows, and a 2-story gallery around three sides. Built by the Wilkesboro Hotel Co., after 1906 it was operated by N. B. Smithey, who began his regional chain of Smithey Department Stores here.

WK 6 J. T. Ferguson Store

Ca. 1890; 111 E. Main St.

The 2-story brick commercial building displays a fine example of the ornate metal facades manufactured by Mesker Bros. of St. Louis.

WK 7 Johnson-Hubbard House

1855–57, ca. 1885; 113 E. Main St.

Built for merchant Stephen Johnson near his Main St. store, the symmetrical 2-story house with simple Greek Revival finish was expanded about 1885 with a 1-story rear ell by Julius and Lula Hubbard, who probably also added the broad central gable and latticed front porch with sheaf-of-wheat balustrade.

WK 2 *Old Wilkes Co. Jail*

WK 8 Brown-Cowles House and Cowles Law Office

Ca. 1830, late 19th c.; 200 E. Main St.

Occupying a large lot near the center of town, the big frame house was built for county sheriff Hamilton Brown as a 2-story central block with simple Federal style finish. It gained a 2-story west wing before 1885, then a 1-story east wing and other additions ca. 1900. On the sw corner of the property stands the **W. H. H. Cowles Law Office** (1870s; 106 E. Main St.), a small frame building with gable roof, wraparound porch, and Tudor-arch labels over the front door and windows; it was built for Cowles, longtime congressman and resident of the house. Like the nearby *Thomas B. Finley

WK 1, 5 *Wilkes Co. Courthouse and Wilkesboro-Smithey Hotel*

Law Office, it represents a once-common building type in county seats.

WK 9 Wilkesboro Presbyterian Church

1849–50; D. Dameron, builder;
205 E. Main St.

The tiny, austere Greek Revival temple-form church of dark red common-bond brick features a portico of stout columns in contrasting smooth white stucco. The interior is equally simple, with plastered walls and a flush-board ceiling. The small belfry dates from the late 19th c. The congregation, established in 1837, is said to be the oldest Presbyterian congregation in 21 western N.C. counties. A member's letter reported in 1849, "The contract for the Presbyterian Church at Wilkesboro was let to old Dameron for one thousand and forty dollars. It is to be a brick building, with big pillars in front." Dameron also built Wilkesboro's *St. Paul's Episcopal Church.

WK 9 *Wilkesboro Presbyterian Church*

WK 10 Federal Building (Wilkes Co. Board of Education Building)

1915; James A. Wetmore, supervising architect of the Treasury; 201 W. Main St.

The small-town courthouse and post office reflects the federal government's commitment to excellence in local building projects in the early 20th c. The yellow brick building has a 5-part, Palladian-inspired plan and delicate classical detailing, rendered in terracotta, brick, wood, marble, and plaster. Since 1970 it has housed county offices.

WK 10 *Federal Building*

WK 11 Wilkesboro Methodist Church

1896; S side W. Main St. between Woodland Blvd. and Pine St.

The prominent Gothic Revival church has a steep gable roof, lancet-arched doors and windows, corner buttresses, and corner tower with spire that dominates W. Main St.

WK 12 St. Paul's Episcopal Church

1848–49; William Gries, designer;
D. Dameron, builder; N side Cowles St.,
between Woodland Blvd. and West St.

Located on a hilltop amid its graveyard, the compact brick church is one of a very few antebellum Gothic Revival churches in western N.C. With its steep gabled nave and chancel, lancet-arched openings, and side portal, it embodies a unique chapter in Episcopal church history: the influence of the Ecclesiological movement, with its emphasis on authentic Early English church precedents and high-church liturgical forms such as the deep, clearly defined chancel.

The brick church was designed by its minister, William Gries, a student at the *Valle Crucis seminary established by Bishop Levi Silliman Ives in Watauga Co. An ardent proponent of Ecclesiological practices and Gothic Revival architecture, Ives generated controversy in the traditionally low-church diocese and raised fears of Roman Catholic influences. An eyewitness to the 1849 consecration of St. Paul's reported that the students and faculty of Valle Crucis "walked the entire distance of forty-five miles" for the event and "marched into town bearing pilgrims' staffs, and with religious fervor and in well-trained unison chanting the Gloria in Excelsis." The *New*

York Ecclesiologist magazine (1851) commended St. Paul's "very satisfactory liturgical arrangement," and Ives described it as "a beautiful Gothic structure of brick erected at small expense, with small means, applied with directed zeal." To low churchman William H. Battle of Chapel Hill, however, who visited in 1851 in the midst of the Ives controversy, it was "quite a quaint looking building, being the extreme of the Gothic style with quite a sufficiency of crosses." The Ives furor came to a head when he converted to Catholicism in 1852, but N.C. Episcopalians never abandoned the Gothic Revival style he had promoted.

WK 12 *St. Paul's Episcopal Church*

WK 13 J. L. Hemphill House
1899; 203 N. Brook St.; private

The town's finest Queen Anne style house features the irregular massing and rich texture and ornamentation that characterize the style, here with a bold corner tower, bay window, and wraparound porch with turned posts and balustrade and spindle frieze.

WK 14 Lincoln Heights Rosenwald School
1924; end of Lincoln Heights Rd.

Between 1915 and 1932 the Julius Rosenwald Fund assisted construction of some 5,300 schools for black children in the rural South. Over 800 were constructed in N.C., more than in any other state. The idea of a public-private partnership for school construction was conceived by Booker T. Washington and supported by Rosenwald, philanthropist and chief executive of Sears, Roebuck & Co. The fund provided seed money for construction and required commitments of cash and labor from both the local school boards and the black community.

Because of the relatively small African American population in western N.C., mountain counties usually had only one Rosenwald school, and several had none; foothills counties typically had four or five. Six were built in Wilkes Co. The schools followed standard plans for buildings of one to seven classrooms supplied by the fund. The Lincoln Heights School is one of the largest of the Rosenwald schools in the state, a seven-teacher school built on an H-plan, and one of the few constructed of brick. It now serves a charter school.

North Wilkesboro (WK 15–16)

North Wilkesboro is a classic illustration of the railroad boomtown that overshadowed an older neighbor. It began in 1890 as a planned development at the western terminus of the newly constructed Northwestern N.C. Railroad from Winston, built to tap the timber and agricultural wealth of the verdant upper Yadkin River valley. (Controlled by the Richmond & Danville Railroad, the line became a branch of the successor Southern Railway in 1894 and since 1989 has operated independently as the Yadkin Valley Railroad.) The line was conceived by Winston businessmen in response to Greensboro's new rail link to Mount Airy in Surry Co. and the threat of the rival city's dominance over the region's resources. The Winston Land and Improvement Co., a consortium led by Winston businessmen Willard Franklin Trogdon and George Washington Hinshaw, purchased farmlands owned by the long-prominent Finley family on the north side of the river opposite Wilkesboro, built a depot in 1890, and laid out the town in 1891.

The town was incorporated the same year. Its plan is a grid draping the hillside above the river. Streets were efficiently named: those parallel to the river follow the alphabet, beginning with A St. nearest the river, and perpendicular streets are named 1st, 2nd, etc., from east to west. Within ten years the population reached 1,000, and the grid was expanded in 1904 to accommodate further growth. By 1920 the population had reached 4,000, after which growth began to level off. Some street sections within the ambitious grid plan were never actually constructed, though the town retains their right-of-way dedications. Unwary visitors can find themselves in dead ends or cut off from their intended destination.

North Wilkesboro quickly developed as the region's principal shipping point for timber, fruit, chickens, eggs, furs, and a market in wild herbs and roots. The Wilkesboro Manufacturing Co., a sash and blind factory, opened in 1896 and supplied materials to build the town. C. C. Smoot and Sons Tannery came in 1897 and built a 35-acre complex by the river that made the town a collection point for tanbark and raw hides brought to town in wagons as well as a shipping point for finished leather. Furniture and textile factories were also established. Today the community is headquarters of Lowe's, one of the nation's largest building supply chains, which grew out of a downtown family business, North Wilkesboro Hardware.

Industrial development first concentrated along the railroad along the Yadkin River, where high waters occasionally washed out entire businesses, and few vestiges of the earliest industries remain. Completion of the W. Kerr Scott Reservoir upstream in 1962 controlled floods and opened the way for industrial and retail development in the floodplain. Just above the plain are the commercial blocks, with B St.—also called Main St.—having the principal collection of early commercial buildings. Residential blocks climb to the top of the hill. Commercial, residential, and institutional architecture follows nationally popular styles of the late 19th and especially the early 20th c.

WK 15 Downtown North Wilkesboro

The chief landmark near the river is the **North Wilkesboro Depot** (ca. 1912; N side of tracks just E of 9th St.), a long, low brick depot with low hip roof with bracketed eaves and segmental-arched windows and doors; it replaced the original 1890 wooden depot after a fire.

WK 15 *Bank of North Wilkesboro and Hotel Wilkes*

Developed within a relatively short period, the commercial district has an unusually homogeneous quality, with standard 2-story, early 20th-c. brick storefronts predominating. Key buildings cluster at the intersection of B (Main) St. and 9th St. The **Brame Drugstore** (1891; 833 B St.) at the southeast corner is the oldest downtown store, a 2-story brick building with corbeled cornice, corner pilasters, and segmental-arched windows with brick hood molds. On the southwest corner is the first former **Bank of North Wilkesboro** (ca. 1895; 901 B St.), a decorative, 1-story brick building with a multilayered corbeled cornice, bands of terra-cotta tile trim, and windows with fanlights. At the northeast corner stands the second former **Bank of North Wilkesboro** (1923; Charles C. Benton [Wilson], architect; 832 B St.), a grand, 2-story Neoclassical Revival brick and stone bank with inset Doric columns. This rendition of a popular form for banks of the 1920s marked a long-distance foray into western N.C. by the prolific eastern N.C. architect Benton, who also gained commissions in Lenoir and Morganton. He probably also designed the adjoining **Hotel Wilkes** (1926; Charles C. Benton [Wilson], attributed architect; 822–830 B St.). The largest building downtown, the 5-story hotel has a stone-faced base and projecting cornice enhancing a simply detailed shaft of dark red brick.

Eastward on B St. the 2-story brick store at **823 B St.** (ca. 1895) displays the sole surviving cast-iron and pressed-metal upper storefront; like that of the *J. T. Ferguson Store across the river in Wilkesboro, it was probably manufactured by the Mesker Bros. of St. Louis. Charles C. Benton's work continued in the **North Wilkesboro Town Hall** (1939; Charles C. Benton & Son [Wilson], architects; s side B St. at foot of Kensington Dr.); the rectilinear composition of buff-colored brick and concrete trim is a work in small-town modernism by an architect best known for his Colonial Revival designs; it was built with the assistance of the Works Progress Administration (WPA). In a park above the street is the **Sharpie McNeil Texaco Station** (ca. 1925; B St. Park), a tiny board-and-batten filling station that once stood at 10th and D Sts. This survivor of the early automotive era, complete with an early gas pump and hip-roofed canopy on heavy, bracketed posts, was moved and adapted as restrooms for the park.

On the next street the 1-story, red brick Colonial Revival style former **U.S. Post Office** (1934; Louis A. Simon, supervising architect of the Treasury; C St.) repeats the use of regional revival styles typical of WPA public buildings; it now houses the library.

WK 16 Residential District

The oldest residential development overlooks the downtown and the river from the hillside. Predating the founding of the town is **Fairmont** (early 19th c., 1912 and later; 707 Kensington Ave.), a 2-story frame plantation house built for Chapman Gordon. It was occupied through most of the 19th c. by the Finley family, from whom the Winston Land and Improvement Co. purchased the land to develop the town in 1890. Moved from the hilltop and remodeled in 1912, it retains its Federal style dentil cornice and 9/9 and 9/6 sash windows.

WK 16 *Thomas B. Finley House*

A concentration of turn-of-century houses flanks **E St.**, including several built for Finley family members. The town's grandest Queen Anne style house is the **Thomas B. Finley House** (1893; 1014 E St.); built for a leading lawyer and judge, it is a lavish composition of porches, balconies, and corner tower embellished with shingles, diagonal sheathing, stained glass, and ironwork, meticulously maintained on a big corner lot.

Later examples of the Queen Anne style along the street include the **J. Robert Finley House** (1907; 1107 E St.) and the **E. M. Blackburn House** (1905; 1015 E St.), big frame houses with hip roofs, projecting gables, wraparound porches, and touches of Colonial Revival detail. At the west end of the street, the **Arthur A. Finley House** (1890s; 1208 E St.) is a 2-story frame house of traditional form with ornate detail on its wraparound porch, no doubt milled at the Wilkesboro Manufacturing Co., the sash and blind factory established by Finley.

Notable 1-story Queen Anne residences include the **Carrie W. Foote House** (ca. 1905; 703 9th St.) and the nearby **Caudill House** (ca. 1900; 710 9th St.). The **Dan Brookshire House** (ca. 1910; 1001 Trogdon St.) at the crest of the hill is a brick house of Queen Anne massing, with a 3-story corner tower and Colonial Revival detail. Closer to downtown the **W. F. Trogdon House** (ca. 1910; NW corner D and 8th Sts.), home of a town founder, is a large, somewhat altered 2-story frame house with portico.

Overlooking downtown from a perch on the east side of the old residential area, the **North Wilkesboro Graded School** (1913; J. H. Burcham, architect; R. L. Poindexter, builder; NW corner D and 3rd Sts.) is a handsome 2-story school building of dark red brick featuring curvilinear gable parapets and a wooden belfry. The adjacent **North Wilkesboro High School** (1926; SW corner E and 3rd Sts.) displays a more classical mode typical of 1920s public school construction, with projecting end pavilions and central entrance bay. **North Wilkesboro Presbyterian Church** (1949; NW corner E and 8th Sts.) is the town's most prominent church, rendered in Gothic Revival style in gray stone with a tall entrance tower with spire.

WK 17 North Wilkesboro Speedway

1946, with various later improvements; S side SR 2355 (Speedway Rd.), 1.8 mi. E of NC 115 (also visible on N side US 421)

Organized stock car racing has deep roots in rural areas of N.C. and the Southeast. Regional legends recount how the sport originated with moonshine whiskey haulers who supercharged their engines and honed the art of high-speed driving on country roads to outrun the law. One such alleged moonshiner-turned-racer was Junior Johnson, a native of the Brushy Mountain area of southeastern Wilkes Co. and one of the first major stars of the sport. Johnson was said to be a master of the "bootleg turn"—a skidding 180-degree about-face—and other driving feats that confounded his pursuers. Such skills found popularly accepted—and legal—expression in organized competitions on dirt tracks across the South.

The North Wilkesboro Speedway was developed by Wilkes Countians Charlie Combs, Calvin Combs, Lawson Curry, and Enoch Staley. When the track was completed near the end of 1946, the local newspaper hailed its five-eighths mile of oval as "one of the fastest dirt tracks in automobile racing." The first official race was run on May 18, 1947, with the field made up primarily of modified 1939 and 1940 Ford coupes.

The National Association for Stock Car Auto Racing (NASCAR) was incorporated in 1948, placing an emphasis on races of late-model cars, theoretically "stock" cars just out of the showroom. Fueled by postwar prosperity and the public's love for automobiles, the sport soon grew into a multimillion-dollar business, with a brotherhood of highly skilled drivers supported by specialized teams of mechanics and pit crews. Over time the cars became less and less "stock" and are now built by the racing teams along NASCAR-governed templates. In races on the largest tracks, cars sustain speeds approaching 200 miles per hour, though speeds on smaller tracks such as North Wilkesboro's are considerably less. NASCAR has built an enormous following of fans drawn to the excitement of the roaring engines and blinding speed, and perennial winners such as North Carolinians Junior Johnson and Richard Petty are revered as folk heroes.

The North Wilkesboro Speedway became one of three N.C. tracks on the NASCAR Grand National Division circuit and later hosted twice-annual races in the Winston Cup series, which superseded the Grand National as the highest echelon of NASCAR racing. Over the years the track was paved, and press boxes and grandstands were added, enlarged, or improved. Nevertheless, the speedway was one of the two smallest tracks on the Winston Cup circuit, and since 1996 the major events moved to larger facilities in other states. The track remains actively used for the races of the now second-tier Grand National circuit and for the emerging corollary sport of truck racing.

WK 18 Traphill

Jct. of SR 1002 and SR 1749

The crossroads community at the foot of the Blue Ridge was once a busy rural trading and educational center with several stores and two academies. A cluster of simple frame structures grew around the crossroads from the early 19th c. onward. Vestiges of its late 19th-c. prime flank SR 1749 south of the intersection: the **Traphill Bargain House** (ca. 1885; E side SR 1749), a 2-story frame general store with 2-story porch under the projecting gable roof, now used as a branch library; the **White-Hinson House** (ca. 1882; W side SR 1749; private) across the road, a 2-story frame house with decorative vergeboards; **Traphill Baptist Church** (1887; E side SR 1749), a plain, gable-fronted frame church with later vestibule and steeple; and the **Traphill Institute** (1891; E side SR 1749), a 2-story frame, gable-fronted school building that serves as a Masonic lodge.

WK 19 Hutchinson Farmstead

Mid- and late 19th c.; Stone Mountain State Park off SR 1739 (turn at "Stone Mountain Hiking and Picnicking" sign), at base of

Stone Mountain adjacent to handicapped parking area; accessible during park hours

The dramatically sited log house at the base of the towering, sheer stone face recalls 19th-c. life in remote farmsteads along the Blue Ridge. Two log pens of roughly equal size meet at right angles to form an L plan. Each section is composed of hewn logs joined in half-dovetailed notches, and each has a fieldstone foundation and gable-end chimney. The oldest (west) section, which is divided by a central board partition into 2 rooms, was built ca. 1852 by John and Sidney Brown Hutchinson, who raised eight children here. A generation later their son John Ely Hutchinson added the east section, and he and his wife, Carrie, likewise raised eight children in the house. A third generation of Hutchinsons lived at the site in a newer house until 1977, when the property was acquired by the state. A log corncrib and a frame barn from the Hutchinsons' farming operations also survive at the site.

WK 20 Ronda

Set amid beautiful farming country, the little town on the north bank of the Yadkin River takes its name from "Round About," the 18th-c. plantation of Revolutionary leader Benjamin Cleveland, which lay in a nearby big horseshoe bend of the river. The name Round About is also said to have come from Cleveland's wandering adventures as a Tory hunter and from his enormous girth: he reportedly weighed almost 400 pounds at the time of his death. His brother's 18th-c. log house, the *Robert Cleveland House, now stands in Wilkesboro. The present house at **Round About** (mid-19th c.; private, no public visibility) is a brick Greek Revival house built for a later owner.

An academy was established at Ronda soon after the Civil War, and a small community grew up around it. The completion of the Northwestern N.C. Railroad (Yadkin Valley Railroad) from Winston to North Wilkesboro in 1890 promoted a few small industries. The building housing the **Home Chair Company** (ca. 1920; N side NC 268) was originally Ronda Cotton Mills but has been occupied by the chair company since 1940. The big 3-story frame building with a corner stair tower may be the state's largest surviving wooden textile mill building. Three early 20th-c. 2-story brick commercial buildings with corbeled cornices and segmental-arched windows stand on the west side of Main St., and around the town

WK 19 *Hutchinson Farmstead*

are 1- and 2-story frame houses from the turn of the century, some with simple Queen Anne motifs.

WK 21 Claymont Hill
1870; W side SR 2303, 0.8 mi. S of NC 268, Ronda vic.; private, visible from road

The county's best-preserved 19th-c. farm complex occupies a prominent, unspoiled site above the Yadkin River south of Ronda. The centerpiece is a large, 2-story, L-plan frame farmhouse with multiple gables and decorated 2-story porches on 3 sides. It was built for Albert Hendrix, a farmer, merchant, and legislator, soon after his purchase of the property in 1870, and incorporates an early 19th-c. log house built by the Martin family. The unusual Gothic Revival–influenced porch has sawnwork posts, brackets, and balustrades cut to mimic the profiles of elements turned on a lathe. Outbuildings form a domestic compound within a fenced yard and include a weatherboarded log kitchen, well house, flower house, wood house, and smokehouse. A springhouse is nearby, and two barns, a crib, and a granary stand across the road. The farm is maintained by descendants.

WK 22 Martin-Pardue Farm
Ca. 1865, ca. 1910; NE corner US 421 and SR 2316 just N of US 421; private, visible from road

A landmark to travelers along the county's main highway, the 2-story, L-plan farmhouse near the edge of the Brushy Mountains captures the county's late 19th- and early 20th-c. rural vernacular character and has been a popular subject for artists. The rear ell was the original house, a 2-story log dwelling built around the end of the Civil War by Willie and Dicie Martin, who raised corn, wheat, and oats on their farm. About 1910 the Martins added the east-facing main block, a frame I-house with end chimneys and center-passage plan, adorned with stylish central front gable, pressed-tin shingle roof, and wraparound porch. Contemporary outbuildings include an 1890 livestock barn and a granary east of the house. Martin's sons continued the grain-farming operation until the 1950s, when new owners James and Nellie Pardue, like many other Wilkes Co. farmers after World War II, turned to chicken farming and erected the long chicken houses to the north.

WK 22 *Martin-Pardue Farm*

wk 24 *Wade Hampton Harris Memorial Bridge*

WK 23 Ready Branch Community

A few houses and a country store along sr 1155 recall the farming community that once had its own post address. The focus is the **Linsy Lafayette Church Store** (ca. 1880; NE side sr 1155), a long, unpainted, 2-story, gable-fronted frame general store that operated until 1958; it also served as the Ready Branch, N.C., Post Office. Just east of the store is the **Church-McGee House** (ca. 1900; private), a 2-story, L-plan frame farmhouse with central gable and decorative double-gallery, hip-roofed porch, home to store proprietors Gerald and Estelle Church McGee. West of the store stands the similar **Dr. A. J. Eller House** (ca. 1900; private), with sinuous sawnwork porch post brackets and balustrade.

WK 24 Wade Hampton Harris Memorial Bridge
1931; SR 1389 (old US 421) over South Prong Lewis Fork Creek, just N of US 421; visible in winter from US 421

One of the state's most dramatic reinforced concrete arch bridges, the single rib-arched open spandrel structure is 312 feet long and 114 feet high, with the arch spanning 150 feet. The second highest bridge in the state when completed (cf. *High Bridge, Henderson Co.), it improved automobile access to Boone and northwestern N.C. along old US 421. It was named for a Charlotte newspaper publisher and promoter of improved roads and mountain tourism. With the completion of a new highway and bridge in the late 20th c., it now carries a secondary road and can be viewed broadside north of the new bridge.

WK 25 Reddies River Baptist Church
Early 20th c.; NE side SR 1559 (Old NC 16), 0.3 mi. NW of SR 1570, Wilbar vic.

Though no longer serving an active congregation, the simple gable-fronted frame church and its adjacent cemetery are maintained on its hillside by nearby residents as one of the county's few country churches dating from before the mid-20th c.

Alexander County (AX)

AX 1 Taylorsville

The county seat, probably named for Gen. Zachary Taylor, was established along with Alexander Co. in 1847 and grew into a small manufacturing town. In the late 19th and early 20th centuries visitors came to Taylorsville on their way to nearby resorts, including the Sulphur Springs Hotel and All Healing Springs Hotel. Many arrived on the Statesville & Western Railroad, which was built in 1887, was later absorbed into the Southern Railway, and is now the independent Alexander Railroad.

Taylorsville's downtown includes several turn-of-the-century brick commercial buildings along Main Ave. and Center St. The initial 1848 courthouse was succeeded ca. 1902 by a brick building erected by the B. F. Smith Fireproof Construction Co. After it burned in 1967, it was replaced by the present facility. The former **Alexander County Jail** (1913, Camden Iron Works; 1930, Manly Jail Works; Main Ave. Dr. SE at 1st St.) is a 2-story brick building with a low hip roof, which takes the essentially domestic form of many jails and once housed the jailer and his family as well as prisoners.

AX 2 "Diamond Jim" Lucas Mansion (Hiddenite Center)

Ca. 1900, ca. 1928; E side SR 1503 (Hiddenite Church Rd.), 0.3 mi. N of NC 90, Hiddenite; open regular hours

The eccentric 3-story house, cruciform in plan and bedecked with decorated porches, is the architectural curiosity and landmark of the county. James Paul Lucas of South Carolina began his career as an umbrella and walking-stick salesman but soon entered the diamond import business in New York. After traveling the world in the trade, he became known as "Diamond Jim." In the early 20th c. he visited the Sulphur Springs resort near Hiddenite, liked the countryside, and in 1908 bought property for his retirement, to which he moved his parents. Hiddenite was named for mineralogist W. E. Hidden, who investigated local minerals ca. 1880. The green gem called hiddenite is found only in this area, along with emeralds, rubies, and other stones. (Emerald Hollow Mine nearby is open to the public.)

Lucas soon enlarged the existing house. As an old photograph shows, he first raised the old house on cribs and built a new first story beneath it; later he raised the upper story again and inserted a new second story. The interior is simply finished with beadboard and paneled doors, some of which are grained. After retiring here ca. 1929, Lucas entertained visitors from far and wide and filled the house with objects he had collected in his travels or received as gifts from celebrities. The upper balustrade of the 2-tier wraparound porch is hinged at intervals, supposedly to admit objects too big to get up the stair inside. With attractions such as General Pershing's World War I helmet, clothing worn by Buffalo Bill, and Czar Nicholas's pipe, the place became something of a local museum. Following Lucas's death in 1952, his possessions were auctioned off. After a period of neglect, the house has been restored as a house museum and cultural center, with displays on local history, arts, and mineralogy.

AX 3 Linney House

Ca. 1880; W side SR 1001, 1.2 mi. S of SR 1442, Vashti vic.; private, visible from road

The Brushy Mountains are a spur of hills off the Blue Ridge that rise to considerable heights along the border between Alexander and Wilkes counties. Though little survives from early settlement, the rolling landscape harbors a number of farmsteads developed in the late 19th and early 20th centuries. Among the most prominent farmhouses in this section is this frame I-house with a 2-story gabled porch, sawnwork bargeboards in the gables, and massive gable-end brick chimneys. Outbuildings include an early 20th-c. gambrel-roofed barn.

AX 4 Linney's Mill
1937; S side SR 1446 at Rocky Creek, 2 mi. E of SR 1001, Linney's Grove community

The frame millhouse, covered with metal sheathing, stands beside its pond in a rural setting that has long been a favorite picnicking spot. Although gristmills operated along the swift waters of the region's streams well into the 20th c., few still survive, and even fewer remain in operation. Linney's Feed Mill on Rocky Creek is the only operating waterpowered mill in the county, where once as many as eleven mills stood along Rocky Creek alone. Miller William Linney's father, W. T. Linney, established the mill in 1937 on the site of the 19th-c. Mayberry Mill and installed a waterwheel that another local businessman had acquired in 1927 from the Fitz Water Wheel Co. of Hanover, Pa. With the millrace rebuilt in 1971 to increase production, the facility grinds cornmeal and operates as a low-head hydroelectric plant.

AX 5 Childers House
Ca. 1885; S side SR 1403, 2.6 mi. E of NC 16, Vashti vic.; private, visible from road

Several late 19th-c. farmhouses across the county repeat this 1½-story form with a trio of gables across the front. Here the gables and eaves are trimmed with decorative bargeboards, emphasizing the Gothic Revival character.

AX 6 Lewis Foote Davis Farm
1879, ca. 1900; Johnny Davidson and Johnny Price, builders; NW side SR 1334, 0.5 mi. W of NC 16, Kilby vic.; private, visible from road

One of the most beautifully sited and best preserved of the late 19th-c. farmsteads in the Brushy Mountains, the 2-story frame house with 2-story rear ell occupies a knoll overlooking the valley of the East Prong Lower Little River. The rear ell is the older section, built about the time of Davis's marriage to Mary Bumgarner in 1879. In 1900 carpenters Davidson and Price added the 2-story front section with separate front doors opening into the 2-room plan. Both front and rear 1-story porches have latticed porch posts. Contemporary outbuildings include a washhouse, a crib, and a distinctive

AX 2 *"Diamond Jim" Lucas Mansion*

gable-roofed barn with louvered, segmental-arched ventilator windows along the sides. Davis operated a successful apple orchard business, and the orchards on the farm remain in production.

AX 7 Oxford Hydroelectric Plant
1927–28; NC 16 at Catawba River,
9 mi. S of Taylorsville

A dramatic sight from the highway that crosses the Catawba River just below it, the power plant and dam were built for the Southern Power Co. as part of industrialist James B. Duke's long-range plan of "electrifying an entire river." Construction of the 91-foot-high concrete dam forming Lake Hickory took more than two years and required special railroad tracks built to the site from Newton and a quarry upriver. On the south (Catawba Co.) side of the river stands the large brick powerhouse atop an arcaded base.

Caldwell County (CW)

Lenoir (CW 1–8)

The town began in 1841 as seat of newly formed Caldwell Co., which had been carved from Burke and Wilkes counties and named for Joseph Caldwell, first president of the University of North Carolina. The county seat, located at the site of James Harper's plantation and store, was named for local political leader William Lenoir. The county combines broad, arable valleys and relatively rugged mountains. White families settled in the county in the mid-18th c., initially in the fertile valleys of the Yadkin River, which traverses the northern part of the county, and the Catawba River, which runs along its southern boundary.

Growth of Lenoir, centrally located in the county beyond either river, was slow until the 1880s. The much-anticipated and relatively late arrival of the Chester & Lenoir Railroad in 1884 boosted trade and industrial development, especially furniture manufacturing, which has continued as a mainstay of the economy. The industrial era brought extensive rebuilding from the 1890s into the 1920s. Two- and 3-story brick Italianate buildings of the late 19th c. and various renditions of brick and stone Neoclassicism from the early 20th c. dominate the commercial district. Although development

has eliminated most of the 19th-c. residential areas near the town center, along **Harper Ave.** (NC 18) west of downtown are pleasant early 20th-c. residential sections and, near the railroad, clusters of early 20th-c. and later industrial development.

Lenoir was home to Davenport College, which operated from 1857 to 1933. A local museum occupies the brick, Neoclassical **Music Building** (1926; 901 College Ave.), the last remaining building associated with the college.

CW 1 Downtown Lenoir

The heart of the town is the spacious intersection of Main St. and West Ave., called the Square, with small public spaces at the four corners. In the 19th c. an island at the center of the intersection held the antebellum brick courthouse. After a new courthouse was built adjoining the northeast corner, the island became the hub of a traffic circle and site of the **Confederate Monument** (1910). In 1964 the island was removed to improve traffic flow, and the monument was moved to the northeast corner beside the courthouse. Commercial and institutional architecture surrounds the square and extends along the axial streets.

The **Caldwell County Courthouse**

CW 1 *Caldwell Co. Courthouse*

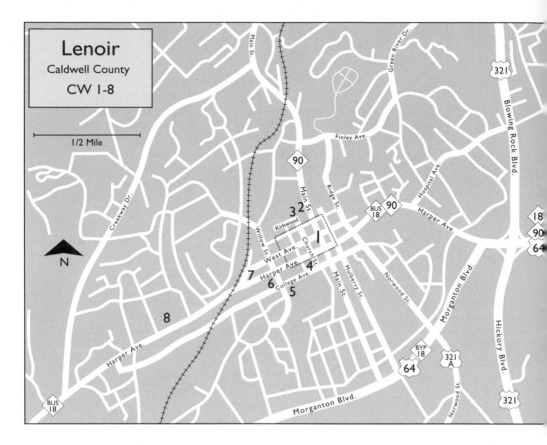

1/2 Mile

N

(1928; Martin L. Hampton, architect; NE of Square, 208 Main St., at West Ave.) is a stylized Neoclassical building in tan brick and stone, with Art Deco influence evident in its geometric motifs. On the adjoining square, facing the Confederate monument, is a stone bench with a fountain in a niche and curving seats ending in griffins.

The imposing 3-story brick commercial block that turns the northwest corner of West and Main was the pride of the town in the early 20th c. At the corner the **Lenoir Building** (ca. 1908; Hook & Rogers [Charlotte], architects; 808 West Ave.) is a well-crafted edifice of pressed brick, with rectangular windows with granite lintels at the second story, clean-cut arched windows at the third, and a modillion cornice. Built for the Lenoir family and designed by the prominent Charlotte firm established by C. C. Hook, it housed the Lenoir Hardware and Furniture Co., a bank, and professional offices.

The adjoining **Courtney Building** (1907–8; 814 West Ave.) features corbeled brickwork and pressed-metal ornament creating a pair of 2-story arches. In 1882 Marshall M. Courtney, founder of a successful crossroads store in the county, moved his business to Lenoir and with his brother R. G. Courtney opened a large dry goods and hardware store that traded in local produce, roots, and herbs. In 1897 M. M. Courtney built the store on West Ave. and opened a department store selling ready-made ladies' clothing and custom millinery. The business continued into the mid-20th c. The **Courtney Block** (1897; 818 West Ave.) retains its Italianate cornice and name/date parapet rising above a late 20th-c. covering; on the side the painted motto proclaims the store has "everything for everybody." On Church St. adjoining the rear of the Courtney Block is a small gabled and bracketed **Commercial Building** (late 19th c.), an unusually intact example of the Italianate mode.

CW 1 *Courtney Block and Building and Lenoir Building*

Across the street the **Lenoir City Hall** (ca. 1930; 801 West Ave., sw corner of the Square) is a streamlined Neoclassical composition. Farther down West Ave. the former **U.S. Post Office** (1930; James A. Wetmore, supervising architect of the Treasury; 1002 West Ave.) exemplifies the restrained Georgian Revival style in red brick with a pedimented central pavilion. South on Main, the **Ballew Arcade** (early 20th c.; 118 S. Main St.) presents a fine moderne facade and lettering of carrera glass.

CW 2 American Legion Post 29
1949–50; Clarence Coffey (Lenoir), architect; 401 Main St. NW

The simply detailed, modernist brick building with a central geometric tower features an unusually powerful World War memorial sculpture. It depicts in low relief a kneeling soldier, rendered in the muscular classicism characteristic of public art of the 1930s and 1940s. Local architect Coffey had studied and worked in Chicago before returning home.

CW 3 Kirkwood
Mid-19th c., ca. 1913; 902 Kirkwood Dr. at N end of Church St.

The hilltop house was for many years the Kirkwood School, a girls' academy begun in 1857 by Presbyterian minister Jesse Rankin and later run by his daughters. After the school closed, the building was enlarged as a residence by G. W. F. Harper. The large classical portico was added ca. 1913. The house remained in the Harper family until 1984, when Miss Margaret Harper, longtime local preservationist, willed it to the First Presbyterian Church; it is now the county hospice.

CW 4 St. James Episcopal Church
1851, 1920s, 1962; 806 College Ave.

The Gothic Revival style church, changed over the years from a small, wooden building to a larger, stuccoed one, is notable for its religious paintings by artist and priest

CW 2 *American Legion Post 29*

J. A. S. Oertel. The altar painting was executed and installed in 1872 while Oertel was rector; others were donated by his son in 1936.

CW 5 St. Francis of Assisi Catholic Church

1936; Frederick G. Necker (New York), architect; A. J. Durner (Asheville), contractor; 1025 College Ave., at Willow St.

The church is among the few Catholic churches in strongly Protestant western N.C. The parish was organized in 1932 by the Franciscan order at the invitation of the Catholic bishop of the Diocese of Raleigh. The parish started with only four members but grew sufficiently to erect the church despite the Great Depression. The long, gable-fronted church is built of rough stone blocks and sits high on a raised basement; the facade is pierced by deep, round-arched entrances and rises to a curved parapet and arcaded belfry with a Spanish mission flavor. At the rear is the parish house that held early services—the **Leffington House** (ca. 1900; 1025 College Ave.), one of the town's best examples of the Queen Anne style, built in brick with a wraparound porch and corner turret.

CW 6 Lenoir High School

1922; Benton & Benton (Wilson), architects; Joe W. Stout, Sanford, contractor; 1937, band building, Robert Clemmer (Hickory), architect; 100 Willow St.

The large, 2-story brick high school typifies the consolidated high schools that were the pride of their communities in the early 20th-c. public education campaign. The 220-foot facade is broken by pavilions projecting at the ends and in the center; classical detailing in cast stone contrasts with the red brick walls. The school gained fame for the early excellence and longevity (1924–77) of the Lenoir High School Band, founded by principal and bandleader Capt. James C. Harper. From the late 1920s on, the band won many state and national contests and competed successfully against much larger schools. The purpose-built **Band Building**

was erected in 1937. Like many others, the school (closed in 1977) has been converted to residential use.

CW 7 Lenoir Mills

Ca. 1900; jct. of West Ave. NW and W. Harper Ave., Lenoir vic.

Part of an industrial area around the railroad, the 3- and 4-story structure typifies the form and scale of many turn-of-the-century roller mill plants. Stepped parapets define the 3-story gable ends, while the center section, also gabled, rises 4 stories. The weathered sign still proclaims, "FEEDS. LENOIR MILL. QUALITY FLOUR. PERFECTION." Roller mills—typically steam-powered and using iron rollers instead of millstones to produce finer flour at greater speed—began to replace gristmills in the late 19th c. The railside location allowed the facility to receive wheat and ship out bags of flour and feed in quantity.

CW 8 Fairfield

1825–29, 1843, 1869, 1923, 1968; 1436 Harper Ave.

At the core of the brick, Colonial Revival style house stands the Federal era brick dwelling built for James Harper, Pennsylvania immigrant and founder of the plantation and store that eventually became the town of Lenoir. After the Civil War the property was inherited by his daughter Mary, wife of Dr. Robert Beall. Harper and Beall family history records each generation's expansions through a long continuity of family prominence and occupancy. Originally there were some two dozen outbuildings.

CW 9 Corpening House

1880s; E side SR 1142, 0.4 mi. S of NC 18, Gamewell vic.

This late version of the traditional piedmont brick house has exterior end chimneys and a slightly asymmetrical 3-bay facade that recall early 19th-c. patterns, while the center-passage plan one room deep, transomed doorway, and broad mantels and moldings are more typical of the mid-19th c.

CW 10 John E. Corpening House

1856; S side SR 1142, 1.8 mi. S of NC 18, Gamewell vic.

Also known as "Calico," the large brick house was built in Greek Revival style for John Eli Corpening, who owned a plantation and is said to have discovered gold nearby, which permitted him to build such a substantial and stylish dwelling. It has a pedimented, 2-tier entrance portico sheltering double doors with sidelights and transoms at both levels. Until a 1955 fire, the plantation also had a number of log agricultural and rural industrial buildings.

cw 10 *John E. Corpening House*

Happy Valley (CW 11–19):
The pioneer's heart must have leaped at the sight of this generous valley, where the Yadkin River and its fertile bottomlands extend for miles between mountain ranges. Characteristically, ambitious early settlers took up these productive lands and created a plantation economy. Interrelated valley planter families dominated the local political and economic structure and erected substantial buildings that have outlasted the modest dwellings of the far more numerous small farmers of the region. Along the Yadkin River the Lenoir and Jones families assumed early prominence in manufacturing—founding an antebellum textile mill at Patterson—as well as farming and politics. Their prosperity and congenial social life gave rise to the beatific name of the valley. Happy Valley's relatively unspoiled rural character, with farmsteads and buildings from the late 18th through the early 20th centuries, makes this a worthwhile detour.

CW 11 Harper's Chapel Methodist Church

1872; W side SR 1560, 0.6 mi. N of jct. w/NC 268, Patterson vic.

The spare, well-maintained country church has a broad pedimented facade with gallery windows and a central entry. The shingled tower at the side may be a later addition. The church was built by James C. Harper in memory of his son, John, killed during the Civil War. He donated the church and the land to a Methodist congregation that had begun in a log building in the area. The Patterson community was the site of the Patterson Mill, founded in 1850 by Samuel F. Patterson, Edmund W. Jones, and others; it was burned during the Civil War.

CW 12 Clover Hill

1846; E side SR 1514, 0.5 mi. SE of NC 268, Patterson vic.; private, barely visible from road in winter

The plantation complex epitomizes the antebellum river valley gentry. Col. Edmund W. Jones built Clover Hill for his bride Sophia C. Davenport. Jones, son of Ann Lenoir (only daughter of William Lenoir) and planter Edmund Jones, was a cofounder of Yadkin Valley school in 1852 and the first cotton factory in Caldwell Co. The big Greek Revival brick house, 5 bays wide with a double-pile plan, displays a locally unusual use of the Ionic order on the 3-bay porch and at the upper and lower doorways. Flemish-bond brickwork is employed on the front and (visible) southwest side, and common bond on the rear and southeast. Log

cw 12 *Clover Hill*

and brick outbuildings and a ca. 1918 round brick barn survive. Clover Hill enjoys a view across Happy Valley toward the distant mountains.

CW 13 Chapel of Rest
Late 19th c.; NW side NC 268,
0.8 mi. NE of SR 1514

The picturesque Episcopal chapel in Carpenter Gothic style was located on the property of Samuel L. Patterson, who donated his estate to the Episcopal diocese of western N.C. for conversion to the *Patterson School.

CW 14 Patterson School
1908 and later; NW side NC 268,
1.2 mi. NE of SR 1514

Samuel L. Patterson, longtime state legislator and commissioner of agriculture, sought to aid educational opportunities for the youth of his native Happy Valley. He left his plantation, Palmyra, to the Episcopal church to serve as an industrial and agricultural school for boys; his residence served for a time until it burned in 1922. A few early 20th-c. brick buildings stand in the oldest section of the campus, which is now a preparatory school.

CW 15 Walter Lenoir House
1893; SE side NC 268, 0.6 mi. E of SR 1504

The frame house illustrates the adaptability of traditional building forms. When this branch of the local squirearchy erected his house in 1893, the builder relied on the familiar 2-story, gable-roofed form with end chimneys but accommodated current taste

cw 15 *Walter Lenoir House*

in the double porch with its spindle frieze, sawn balustrade, and giant sunburst in the gable. After years of neglect, the house has been carefully restored from a ca. 1895 photograph.

CW 16 Fort Defiance
1788–92, Thomas Fields, builder;
1974, restoration; S side NC 268,
1.1 mi. E of SR 1504; open limited hours

Constructed over a 4-year period for Revolutionary War leader William Lenoir, the plantation house takes its name from a frontier fort that once stood here. Born in Virginia, Lenoir moved as a child with his family to Tarboro and married Ann Ballard of Halifax Co., N.C.; on the eve of the American Revolution he moved to the Yadkin Valley in present-day Wilkes Co. Active in the patriot cause, Lenoir fought in Gen. Griffith Rutherford's expedition against the Cherokees and in the Battle of Kings Mountain. After the war he was a leader in the new state's political circles and president of the first board of trustees of the University of North Carolina.

cw 16 *Fort Defiance*

Lenoir and his family settled in Happy Valley shortly after the war. After a brief stint in a log house, he contracted with workmen to erect a substantial frame house suitable to a valley planter—a 2-story block with interior end chimneys, Georgian finish, and an irregular 4-room plan. In his papers at the Southern Historical Collection, Lenoir's sketches of various layouts survive, along with agreements with his workmen. In 1823 the west wing was added, providing two more rooms on the first floor and one in the finished attic as private chambers for General Lenoir, while his adult son and his family occupied the older section. The late 20th-c. restoration removed subsequent alterations, reconstructed woodwork and graining, and rebuilt the porch.

CW 17 Shuford Farm and Blackstone Post Office

1920s, 1970s; NW side NC 268,
0.6 mi. SW of SR 1552 (Grandin Rd.)

William H. Shuford, farmer and carpenter, erected the farmhouse in the 1920s in front of an earlier log house that became the kitchen. He built the small post office in the 1920s for his wife, Harriet, who served as postmistress from 1920 to 1949. In 1938 he built the gambrel-roofed barn for hay, grain, and livestock, set into the hillside with entrances and levels arranged for convenience in unloading and good circulation. Shuford is also credited with erecting other similar barns in the area. A hillside potato house and other storage structures complete the complex. The residence was remodeled in the 1970s.

cw 17 *Blackstone Post Office*

CW 18 Riverside

1840, 1850s; SW side SR 1552 (Grandin Rd.),
0.2 mi. S of NC 268

The beautifully sited, T-shaped brick house near the banks of the Yadkin River blends two threads of stylish mid-19th-c. architecture. The Greek Revival taste predominates in the clean boxy forms and pedimented gables, while the influence of the pic-turesque cottage style of Downing and Vaux appears in the latticed supports and lacy swags of the double porch. Notable outbuildings also survive. The house is said to have been built in 1840 for John Langdon Jones, using bricks made on the premises. In 1882 the property was sold to Col. George N. Folk, who taught law here to many young men from nearby counties and called his law school "Blackstone" after the English jurist.

CW 19 Mariah's Chapel

1875; NE side SR 1552 (Grandin Rd.),
0.2 mi. S of NC 268

This simple frame church on its picturesque knoll recalls the character of many 19th-c. churches that once stood in the county. The gable-fronted rectangular building has two front doorways and a belfry atop the front gable; sash windows along the sides light the sanctuary. The chapel was built to serve both Methodists and Episcopalians in Happy Valley and was named for Mariah Earnest, at whose nearby home services had been held.

CW 20 William Hagler House (Beech Hill)

Ca. 1838; Mr. Hopkins, attributed bricklayer; no public access or visibility

The 2-story brick house is similar to dwellings constructed by settlers of German stock in the western piedmont in the early 19th c. Hagler was a farmer and the son of Swiss immigrant John Hagler and Elizabeth Van Hoose, of a Dutch family. John and

cw 20 *William Hagler House*

CW 19 *Mariah's Chapel*

CW 21 *Rhodhiss Dam and Power Plant*

Elizabeth met in New York, married, and moved first to South Carolina, then to the western N.C. frontier, where they eventually purchased this farm near the Yadkin River and built a log house. Their older sons moved to Tennessee, but William, the sixth son, married Elizabeth Mullens and remained here, building the brick house and using the old log house as a kitchen. Walls are of 1:7 common-bond brick over a fieldstone foundation; family tradition cites a Mr. Hopkins as builder of this and four other local brick houses. The front has a slightly asymmetrical 3-bay facade; the rear has a pair of entrances.

CW 21 Rhodhiss

The mill town flanks the Catawba River, with the large, brick **Rhodhiss Manufacturing Company Mill** (1900–1901) and an extensive collection of mill houses on the Caldwell Co. side. Spaced along Caldwell, Hickory, Cedar, and other streets that wind up the hillside, the workers' houses are predominantly 1-story frame dwellings, most with gable roofs, some with pyramidal roofs. Many perch on steep slopes. A few 2-story houses are interspersed among the smaller ones.

The town was named for founders John Rhodes of Cherryville and George Hiss of Charlotte, textile entrepreneurs who built the dam to power their mill in 1900. In 1914 the **E. A. Smith Manufacturing Company Mill** was built on the Burke Co. side of the river. The Southern Power Co. bought the mills and dam in 1919, rebuilt the dam, and in 1925 erected a hydroelectric plant, which provided power to nearby communities. The **Power Plant** (1925) beside the dam is an imposing masonry building, a 2-story brick block atop a high, arcaded base. Rhodhiss continues as a textile production town, where, as the town sign proclaims, the U.S. moon flags (1969) were woven.

CW 22 Edgemont

The community on the headwaters of Wilson Creek in the shadow of the Blue Ridge was the western terminus of the Caldwell & Northern Railroad, constructed between Lenoir and Edgemont from 1893 to 1906. In 1910 the line merged with the Carolina & North-Western Railway, which extended from Lenoir into South Carolina via Hickory and Gastonia. Ambitions to lay mainline tracks over the Blue Ridge from Edgemont to Pineola or from Lenoir to Boone never materialized, and the C&N-W earned the playful nickname "Can't and Never Will."

At Edgemont, logging spurs fanned out up the slopes of the Blue Ridge to pull out timber for the big W. M. Ritter Co. sawmill at Mortimer, 2 miles down the line, from which sawn lumber was shipped to Lenoir and beyond. A popular resort hotel, the Edgemont Inn, was a draw for tourists. The great flood of 1916 destroyed the sawmill at Mortimer, and within a decade the logging ventures in the area played out. But freight and passenger service continued until the late 1930s when the line was abandoned back to Lenoir.

A few early 20th-c. vestiges of Edgemont's heyday as a logging center and resort remain. The chief survivor is the **Edgemont Depot** (W side NC 90, 0.1 mi. S of SR 1358), which was moved a short distance and adapted as a private residence when passenger service ended in 1937. The well-crafted, gable-roofed station has deep bracketed overhangs on all four sides and is clad with German siding and sawn shingles. **Edgemont Baptist Church** (end of SR 1358) is a small frame church with round-arched windows and a combination belltower–entrance vestibule on one side. **Coffey's General Store** (W side SR 1420, 0.2 mi. N of NC 90), a frame store with a parapet front gable and recessed entrance, has been in operation since the community's early boom years. Remnants of the railroad bed and bridge abutments may be seen in a few places, and the secondary road south of Mortimer (SR 1328) follows the old bed of the C&N-W up Wilson Creek Gorge on its long slow climb to Edgemont.

Burke County (BK)

See J. Randall Cotton, Suzanne Pickens Wylie, and Millie M. Barbee, Historic Burke: An Architectural Inventory of Burke County, North Carolina *(1987).*

Morganton (BK 1–16)

Incorporated in 1784, Morganton was the earliest town in western N.C. and served as the principal trading and political center as settlement proceeded westward. The community was founded by families who assumed early prominence among the planters and manufacturers of the broad Catawba River valley. Because of the southward direction of the river, which becomes the Santee, then the Cooper River, Morganton traded chiefly with South Carolina and formed architectural as well as economic connections with the low country.

Around Morganton a plantation culture emerged among the interconnected families whose progenitors came as ambitious pioneers and took up the prime river valley lands. These families thrived as planters and merchants, lawyers and physicians, and diverse entrepreneurs who took good advantage of their river and road access to distant markets. They operated in a state or national context in architecture as well as in social and political matters. Their substantial antebellum houses, many built of brick, survive in far greater proportions than do the small log and frame houses of the smaller farmers who dominated the population numerically. Particularly distinctive are several early 19th-c. plantation houses such as *Quaker Meadows, *Bellevue, and *Cedar Grove, members of a regional group of 2-story brick dwellings, with 3-room plans served by paired front doors.

Supported by economically progressive Burke planters and lawyers, the Western North Carolina Railroad (WNCRR) was built nearly to Morganton by the eve of the Civil War. After long delays it was completed across the Blue Ridge to Asheville in 1880. During the postwar era Morganton's Samuel McDowell Tate, legislator and former president of the WNCRR, secured for Morganton major new state institutions: the Western N.C. Insane Asylum (*Broughton Hospital) and the *N.C. School for the Deaf. The prominence of the town's political leaders, plus the railroad and the arrival of physicians, teachers, and other professionals for the state institutions, gave Morganton a wider window on the world and a more cosmopolitan outlook than many small county seat towns. Local leaders, many of whom were scions of old planter families, turned their energies to building furniture and woodworking factories, textile mills, and tanneries in the railroad era, and industrialization has continued to the present.

Morganton's irregular grid of streets stretches from a central courthouse square along several hills. Scattered antebellum buildings survive, but the principal concentrations of notable architecture date from 1870–1930, including work by architects from Charlotte, Wilson, Philadelphia, and New York. These focus in the central business district and adjoining neighborhoods, and on the southern edge of town where the two huge Victorian institutional buildings preside over neighboring hilltops.

BK 1 Burke County Courthouse
1830s, James Binnie, builder;
1903 remodeling, Frank P. Milburn,
architect; Courthouse Square

The oldest courthouse in western N.C. occupies a large, central square bounded by Union, Sterling, Meeting, and Green Sts. Morganton was the center of the oldest established district court system in the western region. Many traditions surround its construction, including the story that its builder, a Scotsman named James Binnie, hauled the stone by oxen from a quarry 5 miles away and went bankrupt in the pro-

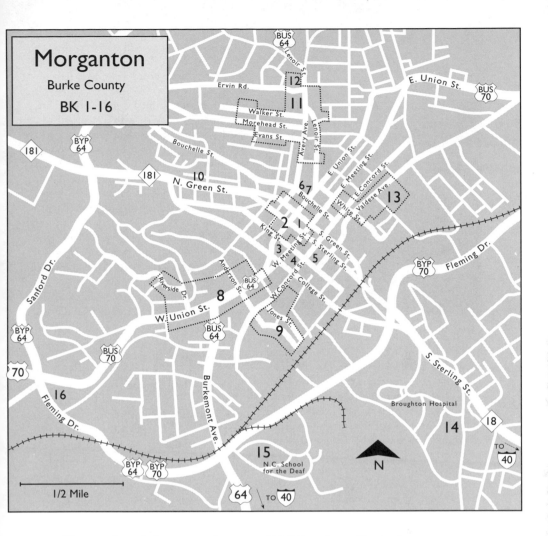

Ervin Rd.

BUS 64

E. Union St.

BUS 70

Lenoir St.

12

11

Walker St.

Morehead St.

Evans St.

Avery Ave.

Lenoir St.

181

BYP 64

Bouchelle St.

181

10

N. Green St.

E. Union St.

E. Meeting St.

E. Concord St.

Valdese Ave.

13

6 7

Bouchelle St.

White St.

2 1

King St.

W. Meeting St.

S. Green St.

S. Sterling St.

3

4 5

Anderson St.

Riverside Dr.

BUS 64

8

W. Concord St. College St.

BYP 70

Fleming Dr.

Sanford Dr.

W. Union St.

Jones St.

9

BYP 64

BUS 64

S. Sterling St.

BUS 70

Broughton Hospital

70

16

Fleming Dr.

Burkemont Ave.

14

18

15

N.C. School for the Deaf

N

TO 40

BYP 64

BYP 70

64

TO 40

1/2 Mile

cess. The severity of the stuccoed stone structure, still evident in the four-square proportions and opposing Doric porticoes, contrasts with the Baroque cupola, cast-iron porch railings, and elaborate cornices of Frank Milburn's Neoclassical remodeling. From 1847 to 1861 the N.C. Supreme Court escaped the summer heat of Raleigh to meet here. In April 1865 a contingent of Stoneman's cavalry raided the building and destroyed most of the county records—a loss that still plagues researchers. In 1976 the county moved to a new facility one block east (J. T. Peagram [Statesville], architect); the old courthouse has been restored as a heritage museum and cultural center.

BK 2 Downtown Morganton

Extending along E. and W. Union Sts. and the intersecting blocks of Green and King, the central business district maintains consistent rows of primarily 2-story brick commercial buildings of the late 19th and early 20th centuries. After an 1893 fire destroyed much of the downtown, in 1894 the local paper reported new stores built and stated, "Every brick at the Catawba River brick yards has already been purchased, and there are orders enough in sight to keep them all running on full time during next season. Workmen of all kinds will be kept busy during the year and Morganton will look like another town before next winter sets in."

BK 1 *Burke Co. Courthouse*

On the north side of the 100 block of W. Union St., diverse treatments of facades date from 1894 into the early 20th c., including the old **Tulls Drugstore** (1894; 136 W. Union St.), with its arched windows and clipped corner. A cohesive row of six brick buildings with corbeled brick cornices and pilasters occupies the 100 block of E. Union St., with some pre-fire survivors from the late 1880s and others from 1894 and after. From a later era, on the corner of E. Union and N. Sterling Sts. is the striking **Tate Block** (1941; Charles C. Benton [Wilson], architect), a stuccoed brick building in Art Deco style. The **Alva Theater** (1929; NE corner Sterling and Avery) is a vividly eclectic movie palace in brick with Spanish touches, including a tiled pent roof. The **Mimosa Theater** (ca. 1939, attributed to Charles C. Benton [Wilson], architect; 103 S. Green St.) presents a simplified Art Deco image in its blocky stuccoed forms.

BK 3 The Cedars (Tate House)

1850s, ca. 1875; 100 S. King St.; private

Family tradition recalls that shortly before the Civil War Samuel McDowell Tate bought the large Greek Revival style brick house (begun for Dr. William L. McRee, who died

in 1855) and completed it in anticipation of his marriage to Jennie Pearson, but his service in the war delayed the wedding until 1866. The couple raised a family of ten children. About 1875 the Tates enlarged the house and transformed it into a stylish Second Empire mansion with a mansard roof and big central tower. Corbeled brickwork panels in the octagonal tower complement the brick pilasters and frieze of the Greek Revival main block. Ornate turned and sawn millwork adorns the porches, tower, and dormers of the mansard roof of tower and main block.

The house epitomizes the vigor with which Tate moved into the thick of postwar developments. In the 1850s Tate had worked as an agent in construction of the WNCRR from Salisbury west to Morganton. After serving as a colonel commanding the 6th N.C. Regiment from Gettysburg until the end of the war, he returned to Morganton and was elected president of the WNCRR. During the political strife and financial problems of building the WNCRR, Tate took various roles in its governance. In 1874 he resigned from the railroad and was elected to the state legislature, where he promoted state construction of the railroad with convict workers and succeeded in locating two major state institutions at Morganton, the Western N.C. Insane Asylum (*Broughton Hospital) and the *N.C. School for the Deaf. It is tempting to look for the hand of asylum architect Samuel Sloan in the remodeling of Tate's residence, but evidence is lacking.

BK 3 *The Cedars*

BK 4 Morganton Library

1935; M. R. Marsh (Charlotte), architect;
J. J. McDevitt (Charlotte), contractor;
204 S. King St.

As early as 1921 the Morganton Woman's Club pushed for establishment of a local library, and by 1923 a library with a yearly circulation of 12,000 books was operating in a downtown building. By the 1930s circulation of 112,000 required new space, and with donations from the Kistler family, architect Marsh of Charlotte was commissioned to design this Colonial Revival facility. Built of red brick with delicate classical portico and trim, its interior continues the Colonial Revival aura in a bright paneled and columned space.

BK 5 Grace Episcopal Church

1894; William Milne, builder;
303 S. King St.

The oldest church building in Morganton, the simple Gothic Revival church is built of irregularly coursed stone quarried near *Broughton Hospital. Its builder, William Milne, is described as a Scottish artisan. Rendered in restrained Early English style, it has pointed arched openings cut cleanly into the stone walls and a corner entrance tower with crenellated parapet.

BK 6 Avery Avenue School

1921; attributed to Charles Christian Hook (Charlotte), architect; Goode Construction Co. (Charlotte), contractors; 200 Avery Ave.

The unusual form of Morganton's first high school dramatizes its corner site, with its central, polygonal entrance pavilion set at a

BK 6 *Avery Ave. School*

diagonal and its wings extending at angles along the intersecting streets. Although the classroom wings are rendered in standard brickwork with typical schoolhouse banks of windows, the entrance pavilion combines classical elements with an Art Deco spirit, with a wide frieze underlining a polygonal roof.

BK 7 Gaston Chapel A.M.E. Church

1900–1911; Philo G. Harbison and others, builders; 100 Bouchelle St., at Union St.

The oldest church in the county built for a black congregation, this is the second oldest church building in Morganton. The substantial brick church features a pair of entrance towers flanking a central gable; characteristic of many African American churches, the towers are of unequal size. Corbeled brickwork emphasizes the towers and outlines the pointed openings.

BK 7 *Gaston Chapel A.M.E. Church*

The congregation grew out of an African Methodist Episcopal congregation organized in Morganton ca. 1872, from which Slades Chapel A.M.E. Zion Church and Gaston Chapel A.M.E. Church developed ca. 1881. Named for the Reverend Moses Gaston, a local black minister in the mid-1860s, the congregation worshiped for a time in a small frame building. Church members, including local builder Philo G. Harbison and several artisans, erected the brick edifice at a time of widespread church rebuilding in Morganton. Of Morganton's turn-of-the-century churches, only this and *Grace Episcopal Church (1894) still stand.

BK 8 West Union St. Neighborhood

The deluxe residential avenue of Morganton's late 19th- and early 20th-c. entrepreneurial and lawyer class features large lots, towering trees, and architect-designed houses in various Victorian and Colonial Revival styles. Indicative of Morganton's stature, many are unusually large and opulent for a town of its size. The **A. C. Chafee House** (1919; Louis Asbury [Charlotte]; 310 W. Union St.) is a Colonial Revival brick house by a leading Charlotte architect. The **B. S. Gaither III House** (ca. 1935; M. R. Marsh [Charlotte]; 314 W. Union St.) is a notable bungalow with Colonial Revival detail. Moved from its former position on W. Union St. to an adjoining street is the **Burgess S. Gaither House** (ca. 1840; 102 N. Anderson St.), an expansive, 1-story Greek Revival house built for Gaither, an attorney active in state politics and superintendent of the U.S. Mint at Charlotte.

BK 8 *Burgess S. Gaither House*

BK 8 *Franklin Pierce Tate House*

The **Franklin Pierce Tate House** (1928; Electus D. Litchfield [New York]; 410 W. Union St.), a very large Colonial Revival house of Mount Airy granite, was designed by a New York architect for Franklin Pierce Tate, son of 19th-c. railroad and political leader Samuel McDowell Tate; director of the Bank of Morganton, F. P. Tate married Martha Thomason, principal of the *N.C. School for the Deaf. The **Dr. Joseph B. Riddle House** (ca. 1892; 411 W. Union St.), which is among the street's most elaborate Queen Anne style houses, was built for a physician at the local Grace Hospital.

The **A. M. Kistler House** (ca. 1927; attributed to Louis Asbury [Charlotte], architect; 502 W. Union St.) is a symmetrical Colonial Revival house with fanlit entrances; Kistler was a banker and operated the family's Burke Tannery. The **Kistler-Stoney House** (1936; M. R. Marsh, architect; J. J. McDevitt [Charlotte], contractors; 509 W. Union St.) is a massive red brick Colonial Revival house built during the Great Depression for Charles E. Kistler, son of A. M. Kistler. The **Henry J. Gaston House** (ca. 1926; E. E. Bolick, builder; 602 W. Union St.) is a formal Colonial Revival brick dwelling.

A few antebellum houses recall the initial development of the avenue, together with the changes it has seen. A vestige of early Morganton stands at **Mountain View** (1815 and later; 604 W. Union St.), a Federal style former plantation house of brick, with Victorian and Colonial Revival embellishments. It was built for Samuel Greenlee, one of the county's largest planters, and was later owned by the Walton and Avery families.

BK 9 Jonesboro Neighborhood

Southeast of the business district on Jones, W. Concord, S. Anderson, and Bay Sts., the residential section of approximately 50 houses is Morganton's most intact historically black neighborhood. Winding streets lead through an irregular terrain, where open spaces and garden plots remain among the houses. Among the houses that date from ca. 1895 to ca. 1935, residences range from substantial 2-story houses to small bungalows, cottages, and a few shotgun dwellings. Contractor Philo G. Harbison built several of the large and small dwellings, including shotgun houses on Jones and Anderson Sts. and his own large, 2-story frame dwelling, the **Philo G. Harbison House** (305 W. Concord St.).

BK 10 Avery House
Ca. 1876; 408 N. Green St.

The brick house, which combines Italianate massing, corbeling, and window hoods with a Second Empire tower reminiscent of the *Tate House, likewise exemplifies an Old South family's adoption of the New South architectural idiom. It was built for Alphonso Calhoun Avery and Susan Morrison Avery. Born into a leading planter family at *Swan Ponds, he survived the Civil War to move into town and become a lawyer, conservative political leader, judge, and amateur Civil War historian.

BK 11 Avery Avenue Neighborhood

North of the commercial district, the largest residential section from ca. 1875–1935 presents many architectural styles on Avery, Lenoir, Morehead, Evans, Walker, and Short Sts. Notable is the era's mix of large and small residences, a contrast to the more uniform scale and economic status represented in early 20th-c. suburban developments. The neighborhood includes homes of textile executives and workers, bankers and schoolteachers, and large Queen Anne style and Colonial Revival residences as well as smaller, tri-gabled cottages and bungalows.

BK 12 Ervin House
1878–1955; 517 Lenoir St.; open regular hours

A local history museum, the house was the birthplace and boyhood home of Samuel J. Ervin Jr. the brilliant, conservative, storytelling U.S. senator who captured national attention as chairman of the Watergate hearings in 1973–74. The frame dwelling began as a simple I-house; in 1885 Samuel J. Ervin Sr., an attorney who came from South Carolina, contracted with John R. Martin to add three rooms and the front "piazza" in "a

strong workmanlike manner." Other alterations including a new porch came in the 1920s. Ervin Sr. and his wife, Laura Powe, raised their ten children here.

BK 13 Valdese Ave. Neighborhood

While the most prestigious residential development extended west on *West Union St., eastward growth was also important. One especially intact area extends along Valdese Ave. and White St. As was true in several Morganton neighborhoods, large houses were built first—including several Queen Anne style residences from the 1880s and 1890s—and smaller ones subsequently filled in the blocks, such as the **Kibler House** (ca. 1925; 100 Valdese Ave.), a brick bungalow with stickwork in the stuccoed gables. An important vestige of early medical practice in the area survives at the **Broad Oaks Sanatorium** (early 20th c.; 210 Valdese Ave.), a large, 2-story brick building with columned portico, which was once the main building of a private psychiatric asylum and sanatorium established in 1901 by a former psychiatrist at *Broughton Hospital.

BK 13 *Kibler House*

Morganton Outskirts

BK 14 Broughton Hospital (Western N.C. Insane Asylum, later State Hospital)
1877–86; Samuel Sloan and Adolphus Gustavus Bauer (Philadelphia and Raleigh), architects; James Walker (Wilmington), builder; Broughton Rd. at NC 18

One of the few grand late 19th-c. institutional buildings still in use in the state, the massive red brick building is a powerful landmark. Its dramatically picturesque form is enriched with eclectic detail—heavy modillions, quoins, dramatic domes and dormers, and porticoes stacked three high. The landscaped campus borders NC 18.

The hospital was authorized by the legislature in 1875 to relieve overcrowding of the state's original insane asylum in Raleigh (now Dorothea Dix Hospital); some observers attributed the growing numbers of the insane to the stresses of the Civil War and its aftermath. Locating an asylum in the west would enable family members to visit patients more easily. The asylum was sited in Morganton through the influence of Samuel McDowell Tate, an enterprising legislator from Morganton, and substantial town contributions. Samuel Sloan, the Philadelphia architect known for his expertise in hospital and church design and the veteran of antebellum commissions in Wilmington, N.C., was recommended by leading hospital planner Thomas Kirkbride.

Like the antebellum asylum in Raleigh (designed by architect Alexander Jackson Davis), the facility followed Kirkbride's concepts: it was located on a spacious rural site convenient to town and rail line; the grounds allowed for therapeutic outdoor activity; and its plan featured a central administration section flanked by long wings containing rooms for patients, who were originally segregated by sex—men on the north end, women on the south.

Builder James Walker of Wilmington undertook construction, using brick supplied by convict labor—a practice common in the postwar era. Money ran out, delaying completion, and the first patient was not admitted until 1883. Sloan also gained the commission to design the Executive Mansion in Raleigh, another major state undertaking. He died in 1884 before it was completed, and both projects were completed under the supervision of Sloan's assistant, Adolphus Gustavus Bauer. The new hospital filled so quickly that expansion was required almost immediately. In 1886 a wing was built from designs by Bauer.

Early in the 20th c. new ideas about treatment of mental illness produced the Colony Program, with smaller, more home-like quarters for patients southwest of the main complex. This was one of several innovations by longtime superintendent Patrick Livingston Murphy, nationally known for his progressive and humane work. Opposite the Center Building stands a series of red brick buildings in Colonial Revival style erected in the 1920s and 1930s. Dwellings for staff were built on streets adjoining the campus. The facility was renamed in 1959 in honor of former governor Melville Broughton. (See Introduction, Fig. 39.)

BK 15 North Carolina School for the Deaf

1892–94; Adolphus Gustavus Bauer, architect; entrance at SE corner of US 64 and Fleming Dr.

The spectacular Victorian institutional building is architect Bauer's last surviving major work in N.C. With its companion *Broughton Hospital, it is a landmark of late 19th-c. social and architectural history. The dramatic roofline of the 4-story, E-shaped main building centers on a great turreted, towered entrance pavilion. Although modernization stripped off the skirt of Eastlake porches and replaced the windows, the edifice maintains its monumental presence.

BK 15 *N.C. School for the Deaf*

The state had built a school for the deaf and blind in the 1840s in Raleigh, and in 1891 the legislature authorized a school for the deaf. The town of Morganton donated funds and land to win the institution.

Architect A. G. Bauer came to N.C. as assistant to Samuel Sloan of Philadelphia, and after Sloan's death in 1884, Bauer finished up the *Executive Mansion in Raleigh and other projects. He also began to win commissions on his own, which included some of the state's grandest Queen Anne style buildings. He ended his own life in 1898 and was buried in Raleigh's Oakwood Cemetery, along with his wife Rachel.

In Morganton Bauer expanded the Western N.C. Insane Asylum (*Broughton Hospital) and was selected from among several candidates to design the School for the Deaf. His plan, it was reported, was modeled on the Philadelphia Institution for the deaf. Construction was slowed by tardy funding, but the school opened in 1894 and soon required additional buildings. West Hall (1898) burned, but the campus still includes several early 20th-c. red brick buildings in simplified Colonial Revival styles.

BK 16 Creekside
Ca. 1836; 825 Union St.

Creekside has long served as an icon of the river valley planter class of western N.C. Now encompassed within the town, it was described by Thomas T. Waterman in *The Early Architecture of North Carolina* as the "most monumental mansion of the Piedmont." An early and full-blown example of the Greek Revival style, it marked a bold departure from the prevailing Federal style. Family tradition claims that planter Thomas George Walton, drawing on houses he had seen while traveling in Virginia, planned the big brick house and had it built shortly before his 1837 marriage to Elizabeth Murphy.

Heavy pilasters articulate the walls, and the portico features full-height Doric columns of stuccoed brick. The forceful if unacademic entablature is adorned with wooden blocks, each with a leaf design. In a motif retained from the earlier Federal style, the entrance is topped by a delicate fanlight. It opens into a spacious center-passage plan two rooms deep. The combination of late Federal and Greek Revival devices continues inside, where mantels and other elements show derivation from Asher Benjamin's

widely popular book, *The Practical House Carpenter* (1830), which introduced the Greek Revival style into many regions. (See Introduction, Fig. 21.)

BK 17 Hunting Creek Railroad Bridges
Ca. 1860, 1910; Hunting Creek, just W of jct. of US 70 BUS and BYP; not readily visible or accessible

Characteristic bridges of two important eras of bridge construction cross the creek. The first, built ca. 1860 during construction of the WNCRR, is an important survivor of that vital and demanding project. It is believed that the bridge was built before the war, although the track was not laid across it to Morganton until after the Civil War. It is a 2-span arched bridge of cut stone, similar to the antebellum WNCRR bridges east of Morganton—Grant's Creek Bridge (1857) and Bostians Bridge (1858) in Iredell Co. It may have been built by contractor William Murdoch, who built a similar bridge near Salisbury and was associated with this segment of the railroad as well. The ca. 1910 metal truss bridge dates from a regrading of the line. It is a modified Warren truss made by the Phoenix Bridge Co. of Phoenixville, Pa., and is among the few surviving truss bridges in a county that once had many.

BK 18 Magnolia Place
Ca. 1818, 1847; SE corner I-40 and US 64, Morganton vic.; private, visible from road

Standing near the interstate highway, the former plantation house combines elements from two eras of prosperity in the Catawba River valley. John Henry Stevelie, a native of Switzerland, moved to the Morganton area ca. 1818 and built a simple Federal style brick house. The property was later acquired by Thomas Walton of *Creekside, who sold it in 1847 to his son-in-law, Clarke Moulton Avery, son of Isaac Avery of *Swan Ponds. Perhaps in emulation of their parents' dwellings, Elizabeth and Moulton Avery expanded the brick house to twice its original size. The remodeling produced an impressive Greek Revival house in a variation of the pedimented temple form, with a rectangular plan incorporating an inset porch with full-height Doric columns. Avery joined others of his family and class in local politics, in the organization of the WNCRR, and in the secessionist cause. With two of his brothers, he lost his life in the war. Although surrounded by commercial development, the house is still a private residence.

BK 18 *Magnolia Place*

BK 19 Swan Ponds

1848; end of SR 1222, 0.5 mi. S of NC 126, Morganton vic.; private, visible from road

A fine rendition of the Greek Revival style, the brick house has the low-pitched hip roof and the boxy proportions typical of the mid-19th c., enhanced by Flemish-bond brickwork and carefully treated classical detail. The house was built for planter and banker Isaac Avery, son of state attorney general Waightsill Avery, who had established the plantation in the 1770s. Of Isaac's six sons, three were killed in the war.

BK 19 *Swan Ponds*

BK 20 Quaker Meadows

1812; NW side SR 1414, 0.1 mi. NE of NC 181, Morganton vic.; open limited hours

The sturdy, severely plain brick house is a key member of the brick plantation houses of the Catawba River valley, a group of houses that represents the first surviving generation of architecture in the region and suggests links with Pennsylvania architectural traditions. Like *Bellevue and *Cedar Grove, the 2-story house is of Flemish-bond brickwork with a corbeled cornice. Like most of the group, it follows a 3-room plan with two front doorways; one door opens into the large room that extends the depth of the house, the other into the small front room, behind which is another small room. An enclosed stair separates the two front rooms, which have vernacular Federal style finish and reeded mantels. A 19th-c. log barn has typical half-dovetailed notching.

The site in the bottomland north of the Catawba River was settled by Joseph McDowell in the 1760s. His sons, Col. Charles and Joseph McDowell, met here with militia leaders on Sept. 30, 1780, to lay plans that led to the defeat of the British at the Battle of Kings Mountain on Oct. 7. The present house was built about 1812 for Col. Charles McDowell's son, Capt. Charles McDowell. The place name traces back to as early as 1751 and may refer to Quakers who traded with Indians in the area. The nearby **Quaker Meadows Cemetery** is among the oldest in the region, with marked graves from 1767 — that of David McDowell, 2-year-old grandson of Joseph McDowell. The house is under restoration by the Historic Burke Foundation. (See Introduction, Fig. 13.)

BK 21 Bellevue

1823–26; woodwork by Jonas Bost; E side SR 1419, 0.3 mi. N of SR 1421, Morganton vic.; private, visible from road

Named for its position on a knoll overlooking the broad valley where Warrior Fork meets the Catawba River, Bellevue is among the most elegantly finished of the early 19th-c. plantation houses of the Catawba River valley. Built of brick laid in Flemish bond, the main block of the house contains a 3-room plan with two front doors, one opening into the large room that extends through the house, the other into the smaller front room. Likewise unusual is the full-height rear recessed porch behind the large room. The ornate and robust Federal style woodwork is documented as the handiwork of local artisan Jonas Bost, who may also have executed the finish at other contemporary houses. Notable among the outbuildings is the half-dovetailed log **Smokehouse** (early 19th c.), with characteristic projecting front gable. The house was built for James Erwin on land he received from his father, Alexander, who served in the Revolution and was a commissioner to lay out Morganton. James's grandson, William Allen Erwin, became one of the state's leading textile manufacturers in the late 19th c.

BK 22 Cedar Grove
(Jacob Forney Jr. House)
1825–26; W side SR 1419, 0.3 mi. N of SR 1440, Morganton vic.; private, visible from road

One of the best documented of the regional group of early 19th-c. brick houses of the Catawba Valley, Cedar Grove shares such features as twin central entrances serving the 3-room plan, Flemish-bond brickwork, and Federal style woodwork. The journal notation of Jacob Forney Jr. recorded, "On the 4 day of May 1825 we begun build our house." Forney was then age 71, at a later stage of life than is usually assumed in linking construction dates and family ownership. He was the son of a Lincoln Co. family who were pioneers in the region's iron-manufacturing industry. There are several important log agricultural buildings, including a smokehouse, a corncrib and granary, and a large, early 20th-c. frame barn.

BK 23 Worry

The crossroads on SR 1423, so the story goes, was named by Jane Elizabeth Caldwell, who had proposed several community names that were rejected by the authorities and, thus troubled, suggested Worry, which was accepted. The principal landmark is **Arney's Chapel** (1900; E side SR 1423, just S of SR 1439), a simple frame church with steep gable roof, a double door with lancet fanlight in the gable front, and graceful lancet windows along the sides. One of the few county churches that retains its traditional character, it was built for a Methodist congregation established in 1900, on land donated by William J. Arney. The **William J. Arney House** (ca. 1895; NW corner SR 1438 and SR 1424) nearby is a T-shaped, 2-story frame house built for storekeeper and farmer Arney and his wife Margaret McCall. The house of his son is similar, the **Marshall Arney House** (ca. 1900; W side SR 1424, 0.5 mi. N of SR 1438).

Valdese (BK 24–29)

At the center of town a street sign marking the corner of Main and Italy Sts. suggests the special history of the community. In contrast to much of the nation, N.C. received relatively little European immigration in the late 19th and early 20th centuries. The Waldensian colonists, who came from the Cottian Alps in western Italy near the French border and settled around Valdese in 1893, represent a unique element in the state's history. The architecture they erected is, like the Moravian buildings of Old Salem in Winston-Salem, a rare example in the state of direct replication and adaptation of an Old World building tradition.

The Waldenses or Waldensians, as they are called after early martyr Peter Waldo, were an evangelical sect as early as the 12th c. and were persecuted by the Catholic Church for 600 years. They found common ground with Protestants in the Reformation period. By the late 19th c., persecution had ended, and as the people who farmed the valleys and slopes became too numerous for the stony land to support, several groups established colonies in various countries, including North and South America. One group was drawn to the foothills of Burke Co. after Marvin Scaife, a Pittsburgh and Morganton industrialist, met Waldensian pastor M. Buffa in Rome and made an offer of land.

The first group of 29 colonists arrived in

the spring of 1893, and 178 more came in the fall, disembarking from the train to begin a new life. The first years of settlement were hard, but soon the families gained footholds in agriculture and wine production and established textile mills and a bakery. The community of Valdese and the farms around it maintain a distinctive cultural identity seen in the family names, the neat farmsteads, the names of streets, and most obviously, the Waldensian Church. The Waldenses celebrate their heritage through a museum; an annual celebration; an outdoor drama, *From This Day Forward*; and continued contact with the valleys of their origin.

Architecturally the Waldensian heritage is represented in several phases. A few buildings survive as vestiges of the initial (1890s) replication in local fieldstone of the traditional stone architecture of their rural Alpine valleys. Besides stone houses set into slopes are bake ovens and farm buildings, including wine storage structures. The colonists also repeated the more formal stuccoed style of town and public architecture in their homeland in several houses and, especially, the *Waldensian Presbyterian Church.

In the early 20th c. the Waldensian stonemasons applied their traditional skills to Americanized building forms, including bungalows and public buildings in Valdese and elsewhere. Tradition reports that a number of Waldensian craftsmen were employed in executing stonework along the *Blue Ridge Parkway during the Great Depression.

BK 24 Waldensian Presbyterian Church

1896–99; Mr. Munsch, architect;
109 Main St. East

The stuccoed masonry structure embodies 19th-c. architectural patterns from the Waldensian valleys of northwestern Italy and bears a strong resemblance to the churches of that region. The severe form is dramatized by buttresses, a tall tower, and Romanesque and Gothic openings. The architectural dominance of the church in the town parallels its centrality to the life of the Waldensian community. The church is Presbyterian because in N.C. the Waldenses found the denominational structure most

resembled their own and thus allied with that group. The church plans were obtained by pastor Barthelemy Soulier from an architect named Munsch (unidentified). Construction was led by Waldensian masons James H. Tron, Eli Bertalot, and Henry J. Long; the carpenter was Henry Vinay Sr. Many men donated several days' work. The sanctuary was lengthened in the 1990s.

BK 24 *Waldensian Presbyterian Church*

BK 25 Valdese Elementary School (The Rock School)

1921–23; Quince Edward Herman (Hickory), architect; 402 Main St. West

Constructed of native stone by members of the Waldensian community, the school exhibits complex massing and free classical detailing. The importance of the school in the community embodies the Waldenses' longstanding emphasis on education. The school was designed by Hickory architect Herman, who had produced many schools in the area; money was raised by a self-imposed local tax and bond issue; and local workmen led construction, in which community artisans worked for 30 cents an hour to reduce the cost of the building. The school was dedicated at a trilingual ceremony in 1923. J. H. Pascal, J. P. Dalmas, Oscar and August Pascal, Henry Perrou, and others were stonemasons, and James Powell supervised carpentry.

BK 26 Waldensian Baking Company

1929 and later; 320 Main St. East

Established by John P. Rostan and Fillippe Ghigo in 1915 in a small brick building, the Waldensian Baking Co. continues as an im-

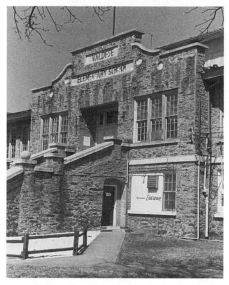

BK 25 *Valdese Elementary School*

BK 27 *Dalmas House*

portant regional bakery to the present, with its trucks delivering bread through much of western N.C. Although this facility, begun in 1929, has been expanded over the years, the central portion of the 1-story brick structure remains, with its distinctive arcaded and columned entrance recess.

BK 27 Laurel Street Houses

Along Laurel St. between Bouchard and Forest Sts. is a concentration of houses of Waldensian character that display the acculturation that took place in the period ca. 1895 to 1940. Probably the earliest is the **Henri Grill House** off Philippe St., a massive stone house of foursquare form, reminiscent of the town architecture of the Waldensian valleys. The **Dalmas House** (not visible from road) is an eccentric blend of Waldensian stonework and the traditional hillside location and balconies with Bungalow and Stick-style details; a lamp-stand motif in stone illustrates the Waldensian symbol of the lamp shedding light on the gospel. Along Laurel St. and on Main St. are several ca. 1920 typically American bungalows, rendered in traditional Waldensian fieldstone. Less distinctive are several probably ca. 1930 houses of stucco and stone in the popular "English cottage" mode.

BK 28 Tron House

1893; E side Church St. opp. Lincoln Ave.; open limited hours

The tiny board-and-batten dwelling is an important vestige of the temporary housing settlers built upon arrival in their new home. More than one family tradition recalls starting with a "sawmill shack" while building a permanent dwelling. This little house, built for Pierre Tron, stood on nearby Praley St. and was moved in the late 20th c. to the Old Colony Amphitheater for use as a museum; a traditional Waldensian bake oven has been reconstructed adjacent.

BK 29 Refour Houses

Ca. 1894, ca. 1925; private, no public access or visibility

Located on a private farm, the 1894 Refour House is an extraordinary building, a pure manifestation of the Waldensian culture and the building traditions of the upper slopes of the Waldensian valleys. Soon after their arrival in 1893, the Refour family gathered stone from the hillsides and erected a farmhouse in the traditions they knew at home. Built into an embankment, the fieldstone structure combines dwelling space on the upper level with a stable area for farm animals below, making it a true "house barn," a usage brought to this country by various European cultural groups but quickly abandoned. These features, like the balcony on the tall side of the house, repeat traditional practices in Alpine valley houses. Farther down the hillside is a barn of stone and frame. In about 1925 Frank Refour, who had grown up in the first house, married

BK 29 *1894 Refour House*

Anna Bounous and built a larger 2-story house nearby, which displays the balcony and the stuccoed masonry of Waldensian town architecture.

BK 30 Rutherford College

The community grew up around Rutherford College, a Methodist school that was established here in 1853 and had a strong regional presence until it was closed during the Great Depression. The most striking building is **Abernethy Memorial Methodist Church** (1930; attributed stonemasons Albert Bleynat, John Henry Pascal, John Pons, and Henry Perrou; E side SR 1001, just N of SR 1575), named for college founder R. L. Abernethy. A particularly fine example of Waldensian stonework, the Gothic Revival building with corner tower was built of irregularly coursed stone by craftsmen from Valdese. Also on SR 1001 (Malcolm Blvd.) stand several late 19th- and early 20th-c. frame houses that were the homes of professors or boardinghouses for students. Valdese General Hospital (Malcolm Blvd.) now occupies the college site, where a 3-story brick **Boys' Dormitory** (1927), converted to serve as the hospital in 1939, is now an annex.

BK 31 Connelly Springs

Almost a ghost town, a small commercial district recalls the community's heyday as a railroad-born resort town around a mineral spring. Brick and frame stores of the late 19th and early 20th centuries stand near the rail line. The **J. M. Sides Boarding House** (ca. 1880; SE corner SR 1607 and SR 1755) ex-

emplifies the many boardinghouses that once accommodated rail travelers who came to enjoy the springs. The 12-room boardinghouse is a traditional, 2-story frame dwelling with end chimneys, a rear ell, and a 2-story entrance porch trimmed with sawnwork. "Mort" Sides and his family moved here from Mitchell Co. so the children could attend nearby *Rutherford College; in addition to accommodating boarders, the family sold box lunches to rail passengers.

BK 32 Henry River Mill Village

This classic mill village is the county's only planned village, having been laid out in 1905 by owners Michael Erastus Rudisell and Albert Pinkney Rudisell. Its location along a gorge created by the Henry River, which powered the cotton yarn mill, employs a topography that makes its social and economic hierarchy especially clear. The mill produced fine cotton yarn. Down beside the river are the ca. 1905 dam, the ruins of the main brick mill (burned 1977), a machine shop, and other secondary buildings. On the northern bank rise the curving streets of the village, where about twenty of the original thirty-five **Workers' Houses** range up the steep slope; typically these are 1½-story, gabled duplex dwellings covered in board and batten or weatherboards, usually with a central chimney and a symmetrically disposed door and window to either side. Across the river, on the southern bank (N end SR 1854) stand the two, big, columned, Colonial Revival style residences of the founders, the **Miles and Michael Rudisell Houses** (ca. 1907 and ca. 1910), built with views down into the mill and across to the homes of the workers.

BK 33 Gilboa Methodist Church
1879; access road W side US 64, at 0.2 mi. N of SR 1102, Salem vic.

The frame church epitomizes the eloquent simplicity of country churches of the 19th c. The gable front features two sets of double-leaf entry doors beneath a lunette vent inscribed with the church name and date. The cemetery contains markers dating from the

BK 32 *Henry River Mill Village, Workers' Houses*

early 1800s. Inside, a stylized wooden dove above the chancel invokes the Holy Spirit. The congregation traces its origins to the missionary work of Bishop Francis Asbury in 1793 and appeared in conference records by 1800. After worshiping in log meeting-houses, the congregation built the present frame church. At its dedication it was praised as "a splendid building" that would "compare favorably with many village churches."

BK 34 Walker Top Church

Ca. 1845; SR 1957, Burkemont vic.

The small log church is located in the South Mountains up a long, rough road. Very few buildings still stand in Burke Co. to recall the upland farmers who carved out a life on steep farmsteads and built small log buildings. This small, revered church represents the meetinghouses that once served hun-

BK 33 *Gilboa Methodist Church*

dreds of mountain farm families. Built by Joseph Alexander Walker, who owned much of the mountain, it served also as a schoolhouse for children of the twenty-seven families who once populated the mountain. It is a 1-room, utterly plain, rectangular half-dovetailed structure, with a frame apse added ca. 1850.

BK 34 *Walker Top Church*

BK 35 Glen Alpine

The community on US 70 began as Turkey Tail when the WNCRR was built through this section. It soon took the name of the Glen Alpine Springs Hotel, a resort established in the 1870s at a nearby healing spring. After the hotel closed, a boarding school operated at the site. In 1920 the **Glen Alpine Knitting Mill** was founded to produce hosiery "impregnable as the Blue Ridge Moun-tains." The mill is a typical brick structure with segmental-arched windows. The business district on Linville St. contains several early 20th-c. corbeled brick stores. The earliest residential areas (E. Allen and E. Main Sts.) have bungalows and Colonial Revival houses. Notable is **The Aerie** (SW corner Church and London Sts.), a ca. 1905 towered stone house with Tudor and Queen Anne details, built for a local physician, E. A. Hennessee.

BK 36 Bridgewater Hydroelectric Power Complex
1916–23; SR 1233, 2.6 mi. NE of US 70, Bridgewater vic.

The hydroelectric complex consists of three concrete gravity dams that together form Lake James: the Catawba River Dam in McDowell Co. (3,155 feet overall length), and the Paddy Creek Dam (1,610 feet) and the Linville River Dam (1,325 feet) in Burke Co. The brick power station, located at the base of the Linville Dam, can be seen from above along SR 1233, which crosses the dam, or from SR 1223 below. The complex was built between 1916 and 1923 by James B. Duke's Southern Power Co. (now Duke Power Co.) as one of a series of hydroelectric stations along the Catawba River.

McDowell County (MC)

Marion (MC 1–4)

The town was founded in 1843 as the seat of the newly formed county of McDowell, where piedmont settlement and mountain frontier intersected. Located on land given by John L. Carson, the county seat was named for Revolutionary general Francis Marion. The community remained small until the 1870 arrival of the Western North Carolina Railroad (WNCRR) on its way west toward the Blue Ridge. The Charleston, Cincinnati & Chicago came from the south in 1890, and the Clinchfield arrived in 1908, giving Marion rail connections in five directions. Marion thrived as a gateway to the mountain region and had many hotels as well as industries, including tanneries, furniture manufactories, and three textile mills established in the early 20th c. The railroad boom era is reflected most strongly in the central business district and the outlying mill villages.

MC 1 Downtown Marion

Main St. and Court St. (US 221 and US 70) cross at the heart of the business district. After an 1894 fire destroyed most of the commercial section, the town soon rebuilt, producing handsome brick buildings dating from the mid-1890s onward, typically in solid, conservative versions of mainstream national styles. Major buildings stand at the four corners of the intersection.

Prime among them is the **McDowell County Courthouse** (1922; Erle Stillwell [Hendersonville], architect; Southern Ferro Concrete Co., builders) (**a**), located on the southeast corner. The severity of the 3-story yellow brick courthouse contrasts with the more elaborate classicism of most public buildings of its era; it seems to presage the Works Progress Administration (WPA) moderne of the 1930s, which married Beaux Arts Neoclassical authority to the clean lines of streamlined moderne. The second level of the 7-bay central pavilion contains tall court-room windows framed by brick pilasters with stylized capitals. This is the only N.C. courthouse by Stillwell, one of western N.C.'s most prolific and versatile 20th-c. architects.

MC 1 *McDowell Co. Courthouse*

Completing the square are the **First National Bank** (1903) (**b**), on the southwest, with its curved parapet and domed corner tower; the 3-story, yellow brick **Marianna (James) Hotel** (ca. 1910; J. M. McMichael [Charlotte], attributed architect) (**c**), on the northeast, which once had bay windows and a tall porch; and the Italianate, brick **Merchant's and Farmer's Bank** (ca. 1902) (**d**) on the northwest.

Nearby blocks of Main St. continue the brick commercial architecture, with lower facades altered but with corbeled brick facades in the upper stories. Especially striking is the former **McDowell Hotel** (ca. 1894; 9–11 N. Main) (**e**), with a grand display of corbeled brick, terra-cotta ornament, and great arched windows rising to 4 stories. Originally the Eagle Hotel, it is apparently the only downtown building surviving from before the 1894 fire.

Key churches stand within a few blocks of the central business district. The **First Baptist Church** (1912–14; Chesley Buchanan, construction supervisor; NW corner N. Main and Fort Sts.) (**f**) is a prominent and robustly designed Gothic Revival church from the prime building era. The corner entrance tower anchors the composition of broad gables and secondary towers; basket arches, corbel tables, buttresses, and bartizans are boldly treated and beautifully pre-

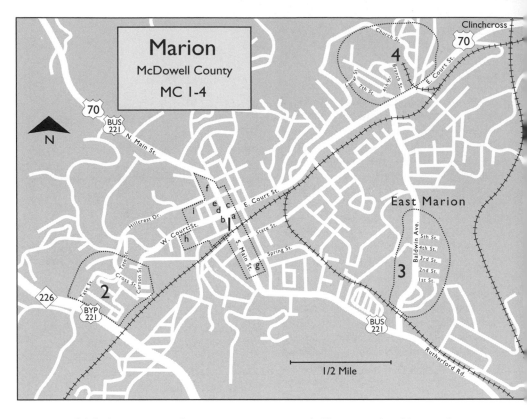

served. The harmonizing education wing was designed by Henry I. Gaines of Asheville.

The oldest church in town is **St. John's Episcopal Church** (1883–84; SE corner S. Main and Spring Sts.) (**g**), a picturesque Gothic Revival church in the board-and-batten mode promoted by Richard Upjohn's *Rural Architecture*. It was built by the minister, Charles T. Bland, and local carpenter William Dellinger with the style's characteristically steep gables and lancet windows, with exposed trusswork in the sanctuary. The original, simple entrance tower with

open belfry was replaced in 1903 by a more elaborate belltower; subsequent changes were made in harmonizing materials.

St. Matthew's Lutheran Church (1935; Q. E. Herman [Hickory], architect; Pink Williams, builder; 307 W. Court St.) (**h**) is a simple Gothic Revival building with fine stonework in local, yellow-hued river rock. Local stonemason Pink Williams is also credited with building several local retaining walls of the same stone. **First Presbyterian Church** (1923; James W. Greene [Birmingham, Ala.], architect; 12 W. Fort St.) (**i**) is a

MC 1 *First Baptist Church*

MC 1 *St. John's Episcopal Church*

MC 1 *First National Bank*

large, tan brick building in Neoclassical Revival style with an Ionic portico. It was built for a congregation founded in 1845.

Marion Mill Villages:
On the outskirts of Marion are mill villages where workers' housing, churches, schools, and brick textile mills of ca. 1900–1930 vintage recall the industrial and social history of the town. Characteristically, tight ranks of 1- and 2-story frame, simply finished dwellings line the streets; most were built by the textile companies and rented to millworkers as part of an established system of paternalism. As elsewhere, many of the houses have been sold to residents over the years as business practices changed.

MC 2 Cross Mill Village
1916, 1925; area bounded by SR 1195, SR 1201–1205, Marion

The mill village of frame housing was built for the newly formed Cross Cotton Mills in 1916. The third large mill established in Marion in the early 20th c., the village retains elements of its original layout and buildings. The village design is credited to Eugene Cross Sr., founder of the mill. Streets were named for Cross family members and others involved in the mill operation. A Mr. Ferguson of the Gaston Construction Co. in Gastonia (an important

piedmont mill community) reportedly built many of the houses. The grid plan and curved streets are lined with 1-story frame houses of a few basic types, with gable or pyramidal roofs and L and T plans. Many have shed porches and exposed rafter tips in an echo of the Craftsman style. In 1925, when the mill expanded, "New Hill" was developed for additional housing, with dwellings of similar design on Roane, Thole, and Hoyle Sts.

MC 3 Marion Manufacturing Company
1906–10; 700 Baldwin Ave., East Marion

A rare surviving example of an independent small textile mill, the factory is still surrounded by its associated housing. The 3-story brick mill is the oldest in Marion, with its original block erected in 1910 for the Marion Manufacturing Co., which had been organized the previous year by thirty-five investors led by Carroll Baldwin of Baltimore. The well-detailed brick structure combines broad, segmental-arched windows later filled with glass block; deep, bracketed eaves; and slightly later facade treatments with stepped parapets. The mill village included several blocks of small, gable-roofed, frame dwellings on 1st through 5th Sts., Baptist and Methodist churches, a store, and a community building. The mill attracted attention during the textile strike of 1929, which was covered by reporter Sinclair Lewis for the *Literary Digest* and featured in Tom Tippett's *When Southern Labor Stirred* (1931).

MC 3 *Marion Manufacturing Co. Mill*

MC 4 Clinchfield Manufacturing Company Mill and Village

1914; bounded by Hill, 4th, 7th, and Lamar Sts., East Marion

The Clinchfield Manufacturing Co., established in 1914, developed into the county's largest manufacturer, including carding, spinning, weaving, and production of printed cloth. Plant #1 was completed in 1915, and growth required construction of a second building in 1917–18. Both are typical brick industrial buildings with low-pitched gable roofs, arched windows, and various expansions. By the mid-20th c. the plant employed 1,000 workers and had 81,000 spindles and 1,900 looms. In 1955 the factory was acquired by Burlington Industries, which constructed a new mill in 1978 and switched to corduroy production. The mill village, one of the largest in the region, at one time had about 235 frame houses, 3 churches, a commissary, and a school. After Burlington purchased the property, the houses were sold to individuals. The surviving mill houses are 1- and 2-story, side-gabled frame dwellings, located on the hillsides encircling the mill.

MC 5 Pleasant Gardens (Joseph McDowell House)

Late 1780s and later; N side US 70, 0.1 mi. E of US 221/US 70 jct.

The ancient east-west route of present-day US 70 is marked by some of the region's oldest houses facing the road. Despite changes over the years, this prominent house beside the road is a landmark in local history. Joseph McDowell, born near present-day Marion in 1758, was cousin to Charles and Joseph McDowell of *Quaker Meadows (Burke Co.) and part of a network of families who were early settlers in the Catawba River bottomlands. After serving during the American Revolution in Indian campaigns and at Kings Mountain, he became a state legislator and congressman. If its traditional date of 1780s is accurate, the house he and his wife Mary Moffitt built on land granted to his father is one of the oldest frame houses in western N.C. It is a 2-story house with end chimneys of brick, two front doors, and irregular fenestration.

MC 6 Carson House

1793, ca. 1800, 1840s; S side US 70, 0.2 mi. E of NC 80, Marion vic.; open limited hours

One of the region's most impressive and evocative 19th-c. houses open to the public, this grand house built for the riverbottom gentry combines traditional and popular elements on a large scale. It faces the old east-west road through a lane of immense boxwoods. The massive 2-story-plus-attic structure has a full-length, 2-story front porch and balancing rear shed rooms. It developed in several phases. It began as a one-room log dwelling to which another 1-room unit was added with an open dogtrot passage between the two sections. The building reached essentially its present form near the middle of the 19th c., when it was enlarged with the engaged 2-tier front porch and 2-story, rear shed rooms, all covered with a broad, tall gable roof, with the end gables treated as pediments. The interior contains simple Greek Revival trim; the dining room is enriched by painted marbling of the later 19th c. Curiously, the dogtrot passage remained open for many years after the house was enlarged and formalized.

The log house was built ca. 1810 for Col. John Carson, an Irish immigrant and pioneer in the upper Catawba Valley, who came to the Pleasant Garden area ca. 1769 and married Rachel McDowell, sister of Joseph

MC 6 *Carson House*

McDowell of *Pleasant Gardens. Carson served as representative to the Fayetteville constitutional convention of 1789. After Rachel's death, he married Mary Moffitt McDowell, widow of Joseph. Among John Carson's twelve children, Joseph McDowell Carson, Samuel Price Carson, and William Carson were also active in political affairs. After John Carson's death in 1841, his youngest son, Jonathan Logan Carson, inherited the homeplace. In 1843 when McDowell Co. was formed, the Carson home served as the seat of government until a courthouse was constructed. For many years the house served as a popular stopping place for travelers and is now a local museum.

MC 7 William Carson House
Early 19th c.; Mr. Ballew, bricklayer;
E side NC 80, 1.5 mi. N of US 70,
Marion vic.; private, visible from road

The symmetrical, 2-story brick house was built for William Carson, son of the pioneer Col. John Carson. Construction is credited to a bricklayer named Ballew, and the brickwork is handsomely executed in Flemish bond. Like his father's house, William Car-

son's residence is fronted by great boxwoods, evocative of the tastes of the region's bottomland gentry. After 1930 it was the home of George Chapman, local businessman and developer of *Lake Tahoma.

MC 8 Lake Tahoma Casino and Office
Ca. 1925; Earle S. Draper, planner; E side
NC 80, 1 mi. NW of SR 1434, Lake Tahoma

As in Asheville and other Roaring Twenties resorts, the boom era brought ambitious development and created a naturalistic, rustic architecture. The small, hip-roofed **Office** was used as the field office of the initial Buck Creek Development Co., established by local businessmen to dam the creek for the lake as the center of a planned resort community. The dam also provided electricity for the resort. The company employed nationally recognized city planner Earle S. Draper to design the development.

Draper probably suggested the placement of the rustic, stone **Casino** pavilion out in the lake—the principal building surviving from the early days. Waldensian stonemasons from Valdese are credited with construction of the stone structure. Ap-

MC 8 *Lake Tahoma Casino*

proached by a long pier, the circular dance pavilion has a bold, conical roof, and the adjoining dock area has multisloped jerkinhead roofs. Kay Kyser, Hal Kemp, and Jan Garber played for dances, which drew crowds from as far away as Asheville and Morganton. Even today it is not hard to imagine the big-band melodies and the late-night laughter of flappers and their beaux wafting across the water from the pavilion. The development failed during the Great Depression, and construction of the hotel halted. After 1945 local stockholders continued the private development.

MC 9 Ransom-Moore House

Ca. 1890; S side I-40 at Old Fort;
private, visible from a distance at exit 73

The farmhouse typifies substantial rural houses of the era in its conservative, symmetrical 2-story form, adorned with stylish bracket cornice, polygonal bay, patterned tin shingle roof, and double porch with fancy sawnwork.

MC 10 Old Fort

Named after a Revolutionary period frontier fort, the small community developed in the early 19th c. at the foot of the Blue Ridge. At the center of town is the **Arrowhead Monument** (1929–30), an arrowhead 14½ feet tall

chiseled from Salisbury granite, standing atop a 15-foot stone base. Its plaque claimed that it "marks the site of the Old Indian Fort built A.D. 1756, the western outpost of the United States and North Carolina until 1776," though the actual site of Fort Davidson is a short distance away. Some 6,000 people attended its dedication, which involved Cherokee and Catawba leaders as well as white religious and political dignitaries.

Old Fort's typical small-town architecture dates from the half-century after a northern land company purchased the surrounding land for development in 1872. The WNCRR track was completed to Old Fort in 1873, but construction farther west suffered long delays. Until 1879 Old Fort was the end of the railroad line, where hotels were built and many visitors stayed before taking stagecoaches up the steep and difficult road across the Blue Ridge, a scene depicted in Christian Reid's *"Land of the Sky"* (1876).

MC 10 *Arrowhead Monument*

Construction of track from Old Fort up to the Swannanoa Gap during the 1870s was a trying and costly endeavor. An 1885 brochure described the accomplishment: "Here the railroad climbs by a tortuous path, winding over trestles, through tunnels and along shelving rocks in its panting journey to the summit, where the waters part which flow to the Atlantic shores and to the Gulf. The line winds and doubles upon itself in such a manner that in places a series of four tracks may be seen one above another." The dramatic railroad route is still in use. The modern highway up from Old Fort, the impressive sweep of I-40 across the Continental Divide, replaced an old and circuitous route of the 1950s.

The town's centerpiece is the **Old Fort Depot** (ca. 1910), a frame building with the characteristic stick-bracketed eaves and generous windows, with its waiting rooms, offices, and freight areas intact (see Introduction, Fig. 26). One- and 2-story brick commercial buildings with corbeled cornices and plain storefronts concentrate around the junction of Main St. (SR 1400) and Catawba Ave.

On a hillside overlooking the railroad stands the **Westerman House** (1880s; W. Main St. NW of depot), a gabled Gothic Revival cottage with lancet-arched windows and matching blinds. Queen Anne and Colonial Revival style frame houses stand on E. Main St. and along Thompson St.

Near the town center stands the **Mountain Gateway Museum and Log Houses** (E side SR 1103, 0.1 mi. S of US 70). The **Museum and Visitor Center** (1937) is a stone building constructed as a community building with WPA assistance; it contains exhibits on frontier life. The two log houses provide reasonably accurate and publicly accessible versions of the house type that long dominated the region. The **Allison-Stepp House** (ca. 1860) is roughly square in plan and built of half-dovetailed logs. The weatherboarded gables, the unglazed shuttered window, and the eave extending over the chimney are typical elements. The floors, logs, and doors are original. The **Morgan House** (ca. 1880), also half-dovetailed, is rectangular in plan and has a corner stair. The masonry chim-

MC 10 *Allison-Stepp and Morgan Houses*

neys are new. Both houses were moved ca. 1978 from sites about 3 miles east.

MC 11 Westerman-Adams House
1887, early 20th c.; W side SR 1119, 0.3 mi. S of SR 1400, Old Fort vic.; private, visible from road

The turreted, gabled Queen Anne cottage with spreading porches stands amid the vestiges of an ambitious early 20th-c. resort development—hunting lodge, riding stable, and fishing lodge—which ended with the crash in 1929. The house was built ca. 1887 for Henry and Ella Dula Westerman. In 1914 it was purchased by Col. Daniel W. Adams, a flamboyant figure whose occupations included inventor, miner, author, forester, and engineer; he is credited with building the nation's first forest fire tower, in Arkansas. He also founded the town of Glendale Springs in Ashe Co. and built its *Glendale Springs Inn. At his residence in Old Fort, Adams undertook several projects, including rock pools and a trout farm that still survive near the railroad.

MC 11 *Westerman-Adams House*

MC 12 James W. Wilson House

Ca. 1875; N side SR 1400, 0.5 mi.
W of SR 1119, Old Fort vic.; private,
visible from road

The small, T-plan, 1-story frame house, originally covered with board and batten, is notable as the residence of Wilson, chief engineer for the construction of the WNCRR for a long stretch of the line, including the heroic climb from Old Fort to Asheville, and the drilling of the *Swannanoa and other tunnels. He was also president of the WNCRR for four years. Wilson, who was responsible for planning, surveying, and management on site, lived here during the project. A historical marker "erected by the Southern Railway as a tribute to a Master Builder" commemorated his work.

MC 13 Andrews Geyser

Ca. 1885, 1911; W side SR 1407, 2.1 mi.
N of SR 1400, Old Fort vic.

The 70-foot manmade fountain is in a park amid the series of switchbacks of the spectacular climb of the railroad track to the Blue Ridge. It is fed by a stream farther up the mountain. The fountain was originally created ca. 1885 near the Round Knob Hotel, a popular railroad stop established by leading WNCRR men. The "geyser" in its unique setting was a great tourist attraction on the WNCRR. For travel writer Charles Dudley Warner it was "a column of water . . . stiff as a flagstaff, with its feathery head of mist gleaming like silver." As his train circled down, the fountain repeatedly "disappeared and came to view, now on one side and now on the other, until our train seemed bewitched." After the hotel burned in 1903, the geyser was moved a short distance and rebuilt in 1911 as a tribute to A. B. Andrews, a president of the WNCRR. It was restored in 1976 through local efforts in a park with a fine view of trains ascending and descending. (See Introduction, Fig. 24.)

North Cove:
The farmlands beside the North Fork of the Catawba are framed by higher, forested foothills. The agricultural valley contains several

well-maintained 19th- and early 20th-c. farmsteads and farmhouses whose substance and stylishness suggest the prosperity of the area's diversified farms.

MC 14 Reid-Brinkley House

Mid- to late 19th c.; S side NC 226-A,
0.2 mi. W of NC 226, Cox Creek vic.;
private, visible from road

The prominently positioned 2-story brick house is built of 1:7 common bond with a coved brick cornice. Decorated interior chimneys suggest the central-passage plan, and the broad, 2-tier front porch retains its Victorian sawnwork trim. Two log outbuildings survive. It was built for Joseph Reid, owner of several hundred acres in the vicinity, and was later owned by the Brinkley family.

MC 14 *Reid-Brinkley House*

MC 15 North Catawba Methodist Church

Ca. 1900; W side SR 1560, 0.1 mi.
N of SR 1569, North Cove

One of a dwindling number of simple country churches important to the region's rural communities, the utterly plain little building has a double door with transom and three 6/6 sash windows with shutters on each side, and it rests on a low, fieldstone foundation.

MC 16 McCall Farm

Late 19th–early 20th c.; private,
no public visibility or access

The classic valley farmstead was established by Catherine and William McCall. Soon

MC 15 *North Catawba Methodist Church*　　　MC 16 *McCall Farm*

after their marriage in 1871, they built the 2-story frame house, a weatherboarded structure with simple finish, exterior end chimneys, and a lacily decorated double piazza — a form seen in western as well as coastal N.C. McCall was a farmer, surveyor, and partner in a general store. His red, gable-fronted **Store** remains, as does a stand of red **Barns** with various patterns of gridded and herringbone weatherboards and venting. The farm retains venerable boxwoods and neat rail fences against a backdrop of forested slopes.

MC 17 Little Switzerland

Several resort communities along the Blue Ridge have ties to piedmont and low-country towns whose wealthy families established private, tightly knit summer colonies. Beginning with antebellum Flat Rock, the summer refuge of Charleston's elite, the trend continued with Lenoir's Blowing Rock, Wilmington's Linville, and Winston-Salem's Roaring Gap. In 1909 Charlotte attorney Heriot Clarkson visited Grassy Mountain on the McDowell and Mitchell Co. line and was so taken by the spectacular views he quickly enlisted Charlotte associates to purchase 1,100 acres and develop "the Beauty Spot of the Blue Ridge." Investors included industrialist and publisher D. A. Tompkins, whose secretary, Anna Twelvetrees, suggested the name for the resort. The completion of the Clinchfield Railroad over the Blue Ridge from Spartanburg, S.C., to Spruce Pine brought rail transportation within 4 miles of the site, and construction began almost immediately.

A 25-room hotel called the Switzerland Inn opened in 1910; designed by Charlotte architect Louis H. Asbury, the chestnut-bark-shingled structure was torn down in 1970 to make way for the present chalet-style lodge of the same name. Cottages were constructed on lots of a minimum of one acre each; most were rustic bungalows clad with bark or wood shingles. Many have been replaced, and most that remain are shielded from public view. The most prominent is **Echo Cottage** (1911; W side SR 1446, 0.25 mi. SW of NC 226A; private), a rambling bungalow with deep porches adapted from a plan published in *Ladies Home Journal.* It was built for the family of Charles H. Duls Sr., one of the resort's original stockholders.

A key building from the early years is the Episcopal **Church of the Resurrection** (1913; Adlai Osborne, architect; Ridge Rd.), a simple board-and-batten church of cruciform plan with steep gables, moved to its present site out of the path of the Blue Ridge Parkway in 1939. The **Switzerland Store** (1927; E side NC 226A at Bearwallow Rd.) is a stone commercial building that housed the post office for many years and still functions as "downtown Little Switzerland."

In the early 1920s Charlotte lawyer and novelist Thomas Dixon, author of *The Clansman,* purchased 1,400 acres on nearby Pompey's Knob and built a hotel and other structures for a proposed artists' and writers' colony, called **Wildacres** (SR 1421, S of NC 226A; private). After the venture collapsed in the Great Depression, Charlotte businessman and philanthropist I. D. Blumenthal opened the facility in 1946 as a retreat center for nonprofit organizations, dedicated to "the betterment of human relations and inter-faith amity." Dixon's original buildings were all replaced by the 1970s. See Louisa DeSaussure Duls, *The Story of Little Switzerland* (1982).

MC 18 Catawba River Dam Spillway Bridge (N.C. Bridge #126-87-10)

1919; Virginia Bridge and Iron Company (Roanoke, Va.); end of SR 1595; spanning Catawba River Dam spillway at Lake James

The two 8-panel Pratt through-trusses composing this bridge are each 152 feet long—the longest Pratts in N.C. and the maximum length for this span type. Like the nearby Lake James Canal Bridge in Burke Co. (destroyed), it was built for the Southern (later Duke) Power Co. as part of the *Bridgewater Hydroelectric Complex in Burke Co. Now bypassed by NC 126 below the dam, the bridge and spillway remain visible to travelers on the road below. Its construction was considered a feat at the time, for unimproved roads required the bridges at Lake James to be made of relatively short members that could be trucked to the site, assembled, and field riveted.

Rutherford County (RF)

See Kimberly I. Merkel, The Historic Architecture of Rutherford County *(1983).*

Rutherfordton (RF 1–5)

The county seat was incorporated in 1787 and, like the county established in 1779, named in honor of Revolutionary War general Griffith Rutherford. Traversed by the Broad and Second Broad rivers, the county supported diverse agriculture. After gold was discovered in the South Mountain belt that runs from Morganton to Rutherfordton, from 1814 into the 1840s Rutherford Co. flourished as part of a national gold production center. The Bechtler mint was established near Rutherfordton in 1831 by a German immigrant family expert in gold working. The mint coined the first U.S. gold dollars in 1832 and by 1840 had produced over $2 million in gold coins, operating even after an official U.S. mint was opened in Charlotte in 1837. Local gold mining declined after the California gold strikes.

With the arrival of the Wilmington, Charlotte & Rutherfordton Railroad in 1887 (later the Carolina Central and the Seaboard Air Line), the county and its towns entered an era of textile mill and resort development. Although Rutherfordton was outstripped by its more industrialized neighbor Forest City, in the railroad era the town grew to about 1,000 people by 1910, with accompanying building and rebuilding. With its compact downtown flanked by old residential and textile neighborhoods across ravines, the community reflects its post-railroad growth, with commercial, public, and residential buildings in popular late 19th- and early 20th-c. modes, along with a few survivors from antebellum years.

RF 1 Downtown Rutherfordton

The grid of streets draped across the hilly terrain encompasses several blocks of 1- and 2-story commercial buildings with simplified classical and Italianate motifs, dating from the late 19th and early 20th centuries. A restrained Neoclassical demeanor informs the **Rutherford County Courthouse** (1926; Louis H. Asbury [Charlotte], architect; w side N. Main St.) (**a**), which is sheathed in a smooth stone veneer and faced with a hexastyle portico in antis. It displays the prolific Charlotte architect Asbury's sure-handedness as a designer of conservative, generally classical public buildings. (Asbury, a graduate of MIT who had worked in the office of Cram, Goodhue & Ferguson in New York, established his Charlotte firm in 1908 and designed hundreds of buildings in North and South Carolina, including several in Rutherford Co.) This courthouse is the county's third, succeeding those of the 1830s and 1908; the clock from the 1908 courthouse is atop the entrance.

The freer, more exuberant classicism of a slightly earlier era appears in the **Rutherfordton City Hall** (ca. 1900; 138 N. Washington St.) (**b**), a big, boldly treated red brick building dramatized by its sloping site and corner position. Its architect has not been identified. Broad pilasters define both stories: those of the sloping lower story flank large rectangular windows and carry a molded belt course; from it rise the pilasters of the second story, which separate round-arched windows and carry a full entablature.

The **Federal Building** (1931; James A. Wetmore, supervising architect of the Treasury; 146 N. Main St. at Court St.) (**c**) is an unassuming Flemish-bond brick version of Treasury Department Colonial Revival. Aid from the Civil Works and Emergency Relief Administration supported construction of the **Norris Public Library** (1933; Louis H. Asbury [Charlotte], architect; 132 N. Main St.) (**d**), a 1½-story red brick building with a restrained classical detailing including a stone entrance portico of slender Tuscan columns, an example of the Charlotte architect's depression-era work.

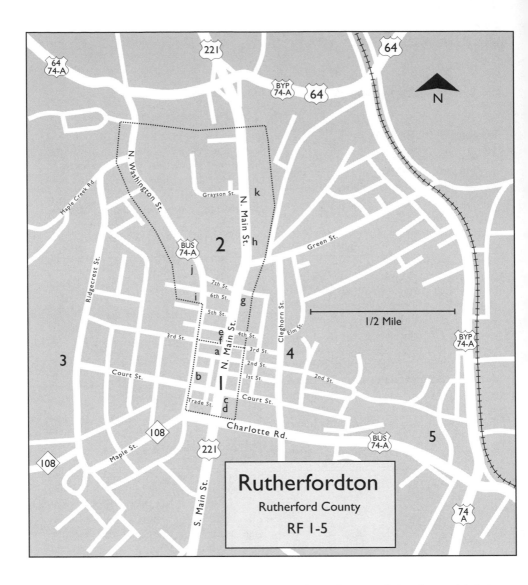

Rutherfordton

Rutherford County

RF 1-5

RF 2 N. Main St. and N. Washington St.

The largely residential section north of the business district contains the prime concentration of late 19th- and early 20th-c. domestic architecture. Two especially ornate frame houses were built for a local mercantile leader. The **Carrier-McBrayer House** (ca. 1835, late 19th c.; 255 N. Main St.; B&B) (**e**) began as a Federal–Greek Revival style dwelling, built for tinner Harvey Carrier of Massachusetts, who came to Rutherfordton during the gold-mining boom era and became a manufacturer and builder; after the

Civil War he expanded and remodeled the house with gables, sawnwork, and shingling. About the same time, apparently for his daughter Margaret, Carrier erected the **Carrier-Ward House** (1879; 249 N. Main St.; B&B) (**f**), a stylish Queen Anne house with front-facing ell and a peaked tower in the elbow, reflecting a new industrializing era.

A vestige of antebellum Rutherfordton appears in **St. John's Episcopal Church** (ca. 1848; E side N. Main St. opp. W. 6th St.) (**g**), built as a mission during Bishop Levi Silliman Ives's efforts to expand the Episcopal church in western N.C., for an Episcopal

RF 1 *Rutherford Co. Courthouse*

RF 2 *St. John's Episcopal Church*

RF 1 *Rutherfordton City Hall*

congregation that was one of the first in the area. Large-scale Greek Revival detail on such a tiny frame church gives it unusual presence. Corner pilasters carry the front pediment, and generous 12/12 windows flank the lancet entrance and mark the 2-bay sides. The square, louvered belfry has a low pyramidal roof. **St. Francis Episcopal Church** (ca. 1898; 408 N. Main St.) (**h**) is a prominent Gothic Revival edifice in stone, which succeeded the smaller church after funds for construction were given by Franklin Coxe, Asheville and Philadelphia businessman.

The neighborhood includes large and small versions of the Queen Anne style, Colonial Revival dwellings, and several fine bungalows and other Craftsman style houses. In the late 19th c. the picturesque cottage mode exerted an especially strong influence in Rutherfordton as well as in the county's rural architecture. The **Rucker-Eaves House** (ca. 1870; 257 N. Washington St.) (**i**), among the earliest examples, is a steep-gabled house in the Downing mode. An unexpectedly exotic note appears in the work of the Monfredo brothers, Italian builders credited with several boldly decorated, picturesque frame

houses from the 1870s through the 1890s. The **Dr. W. A. Thompson House** (ca. 1897; Monfredo Brothers, builders; 723 N. Washington St.) (**j**) displays an asymmetrical cottage form with its steep-pitched, front-facing gable wing and bay window, flanked by decorated porches. A later era's sense of the picturesque appears in the **Leslie L. Taylor House** (1939; 560 N. Main St.) (**k**), an ambitious recovery-era venture in the Tudor style with irregular massing and intricate brick and half-timber motifs. Its construction is credited to a Mr. Shytles, but the architect has not been identified.

RF 3 St. John's A.M.E. Zion Church
Early 20th c.; W side Ridgecrest St. at W end of Court St.

Rutherfordton's black Methodists formed a congregation soon after emancipation. The A.M.E. Zion congregation was organized in 1871 by Bishop J. W. Wood and, with Ezeral Payne as the first pastor, built a church of logs. The brick church the congregation erected in the early 20th c. features contrasting twin towers flanking a pedimented entrance and containing arched windows, characteristics favored by many African American congregations.

RF 4 Cleghorn Mill
Late 19th c., 1895; E side Cleghorn St. between 2nd and Elm Sts.

The brick industrial complex stands in a ravine east of the business district. The early history of the mill is uncertain, but a portion of the mill is said to date from ca. 1850. The factory operated for a time as Rutherford Cotton Mill Co. and was expanded in 1895 under M. Levi before being incorporated into the system of mills owned by S. B. Tanner and R. R. Haynes and renamed Cleghorn. Reflecting growth over the years, the mill's most prominent sections exhibit standard brick construction, arched windows, and a shallow roof. Mill housing—principally 1-story gabled cottages and small bungalows of ca. 1910–25—reaches up Cleghorn St. northward and on side streets to the east.

RF 5 Rutherfordton-Spindale Central High (Middle) School
1924–25; 1939, Hugh White (Gastonia), architect; Earle Sumner Draper, landscape designer; NW corner of US 74A BUS and BYP, Rutherfordton

In the era of great public school building, some of the state's finest high schools were built in leading industrial towns, with those in Roanoke Rapids and Gastonia being prime examples. For Rutherfordton-Spindale's large facility, architect Hugh White, who had recently designed the model Gastonia High School, was selected. Capitalizing on the hilltop site, he designed a formal composition in red brick with simple classical detail, with wings angling back from an entrance pavilion. Landscape designer Draper emphasized the public presence of the school with his approach drive.

Textile Mills:
*Southeast of Rutherfordton an important series of textile mills grew up, first along the winding course of the Second Broad River, then along the railroad line. The first was *Henrietta, established in 1887 by county native Raleigh Rutherford Haynes and associates Simpson Bobo Tanner and J. S. Spencer of Charlotte. Together and then separately R. R. Haynes and S. B. Tanner created the county's major cotton mills and villages, including Henrietta (1887), Caroleen (1895), Florence (1897) at Forest City, Cliffside (1899), Avondale (1916), and Spindale (1916). With changes in the mid- and late*

20th c., none of these once-extensive mill communities retains its full complement of facilities from the early 20th c., but different components—mill, housing, schools, and churches—survive at various sites.

RF 6 Spindale

In this important textile community, continued growth and modernization have left only scattered evidence of its early 20th-c. beginnings. Spindale was established in 1916 by Simpson Bobo Tanner, leader in the county's industrialization. In contrast to the earlier waterpowered mills, it stood by the railroad line and was steam powered. The mill village was planned by Earle S. Draper, but little of his curvilinear plan survives. Now the largest industrial center in the county, the community is dominated visually by the massive **Stonecutter Mill**, a firm organized in 1920, with an industrial complex greatly expanded over the years. Some early 20th-c. mill housing extends northeast from the railroad. The **Spindale House** (19th c.; 100 E. Main, at Tanner St.) near the mill is a 1½-story brick building described as the 19th-c. residence of Frank Coxe, which was given to the town in 1926 as a memorial to founder Tanner.

RF 7 James D. Ledbetter House
1914; James Andrew Baynard, builder; N side US 74 BUS, 0.1 mi. W of SR 1551, Forest City vic.; private, visible from road

The grand, inventive interpretation of the Southern Colonial Revival style presents a dramatic interplay of 1- and 2-story porches engaged under the broad, deep hip roof.

RF 7 *James D. Ledbetter House*

Built for a founder of the National Bank of Forest City, the house stands on a wooded 15-acre tract west of town and provides an oasis amid the dense highway development.

RF 8 Forest City

Incorporated in 1877 and winner of a 1927 prize for its downtown layout around a central public square, Forest City has diverse early 20th-c. residential and industrial architecture. A broad boulevard gives the downtown unusual spaciousness. Facing the main street are early 20th-c. commercial buildings, some with handsome corbeled brickwork; the most ornate is **121 E. Main St.**, with intricate recessed panels and arched windows beneath a stepped parapet. **First Baptist Church** (1915, 1927; James M. McMichael [Charlotte], architect; 301 W. Main St.) is a big red brick edifice with hefty Ionic portico, intersecting wings, and a tall central auditorium beneath a peaked roof—forms typical of McMichael's popular Protestant classicism. **Florence Mill** (1897 and later; Depot St., 1 block s of Main St.) was begun by industrialists R. R. Haynes and S. B. Tanner, who bought the existing Forest City Cotton Mills in 1892 but soon razed that factory and built new. The typical 2-story brick mill has arched windows and a low-pitched roof.

RF 9 Caroleen Mill Village
US 221-A at Second Broad River

The second major project of local textile pioneers R. R. Haynes and S. B. Tanner, the cotton mill and village on the Second Broad River were named after Tanner's wife Caroline. Development began in 1895 under Haynes's supervision. The rail line that served the cotton industry is gone, but the small frame **Caroleen Depot** stands. The **Caroleen Cotton Mill** is a characteristic turn-of-the-century brick mill of restrained Italianate style, with arched windows, a tower, and some alterations. The village climbing nearby hillsides retains 1- and 2-story workers' houses, principally duplexes, with some board-and-batten duplex cottages along the ridge. A predominant form is a 1-story du-

plex with central chimney flanked by a door and a window to each side, plus a rear ell.

RF 10 Avondale Methodist Church
1924; W side US 221-A, Avondale

The last venture of Rutherford Co. mill developer R. R. Haynes was a mill to be named Avondale after his Florida winter home. Construction began in 1916, linked by a new rail spur to Cliffside. After Haynes's death in 1917, his son Charles continued the work. Avondale's Methodists and Baptists met in a knitting mill until they could erect their own churches. Most of the village has vanished, leaving the imposing Methodist church as its principal landmark. The tan brick church, in the spirit of Charlotte church architect J. M. McMichael, has a domed central mass, elaborate Neoclassical details, and a spacious auditorium-plan sanctuary.

RF 11 Henrietta Mill Village
US 221-A at Second Broad River

Henrietta was once among the state's largest mill villages, but only remnants still stand. It was the first of the local mill projects initiated by R. R. Haynes, a native of the county, who in 1887 joined forces with S. B. Tanner and J. S. Spencer of Charlotte to form Henrietta Mills, Inc.—named for Tanner's mother—and to develop the promising waterpower site at High Shoals. In its time Henrietta No. 1 was the biggest cotton mill in the state. In 1895 it had 2,000 looms and 62,000 spindles, while its nearest competitor, in Concord, had 1,328 looms and 25,000 spindles. The chief early product was a coarse white "factory cloth."

The mill on the north side of the river was razed in the late 20th c. Remaining at the center of Henrietta (jct. US 221-A and SR 1920) is the **Haynes Brick Store** (ca. 1895–1907), a brick block of 1- and 2-story commercial buildings with arched openings and bracket cornices, built to trade with the growing number of workers in the communities. Also still standing are many of the large and unusually uniform 2-story workers' duplexes along narrow roads up the hillsides. They display modest changes made by

RF 11 *Henrietta Mill Village, Workers' Houses*

occupants who were allowed to buy them in the mid-20th c.

RF 12 Cliffside
US 221-A at Second Broad River

The magnificent mill on its namesake cliff above the river is among the most striking textile mills in the state. The steep site holds a great pile of brick mill buildings, towers, smokestacks, and chutes, combining long rows of arched windows, stonework, and a multitude of rooflines. The main mill is a 4-story brick building in 1:5 bond, with segmental-arched windows and a 6-story stair tower.

R. R. Haynes, who had developed other waterpower sites in the county, saw the horseshoe bend of the Second Broad River as a prime site for a manufacturing town with a large mill and an extensive village with model community facilities. He sold his interest in the *Florence Mill to invest in Cliffside. Kelly Moore was "chief building engineer." Construction began in 1899 and continued into 1902; until a 3-mile rail spur was built in 1903–5, materials and equipment had to be hauled from the main line by wagon. The waterpowered mill, one of the last and largest of its kind built in the state, was in operation by 1902 and grew over the years. In 1908 Haynes claimed it was "the largest gingham mill in the south." Haynes also built schools and seven churches and encouraged a high "moral tone," assuring that the "inviting and attractive streets [are] laid out with such taste and the pretty cottages flanking them are as neat as a pin."

After Haynes's death in 1917, the mill continued under his son Charles, who carried forward his ideas and built several important community facilities. The mill was retooled to produce cotton terry toweling. In 1945 Cliffside became part of Greensboro's Cone Mills system (R. R. Haynes and the Cone brothers had been friends since the 1880s). Although the mill was retained, the millworkers' houses and most community facilities were razed in the 1960s and 1970s. A few landmarks besides the mill survive. **Cliffside Baptist Church** (1940s) is a large, red brick church in classical temple form, replacing an earlier frame church. Only the tower is preserved of the **R. R. Haynes Memorial** (1919–22; SR 2111), the community building erected in honor of the founder. Perched on a nearby outcropping is **Cliffside Methodist Church** (1926; NW corner of jct. of US 221-A and SR 1003), a crossgabled brick church with Gothic detail. **Cliffside School** (1920–21, Louis H. Asbury [Charlotte], architect; 1931–32, Earle S. Draper [Charlotte] landscape designer; N. Main St.) is a symmetrical, 2-story, red brick building with restrained classical details. It was built at a cost of a quarter-million dollars by Charles H. Haynes to carry out his father's interest in education. The county's

RF 12 *Cliffside Mill*

first modern school building, it initially housed grades 1–11; in 1933 it was sold to the county.

RF 13 Henry Jenkins House
Ca. 1900; S side SR 2117, 1.5 mi.
W of US 221-A, Cliffside vic.;
private, visible from road

The expansive 1-story frame house was constructed for Civil War veteran Jenkins as the seat of his 1,400-acre farm. Featuring sawn and turned trim on the wraparound porch and shingled gables with sawn inserts, the house is similar to those built in the western part of the county by carpenter Guilford Nanney.

RF 14 Cleghorn
1830s; NE corner SR 1005 and SR 1148,
Rutherfordton vic.; private, visible from road

Poised above the valley where Cleghorn Creek joins the Broad River, the stuccoed brick plantation house retains its distinctive and locally unique form. The second story of the hip-roofed house is treated as a piano nobile, with broad windows marking the 3-bay main facade and 2-bay sides. The plan

has four rooms flanking the central passage. Tradition attributes the design to David Paton, Scots-born supervising architect of the State Capitol in Raleigh. The house was apparently erected for Scotsman Thomas McEntire in the 1830s, during the capitol project, but the Paton connection is undocumented. It is now the clubhouse for a country club.

RF 15 Miller-Whiteside House
Early to mid-19th c., ca. 1900; SW side
SR 1149, 1.1 mi. SE of SR NC 108;
private, visible from road

The big frame house, among the oldest in the county, was built for Andrew Miller in

RF 14 *Cleghorn*

the early to mid-19th c. The 2-story, 5-bay dwelling has pedimented ends and brick end chimneys in 1:5 bond. This form is common among early 19th-c. houses to the east but rare in western N.C. The overall simplicity is complemented by Federal and Greek Revival details, including bold patternbook Greek key and cornerblock motifs at doors and windows. After 1900 it was the home of Jefferson Davis and Flora Bryan Whiteside, who added the wraparound porch in Colonial Revival style. Among the several outbuildings is a large log barn with gable front and paired log cribs.

RF 16 William G. Miller House

1880s; Monfredo Brothers (Rutherfordton); NE side SR 1149, 0.5 mi. S of NC 108; private, visible from road

The steeply pitched multiple gables, projecting central gable, and sawnwork bargeboards repeat the A. J. Downing influence seen in the Italian Monfredo brothers' work in Rutherfordton. It was built for William Miller, whose wife ran the post office in a nearby log building.

RF 16 *William G. Miller House*

RF 17 Grays Chapel Methodist Church

Mid-19th, early 20th c.; end of SR 1192, 0.2 mi. SE of SR 1155

Located in a quiet wooded setting, the frame church with its entrance tower at the gable front is among the oldest churches in the county. It evidently reflects an early 20th-c. rebuilding of a meetinghouse thought to have been built in 1852. Tradition recalls that a log structure was erected here about 1825 to serve a Methodist congregation named for church leader David Gray. In 1861 he deeded to the congregation the land "whereon the Church house now stands, known as Gray's Chapel Church by name." The origins of the congregation trace back to an 1802 camp meeting.

RF 18 Fox Haven

Ca. 1823; N side SR 1157, 1 mi. NW of NC 108; private, visible from road

The elegant 2-story, 5-bay brick house is one of the finest early 19th-c. plantation houses in western N.C., with Flemish-bond brickwork and Federal style finish in its center-hall plan interior. The placement of interior chimneys on the rear wall and the segmental-arched lunettes in the pedimented side gables are unusual. Located in the beautiful rolling farmland overlooking the Broad River, the house was built for Revolutionary War veteran James Morris on land his father had begun acquiring in the 1760s.

RF 19 J. W. Whiteside House (Pumpkin Center)

Late 18th c.?, ca. 1884; S side US 64/74A, 0.5 mi. W of SR 1184, Lake Lure vic.; private, visible from road

A picturesque landmark between the old road and the Broad River, the weatherboarded, 2-story house began as a log dwelling and was enlarged over the years—on the south front with two shed additions, and on the north, toward the road, with an ell with 2-tier engaged porches on each side. As early as the 1780s the Whiteside family owned this property, but it is not certain when the house was built; it is said to have served as a stage stop for a time. Zackery Taylor White-side, a farmer, teacher, and Baptist preacher, moved into the house ca. 1884 and added the rear ell; subsequent generations gave the farm its fame as "Pumpkin Center," displaying an immense harvest of pumpkins.

RF 20 Davenport-Edgerton House
Ca. 1800, 1870, 1900; N side US 64/74A,
0.1 mi. E of SR 1008, Lake Lure vic.;
private, visible from road

The distinctive house at the base of US 64's long climb into the Blue Ridge was built in at least three stages. The 1-story rear ell was a dwelling built for John Davenport ca. 1800; the 2-story front section was added for Benjamin F. Edgerton after the Civil War; and the 2-story, full-width sawnwork porch was probably the work of local carpenter Guilford Nanney, who is credited with several elaborately finished houses in the county.

RF 21 Lake Lure

In a spectacular setting that combines a placid lake with forested mountains, the Spanish Mission style resort buildings of the mid-1920s seem oddly at home in the curve of the lakeside road. An unidentified Philadelphia architectural firm is credited with the design of the simply detailed stuccoed buildings with their arcades and red tile

RF 21 *Lake Lure Inn*

roofs, and planner Earle Sumner Draper of Charlotte created the naturalistic plan.

Like many mountain resorts begun in the land boom of the 1920s, the Lake Lure complex was part of a development scheme stopped midway by the Great Depression. Dr. Lucius B. Morse, a physician from Illinois who came to Asheville for his health, envisioned a $10 million resort—"America's greatest mountain playground resort"—linked with nearby *Chimney Rock. At this scenic "portal to the Western North Carolina mountains," Morse foresaw "great villas and pretty bungalows overlooking a great inland lake."

In 1923 he and his brothers enlisted local bankers, mill owners, and other investors to form Chimney Rock Mountains, Inc. As the *Lake Lure News* reported in 1926, the "landscape visualizer" was the "famous landscape engineer" Earle Sumner Draper, who also designed the mill village of Spindale. Draper, who had come to Charlotte in 1915 to execute planner John Nolen's design of the Myers Park suburb, established offices in Charlotte and designed more than 100 suburbs, about 150 mill villages, and other projects.

By 1926 the company had acquired 8,500 acres, built a 3-mile toll road to Chimney Rock, constructed the concrete dam to create the 1,500-acre Lake Lure, erected a hotel and other buildings, installed "ornamental bridges and illuminated highways," and begun other improvements before financial problems halted work. The hydroelectric dam was used first by the Blue Ridge Power Co. and later Duke Power Co. The inn and its complex hosted celebrities including F. Scott Fitzgerald and Franklin D. Roosevelt, served as a rest and recreation facility for air force officers during World War II, and later housed the cast and crew during local filming of *Dirty Dancing* (1987). *The Last of the Mohicans* was also shot in the vicinity.

Set against the sheer mountainside backdrop, the original hotel, **Lake Lure Inn** (open as an inn) is a long, 3-story stuccoed building with red tile roof and simple details; an arcaded first-story loggia carries across the central 9 bays, flanked by end pavilions. Also from 1925–26, and continuing the architectural ensemble in stuccoed Spanish style, are the **Administration Building** and even the **Lakeview Service Center** filling station with arcaded bays, recalling the early importance of automobile tourism. Part of the same development were distinctive concrete bridges with classical balustrades. These "ornamental bridges" carried the state highway—now US 64—built at that time to the resort: **Broad River Bridge #26** (1925; US 64 at Broad River, 4.1 mi. w of NC 9), which has 3 spans of about 50 feet, with reinforced concrete Luten arches; **Pool Creek Bridge #34** (1925; US 64 over Broad River, 3.4 mi. w of NC 9), with a single arched span and Ionic column lampposts; and **Lake Lure Bridge #52** (1926; 0.1 mi. w of NC 9), also with a single arched span.

RF 22 Pine Gables

*Late 18th–early 19th c., late 19th c.;
S side SR 1305, 0.5 mi. E of US 64/74A,
Lake Lure vic.; private, visible from road*

The picturesque inn has a venerable history as a popular stop on the old Hickory Nut Turnpike that crossed the mountain and ran past *Sherrill's Inn in Buncombe Co. The original section, believed to have been built in the late 18th or early 19th c. for Dr. John

Washington Harris, consists of two square log houses, later weatherboarded. After the Civil War, George W. Logan acquired the inn, which became known as the Logan House, and about 1880 the building gained its distinctive ornate gables and porches in the picturesque cottage mode. Many travelers and writers stopped here to enjoy the inn and the magnificent scenery of the Rocky Broad River, as this stretch of the Broad is known. In the 20th c. it served as headquarters for the Chimney Rock Mountains development project and for a Civilian Conservation Corps camp. It is now a private residence with vacation cabins.

RF 23 Chimney Rock Park

*1920s; Gateway, Douglas Ellington
(Asheville), architect; S side US 64/74A,
Chimney Rock*

Chimney Rock, an unusual freestanding monolithic granite formation towering some 1,000 feet above Hickory Nut Gorge, with splendid views of diverse and distant mountain scenes, attracted various tourism development campaigns from the 1880s through the 1940s. Purchased by Dr. Lucius B. Morse, in the 1920s the site was part of his ambitious Chimney Rock Mountains project, which also produced *Lake Lure and its

RF 23 *Chimney Rock Park Gateway*

resort facilities. The park remains in the Morse family. The chief architectural element dates from this era: the massive stone entrance **Gateway**, designed ca. 1926 by Asheville architect Douglas Ellington.

RF 24 John Logan House

1906; Guilford Nanney, builder;
W side SR 1008, 2 mi. N of US 64/74A,
Lake Lure vic.; private, visible from road

One of several late Queen Anne style houses credited to local builder Guilford Nanney, the prominent 2-story frame dwelling has irregular massing with a projecting 2-story bay and a decorated wraparound porch.

RF 25 Antioch Baptist Church

Late 19th c.; E side SR 1008, 3.3 mi. S of
SR 1001, Bills Creek, Whitehouse vic.

The simple frame chapel in the woods is remarkably unchanged and well kept. A double door with transom opens into the gable front, and plain 6/6 windows light the sanctuary. There was a Baptist congregation on Bills Creek by the early 19th c., when the pioneer Baptist minister Humphrey Posey preached there. The congregation evidently dates from the mid-19th c.

RF 26 Union Mills

SR 1510 between SR 1504 and US 221

The old farming community of Crabapple Gap developed into a little town after railroad lines arrived in 1890 and 1906. The amalgamation of several area lumber mills evidently brought the name Union Mills. Recalling the railroad era are a row of small, 1-story brick commercial buildings, including the post office, and several 1- and 2-story frame houses in the Queen Anne, Italianate, and other modes. **Union Mills Presbyterian Church** (ca. 1902) is a frame building with pedimented entrance vestibule, tall belfry, and lancet windows.

RF 27 James Harvey Forney House

1859; N side SR 1504, 1.0 mi. E of SR 1510,
Union Mills vic.; private, visible from road

The striking house captures the picturesque spirit in unusual form: a 2-story entrance porch features 2 tiers of lancet-arched latticework beneath a peaked roof, and scalloped bargeboards outline the porch and house eaves. This concoction adorns an otherwise standard 2-story frame house. Family tradition recalls that Forney completed his house in 1859; whether the Gothic treatment came then or slightly later is uncertain. The

RF 25 *Antioch Baptist Church*

RF 27 *James Harvey Forney House*

farm complex includes two log barns and a log smokehouse.

RF 28 Black House
19th c.; W side SR 1514, 0.7 mi. N of SR 1504; private, visible from road

Typical of many that once stood in the county, the 1-room log house has half-dovetailed notching and a stone chimney; a rear shed porch encloses a small shed room. Family tradition reports that the house was built about 1800 for Hugh and Margaret Smart Black (m. 1799) on a 100-acre tract given her by her parents, William and Jane Smart, early settlers in the area. The place descended to their son John R. Black and his wife Isabella Carson (daughter of Gen. John Carson), members of nearby *Brittain Presbyterian Church, an important center for the largely Scotch-Irish families in the locale. The house was restored in the mid-20th c.

RF 29 Hamilton-Andrews House
Ca. 1850; E side SR 1713, 1.0 mi. E of US 64, Lanes Store; private, visible from road

The big, 2-story brick house surveys the bottomlands of Cane Creek from its hillside. It was evidently built for Benjamin Hamilton as the center of a large farm. The 2-tier porch of ornate sawnwork was added by James and Lucy Melton Andrews probably in the 1880s, about the time they built the rear dining-kitchen ell to replace a freestanding kitchen. The Andrews family settled in the area in the mid-18th c. and helped estab-

lish *Brittain Presbyterian Church. James had joined the California gold rush as a young man and returned sufficiently prosperous to buy the large farm with its brick house. He and Lucy named the first of their nine children Sarah Elizabeth California.

RF 30 Albert G. Thompson House
Ca. 1874; W side SR 1713, 1.5 mi. E of US 64, Lanes Store vic.; private, visible from road

The Italianate style rarely appears in such full-blown form in rural settings in the region, but Albert G. and Mary Andrews Thompson built their 2-story frame farmhouse with all the hallmarks of the mode: a low hip roof with bracketed eaves, peaked window hoods, interior chimneys with corbeled caps, and elaborate sawnwork porch brackets. A large, decorated barn with cupola stands nearby. The couple, descendants of early settlers and founders of *Brittain Presbyterian Church, married in 1852 and had seven children. Albert lost a leg during service in the Civil War, then returned to operate the large farm, build a stylish house, and run a store. His 1-story, gable-fronted store still stands by the road.

RF 31 Mooney-McCurry House
Mid-19th c.; E side SR 1006, 2.9 mi. S of NC 226, Sunshine vic.; private, visible from road

Although 1-story houses with engaged and inset porches are often associated with the coastal region, the form also appears in scattered examples in the piedmont and mountains. In this small frame house set on a high basement, the inset porch is enclosed with shed rooms on two sides, creating a recessed central porch. A large double-crib barn and several 20th-c. frame outbuildings are also located on the farm. The house was probably standing when M. S. McCurry, member of a large local family, bought the property from J. Mooney in 1874.

RF 32 Brittain Presbyterian Church
1850s, 1940; E side US 64, 0.2 mi. S of SR 1007, Westminster

The gable-fronted church was built in frame with a modest belfry in 1852 and was brick-veneered in 1940. The congregation, the oldest in the county and one of the oldest west of the Catawba River in N.C., was established in 1768 by Scotch-Irish settlers who came mainly from Pennsylvania. It served as an important community focus over the years. The large cemetery contains some of the oldest gravestones in the county.

RF 33 Andrews Mill Complex

1830, ca. 1907; SW side SR 1007,
1.8 mi. NW of SR 1006, Washburn vic.;
private, visible from road

A grand 2-story frame house with Colonial Revival detail and a deep wraparound porch overlooks the creek from its shaded slope. A mill was begun here ca. 1830 for John Cansalor. In 1878 it was sold to James M. Andrews (cf. *Hamilton-Andrews House). He left it to his son Benjamin, who moved the miller's house to another site and erected the present large house in 1907. The frame mill house by the creek may contain elements of the 1830

gristmill that operated at the site, enlarged and outfitted with a small cupola in the 1870s by James M. Andrews.

RF 34 E. N. Washburn House

Ca. 1915; W side SR 1006,
0.1 mi. S of SR 1007, Washburn;
private, visible from road

Family tradition says that the form of the Southern Colonial Revival house is based on a residence Washburn had seen in Spartanburg, but the house also appears to be a brick version of the *James D. Ledbetter House near Forest City. Both are unusual in having a massive hip roof that encompasses the full-height portico, plus a pedimented entrance portico and wraparound 1-story porch. The house was built for Edgar Nollie and Grace Harton Washburn, just across the road from the brick **Store** he had erected in 1904 to expand the mercantile business begun by his father, Reuben, a circuit-riding Methodist minister. Edgar also sold caskets, founded the Bostic Bank, and served as a civic and church leader.

Polk County (PL)

One of the state's smallest counties in population, Polk is also one of the most prosperous, with its location on the unusually temperate south slope of the Blue Ridge making it a year-round resort and retirement center. In the antebellum period the Mills family, originally of South Carolina, owned several large plantations and dominated local society and politics. Because of its plantation culture, Polk Co. included a small but significant black population before and after the Civil War. With the arrival of the railroad from South Carolina in the 1870s, the county quickly became a tourist mecca. In the 1890s a Pennsylvania visitor exulted, "It was my good fortune, while in search of a health-restoring climate, to hear of Polk County, N.C.," where an "encircling mountain range gives . . . a freedom from coldness and dampness that can only be appreciated by those who have felt its exhilarating influence." "While the Creator could have made a more delightful climate . . . surely He has never done so." The county comprises diverse elements: hardscrabble farms on rough terrain where few early buildings survive; large 19th-c. houses—including three Mills family plantations—of a small planter class that farmed the riverbottoms; and more recent, resort communities attracting South Carolina and northern horse people.

PL 1 Columbus

Established when Polk Co. was formed in 1855 and named for Col. William Polk of Mecklenburg Co. (d. 1834), who was N.C.'s last living field officer of the American Revolution, the tiny county seat was named for Dr. Columbus Mills, of the area's dominant planter family and legislator instrumental in creating the county. The principal landmark is the **Polk County Courthouse** (1859; Ephraim Clayton and George W. Shackleford [Asheville], contractors), one of the state's finest Greek Revival courthouses. Standing alone in its central square, the 2-story brick edifice features a massive portico with four square pillars and is crowned with a cupola; inside is a graceful double spiral stair. Unusual in being the only courthouse the county has built, it is also the oldest courthouse in western N.C. still serving its original function. The bell in the belfry has been rung every day that court has been in session. Clayton was a leading western N.C. builder who also built *St. John-in-the-Wilderness Episcopal Church in Flat Rock.

Also notable is the brick Neoclassical Revival **Columbus School** (1922; NW corner E. Mills St. [NC 108] and N. Peak St.), which

PL 1 *Polk Co. Courthouse, Columbus*

houses a school begun in 1891 by Frank Stearns, who settled in the area ca. 1888 and aided local civic causes. The **J. G. Hughes House** (1896; 202 N. Peak St.; private) is a sprightly 1½-story Queen Anne house with wraparound porch, shingled and half-timbered gables, and a cutaway bay window. It was built for a city councilman and president of the Polk Co. Telephone Company; the deed required construction of a frame building with not less than 5 rooms, "properly finished," and to cost not less than $800.

PL 2 Stony Knoll

Soon after the Civil War the African American community was established just over a wooded hill from Mill Spring. The **Rev. Joshua D. Jones House** (ca 1884, 1897; SW side SR 1531, 0.4 mi. SE of NC 108; private), a plainly finished, 2-story frame house, belonged to a teacher, merchant, farmer, carpenter, and pastor of the community's C.M.E. (Colored Methodist Episcopal) Church. The **Stony Knoll Library** (1940; N side SR 1531, 0.5 mi. E of NC 108) succeeded the Jones House as the site of the library. A young black teacher, Della Hayden Davenport, who convinced the county to fund the institution in 1937, designed the building. A local carpenter laid the rough-faced cement blocks, which were made on a machine owned by Mrs. Davenport's cousin.

PL 2 *Rev. Joshua D. Jones House*

PL 3 Mill Spring

Originally known as Basin Springs, Mill Spring developed into a thriving turn-of-the-century resort town with several hotels, boardinghouses, and retail businesses. During the town's earlier years it was the site of the first two county court sessions. Northwest of the main intersection, the **Baynard House** (ca. 1895; N side SR 1138, 0.2 mi. W of NC 9) is a large frame house with central chimney and double porch, built as a vacation house for a South Carolina family.

PL 4 "Toddy Joe" Waldrop House

Early and late 19th c.; NW corner NC 9 and SR 1330, 0.2 mi. N of US 74, Beulah; private, visible from road

Presiding over a hilly pasture, the picturesque farmhouse with twin front gables contains an early 19th-c. dwelling—probably a 1-room log house—and a larger ca. 1830 section with Federal and Greek Revival elements. Thomas Joseph "Toddy Joe" Waldrop, a prominent farmer and county commissioner, added the second story that brought the house to its present appearance. A log smokehouse, barns, and a cemetery are nearby.

PL 5 Richard Whitesides House

1859; Tolliver Lewis, attributed carpenter; E side SR 1311, 1.4 mi. N of SR 1161, Sunnyview vic.; private, visible from road

The typical mid-19th-c. frame farmhouse has a center-passage plan and simple Greek Revival detail. The fine brick chimneys were laid by a mason from Charleston. Whitesides, a member of the school board and a superior court justice, operated the Poplar Grove post office in the front ell; upon his death his son, Harvey, succeeded him as postmaster. The house also served as a weaving school.

PL 6 Green River Plantation

Early and mid-19th c., late 20th c.; N side SR 1005, 1.4 mi. E of SR 1326, Cox Store vic.; open by appointment

The finest of the county's antebellum houses is a prominent sight on the bank of the beautiful Green River. The 2-story frame Federal style block of this complex house may have been standing when Joseph McDowell Carson (son of John Carson of Mc-

Dowell Co.; see *Carson House) settled here in the early 19th c. Carson later added the 2-story brick Greek Revival section. As in other Polk Co. plantation houses, the high-quality finish demonstrates the owner's ability to import skilled craftsmen (and perhaps finished woodwork) into a remote area. Asheville developer Franklin Coxe, builder of the original Battery Park Hotel in that city, owned the property after 1878. Outbuildings include log buildings and a Gothic Revival family chapel.

PL 6 *Green River Plantation*

Tryon (PL 7–13)

See Diane E. Lea and Claudia Roberts, *An Architectural and Historical Survey of Tryon, North Carolina* (1979).

The uniquely equable weather of the "thermal belt" makes Tryon attractive as a vineyard area and year-round residential resort. Located near the South Carolina line, the community had its beginnings in 1839 when a post office was established on the old Howard Gap Road, which followed an Indian trading route between the Block House—a trading post south of present-day Tryon—and the western mountains.

Growth began with the arrival of the Asheville & Spartanburg Railroad in 1877. In the early years the McAboy House inn welcomed train passengers to the hamlet; many of the early guests, including the famed southern poet Sidney Lanier, came seeking relief from tuberculosis. By the time Tryon was incorporated in 1885 and laid out in a circle around the depot, six daily trains were bringing visitors, some of whom purchased land and built vacation homes. Cultivation of grapes and peaches began before

the end of the century, and the fruit was shipped by rail to distant markets.

Tryon residents found a market for traditional handicrafts in the influx of out-of-state visitors. In 1915 Eleanor Vance and Charlotte Yale moved to Tryon from Asheville, where they had begun the *Biltmore Industries' handicrafts shop under the aegis of Edith Vanderbilt, and soon established the Tryon Toy Makers, training local people in various crafts.

Tryon's architecture dates from the railroad and automobile era, with a range of popular styles enlivened by picturesque compositions in cottage, chalet, Tudor, and rustic modes. Many of the finest houses lie beyond public view, but some are visible from the street.

PL 7 Trade St. Commercial District

The small business district facing the railroad has brick commercial buildings with the corbeled detail typical of ca. 1900 construction, graced by well-modulated renovations. The former **Bank of Tryon** (1905; 106 N. Trade St.) has classical quoins and Palladian windows outlined in granite. The **Tryon Depot** is a modest frame structure erected ca. 1915 and renovated in the 1950s. Local lore recalls that in 1889 the actor William Gillette (famed for his portrayal of Sherlock Holmes) stopped to make a connection at Tryon. While awaiting a delayed train to Charleston, Gillette explored the community and was so impressed by the beauty of its setting that he claimed his luggage and remained in the town, where he established a home, "Thousand Pines." (See Introduction, Fig. 42.)

PL 8 Melrose Ave.

As Tryon developed in the early 20th c., Melrose Ave. emerged as the preferred address of prosperous citizens involved in medicine, law, and local vineyards. The houses exhibit local expressions of Queen Anne, Colonial Revival, or Craftsman Bungalow style, many with shingled or stuccoed wall surfaces. A striking example of the Tudor Revival style appears in the **Woodcarver's**

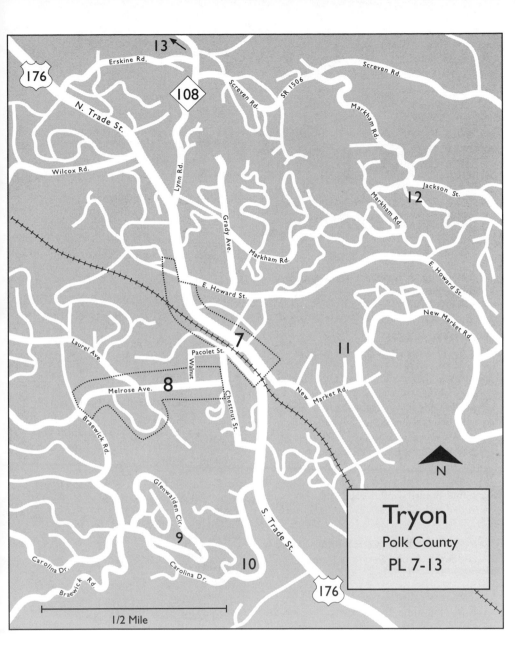

Tryon

Polk County

PL 7-13

1/2 Mile

House (1920s; J. Foster Searles, architect; 331 Melrose Ave.), a cottage with curved raking boards and applied half-timbering. Local architect Searles designed the house for Frank Arthur, a woodcarver associated with the Tryon Toy Makers. Arthur did all of the carving, including the two gargoyles in the entrance gable. His studio is lit by the band of windows facing the street.

An exotic Mediterranean character defines the **Spanish Court** (1927; 219 Melrose Ave.), a 5-unit apartment building embellished with stuccoed walls, terra-cotta roof tiles, wrought-iron balconies, and arch-framed windows. Uncoursed local stone combines with a Gothic Revival design in the **Congregational Church of Christ** (1908; 328 Melrose Ave.), attributed to local bene-

PL 8 *Woodcarver's House*

factor Charles Erskine and his son Harold, the latter having attended the École des Beaux Arts in Paris.

PL 9 The Tower
Early 1920s; 606 Glenwalden Cir.

Inspired by medieval castles, Norwegian-born artist Homer Ellertson designed the half-round, half-polygonal turret as a free-standing building, which was originally concrete covered with stucco. Each floor of the 3-story structure contains 1 room connected to the other levels by spiral staircases. In the 1950s a complementary 3-story wing with round-headed windows and Tudor doors was added and the tower was brick-veneered.

PL 10 Old St. Luke's Hospital (Polk Co. Social Services Center)
1929; Wright J. Gaines, builder; Carolina Dr.

The most distinctive public building in town, the stone Tudor Revival hospital displays a polygonal tower and applied half-timbering in its gables. For years the county's only hospital, since 1972 it has served as a social center for the elderly.

PL 11 Pine Crest Inn
1906–7 and later; 200 Pine Crest Lane; B&B

Pine Crest is the last of the early 20th-c. inns from Tryon's emergence as a resort community. The 2-story frame main building and three of the surrounding cottages—all with simple Colonial Revival detail—were built as a sanatorium for tuberculosis patients. In 1917 Carter Brown, a developer from Michigan instrumental in promoting Tryon as a resort and equestrian center, converted the facility into an inn and added cottages.

PL 12 Church of the Good Shepherd
Mid-19th c.; E corner Markham Rd. and Jackson St.

An African American neighborhood developed in the Markham Rd. area in the late 19th c. The focal point of the community is this simple frame chapel with Gothic Revival lancet windows and enclosed porch. It was moved to its present site in 1955 from *Green River Plantation to replace an early 20th-c. chapel. The building is believed to have been a slave chapel on the plantation. If so, it is one of only two known surviving church buildings in the state built for blacks before the Civil War, the other being St. Philip's Moravian Church at Old Salem. The most distinctive residence in the neighborhood is **Stony Crest** (ca. 1910; 101 Jackson St.), a large, lavishly decorated Queen Anne–Colonial Revival house built for Prof. Scotland Harris, principal of the Good Shepherd School.

PL 12 *Church of the Good Shepherd*

PL 13 Lynncote
1893–97, 1927; Richard Sharp Smith (Asheville), attributed architect; Erle Stillwell (Hendersonville), architect; W side NC 108, 0.3 mi. N of SR 1506 (Screven Rd.), Tryon vic.; private, visible in winter from road

One of the state's finest Tudor Revival style houses, Lynncote combines massive stone rubble walls and half-timbered gables. Matching accessory buildings and winding rock-walled terraces share the wooded hillside. Built for Charles B. and Emma Erskine of Racine, Wis., community leaders in Tryon, it is said to have been designed by Erskine with assistance from an architect working at *Biltmore Village, probably R. S. Smith. Gutted by fire in 1916, the house was rebuilt for the Erskines' daughter Susan Rogers in 1927 under Hendersonville architect Stillwell's direction.

PL 13 *Lynncote*

PL 14 Mills-Screven Plantation

Ca. 1820, 1840, ca. 1900; S side SR 1506 (Screven Rd.), opp. SR 1509, Tryon vic.; private, visible from road

Situated on a rise among tall trees and 19th-c. outbuildings just northeast of Tryon near the Pacolet River, this is one of the largest antebellum houses in western N.C. The complex 2-story frame house comprises an earlier dwelling expanded with Federal–Greek Revival additions by Goven Mills (descendant of Ambrose Mills of *Blackberry Hill), who acquired the property in 1839. Porches include a pedimented double gallery centered on the long 7-bay south front, a 1-story shed porch on the north, and a full-height Ionic portico added to the west gable end after 1900. Outbuildings include an 1850 stone springhouse, a double-crib log corncrib, and a 20th-c. barn.

PL 15 Seven Hearths

Early 19th c.; NE corner US 176 and SR 1121, Tryon vic.; private; visible from road

PL 14 *Mills-Screven Plantation*

The plantation house was probably built for a grandson of Ambrose Mills (see *Blackberry Hill), Marvell Mills, who settled in the Mills River section in the early 19th c. and was a prominent political figure; the commissioners who laid out Polk Co. met at his home in 1847. The 2-story frame house has a low hip roof that shelters a recessed 2-tier porch in the central 3 bays of the 5-bay facade. In 1935 the house was dismantled, moved to its present spot near Tryon, and restored.

PL 16 Blackberry Hill (Mills House)

Early 19th c.; moved, 1930s; private, no public visibility or access

Though traditionally associated with Col. Ambrose Mills, a Tory who was hanged by patriots after the battle of Kings Mountain in 1780, the house was probably built (or substantially overbuilt) for his son of the same name. The 5-bay, 2-story frame house follows a center-hall plan and has Federal style details. The 2-tier porch dates from the 20th c.

Saluda (PL 17–23)

The pleasant resort town is the first rail stop on the Blue Ridge coming from South Carolina. Dramatized by the steep terrain, its architecture embodies the town's blossoming in the 1880s, the resort boom of the 1910s and 1920s, and the retirement home prosperity of the late 20th c.

Originally called Pace's Gap, the town owes its development to the Asheville & Spartanburg Railroad, which scaled the Blue Ridge with **Saluda Grade**, a 3-mile climb between Melrose and Saluda that rises 600 feet in a 4.7 percent grade—the steepest mainline, standard-gauge grade in the United States. The first train reached the top at Saluda on July 4, 1878, eight months before the Western North Carolina Railroad completed its climb over the Blue Ridge with the opening of *Swannanoa Tunnel. The Asheville & Spartanburg became part of the Southern Railway system in 1894. In the early years the grade was the site of frequent accidents, and extra engines worked the grade as helpers or pushers to get trains up the ascent. Once the railroad was completed, inns, boardinghouses, and resort homes sprang up along the tracks, and Saluda became a summer retreat for people primarily from South Carolina.

PL 17 Downtown Saluda

The tidy Main St. commercial district faces the railroad that gave the town its life. The **Saluda Depot** (ca. 1900–1910; N side Main St., between Carolina and Church Sts.) was moved from the tracks to a site near the west end of the commercial row. The German-sided building has a flared hip roof with eyelid vents and broad eaves with braces.

Railroad-era prosperity is reflected in the compact row of early 20th-c. 1- and 2-story commercial buildings with decorative brickwork. Among the best preserved is the **M. A.**

Pace Store (1905–10; NE side Main St. between Cullipher and Greenville Sts.), which displays an intact exterior and an interior evocative of the early 20th-c. general mercantile business. Well-worn wood finishes the floor, ceilings, and walls, while original shelving, display cases, scales, an antique cash register, and a pot-bellied stove still serve the family-owned business. **Saluda City Hall** (1897–1906; NE corner Main and Church Sts.) displays classical motifs in its pressed-metal facade. With its rough stucco exterior, the 2-story **Pebbledash Building** (between 1911 and 1916; SE side Church St. between Main and Henderson Sts.) attests to the influence of Asheville architect Richard Sharp Smith, who popularized this surface treatment for buildings throughout western N.C. in the early 20th c.

Up the hill from Main St. is the **Saluda Presbyterian Church** (1895–96; SE side Carolina St. between Main and Henderson Sts.), a frame Gothic Revival chapel built with funds raised by the joint efforts of summer people and permanent residents. The gable-fronted building features a 2-tier corner tower with brackets and a carved pediment.

PL 18 Ivy Terrace
1890; S side E. Main Street (US 176), 0.5 mi. W of SR 1181

PL 17 *Main St., Saluda*

The 2-story frame house was built for Charleston attorney Capt. W. G. Hinson as a summer retreat on "Shand Hill," Saluda's earliest resort neighborhood. Subsequent owners operated it as a boardinghouse and until recently as an inn, one of the town's few vestiges of its early tourist days.

PL 19 Saluda High School
1940; N side E. Main St.

Situated prominently on a hill, the 2-story stone school has brick window and door surrounds and a full-height portico. It was built to replace a school erected in 1927.

PL 20 Church of the Transfiguration
1889; Rev. John DeWitt McCullough, architect; S corner of Henderson and Charles Sts.

With the help of his sons, townspeople, and students from Sewannee Seminary, summer visitor and Episcopal priest John D. McCullough of Spartanburg designed and constructed the Gothic Revival chapel to serve his fellow Episcopalians who came by rail from South Carolina for the summer. After the church on the hill above Main St. was consecrated, its new rector, William S. Barrows, noted in 1892 that the "beautiful little church" was "virtually a gift from the Diocese of South Carolina to that of North Carolina." Reflecting the lasting influence of Richard Upjohn's patternbook on the denomination, the board-and-batten church features a steep gable roof and a corner bell-tower with spire.

PL 21 Infants' and Children's Sanitarium (Smith Hill)
Early 20th c.; bounded by Smith and Carver Drs., W side of Greenville Rd.

In 1914 pediatrician Dr. Daniel Lesene Smith, hoping to save his young Spartanburg patients from the "summer complaint" of fever and diarrhea, opened a private children's sanitarium in Saluda near his summer home. That same year, in response to an editorial in the *Spartanburg Herald* that called for a similar institution for poor families, Dr. Smith established the Spartanburg Baby Hospital nearby, to treat babies and to educate area mothers in infant care. In 1921 the reputation of the two institutions spawned the Southern Pediatric Seminar, a professional retreat held every July until 1958, which attracted renowned specialists from across the country. Several buildings associated with the original 13-acre medical campus survive on the ½-mi. loop on Smith Hill. These include frame cottages, many used to house sanitarium employees and seminar participants; **Bon Aire** (1896; N side of lower loop of Smith Dr.), a rambling 2-story frame boardinghouse; and the **Children's Dining Hall** (early 20th c.).

PL 22 Greenville Rd.

A few examples of late 19th- and early 20th-c. residential architecture stand along Greenville Rd. south of the commercial district, with renditions of Victorian and Craftsman styles. The **H. L. Capps House** (1895; sw corner Greenville Rd. and Chestnut St.) is a 2-story clipped-gable house with sawnwork porch posts. Across Chestnut St. is the **Saluda Inn** (late 19th c.; NW corner Greenville Rd. and Chestnut St.), a 2-story Victorian house with a wraparound porch. **The Oaks** (1908; William Luther Thomp-

PL 20 *Church of the Transfiguration*

son, builder; w side Greenville Rd., 0.1 mi. s of Chestnut St.; B&B), operated by Mrs. H. B. Lane as a boardinghouse in the first half of the 20th c., is Saluda's most ornate Queen Anne style dwelling, with a high hip roof, a conical corner turret, and a wraparound porch. Dominating the neighborhood is **Saluda Methodist Church** (early 20th c.; E side Greenville Rd.), a big frame church with a tall combination belltower–entrance vestibule on the front gable.

PL 23 Estes-Coates House

Ca. 1890; W side Coates St.,
between Gaffney and Main Sts.

Adorned with bold vergeboards and square porch posts with intricate brackets, the Gothic Revival cottage was built as an auxiliary to Breezepoint Cottage, a boardinghouse that no longer stands; among its early owners were Charles Estes, the mayor of Augusta, Ga., and John Thomas Coates Jr.

Mountains

(Overleaf) MD 1 *Marshall*

Alleghany County (AL)

See Jean Sizemore, Alleghany Architecture: A Pictorial Survey, Alleghany County, North Carolina *(1983).*

Bounded on the south by the Blue Ridge and on the north by the Virginia line, the sparsely populated and scenic agricultural county harbors a fine collection of late 19th- and early 20th-c. rural vernacular architecture. Late 19th- and early 20th-c. decorated farmhouses, often sited against the hillsides with long prospects across the valleys, were erected during a period of agricultural prosperity. In a rolling landscape drained by the New River and its tributaries, the lush, gentle hillsides were well suited for grazing, but the difficulties of transporting perishable commodities to distant markets—no railroad ever entered Alleghany—encouraged sheep farming and the conversion of milk to cheese, which keeps and travels well. In the decades before and after the turn of the century, Alleghany was third in the state in cheese production (after its larger neighbors Ashe and Watauga counties) and fifth in the production of wool.

AL 1 Sparta

The county seat was settled by 1825 as Bowers Store, renamed Gap Civil in 1846, and renamed again, for the ancient Grecian city, when incorporated in 1879. Sparta remained a small village well into the 20th c., and a 1932 fire destroyed the courthouse and much of the old commercial district. The principal edifice is the **Alleghany County Courthouse** (1933; Harry Barton [Greensboro], architect; N. Main St.), a simple Neoclassical building in red brick designed by the prominent Greensboro architect to suit the county's depression-era budget of $17,000.

AL 1 *Alleghany Co. Courthouse*

AL 2 Whitehead

The community on NC 18 retains churches, a school, and several houses from its early

20th-c. heyday as an agricultural trading community and the site of a gristmill. Three Baptist churches reflect differences in points of doctrine. **Union Primitive Baptist Church** (SE corner NC 18 and SR 1193) is an austere early 20th-c. frame building with a deep roof overhang supported by bungalow-type brackets. The altered **Landmark Union Baptist Church** (E side SR 1193, 0.4 mi. S of NC 18) was formerly its near-twin. **Liberty Baptist Church** (1908; E side SR 1193, 0.5 mi. S of NC 18) has a Gothic flavor with lancet windows and a corner entrance tower with belfry under a bellcast tin roof. Now a community center, the former **Whitehead School** (1917; Monroe Estep, carpenter; N side NC 18 at end of SR 1194) is a T-plan frame schoolhouse with a hexagonal belfry, erected by local carpenter Estep and identical to his *Second Elk Creek Academy a few miles away. The most prominent dwelling is the **Reeves-Hoppers House** (1900; N side NC 18 at SR 1193; private), a 2-story frame house with a strikingly tall pyramidal hip roof punctuated by two sawtooth-shingled gable dormers. Other turn-of-the-century houses appear along NC 18 toward Laurel Springs.

AL 3 Brinegar House

1880s; milepost 238.5 on the Blue Ridge Parkway; open regular hours in season

Perched on the Continental Divide at an elevation of 3,500 feet, the weatherboarded, 1-room log house with rear kitchen shed and fieldstone chimneys is one of the best and most accessible examples of the Appalachian log dwelling. Martin Brinegar (d. 1925), a farmer and cobbler, is said to have built the almost windowless house himself, with friends helping place the logs; his widow, Caroline, lived here until the mid-1930s. Maintained by the Park Service as one of a series of sites along the Blue Ridge Parkway that commemorate 19th-c. mountain life and culture, it houses a mountain crafts shop and weaving display. A springhouse and a shed with full stone basement stand nearby.

AL 4 Caudill House

Late 19th c.; visible from Wildcat Rock Overlook at Doughton Park; exit the Blue Ridge Parkway opp. The Bluffs Lodge (milepost 241.5)

In a forested cove 1,000 feet below the overlook, the small log house is the last survivor of the Basin Cove settlement, which was largely wiped out in the flood of 1916. The house evokes the relative isolation of many 19th-c. small farmers along the Blue Ridge.

Martin and Janie Caudill raised fourteen children here. Not accessible to the public, the house is preserved by the Park Service for viewing from Wildcat Rock.

AL 5 John Jackson Miller House

1897; Will Hendrix and Tom Bowers, carpenters; N side Blue Ridge Parkway at SR 1145 (Elk Knob Rd.); private, visible from road

The 2-story frame farmhouse is one of the few examples of the regionally prevalent, decorated late 19th-c. farmhouses that remain along the parkway. With a shingled front gable with a sawnwork insert and a 2-story rear ell, its size and decorative touches pro-

AL 5 *John Jackson Miller House*

AL 3 *Brinegar House*

vide a contrast to the *Brinegar and *Caudill houses and reflect an era of relative prosperity even at this remote Blue Ridge site.

AL 6 Robert Lee Doughton House
Late 19th/early 20th c.; W side NC 18, 0.2 mi. S of NC 88, Cranberry; private, visible from road; B&B

Representative of a number of houses from the county's early 20th-c. agricultural prosperity, the rambling 2-story farmhouse is a simplified version of the Queen Anne style with characteristic irregular massing, complex roofline, and a double-pile, center-hall plan interior. It was the home of Robert Lee "Muley Bob" Doughton, U.S. congressman for 42 years and powerful chairman of the House Ways and Means Committee from 1933 to 1945.

AL 6 *Robert Lee Doughton House*

AL 7 Jones Waddell House
1889; S side US 221, 1.6 mi. W of NC 113, Scottville vic.; private, visible from road

One of several late 19th-c. houses around the post office community of Scottville on the Alleghany-Ashe line, this is an especially well-preserved example of the decorated farmhouses plentiful in the New River area. The gable-roofed I-house is dressed with a 2-story porch with delicate sawn balustrade, brackets, and a half-circle gable insert. The date 1889 is sawn into the triangular window hood of the porch gable. A 1-story rear wing, a dwelling predating the front block by 10 or 20 years, forms a T-plan.

AL 7 *Jones Waddell House*

AL 8 William Weaver House
1848, 1890, 1895; private, public visibility only from South Fork New River or from SR 1549 in Ashe Co.

Not publicly accessible by automobile but a landmark for canoers and rafters on the South Fork New River, the picturesque riverside house reached its present form through three generations of Weaver family ownership. William Weaver built the original 1848 house as a 2-story main block with hall-parlor plan and 1-story rear ell. In 1890 and 1895 Weaver's son, Andrew, a blacksmith, carpenter, and furniture maker, extended and raised the ell and added the 2-story, full-width shed porch rich with sawnwork ornament. Outbuildings, some log, survive from each generation.

Piney Creek:
Though miles from the nearest railhead, the Piney Creek section in the northwestern corner of the county above the New River enjoyed a prosperity around the turn of the century comparable to that of the Grassy Creek and Helton communities across the river in Ashe Co., supported in part by cheese production. A striking number of large 2-story frame farmhouses, many with decorated porches and Queen Anne style details, may be seen along NC 93 and NC 113 and secondary roads adjoining them. Unfortunately, many are now abandoned and deteriorated, victims of changing economies and attitudes.

AL 9 Piney Creek Primitive Baptist Church
1875; N side NC 93 at SR 1317, Piney Creek

Thought to be the oldest standing church building in the county, the plain frame structure reflects the conservative doctrine of the denomination and differs little from churches in Primitive Baptist strongholds elsewhere in the state. The sole decoration is an arched panel over the separate front entrance doors for men and women. Organized by 1825, the congregation was one of the first established in the county.

AL 10 Second Elk Creek Academy

Ca. 1915; Monroe Estep, builder; E side SR 1167 at US 221, Stratford; private, visible from road

The early 20th-c. frame rural school is nearly identical in its T-plan and octagonal belfry to the *Whitehead School, also attributed to local carpenter Estep.

AL 11 W. E. Cox House

Ca. 1900; Joe T. Finney, builder; E side SR 1167, 0.2 mi. S of US 221; private, visible from road

The 2-story farmhouse with Queen Anne detail displays the curving wraparound porch that is a common feature in the area. The curve repeats in the window at the rounded corner of the main block.

AL 12 William R. Gentry House

Ca. 1909; N side NC 18, 0.1 mi. E of SR 1426, Edwards Crossroads; private, visible from road

One of the largest and most stylish Queen Anne houses ever built in Alleghany Co. has fallen on hard times but retains its prominence on NC 18. Its complexity of form and richness of ornament—even with its Eastlake porch removed to a nearby house—reflect the prosperity, ambitions, and style-consciousness of Gentry, a rural entrepreneur who operated a large mill and a furniture and coffin shop nearby.

AL 13 Clark Higgins House

Late 19th c.; NW side NC 18, 0.6 mi. NE of SR 1450; private, visible from road

Standing on a high fieldstone foundation that accommodates the hillside site, the prominent I-house is representative of scores in the area. Sawnwork adorns the full-width shed porch. Outbuildings include a board-and-batten barn with a latticed cupola in the meadow across the road.

AL 14 Laurel Glen Regular Baptist Church

Late 19th c.; W side SR 1428 just N of SR 1422, Glade Valley vic.

The starkly plain, weatherboarded country church is a rare and important western N.C. example of the traditional meetinghouse plan. The main entrance is centered on the long side rather than the gable end, and old wooden bench pews are arranged in a U around the pulpit opposite the entrance, with a wood stove at the center. Many early meetinghouses with such a plan were later modified to place the main entrance on the gable end, with a long aisle leading to the pulpit; by the late 19th c. virtually all new churches of every denomination followed the gable-end-entry plan, and many old ones were reworked in that arrangement.

AL 14 *Laurel Glen Regular Baptist Church*

AL 15 Glade Valley

Jct. of SR 1444 and SR 1431, 0.3 mi. E of US 21

Located in one of the first sections settled in the county when the region was opened up after the American Revolution, the community retains two 19th-c. houses of interest. East of the town's main intersection is the **Abram Bryan House** (W side SR 1440, 0.6 mi. E of SR 1431; private), the county's oldest

AL 17 *Graystone Inn*

house and one of the very few antebellum houses in the state west of the Blue Ridge. Its engaged porch with flush sheathing and engaged rear shed demonstrate the wide distribution of the so-called coastal cottage form in the first half of the 19th c. Though 1840 is traditionally cited as the construction date, the off-center interior chimney and the mix of late Georgian and Greek Revival elements suggest two construction phases, one perhaps predating 1840. Nearby is the **Clarence C. Thompson House** (1906; W side SR 1467, 0.2 mi. S of SR 1444; private), a Queen Anne cottage with sawn shingles and a unusual recessed porch. Thompson was proprietor of the (former) **C. C. Thompson and Son Store** (ca. 1920; corner of SR 1444 and SR 1431), a late version of the parapet-fronted frame general store; it contained the post office and a market where local people sold small game and marketable wild plants to supplement cash income.

AL 15 *Abram Bryan House*

AL 16 Antioch Methodist Church

Ca. 1895; E side US 21, 0.6 mi. N of SR 1478, Roaring Gap vic.

The simple country church is a landmark along the well-traveled highway, its austere form alleviated by the tall steeple on the front peak of the gable roof. The congregation was established in 1848.

AL 17 Roaring Gap

The resort community on the Blue Ridge was established in the 1890s by Hugh Gwyn Chatham, blanket manufacturer and mill owner of Elkin, and became the exclusive summer retreat for families of leading industrialists of piedmont cities, chiefly Winston-Salem and Greensboro. By 1915 the Elkin & Alleghany Railroad, of which Chatham was president, reached the foot of the Blue Ridge below Roaring Gap, and though the line never scaled the mountain as planned, Roaring Gap flourished as a private resort. It remains an intensely private place, though visitors can view the area from the state-maintained roads. The prime house sites are on the crest of the ridge, giving magnificent views into the Yadkin Valley to the south; on clear days in leafless winter the traveler ascending US 21 can see cottages on the rim high above. A few simple frame cottages with deep wraparound porches date from the early 20th c.; later cottages are a mix of informal styles, many shingled or stuccoed.

The centerpiece is the **Graystone Inn** (1926; Charles Barton Keen [Philadelphia], architect; E corner SR 1476 and 1477; private, not a commercial hotel), a grand 3-story, 55-room Colonial Revival building of random gray ashlar designed by Keen, the Philadelphia Beaux Arts architect patronized by the Reynolds and other wealthy Winston-Salem families. From the rectangular main block project two wings connected by a 2-story porch, sheltering French doors beneath blind arches. The interdenominational **Roaring Gap Church** (1927; W side SR 1478 at SR 1475) is a small Gothic Revival sanctuary of coursed rubble, also believed to be Keen's work.

Ashe County (AH)

One of the "lost provinces" beyond the Blue Ridge in the northwest corner of the state, Ashe Co. was formed in 1799 and named for Governor Samuel Ashe. After a visit in 1828, Professor Elisha Mitchell of the University of North Carolina, who once compared western N.C. to "ancient Arcadia—the country of herdsmen and shepherds," predicted that the county would become a land of "extensive pastures on which will be fed vast herds of cattle and flocks of sheep." The New England–born Mitchell also observed that "if the inhabitants would be industrious . . . they might have painted frame houses instead of the present unsightly log hovels." His vision was at least partly realized. In 1890 a Tennessee vacationer at *Thompson's Bromine Arsenic Springs described the county for the Knoxville Journal: *"Kentucky thoroughbreds graze in peaceful pastures, and short horns and Jerseys stand knee deep in the crystal springs or graze in meadows as rich in herbage as the blue grass fields of central Kentucky. Many of the farm houses we saw are veritable mansions, all of them neat and comfortable." Other travelers remarked on the county's bounteous apple orchards and groves of cherry trees.*

Drained by the north and south forks of the New River, which is the headwaters of the Kanawha and Ohio River system, Ashe is a county of rolling, bucolic landscapes. In spite of its isolation from major markets, it enjoyed a period of agrarian prosperity reflected in the many well-built, often richly decorated late 19th-c. farmhouses, of which only a sampling can be presented here. With neighboring Watauga and Alleghany counties, Ashe was long among the state's leaders in cheese and wool production. Iron and copper mining also were important industries through the 19th c., and the copper mine at Ore Knob (once the county's largest town but now vanished) was one of the nation's major producers of that metal. In the mid-1970s the county was the focus of an extended controversy over the Appalachian Power Co.'s proposal to construct pump storage dams on the New River in Virginia, which would have impounded much of the river on the N.C. side. The proposal was abandoned following Congress's designation of part of the New as a Wild and Scenic River. Rafting down the New River has since become a popular recreation, and the valley has seen a surge in second home development.

AH 1 Jefferson

The county seat at the base of looming Mount Jefferson was incorporated in 1803 and named for Thomas Jefferson. A few scattered late 19th- and early 20th-c. frame buildings survive, but the railroad town of West Jefferson drained away the village's commerce in the early 20th c. Demolitions have left little of the character of what a 19th-c. visitor called "dreamy Jefferson," where cherry trees once lined Main St. The **Ashe County Courthouse** (1904; Wheeler & Runge, architects; Main St.) is one of six similar Neoclassical Revival courthouses in N.C. designed by Oliver Wheeler of Charlotte with various associates; all feature distinctive mansard-like domes and Ionic porticoes. Across the street the former **Jefferson Presbyterian Church** (now St. Francis of Assisi Catholic Church) (ca. 1900; sw corner of Main and Ivey Sts.) is a shingled Gothic Revival church with corner bell-tower. Nearby the little **William B. Austin Law Office** (ca. 1900: s side Main St.), with its recessed porch with bracketed posts and

AH 1 *Ashe Co. Courthouse*

AH 2 *West Jefferson Hotel*

spindle frieze, exemplifies the 1- and 2-room freestanding law offices once common in courthouse towns.

AH 2 West Jefferson

Like North Wilkesboro and Sylva, West Jefferson is an early 20th-c. railroad town that usurped a nearby older county seat as focus of its county's commerce. Ambitious 19th-c. plans for rail connections in northwestern N.C. never materialized, but in 1915 the Virginia-Carolina Railroad, a subsidiary of the Norfolk and Western, came down from Abingdon, Va., established a depot 2 miles southwest of Jefferson, and continued south to Todd at the Watauga Co. line. The new town that grew up at the depot of the "Virginia Creeper," as the railroad line came to be called, quickly became the county's shipping center, with a burley tobacco warehouse, a cheese factory, a chair factory, and other industries. Though the line from West Jefferson to Abingdon was abandoned in the late 1970s and the tracks have been removed, the **West Jefferson Depot** (ca. 1915; W. Main St. at S. Second Ave.) still stands, a small board-and-batten depot under a broad gable roof with deep overhangs, moved a short distance from the old track bed.

Long rows of simple 1- and 2-story brick commercial buildings of the 1920s to 1940s line Jefferson Ave. for several blocks. On a principal corner is the **West Jefferson Hotel** (1917–18; sw corner S. Jefferson Ave. and W. Main St.), a 2-story brick building stretching the depth of the block; the rear 2-story porch faced the tracks and greeted passengers and train crews disembarking at

the depot. **Mount Jefferson Presbyterian Church** (1927; se corner S. Jefferson Ave. and E. Ashe St.) is a distinctive, small Gothic Revival church in stone.

After burley tobacco was introduced in the region in the early 20th c., farmers brought their leaf to town for sale. **Farmers Burley Warehouse #1** (1947; corner of Long St. and Graybeal Ave.) is a building occupying a full block, with its cavernous interior lit by skylights. The **Ashe County Cheese Company** (1930; 106 E. Main St.) is a utilitarian brick building housing the last active operation of an industry once widespread across the county and region. The **Ashe County Arts Center** (1938; Works Progress Administration [WPA]; 303 School St.) is a compact, 1-story, T-plan stone building built by the WPA for a community center and later used by the 4-H and other agencies. A cluster of early 20th-c. houses overlooks the town from College Ave. and Terrace St. on Paddy Mountain.

AH 3 St. Mary's Episcopal Church

1904–5; N side US 221, 0.1 mi. W of SR 1147, Beaver Creek

The Gothic Revival frame church, featuring a side vestibule with belfry and a projecting apse, stands within a picket fence alongside its small graveyard. Inside are three frescoes painted in the mid-1970s by N.C. artist Ben Long—a crucifixion, the expectant Mary, and St. John the Baptist. These have made the little church a popular attraction along with *Holy Trinity Episcopal Church at Glendale Springs, which also contains fresco work by Long. Originally called Church of

St. Simon the Zealot, the church was established in 1897 during a period of Episcopalian outreach through northwestern N.C. In 1984 this church, Holy Trinity, and *St. Matthews near Todd were united into the Parish of the Holy Communion.

AH 3 *St. Mary's Episcopal Church*

AH 4 Todd

First known as Elks Crossroads, the village on South Fork New River at the Watauga Co. line became the southern terminus of the Virginia-Carolina Railroad when the line, known as the "Virginia Creeper," arrived in 1915. The town was incorporated as Todd, after Capt. Joseph W. Todd, a local attorney, but the railroad called the station Elkland, in reference to the older name or to Elk Township. For about two decades the community was a railhead for shipment of agricultural products and timber from southern Ashe and northern Watauga counties. After the original depot burned in 1920, the railroad replaced it with an older depot brought down from Virginia. Though the line from Todd to West Jefferson was abandoned in 1933 and the tracks were removed, the **Elkland (Todd) Depot** (late 19th c., 1920) has been preserved for private business

AH 4 *Todd Depot*

use. The gabled board-and-batten building has deep eaves supported by corner braces, and a gabled, 3-sided bay that gave the stationmasters a view down the tracks. An early diesel engine and two cabooses embellish the railroad atmosphere.

Among several frame commercial buildings now clad in pressed-tin siding, a standout is the **Todd General Store** (1914, 1920), built by brothers Walter and Monroe Cook in anticipation of the railroad's arrival and enlarged as business grew. The big 2-story, gable-fronted store with shed porch has operated continuously since its construction and still stocks general merchandise for local residents as well as items for the growing tourist trade. Other tin-clad buildings include an old bank and a Ford car assembly building, where Model A Fords were unloaded from the railroad, assembled, and transported by road to the dealership in Boone.

AH 4 *Todd General Store*

A landmark in the village is the **McGuire House** (mid- and late 19th c., ca. 1915; private), a 2-story frame house said to have been built by the Brown family in the 1840s and ornamented and expanded by subsequent owners to its present turn-of-the-century form. It has a facade gable, sawn bargeboard trim, and a gable-end bay window; the long 2-story rear wing with double porch was added by Felix McGuire about 1915 to provide lodging for travelers on the new railroad.

AH 5 Felix McGuire House
Late 19th c.; NE side SR 1100, 2.5 mi.
SE of Todd; private, visible from road

The drive along SR 1100 beside the South Fork New River follows the abandoned track bed of the "Virginia Creeper" past riverbottom farms. In a county and region of decorated late 19th-c. farmhouses, this distinctive 2-story frame house presents uniquely individualized forms. A pair of steep gables—said to have been designed in an M after the family name—dominates the tall facade, and a 2-tier porch shelters the central entrance. The weatherboards are applied diagonally to echo the facade gables. McGuire was a successful farmer, merchant, and lumber dealer.

and the **Thomas A. "Red Tom" Sutherland House** (ca. 1885), a frame I-house with a decorated 2-story porch; the rear ell is an older log house, and log and frame outbuildings stand nearby. Back on NC 88 the **Donnelly Farm** (late 19th and early 20th c.; S side NC 88, 0.4 mi. w of SR 1118) epitomizes the prosperous mountain farmstead: a big rambling frame house with multiple gables and deep porches, nestled partway up the hillside above the broad creek bottom, surrounded by frame barns and other outbuildings. (See Introduction, Figs. 52 and 53.)

AH 6 *Sutherland Methodist Church*

AH 5 *Felix McGuire House*

AH 6 Sutherland

Like Grassy Creek, Sutherland is a mountain community rich in scenic beauty and ambitious late 19th- and early 20th-c. vernacular architecture. The North Fork New River hamlet takes its name from the family whose progenitor Thomas Sutherland settled here near the mouth of Hoskins Fork in 1807. A popular academy operated in the late 19th c., along with grist- and sawmills, stores, and a cheese factory. **Sutherland Methodist Church** (ca. 1885; NE side SR 1118, E of NC 88) presides from a hilltop site, a white frame country Gothic Revival church with tapered belfry, kingpost ornament, and stained glass windows with triangular heads. Just east on SR 1118 is the **J. H. Hardin House** (ca. 1880), a brick I-house with exceptionally bold curvilinear sawnwork in its 2-story central porch. Farther east and across the road are the **Wilson House** (ca. 1900), a big, frame foursquare with pyramidal roof,

AH 6 *Thomas A. Sutherland House*

AH 7 Osborne-Brown House

*Mid-19th c.; SE side NC 88, 0.1 mi.
S of SR 1122, Creston vic.; private,
visible from road*

Highway NC 88 along the North Fork New River offers a pastoral drive among bottomland farms, several with big frame barns and late 19th- or early 20th-c. farmhouses. A rarity among the predominantly frame houses is this simply finished but solidly built I-house of dark red, handmade brick. Poised on a knoll, the house was probably built for John Osborne about 1860. Later owners grew apples on the hillsides and truck crops in the bottomlands.

AH 8 Creston

Known as North Fork until 1882 for its site along that branch of the New River, Creston was a center of rural enterprise through the 19th c. that included a major regional store, grist- and sawmills, a tannery, a wool carding operation, and a furniture and wagon factory. All were ventures of David Worth, a Quaker from Guilford Co. who came to Ashe Co. as a young man in about 1830. He formed a partnership with storekeeper Stephen Thomas, in time marrying Thomas's daughter and raising a big family.

The **David Worth House** (ca. 1840, ca. 1860?; S side SR 1100; private), one of the largest antebellum houses surviving in northwestern N.C., is a 2-story frame house that began as an I-house with end chimneys and was later doubled in size to create a double-pile house under a hip roof. In 1888 travel writer Charles Dudley Warner described a restful stay with the Worth family, in "a dwelling not unlike a roomy New England country house," where he was delighted to find "two pianos and a bevy of young ladies," probably the Worths' granddaughters, attired in fashionable dress and reading the latest novel.

Nearby is one of the most ambitious rural Gothic Revival churches in the region, **Creston Methodist Church** (1903; E side SR 1100, 0.1 mi. S of NC 88), a vigorous composition with the upper sections of its massive, pinnacled 3-stage corner tower enlivened

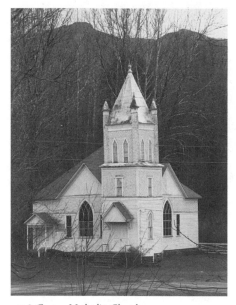

AH 8 *Creston Methodist Church*

with diamond-patterned shingles. It is the second building of a congregation founded in 1852 on land donated by David Worth.

AH 9 Lansing

The town on Big Horse Creek grew up beside the Virginia-Carolina (Virginia Creeper) Railroad and was incorporated in 1928. The **Lansing School** (1935–38; E side NC 194, just N of SR 1517) is a long, 2-story stone building with simple Colonial Revival detail including fanlight windows in the parapeted end gables. It is one of the largest of several public schools in the mountains built of native stone with the assistance of the WPA, reflecting the agency's policy to build in regionally appropriate styles and materials.

AH 9 *Lansing School*

AH 10 Helton

Like Creston, the community on Helton's Creek was a scene of diversified rural industry through the 19th c.: small-scale iron mines and forges, gristmills, a woolen mill, and other enterprises. **Helton Methodist Church** (1856, 1939; N side NC 194, 0.2 mi. W of SR 1526) is one of the oldest church buildings in the region; it retains a simplified Greek Revival, pedimented gable-fronted form, with a small belfry and pedimented vestibule added in the 1930s. The **Helton Roller Mill** (ca. 1885; SE corner NC 194 and SR 1526; private), which produced flour, feed, and cornmeal, is the last vestige of the community's industrial ventures; the tall frame structure, built by brothers Winfield and Will Perkins beside Helton Creek, has been converted into a residence. The **Winfield Perkins House** (1898; N side NC 194, 0.2 mi. E of SR 1526; private) is another of the county's many fine, late 19th-c. decorated frame houses, here with asymmetrical massing and a wraparound porch with delicate turned posts; a contingent of frame barns stands near the highway. The **Gert Perkins House** (ca. 1885; N side NC 194, opp. SR 1523; private) is of a simpler I-house form with sawnwork spandrels between the porch posts and a gable-end bay window.

AH 10 *Winfield Perkins House*

AH 11 Grassy Creek

This creek valley is among the region's loveliest agrarian landscapes, with old farmsteads sheltered among gentle hills where cattle grazed for two centuries. Prominent among the early families were the Greers, who cultivated the bottomland, raised cattle, and manufactured cheese through four generations at six individual farms. After 1920 the Greers and other families here and across the county transferred their cheese-making industry to Bel Air, Maryland. Today the community is little changed from its early 20th-c. appearance, with several fine farmhouses surrounded by outbuildings dotting the folded hillsides sloping down to the creek. Most lie east and south of the intersection of SR 1535 and SR 1573.

AH 11 *Greer Farm*

Grassy Creek Methodist Church (1904; N side SR 1535, 0.1 mi. W of SR 1573) surveys the community from a hilltop site; the frame, gable-fronted Gothic Revival church has a tall corner tower with belfry, and wood shingles cover the gable and the second stage of the tower. The sanctuary is turned to form an auditorium plan. (See Introduction, Fig. 57.)

Farther east along SR 1535, the **Greer Farm** (1890s; N side SR 1535, 0.25 mi. E of SR 1573; private) includes a big T-plan, 2-story house with decorated porches and bracketed eaves; notable among many outbuildings and standing near the road is a contemporary small frame schoolhouse with shingled gables, where a private tutor instructed neighborhood children. The **John Jones Farm** (1904; N side SR 1535, 0.4 mi. E of SR 1573; private) centers on a 2-story, T-plan frame house with decorative gables and window surrounds.

Across the valley from the Jones House, the beautifully sited **Robert Livesay House** (1904; S side SR 1535; 0.4 mi. W of SR 1573; private) is a 2-story house of foursquare form with simple Colonial Revival detail; among several barns and other outbuildings is an octagonal woodshed (see Introduction,

Fig. 5). On SR 1573 south of the main intersection is the **L. F. Young Farm** (1840s, 1893; NE corner SR 1573 and SR 1551; private), where an early 2-story log house was expanded with frame additions and ornamented porches at the end of the 19th c. Many other houses of this period and tradition may be seen along the winding secondary roads flanking the New River in this section.

AH 12 Ballou House (River House)

1870, 1943–44; N side SR 1539, 0.4 mi. W of NC 16, Grassy Creek vic.; inn and restaurant open to public

The 2-story frame farmhouse of traditional form and finish overlooks the North Fork of the New River, an inviting sight to travelers looking down from NC 16 along the ridge to its east. It was built in 1870 by Uriah Ballou, grandson of Meredith Ballou, a pioneer in the region's copper and iron industries, on part of a state grant of 10,000 acres that Meredith received in 1800. Uriah's son, Dr. James Ballou, remodeled and enlarged the house in the mid-20th c.

AH 13 Thompson's Bromine Arsenic Springs (Healing Springs)

Ca. 1887, ca. 1900, ca. 1920; S side SR 1542, 1.2 mi. E of NC 16, Crumpler vic.; open in season

A small octagonal springhouse (ca. 1900) and a row of simple frame guest houses (ca. 1920) survive at this once-popular health spa, evocative of the importance of health resorts in the social history of the Appalachians. William Barker discovered the springs in 1885, and before long, he recalled, "it had cured a power of folks." H. V. Thompson of Virginia soon acquired the property and advertised the water, which contains sodium arseniate and sodium bromide, as "the most remarkable discovery of the nineteenth century." In 1887 Thompson built a fashionable hotel with long, 2-story porches and bottled and shipped quantities of water from the springs. His enterprise flourished, and the hotel operated continuously under subsequent owners until it burned in 1962. After a period of disuse, the remaining buildings have been rehabilitated and reopened for business.

AH 14 Shatley Springs

1930s; W side NC 16 at SR 1574, Shatley Springs; open in season

The complex of freestanding tourist cabins, dining hall, and other buildings, all painted a deep red, is one of the state's best-known traditional mineral springs resorts. About 1890 farmer Martin Shatley, long suffering a painful skin ailment, discovered a spring on his property whose waters effected a miracu-

AH 13 *Thompson's Bromine Arsenic Springs Cottages*

lous cure. In time Shatley built a bathhouse for guests, but it was a small operation until 1930, when he sold the place to a group of local investors who began the present complex. It is famed today for its generous country cooking served family style.

AH 15 New River General Store (Joins-Huffman Store)

1930s; N side jct. US 221 and SR 1567, Scottville vic.

The 2-story frame, hip-roofed store with front porch and 1-story side addition has served the neighboring farm community for much of the century. The interior retains narrow beaded sheathing, old shelves, and counters with bins for flour and cornmeal. Unlike its counterparts that have fallen to changing times, this store has taken advantage of its location by the New River, providing provisions and equipment to raft and canoe enthusiasts on the scenic waterway.

AH 15 *New River General Store*

AH 16 McMillan House Ruin

Mid-19th c.; S side US 221, 1.2 mi. E of SR 1595, Nathans Creek vic.; private, visible from road

Little remains from the antebellum period in the New River valley. Though slavery was not as widespread here as along the French Broad River, in 1860 there were more than 500 slaves in Ashe Co. working farms, mines, and industries. The largest slaveholder was George Bower, with 34 slaves. Until the mid-1970s three mid-19th-c., 2-story brick plantation houses were still standing in this area—the Solomon Edwards House in Alleghany Co. and the Aquilla Greer House and McMillan House in Ashe. All have now vanished with no trace except for a few sec-

tions of brick wall of this 2-story house probably built for Andrew McMillan, a planter and Confederate officer.

AH 17 Dr. Aras B. Cox House

Mid-19th c., ca. 1875; NE side SR 1595, 1.2 mi. S of US 221, Nathans Creek vic.; private, visible from road

Probably the oldest house standing in the county, the compact 2-story, 2-bay, frame-front block has simple Federal style finish and an original Flemish-bond brick chimney on the west gable end. Dr. Aras B. Cox, a prominent physician, civic leader, and historian, purchased the property in 1852 from George Bower, one of the county's largest landowners and slaveholders in 1860, but it is uncertain whether Bower himself ever occupied the house. Cox owned 8 slaves in 1860 and commanded a company of Confederate infantry during the Civil War. About 1875 he doubled the size of the house with a 2-story rear wing with double-gallery porch. Here Cox authored *Footprints in the Sands of Time* (1900), a history of the New River region.

AH 18 Glendale Springs Inn

1895, 1902, 1905; SW corner NC 16 and SR 1632, Glendale Springs; B&B

Recalling the region's many 19th- and early 20th-c. resort spas, the picturesque inn occupies a shaded lot at the center of the community. Constructed in 1895 by Col. Daniel W. Adams (see Old Fort) as a 1-story structure, the frame building grew through a series of additions and gained a simple Neoclassical character when the porches were

AH 18 *Glendale Springs Inn*

enlarged about 1905. Early in the century the resort inn flourished, with its mineral water bathing pools a major attraction. From 1935 to 1938 the inn served as headquarters and workers' dormitory for construction of a section of the Blue Ridge Parkway.

AH 19 Holy Trinity Episcopal Church
1901; E side SR 1161 opp. SR 1160, Glendale Springs

The small frame Gothic Revival church, like *St. Mary's at Beaver Creek, was home of a congregation established in the late 19th c. during a period of Episcopal outreach. And like St. Mary's, it has become a shrine for pilgrims coming to view the frescoes of N.C. native Ben Long, whose depiction of the Lord's Supper, painted in 1980, fills the back wall of the apse. Though the massing of this church is similar to St. Mary's, here the main entrance is on the gable end, and the side vestibule with belfry is a secondary entrance and vestry room.

Watauga County (WT)

Boone (WT 1–3)

The largest town in the northwestern N.C. mountains, with a permanent population of 12,915 in 1990, Boone owes its size to the presence of *Appalachian State University (ASU). Most of the growth of the school and the town have come since World War II. Until the school was established in 1903 and for some time thereafter, Boone was a mountain village, described in 1888 as having "a gaunt, shaky courthouse and jail, a store or two, and two taverns." Its population in 1900 was only 155, and even with the 1918 arrival of the narrow-gauge railroad, in 1920 it had grown to only 374.

First called Councill's Store, the site was designated as county seat when Watauga Co. was formed in 1849. The post office and later the town, incorporated in 1871, were named for pioneer Daniel Boone, who frequented the area in the 1760s during extended hunting trips from his home down the Yadkin River. One story holds that a man named Burrell, a slave and cattle-drover of local farmer Benjamin Howard, for whom nearby Howard Knob is named, was the first to lead Boone over the Blue Ridge along a buffalo trace to this site near the headwaters of the Yadkin, New, and Watauga rivers. Boone is said to have stayed in a herdsman's cabin built by Howard that stood on the site of present-day ASU. The rocks of its chimney still lay at the spot in 1912, when Col. William Lewis Bryan, the town's first mayor, incorporated them into an 18-foot **Daniel Boone Cabin Monument** (1912, 1969; Faculty St. at Justice Hall, ASU). When Faculty St. was widened in 1969 and covered the original cabin site, the monument was taken down and rebuilt nearby.

WT 1 Downtown Boone

The mid- to late 20th-c. college and resort town has few survivors from earlier days. The 1904 Neoclassical courthouse by Charlotte architect Oliver Wheeler—razed in 1968—was similar to other Wheeler courthouses, including those in Wilkes and Avery counties. A block south of King St. the former **Watauga County Jail** (1889; William Stephenson [Mayesville, Ky.], builder; 155 S. Water St.) (**a**) is a 2-story, hip-roofed brick building of domestic form that held the jailer's residence as well as cells for men and women prisoners.

WT 1 *U.S. Post Office*

King St. is lined by simple 1- and 2-story brick commercial buildings of the 1920s to 1940s, some with ornamental brickwork or classical detail, and many with late 20th-c. "mountain rustic" storefronts. A downtown landmark is the **U.S. Post Office** (1938; Louis A. Simon, supervising architect of the Treasury; Leslie, Clarence, and Earl Lyons, stonemasons; 679 W. King St.) (**b**), a compact, Colonial Revival style Works Progress Administration (WPA) building of dressed stone with a louvered cupola. The local stonemasons also worked on the *Blue Ridge Parkway, the *Cove Creek School, and buildings at Duke University in Durham. The mural inside, painted in 1940 by Connecticut artist Alan Tompkins, depicts Daniel Boone with two companions on a mountain hunting trip. The last of the early 20th-c. residences that once faced King St. is the **Jones House** (1908; 124 E. King St.) (**c**), a 2-story frame Queen Anne and Colonial Revival blend on a large lot, now a community center. The oldest residential section, on hillsides north of King St., includes handsome stone bungalows of the 1920s and 1930s.

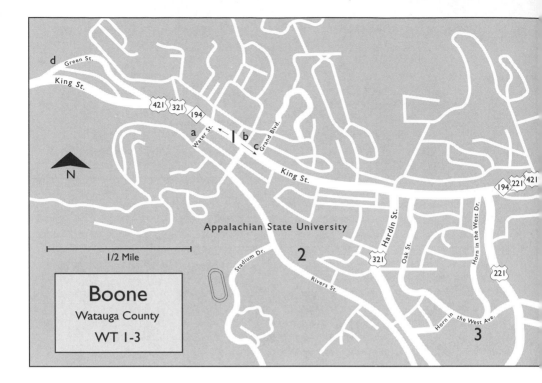

Of the late 19th-c. frame houses on the fringes of the town, the best preserved is the **Lovill House** (1875; Green St. at Old Bristol Rd.; B&B) (**d**), a 2-story farmhouse with a wraparound porch and sawn bargeboards. A frame barn and other outbuildings remain on the 11-acre lot. It was built for Civil War veteran and attorney Capt. Edward F. Lovill, an early supporter of what would become ASU, and was later the home of his son, noted criminal lawyer William R. Lovill. Here one night in 1903 the Lovills, father and son, assisted B. B. Dougherty in drafting the bill that would create the institution. E. F. Lovill served as chairman of the school's board of trustees until 1925.

WT 2 Appalachian State University

Now part of the 16-campus state university system, ASU began as Watauga Academy, founded in 1899 by two brothers, Boone natives Dauphin Disco Dougherty and Blanford Barnard Dougherty. When B. B. Dougherty successfully lobbied the legislature in 1903 for a teacher training school in

northwestern N.C., Boone was selected as the site because the town offered both the required $1,500 match to the state appropriation and use of Watauga Academy's new 2-story, 5-classroom building with auditorium and library. B. B. Dougherty became first superintendent and, later, president and led the school for over half a century. First called Appalachian Training School, it grew from 325 students in 1903 to over 1,000 in 1925 and became Appalachian State Teachers College in 1929, and Appalachian State University in 1968. In 1998 there were 12,000 students and over 700 faculty members.

The modern campus sprawls over a saddle of land south of downtown at Boone Creek. It is largely of post–World War II character, dominated by red brick buildings in institutional fashions popular from the 1950s to the present. The old Watauga Academy burned in 1946. The oldest buildings date from a 1930s expansion, several constructed with WPA assistance. Survivors from this era scattered among the newer buildings include **Dauphin Disco Dougherty Library** (1935), **Smith-Wright Hall** (1937), and **Founders Hall** (1937), the latter built as Watauga Hospital. These are rectilinear brick buildings with quoined corners and other simple classical detail. **Chappell Wilson Hall** (1938) is a long, 2-story stone building built as a demonstration high school for training teachers, originally called Appalachian High School.

WT 3 Horn in the West Amphitheater and Hickory Ridge Homestead
1950s; 591 Horn in the West Dr.

Boone's image as a tourist destination was boosted by the creation of *Horn in the West*, one of the oldest outdoor dramas in the state, presenting a saga of frontier life along the Blue Ridge. Following the success of a locally produced outdoor pageant in 1950, the Southern Appalachian Historical Association commissioned Kermit Hunter, author of the outdoor drama *Unto These Hills* at Cherokee, to write the play, and since 1952 it has been produced in the **Horn in the West Amphitheater**. Near the entrance is **Hickory Ridge Homestead**, where several log buildings have been moved in from the region to commemorate frontier life. The **Tatum Cabin** is a windowless, 1-room log house with half-dovetailed notches, traditionally dated to 1785. Other buildings include the **Coffey House** (1875), with shallow full-dovetailed notches, and a **Weaving House** with V-notches and a gable-end entrance.

WT 3 *Tatum Cabin*

WT 4 Tweetsie Railroad
W side US 221/321 midway between Boone and Blowing Rock

Although the popular tourist park projects a "wild West" image to attract visitors, it features an authentic early 20th-c. locomotive from a line that once operated nearby and offers a taste of old-time mountain railroading. The challenge of building railroads through mountain terrain was met by narrow-gauge lines, with tracks 3 feet apart instead of the standard 5 feet, 8½ inches, allowing tighter curves and steeper grades and reducing construction and equipment costs. One of the first such lines in western N.C. was the East Tennessee & Western N.C. Railroad, completed in 1882 from Johnson City, Tenn., to the iron mines at Cranberry in Avery Co. Its subsidiary, the Linville River Railway, extended the line across Avery Co. in the 1890s and to Boone in 1918. The railroads operated as a single line, hauling freight and passengers through the mountains. They were generally simply called "the narrow gauge" until about 1930, when someone coined "Tweetsie" after the shrill whistle of the small steam engines. After the floods of 1940 washed out much of the track, the line was abandoned back to Cranberry, and back to Tennessee in 1950.

The railroad line maintained a small fleet of "ten-wheeler" locomotives manufactured by Baldwin Locomotive Works of Philadelphia. A mainstay of American railroading in both standard and narrow-gauge versions, these general-purpose engines had a short, rigid wheelbase, with three large driving wheels on either side and four small pilot wheels in front. After the line's abandonment, **Locomotive No. 12** (1917; Baldwin Locomotive Works) escaped the scrap pile; it was owned for a time by movie star Gene Autry and saw brief service at a tourist park in Harrisonburg, Va. In 1955 Blowing Rock businessman Grover C. Robbins Jr. (whose father developed tourism at the Blowing Rock site) acquired and restored the engine. On July 4, 1957, No. 12 made its first run on the 3-mile oval at Robbins's new Tweetsie Railroad theme park—one of the first in the state—located a few miles east of the old Tweetsie's right-of-way. The engine has now seen longer service on the family-run tourist line than on its original railroad.

WT 5 Dougherty House (Appalachian Heritage Museum)

1903; Adolphus Cook, carpenter; W side US 221/321, at Mystery Hill Park just S of Tweetsie Railroad between Boone and Blowing Rock; open regular hours

Though its present location within a roadside tourist park bears no relation to its original setting, the 2-story frame house is notable both as an example of a turn-of-the-century mountain residence that is open to the public and for its associations with the founding of *ASU. The house was built on Rivers St. in Boone for Dauphin Disco Dougherty and his wife Lillie. Dougherty and his brother Blanford Barnard Dougherty were the founders of what became ASU, and B. B. Dougherty, a bachelor who lived with his brother's family, led the school for a half-century. Standing in the path of campus expansion plans in the 1980s and unwanted by the school, the house was moved here by a nonprofit group for restoration as a museum. The house is typical of many spacious but simply finished frame houses of the period in the northwest mountains, here with a gabled and recessed second-floor central balcony; a 1-story wraparound porch was later enclosed on one side.

WT 6 Blowing Rock

One of the state's largest and most popular mountain resorts, the thriving ridge-top town differs from other turn-of-the-century resorts such as Linville and Roaring Gap in that it has actively courted tourism by the general public while maintaining elements of an exclusive summer community. The name comes from a rock formation 2 miles south of the town center that juts 2,000 feet above the John's River gorge. The steep walls of the gorge sometimes act like a flume that carries winds up the mountainside with such force that light objects cast from the rock are lifted back up to the sender.

Development of Blowing Rock began with construction of a 20-mile turnpike up the Blue Ridge from Lenoir in 1846–47 by Lenoir industrialist James C. Harper, giving access to one of the most scenic areas in the mountains. Harper's uncle, James Harper, built a cottage at the summit called Summerville, and the Harper family continued to lead the resort in the ensuing decades, joined over time by textile and furniture industrialists of Lenoir, Statesville, Concord, Salisbury, Greensboro, Rockingham, and other piedmont cities.

During the 1870s a few private houses provided lodging for visitors, but development intensified with completion of a rail line from Hickory to Lenoir in 1884. Hotels were constructed in 1884 and 1888, and the village was incorporated in 1889. In the 1890s a second development, called Green Park, grew up near the rock formation from which the original village took its name. As automobile access increased, a third community, Mayview Park, was established west of the old town center in the 1910s and 1920s. In 1926 both Green Park and Mayview Park were incorporated into the town limits of Blowing Rock. Proximity to the *Blue Ridge Parkway boosted the community's tourism appeal in the mid-20th c. It has become a popular resort and retirement community and the setting of Jan Karon's bestselling "Mitford" novels of the late 20th c.

The **Main Street Commercial District** at the center of the original village is a lively and prosperous blend of new construction with early 20th-c. commercial and residential buildings adapted as shops and restaurants. Gothic Revival churches punctuate S. Main St. and reflect the importance religious institutions had in this and other summer resort colonies. **St. Mary's of the Hills Episcopal Church** (1918–21; Delancey Robinson [New York], architect; 121 S. Main St.) is a picturesque Gothic Revival stone church in the manner of an English country parish church, with a massive belltower with crenellated parapets; it was built for a congregation founded in 1890. **Rumple Memorial Presbyterian Church** (1905–12) across the street is a simpler Gothic Revival stone edifice sheltered under a long, deep gable roof. A block south is **Blowing Rock Methodist Church** (1900), a small gable-fronted frame church clad in chestnut-bark shingles and nestled in a grove of rhododendron.

North of the commercial district is

Chetola Manor (1890s; w side N. Main St.), a big, Shingle style house with sweeping gables, constructed as a summer home for the family of Alabama businessman William W. Stringfellow, who also created a man-made lake on the property. The house is said to incorporate an older boardinghouse built by the Estes family. It is the core of a late 20th-c. resort development, with condominiums and lodges taking architectural cues from the manor.

WT 6 *Chetola Manor*

WT 6 *Green Park Inn*

The centerpiece of the Green Park development south of the town center and near the Blowing Rock is the **Green Park Inn** (1891; later additions; N side US 321 opp. the entrance to the Blowing Rock; public hotel), one of the oldest resort hotels in the mountains. It was built by G. W. F. Harper and other Lenoir businessmen to cater to the growing mountain tourist trade and has never lost its status as one of the region's outstanding resort facilities. Despite major additions in the 1910s and remodelings in a simpler Colonial Revival image, the Queen Anne form of the building survives, with a shingled third floor, shingled gables, long porches, and curving brackets.

Informally arrayed on the curvilinear lanes around the inn are picturesque private summer cottages built for families of piedmont industrialists from the late 19th c. to the 1940s, with a majority from the 1920s reflecting Craftsman Bungalow influences. Several were erected by local builders J. Lee Hayes and Charles Moody. Chestnut-bark shingles are used on several houses, and stone retaining walls, terraces, and informal native plantings unify the landscape. The **Blowing Rock Country Club Golf Course** north of the inn was first developed as a 9-hole course in 1915 under the supervision of Lute Nelson, a landscaping contractor; it was expanded in 1922 to 18 holes, possibly under the direction of golf course designer Donald Ross.

Among the piedmont industrialists who first summered at Blowing Rock were prosperous descendants of German Reformed settlers of Cabarrus, Rowan, and Catawba counties, including the Klutz, Lentz, Bollinger, Bernhardt, Shuford, and Holshauser families, whose early presence at the resort is reflected in **Mount Bethel Reformed Church** (1893; Goforth Rd.). The simple, white frame, gable-fronted building with triangular window heads is the community's oldest church.

The Blowing Rock itself has long been privately owned by the Bernhardt family of Lenoir, who began leasing it in 1933 to Blowing Rock entrepreneur and mayor Grover C. Robbins Sr. He promoted the feature as an attraction to automobile tourists, whose numbers grew with construction of the Blue Ridge Parkway nearby, and soon built the **Blowing Rock Reception Center and Gift Shop** (1935), a rustic, 1-story stone building containing a massive fireplace, beamed ceiling, and copper chandeliers. See Barry M. Buxton, *A Village Tapestry: The History of Blowing Rock* (1989).

WT 7 Flat Top Manor (Moses and Bertha Cone Estate; Moses H. Cone Memorial Park)

1899–1901; Orlo Epps, architect; W. A. Fries, contractor; S side Blue Ridge Parkway, milepost 294, 2.0 mi. W of jct. w/US 321 (take Parkway South from US 321), Blowing Rock vic.; open regular hours in season

Commanding magnificent views across a broad valley south toward Blowing Rock, the big Colonial Revival house was the centerpiece of the mountain retreat of Greensboro textile baron Moses H. Cone and his wife, Bertha, who established here an estate described in 1921 as "the finest, except one, in North Carolina." Cone was the son of an immigrant German Jewish peddler who settled in Jonesborough, Tenn., where Moses was born, and later in Baltimore. Moses and his brother Ceasar were phenomenally successful businessmen, working their way from "drumming" for their father's wholesale operation into textile manufacturing. In 1893 the brothers built a textile finishing plant in Greensboro, and by 1905 they had built there three of the state's largest textile mills, becoming world leaders in production of denim.

WT 7 *Flat Top Manor*

By the early 1890s Moses and Bertha Cone began buying land near Blowing Rock, which was becoming a fashionable summer retreat for industrialists of the piedmont. Over time the Cones assembled 3,600 acres for their Flat Top estate, named for a mountain on the property. After negotiations with architect Stanford White of New York fell through for reasons of cost, the Cones selected Orlo Epps of Washington, D.C., to design a house and support buildings. Epps had practiced architecture in Greensboro in the mid-1890s and designed Cone's Proximity Mill.

The 2½-story frame house of 23 rooms is one of the state's earliest and largest exam-

ples of the Colonial Revival idiom. In contrast to the Southern Colonial houses with great porticoes more typical of the early Colonial Revival in the South, it is of a more academic, largely Neofederal character. The symmetrical facade has a projecting central pavilion, pedimented frontispiece, and a 1-story porch with Ionic columns that breaks into a curve at the entrance. Flanking a broad central passage, the large rooms have Neofederal mantels and other woodwork. The cool formality sets it apart from the generally more informal, Craftsman-influenced resort and summer home architecture of the mountains. Support buildings near the manor house included a laundry house and a bowling alley, both now lost.

Influenced by the Biltmore example, the Cones gave attention to landscaping, land management, horticulture, animal husbandry, and scientific farming. They developed extensive gardens, trout and bass lakes, deer parks, and 20 miles of bridle paths and carriage roads with scenic lookouts. To make the property self-supporting insofar as possible, Cone planted and carefully managed apple orchards, installed a dairy, and raised beef cattle, sheep, and poultry. At the peak of its operation, the estate employed some 30 tenants and their families, who like workers at Cone's textile mills, earned a modest wage and lived rent-free in small frame houses on the property.

In their mountaintop manor the Cones entertained friends and dignitaries with formal dinners, carriage rides, billiards, bowling, and other amusements. Frequent visitors were Cone's unmarried sisters, Claribel and Etta, art collectors and friends of Gertrude Stein since their youth in Baltimore. Through Stein—also a guest at Flat Top—in Paris the Cone sisters met Picasso, Matisse, and other giants of the early 20th-c. art world. Most of the sisters' collection was bequeathed to the Baltimore Museum of Art and housed in the Cone Wing.

After Moses Cone's unexpected death in 1908 at age fifty-one, his widow, Bertha, maintained the estate until her death in 1947 and blocked construction of the *Blue Ridge Parkway through the property until after her death. The couple had no children. Mrs.

Cone willed the property to Cone Memorial Hospital in Greensboro for a "park and pleasure-ground for the public," with the stipulation, later ignored, that the house not be open to the public.

The hospital quickly transferred the estate to the National Park Service for use in conjunction with the parkway. With a limited budget and a programmatic emphasis on natural scenery and the more rustic aspects of the local culture, the Park Service had neither means for nor interest in preserving an industrialist's tightly managed and well-manicured estate. Most of the 50 support buildings and tenant houses were razed in the 1950s, though the carriage house and a few others were retained for park operations. Gardens, pastures, and orchards were allowed to regenerate with native plants. Ironically, the elegant manor house, home to the urbane, entrepreneurial children of immigrants who hosted the likes of Gertrude Stein, came to shelter a pioneer museum and displays of mountain crafts. See Philip T. Noblitt, *A Mansion in the Mountains* (1996).

WT 8 Sandy Flat Missionary Baptist Church
1905–6; N side US 221, 0.1 mi. W of Blue Ridge Parkway connector at SR 1571

The weatherboarded, T-plan frame building with pedimented, shingled gables was constructed as a 2-room public school, partly funded by Moses and Bertha Cone of *Flat Top Manor. The Cones transferred a 3-acre tract to the county for $1 and contributed $1,500—which included donations from their tenants on the manor—toward the $1,800 project. They also subsidized teachers' salaries to extend the school year from four to eight months. Deemed "the best public school in the county," it had a sliding door between the classrooms that opened to provide an auditorium for public events. After the consolidation of rural schools closed the school in 1927, Mrs. Cone repurchased the property and made the school into Sandy Flat Missionary Baptist Church in 1928, with over half the congregation tenants on the Cone estate.

WT 9 Westglow (Elliot Daingerfield House)
1916; Mr. Smythe (New York), architect; J. Lee Hayes, builder; SE side US 221, 2.6 mi. W of BUS 321, Blowing Rock vic.; open as private spa, visible from road

Dominated by a monumental Ionic portico, the big Colonial Revival frame house enjoys an unobstructed view into the valley to the west. It was built as a summer home and studio for landscape painter Elliot Daingerfield of Fayetteville, often considered the state's greatest early 20th-c. painter. Like *Flat Top Manor, it is a relatively rare appearance of the grand Colonial Revival style in a summer home in the mountains. It remained in the family until the 1970s. To the rear stands a small frame artist's studio with a pair of 30-light windows in the north wall. The artist's daughter recalled that Daingerfield provided a rough design for the house and had drawings prepared by a Mr. Smythe of New York. Contractor Hayes also built the 1916 additions to the *Green Park Inn and several cottages in Blowing Rock.

WT 9 *Westglow*

WT 10 Gragg House
Mid-19th c.; N side US 221, 0.6 mi. N of Watauga-Caldwell line; private, visible from road

The exacting craftsmanship in the saddlebag-plan house with 2 pens flanking a central stone chimney makes it one of the state's finest examples of dovetail plank construction, the more remarkable for its once-remote mountain location. The carefully hewn timbers are of exceptional width and joined tightly with full-dovetailed corner notches so that daubing was unnecessary. Tradition holds that it was built in the mid-19th c. by Burton Gragg and his son Finley. In the mid-20th c. it was adapted as part of a small roadside tourist complex.

WT 10 *Gragg House*

WT 11 Valle Crucis

Meaning "Vale of the Cross," the name reflects the shape of the valley formed by the confluence of three creeks with the Watauga River and was proffered by Episcopal bishop Levi Silliman Ives, founder of *Valle Crucis Mission in 1844. From the early 19th c. onward, a few families—mainly Masts, Shulls, Bairds, Churches, and Taylors—acquired the exceptionally rich bottomlands of the broad and beautiful valley, maintained their holdings, and prospered. Boosted by the presence of the Episcopal mission, the community became a social, commercial, and educational center for the surrounding area.

The centerpiece is the **Mast Store** (late 19th c.; N side NC 194, 0.2 mi. W of SR 1112), perhaps the state's best-known country store, still thriving as a supply center for both farmers and tourists and housing the post office. The business grew out of a store established by Henry Taylor in the early 1880s, and the central portion of the present building was apparently erected by the time he formed a partnership with W. W. Mast in 1898. Mast became sole owner in 1913. The 2-story central block of the weatherboarded building has a broad gable front flanked by

false-front wings with raised arch parapets. Inside, the old wooden shelves and glass display cases are filled with an array of merchandise, though the focus today is on outdoor clothing and camping equipment. East of the store a simpler, 2-story, gable-fronted frame store, the former **Valle Crucis Company Store** (1909; N side NC 194), serves as an annex.

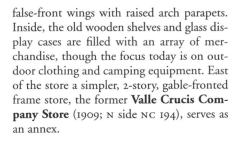

WT 11 *Mast Store*

WT 12 Mast Farm
Ca. 1812; 1885, M. C. Church, carpenter; early 20th c.; S side SR 1112, 0.5 mi. E of NC 194; B&B

The farm complex beside the road comprises one of the most complete and best-preserved examples of a 19th-c. farm in western N.C., with a history that combines agriculture, tourism, and handicrafts. The farmstead was established by David and Mary Shull Mast, descendants of Swiss and German settlers who came to the region in the late 18th c. They are believed to have built the oldest structure on the farm as their home: a small, 2-story log building with dovetailed notches, a gable-end stone chimney, and exterior stair. After their son Andrew inherited the farm in 1873, he moved the old log house across the yard, so that he and his wife Caroline could have the present large frame **Mast House** erected about 1885 by carpenter M. C. Church.

In 1880 their son David Finley Mast married Allie Josephine Mast of nearby Cove Creek, and the couple made their home at the farm. To accommodate growing tourism, about 1900 they began accepting overnight guests and soon expanded their house with a large rear section to create 13 bed-

WT 12 *Mast House*

WT 12 *Mast Weaving House*

rooms. The full-length, 1-story shed porch, extended to wrap the sides, has a gabled 2-story section that was enclosed as a sun room, a typical practice in the region.

Josephine (Josie) Mast also profited from the tourist trade by developing a handweaving operation. She worked in the old log house—now called the **Weaving House** or Loom House—and used an old loom said to have been built by Mary Mast. A respected participant in the regional crafts revival, Josie Mast gained fame when First Lady Ellen Wilson ordered a carpet and other textiles for the White House from her in 1913; Mast also taught weaving at the nearby *Valle Crucis Episcopal Mission, gave weaving demonstrations in other states, and evidently influenced such crafts revival leaders as Lucy Morgan and Dr. Mary Sloop.

Other farm buildings include an octagonal gazebo, a springhouse, a meathouse, a blacksmith's shop, and, across the road, a large frame barn with gambrel roof and vented cupolas, built for Andrew Mast. Continuing to serve tourists, the farm is a popular bed and breakfast inn. (See Kathleen Curtis Wilson, "The Handweaving of

Allie Josephine Mast, 1861–1936," in *May We All Remember Well*, edited by Robert S. Brunk (1997.)

WT 13 Baird Farm
Late 19th c.; N side NC 194, 0.5 mi.
W of SR 1112; private, visible from road

The well-kept farm west of the Mast Store centers on a frame farmhouse of traditional I-house form with a 2-story rear ell; the front section is said to incorporate a mid-19th-c. log house. In a typical decorative flourish, the 2-story porch at the entrance has delicate sawnwork balustrades and porch post brackets. Among the outbuildings is an unusual frame barn with a broad clipped gable roof that projects forward to create a wagon shelter, and diagonally slatted eaves ventilate the hayloft. (See Introduction, Fig. 54.)

WT 14 Valle Crucis Episcopal Mission (Valle Crucis Conference Center)
NW side NC 194, 1.0 mi. S of Valle Crucis

The early 20th-c. farm school complex traces its origins to the mission founded in 1844 by Levi Silliman Ives, bishop of the diocese of N.C., who worked to establish an Episcopal presence in northwestern N.C. After visiting the site, he purchased farmlands and buildings, apparently in his own name, and directed construction of log and frame buildings to serve a classical and agricultural school for laity, a seminary, and a model farm. By 1848 Ives had also founded a secret monastic order, the Order of the Holy Cross, inspired by the principles of tractarianism, a movement calling for a return to piety through ritual. When its existence became public, many N.C. Episcopalians believed the order dangerously resembled Catholicism. Ives was at the center of a storm over this and other of his tractarian policies and statements. The controversy culminated in his conversion to Catholicism during a journey to Rome in 1852.

In its brief existence from 1848 to 1851, the seminary produced eight ministers active in the expansion of the church in western N.C., including William Gries, rector and designer of *St. Paul's Episcopal Church in Wilkesboro, and William West Skiles, founder of nearby *St. John's of Lower Watauga. The diocese lost title to the land when Bishop Ives left the state, but Skiles provided religious, educational, and medical services to the area for a decade after the seminary closed. Only one building survives from this era, now called the **Bishop Ives House**, a twice-moved and heavily altered log structure.

Under the direction of Bishop Joseph Blount Cheshire Jr. in the late 19th c. and of Bishop Junius J. Horner of the newly established Jurisdiction of Western N.C. in the early 20th c., the church reacquired some of the mission lands and began a rebuilding program that established the present character of the hillside campus. By 1911 over 700 acres had been acquired for an agricultural and industrial school serving 100 students. The working farm included apple orchards, dairy cattle, a cheese factory, a blacksmith shop, a wagon factory, and a sawmill. A waterpowered generator provided the first electric power in the county. The school flourished until 1943, when financial stresses, shortages, and depleted enrollment during World War II forced its closing. After the war the campus returned to use as a training and conference center.

WT 14 *Auchmuty Hall, Valle Crucis Episcopal Mission*

The first structure erected during the rebuilding was the dormitory or **Mission House** (1896), a frame 2-story house of foursquare form, with a gable-fronted entrance and shingled gables. Dominating the view of the campus from NC 194 is **Auchmuty Hall** (1910–11), a 2½-story dormitory set in the slope of the hill over a raised basement; with its high hip-on-gable roof with multiple

dormers, it gives an imposing 4-story appearance on the south. It is built of concrete block, with rusticated block used in stringcourses and quoins; a broad 1-story porch wraps three sides. The **Annex** (ca. 1920), a 2-story building of hollow ceramic block stuccoed at the basement and first-floor levels, has a similar wraparound porch. The **Church of the Holy Cross** (1924) is a compact gable-fronted Gothic Revival church of irregular rough-cut stone with parapeted gable front and side narthex. Other buildings include **Farm House** (1915), a frame bungalow with recessed porches, and barns and sheds from the farming operation. A few post–World War II buildings were added to serve the conference center. The broad valley of Dutch Creek spreads below the campus, and forested hills rise above.

WT 15 St. John's of Lower Watauga Episcopal Church
1860?, late 19th c.; end of SR 1118, 0.6 mi. W of SR 1117; Valle Crucis vic.

The tiny white frame mission church gains presence from its hillside site overlooking the broad Watauga River valley. For all its rural simplicity, it embodies the spirit of Gothic Revival, with steeply vertical proportions, triangular window heads, and projecting vestibule and apse. Board and batten covers the upper half of the walls, with sawn shingles below and on the gables and belfry. The beaded tongue-and-grove sheathing of the interior rises into a vaulted ceiling, and Gothic Revival moldings and furnishings remain intact. William West Skiles of the *Valle Crucis Episcopal Mission established St. John's at a site 6 miles down the Watauga River in 1860, and a church he erected at his expense was consecrated in 1862, shortly before his death. Tradition recalls that following years of disuse, in 1882 the mission was renewed and the church was moved to this location closer to Valle Crucis. It is unclear how much of the present building is Skiles's church. Possibly it was disassembled and rebuilt with old and new materials, with shingles replacing damaged board and batten on the lower walls. Skiles's remains were reinterred in the new churchyard.

WT 15 *St. John's of Lower Watauga*

WT 16 Tom Ward House

1897–1900; S side US 321 at SR 1121; private, visible from road

Located on a major highway into Tennessee, the 2-story, frame, T-plan house uses elements familiar in the region's ornamented late 19th-c. farmhouses to create an unusually full-blown Queen Anne composition, with projecting bays, sawtooth shingles, elaborately sawn spandrels in the gables, and a large cupola. It was built for farmer Tom Ward, descendant of early settlers in this section, and remained in the Ward family until 1974.

WT 16 *Tom Ward House*

WT 17 Cove Creek School

1941; WPA, Clarence Coffey [Lenoir], architect; Charlie Hartley and Orville Hagaman, supervisors; Leslie, Clarence, and Earl Lyons, stonemasons; Alfred Howard Ward, cast stone work; W side SR 1233, 0.75 mi. N of US 321, Sugar Grove/Sherwood vic.

One of the largest of several WPA schools constructed of native stone in the mountain region, Cove Creek exemplifies the agency's policy to build in regionally adapted styles and materials. The large 2-story building has stone walls in a mosaic pattern, using stone from two nearby farms. The cast stone entrance and other details blend Tudor and moderne motifs. Located in a fertile valley known as "the Egypt of Watauga County," the school was the pride of the community and the local men who built it. Construction supervisor Hartley recalled, "I wonder lots of times, 'Did I do this?' But there's a building to show. I guess I could pick out a hundred buildings around Boone that I was the boss on. But Cove Creek is my pride." The stonemasons also worked on the *U.S. Post Office in Boone, the *Blue Ridge Parkway, and Duke University in Durham. The school is under development as a community center.

WT 17 *Cove Creek School*

WT 18 Henson Chapel Methodist Church and Parsonage

1926–31; Mr. Hartzog (Boone), contractor; W side SR 1233, just E of SR 1217, Amantha

In size, form, and materials the red brick church is a departure from the region's frame country churches. The Gothic Revival building is organized around a steep pyramidal roof, with projecting gables and side wings and unequal, crenellated corner towers. The auditorium plan is typical of urban Methodist churches of the period. Its design is reportedly based on another (unidentified) church planned by architect James M. McMichael of Charlotte. It is the third sanctuary of a congregation founded in 1858.

WT 19 Wilson-Vines House

Ca. 1895; E side SR 1209, 0.3 mi. S of SR 1201; private, visible from road

The Bethel community, located at the confluence of Rube and Beaverdam creeks near the Tennessee line, retains several late 19th-c., 2-story frame farmhouses in an unspoiled agricultural landscape. Most notable is the Wilson-Vines House, a well-preserved L-plan house with exceptionally lavish decoration: chamfered posts with curved spandrels and brackets carry the 2-tier porch and are connected by sawnwork balustrades. A pair of decorative gables rise above the porch, each with a roundel medallion, and the gables have sawn kingpost-and-collar inserts.

WT 19 *Wilson-Vines House*

WT 20 Greene Farm

Ca. 1875, early 20th c.; W side NC 194, just S of SR 1335, Boone vic.; private, visible from road

The fine example of a prosperous bottomland farm lies along a major highway in the valley of Meat Camp Creek. The 2-story frame farmhouse, which evolved in sections, presents a long, asymmetrical, 3-part facade with a gable-fronted central block and flanking wings. A 1-story porch wraps across the front, and covered balconies break out above the porch at the wings, all adorned with delicate sawnwork. Outbuildings to the east include two gambrel-roofed barns, one with diagonal sheathing.

WT 21 Meat Camp Baptist Church

1927; NW corner NC 194 and SR 1364

Like many Baptist and Methodist churches in the region, the little gable-fronted building with vestibule and belltower now has vinyl siding and other late 20th-c. remodelings. But it maintains a strong presence on its lofty site above the valley of Meat Camp Creek, with generations of church members buried in the hillside cemetery below. The congregation, which began in 1851 in a schoolhouse before building a frame church in 1854, erected this church in 1927 during a period of widespread local church building. The creek, church, and community take their name from an early campsite where hunters brought hides and salted meat.

WT 22 St. Matthews Episcopal Church

Ca. 1900; SW side NC 194, 0.5 mi. W of Todd

WT 22 *St. Matthews Episcopal Church*

Several Episcopal mission churches in the northwest mountains were established around 1900 following creation of the Jurisdiction of Western N.C., including *St. Mary's near West Jefferson and *Holy Trinity at Glendale Springs. All are simply rendered variations of the Gothic Revival in frame. Small as it is, the weatherboarded building has all the essentials of a liturgical church: lancet-arched openings, a front vestibule, a corner belltower, and an apse at the rear.

Avery County (AV)

Avery, one of the state's two youngest counties, was formed in 1911 and named for Revolutionary leader Waightsill Avery, progenitor of an influential western N.C. family. In earlier times its rugged terrain harbored isolated small farms with few slave owners, and many citizens maintained Unionist sympathies during the Civil War and remained staunchly Republican thereafter. A narrow-gauge railroad entered from Tennessee in the 1880s to fetch iron from mines at Cranberry and virgin timber from throughout the area. The simultaneous establishment of a resort for industrialists and their families at Linville heralded the tourism to come in the 20th c. An unusually strong Presbyterian presence grew out of denominational mission schools and hospitals established in the early 20th c. at Banner Elk and Crossnore. These resorts and schools are distinguished by some of the region's best examples of rustic chestnut-bark and native stone buildings.

AV 1 Newland

This site by the North Toe River and the railroad was selected as county seat for its central location and named for Lieutenant Governor William C. Newland of Lenoir, who helped establish the new county. The **Avery County Courthouse** (1913; Wheeler & Runge [Charlotte], architect; R. C. Campbell, builder) is the county's first and only courthouse, and one of six surviving N.C. courthouses of similar form designed by Oliver Wheeler of Charlotte with various associates. The 2-story brick Neoclassical Revival building has the 3-story, hip-roofed central core, Ionic portico, and oblong mansard-like dome characteristic of the group. The nearby **Avery County Jail** (1913) takes a domestic form common to jails in small county seats through the early 20th c.; the 2-story, hip-roofed brick building now houses the county museum.

AV 1 *Avery Co. Courthouse*

AV 2 Linville

Access to private residential sections is largely restricted.

One of the most exclusive and architecturally distinctive resort communities in the mountains, Linville has an important collection of sophisticated rustic vacation architecture of the late 19th and early 20th centuries, including work by nationally renowned architect Henry Bacon. The community was developed for "cottagers" principally from Wilmington and Charlotte, N.C.; Nashville, Tenn.; and Birmingham, Ala., who have summered here for generations.

In 1888 a group of investors headed by the MacRae family of Wilmington purchased about 16,000 acres, including nearby *Grandfather Mountain, with an eye to developing the timber and mineral resources. The site's potential had been identified by S. T. Kelsey, developer of Highlands, who was surveying for a railroad line planned along the Blue Ridge. Recognizing that the plateau near iron deposits and old-growth forests was an ideal site for an industrial town, Kelsey joined with a Highlands associate, S. P. Ravenel, and Donald MacRae of Wilmington, a businessman involved in diverse real estate and industrial enterprises. MacRae brought in his sons Donald Jr. and Hugh; the latter, a recent graduate of the engineering program at MIT, was overseeing family mica works near Burnsville.

The investors organized the Linville Improvement Co., which soon had the town site "cleared and stumped so clean that it looked like a desert bordered with trees" and built a small hotel. The story is told that when the company's directors held a meeting at the site, their wives were so struck by the tract's natural beauty that they urged their husbands to develop a resort for their families and friends. Other accounts indicate that the investors disagreed about the purpose of the project, and that lawsuits ensued.

With their plans redefined, the company, under the leadership of Hugh MacRae, began development of a resort. To improve access to the remote site, in 1892 the company built the *Yonahlossee Road to Blowing Rock, the winding route of present-day NC 221. Visitors from Tennessee arrived by train on the *Tweetsie Railroad, then took a hack from the line's terminus as it extended across the county until it reached Linville about 1915. The company promoted the benefits of the altitude and good air, claiming that "literary people and brain-workers, especially" would benefit from the "invigorating atmosphere."

Indeed, as early as 1891 a visiting Harvard professor rhapsodized, "At last, I have struck it rich here in North Carolina and am in the most peculiar and one of the most poetic places I have ever been in." At the partially finished resort on its plateau, he reveled in the "peculiar combination of virgin wilderness with perfectly planned roads, Queen Anne cottages, and a sweet little modern hotel." He believed "the serpent has not yet made his appearance in this Eden, around which stand the hills covered with primeval forest of the most beautiful description, filled with rhododendrons, laurels and azaleas which, through the month of July, must make it ablaze with glory."

During an initial expansion that lasted until about 1920, the character of the village was established, with cottages and support buildings covered in chestnut-bark shingles. The original hotel, the Eseeola Inn built in 1891–92, burned in 1936, but its rambling form, long veranda, and shingled walls set the tone for the community.

Of several Shingle style houses erected in the early period, especially notable is **Dormiecroft** (ca. 1897; E side Carolina Ave.; private), the summer home of Hugh MacRae, Linville's leading developer, a complex wood-shingled mass of steep gables, pents, and porches. Evidently its design came from architect William L. Price's "Model Suburban House" published in the *Ladies' Home Journal* (July 1897).

Among the finest buildings in the chestnut-shingled mode are those designed by architect Henry Bacon, friend of the MacRae family from his childhood days in Wilmington and best known as the architect of the Lincoln Memorial. He made visits to Linville over the years from 1895 to 1910. Three private cottages dating from the early years are credited to Bacon, including a remodeling of a farmhouse as the **Donald MacRae Cottage** (1890s; Henry Bacon, architect; Watauga Ave.), a gable-fronted, deep-porched house, where Bacon introduced the chestnut-bark shingles; the somewhat altered **VanLandingham Cottage** (ca. 1900; Henry Bacon, architect; Watauga Ave.), originally a T-shaped house, with chestnut-bark shingles in the oldest portions; and **The Studio** (ca. 1895; Henry Bacon, architect; Beech St.), a 1½-story bungalow with chestnut-bark shingles inside and out. All are simple bark-clad buildings with logs left in the round for structural and decorative elements. The informal, rustic artistry of his Linville work contrasts with Bacon's better-known Neoclassicism.

Most visible and accessible of Bacon's work in Linville is **All Saints Episcopal Church** (1910–13; Henry Bacon, architect;

AV 2 *Dormiecroft*

AV 2 *Donald MacRae Cottage*

E side Carolina Ave.), built with funds donated by Agnes MacRae Parsley. This gem of
a church takes a simple gable-fronted form,
with its walls covered with thick chestnut-
bark shingles and exposed log timbers in the
eaves. A roundel window accentuates the
front gable, and above it the bark-clad, gabled belfry rises to a cross of branches. The
interior is a gloriously subtle creation in
which high-church Episcopalian motifs are
rendered in rustic, natural materials, from
the bark-clad interior walls and ceiling to
the roof truss of saplings, the rood screen of
arcaded branches, and the chancel furnishings of beautifully wrought branches and
twigs. (See Introduction, Fig. 40.)

Linville's centerpiece is the **Eseeola
Lodge** (1920s, 1937; SE corner Linville Ave.
and Beech St.; open to guests), the grandest
building in the bark-shingle mode, with
2-story gable-end porches with log supports.
It was built as Chestnut Lodge, a supple-
mentary building for the original Eseeola
Inn built in the 1890s, but after the old inn
burned in 1936, this building was expanded
to serve as the main inn.

Between 1920 and World War II, Hugh
MacRae's son Nelson inaugurated a phase of
development centered on a growing interest
in golf. He oversaw the creation of a professional golf course (1924–26) designed by the
famed Donald Ross. He also employed architect Harry Stearns, an architect remembered locally as having been from New York
or Connecticut, to design the 1927 bark-
shingled clubhouse for the golf course. Although the clubhouse burned in 1952, it was

but the first of many Stearns commissions in
Linville.

The 1920s and 1930s expansion also produced many large, Tudor Revival houses,
which can hardly be called cottages, employing rustic stonework, chestnut-bark shingles, and applied half-timbering, sometimes
rendered in rustic logs. Ten of these are credited to Harry Stearns and were built in the
late 1920s. Several handsome Stearns cottages stand along Linville Ave., while others
line the west side of Watauga Ave. along the
golf course. Typical is the **Calhoun House**
(1928; Harry Stearns, architect; Watauga
Ave.), which displays such Stearns hallmarks
as a stone entrance tower, bark-clad lower
walls, and half-timbering and porch posts
rendered in round logs. Among smaller
houses the log-and-bark vocabulary was combined with the Craftsman bungalow, as in
the **Stedman House** (1920s; Mr. Billingsly,
builder; Linville Ave.).

AV 2 *Calhoun House*

The chestnut blight of the 1930s ended
the tradition of building with chestnut-bark
shingles, but modern construction, usually
faced in vertical board-and-batten siding,
has been well integrated with the older
buildings.

AV 3 Grandfather Mountain

At 5,964 feet, Grandfather Mountain is the
highest peak along the Blue Ridge and one
of the state's most popular tourist destinations. It has been known as Grandfather
since early settlement, apparently from the
profile of a bearded man that can be imag-
ined in the rock formations. In 1794 the
French naturalist André Michaux explored

the region to collect botanical specimens. Believing Grandfather Mountain to be "the highest mountain of all North America," he recorded in his journal that he "climbed to the summit . . . and with my companion and guide, sang the Marseillaise Hymn and cried: Long Live America and the French Republic! Long live Liberty!"

Nearly a century later the mountain was part of the 16,000-acre tract acquired by the consortium of businessmen who developed Linville, including Hugh MacRae of Wilmington. When the Linville Improvement Co. dissolved in 1952, ownership of the mountain went to MacRae's grandson, Hugh MacRae Morton. Though a toll road for visitors had long been in place, Morton stepped up promotion of the mountain as "Carolina's Top Scenic Attraction," with emphasis on its natural character, improving the roads, opening hiking trails and wildlife "environmental habitats," and spanning two of the mountain's seven crags with the **Mile-High Swinging Bridge** (1952), a 228-foot suspension footbridge. Grandfather Mountain hosts the annual "Singing on the Mountain," a festival of gospel music, and the "Gathering of the Scottish Clans," one of the largest Highland games events celebrating Scots heritage.

AV 4 Linn Cove Viaduct

1978–83; opened 1987; Figg and Muller, Inc. (Tallahassee, Fla.), engineers; Jasper Construction Co. (Plymouth, Minn.), contractors; Rex Cocroft, Federal Highway Administration, chief supervising engineer; Blue Ridge Parkway on East Face of Grandfather Mountain

The last link to be completed on the 469-mile-long scenic parkway that began in 1935 includes the viaduct, an innovative 1,243-foot ribbon of concrete that gracefully skirts the side of *Grandfather Mountain and rests on concrete piers built to minimize cuts into the slope.

Right-of-way acquired in 1939–40 ran along the base of the mountains, but in the 1950s a new parkway route was designed to cut across higher ridges of the mountain. Hugh MacRae Morton, owner of Grand-

father Mountain, refused to give up the land. He fought the higher route "every way we could," arguing that cutting and blasting a road across Grandfather Mountain would be "like taking a switchblade to the Mona Lisa." Morton's campaign delayed the project for more than twenty years. After intervention by Governor Dan K. Moore, park service officials agreed to consider alternate routes and, with Morton, settled on a middle route.

By that time, engineering developments had emerged in Europe that allowed a revolutionary approach in which the road appears to float beside the mountain. The structure literally and figuratively completes the original vision of the parkway in a marriage of aesthetics, environmental sensitivity, and spectacular engineering. The roadway is composed of 153 pie-shaped sections—no two the same shape, and only one straight—compressed into a continuous S-curve by internal tension cables. It was built from south to north with precast segments progressively lowered into place by a stiff-leg crane. The seven piers are set on microshaft piles drilled into the rock—the only disturbance of the mountainside of massive boulders. (A principal concern was to avoid methods that would destabilize the mountainside—a problem evident in landslides along other mountain highways, including I-40 in recent years.)

Although comparable structures had been built in Europe, this was the first of its type in the United States. The French engineering firm of Figg and Muller was the only one in the world that had successfully used the techniques required. The project was bid at $7.9 million, but final cost rose to $9.8 million. The work crew was almost entirely from the Grandfather Mountain area. Becoming a tourist attraction for its novel construction long before the other segments of the parkway were completed to permit its opening in 1987, the viaduct won national awards from the American Society of Civil Engineers and the Prestressed Concrete Institute. (See Introduction, Fig. 65.)

AV 5 Yonahlossee Road

Along US 221 between Linville and Blowing Rock

Now considered by many a carsick motorist to be a treacherous section of old mountain highway, the 16-mile stretch of US 221 between Linville and Blowing Rock winds along the roadbed of the Yonahlossee Rd., created in 1892 by the Linville Improvement Co. against the southern slope of *Grandfather Mountain to connect the two growing resort towns. The name is said to be an Indian word for "passing bear." In its day the road was as great a wonder as the *Linn Cove Viaduct became in the late 20th c. An account of 1896 reported that before construction of the Yonahlossee Rd., a traveler attempting to traverse the distance "started, trembled, and went back; [but] now a road, the most beautiful and easy grade in all the hill-country woos the traveler over its broad ribbon-like track. . . . To whirl along at the horses' best speed, as smoothly as if bowling along a drive in Central Park, is to enjoy the utmost luxury of locomotion through an exhilarating atmosphere scented with pine and balsam on the most stony mountain of the Appalachian chain." Two decades later it was still termed "the most picturesque and durable highway in the mountains or in the state." Until the opening of the Linn Cove Viaduct in 1987, the road served as a link of the Blue Ridge Parkway around Grandfather Mountain.

AV 6 Pineola Presbyterian Church

1927, Bob Hughes, supervising carpenter; 1968; E side US 221 at NC 181, Pineola

Clad in dark brown cedar shingles, the church blends sophistication with rustic informality also seen at Linville, here with a big square belltower rising from an assemblage of intersecting and parallel gables. The congregation was founded in 1898 by Edgar Tufts of Banner Elk, whose mission work ensured a strong Presbyterian presence across the county. The present building was begun during the pastorate of E. Frank Camp; carpenter Hughes, who may have constructed some of the cottages at Linville, supervised volunteers from the congregation. The church was expanded in the 1960s with a compatible wing. The sanctuary retains an exposed truss of bark-covered saplings similar to that at *All Saints Episcopal Church in Linville.

AV 6 *Pineola Presbyterian Church*

AV 7 Crossnore

Named for a 19th-c. storekeeper, Crossnore was a Linville River village with three houses, a store, and an old combination church-schoolhouse in 1911 when Presbyterian mission workers Dr. Eustace H. Sloop and Dr. Mary Martin Sloop relocated their medical practice here from *Plumtree in order to be more central to their service area. The Sloops, natives of the western piedmont of N.C. and graduates of Davidson College, had come to the area after their marriage in 1908 and devoted their lives to medical, educational, and religious work in Avery and surrounding counties. Over the next half-century the Sloops built a boarding school and hospital complex on a 250-acre campus. A secondhand clothing store, a working farm, and a crafts and weaving program helped support the endeavor, and further assistance came from the Daughters of the American Revolution and private donors. The Sloops also built a stone dam and powerhouse on the Linville River that provided power to the hospital and surrounding community until 1945.

School and hospital buildings, several in stone or stucco, are simple, functional structures built by local workmen. Garrett Memorial Hospital was a stone building constructed in 1928–29 by "Uncle Will" Franklin, mason of nearby *Crossnore Presbyterian Church; it is encased within Sloop Memorial Hospital. **Sloop Chapel** (1954), at the entrance to the complex, is a simple Gothic Revival church with buttressed walls, designed and built by staff of the school. Reflecting the long association of the D.A.R. with the school, the **D.A.R. Chapter House** is a small log house with half-dovetailed notches moved from near Plumtree and restored in the late 1950s; it was one pen of a dogtrot house built ca. 1906 for Thomas and Lola Webb, who raised eight children in the house.

AV 7 *D.A.R. Chapter House, Crossnore*

AV 8 Crossnore Presbyterian Church

1924–26; William E. Franklin, builder; E side US 221/NC 194 opp. Dellinger Rd.

One of several buildings of native stone associated with the Presbyterian missions at Crossnore and Banner Elk, the church was built by Eustace and Mary Sloop, founders of the school and hospital at Crossnore, for their students. The church combines Craftsman style influences with traditional church planning, rendered in water-smoothed rock taken from the nearby Linville River and laid by local workmen. It follows a T-plan, with stout towers of unequal height at the front corners of the T, linked by a porch with tapered rock piers. Inside, exposed rock walls rise to an open beam ceiling where strips of chestnut bark form a herringbone pattern between the rafters. Construction was supervised by "Uncle Will" Franklin, an illiterate but resourceful farmer, millwright, carpenter, and mason who did most of the rock work himself. Dr. Mary Sloop recalled that the church "was built according to Uncle Will's ideas, for none of the rest of us

AV 8 *Crossnore Presbyterian Church*

could conceive of the beauty of that structure." Leonard White Jr., a relative of Dr. Sloop and an associate of Greensboro architect Harry Barton, may also have had a hand in the design.

AV 9 George and Anna Watkins House

Ca. 1890; Henry Poteat, builder; E side US 221, 0.1 mi. N of SR 1525, Altamont; private, visible from road

The county's most ambitious late 19th-c. house is a 2-story, 5-bay frame dwelling of traditional form with Eastlake and Gothic Revival touches, including decoratively shingled walls, a full-width, 2-story shed porch with scrollwork, and sinuous vergeboards. After long neglect and loss of its interiors, it was stabilized as headquarters for a Christmas tree farm.

AV 10 Plumtree

The community on the North Toe River has been a mica processing center since the late 19th c. The **Tar Heel Mica Building** (1912, 1919) stretches alongside the highway; the 2-story, 16-bay structure of rusticated concrete block was expanded with an even longer 1-story addition in 1919. The company continues to grind and bond mica into sheets and rolls for industrial use even though the material is no longer mined locally and is imported from abroad.

Across the river is **Plumtree Presbyterian Church** (1914; E side US 19E at SR 1122), one of several substantial Presbyterian churches in the county that arose out of the mission work of Edgar Tufts of Banner Elk, Drs. Eustace and Mary Sloop of Crossnore, and others. This church was founded by Rev. Joseph P. Hall, who was associated with a boys' school at Plumtree founded by Tufts and later merged with *Lees-McRae College. The Sloops were members of this congregation for a time. The unusually large frame church stands 2 stories under a hip roof with cross gables; a 3-story corner tower contains an open belfry under a bracketed pyramidal roof. Nearby stands the **C. W. Burleson Store** (late 19th c.; w side US 19E at SR 1122), a 2-story frame general store with a stepped parapet facade and a 1-story gable-fronted side addition. Plumtree was used as a location for the film *The Winter People* (1989), based on John Ehle's novel. Sets left after the filming include a stone clock tower in front of the store. West of the store is the **Wilkins House** (early to mid-19th c.), a double-pen, half-dovetailed log house original to the site and believed to be the oldest structure in the county.

AV 10 *Plumtree Presbyterian Church and Burleson Store*

AV 11 Minneapolis Christian Church

1932; Charley Hartley, designer;
Will Cook and Walt Mitchell, stonemasons;
E side US 19E at Minneapolis

The village, named for the Minnesota city, is near what was once the largest asbestos mine in N.C., no longer active. Standing out among simple frame buildings, the compact church of neatly dressed stone features a porch and belltower with steeple at the gable front. The church history recalls that when the old frame church burned in early 1932, the congregation rallied to erect a new building. Member Pink Young hauled rock off his father's farm on a sled pulled by his

mule, "Ole Kate"; other members donated equipment, materials, and labor, and the women cooked every day "to provide a bountiful meal for the working men." In September "the beautiful bell in its steeple rang out to announce the completion of the lovely building."

AV 12 Cranberry

Cranberry was the site of N.C.'s largest iron-ore deposit, where iron mines and forges operated between 1826 and about 1930. The high quality ore was first mined on a small scale, but production boomed when the narrow-gauge East Tennessee & Western N.C. Railroad arrived from Johnson City, Tenn., in 1882 (see *Tweetsie Railroad, Watauga Co.). In 1888 travel writer Charles Dudley Warner described Cranberry as "the first wedge of civilization fairly driven into the northwest mountains of North Carolina . . . where a big company store, rows of tenement houses, heaps of slag and refuse ore, interlacing tracks, raw embankments, denuded hillsides, and a blackened landscape are the signs of a great devastating American enterprise." Today there is little public evidence of that enterprise. The principal landmark from the iron heyday is **Cranberry School** (1923; SE corner US 19E and NC 194), a big 2-story red brick school on a raised basement cut into the hillside, with long rows of paired windows and a small central entrance porch with Tuscan columns.

AV 12 *Cranberry School*

AV 13 Banner Elk

Named for a local family, the village on the Elk River is the home of **Lees-McRae Col-**

lege, a junior college with a campus of remarkably fine stone buildings. It began in the 1890s as a summer mission school conducted by Elizabeth McRae, a Presbyterian teacher and activist from Robeson Co. in southeastern N.C., who was nearly seventy when she began her work in the mountains. The present school was founded about 1900 by the Reverend Edgar Tufts, who named it for Mrs. McRae and a donor who assisted the school. Tufts also established a hospital and orphanage. The campus dates from about 1920 onward and is distinguished by several stone buildings of the mid-1920s planned by architect Donald R. Beeson of Johnson City, Tenn. Beeson's association with the school began in 1917 with the design of a small brick hospital and continued for over a decade.

Along a ridge at the highest point of the campus are five Beeson buildings that combine formal plans with irregular stonework to achieve a rustic monumentality. The **Virginia Dormitory** and the **Tennessee Dormitory** are similar 2½-story, U-shaped buildings with arcaded stone porches between the arms of the U. These flank the **North Carolina Building** with a central tower, built as an administration building and later converted to classrooms. The

Water Tower (Tufts Tower) just east of the Virginia Dormitory is a five-sided stone structure with buttressed corners. **Banner Elk Presbyterian Church** to its east features a massive corner tower with belfry under a pyramidal roof. Architect Beeson later wrote that the buildings were "all of river rock picked up along the creek and set by the local farmers who were rock masons in their spare time."

AV 14 Sugar Top Condominiums
1981–85; Stevens-Wilkinson (Columbia, S.C.), architects; 303 Sugartop Rd., Sugar Village; private resort

Skiing was an on-again, off-again sport for relatively few enthusiasts in western N.C., subject to the whims of winter weather, until practical snow-making machines developed in the mid-1950s enabled entrepreneurs to offer snowy slopes to paying guests for most of the season. The first commercial ski slope in N.C. opened at Cataloochee in 1961. Seven such resorts now operate in the state. Even with machine-made snow, it has proven to be a slippery business, with several bankruptcies and closings. The slopes on Sugar Mountain, one of the largest and most successful resorts, opened in 1969.

AV 13 *Lees-McRae College: Virginia Dormitory and North Carolina Building*

A highly visible—and controversial—symbol of this phase of recreational tourism is Sugar Top, a 10-story, 320-unit high-rise condominium of gray concrete crowning Sugar Mountain. It is heavily built like a bunker with bands of concrete balconies to withstand storms and icy winds. Visible on the horizon for miles in all directions, the building ignited controversy over the direction of development in the mountains. Its friends love the magnificent views from their private balconies; detractors call the gray, slab-like mass "Western North Carolina's Tombstone" that heralds despoliation of the region's natural beauty. The building prompted the state legislature to enact a "ridge law" in 1984 that enables local governments to monitor and regulate construction on mountain ridges. Thus far there have been no repeat performances on this scale.

Mitchell County (ML)

ML 1 Bakersville

One of the state's smallest counties, Mitchell is a land of steep slopes and narrow river valleys that supported only small farms until the commercial extraction of its mineral resources, chiefly mica, began on a large scale in the 1870s. With few slave owners or large farms, its populace was strongly pro-Union before and during the Civil War, and the county was formed in 1861 amid secessionist controversies. Its politically neutral name honors Elisha Mitchell, professor at the University of North Carolina who died in 1857 exploring the mountain in neighboring Yancey Co., tallest in the eastern U.S., that also bears his name. The centrally located county seat was first called Davis after the Confederate president, but after objections from the Unionist citizenry, it was renamed for David Baker, an early settler. Bakersville's isolation and lack of a railroad restricted its growth, though it flourished during the late 19th-c. mica-mining boom; in 1888 travel writer Charles Dudley Warner called it "a pretty place in the hills, of some six hundred inhabitants." With a 1990 population of about 300, it is smaller today than a century ago.

At the center of town is the **Mitchell County Courthouse** (1907; N. Mitchell Ave.), a compact Neoclassical Revival building of stuccoed concrete block with a 2-stage cupola, polygonal corner bays, and a pediment displaying the construction date. It is almost identical to the former *Yancey County Courthouse erected about the same time; though no architect has been identified for either building, local carpenter Moses Albert Blanton was instrumental in the Mitchell version.

A few brick and frame commercial buildings cluster about the courthouse. Behind it is the **McBee Building** (1880s), a simple 1-story, gable-fronted frame building that became the law office of John C. McBee, advocate of better roads in the mountains during the 1920s; it houses the Mitchell Co. Historical Society Museum. Across the street is the **Greene Building** (ca. 1900), a 2-story frame commercial building covered in stamped metal siding.

Among the few late 19th- and early 20th-c. houses are two substantial brick residences from the early years of the mica boom. According to local legend, the fiancée of businessman John Gudger would not marry him until he had a big brick house on a hill. The Gudgers married in 1880, by which time the **Gudger House** (1880; private) was perched on its hillside behind the courthouse. It is a hip-roofed I-house with mousetooth corbeled cornice, 2-story porch, and later rear additions. Mrs. Gudger's inspiration may have been the similar, slightly older **Greene-Sharpe House** (ca. 1875; visible looking s from NC 226 w of courthouse; private) on a hilltop southwest of town. Built for Tom Greene, a pioneer in the mica industry, it once featured double-

ML 1 *Mitchell Co. Courthouse*

ML 1 *Greene-Sharpe House, Bakersville*

gallery porches with sawnwork balustrades on three sides, offering long views down on the town and north to Roan Mountain; the porch survives only on the east side.

ML 2 Loafers Glory

The community's name alone, proposed by a disgruntled wife, makes it worthy of admiration. A little industriousness on the part of the menfolk is evident in **Master's Mill** (1920s; NC 80 at SR 1187 on Cane Creek), a 3-story frame building with gabled monitor roof, now covered with stamped metal siding. The mill site, believed to date from the 1860s, includes a broken stone dam and wheel.

ML 3 Penland School of Crafts
Late 19th c. to present; N side SR 1164, 1.0 mi. N of SR 1162, Penland

An important mountain institution on a lofty site above the railroad village of Penland, the crafts school campus embodies a complex history rooted in the missionary and crafts revival work of the late 19th and early 20th centuries. Penland began in the 1920s as a mountain crafts school founded by educator Lucy Morgan, a native of Macon Co. who had taught school in Michigan, Montana, and Illinois and studied at the University of Chicago. From 1920 to 1923 Miss Morgan served as principal of the Appalachian Industrial School, where her brother, Episcopal priest Rufus Morgan, had been director in the 1910s, at the site of the former Seven Springs Baptist Industrial School.

In 1924, after studying weaving at the crafts training program at Berea College in Kentucky, Lucy Morgan founded the Appalachian Department of Fireside Industries, with a few local women to revive traditional handweaving. She added pottery making in 1928 and changed the name to the Penland Weavers and Potters School. Like other crafts centers elsewhere in the Appalachians and in Scandinavia, the school incorporated local traditional methods and arts and crafts ideas to produce goods for local and regional markets. The center also attracted students and teachers from distant communities and schools for summer programs.

In 1928 the school hosted a meeting of eight Southern Appalachian schools and craft center leaders, including Olive Campbell of *John C. Campbell Folk School at Brasstown, Mary Sloop of the *Crossnore School, Clementine Douglas of the *Spinning Wheel in Asheville, and representatives from the Russell Sage Foundation and Berea College. From this meeting developed the founding of the Southern Mountain Handicraft Guild, the present Southern Highland Craft Guild, which became a strong force in the shaping of the crafts revival and marketing. Under Lucy Morgan's guidance, the Penland School of Handicrafts was incorporated in 1938 and developed into one of the largest and best-known crafts schools in the nation. After Morgan's retirement in 1962, director William J. Brown expanded the emphasis on contemporary crafts; the school absorbed the adjacent campus of its parent institution in 1965.

Campus buildings range from the utilitarian facilities of the original vocational school to the self-consciously rustic buildings of the crafts center executed in log, stone, and wood shingles. The **Weaving Cabin** (Visitors' Center; 1926), the first building erected for the crafts school, was a cooperative project of the weavers and their husbands. The 18-by-30-foot log structure was built by local men familiar with traditional log construction methods, and the logs were donated from the weavers' farms. The log raising took place May 5, 1926. The building, scene of the 1928 meeting of crafts leaders, served the weavers and potters until the Crafts House was erected in 1935, then as offices.

The centerpiece of the campus is the **Edward F. Worst Craft House** (1935; D. R. Beeson [Johnson City, Tenn.], architect), a 2½-story log building, 84 feet long, said to be the largest log structure in N.C., designed by a Tennessee architect active throughout the Southern Appalachians (cf. *Lees-McRae College, Avery Co.). It was named for Worst, a famed weaving teacher from Chicago, and built with contributions ($2.50 for a log) from donors throughout the eastern

United States. The use of locally available materials—including native stone and poplar logs left in the round with their bark—and volunteer labor permitted completion of the project on a depression budget. The raising took place in May 1935, and the building was occupied, with 48 looms in place, in August. With its dormered gable roof and full-width shed porch, the building is one of the region's prime examples of the log building revival of the early 20th c. (See Introduction, Fig. 60.)

ML 3 *Weaving Cabin*

ML 3 *Carolina Cabin (the Travelog), 1933*

A unique element in the school's history is the **Carolina Cabin** or Travelog (1933), a small log cabin that Lucy Morgan had built to fit on the back of a truck; it was driven to Chicago's Century of Progress fair of 1933 to boost sales of the school's crafts during the Great Depression. Brought back and eventually restored, it is currently on loan to *Appalachian State University in Boone. Among more than 30 other buildings are the **Dye Shed** (19th c.), originally a barn, and the 2-story frame **Farm House** (19th c.), part of the farmstead that predated the school; the **Lily Loom House** (1947–49;

Van Wageningen & Cothran [Shelby], architects), a large 2½-story, multiwindowed building of stone, funded in part by the Lily Mills Co. of Shelby. Connected to the loom house on the ridge are the **Pottery Shop** (1947–48), built of stone with the assistance of the American Friends Service Committee, and the linking **Metal Shop** (1960s).

ML 4 Spruce Pine

Although a 19th-c. settlement gathered here around the *English Inn on the south side of the North Toe River, the town, the largest in the county, is an industrial community born of the 1903 arrival of the Clinchfield Railroad and raised on the mica, feldspar, and kaolin mined and processed in the vicinity. The streets are named for minerals and trees to reflect the town's origins in mining and lumbering. It was incorporated in 1907 and named for a tree on the grounds of the English Inn.

The commercial district of plain 1- and 2-story early 20th-c. brick stores is stacked on the steep north bank above the river on two parallel streets, Oak St. above and Locust St. below. The **Spruce Pine Depot** (ca. 1909; Locust St.), a bracketed frame station with stucco between its exposed exterior framing, is the last of the Clinchfield depots in the mountains.

Two stone buildings built by two local stonemasons stand out among the conventional brick structures. The **Gunter Building** (early 1930s; Dave Greene and Charlie Mitchell, stonemasons; 336 Oak St.) is a 2-story building of biotite (black mica) rock, an expressive use of a native material by local stonemasons Greene and Mitchell for mica industrialist Charles S. Gunter. **Crystal Place** (1937; 108 Crystal St.), a 3-story stone building on a steep side street, was also erected for Gunter by masons Greene and Mitchell. **Central Baptist Church** (ca. 1935; Oak St.), a church of otherwise simple conventional form, is another of their works in stone.

An unusual feature of the downtown is the **Spruce Pine Footbridge** (1929; near E end Locust St.), a 400-foot-long structure combining a steel deck truss and steel pylons, spanning the river and the railroad.

ML 4 *Spruce Pine Depot and Locust St.*

The state's longest pedestrian bridge, it was built as a joint project of the town and the Clinchfield Railroad to give students safe access to Harris School on the south side of the river.

The oldest residential neighborhood is on the hillsides above the commercial district. Standing out from the typical bungalows and other early to mid-20th-c. frame houses is the **Dr. Charles Peterson House** (1928–29; D. R. Beeson [Johnson City, Tenn.], architect; 101 Hazel Ave. at Diamond St.; private), a big red brick Colonial Revival residence with sunburst panels over the first floor windows, designed for a physician and state legislator by the Tennessee architect who also designed buildings at *Penland School and *Lees-McRae College. As in the Gunter Building they constructed downtown, for the **Charles S. Gunter House** (1928; Dave Greene and Charlie Mitchell, stonemasons; Elm St.; private) the masons used black mica, here to fashion a bungalow for the mining entrepreneur's residence out of the material that gave him his livelihood.

tions and connected by open breezeways. The components are gathered under a common roof and unified with a full-width 2-story porch. The oldest, V-notched section may have been standing when Isaac English, an immigrant from England via Rhode Island, acquired the property in 1860. His home was a favorite stop for travelers through the Toe River valley. He and his son Thomas expanded the structure with half-dovetailed log sections that produced its present form by the 1920s. Father and son were pioneers in the local mica-mining industry.

ML 4 *The English Inn*

ML 5 The English Inn

Early 19th c.–1920s; S side of N. Toe River on English St., at SW corner with Hillcrest St., Spruce Pine; private residence, visible from road

Now surrounded by mid-20th-c. residential development, Spruce Pine's oldest landmark is a long, L-shaped, 2-story log building in multiple sections added over several genera-

ML 6 Museum of North Carolina Minerals

1955; NW jct. of Blue Ridge Parkway and US 226, Spruce Pine vic.; open regular hours

The simple gable-roofed stone structure, built by the state of N.C. to showcase its mineral resources, was donated to the National Park Service, which operates it as part of the Blue Ridge Parkway. The site was selected because of the importance of mining in Mitchell and surrounding counties. The museum houses exhibits on mica, feldspar, kaolin, and other minerals.

ML 7 Little Poplar Schoolhouse
Ca. 1880; end of SR 1193 on grounds of Mitchell High School, Ledger vic.

The county's last surviving 19th-c. 1-room schoolhouse was moved from the Poplar community in northwest Mitchell Co. and restored by a group of retired schoolteachers in 1980. The tiny, unpainted board-and-batten building has a small belfry, batten shutters, and a wood-shingled roof. It sits in an oak grove on the grounds of the large, late 20th-c. Mitchell High School—a contrast bespeaking a century of change in public education. Inside are a pot-bellied stove, a wooden bench, and exhibits on local school history.

ML 7 *Little Poplar Schoolhouse*

Toe River Communities:
The Toe River begins at the confluence of the North and South Toe rivers at Kona and flows northwesterly to mark the boundary between Mitchell and Yancey counties. At Huntdale it joins the Cane River and becomes the No-

lichucky before continuing into Tennessee. Its narrow valley was settled from the early 19th c. with scattered farmsteads wherever the bottomlands widened enough to allow a crop. In the first years of the 20th c. the Clinchfield Railroad snaked its way along the north bank of the river from Tennessee, reaching Spruce Pine on the North Toe in 1903. It continued down over the Blue Ridge to connect Kentucky with South Carolina and become a major trans-Appalachian route that still carries heavy rail traffic. When the railroad was new, a few depots and stores were established at key points along the river, creating focal points for local trade. Though the Clinchfield's successor, CSX, has removed the last of the riverside depots, other traces of these railroad communities remain at Kona, Lunday, Toecane, Green Mountain (in Yancey Co.), Relief, and Huntdale.

ML 8 Kona

The confluence of the North and South Toe rivers was the site of one of the county's earliest settlements, evidenced by the **George Silver House** (early 19th c.; SR 1175; private), a 2-story log house of dogtrot form with stone gable-end chimneys. It is believed to be among the oldest houses in the region. Silver was the father-in-law of Frankie Silver, the first woman hanged by the state (1833) following her conviction for the murder of her husband, Charlie, at their home nearby.

The present community dates from the railroad era, and the name Kona was reportedly conferred by the line's first dispatcher because it was easy to spell and understand. **Kona Baptist Church** (1943; N side NC 80) surveys the community from a hilltop, a late version of a common rural church form in the mountains, with the gable-front entrance under a central belltower with an open base. It houses a local history museum. Behind it are the graves of some of the county's first settlers.

A sprawling facility for processing kaolin, a clay used in china and industrial ceramics, was established along the tracks by the river. But the public road no longer extends to the river, and the Clinchfield depot there was removed in recent years. At Kona the Black Mountain Railroad (later Yancey Railroad) joined the Clinchfield, crossed the river, and followed the South Toe River to Micaville, Burnsville, and points beyond. That line has been abandoned.

ML 9 Lunday

For several decades the **W. Bristo Ellis Store** (1910; end of SR 1178; private) provided goods shipped via rail to farm families on both sides of the river and served as the post office for Lunday, once a busy rail stop. Poised on a rock outcrop above the river, the simple 1-story frame store has full-width shed porches front and back. Suspension footbridges are found throughout the mountains where pedestrian access is required to property not reached by roads, and the Ellis Store is reached from the Yancey Co. side of the river by the **Lunday Footbridge**. Most of these bridges, including this one, date from the mid-20th c. but replace older

bridges; many were built by the state Department of Transportation's Division of Bridge Maintenance.

ML 10 Toecane

The community at the confluence of the Toe River and Cane Creek was the station for passengers and freight bound for the county seat of Bakersville, 3 miles up Cane Creek. **Garvin's Hotel** (early 20th c.; SR 1187; private) is the last of the small early 20th-c. railroad hotels on the river, once an essential feature at every depot. The 2-story, T-plan frame building has a 2-story wrap-around porch overlooking the river. A 1917 listing of accommodations along the Clinchfield reported the hotel could provide for up to twenty guests at $1.50 per day. On the winding road down to the river from the hotel are three brick commercial buildings of the 1920s.

ML 9 *Lunday Footbridge and Ellis Store*

ML 11 Relief

The community predates the railroad era and is said to be named for Hart's Relief, a popular patent medicine with a high alcohol content that was sold at the store here in the late 19th c. The present buildings postdate a 1902 flood. The **Relief Post Office and Store** (1925; Kimsey Bryant, carpenter; SR 1315; private) is a frame, false-fronted commercial building that served as the community center for a half-century. The **J. D. Bradshaw House** (ca. 1905; private) behind the store, home of the storekeeper and postmaster, is a 2-story frame house with a trio of gables across the front, a form seen frequently in this section of the mountains. West of the store is the **Dr. J. W. Bradshaw House** (1902; private), a plain 2-story frame house of hip-roofed and foursquare form, with a 1-story porch wrapping 2 sides; it was home to a physician who is said to have delivered over 3,000 babies in the surrounding communities during his long career.

ML 12 Huntdale

At Huntdale the Toe River joins the Cane River flowing north from the Yancey Co. interior to form the Nolichucky River. An early 20th-c. photograph shows a busy trackside community with stores, one or two

ML 12 *Toe River Free Will Baptist Church*

frame hotels, houses, and other buildings. Surviving from that era is the **Robert Griffith House** (1903–5; N side SR 1304; private), a 2-story frame house with a gabled central bay, a 1-story porch, and a 2-story rear ell; it was the home of the owner of the community store and hotel. Also remaining from the time are the **Phin Peterson Store** (early 20th c.), a frame building with a broad 5-bay gable front, and **Toe River Free Will Baptist Church** (early 20th c.), a simple frame building with a gable-fronted entrance, tucked against a hillside above the railroad tracks.

Yancey County (YC)

The Black Mountains in southern Yancey Co. are the highest in the eastern U.S. (see *Mount Mitchell State Park), but elsewhere the terrain is less forbidding as the ridges and streams drop toward the Toe River at the county's northern boundary. The valleys of the Cane River, the South Toe River, Jacks Creek, Price Creek, Possumtrot Creek, Little Crabtree Creek, and others widen in places with bottomlands that have supported a productive agriculture since the early 19th c. and still harbor unspoiled farming landscapes. Many turn-of-the-century farmhouses are decorated with sawn ornament, and everywhere are big frame hay and burley tobacco barns with vertical or diagonal siding. Burley tobacco, an air-cured leaf, has been an important crop in the county since the early 20th c.

YC 1 Burnsville

Several western N.C. counties were named for eastern N.C. statesmen, to honor those who supported western causes but also to secure political support in the east-dominated legislature when new counties were proposed in the west. Established in 1833, Yancey Co. honored Bartlett Yancey, a Caswell Co. legislator, and the county seat was named for Otway Burns of Carteret Co., a naval hero in the War of 1812 and a state senator. Both men championed greater political representation for the west, a position that cost Burns his senate career.

Burnsville occupies a central, elevated site by Little Crabtree Creek on the divide between the Cane River and the South Toe River. In 1888 travel writer Charles Dudley Warner found it "more like a New England village than any hitherto seen" on his journey through the region. The village gathers around the **Burnsville Town Square** (laid out 1834), which held the first two courthouses but has been an open green since 1908. Its **Otway Burns Statue** (1909; W. H. Mullins Co. [Salem, Ohio]) is a 6-foot copper likeness of the sea captain in naval uniform, 300 miles from the sea, donated to the town by Burns's grandson, Walter Francis Burns Sr.

Around the square stand the principal public and commercial buildings. The **Nu-Wray Inn** (1830s, ca. 1870, ca. 1915; s side of Town Square; B&B) is a 2½-story frame inn, a landmark since the earliest years of the county and town. Tradition holds that the oldest (western) section of the structure was built by innkeeper Backhaus Smith in the 1830s, and such elements as two raised-panel interior doors and an early mantel suggest a portion of the building could date from that period. Purchased after the Civil War by Garrett and Elizabeth Ray, the inn gained extensive Victorian additions in the 1870s and became known as Ray's Inn. In 1888 Warner enjoyed the "inviting tavern, with a long veranda," and praised the proprietor as "a very intelligent and enterprising man, who had traveled often in the North" and was "full of projects for the development of his region and foremost in its enterprises, and had formed a considerable collection of minerals." Ray was active in the local development of mica mining and other endeavors. The Rays' daughter Julia and her husband William B. Wray took possession of the inn in 1915 and made numerous alterations under the sway of the Colonial Revival, giving it its present name and appearance, with a big portico on brick columns and a long porch for enjoying mountain breezes and watching the activity around the town square.

The **Old Yancey County Courthouse** (now Burnsville Town Hall; 1908; sw corner Town Square), the county's third courthouse, is a 2-story Neoclassical Revival building of stuccoed concrete block with a central pedimented entrance pavilion surmounted by a

YC 1 *Nu-Wray Inn*

YC 1 *Jarrett House*

YC 1 *Watson-Whisnant House*

square cupola. The 5 center bays of the facade are divided by Corinthian pilasters, and the corners break into polygonal projections like those on the 1907 *Mitchell County Courthouse. The common design source has not been identified. After serving the county until a new Neocolonial courthouse was constructed on the east end of the square in 1965, it is now the town hall.

An ambitious statement among the otherwise plain brick early 20th-c. commercial buildings near the square is the former **Citizens Bank Building** (Yancey Co. Public Library; 1925; s side Town Square), a 3-story Neoclassical Revival building of yellow brick erected during the real estate boom of the 1920s.

The oldest house in town is the **John Wesley McElroy House** (Rush Wray Museum; ca. 1845; Ephraim Clayton, attributed builder; 11 Academy St.; open limited hours). Perched on a hillside near the town square above W. Main St., the frame I-house has brick end chimneys and simple Greek Revival interiors. Builder Clayton of Henderson Co. and Asheville, who also erected other buildings in Burnsville, was merchant McElroy's brother-in-law.

Burnsville's late 19th- and early 20th-c. residential development was dispersed around the square, so that Victorian cottages and Craftsman bungalows share streetscapes with ranch houses and other more recent infill. The finest of several late Victorian houses is the **Watson-Whisnant House** (1898; 11 E. Main St.; private), a rambling, bracketed frame cottage with projecting gables, bay window, and porch gazebo under a conical roof. The **Jarrett House** (1918; Sears, Roebuck & Co.; 105 Swiss St.; private) is a shingled bungalow, a Sears mail-order house featuring deep front and side porches with exposed tie beams and plates carried by quartets of stocky posts on brick plinths.

On a hillside north of the square overlooking the town, the **Yancey Collegiate Institute Building** (1922; Green Mountain Dr.) was the main building of a Baptist school established in 1901. The 2-story brick structure has broad pedimented gables with modillion cornices and a matching pedimented portico. The institute became part of the public school system in 1926. Across the street is the former **Burnsville High School** (1936), now offices for the county Board of Education; the long 1-story building was one of five schools in Yancey Co. built of native rock during the Great Depression with the assistance of the Works Progress Administration (WPA).

YC 2 Micaville

The community on Little Crabtree Creek near its confluence with the South Toe River was once a center for the mica industry, which began in this section in the late 19th c. and increased after 1911 when the Black

Mountain (later Yancey) Railroad followed the river up from Kona to extract minerals and lumber from Yancey Co. A few buildings from the mica heyday cluster at the junction of NC 80 and SR 1186. The former **Harris Clay Company Office and General Store** (ca. 1916), later known as the Robinson Store, is a gable-fronted building covered in pebbledash, with a circular window in the gable and a recessed entrance flanked by big windows. It was part of a larger kaolin-mining enterprise established by industrialist C. J. Harris of Sylva. A few other frame stores and houses survive from the 1920s and 1930s. The **Micaville School** (late 1930s; w side NC 80, 0.1 mi. s of SR 1186) is one of the largest of five similar rock schools built by the WPA in the county—a long, 1-story building with a central, gabled entrance porch. (See Introduction, Fig. 62.)

YC 3 Mount Mitchell State Park

The Black Mountain range in southern Yancey Co. is a spur of the Blue Ridge with a dozen peaks over 6,000 feet. They are named for the dark green balsam firs that blanket their upper slopes. At 6,684 feet, Mount Mitchell is the tallest mountain east of the Mississippi. Dr. Elisha Mitchell, a Presbyterian minister, scientist, and esteemed professor at the University of North Carolina in Chapel Hill, fell to his death here in 1857 during an expedition to prove that "Black Dome," as the mountain was previously known, was indeed the tallest in eastern America. First buried in Asheville, Mitchell was reinterred a year later atop the mountain, which officially became Mount Mitchell in 1882 when the U.S. Geological Survey confirmed his claim.

The mountain, long a source of wonder, has been a tourist destination since the 19th c. In his 1888 book *On Horseback*, Charles Dudley Warner described his ascent up the mountain guided by "Big Tom" Wilson, the legendary hunter who had discovered Dr. Mitchell's body after his disappearance. Of Mitchell's gravesite, then marked only with a cairn-like pile of loose stones "to which each visitor adds one," Warner said, "The mountain is his monument. . . . It is the most majestic, the most lonesome grave on earth." The **Dr. Elisha Mitchell Gravesite** is still treated as a cairn, now surrounded by a wrought-iron fence, with a bronze plaque describing Dr. Mitchell's contributions placed over the grave.

Industrial logging came to the Black Mountains in the late 19th c., and by 1914 a private narrow-gauge logging railroad known as the Mount Mitchell Railroad had reached Camp Alice near the summit, ascending from the town of Black Mountain in Buncombe Co. The line hauled tourist excursions as well as timber until 1921, when the tracks were replaced with an automobile toll road. For a time Camp Alice had a rustic dining hall and rental cottages for tourists. A second private toll road approached from Pensacola. A free public road was not constructed until 1940.

Public concern over clear-cut logging on the mountain led to the state's purchase of the summit in 1915 and the creation of Mount Mitchell State Park, the first state park in N.C. The park now totals 1,677 acres. None of the early tourist facilities remain. The **Mount Mitchell Observation Tower** (1960) is a 43-foot stone tower with a cast-concrete balcony. On a clear day the visitor can see over 100 miles. In the late 20th c., air pollution threatens the mountain's high forests once rescued from the loggers.

YC 4 Upper Cane River Valley
NC 197 S of Burnsville

The Cane River rises on the northern slopes of the great Black Mountain range and meanders northward across the breadth of the county to the Yancey-Mitchell line, where it joins the Toe River to form the Nolichucky. Even in its upper reaches the valley widens in places with fertile bottomlands that have supported productive farms since the 19th c. In 1913 a branch of the Black Mountain Railroad crept alongside the river south from Burnsville to draw out timber from lumber camps at Pensacola, Murchison, and Eskota; this line operated only until the timber was depleted in the late 1920s.

Striking evidence of the early settlement and prosperity of this part of the valley is the

Nathan Ray House (mid-19th c.; visible across fields on w side NC 197 just s of SR 1112; private) (**a**), a rare surviving bottomland farmhouse of unusual scale for the region, commanding a long view across a broad section of the valley. The big 2-story, 5-bay, weatherboarded log house has stuccoed stone gable-end chimneys.

Several communities cluster around stores and churches along the river. At Vixen is the **Ray Store** (ca. 1910; w side NC 197, just s of SR 1109; private) (**b**), one of several traditional general stores still standing in the county, a 2-story, gable-fronted frame building, here sheathed in board and batten instead of the more common horizontal weatherboards.

Up Low Gap Hollow near Vixen, the **Hensley Farm** (late 19th c.; s side SR 1109, 0.7 mi. NE of NC 197; private) (**c**) typifies small 19th-c. farms once found up coves and hollows but now largely vanished from the landscape or inaccessible to public view. A small 1-story log house of half-dovetailed notches with a frame rear ell overlooks the narrow fields, with two small log outbuildings nearby. On the edge of the lower field are two big log barns, one with extensive latticework to ventilate the hay loft.

The **Pearson Riddle House** (ca. 1900; w side SR 1184, 0.1 mi. w of NC 197, Pensacola vic.; private) (**d**) is one of the best preserved of several turn-of-the-century farmhouses along this section of the river. The facade gable of the modest 1-story frame house has herringbone-pattern sheathing and a delicate gable insert in a sunburst pattern.

Pensacola was the center of a major lumbering operation in the early 20th c. and a depot on the Black Mountain Railroad. From this point the Carolina Spruce Lumber Co. reportedly constructed a web of narrow-gauge tracks up the mountainsides totaling 17 miles to log 5,000 acres of timberland. Predating the arrival of the railroad and lumber company is **Laurel Branch Baptist Church** (1904; w side NC 197, opp. SR 1102, Pensacola) (**e**), a frame church built by members of the Riddle family. In a treatment seen elsewhere in the mountains, the first stage of the 4-stage belltower at the front gable is open like a porch to shelter the pair of entrances. (See Introduction, Fig. 25.)

YC 5 Price Creek Valley
SR 1136 and SR 1126 S of US 19E

A landmark in this farming valley along tributaries of the Cane River is **Wray Villa** (ca. 1900; N side SR 1126, 0.1 mi. w of SR 1136; private) (**f**). The big, unusual 2-story house of late Queen Anne form is covered in pebbledash, a rough stucco common in Asheville but rare in rural areas. An oversized octagonal corner tower with a conical roof dominates the complex composition of broad gables and wraparound porch. The house was seat of the farm of William B. Wray (later the owner of the *Nu-Wray Inn) and operated for a while as a small resort

YC 4 *Hensley Farm*

YC 5 *Wray Villa*

YC 5 *A. O. England Store, Paint Gap*

YC 5 *Henry Holcombe House, Paint Gap*

hotel. A barn with a gambrel roof stands to its north.

The **Dr. Peterson House** (ca. 1905; w side SR 1126 opp. SR 1121; private) (**g**) was the seat of another thriving Price Creek farm. The 2-story frame house is representative of Queen Anne style farmhouses across the region, with gables projecting from a high hip roof and a deep 1-story front porch.

Paint Gap (jct. SR 1126 and SR 1124, 3.2 mi. s of US 19E) (**h**) is a highlight of the area,

an unusually well-preserved and picturesque cluster of turn-of-the-century frame buildings on Horton and Indian creeks, tributaries of Price Creek. It centers on the **A. O. England General Store** (ca. 1900), a weatherboarded 2-story, gable-fronted general store with a 2-story, hip-roofed porch that is enclosed on the second level, creating a recessed entrance below. The local Oddfellows chapter used the second floor as a meeting hall. At the **Paint Gap Presbyterian Church** (1901) on the hill just east of the store, the gabled entrance vestibule, capped by a small belfry, is on the long side instead of the more usual gable end. Notable among several 1-story frame houses, the **Horton-Maney House** (1899; William Horton, carpenter; w side SR 1126, s of SR 1124; private) features a deep porch projecting from under a broad central gable and triangular paneled heads over the windows. It was built by carpenter Horton as his residence and has been pristinely maintained by descendants. Its neighbor on the south, the **Henry Holcombe House** (ca. 1905; private), is of the more typical tri-gable form, with a porch decorated with scrollwork brackets and balustrade; its center chimney and two front doors may derive from the saddlebag plan. (See Introduction, Fig. 50.)

YC 6 Possumtrot Creek Valley
SR 1128 S of US 19

Possumtrot Creek is a fertile farming valley with one of several whimsical creek names in this section of the county; other nearby tributaries of the Cane River are Lickskillet Creek, Hardscrabble Creek, and Nubbinscuffle Creek. Especially notable is the **McPeters House** (ca. 1900; N side SR 1128, 1.1 mi. sw of US 19E; private), an enormous Queen Anne frame house similar in contour to *Wray Villa on Price Creek, with a massive octagonal corner tower, broad gables, and a wraparound porch. The story goes that Charles McPeters built the house for a hotel in anticipation of a railroad up Possumtrot Creek that never came, so he established a cannery here for local fruit and produce. Up and down the valley are several big, frame, gable- and gambrel-roofed barns,

YC 6 *McPeters House*

some with latticework ventilation, and stone bungalows from the 1920s and 1930s.

YC 7 Bald Creek Valley

Because busy US 19 now runs alongside Bald Creek, its valley has been subject to more development than less-traveled ones. But the valley here is one of the broadest and was once among the most prosperous in the county, evidenced by three decorated, 2-story late 19th-c. farmhouses familiar to regular travelers along the highway. Located near the junction of US 19E and US 19W, the **Wilkes Hensley House** (N side US 19, 0.3 mi. W of SR 1128; private) has a 2-story shed roof porch with intricately sawn balustrades and porch post brackets. Among the outbuildings of this working farm are two frame barns with shallow gambrel roofs. To the

west the **Ed and Lizzie Neal House** (SW corner US 19 and SR 1393 opp. Bald Creek School; private) has a similar porch, with Italianate bracketed eaves, and corbeled chimney stacks set at a 45-degree angle to the roof ridge. A log smokehouse stands in the side yard. Farther west, the most elaborately ornamented of the three is the **Sam Byrd House** (1897; NW corner US 19 and SR 1393), with a projecting 2-story central bay, shingled gables, bracketed eaves, and scrolled gables.

At the center of the Bald Creek community is **Bald Creek School** (late 1930s; S side US 19, Bald Creek), one of five similar rock schools in the county built with WPA assistance. The long, 1-story building has parapeted entrance and end bays. A rock gymnasium building stands nearby.

YC 8 Lower Cane River Valley
US 19W and secondary roads along Cane River

The lower (northern) Cane River cuts through a gorge steeper than that of its upper section, with less open bottomland for farming. At Higgins is the **Markle School** (1929; E side US 19W at SR 1383; private) (i). Built as a religious mission and school of mountain handicrafts, the ambitious complex of five stone buildings was created under the aus-

YC 7 *Ed and Lizzie Neal House*

YC 8 *Markle School Workshop*

pices of the Presbyterian Church by Penn-sylvanian Martha Robinson and named to honor her sister-in-law. The school survived the Great Depression but closed when the war began and Robinson returned to Penn-sylvania. Part of the complex was later used as a medical clinic. All five buildings are of coursed rubble stonework. The main build-ing, called the **Workshop**, is a long, 2-story, 9-bay building with a projecting 3-bay gabled pavilion and a high hip roof. The pointed arch entrance imparts a Gothic touch. On the hill is **Bethel Presbyterian Church** (1933), a simple Gothic Revival building with an arched belltower.

The riverside community of **Lewisburg** is the site of the **Phillips and Son Texaco Station** (1930s; E side US 19W; private) (**j**). The diminutive survivor of the early auto-motive era is built of smooth river rock with

segmental-arched windows and doors and a cantilevered front canopy. Downriver, a number of **Cane River Suspension Foot-bridges** provide access from the highway on the east bank across to houses on the west.

The community of **Bee Log** on Bald Mountain Creek is said to be named for a fallen tree full of bees and honey. **Bee Log School** (1936; S side SR 1395 at SR 1408) (**k**) is one of five similar 1-story stone schools built in the county by the WPA. The school burned about 1949 and was rebuilt within the walls. Across the road is the **A. J. Ed-wards General Store** (early 20th c.; N side SR 1395) (**l**), one of several well-preserved but vacant 2-story frame general stores in the county.

YC 9 Jacks Creek Valley
SR 1336 N of US 19E along Jacks Creek

Jacks Creek rises at Wolfpit Gap west of Burnsville and flows northeast about 8 miles to the Toe River. Its valley provided suffi-ciently broad bottomlands to support farm-ing and community life since the early 19th c. and offers a pleasant rural mountain drive past farmhouses, frame barns, and churches of various eras.

North from US 19E on SR 1336, **Boring's Chapel Free Will Baptist Church** (early 20th c.; E side SR 1336, 3.9 mi. NE of US 19E)

YC 9 *Horton-Laughrun Farm*

(**m**) is a small gable-fronted frame church, utterly plain except for a touch of curvilinear sawn bargeboard along the eaves. **Jacks Creek Baptist Church** (early 20th c.; W corner jct. SR 1336 and SR 1354) (**n**) is another simple rural church, with a 3-stage combination vestibule and belltower.

The best preserved of several late 19th-c. and early 20th-c. farms is the **Horton-Laughrun Farm** (late 19th c.; 1904; SE side SR 1336, 0.3 mi. NE of SR 1354; private) (**o**), which enjoys an especially wide section of bottomland beside the creek. The 1½-story frame farmhouse, said to be a 1904 enlargement of an older house, has a trio of gables across the front—a common treatment in this section—covered with fish-scale shingles. Two big shed-roofed hay and tobacco barns, a type common in this valley and across the county, stand to the rear.

At the Day Book community, said to have been site of a post office from the early 19th c. and probably named for a record book kept by a local store or lumber company, is **Clearmont School** (late 1930s) (**p**), one of five stone schools in the county built by the WPA. All are long, 2-story buildings with projecting entrance and end bays; this one differs with the curvilinear parapet over the entrance bay.

YC 10 Green Mountain

Settled from the 19th c., the community became one of several depots established in the early 20th c. on the Clinchfield Railroad, which hugs the north bank of the Toe River on the Mitchell Co. side of the river (see *Toe River Communities, Mitchell Co.). Since the 1930s the community's center has been on the Yancey Co. side, focusing on the **J. W. Howell Store** (now O. C. Whitson and Sons Store; 1932; SW side SR 1338 NW of NC 197), a big 2-story brick general store that remains in business. The adjacent **Green Mountain Presbyterian Church** (1942; D. R. Beeson [Johnson City], architect) is a simple Gothic Revival building with a corner tower. Tennessee architect Beeson, who worked widely across the mountains, is said to have donated his services. Carpenter Ernest Canipe and mason George Green supervised construction.

The narrow Toe River valley has been settled with small farms since the early 19th c. The oldest house on the Yancey side is the **Peterson House** ("River House") (mid-19th c. and later; W corner SR 1336 and NC 197; private), a log and frame house that apparently began as 2 log pens with half-dovetailed corner notching and separated by a dogtrot. About the turn of the century it gained a frame second story and was covered in weatherboards, though one account suggests the frame story replaced an out-of-kilter log second story. Its recent rehabilitation left the first floor logs exposed. Big stone chimneys stand at the gable ends.

Madison County (MD)

Once known as "the Kingdom of Madison" for its isolation and the independence of its people, the county has a dual heritage that encompasses rural mountain culture and a once-great mineral springs resort at Hot Springs. Bisecting the steep terrain, the French Broad River courses through its narrow gorge from Asheville to Paint Rock at the Tennessee state line. The southeast part of the county traded with Asheville, while the north and west sections were oriented to Greeneville, Tenn. Along the ledge on the right bank of the river, early roadbuilders hacked the route of the Buncombe Turnpike in the 1820s. Drovers herding livestock down the turnpike from Tennessee to the coastal lowlands created a market for local farmers' corn and other feed crops, and the low-country elite came in their carriages up the turnpike for summer stays at the famous springs.

The turnpike was followed by the Western North Carolina Railroad (WNCRR) along the same route where, as an 1885 booster booklet observed, "the train enters the canon [sic] of the French Broad, so narrow in places that the jealous river will scarcely permit the passage of the iron horse." In the 20th c. the paved road followed the river as far as Marshall, then took a higher route. The railroad still runs along the French Broad, which has become a prime canoeing and kayaking stream. In the late 1990s, construction of I-26 is transforming a swath of the rural county.

MD 1 Marshall

The county seat, with its single main street paralleling the WNCRR track between the French Broad River and the precipice behind it, has been called "one mile long, one block wide, and sky high." Originally named Lapland, the community began as one of many drovers' stands along the Buncombe Turnpike, providing lodging for the drovers and pens and feed for the thousands of cattle, pigs, turkeys, and other animals they walked to market. David Vance, father of Governor Zebulon Vance, ran a stand here. After the county was formed from portions of Buncombe and Yancey counties in 1851 and named for former president James Madison, the county seat was authorized at this location and named for Chief Justice John Marshall. Debate delayed its founding until 1855, and court met at Jewel Hill, now Walnut.

During the Civil War, Marshall found itself at the center of bitter conflict, as the internal war raged among Union and Confederate sympathizers, troops from both sides, guerrilla bands, draft resisters and deserters, and local citizens grown desperate for essential supplies. The divided loyalties that troubled much of the state and region were especially intense in Madison Co., in part because of the presence of Unionist strongholds in neighboring east Tennessee. Confederate troops' killing of civilians at Shelton Laurel in 1863 horrified the state.

Rebuilding after the war came slowly. The popular travel book *"Land of the Sky"* (1876) touted the county's scenic wonders and boosted tourism. Trade blossomed with the completion of the WNCRR from Asheville to the Tennessee line at Paint Rock in 1882. Although most had considered the French Broad impossible as a waterpower site, in 1903 local businessmen organized to dam the river and establish a textile mill, and other small industries followed. Severely damaged by the flood of 1916, Marshall recovered from its losses. It possesses a notable collection of early 20th-c. architecture framed by its spectacular riverside setting.

The centerpiece of Marshall is the **Madison County Courthouse** (1907; Smith & Carrier [Asheville], architects), which backs up to the mountainside and faces across the

French Broad River bridge. Crowned by a domed, polygonal cupola and fronted by a Corinthian portico, the Neoclassical, red brick courthouse is similar to the *Jackson County Courthouse (1914), also by the firm of Richard Sharp Smith, supervising architect of *Biltmore. The Marshall design came soon after Smith and Carrier's partnership was established in 1906; the firm also planned courthouses in Swain and Henderson counties.

Flanking the courthouse, the compact business district along Main St. contains 2- and 3-story masonry buildings in simplified Neoclassical and Italianate designs unified by dark red brick and stone trim, as well as several structures of river rock or rock-faced concrete block. Just north of the courthouse is the **Rock Cafe** (1947; Main St.), a small, square building faced in local river rock. It was erected by Page and Pricey Brigman in front of Mrs. Brigman's mother's late 19th-c. residence. The Brigmans lived over their restaurant, which was a local gathering place and housed the Greyhound bus station. It was featured in the movie *My Fellow Americans* (1996). South of the courthouse stands the **Roberts Building** (Main St.; 1922), boldly treated with Neoclassical cast stone detail and round arches marking the storefronts and courthouse side. Across Main St. the 3-story Italianate **Commercial Building**, with corbeling and pressed-metal trim, is probably the town's oldest commercial building.

A few doors south of the courthouse on Main St. is the **Allen-McElroy House** (ca. 1854 and later), a 2-story frame house with broad 2-tier front porch. It was built for Col. Lawrence Allen, who with Lt. Col. James Keith led the Confederate troops involved in the Shelton Laurel massacre, which occurred after civilians in search of salt raided the town and looted Allen's home. The home of Judge Pender McElroy and his descendants from 1899 to 1993, it is evidently the oldest building in Marshall.

Above the downtown, early 20th-c. residences mount the steep hill behind the courthouse. Notable is the **J. H. White House**

MD 1 *Madison Co. Courthouse*

(Hill House; 1903; Richard Sharp Smith [Asheville], architect; 5 Hill St.; B&B), visible from Main St. above the south shoulder of the courthouse. Featuring architect Smith's favored pebbledash stuccoed walls, the 2-story house atop a stone terrace has a long porch with a turreted corner "tearoom," as Smith called it, with views of the river and mountains. It was built for J. H. and Anna May White; he was a tobacco businessman, newspaper publisher, postmaster, banker, clerk of court, and proponent of construction of Smith's 1907 *Madison County Courthouse.

A block south on Main St. is the **Marshall Depot** (early 20th c.), a 1-story frame structure with broad eaves and simple detailing; it was swept off its foundations in the floods of 1916 and 1940, then put back or rebuilt. Across the street stands the **Teague Milling Company** (early 20th c.), built of rock-faced concrete block as a feed mill served by the railroad.

The bridge from downtown has a spur to Blennerhassett Island in the middle of the river, site of the **Marshall School** (early 20th c.; E side SR 1001), an extensive, 2-story brick school with generous bands of windows and parapeted entrance bays. On the opposite bank of the river stands a large brick warehouse that survives from the **Capitola Manufacturing Company** (ca. 1910), a textile plant established by local businessmen, including political figure Charles B. Mashburn, newspaper editor J. R. Swann, and W. J. McLendon, who built a low concrete dam (part of which remains), a brick power plant (now gone), and a textile mill.

MD 2 Charles B. Mashburn House

1925; W side SR 1395 at US 25/70 BUS; private, visible from road

Set on a knoll, the brick bungalow with tile roof and Craftsman detail is among the most substantial of the county's many bungalows. It was built for Mashburn, an attorney, farmer, and businessman active in the Republican party, who was mayor, legislator, and organizer of the *Capitola Manufacturing Co.

MD 3 Enon Baptist Church

1918; S side SR 1399, 0.1 mi. E of SR 1395, Marshall vic.

Prominently sited on its hill, the T-plan frame church has a central entrance vestibule and belfry flanked by simple lancet openings.

MD 4 Jefferson J. White Jr. House

Ca. 1880; Mr. Campbell, attributed builder; N side NC 213 at SR 1388, Marshall vic.; private, visible from road; B&B

The 2-story frame farmhouse is made extraordinary by the application of luxuriant wooden ornament perhaps seldom rivaled in the state. The 2-tier, gabled front porch drips with sawn and turned work, including a sinuous comet-like motif, and features a Masonic emblem in the decoratively shingled gable. Bay windows and porches on each end repeat the lavish millwork; the upper balconies were probably added in the 1890s. Ornate mantels adorn the two parlors flanking the center passage. The house was built for Jefferson and Harriet Keith White, and family tradition recalls a Mr. Campbell as builder, possibly Henry Campbell, who built the *Stackhouse House. White was clerk of court and presumably a Mason, but it is not certain why he and other local citizens installed Masonic emblems so prominently on their houses.

MD 4 *Jefferson J. White Jr. House*

MD 5 Mars Hill

The college town has a small early 20th-c. brick commercial district and neighborhoods with brick and frame houses of the era, including several notable bungalows. It is best known as the home of **Mars Hill College**, a Baptist institution founded in 1856 and the source of the town's classical name. After the Civil War the school struggled to survive; the long presidency of Robert Lee Moore (1897–1938) brought a strong resurgence and a building campaign. Mars Hill became a junior college in 1921 and a 4-year college in the 1960s.

The 180-acre campus comprises buildings of brick and stone from the late 19th c. to the recent past. The oldest structures frame a small central quad. The original 1856 brick college building is gone, but the second campus structure still stands: **Founders Hall** (1891–95), a plain 2-story building of handmade red brick with segmental-arched windows.

Several other red brick buildings date from the early 20th c. **Owen Theatre** (dedicated 1918; M. E. Parmelee [Knoxville], architect) was built as Mars Hill Baptist Church and was acquired by the college in 1953 and renovated as a theater in 1968. The 2-story building features a broad, arched, stained glass window in its gabled entrance pavilion and a cupola on the cross-gabled roof. Others include **Spilman Hall** (1902), with its broad gambrel roof and dormers; **Marshbanks Hall** (1910), with arched openings, quoins, and a cupola; and **McConnell Gymnasium** (1924; Smith & Carrier, architects), a large brick structure fronted with columns.

The architectural gem of the quad is the **Estella Nissen Montague Building** (1918; C. Gilbert Humphries [Winston-Salem], architect), a striking little building of expressive stonework, with large, irregular stones arranged to resemble dry-laid work. Erected as the college library, the building was funded in part by a gift from Col. Henry Montague of Winston-Salem in honor of his wife; the college matched his donation with local volunteer workers and local stone, hauled by wagon from nearby Bailey's Mountain. Architect Humphries designed a number of major houses in Winston-Salem. A matching wing was added in the 1930s.

Similar stonework appears in the **Dr. W. F. Robinson Memorial Infirmary** (early 20th c.), a simple, rectilinear structure.

MD 5 *Estella Nissen Montague Building*

Among the more recent structures is the **Harris Media Center** (Six Associates [Asheville]), a semisubterranean brick and glass composition commended by jurors in its 1983 N.C. American Institute of Architects Award "for its capacity in not becoming object-like" and because it "attempts to be a non-building and succeeds."

MD 6 Forks of Ivy Baptist Church

1917–18; Rev. R. P. McCracken (Clyde), architect; NE corner SR 1610 and 2130, E side US 19/23, at county line

A landmark below US 19/23, the big church on its knoll carries a broad, clipped gable roof whose form echoes the mountains beyond. It is built of rock-faced concrete blocks and features a tall corner entrance tower that rises to a belfry with spire. The spacious sanctuary is open to a "self-supporting" roof. The church takes its name from its position at the joining of Big Ivy and Little Ivy creeks. "Ivy" is used locally to refer to the plant usually called mountain laurel, while "laurel" is applied to the species usually called rhododendron. The congregation began in a log house in 1843 and built two frame churches before erecting this edifice in an era of widespread construction.

MD 7 Beech Glen Baptist Church

1930s; SE side SR 1540, 0.2 mi. SW of SR 1530

In the mid-1930s local residents worked together to build the gable-fronted stone church with its central, crenellated entrance tower. Individuals contributed rocks to create the pale and vivid stonework, using rare

MD 6 *Forks of Ivy Baptist Church*

white quartz, and flat stones were hauled from Flat Top Mountain. Masonry was executed by Jo Sar Ponder, Tom Brigmon, and Kyle Jamerson. The baptismal font in the churchyard reflects a transition from traditional baptisms in the nearby creek. The early 20th-c. brick **Beech Glen School**, now a community center, stands nearby.

Paint Fork area:
Roads through the southeast portion of the county traverse a well-kept agrarian landscape, where rolling hills shelter many farmsteads and country churches. Cows graze the bottomlands and rounded hillside pastures. The rural Paint Fork neighborhood is an especially intact community of small and medium-sized farms linked by family and church ties. Indicative of the tobacco-based agriculture, late 19th-c. dwellings and early 20th-c. bungalows are numerous among the farmhouses, and there are many large log and frame barns where lattice or other decorative vents provide circulation to the hayloft. Farmers used such barns to air-cure the burley tobacco that proved profitable even on small farms from the 1930s onward. Only a few examples survive of the log flue-cured tobacco barns that housed the bright-leaf tobacco grown in the late 19th c.

MD 8 Nelson Anderson Farm

Ca. 1888; Joe Carter, carpenter; W corner jct. SR 1535 and SR 1530, Paint Fork vic.; private, visible from road

At this late 19th-c. farmstead sheltered in a gentle valley, the centerpiece is a substantial 2-story frame farmhouse with a 1-story rear ell, finished with shingled gables, bracketed eaves, and a sawnwork porch balustrade. The house was built for Nelson and Minerva Anderson by carpenter Joe Carter for $300. The Andersons raised eight children here, and the place has remained in the family. Among the several outbuildings is a small log dwelling where Nelson Anderson was born in 1857. Also near the house are a board-and-batten smokehouse and a slatted crib. A large log and latticed frame barn was built in 1903 as a hay barn. Up the hill behind the house, the large log barn was built in 1935 for burley tobacco.

MD 9 Paint Fork Church

1880s; W side SR 1530, 0.1 mi. N of SR 1535, Paint Fork vic.

The country church is an unusually tall, 2-story version of the traditional gable-fronted form, with a belfry and bracketed eaves. Standing on a prominent knoll, it was built to serve both Baptists and Methodists in the locality.

MD 10 California Creek Missionary Baptist Church
1917; George Corn, builder;
E side US 23, 0.3 mi. N of SR 1347

Built on a cruciform plan with asymmetrical belltowers, the frame church has fanlights atop its doors and windows and other Colonial Revival details. It takes its name from the nearby creek, supposedly so named during the California gold rush. The congregation, organized in 1869 from Upper Laurel Baptist Church, completed this, their third building, in time to host the French Broad Baptist Association meeting in August 1917. After the congregation built a fourth church in 1976, the building was converted to private use.

MD 10 *California Creek Baptist Church*

MD 11 Ebbs Chapel School
1940; N of jct. of SR 1502 and SR 1503,
Foust vic.

The stone school, with two levels accommodating the sloping terrain, is one of several public schools built in the mountain region with National Youth Administration and Works Progress Administration assistance, using native rock and local workmen. It now serves as a community center for the Upper Laurel area.

Laurel Section:
In the mountainous terrain of northern and western Madison Co., residents have had strong ties to neighboring Tennessee, as indicated in a barn painted with an old advertisement: "Sell your tobacco on Big Market, Inc. ... Greeneville, Tennessee for better results." The mountainsides and narrow valleys have sheltered a close-knit agricultural society of small farms that line the tumbling creeks. Roads parallel the winding streams, and small wooden bridges, some built of log, span the creeks to give foot or car access to adjoining farms. In this part of the county, Presbyterian missionaries had a strong presence, founding churches, schools, and a hospital in the late 19th and early 20th centuries. Several creeks and the neighborhoods around them bear the name Laurel, including Little Laurel, Shelton Laurel, and Big Laurel. The name "laurel" is used locally for the plant usually called rhododendron, which grows abundantly on the slopes.*

MD 12 Sodom (Revere)

Why this biblical name was given to this mountain community is unclear. Presbyterian missionaries succeeded in having the name officially changed to Revere, but the old designation persists. The area was a center for the survival of traditional music, where in 1916 English folk musicologist Cecil Sharp collected ballads in "the Laurel country" from Jane Hicks Gentry (cf. Hot Springs) and others. In recent years singers Cass Wallin, Doug Wallin, and Della Norton and fiddler Byard Ray and their musical heirs have continued the tradition. The chief architectural landmark is the **Church of the Little Flower** (1932; w side SR 1324

MD 12 *Church of the Little Flower*

at SR 1334), a Catholic mission established by Father Lawrence L. Toups of the Jesuit center at Hot Springs. The little brown-shingled building has a small belfry and vestibule at opposite gable ends, the simplest lancet openings, and gently flared walls.

MD 13 Franklin-Wallin Store

Late 19th c.; SW side SR 1316,
0.5 mi. S of White Rock

Hard by the road, the gable-fronted, board-and-batten store typifies the many country stores that once served local farmers. It was built for Richard Franklin at a hub of the Laurel section, and his son Shad Franklin inherited it. As was usual, the general store sold groceries, clothing, hardware, fertilizer, and seeds as well as serving as a gathering place. Franklin also operated a gristmill and sold coffins.

MD 14 White Rock Presbyterian Church

Ca. 1910; SE corner jct. SR 1316
and SR 1314, White Rock

The unusual frame country church is square in plan under a hip roof, topped with a polygonal, shingled belfry that rises from a shed dormer. Banks of windows suggest its use as a schoolhouse. Frances Goodrich (cf. *Allanstand) and Dr. George Packard founded a hospital here with support from the Presbyterian Board of Home Missions. The ruins of Laurel Hospital (1919), the only hospital the board founded in the mountains, stand nearby. The Presbyterian Church, U.S.A., undertook extensive missionary work in the southern Appalachians in the late 19th and early 20th centuries and had a strong presence in Madison, Buncombe, and Yancey counties. Presbyterian missionaries founded as many as eighteen schools in Madison alone, with Dorland Institute in Hot Springs in 1887 the first and White Rock the last, which operated from 1909 to 1931.

MD 15 Andrew Shelton House

Mid-19th c.; NW side SR 1307,
0.85 mi. N of NC 208, Little Laurel vic.;
private, visible from road

Beside the narrow road and the small stream that wind down the valley, the well-preserved log dwelling represents many that stood in the area until the late 20th c. The single-pen house is built of wide, half-dovetailed logs and has a large, stone chimney. A single entrance marks the front and is sheltered by a shed porch. Nearby fields contain a log and frame barn and well-maintained examples of the long rows of wooden tobacco-drying frames still used in the county. Many barns with slatted vents stand on the small farms along the road.

MD 15 *Andrew Shelton House*

MD 16 Allanstand Complex

Early 20th c.; W side NC 208, 2.8 mi.
N of NC 212, Little Laurel vic.

A simple frame school, a church, and a house, all with clipped gable roofs, cluster at the rural site that was an important early craft center. In 1897 Presbyterian missionary and teacher Frances Goodrich, who established schools and churches in the area, acquired the property on Little Laurel Creek. She soon erected the house, school, church, and outbuildings. Trained as an artist at Yale, Miss Goodrich took special interest in the traditional woven coverlets she was shown by local women, first in Buncombe Co., then in Madison. Adapting the name from Allan's Stand, an old drover's stand in the locality, she began Allanstand Cottage Industries to encourage continuation of the old craft and provide opportunities to rural women.

In 1908 she opened the Allanstand shop in Asheville, where the coverlets and other mountain craft goods were sold to a burgeoning tourist trade. After retiring to Asheville in 1918, she was one of the organizers of the Southern Highland Handicraft Guild in 1930, and the next year she gave her Allanstand shop to the guild. (Both are now located in the Folk Art Center, Blue Ridge Parkway.) She published her influential book *Mountain Homespun* in 1931. Goodrich is regarded as a principal pioneer in the revival of Appalachian handicrafts and their promotion and development.

MD 17 Grady Gahagan House

Ca. 1904–9; E side NC 208,
0.6 mi. N of US 25/70, Big Laurel Creek;
private, visible from road

The unusually large frame farmhouse beside the road is 7 bays wide and 4 deep under a high hip roof. A grand front porch with turned posts and a big rear ell expand the house further. The house was built by Grady Gahagan from carefully selected old-growth timber from local forests; his children Grady and Bonnie Gahagan lived in the house for much of the 20th c.

MD 18 Hot Springs

The community in a wide plateau beside the French Broad River and the route of the Buncombe Turnpike and the WNCRR is one of the oldest health resorts in the state. The Cherokees had enjoyed the benefits of the thermal springs for many years before white travelers learned of them ca. 1788. After the Buncombe Turnpike was completed in 1828, Warm Springs, as it was called, became, along with Flat Rock and Asheville, a famous resort for wealthy southerners, centering on the antebellum hotel operated by James Patton of Asheville. (See Introduction, Fig. 19.)

After the Civil War it continued as a popular destination chiefly among southerners who enjoyed familiar company in their old haunts. Travel writer Charles Dudley Warner commented in the 1880s that even with the arrival of the WNCRR, it was a "sedative and idle resort" with "a certain air of romance and tradition" and "very pleasantly Southern" clientele: "Colonels and politicians stand in groups and tell stories . . . retire occasionally into the saloon, and come

forth reminded of more stories, and all lift their hats elaborately and suspend the narratives when a lady goes past." After Patton's hotel burned in 1884, it was replaced by the 200-room Mountain Park Hotel, which claimed to have the first golf course in the state. With discovery of hotter springs in 1886, the name of the town was warmed up accordingly. Hot Springs also became the home of the Dorland Institute, later the Dorland-Bell School, a Presbyterian facility that occupied several buildings.

During World War I the hotel served as an internment camp for Germans, who built a fanciful German village in intricately wrought branches and twigs; it was razed after the war. Another fire in 1920 destroyed the hotel. A smaller one replaced it, but because of changes wrought by the automobile, the resort never regained its earlier stature. For a time the hotel was used as a Jesuit center, then stood vacant before it too burned in 1977. In the late 20th c. Hot Springs has seen renewal as a vacation spot and a stop along the Appalachian Trail, with a campground offering access to the springs.

Several scattered late 19th- and early 20th-c. dwellings survive from the resort heyday. Prime among these is **Sunnybank** (ca. 1875; sw corner of NC 209 [Bridge St.] and Walnut St.), a decorated 2-story Italianate house with multiple gables, bay windows, and porches, built as a summer residence during the zenith of the springs resort and owned for a time by Col. and Mrs. James Rumbough, who operated the Mountain Park Hotel. After 1919 Sunnybank was the home of Jane Hicks Gentry, the noted mountain ballad singer and storyteller, who moved from her native Watauga Co. to

MD 18 *Sunnybank*

MD 18 *German Internment Camp during World War I, Hot Springs (destroyed)*

Madison Co. as a child and came to Hot Springs with her husband to allow their children to attend Dorland-Bell School. From Gentry the British folk musicologist Cecil Sharp (cf. *John C. Campbell Folk School) collected about seventy songs during his visit in 1916, of which about forty appeared in his *English Folk-Songs from the Southern Appalachians.*

Dorland Memorial Presbyterian Church (1898–1900; Richard Sharp Smith [Asheville], architect; N side Bridge St. [US 25/70] at Meadow Lane) recalls the work of Presbyterian minister Luke Dorland and his wife Juliette, who came to Hot Springs in 1886 to retire but, seeing a local need, founded the Dorland Institute for girls. It gained support from the Woman's Home Mission Board of the Presbyterian Church and developed into the Dorland-Bell School, a predecessor of *Warren Wilson College at Swannanoa. After Dr. Dorland's death in 1897, his widow raised funds for the church, which was dedicated in 1900. The crisply detailed Gothic Revival building takes a cross-gabled form and features the rough stuccoed walls characteristic of Smith's work. The neighboring **White House** (late 19th c.; 81 Bridge St.) is a striking little T-plan, asymmetrical picturesque cottage in board and batten.

Near the river the **Red Bridge** (1910;

Nashville Bridge Co.; end of Andrews Ave.), a Pratt through-truss bridge built across Spring Creek to replace an earlier swinging footbridge, survived the flood of 1916. Across the river the **Bruce House** (1914; NE corner River and Paint Rock Rds.) is a notable Craftsman bungalow with half-timbered motifs and a river rock chimney. It was built for pharmacist Dr. Thomas Jefferson Bruce and his wife Lena. The story goes that the couple built a house in 1912 from a Sears, Roebuck & Co. kit, and when that house burned they ordered an identical new kit—modern home no. 187—and built nearer town and the river as quickly as possible, to "beat the stork." At the other end of town, near the northern edge, the **Lance-Duckett House** (ca. 1900; E side NC 209, 0.4 mi. N of US 27/70; B&B) is a large farmhouse with pebbledash stuccoed walls and a Colonial Revival porch, built for Hot Springs mayor and postmaster Newton Jerome Lance.

MD 19 Ottinger House

Late 1850s; Boys Home Rd., E of US 25/70, 1.5 mi. NW of Hot Springs; private, visible at a distance from road

An imposing sight beside the French Broad River, the house is the largest antebellum brick dwelling in the county and a rare example in N.C. beyond Asheville. Located on bottomland traversed by the Buncombe Turnpike and the WNCRR, it was the home of farmer, ferry operator, and innkeeper Henry Ottinger from 1869 or before. A rope ferry crossed the river here in the turnpike era. For a time the Dorland-Bell School had a second campus here. The 2-story, double-pile house has a hip roof and interior chimneys. A central entrance portico shelters doorways at both levels, and detailing is of simple Greek Revival and Italianate character. Among the outbuildings is a large frame barn approached by an earthen ramp.

MD 20 Amos Stackhouse House

1904; Henry Campbell, builder; N side
SR 1319, 2.7 mi. W of US 25/70, Stackhouse;
private, visible from road

A remarkably elaborate house for its rural site, the large Queen Anne style dwelling features complex massing, a wraparound porch, and a corner turret with conical roof. The house dates from the heyday of rail

travel along the French Broad River between Asheville and Hot Springs. Amos Stackhouse of Philadelphia Quaker origins came to the area at age sixty-five for his wife's health. He soon bought land beside the Buncombe Turnpike and established a community that took his name. He built a store, a sawmill, and then a depot when the WNCRR came through, and he erected the present house in 1900–1904 on a site scooped out of the mountainside. He lived to the age of ninety-nine. Though the businesses are long gone, the house is a prominent sight from river and road.

MD 20 *Amos Stackhouse House*

MD 19 *Ottinger House*

MD 21 Ben Wade Gahagan House

Ca. 1900; W side US 70, 2.5 mi. S of SR 1319; private, visible from road

The substantial Queen Anne style house with front-facing ell and wraparound porch was built for Gahagan, a lumberman who is said to have employed prime woods selected from ancient forests to construct his residence.

MD 22 Walnut

Originally called Jewel Hill (also Duel Hill), the community served as county seat in the 1850s, before debate was finally settled and Marshall became county seat. **Walnut Methodist Church** (early 20th c.; SE corner SR 1439 and SR 1151) is a modest frame church with a shingled corner tower containing the entrance and belfry; its history traces from the Jewel Hill meetinghouse on the site, which served schools and worshipers of "all kinds of professions." Cemeteries extend in three directions from the church, which is sited at the crest of a hill.

MD 23 Meadows House and Store

Early 20th c.; E side NC 209, opp. SR 1165, Spring Creek vic.; private, visible from road

The unusual frame house has a hip and gable roof and multiple porches recessed into its extensive length. Family tradition recalls that Burgin and Mollie Meadows bought the store and a small house in 1919 and moved here with their family of twelve children; they soon extended the dwelling into an 18-room house with 9 outside doors. In the small gable-fronted store, Burgin Meadows operated a post office and general store for many years, followed by his youngest son, Thomas.

MD 24 Malachi Reeves Farm

Ca. 1860; Davis Shackleford, builder; N side NC 63, 0.6 mi. W of SR 1101, Little Sandy Mush Creek vic.; private, visible from road

The well-preserved mid-19th-c. farm complex centers on a 2-story brick house with interior end chimneys and a corbeled cornice. The 1-story front porch came later.

Outbuildings include several log structures and a small gable-fronted frame store by the road. The log barn with half-dovetailed notches is built of logs reused from an earlier Reeves family house on the site. Malachi Reeves Jr. and his wife Elizabeth Robeson Reeves, members of early families in the area and parents of fifteen children, built the brick house ca. 1860. The store by the road was operated by grandson Roscoe Reeves. The farm remains in the family.

MD 24 *Malachi Reeves Farm*

MD 25 Leese B. Reeves Farm

Ca. 1900; E side SR 1100, 0.05 mi. S of NC 63, Little Sandy Mush Creek vic.; private, visible from road

The picturesque grouping of log structures on a hill rising from Little Sandy Mush Creek includes a single-pen house with stone chimney, smokehouse, flue-cured tobacco barn, and burley tobacco barn. Leese Reeves was one of the grandsons of Malachi Reeves and part of a large family in the neighborhood.

MD 26 Bob Ramsey House

19th c.; W side SR 1114, 0.3 mi. S of SR 1116, on Little Sandy Mush Creek at Buncombe Co. line; private, visible from road

Facing the creek, the unusually long, 2-story frame house has a plan resembling two adjoining center-passage-plan dwellings, with the whole front sheltered by a full-length, 2-tier porch.

MD 27 Zeb Jarrett Farm
Late 19th–early 20th c.; E side SR 1116, 0.8 mi. SW of SR 1118, Rector Corner vic.; private, visible from road

Sheltered in a valley beside the road, the farmstead overlooks the lower valley below. The 2-story frame farmhouse (ca. 1897) grew in phases with a series of wings. There are several log and frame outbuildings, including a large log barn with vented hayloft on the hillside by the road.

Buncombe County (BN)

See Douglas Swaim, Cabins and Castles *(1981); David R. Black,* Historic Resources of Downtown Asheville, North Carolina *(1979).*

Asheville (BN 1–83)

The metropolis of western N.C., Asheville possesses the state's most diverse and sophisticated ensemble of early 20th-c. urban architecture. Lying in a superb setting, a sheltered bowl ringed by gentle peaks, the small city's remarkably cosmopolitan architectural character reflects crosscurrents of ambitious clients and architects. The best-known buildings date from resort boom eras of the 1890s through the 1920s, from the romantic eclecticism of *Biltmore to the sparkling collection of Art Deco work. The downtown retains, despite several losses, a wealth of commercial and institutional buildings of striking variety, stylishness, craftsmanship, and coloristic effects. Late 19th- and early 20th-c. suburbs that lap up the surrounding slopes display myriad picturesque responses to the mountain setting, from Queen Anne and Craftsman houses to Swiss chalet, rustic, and English baronial residences.

Architecture in the "little mountain-girt city" evolved in a rapid sequence of ever more expansive phases, each destroying all but a few vestiges of its predecessors. A frontier and turnpike era began in the late 18th c. and extended through the mid-19th c. Because of its favorable location in a broad plateau at the confluence of the French Broad and Swannanoa rivers, the site attracted ambitious settlers when the frontier was opened after the American Revolution. William Davidson, who was granted 640 acres from the state in 1787, hosted the first meetings of the Buncombe Co. court after the county was established in 1792. Zebulon and Bedent Baird opened the first store in 1793, and John Burton, who obtained 200 acres next to Davidson in 1794, laid out Main St. along an old trading path and sold lots on the street. (N. and S. Main were later renamed Broadway and Biltmore Ave., respectively.) Initially called Morristown, the town was incorporated in 1797 as Asheville,

Downtown Asheville, aerial view, looking west

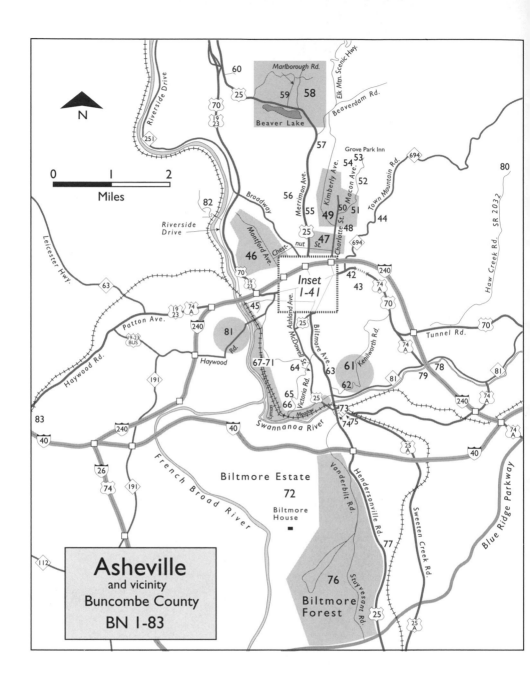

Asheville
and vicinity
Buncombe County
BN 1-83

named in honor of Governor Samuel Ashe.

Although growth was limited by the difficulties of transportation, Asheville nevertheless emerged as a regional trading center. It gained a post office in 1801, a hotel was opened in 1814, and in 1815 a public square (now Pack Square) was created for the courthouse. The 1828 completion of the Buncombe Turnpike through Asheville from South Carolina to Tennessee confirmed the importance of the town. Stagecoaches arrived regularly, and livestock drovers herded thousands of animals through town on their way to southern markets. The cool climate attracted summer tourists, especially from South Carolina, and the first of many hotels

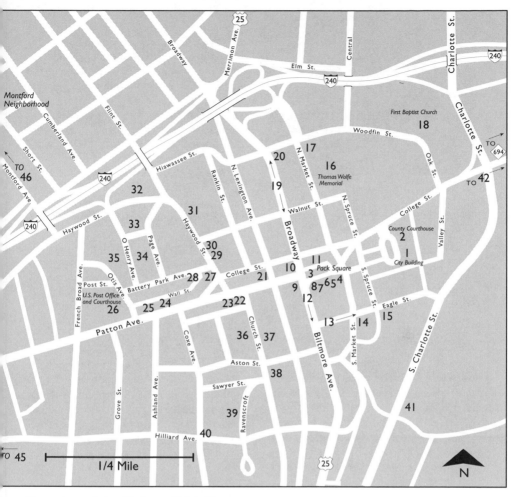

Downtown Asheville Inset BN 1-41

was built. By 1850 the "little hamlet of white-wooden buildings, and a few brick structures" had 520 people and a growing sense of its prospects as a regional trade center. None of the early log buildings survives, but two of the first brick structures still stand, the *Smith-McDowell House and *Ravenscroft School. Leading builders in this period included Ephraim Clayton and George Shackleford, who developed regional building practices that extended into surrounding counties.

Asheville continued to grow during the Civil War and the years afterward, with its population rising from 1,500 in 1870 to 2,600 in 1880. In the postwar era, hopes for

growth and prosperity focused on rail connections. City leaders saw opportunities dashed in the 1870s when their old Buncombe Turnpike markets in Tennessee gained rail links to Atlanta and Mobile. But finally in 1880 the long-anticipated connection of the Western North Carolina Railroad (WNCRR)—begun in the 1850s but interrupted by the Civil War and its aftermath—brought Asheville into the rail network at last. The first train arrived on Oct. 3, 1880.

Completion of the WNCRR across the Blue Ridge opened a new era. Within the first decade the town's population grew from 2,600 to 10,000. Downtown growth extended west along Patton Ave., and in 1889

BN 66 *Smith-McDowell House*

the city began its electric streetcar system, touted as first in the state. The Board of Trade was founded in 1882 to promote tourism and other business, and Asheville's accommodations grew more numerous and more luxurious. Writer Charles Dudley Warner, after traveling through the more remote areas of the region in the early 1880s, arrived in Asheville to find it "in all its watering-place gaiety, as we reined up at the Swannanoa hotel. A band was playing on the balcony. We had reached ice-water, barbers, waiters, civilization." By the mid-1880s as many as 30,000 "summer people" journeyed to Asheville annually, and by 1900 the town had nearly 15,000 residents and an estimated 50,000 annual visitors. One contemporary observer recalled that "Real Estate Boom Number 1 for Asheville" began in 1888 and "fell with the inevitable thud" in 1896.

The chief attraction was the "ozoniferous" climate, which was believed to help prevent some diseases and ease or cure the consumption (tuberculosis) and other lung diseases that were a national health problem. One 1880s report claimed that "Asheville stands today at the head of southern health resorts" and "celebrated physicians . . . name Asheville as pre-eminent in possessing the cool, dry bracing air necessary to health." Summer visitors were soon complemented by "winter people" escaping northern rigors, who made it a year-round resort. Promotion of the city to northerners began soon after the Civil War, when local leaders published *Western North Carolina: Its Resources, Climate, Scenery, and Salubrity* (1870, 1885),

with emphasis on the climate that was pleasant year-round in "The Switzerland of America." The arrival of the railroad meant that "one may be transported in a single day from the crowded cities of the East to the midst of picturesque mountain scenery, clear and rapid streams and evergreen pines and balsam and to a climate so mild as to admit of perpetual enjoyment." A real estate developer's booklet, *Asheville, Nature's Sanitarium*, depicted Asheville as "the mecca of the Southron [*sic*] as he flees from the mosquito, heat and malaria of the Southern Summer, and the dream of the Northerner as he shivers from the blizzards of the North and West."

Big, luxurious resort hotels thrived. The most celebrated were the vast Queen Anne style Battery Park Hotel (1886), designed by Philadelphia architect Edward Hazlehurst and built atop Battery Porter hill, site of an old Confederate breastworks, and the immense and eclectic Kenilworth (1891), designed by Philadelphia architects Francis and William Price. Both hotels have been destroyed. The chief survivor of this romantic hotel era is *The Manor and Cottages, designed by New York architect Bradford Gilbert and sited on a hillside on the northern edge of town. There were also many boardinghouses, one of which gained lasting fame in the novels of Asheville writer Thomas Wolfe — his mother's Old Kentucky Home.

Among the influential newcomers in this era was George Pack, a New Yorker and Michigan lumberman who came here in 1884 with his ailing wife and donated land and money for several civic projects, including the central square that bears his name. Frank Coxe, an engineer instrumental in completing the railroad to Asheville, promoted winter as well as summer visitation, built the Battery Park Hotel, and, with his sons Frank and Tench, developed the section of town near the Battery Park.

A newly sophisticated phase of development began in the 1890s with the creation of the *Biltmore Estate. Industrial heir George Vanderbilt visited Asheville and decided to establish a country retreat nearby. Between 1888 and 1895 he created Biltmore as a vast mountain estate centering on his chateau. The city's architecture repeated or played off the French, English, and other romantic styles introduced by Vanderbilt's architect Richard Morris Hunt and his supervising architect, English-born Richard Sharp Smith.

Several men involved in construction of Biltmore stayed to shape the growing city and benefit from its new Vanderbilt-bestowed cachet. Prominent among these were Rafael Guastavino, who came to execute his celebrated self-supporting tile work at Biltmore and settled permanently near Black Mountain, and stonecarver Fred Miles, whose work graces several local buildings. Most prolific was architect Richard Sharp Smith, a native of Yorkshire who had worked in Chicago and for Bradford Gilbert in New York before joining the firm of Richard Morris Hunt. Smith remained in Asheville and established a large regional practice (with Albert Heath Carrier after 1906), led in forming the N.C. chapter of the American Institute of Architects, and produced a wide range of buildings, many of them in his distinctive, English-influenced Craftsman style vocabulary. Among the leading builders of the era was J. M. Westall, who executed several Smith designs as well as other projects.

Feverish land speculation and growth came in the 1910s and especially the 1920s. In the 1920s the city experienced an unprecedented boom closely tied to the contemporary land rush in Florida: "The real estate men were everywhere," said Asheville novelist Thomas Wolfe in *You Can't Go Home Again*, "and there seemed to be only one rule, universal and infallible—to buy, always to buy, to pay whatever price was asked, and to sell again within two days at any price one chose to fix. It was fantastic." By 1920 the city had 28,000 residents, and by 1930 there were 50,000 and as many as 250,000 visitors annually.

Dominating much of this era was developer Edwin Wiley Grove. The maker of Bromo-Quinine, he, like Vanderbilt, visited the city in 1897 and decided to stay. Before his death in 1927 Grove and others essentially rebuilt the city. He erected a luxury hotel, the *Grove Park Inn, in a burly native stone architecture that contrasted with the

locally dominant eclecticism. He created several residential developments. Grove tore down the old Battery Park Hotel and its hill and erected the tall new *Battery Park Hotel in 1924, and he filled the ravine with earth from the hill as the site of his new commercial sector, centered on the *Grove Arcade. Also in 1924 businessman L. B. Jackson built western N.C.'s first skyscraper, the 13-story *Jackson Building at Pack Square.

On the periphery of the city, Grove and other developers created a ring of stylish, picturesque suburbs that reached up the mountain slopes. Citizens adopted myriad rustic, Craftsman, and Shingle styles, often blended with Tudor, castellated, cottage, and other English-associated styles that seemed to suit the verdant mountain setting. A remarkable series of stone, half-timbered, log, and shingled versions of mountain romanticism appeared in hotels, mansions, suburbs, and schools.

With the city population heading toward 50,000, some civic leaders set their sights on a future city of 200,000 and scaled their plans accordingly. City fathers' grand vision of Asheville's future was both expressed and encouraged when they commissioned famed city planner John Nolen to design a plan for the city, which was published in 1925. Although not all of Nolen's ideas were carried out, many were, including improvement of traffic flow and expansion of the public square. Moreover, the scale and sophistication of Nolen's plan encouraged civic investment in major, costly new public buildings and facilities during the 1920s.

The late 1920s brought still greater growth based on ballooning private and civic debt and soaring real estate prices and profit. Despite a foreboding slump in the real estate boom in 1926, ambitious undertakings continued, with the civic "Program of Progress" supported by bond issues and borrowing against artificially high property evaluations. Towering new structures for the city building (boldly modern Art Deco) and the county courthouse (soberly classical) were erected. Nationally known architects including Bertram Goodhue, Edward Tilton, William Stoddart, and James Gamble Rogers of New York provided designs for Asheville

BN 34 *Grove Arcade and* BN 33 *Battery Park Hotel*

clients. Architects from other cities opened offices in Asheville or moved their practices there, including Beacham & LeGrand of Greenville, S.C.; James Baldwin of Anderson, S.C.; and Albert Wirth of Greensboro, N.C. Beaux Arts-trained, N.C.-born architect Douglas Ellington arrived in the city to design a brilliant sequence of Art Deco buildings, each a different facet of that style, with sumptuous color effects and forms disciplined by Beaux Arts programs.

The crash of 1929 hit Asheville's inflated economy hard and fast. The leading bank closed in 1930, soon followed by five others. The county, city, and public school system lost almost $8 million in unsecured bonds. The president of the bank was sentenced to prison, and the mayor committed suicide. Tourism all but ended. Building came to a halt. The city never regained its 1920s momentum; indeed, between 1930 and 1950 it grew by only 3,000 people. Its civic debt was not repaid until 1978. After renegotiating its debt in the mid-1930s, however, the city witnessed construction of a few important new buildings, which reinvigorated the taste for innovative design: Anthony Lord's elegantly moderne *Citizen-Times Building (1938–39) downtown and, hidden away in a suburb, the unpretentious *Weizenblatt House, de-signed by the leading modernist architect Marcel Breuer and supervised by Lord.

During World War II six local architects—William Waldo Dodge, Henry I. Gaines, Anthony Lord, William Stewart Rogers, Erle G. Stillwell, and Charles Waddell—frustrated in their attempts to get defense jobs, had lunch together at the *S&W Cafeteria and teamed up as Six Associates to bid on wartime projects that required a large office. The firm continued after the war as a prominent modern design office. Architect J. Bertram King and other graduates of the School of Design at present-day North Carolina State University also established offices in Asheville in the mid-20th c. These and other architects developed practices that encompassed both national modernist architectural ideas of their eras and in some cases a sense of regionalism shown in the use of natural woods and rough stonework, such as that at *Warren Wilson College. Late 20th-c. architecture has also included a controversial big-name project on Pack Square, I. M. Pei's *Akzona-Biltmore Building.

At the end of the 20th c., Asheville has weathered economic ups and downs and has entered an intriguing chapter in its history. In part because of the presence of several schools, including the University of North

Carolina at Asheville, as well as the powerful appeal of the mountain setting and the accessibility to interstate highways, the city attracts diverse newcomers and has a growing reputation as an outdoors and arts center of vitality and charm. The population grew from 62,000 in 1990 to approximately 68,000 in 1998. The city has a strong preservation community, with private and public organizations promoting its historic architecture, with special emphasis on its "bull market baronial," Arts and Crafts rustic romantic, and Art Deco work of the glittering half-century before the crash.

Downtown Asheville:
The city spreads gently across the river plateau and reaches up the surrounding mountain slopes, with *Pack Square as its center. In the mid- and late 20th c., urban renewal and the construction of present-day I-240 severed old connections between the city center and the neighborhoods that once extended from it. The commercial district follows an irregular grid from Pack Square west toward Grove's redevelopment of Battery Porter. Commercial and industrial areas line the railroad and the French Broad River. Rising toward the surrounding mountains are the principal late 19th- and early 20th-c. neighborhoods.

Pack Square:
The historic heart of the city is Pack Square, a civic space expanded over the years. It was named for George W. Pack, the New York and Michigan lumber magnate who came to Asheville in 1884 and funded the local library and other projects. Initially the courthouse filled much of the square; in the early 20th c. the square was extended eastward twice. In the mid-20th c. the scale of the square was again redefined by massive buildings on the west and north. (See Introduction, Figs. 45 and 46.)

BN 1 City Building

1926–28; Douglas D. Ellington, architect;
70 Court Plaza Place

The delectable masterpiece of Art Deco displays Ellington's sure handling of geometry and color and his blend of Beaux Arts principles with Art Deco motifs. The powerful

brick mass of pink-orange brick rises from an arcaded base of creamy pink Georgia marble and culminates in an octagonal ziggurat of raspberry and green tile. The main decorative theme, strongest at the jagged roofline, is a stylized feather motif that Ellington described as "lightly reminiscent of the Indian epoch." The lobby continues the Art Deco treatment. The council chamber features stylized classical paneling and chandeliers and murals by artist Clifford Addams. There are Art Deco furnishings in the original mayor's office.

BN 2 Buncombe County Courthouse

1927–28; Milburn & Heister (Washington, D.C.), architects; 60 Court Plaza

The massive public buildings that preside over Pack Square present two stylistic and philosophical poles of 1920s boom-era architecture. Architect Douglas Ellington presented a scheme for a matching pair of Art Deco civic buildings whose forms echoed the mountains. The city proceeded, but the county commissioners rebelled and commissioned an intentionally conservative courthouse on an equally grand scale. Thus Buncombe's eighth courthouse, one of N.C.'s biggest, is a chunky 17-story steel-framed structure clad in brick and limestone in Milburn & Heister's conservative Neoclassical vocabulary, with granite columns at entrance and upper levels. Inside, marble, plaster, and paneled woodwork repeat the classical theme in the lobby and fifth-floor courtroom.

BN 3 Vance Monument

1896; Richard Sharp Smith, architect

The obelisk, designed by architect Smith soon after completion of *Biltmore, is built of granite from the Pacolet quarries in Henderson Co. Erected early in the state's turn-of-the-century memorialization campaign, the monument was funded largely by George Pack to honor Buncombe's native son, former Civil War governor and U.S. senator Zebulon B. Vance, who died in 1894. Within a few years the state placed figures of Vance at Union Square in Raleigh and the U.S. Capitol.

BN 2 *Buncombe Co. Courthouse and* BN 1 *City Building*

BN 4 Jackson Building

1923–24; Ronald Greene (Asheville), architect; 22 S. Pack Square

Epitomizing the venturesome spirit of the era, the spectacularly tall, slim structure (13 stories on a 27-by-60-foot site) was proudly proclaimed as the first skyscraper in western N.C. Originally a searchlight on top illuminated the nearby mountains. It was built for L. B. Jackson, a twenty-seven-year-old real estate developer riding the wave of growth in the city. Architect Ronald Greene clad the steel frame in brick and terra-cotta, with opulent Gothic decorations accentuating its verticality and insouciant gargoyles jutting from the upper story. (This corner was the site of W. O. Wolfe's stonecutting shop.)

BN 5 Westall Building

1925; Ronald Greene (Asheville), architect; 20 S. Pack Square

Planned with the *Jackson Building and sharing its elevators, this narrow, steel-framed structure is clad in brick and accented in orange, blue, and green terra-cotta with Spanish Romanesque motifs.

BN 6 Commerce Building

1904; 16–18H S. Pack Square

The 3-story, simplified Italianate style commercial building typifies the square before the rebuilding of the 1920s.

BN 7 Legal Building

1909; Smith & Carrier, architects; 10–14 S. Pack Square

The spare, elegant office building, exemplifying architect Smith's favored Renaissance palazzo form, is one of the area's first uses of reinforced concrete structure. The heavy overhanging cornice is of sheet metal. The imposing 5-story building was built as the home of the Central Bank and Trust Co., the leading local financial institution that collapsed in 1930.

BN 8 (former) Pack Memorial Library

1925–26; Edward L. Tilton (New York), architect; S. Pack Square

The 3-story Renaissance Revival building repeats the palazzo concept, with its second story dramatized by tall arched windows and the arched entrance rising through the first

and second stories. It is faced in white Georgia marble and adorned with a bas-relief classical cornice. Designed by the New York library specialist architect Tilton and named for donor Pack, the library replaced a castellated predecessor that burned in 1923. It is now the Asheville Art Museum; the successor Pack Memorial Library on Haywood St. has an excellent regional history collection.

BN 9 Pack Square Southwest
Ca. 1890

At the southwest corner of Pack Square stands Asheville's oldest cluster of commercial buildings, brick structures 3 and 4 stories tall with Romanesque and Italianate detail typical of late 19th-c. Asheville. Defining the corner is **1 Biltmore Ave.** (ca. 1887), a 3-story building with its diagonal corner entrance bay emphasized by corbeled brickwork. Tucked into the corner of the square, adjoining commercial buildings recall the late 19th-c. architecture that once framed the square; similar buildings formerly continued along the north side until the 1970s. The 3-story building at **9 Pack Square** sw (ca. 1890), features a pressed-metal cornice and window lintels; a rare survival of the town's 19th-c. hotels, its upper floors were

part of the Western Hotel that once stood at 1 Biltmore Ave. At **7 Pack Square** sw (ca. 1890) the 4-story brick building displays a robust Romanesque Revival character in its corbeled brickwork and rock-faced stone arches. The simpler 3-story building at **5 Pack Square** sw (ca. 1890) typifies the corbeled brickwork and modest Italianate style prevalent in late 19th-c. commercial architecture.

BN 10 BB&T Building
(Northwestern Bank Building)
1964–65; Whittington & Associates (Charlotte), architects; W. Pack Square

The tallest building between Knoxville and Charlotte, and the tallest in western N.C., the 18-story skyscraper is rendered in the rectilinear form and metal grid standard among office towers of the 1960s. The first major downtown commercial building erected after 1929, it was built for Northwestern Bank and has been the BB&T building since the late 1980s.

BN 11 Akzona-Biltmore Building
1978–80; I. M. Pei (New York), architect; 1 N. Pack Square

At a time when occupancy was spotty around Pack Square and the city was eager for investment in downtown redevelopment, Akzona, Inc. (formed in 1970 from a merger of American Enka [cf. *Enka] and other firms) acquired much of the north side of the square, razed the ca. 1890 commercial buildings, and erected this massive, gleaming headquarters block with ribbon windows. Seeking to add a strong, high-quality building to the downtown, Akzona commissioned the design from the nationally prominent firm of I. M. Pei. The building was subsequently acquired by the Biltmore Co.

BN 12 Biltmore Ave.

Several representative early 20th-c. commercial and residential buildings survive in the first blocks of Biltmore Ave. south of Pack Square—known as S. Main St. until 1914. The area has recently been revitalized. The **Latta Block** (1923; 38–48 Biltmore Ave.), a row of four 2-story tan brick buildings with gray terra-cotta trim, was developed by entrepreneur E. D. Latta of Charlotte. In the next block are three 2-story, 4-unit apartment buildings, **130–140 Biltmore Ave.** (ca. 1905; Richard Sharp Smith, architect), with stone and stuccoed facades. Across the street is the **George Mears House** (ca. 1885; 137 Biltmore Ave.), a grand Queen Anne style house of brick, the most distinguished of the few remaining 19th-c. residences near the downtown.

BN 13 Eagle St. Commercial District

During the late 19th and early 20th centuries, as the city's population grew, this area south of Pack Square was the center of the black business district, while S. Main St. (present-day Biltmore Ave.) served a mainly white clientele. Brick buildings replaced frame ones around the turn of the century. Many of the buildings associated with the city's substantial black community of that era were razed in the mid- to late 20th c., but a few remain on this street, recalling its diverse retail enterprises—barbershops, stores, hotels, restaurants, a movie theater, a mica factory, and a foundry. The largest of the remaining brick commercial buildings is the **Asheville Supply and Foundry Building** (ca. 1915; 35 Eagle St.), a 4-story brick building with arched windows, built for a firm that manufactured structural steel for several local buildings, including the *Jackson Building.

BN 14 YMI Building
1892; Richard Sharp Smith, architect; SE corner of S. Market and Eagle Sts.

Under the patronage of George Vanderbilt, R. S. Smith, supervising architect at *Biltmore and architect at *Biltmore Village, used his favored combination of "English cottage" forms in pebbledash and red brick to create a handsome multiuse building. These effects, also used in Hunt's designs at the *Biltmore Estate buildings, repeated trends then popular in English and other northern European architecture, but they were unique to Smith's sphere of influence in

N.C. For black residents of Asheville, including many who worked on Biltmore, Vanderbilt established the Young Men's Institute (YMI) as an equivalent of the Young Men's Christian Association (YMCA). The YMI building served as a social and educational center in the black community and became the Market St. YMCA. It has been renovated as a community center.

BN 14 *YMI Building*

BN 15 Mount Zion Missionary Baptist Church
1919; 47 Eagle St.

The imposing Gothic Revival edifice in dark red brick rises 2½ stories from the stone foundation that accommodates the sloping site. Broad front and side gables are flanked by 3- and 4-story towers. Stained glass fills the many windows. Located on a street that was the heart of the black commercial section at the turn of the century, the massive brick building bears a cornerstone reading, "Mt. Zion Baptist Church, Rebuilt 1919, Rev. J. R. Nelson, Pastor." The church was built for one of the city's largest congregations, which had been established in 1880 and worshiped in various buildings before acquiring this site.

BN 16 Thomas Wolfe Memorial
Ca. 1883 and later; 48 Spruce St.; State Historic Site; National Historic Landmark; open to public regular hours

A memorial to Asheville's great literary genius and prodigal son and known to millions as "Dixieland" in *Look Homeward,*

BN 15 *Mount Zion Missionary Baptist Church*

Angel, the frame, Queen Anne style house is an isolated vestige of 19th-c. Asheville. The house is best known for the early 20th-c. era when Julia Wolfe, Tom's mother, operated it as a boardinghouse, "Old Kentucky Home," for consumptives and others. The irregular plan of the 2-story dwelling developed through a series of additions. Sawn and turned millwork, patterned shingles, and bay windows typify the era.

Its restoration as a state historic site recaptured with rare verisimilitude the threadbare, motley home and boardinghouse filled with Wolfe family furnishings and possessions. During the restoration in the 1970s Thomas Wolfe's brother visited and told staff how to arrange the furniture as it had been in his youth. On a quiet day a visit to this house evokes the spirit of people and times long gone. (See Introduction, Fig. 28.) A fire on July 24, 1998, seriously damaged the house and its contents; restoration is planned.

BN 17 Asheville-Biltmore Hotel
1926; 76 N. Market St.

Built by L. B. Jackson and other investors to accommodate the growing tourist trade, the 8-story brick building contained 100 modern rooms and displayed the restrained classical trim in limestone typical of its era. It is now Altamont Apts.

BN 18 First Baptist Church
1925–27; Douglas D. Ellington, architect; NE corner Oak and Woodfin Sts.

A landmark in Ellington's bold and imaginative style, this was his first design in Ashe-

ville. In this extraordinary church Ellington displayed his innovative combination of concepts, including his resilient Beaux Arts classical massing, the stark forms of early Christian church architecture, and vividly new Art Deco details. The severe brick walls and pillars rise to a large dome, which is covered with tile and rises to a tall Art Deco lantern. Ellington explained that his subtly unifying color program begins with the green of the weathered copper lantern—akin to the green mountainsides in the background—then moves downward through the domed roof of tiles that begin with a similar green, then graduate to warm red akin to the orange bricks, terra-cotta, and pink marble of the walls.

BN 18 *First Baptist Church*

The sanctuary, a great auditorium in the round, is sheltered by the capacious dome. Curved rows of seating on the slanted floor and in the full balcony focus on the pulpit. Behind the pulpit is enframed the raised baptismal pool. The strong detailing throughout continues the Art Deco esthetic. As Ellington observed, the sanctuary was built as part of a unified complex designed to meet the social, educational, and administrative needs of a large, modern congregation; brick support buildings extend beyond the main building.

BN 19 Broadway Commercial Row
1900s–1920s

The blocks of Broadway north of Pack Square contain a representative selection of boom-era commercial architecture, emphasized by the steepness of the street. Polychrome brickwork and stone trim accentuate the diverse styles of the predominantly 2- to 4-story commercial buildings.

BN 20 Scottish Rite Cathedral and Masonic Temple
1913; Smith & Carrier, architects; 80 Broadway

The striking edifice features robust brickwork and is dominated by a tall portico with paired Ionic columns and a 3-story, blind arched window on the Woodfin St. side.

West of Pack Square:
Commercial development extended west along Patton Ave. late in the 19th c. and into the early 20th c.

BN 21 Kress Building
1926–27; E. J. T. Hoffmann, architect; 21 Patton Ave.

The 4-story tan brick and cream glazed terra-cotta building is one of the classically detailed Kress buildings, contrasting with the company's more celebrated Art Deco works. The facade features urns, a parapet, and the company name.

BN 22 Drhumor Building
1895; A. L. Melton, architect; J. M. Westall, builder; 48 Patton Ave.

The Romanesque Revival building is one of the best examples of its style in the state. Architect Melton designed many key buildings of the late 19th c. The 4-story brick edifice has rock-faced limestone at the rounded corner. Ranges of great round-arched and rectangular windows are punched between strong pilaster strips beneath the corbeled cornice. Especially intriguing are the lively first-floor frieze and capitals carved by sculptor Fred Miles (who also worked at *Biltmore), who rendered the robust allegorical images and, some say, the visage of at least one local sidewalk superintendent.

BN 23 S&W Cafeteria
1929; Douglas D. Ellington, architect; 56 Patton Ave.

BN 22 *Drhumor Building*

The small, splendid Art Deco gem displays another face of Ellington's sparkling use of color and his keying of decorative themes to the purpose of the building. The 2-story facade of cream, blue, green, black, and gilt glazed terra-cotta combines geometricized Indian and classical motifs in "festive" fashion. The Charlotte-based S&W chain commissioned the building for one of its first downtown cafeterias. After serving as a cafeteria until 1973, the building endured periods of disuse and loss of its original Art Deco interiors but has recently been renovated.

BN 24 Public Service Building
1929; Beacham & LeGrand (Greenville, S.C.), architects; 89–93 Patton Ave.

The big, boldly handled and eclectically detailed skyscraper, fronting on two streets, was built by the Coxe estate for Carolina Power and Light. The 5 central stories of the shaft are standard brick, but the lower 2 and upper 2 stories dance with Romanesque and Spanish motifs in polychrome terra-cotta, including a Leda-and-the-Swan motif at the second-floor windows. James Beacham and Leon LeGrand of Greenville established an Asheville office (1925–28) and associated with Henry I. Gaines.

BN 23 *S & W Cafeteria*

BN 25 Shell Station
Ca. 1928; W. Stewart Rogers (Green & Rogers), architect; 121 Patton Ave.

The snappy little Art Deco gas station is one of several designed by Rogers for W. C. Shuey's Shell Oil distributorship. Now a retail business, it has been linked to a larger structure but maintains the vividness of the original design.

BN 26 U.S. Post Office and Courthouse
1929–30; James A. Wetmore, supervising architect of the Treasury; 100 Otis St.

One of the state's finest depression-era federal buildings, the post office shows the period's blend of classical massing with Art Deco detail, here producing a powerful composition of great public presence. Art Deco motifs are strongest in the stylized ornament of the limestone-sheathed exterior, which features low relief panels embellished with metal spandrels, doors, and balconies. The interiors have a more classical cast, especially the lobby with its stenciled ceiling.

BN 27 Miles Building
Ca. 1901, 1925; 14–20 Haywood St.

BN 24 *Public Service Building*

The 3-story brick building is vigorously embellished with white glazed terra-cotta classical cornices, trim, and rustication. The polygonal-shaped building faces on both Haywood St. and the shorter Wall St. — named for a wall that once stood here. It was built as the Asheville Club, then remodeled after Herbert Miles bought it. The town plan in this area developed around a triangular slice of land now called Pritchard Park, once the site of the big U.S. Post Office (1892; Peter Demens, builder), which was razed ca. 1930.

BN 28 Flatiron Building

1925–26; Albert C. Wirth (Greensboro and Asheville), architect; 10–20 Battery Park Ave.

A classic urban form, the wedge-shaped 8-story building is faced with limestone and finished with restrained classical detail. It was built as part of the Grove development of the Battery Park area.

BN 29 Woolworth Store

1939; Henry I. Gaines (Asheville), architect; 25 Haywood St.

The late Art Deco building of the recovery era features cream and orange terra-cotta facade with fountain and plant motifs.

BN 30 Loughran Building

1923; Smith & Carrier, architects; SE corner Haywood and Walnut Sts.

One of R. S. Smith's last designs, the 6-story, restrained classical commercial building was among the city's first to use all steel framing. The story is told that Smith, then seventy-one and ailing, inspected the work, took out his watch and chain to use as a plumb bob, found the framing off square, and had the foreman tear it out and begin again.

BN 31 Castenea Building

1921; W. J. East, architect; 57–65 Haywood St.

BN 28 *Flatiron Building*

Handsomely executed, well-preserved 3-story commercial building of richly hued local orange-brown brick, retaining original storefronts.

BN 32 Basilica of St. Lawrence
1905–9; Rafael Guastavino (Asheville) and Richard Sharp Smith, architects; 97 Haywood St.

A major work by internationally known architect-engineer Rafael Guastavino, the Spanish Baroque Revival style Catholic church employs his "cohesive construction" technique in its great self-supporting tiled dome and the Catalan-style vaulting seen in its tower stair. Multihued and Flemish-bond brickwork is complemented by polychrome glazed terra-cotta inserts and carved limestone trim and statuary. The lady chapel, with its blue tile dome and ceiling, shows Guastavino's work at close range, while the elliptical, warm-hued ceiling of the 58-by-85-foot sanctuary features a herringbone tile pattern. Guastavino came to Asheville to execute his self-supporting tile at *Biltmore and decided to settle at nearby Black Mountain (cf. *Rafael Guastavino Estate). He soon declared the city needed a bigger Catholic church and, in association with architect R. S. Smith, whom he knew from their joint work at *Biltmore, planned this spacious and opulently finished edifice. The exact nature of their collaboration is uncertain; Smith's name appears on the plans. Guastavino executed a number of the beautiful tile plaques in the church, and he is interred in a niche in the church. Craftsman Fred Miles (see *Drhumor Building) executed the stone figures on the church. Construction was completed by Guastavino Jr. after his father's death in 1908. The church is similar to Guastavino's St. Mary Church in Wilmington. See Ann Flower, "The Mark of the Builder: Rafael Guastavino's Masonry in Asheville, North Carolina," *Arris* (1991), and Peter Austin, "The Work of Rafael Guastavino in Western North Carolina," in Brunk, ed., *May We All Remember Well* (1997). (See also Introduction, Fig. 6.)

BN 32 *Basilica of St. Lawrence*

BN 33 Battery Park Hotel
1923–24; William L. Stoddart (New York), architect; Battle Square

A proud tower in the city skyline is the 14-story brick hotel erected by E. W. Grove in the 1920s redevelopment project that leveled Battery Porter and redefined this end of town. The Battery Porter hill had been the site of the Queen Anne style Battery Park Hotel from which, tradition claims, George Vanderbilt surveyed Mt. Pisgah. It is said that the rooftop of the old hotel on its hill was as high as the top of the present skyscraper. A colored tile image of the old hotel graces the lobby of the newer one. Grove acquired the old hotel, which burned before he razed it, and graded the hill. He then employed the prolific New York hotel specialist Stoddart to design a luxurious and modern hotel with all the latest amenities, including a grand dining room and a roof garden. Vacant for a time, the hotel has been renovated for apartments for senior citizens.

BN 34 Grove Arcade
1926–29; Charles N. Parker (Asheville), architect; 37 Battery Park Ave.

After E. W. Grove graded and filled the newly cleared block in front of the old Battery Porter, he made it the site of a massive commercial arcade building that was designed as the base of a future office skyscraper. Construction paused when he died but resumed under Walter Taylor and Associates, who finished the arcade section but, with the onset of the Great Depression, decided not to erect the intended skyscraper. Massive in itself, the arcade is a striking building of unusual form, especially at the north end, where ramps to the roof terrace flank the north entrance, watched by large griffins. Tudoresque, ivory-glazed terra-cotta covers the reinforced concrete and steel structure. Among the molded panels in late medieval spirit is a depiction of the architect. Charles N. Parker had worked for Smith & Carrier (1904–18) before setting up his own practice. The skylit 2-level interior contains handsome wooden storefronts in similar Tudor Revival style. Occupied and modified by the federal government in 1942, it is under development for businesses. (Two other early 20th-c. arcades in the state are the Latta Arcade in Charlotte and the Virginia Dare Hotel and Arcade in Elizabeth City.)

BN 35 Citizen-Times Building

1938–39; Anthony Lord (Asheville), architect; 14 O'Henry Ave.

The dignified International style building is subtly composed around the interplay of glass-block window strips and bands of limestone blocks over a reinforced concrete structure. The strong vertical emphasis of the stair tower asserts the asymmetry of the facade. Designed by Asheville architect Anthony Lord with Lockwood, Greene of New York as consulting architect, it is among the region's earliest statements of the expressive rectilinearity of the International style. Lord, trained at Georgia Tech and Yale, joined the Asheville architectural firm of his father, William H. Lord, in 1929. In his long career he became a leader in his profession in the city and the state and was a founder of Six Associates in 1942. Like many architects of his generation, Lord's work spanned a range of styles, from the severe modernism of this building to various revival and regional designs.

BN 36 Central Methodist Church

1902–5; Reuben H. Hunt (Chattanooga), architect; J. M. Westall, builder; 27 Church St.

The large, powerfully composed stone church combines Gothic Revival detailing with massing characteristic of the Romanesque Revival. An arcaded entrance loggia extends between two towers, the north one rising high above the church and topped with pinnacles. The interior has a fine auditorium sanctuary with Art Glass windows. The robust design is characteristic of the architect, Reuben H. Hunt, a widely published and influential church designer.

BN 35 *Citizen-Times Building*

BN 36 *Central Methodist Church*

Builder J. M. Westall was the younger brother of Julia Westall Wolfe, mother of author Thomas Wolfe.

BN 37 First Presbyterian Church
1884, later additions; NE corner Church and Aston Sts.

One of the oldest churches in the city, the brick nave and tower feature corbeled brickwork and Gothic Revival openings; the church has grown with many additions and remodelings over the years.

BN 38 Trinity Episcopal Church
1912, 1961; Bertram Goodhue of Cram, Goodhue & Ferguson (New York and Boston), architect; SE corner Church and Aston Sts.

The Gothic Revival edifice of forceful, almost abstract simplicity was designed by a major American architect who was one of the principals in a firm known nationally as a leader in the Arts and Crafts movement and the renewal of the Gothic Revival style. At the time this church was designed, Bertram Goodhue was operating out of a New York office, while the other two partners were still in the Boston headquarters. The church has red brick walls with granite trim emphasizing the clean-cut openings. Its hefty corner tower rises to a simple gabled belfry. The sanctuary features a fine hammer-beamed ceiling. The parish had a long-standing devotion to leading Gothic Revival architects, for their antebellum church was built from a design by Ecclesiologist Frank Wills.

BN 38 *Trinity Episcopal Church*

BN 39 Ravenscroft School
1840s; Ephraim Clayton (attributed builder); 29 Ravenscroft Dr.

A rare survivor from antebellum Asheville, the towered brick villa indicates the town's growing taste for fashion. The plan and massing of the villa probably come from A. J. Downing's popular patternbook, *Cottage Residences*, but the detail is Greek Revival rather than Italianate. Possibly built for entrepreneur James Osborne in the late 1840s, it was used as an Episcopal school after 1856. When this section of Asheville declined, the villa survived as a rooming house while many of its neighbors vanished. It has been renovated as offices.

BN 40 Coxe Ave. Automotive Buildings

As the automobile rapidly gained preeminence, handsome and substantial buildings

BN 39 *Ravenscroft School*

sprang up on Coxe Ave. to sell, service, and supply the new mode of transportation. The **B and B Motor Company Building** (1925; NE corner Coxe and Hilliard Sts.), the first of the dealerships, is a 2-story, brick-veneered, reinforced-concrete structure with angled corner and limestone trim. The **Sawyer Motor Company Building** (1925–26; SE corner Coxe and Hilliard Sts.) is big, concrete and steel-framed showroom and garage with cast-concrete plaques and pendants, angled to fit its sloping corner site. The most impressive of the group is the **Consbeer Motors Building** (1928; Beacham & LeGrand [Greenville, S.C., and Asheville], architects; 162–64 Coxe Ave.), an orange brick veneered steel-framed building erected by Tench Coxe for a Chrysler agency.

BN 41 St. Matthias Episcopal Church

1894–96; E side Valley St., between Grail and S. Beaumont Sts.

The handsome Gothic style brick structure with elaborate interior woodwork was built for the oldest congregation of black Episcopalians in western N.C. The congregation was established for former slaves as Trinity Chapel in 1865 by the Reverend Jarvis Buxton. When growth required a larger church, the cornerstone was laid by Bishop Joseph Blount Cheshire in 1894, and upon completion of the new building the name was changed to St. Matthias.

BN 41 *St. Matthias Episcopal Church*

BN 42 Hopkins Chapel
A.M.E. Zion Church

1910; Smith & Carrier, architects; James V. Miller, brickmason; 321 College St.

The striking Gothic Revival church with its tall corner tower was built for a congregation that had separated from *Central Methodist Church in 1868 and, like many black Methodist congregations, affiliated with the African Methodist Episcopal Zion faith. They built first a frame church; after that structure burned in 1907, the congregation worshiped for a time at the *YMI Building. For their new church the congregation commissioned a design from the city's leading architect, R. S. Smith, who had designed the YMI under George Vanderbilt's patronage and was practicing in partnership with Albert Carrier. The master brickmason was James V. Miller, a former slave who became a leading local builder. In Smith's powerfully asymmetrical composition, three arched entrances open into three strong forms: a tall central gable flanked by emphatically unequal towers fronting the large sanctuary. A local campaign seeks to preserve the endangered church.

BN 43 Zealandia

1908–20; Smith & Carrier, architects; Vance Cap Rd.; no public access; visible in winter from I-240 W at exit 6, to the left at crest of Beaucatcher Mountain

Another variation on the English manorial theme, this one evokes Tudor splendor. Philip S. Henry, a diplomat, scholar, and businessman whose art collection later formed the basis of Asheville's art museum, had Smith & Carrier design this as an addition to an earlier structure (since demolished). Henry named the estate for his years in New Zealand as a rancher and member of parliament. The 3-story, cruciform-plan house rises from a basement carved out of solid granite; walls are random blue granite ashlar, with the upper half-story and the gables stuccoed and half-timbered.

BN 44 Overlook (Seely's Castle)

Ca. 1915–25; Town Mountain Rd.; no public access, visible at a distance in winter from I-240 W at exit 6, straight ahead at crest of Town Mountain

Asheville's ultimate combination of baronial romanticism and mountain rusticism, the English style stone "castle" was built by Fred Seely as his private residence soon after the *Grove Park Inn was completed for his father-in-law. It contains a great hall with a 32-foot ceiling and incorporates bits of the Blarney Stone, the Tower of London, and other Old World relics beloved of New World capitalists. Seely's home until his death in 1942, and later the site of Asheville-Biltmore College (which evolved into UNC-Asheville), it is now private.

BN 44 *Overlook (Seely's Castle)*

BN 45 Demens-Rumbough-Crawley House

*Ca. 1890; Peter A. Demens
(attributed builder); 31 Park Ave.*

Among the most vivid survivors from Asheville's late 19th-c. boom era, the bizarrely eclectic, towered brick mansion combines the period's Queen Anne, Italianate, and Eastlake motifs in its wide porch, layered cornice, and eccentric multilevel tower. Its energetic, ornate character seems to express the spirit of its colorful builder, Peter A. Demens, a Russian-born entrepreneur who flourished in three American boom cities. After founding St. Petersburg, Fla., which is apparently named for his birthplace, Demens turned up during Asheville's railroad boom and became a contractor for the city's Federal Building (destroyed, formerly located at Pritchard Park) and a similar building in Statesville (now the Statesville City Hall). He left in 1892 for Los Angeles, where he became a fruit grower and a journalist. The house was then occupied by Col. and Mrs. James H. Rumbough, owners of the fa-

mous Mountain Park Hotel at Hot Springs in neighboring Madison Co., and, after 1919, by Ida Jolly Crawley, a Tennessee-born artist who established "The House of Pan" here, the city's first public art museum.

BN 45 *Demens-Rumbough-Crawley House*

North of downtown

BN 46 Montford Neighborhood

Developed as a middle- and upper middle-class suburb during Asheville's early (1890s) boom years, now a downtown neighborhood, Montford is a wooded area with over 600 buildings; the spine and major thoroughfare is Montford Ave. Development was begun by the 1889 Asheville Loan, Construction, and Improvement Co. and others, then invigorated a few years later by lumber tycoon George W. Pack. On its curving streets, leading Asheville citizens built substantial houses, but these were interspersed with smaller dwellings, apartment houses, boardinghouses, schools, and private sanitariums.

The oldest house predates the neighborhood, the **Rankin House** (ca. 1846; 32 Elizabeth Place), a Greek Revival frame house with Italianate touches, seat of one of the estates divided for the suburb. Throughout the neighborhood are robust examples of Queen Anne and Colonial–Queen Anne blends popular at the time of its founding. The **Rumbough House**, now Highland Hospital (ca. 1892; S. S. Gotley [Cincinnati], architect; 49 Zillicoa St.), is a symmetrical Queen Anne–Colonial Revival blend, while the turreted, asymmetrical **Gudger House** (ca. 1890; 89 Montford Ave.) and the **Wright House** (ca. 1900; 235 Pearson Dr.) are among the most ornate and picturesque. The Shingle and Bungalow styles found lively expression in the neighborhoods, seen in the shingled **C. C. Orr House** (early 1890s; 179 Montford Ave.), with its strong forms emerging from broad gables.

BN 46 *Ottis Green House*

Much of the special quality of Montford's architecture comes from the picturesque houses designed or influenced by architect Richard Sharp Smith, complemented by stone walls and informal plantings to create a rich, Craftsman style character unusual among N.C. suburbs of the period. These houses typically combine irregular cottage-style forms; roughcast or pebbledash, stone, and shingled surfaces; and both half-timbered and Colonial Revival detail. Two exemplary Smith houses appear prominently on Montford Ave. and operate as B&Bs. The **Ottis Green House** (ca. 1900; R. S. Smith, architect; 288 Montford Ave.; B&B) offers a full display of Smith hallmarks, from the half-timbered, pebbledash lower walls to the shingled upper stores with cozy recessed balcony and sloping dormers. The neighboring **Jordan House** (ca. 1900; R. S. Smith, architect; 296 Montford Ave.; B&B) was featured in Smith's *My Sketchbook* typifying his "Old English" style, with curved gabled dormers, pebbledash and shingled walls, and a broad porch. Other Smith works dot the neighborhood, such as the **Rutledge House** (1900; R. S. Smith, architect; 209 Cumberland Ave.), which Smith described as a "Cottage," with its roughcast stucco walls and peaked gambrel roof accentuated by heavy brackets.

Early 20th-c. houses continued these motifs and employed the standard Colonial, Tudor, and foursquare styles. Asheville architect William H. Lord designed a number of handsome residences, such as the shingled and stuccoed Bungalow type **Millender House** (1907; William H. Lord, architect; 240 Pearson Dr.) and the Colonial Revival style **Powell House** (1908; William H. Lord, architect; 346 Montford Ave.), a mansion on spacious grounds built for George Powell, president of the firm that began development of Montford. Unusually formal in its refined Colonial Revival style is the **Gay Green House** (ca. 1928; 152 Pearson Dr.), with its pedimented central pavilion.

Several small-scale apartment houses enrich the variety of housing, such as the **Colonial Apartments** (1920s; 111 Cumberland Ave.), suitably rendered in red brick with classical trim, 3 stories high with a tall portico, and the **Frances Apartments** (ca. 1926; 333 Cumberland Ave.), a picturesque gabled composition in rough clinker brickwork. West of Montford lies **Riverside Cemetery**, a large, informal tract with important markers, including those of Thomas Wolfe, O. Henry, and Zebulon B. Vance. In the mid-20th c. the neighborhood underwent a decline, but toward the end of the century it has blossomed in a gradual resurgence. (See Michael T. Southern, ed., *Asheville's Historic Montford District* [1985].)

BN 47 Chestnut Hill (Chestnut Liberty Neighborhood)

Located on a slight rise north of downtown Asheville, the neighborhood recalls the upper-end residential expansion that followed the arrival of the railroad in 1880. It concentrates on E. Chestnut and N. Liberty and adjoining streets. The majority of residences date from 1880 to 1929 and range from simple vernacular dwellings to sophisticated renditions of Queen Anne, Colonial Revival, and Shingle styles.

Beaufort Lodge (1895; A. L. Melton, architect; 61 N. Liberty St.; B&B) is an exuberantly composed and luxuriously detailed Queen Anne style house, built for state attorney general Theodore S. Davidson and designed by the architect of the *Drhumor Building. Several houses in the neighborhood were designed by J. A. Tennent, the architect who designed Asheville's 1876 Second Empire style courthouse and 1892 city hall. U.S. Senator Jeter Pritchard lived for several years in the large Queen Anne style **Tennent-Pritchard House** (ca. 1895; J. A. Tennent, architect; 223 E. Chestnut St.), which architect Tennent had designed for himself.

BN 47 *Beaufort Lodge*

R. S. Smith also designed a number of residences, usually in his hybrid Craftsman modes, and may have designed or influenced many more. The **David Cottages** (1897–99; R. S. Smith, architect; J. M. Westall, builder; 138, 144, 156, and 160 E. Chestnut St.) were designed by Smith as rental dwellings for Dr. J. E. David, typically 1½-story with prominent gables and inset porches. Soon afterward Smith was engaged in a dispute with builder J. M. Westall, who he believed had improperly copied his style in additional buildings. The **Lambert House** (1896; R. S. Smith, architect; J. M. Westall, builder; 166 E. Chestnut St.) is a 2-story, shingled and roughcast residence, one of Smith's first commissions after the Vanderbilt work. The **Annie West House** (ca. 1900; R. S. Smith, architect; 189 E. Chestnut St.), a multigabled cottage, is one of the best examples of his continued use of the pebbledash and half-timbered effects seen in his work at *Biltmore Village. (See Introduction, Fig. 47.)

The **Jefferson Apartments** (1920s; E. Chestnut at Merrimon Ave.) is a prominent small apartment house, with a horseshoe plan and Spanish details. A reminder of the importance of health facilities in the city is the **Karl Von Ruck House** (1904–12; 52 Albemarle Place), a sequence of elaborate frame houses that constituted the residence of the famous tuberculosis specialist who operated a sanitarium on nearby Sunset Mountain.

BN 48 The Manor and Cottages

1898; Bradford L. Gilbert (New York), architect; Samuel Parsons, landscape architect; James A. Tennent, contractor; 265 Charlotte St. and adjacent streets to the E

The splendidly picturesque ensemble from Asheville's turn-of-the-century resort-boom era is among the few reminders of the style of hospitality that reigned in those days. The exuberantly eclectic architecture combines Queen Anne and Shingle styles.

On farmland purchased by his family in 1886 for a summer home, young Thomas W. Raoul built an innovative hotel that he termed his "English inn in America." Raoul had been stricken with tuberculosis while working in Georgia, went west for a rest cure, then joined the family in Asheville. Working with his father, railroad developer William Greene Raoul, Thomas Raoul commissioned New York architect Bradford L. Gilbert to design the inn. Gilbert consulted with landscape architect Samuel Parsons to obtain an overall plan for the site, which the Raouls developed as Albemarle Park.

The first building was the towered, Tudor Revival style **Lodge** or gatehouse, opening off Charlotte St., a main streetcar route. Soon work began on **The Manor**, a long, rambling hotel with a picturesque outline accentuated by multiple shingled gables. Open year-round, it was intended to be homelike in its atmosphere, with rooms offering expansive views of the western mountains. The inn was opened on New Year's Eve 1898. It gained a new wing to accommodate a ballroom and more guests in 1903, and another addition in 1913.

As laid out by Parsons with curvilinear streets hugging the terrain, Albemarle Park also provided for a series of intensely picturesque **Cottages** ranged up the slopes, with their individual designs accommodated to the terrain. Sweetly named Shamrock,

BN 48 *The Manor*

Clematis, Galax, and so on, the series of European-inspired rental cottages and private residences climbed the steep hillside. Fitted deftly into the slopes, the cottages were built from 1898 into the 1910s and display variations on Swiss chalet, Craftsman, Tudor, Rustic, and Shingle themes. Craftsmen are said to have come to work here after finishing *Biltmore Village. Parsons also planned the use of stonework and other naturalistic materials in retaining walls and other features, as well as suggesting various trees, vines, and shrubs harmonious with the "rugged character" of the existing landscape.

In 1920 the inn and several cottages were sold to E. W. Grove, and the inn underwent various uses in the mid-20th c. In the late 20th c., after a long period of uncertainty, the inn was rescued and carefully restored. The cottages, in various ownerships, have been maintained to the present. (See Jane Gianvito Mathews and Richard Mathews, *The Manor and Cottages, Albemarle Park, Asheville, N.C.* [1991].)

BN 49 Grove Park Neighborhood

E. W. Grove, owner of a St. Louis pharmaceutical firm that manufactured Bromo-Quinine, first came to Asheville ca. 1900, reportedly to establish a chemical company. Like Vanderbilt he found the environment so much to his liking that he purchased land and moved his residence; most important, he embarked on some of the area's grandest

boom-period development projects and became a moving force in Asheville's growth. He began planning a quality residence park around 1905, vowing that no property would be sold until "every modern convenience" was provided. In 1908 he offered the first section of the park for sale and in 1913 opened the *Grove Park Inn overlooking the residential area; thereafter sales were brisk.

The landscape design was planned by Chauncey Beadle of *Biltmore Estate. It was the first Asheville suburb, and one of the first in the state, to move from the grid plan to the Olmsted-influenced curvilinear scheme. The Grove Park entrance at **Gertrude Place** and **Charlotte St.** is a curved green space with stone benches and stone gateway with tile roof.

Grove advertised that the suburb would have dwellings "modern and artistic in the highest degree." Distributed throughout the neighborhood are examples of Tudor Revival, Bungalow, and Colonial Revival styles.

BN 49 *Oates House*

Comprising several blocks flanking Charlotte St., the neighborhood remains stable and sought-after.

The most striking of several R. S. Smith works is the beautifully proportioned and detailed **Oates House** (1913; Smith & Carrier, architects; 90 Gertrude Pl.). The crisp and sophisticated design in Smith's English-derived Craftsman style has broad intersecting gables with deep overhangs shading bands of leaded windows. Walls are stuccoed over in fireproof, concrete construction. It was built for J. Rush and Dora Blanton Oates; he was a vice-president of the Central Bank, for which Smith had previously designed the reinforced concrete *Legal Building downtown.

Smith & Carrier also designed a variety of other houses in the neighborhood as well as the small **E. W. Grove Office** (ca. 1912; 324 Charlotte St.), a 1-story stone structure with tile roof and leaded windows.

Neoclassical and Colonial Revival styles, though not exerting the dominance in Asheville they had in many N.C. cities, are well represented. The symmetrical Colonial Revival style **Reuben Robertson House** (ca. 1922; James Gamble Rogers [New York], architect; 1 Evelyn Place) was designed by a noted New York architect for the president of the *Champion Fibre Co. of Canton, one of the region's largest businesses. The restrained Colonial Revival style also appears in the **William Jennings Bryan House** (ca. 1917; Smith & Carrier, architects; 107 Evelyn Place), which was built for the famous political figure as a retirement "cottage" after several visits to Asheville, but Bryan sold the house in 1920 after moving to Florida for his wife's health.

Part of the neighborhood had been developed as Proximity Park before E. W. Grove acquired it for Grove Park. Similar houses were built along its streets. Predating Grove's acquisition of Proximity Park is the big, exuberant Southern Colonial Revival style **Carl V. Reynolds House (Albemarle Inn)** (1909; J. M. Westall, builder; 86 Edgemont Rd.; B&B). It was built for a prominent physician and public health leader and educator who sold much of the land to Grove. He sold this house in 1920 and built one of the first residences in *Biltmore Forest. After serving as a school, the house became the Albemarle Inn, a rooming house, with its most famous resident being Hungarian composer Béla Bartók, who wrote his *Asheville Concerto* here in 1943.

BN 50 St. Mary's Episcopal Church
1914; Smith & Carrier, architects; 337 Charlotte St.

The small Gothic Revival church, built of red brick with stone trim, is a rare if not unique example of Anglo-Catholic architecture in the state. Architect Smith, a member of the vestry, drew on English parish church traditions for its design, with its gabled porch opening into the south side of the nave, and a cruciform plan. The building was intended as a lady chapel, but the larger church was never built.

The parish was founded by the Reverend Charles M. Hall, who had come to Asheville for his health, served briefly as rector of *Trinity Episcopal Church, and soon organized an Anglo-Catholic parish, which, as he explained in the local newspaper, was to be the "exponent of the Principles of the Oxford Movement or Catholic Revival" within the Anglican Church. Such elements as the statues of Jesus and Mary in exterior wall niches and the richly finished interior with its rood screen with crucifixion figures reflect the Anglo-Catholic tradition. The landscape design was provided by Chauncey Beadle of *Biltmore.

BN 51 Sunset Terrace
Ca. 1913–17; Sunset Terrace

Tucked into the slope near the *Grove Park Inn, a series of intensely quaint frame cottages create a picturesque enclave. Variously treated with half-timbering, shingles, and Swiss chalet details, they were built for Rose Mary Byrne and named "Rose Mary," "Primrose," "Rambler," and so on.

BN 52 Longchamps Apartment Building
Ca. 1925; Ronald Greene (Asheville), architect; 185 Macon Ave.

An exotic member of the city's boom-era romantic fantasies, the theatrical 6-story structure combines Chateauesque and Tudoresque elements. With its back to the mountainside, the building is a stage-set-like facade, with a base of stone, a multicolored slate mansard roof, stuccoed end pavilions, and a central frontage of towers, applied half-timbering, brick, slate, and checkering. It accentuates the steep ascent to the *Grove Park Inn.

BN 53 Grove Park Inn

1913; Fred L. Seely, designer; Oscar Mills, engineer and supervisor; Roycrofters, furnishings and fittings; Macon Ave.; expanded late 20th c.

Surely the most architecturally interesting hotel in the state, the Grove Park Inn was the special creation of E. W. Grove. Located on the slope of Sunset Mountain, the great stone building epitomizes the region's use of naturalistic materials and organic forms in the spirit of the Arts and Crafts movement. Inspired by the new Grand Canyon hotel (1911) in Yellowstone Park, developer Grove set out to build a rustic mountain hotel of natural, native stone and timber.

As shown in Bruce Johnson's research, Grove obtained proposals from leading local architects and others from New York, Philadelphia, Los Angeles, and elsewhere. After these failed to satisfy him, in the spring of 1912 Grove turned to prominent New York architect Henry Ives Cobb, who was experienced in working with massive natural stonework in his native Massachusetts. There was extensive consultation on the design with Cobb, and it is not known how much of the final concept is his. Grove gave management of the project to his son-in-law Fred Seely, who broke off relations with Cobb and took over design as well as construction. The simple, massive design incorporates native uncut granite boulders from the mountain, many with moss in place, laid over a reinforced concrete frame. Windows peep from beneath huge boulder lintels surmounted by rough flat arches, and rows of dormers rise from the undulating red clay tile roof.

The interior stone and woodwork, as well as Craftsman style furnishings and lamps by the Roycrofters, the noted Arts and Crafts firm of New York State, continue the rustic grandeur. The big lobby retains its cavernous fireplaces and the elevator that rises in the stone chimney. The guest rooms in the historic section retain Craftsman style fittings, built-in storage pieces, and other furniture made for the hotel, some pieces by the Roycrofters, others by the White Furni-

BN 53 *Grove Park Inn, early 20th c.*

ture Co. of Mebane, N.C. Host to a parade of famous visitors—Thomas A. Edison, Harvey Firestone, and Henry Ford in the early days—the hotel continues to operate as a luxury establishment.

Despite the overbearing late 20th-c. annexes and some interior reworking, it is a grand period piece, and the Sunset Terrace, off the lobby, still offers a spectacular view of the city. (See Bruce E. Johnson, "Built without an Architect: Architectural Inspirations for the Grove Park Inn," in Brunk, ed., *May We All Remember Well* [1997].) (See Introduction, Fig. 48.)

BN 54 Biltmore Industries Complex
*1917; Grovewood Rd., adjacent to
Grove Park Inn*

In 1917 Edith Vanderbilt sold to Fred Seely the handicrafts operation she had sponsored at *Biltmore Village in 1901. Seely reestablished it next to his *Grove Park Inn in a complex of pebbledash, cottage-like shops built to complement the inn's naturalistic architecture.

BN 55 Claxton School
*1922–25; Ronald Greene (Asheville), architect;
241 Merrimon Ave.*

Contemporaneous with his medieval skyscraper the *Jackson Building downtown, architect Ronald Greene employed a classical vocabulary for this suburban school. Fitting its corner site, the 3-story school has a keystone-shaped central entrance block from which wings angle back along the intersecting streets. Cast-concrete veneer over hollow tile is crafted to resemble stone blocks and enriched with pilasters and columns at the entrance bay. The elementary school for "north Asheville" was built to accommodate the city's rapid growth but was filled to capacity upon opening and soon expanded.

BN 56 Merrimon Ave. Fire Station
*Ca. 1927; Douglas D. Ellington, architect;
300 Merrimon Ave.*

The blocky composition is rendered in a soft, rosy brick and enriched with stylized Art Deco motifs, including architect Ellington's favored feather motif. Above the twin arched openings for fire trucks, a small balcony softens the facade. A tall hose-drying tower rises at the rear corner.

BN 57 Grace Episcopal Church
*1905–7; Richard Sharp Smith, architect;
871 Merrimon Ave.*

The small church of rough native stone exemplifies the Early English Gothic Revival style, with simple lancet openings, cruciform plan, and sturdy side tower containing the entrance. The congregation began as a rural mission founded after the Civil War from *Trinity Episcopal Church in Asheville and met for years in a small wooden chapel. The design for the stone church was provided in 1905 by Smith, who brought to Asheville his mastery of a range of English-inspired styles; in 1906 he formed the partnership of Smith & Carrier, which continued until 1924. Within a few years, suburbs such as Lakeview grew up as neighbors to the once-rural church.

BN 58 Lakeview Park
*1920s; John Nolen, planner;
Donald Ross, golf course designer*

Lakeview Park was Asheville's second "residence park" laid out around a golf course designed by the famed Donald Ross; *Biltmore Forest was the other. The nationally known city planner John Nolen, whose 1911 design for Myers Park in Charlotte was one of the state's first curvilinear suburbs, plotted Lakeview's tree-lined streets, which follow the undulating terrain around Beaver Lake. Developers sold lots readily during the early 1920s, but the real estate slowdown of 1926 cooled sales. Still, about 100 residences were built before the stock market crash of 1929. The suburb was built on the soft credit that underlay so much of Asheville's 1920s boom, and many residents lost their property. Hence there is a visible divide between the 1920s boom houses and the renewed construction after World War II.

Prominent from the first phase are elaborate Colonial Revival and Tudor Revival style houses on the "view lots" on Stratford Rd. **Stratford Towers** (1925; 193 Stratford Rd.) is an English manorial pile in brick and stone—built for Wallace Davis, president of the Central Bank and Trust Co., which had provided many Lakeview mortgages and closed in November 1930. The **Campbell House** (ca. 1925; 144 Marlborough Rd.) is a Spanish Colonial Revival concoction with courtyard, built for a partner of developer L. B. Jackson. The eclectic tastes that flowered in such neighborhoods inspired a local newspaper writer to observe in 1926, "They are building so much that they can play at it . . . decide one morning that what they want is a Mexican adobe house, and remember the next morning that it is not that at all—what they really want is a medieval German castle."

BN 59 Dr. Sprinza Weizenblatt House

1940–41; Marcel Breuer, architect; Anthony Lord, supervising architect; 46 Marlborough Rd.; private, visible from street

A quietly monumental work in the International style is set modestly among the trees in the otherwise typically eclectic revival style neighborhood. Dr. Sprinza Weizenblatt, a Viennese ophthalmologist, settled in Asheville in the 1930s. Through connections with activities at *Black Mountain College, she made the acquaintance of the great modernist architect Marcel Breuer, who with Walter Gropius had designed a complex for the college, which was never built. Dr. Weizenblatt asked Breuer to design her residence, a duplex set into the slope of the hill. Anthony Lord of Asheville served as supervising architect.

BN 59 *Dr. Sprinza Weizenblatt House*

Breuer's straightforward and pristine design combines massive blocks of rough native stone with broad, clean bands of stone and glass; the house is oriented to provide privacy from the street, with views of the woods that slope down to the rear. The carefully preserved dwelling is an early statement of the modernist regionalism that gained wider use after World War II.

BN 60 Reynolds House

Ca. 1846, ca. 1905; 100 Reynolds Heights, B&B

The house atop its hill began as a 2-story brick, double-pile structure and probably had a hip roof—one of the largest antebellum residences in the Asheville area. An early 20th-c. remodeling added a mansard roof and a wraparound porch.

South of downtown

BN 61 Kenilworth

Located on the southern end of Beaucatcher Mountain, the boom-era residential development with a lake and curving streets is named for the great Kenilworth Hotel (1891) that once stood nearby and evoked romantic associations with Sir Walter Scott. Started by James Madison Chiles in 1912, the neighborhood was developed through the early and mid-1920s by his Kenilworth Development Co. and annexed by the city in 1929. The city's favored Tudor and other "English cottage" style houses dominate the neighborhood, as seen, for example, at 287 and 309 Kenilworth Rd. and 23–29 Normandy Rd. At the southern end there are some Bungalow and Prairie style houses, such as 107 Kenilworth Rd.

Indicative of the diverse influences in the suburb are the pole log buildings erected as the **Kenilworth Town Hall and Jail** (ca. 1916; 2 Caledonia Rd.); the massive, richly detailed Spanish Colonial style **James Madison Chiles House** (1922–26; 21 Chiles Ave.), built for the development's chief investor; and two fine Chinese-style bungalows (ca. 1920) at 63 Caledonia Rd. and 8 Bowling Park, each with striking, curvilinear detail.

BN 61 *Annie Reed House*

Unusual in the neighborhood and indeed the city is a notable International style house, the **Annie Reed House** (1948; Ronald Greene, architect; 68 Kenilworth Rd.), with clean-lined, rectilinear forms in a quietly asymmetrical composition.

BN 62 Appalachian Hall (former Kenilworth Inn)
1918; Caledonia Rd.

The massive steel-framed building, stuccoed over hollow tile, displays the era's popular Tudor Revival tone in its applied brick quoining and some applied half-timbering. The hotel for 500 guests was built to replace the original 1891 Kenilworth Inn, a concoction of Tudor and other motifs, destroyed by fire in 1909. Since 1931 it has been a private psychiatric hospital.

BN 63 Cedar Crest (William E. Breese Sr. House)
1891; Charles B. Leonard, attributed builder; 674 Biltmore Ave.; B&B

A picturesque, opulent survivor from Asheville's 1890s boom period, the steeply gabled Queen Anne style dwelling features a prominent turret, side and rear porches, and interior woodwork of remarkable elaboration. Breese was a Charleston native who founded the First National Bank of Asheville in 1885. The house later served as a tubercular sanitarium and tourist home.

BN 64 Asheville High School
1929; Douglas D. Ellington, architect; Palmer-Spivey Construction Co., contractors; 419 McDowell St.

Beautifully integrated into its terraced site, the high school displays architect Ellington's blending of Art Deco and Italian Renaissance elements. It is rendered in warm pink stone, chiefly granite from Salisbury, N.C.; the roof is of Ludowici-Celadon tile. The focus of the Y-shaped building is a central rotunda rising through stepped forms to a dramatic ogee roof. Its entrance loggia is approached by a stepped walkway. Three long wings, for classrooms and the auditorium, radiate from the rotunda and lead to additional wings. Consulting on its planning was Dr. Nickolaus Englehardt of Columbia University, public education expert and author of *School Building Program for Cities*. The million-dollar school was intended to be a model facility in its design, quality of materials, and execution, as well as its extensive curriculum in both academic and vocational education.

BN 64 *Asheville High School*

BN 65 Fernihurst

Ca. 1875, 1930s; Henry I. Gaines (Asheville), architect; 279 Victoria Rd.

The villa-style residence stands on a hilltop overlooking the confluence of the Swannanoa and French Broad rivers. Built for Col. John Kerry Connally, it is a rare survivor from the era between the Civil War and the arrival of the railroad. The 2-story brick house features a pedimented central pavilion, arched windows, and a Palladian motif entrance. In the 1930s Mr. and Mrs. John F. Curran employed architect Henry I. Gaines to design Colonial Revival style renovations, including the Tuscan-columned porch that bows at the entrance. Associated with the house are important 19th-c. outbuildings, including a brick structure said to have been a slave house at the nearby *Smith-McDowell House, and a brick carriage house built for Connally. Now part of Asheville-Buncombe Technical Community College.

BN 66 Smith-McDowell House

Ca. 1848; 283 Victoria Rd.;
open regular hours

A rare example of substantial antebellum architecture in the region, the 2-story, double-pile, Flemish-bond brick house has a 2-tier porch engaged beneath an extension of its main gable roof—a feature characteristic of the coastal plain that is seen often in this section of the mountains and thought to reflect South Carolina low-country influences. The first floor received a ca. 1915 Neoclassical remodeling, but Greek Revival woodwork survives on the second floor. The house was constructed for James McConnell Smith, an early entrepreneur and one of the wealthiest and most influential men in antebellum Asheville. Acquired by Asheville-Buncombe Technical Community College, it was leased and restored by the Western N.C. Historical Association.

Riverside Industrial Area:
When the WNCRR extended along the floodplain of the French Broad River, industrial development soon followed. Late 19th-c. factories

made this one of the region's principal industrial zones, complementing an extensive rail yard. Although much has been lost, including the many buildings that were destroyed by the flood of 1916, and the Asheville Cotton Mill lost to fire in 1995, this sector still conveys the importance and variety of the industries that, along with tourism, fueled city growth. The rail yard is, with that in Canton, the most extensive in western N.C. The following are but a few of the many important industrial buildings in this area.

BN 67 Southern Railway Freight Depot

1927; 33 Meadow Rd.

The long, 2-story brick building housed offices and warehouses, with loading docks by the tracks. The public image of the building is emphasized by limestone trim and pilasters carrying an entablature. Southern, which took over many of the region's rail lines in the 1890s, rebuilt extensively in the early 20th c.

BN 68 Southern Railway Roundhouse

1926; E side Meadow Rd.,
just E of Carrier Bridge

The 25-bay roundhouse is among the state's few surviving railroad roundhouses; that at Spencer Shops near Salisbury is the largest. Built as roughly a quarter of a circle, the structure of concrete, hollow tile, and brick served the large rail yard that became central to Asheville's economy.

BN 69 *Hans Rees Tannery*

BN 69 Hans Rees Tannery

Ca. 1900; 191 Lyman St.

Of the tanneries that once flourished in western N.C., this is among the very few of which the principal buildings still stand. This impressive series of brick buildings represents the business that was once among the largest tanneries in the nation. The largest building is a long, 2-story brick structure with arched windows and stepped end gables and firewalls. There are several other buildings of brick, frame, and metal associated with the operation. Various enterprises now occupy the buildings.

BN 70 Carolina Coal and Ice Company
Ca. 1910; Lyman St. at Riverside Dr.

The 2-story brick building rests on a stone foundation and has parapeted end walls and segmental-arched windows. It housed the coal and ice company, a type of joint enterprise usually located beside the tracks. Nearby, on W. Haywood St. at Riverside Dr., stands the burned hulk of the former Asheville Cotton Mills (ca. 1890), along with surviving smokestacks.

BN 71 Depot Street
Early 20th c.

With its name indicating its ties to railroad business, this once-thriving commercial street is lined by 1- and 2-story brick buildings that housed stores, hotels, and small industries in the early 20th-c. railroad heyday.

BN 72 Biltmore Estate
1889–95; Frederick Law Olmsted, landscape architect; Richard Morris Hunt and Richard Howland Hunt, architects; Richard Sharp Smith, supervising architect; entrance US 25 at Lodge St.; National Historic Landmark; open regular hours

This extraordinary place, visited by more than 850,000 people annually, displays the glorious accomplishment of two of America's greatest 19th-c. designers, Frederick Law Olmsted and Richard Morris Hunt. Presented by their young client George Washington Vanderbilt with the opportunity to "design almost without limitations on expenditure" in a vast and challenging natural setting, these two deans of their profession created an American palace. In a richly complex expression of the era, the Gilded Age chateau was equipped with every modern convenience and framed by a formal French garden amid a naturalistic English park, with a manorial village at its gates and, extending into the mountains beyond, some 125,000 acres of forests encompassing a nationally influential scientific forestry program. Still in family hands, the 8,000-acre core of the estate has been meticulously maintained and managed for public visitation, while commercial and other development has accrued on all sides. A prime view, showing the dramatic outline of the chateau against the distant mountain silhouettes, is from the "vista" at the top of the grassy slope above the rampe douce. From here at sunset the hazy blues of roof and mountains merge. (See Introduction, Fig. 4.)

BACKGROUND

George Vanderbilt visited Asheville with his mother and was captivated by a spot overlooking the French Broad River with views of Mount Pisgah. He determined to build a country retreat there. The youngest son of railroad magnate William Henry Vanderbilt, George took little interest in business but had a scholarly and artistic bent. From his father and his grandfather, Commodore Cornelius Vanderbilt, he had inherited some $10 million. His elder siblings had already built lavish residences with their legacies, but as a bachelor George had remained at home. In 1888 he began through an agent to purchase farms in the area, and he began consultation with Olmsted and Hunt to develop plans. He would devote much of his fortune to the creation of the Biltmore Estate.

LANDSCAPE

In 1888 Vanderbilt requested Frederick Law Olmsted, the nation's leading landscape architect, to inspect the property and advise him on its development. Olmsted found the land in deplorable condition. He suggested a park near the house, plus farms and extensive forests. Improvement and management of the forest lands, he said, would be, "a suitable and dignified business for you to engage in," a good long-term investment and a

BN 72 *Biltmore House, Esplanade, and Italian Garden from Ramp Douce*

valuable model for the nation, which had no systematic forestry programs. Vanderbilt employed Olmsted to oversee development of the estate, which by 1891 comprised 6,000 acres. To begin the conversion of cutover farmland into a wooded estate and gardens, Olmsted established a nursery and employed Canadian-trained horticulturalist Chauncey Beadle as its supervisor.

Also at Olmsted's suggestion Vanderbilt hired Gifford Pinchot to direct the forestry program. Son of a wealthy Pennsylvania family and friend of Olmsted and Hunt, the French-trained Pinchot began as Biltmore forester in 1892. Under his guidance Vanderbilt enlarged the estate to some 125,000 acres, of which some 80,000 acres are now in Pisgah National Forest. Pinchot's successor, Carl Schenck, established in 1898 the Biltmore Forest School, now commemorated at the *Cradle of Forestry (Transylvania Co.).

At the estate, Olmsted created a masterpiece of landscape design. From the entrance gate the approach drive winds 3 miles through the naturalistic 250-acre park, punctuated by artfully arranged views and changes in topography. Deer parks and farmlands are interspersed with woodlands. In a sharp transition that Olmsted insisted on, the drive opens suddenly into the formal gardens immediately framing the house. Evidently at Hunt's suggestion, these were modeled after gardens at the Vaux Le Vicomte near Paris. As at that chateau, the house overlooks a level esplanade, from which rises the low *ramp douce* that leads to the long, upward-sloping greensward, to the hilltop "vista"—allowing a suspenseful walk up to the little temple with its view of the house set against faraway peaks. The plateau for the esplanade and chateau was laboriously cut and filled from the steep hillside. The chateau stands at the west edge of the plateau atop the massive stone retaining wall, a vantage from which it overlooks the deer park and river below and commands a magnificent view of Mount Pisgah in the western distance. Terraced gardens southeast of the house include the Italian garden and the walled garden that slopes down to the conservatory, shielded from cold winds.

ARCHITECTURE

At the same time, Vanderbilt commissioned Richard Morris Hunt to design the estate buildings, with suggestions on siting from Olmsted. Hunt had previously designed other Vanderbilt houses, including William K. Vanderbilt's Fifth Avenue mansion. In 1889 architect and client traveled in Europe together for inspiration. Plans evolved quickly from a country lodge to a chateau, apparently at the behest of Hunt, who according to his biographer Paul Baker, "urged him to build on a scale commensurate with the size of the holdings and the natural features of the property." Vanderbilt acquired furnishings and architectural elements in Europe. Hunt produced and revised designs in 1889.

Construction began late in 1889 and continued until 1895. As many as 500 workers were employed in building the house and preparing the gardens, endeavors that proceeded simultaneously. A 3.2-mile rail spur was built to the estate to transport materials, which included immense quantities of steel for the frame of the house, Indiana limestone for its walls, marble from Italy, and endless supplies of machinery, fittings, and equipment for its central heating, electric lights, and elevators. Special tiles were supplied by Spanish engineer and architect Rafael Guastavino, whose unique system for building cohesive, self-supporting tile ceiling vaults was used at Biltmore. Bricks were made in kilns in the village. Throughout the planning and construction, Hunt and Olmsted collaborated, as they did while planning for the 1893 World's Columbian Exposition in Chicago.

As at other Vanderbilt mansions, Hunt drew upon the architecture of the 16th-c. French Renaissance. For Biltmore he adapted ideas from the great François I chateaux of the Loire, Chambord, Chenonceau, and Blois, which Hunt and Vanderbilt had seen during their 1889 journey. The great stair of the entrance facade is modeled on that at Blois, though it spirals in the opposite direction. The mass of the chateau shares something of the drama of Chambord. The asymmetrical but balanced composition, dominated by its dramatically peaked and

BN 72 *Biltmore House, view from west*

turreted roof, is unified by its serene and subtle coloration, the pale limestone of the walls and the gray-blue and green of the slate and copper roof, in hues that warm and cool with changing light.

In contrast to the uniformity of the exterior, the interior displays the diversity as well as the stunning opulence characteristic of Hunt's great houses. The house contains 250 rooms and 4 acres of floor space. A series of octagonal, elliptical, square, and rectangular rooms flows through the principal floor. The entrance hall is flanked by a soaring spiral stair and a glass-roofed winter garden that brings sunlight into the heart of the house. The corridor around the winter garden is one of several spaces with domes and ceiling vaulted with Rafael Guastavino's self-supporting, Catalan tile.

The 90-foot-long tapestry gallery evokes English country house practice, while the long loggia beside it, with a fine view to the west, reflects the period's concern for exposure to sunshine and fresh air also seen in health facilities. The south terrace that extends from the library was a compromise between Hunt and Olmsted, who wanted the house to have a porch or other open-air living space with a view of the mountains.

Vanderbilt's favorite room was the walnut-paneled library in Baroque style, complete with a Pellegrini ceiling painting aswirl with nymphs and clouds. The grandest room is the banquet hall, a medieval conceit with ribbed ceiling 70 feet high and Wagnerian opera figures carved by Karl Bitter. In the bachelor's wing on the north end, a billiard room was the nucleus of a male domain—which also included a smoking room and a gun room—that served as a retreat for Vanderbilt and his friends.

The second and third floors contain sitting rooms, bedchambers, and fabulous bathrooms that repeat the aura of luxury. The fourth floor comprises female servants' quarters plus an observatory. The basement contains a warren of kitchens, pantries, laundries, servants' quarters, and other service rooms rationally organized to dispense hospitality on a heroic scale. Here, too, is a bowling alley and, the *ne plus ultra* of the day, a white-tiled indoor swimming pool—

evidently another use of Guastavino's tile. The subbasement is the heart of technology, with original heating and power equipment, a gas-powered electric generator, a refrigeration plant, and a mammoth ice-maker. Adjoining the house, the matching stables lie beyond a paved courtyard and retain the horse stalls and facilities to house as many as 25 horses and 20 carriages.

Most of the farm buildings were erected within a few years after R. M. Hunt's death in 1895, with plans and supervision carried out by his son, Richard Howland Hunt, or by supervising architect Richard Sharp Smith. In contrast to the stone residence, the estate buildings are rendered primarily in red brick and pebbledash or roughcast stucco, a vocabulary introduced by R. M. Hunt and continued by R. H. Hunt and Smith. The steep-roofed **Lodge Gate**, completed in 1899 by R. H. Hunt after his father's death, epitomizes this mode, with its red brick quoins, arched opening, and high, tiled roof with steep dormers; the ceiling is of Guastavino's self-supporting tile. The **Conservatory** (R. M. Hunt; rebuilt 1957; under restoration) repeats the style with large, arched windows and a glass roof. The **Truck Farmer's Cottage** (1896), likewise completed under R. H. Hunt, is a simpler rendition of the estate style, in pebbledash and red brick, with extended barns outlining a farm courtyard in European fashion. Other farm buildings in the estate mode include the former **Dairy** (R. H. Hunt), a complex that now houses the winery, and **Mule Stable** (R. S. Smith), now a restaurant.

LIFE AT BILTMORE

The house was completed in 1895. In the second-floor living hall of Biltmore House hang John Singer Sargent's full-length portraits of Hunt and Olmsted at Biltmore, which were commissioned by Vanderbilt as the house neared completion. In May 1895 Vanderbilt arranged a house party, and he, Richard Morris and Catherine Hunt, and Sargent came down on Vanderbilt's railway car for the portrait sessions. Olmsted was already at the estate. The portraits, memorializing the completion of the two giants' last great works, also captured a moment nearer

BN 72 *Truck Farmer's Cottage and Farm Building*

the end than anyone anticipated. Olmsted's rapidly failing health and memory forced him to leave Biltmore after only a few sittings and to relinquish operation of his firm to his sons, John and Frederick Jr.; the latter also stood in for completion of the portrait. Olmsted's departure proved to be his departure from a long career. Hunt and his wife enjoyed the visit, but Sargent's keen eye caught a gaunt aspect that proved prophetic. In July, after two years of bad health, Hunt suddenly became gravely ill and died on July 31, within weeks of leaving Biltmore. His son, Richard Howland Hunt, continued the project, and Olmsted's sons carried out the landscape plans. The great house was completed by the end of the year, and on Christmas Eve, Vanderbilt held a grand party that drew guests from far and wide.

George Vanderbilt married Edith Stuyvesant Dresser in 1898, and the couple used Biltmore as their principal home, employing a staff of as many as 50 domestic servants and stable hands and several hundred other estate workers including farmers and foresters. Edith Vanderbilt took special interest in community improvement projects, including creation of *Biltmore Industries to teach handicraft skills, and later she was the first woman president of the N.C. Agricultural Society. After George died unexpectedly in 1914, Edith remained at Biltmore for a time and continued work in the community. In 1915 she sold nearly 87,000 acres to the federal government as part of Pisgah National Forest, and she sold Biltmore Indus-

tries in 1917, *Biltmore Village in 1921, and the land that became the suburban community of *Biltmore Forest in 1920. In 1924 the Vanderbilts' only child, Cornelia, married John Cecil; Edith moved to a new house in Biltmore Forest; and the young couple made their home at Biltmore. At the request of city leaders striving to revitalize tourism, in 1930 the Cecils first opened the house to the public. Under the careful stewardship of the Cecil family, the 8,000-acre estate has thrived as a tourist attraction and productive forest, dairy farm, and more recently, a winery.

Biltmore Estate had a multifaceted and lasting impact on Asheville and the region. In architectural terms, it established a model of romantic, European grandeur to complement the mountain setting. Its supervising architect, Richard Sharp Smith, remained in Asheville and established a distinguished and prolific regional practice. Rafael Guastavino, the Spaniard who came to execute the tilework, likewise stayed in the area and built the *Basilica of St. Lawrence. Several artisans employed at Biltmore also remained in the area, including stonecarver Fred Miles, best known for the *Drhumor Building. Biltmore foresters Gifford Pinchot and Carl Schenck became nationally influential leaders in the nascent forestry movement. And Chauncey Beadle, who came with Olmsted, remained at Biltmore for 60 years as estate superintendent and provided landscape designs in the Olmsted style during Asheville's early 20th-c. boom era.

See John M. Bryan, *G. W. Vanderbilt's*

Biltmore Estate (1994); Paul R. Baker, *Richard Morris Hunt* (1980); Susan R. Stein, ed., *The Architecture of Richard Morris Hunt* (1986); and Elizabeth Stevenson, *Park Maker: A Life of Frederick Law Olmsted* (1977).

Note: Biltmore offers a dizzying wealth of opportunities to study architecture, decorative arts, and elite domestic arrangements—regular tours, behind the scenes, and now rooftop walks—as well as gardens and landscapes that change seasonally. For anyone but the brief one-time sojourner, a year's pass makes sense.

BN 73 Biltmore Village

1889–1910; Frederick Law Olmsted, landscape designer; Richard Morris Hunt, Richard Howland Hunt, and Richard Sharp Smith, architects; area bounded by All Souls Crescent, Lodge St., and Brook St.

When George Washington Vanderbilt began assembling his Biltmore Estate, he planned a picturesque manorial village both as an ornament in the tableau of buildings and grounds and as a practical solution to the problem of housing estate workers. Vanderbilt bought the railroad village of Best, or Asheville Junction, relocated the residents, and had Olmsted, Hunt, and Smith plan Biltmore, N.C., as a model village along with the rest of the estate. By 1896 the streets were laid out in a fan-shaped plan around an axial street linking Hunt's *All Souls Church and Railroad Depot, and these structures, along with the parish house, rectory, and estate office, were completed. Other buildings including the dwellings were added until about 1910. The predominant style of building employed rough pebbledash walls, red brick, and Tudoresque half-timbering to create a picturesque ensemble, generally English in feeling and related to the estate buildings. Some of the later buildings are red brick in Colonial Revival modes.

Richard Morris Hunt set the tone with the principal structures. After his death in 1895, his son Richard Howland Hunt and architect Richard Sharp Smith continued the work. R. M. Hunt's **Railroad Depot** is a pebbledash, half-timbered and brick building with a deep, hipped roof carried on hefty brackets. His **Biltmore Estate Office Building**, a 1½-story structure, has a dormered, hipped roof sheltering an engaged porch; its stuccoed walls, designated on Hunt's 1894 drawing as "rough stucco," lack the pebbles seen in the "roughcast" or pebbledash buildings. The cottages, which continued to be built into the early 20th c., were individually designed by Smith for Vanderbilt, with pebbledash walls, Tudor details, and myriad plans and roof forms.

In addition to dwellings for estate workers and other residents, the village held a post office, hospital, shops, and other facili-

BN 73 *Biltmore Village*

ties. Classes for the Biltmore Forest School (see *Cradle of Forestry) were held here as well as in the field at Pisgah Forest. Eleanor Vance, an artist who rented a cottage in the summer of 1900, and Charlotte Yale began a boys' woodcarving class, affiliated with All Souls Church; the endeavor attracted the interest of Edith Vanderbilt and under her sponsorship developed into *Biltmore Industries, producing homespun and other crafts.

Within a few years after George Vanderbilt's death in 1914 the village was sold. The mid-20th c. saw several changes that detracted from the village quality, particularly the intrusion of franchise restaurants and other roadside businesses. In the late 20th c. the village has undergone a spirited rejuvenation, which has restored much of its original architectural flavor; especially intact sections survive along All Souls Crescent and Boston Way.

BN 74 All Souls Episcopal Cathedral
1895; Richard Morris Hunt, architect;
All Souls Crescent

The powerfully composed and beautifully detailed church was one of Richard Morris Hunt's last works before his death in 1895. Built as the centerpiece of Biltmore Village by George Vanderbilt, the small Romanesque Revival church exemplifies Hunt's idea that the short-naved Greek cross offered a better church plan than the more usual, long-naved Latin cross, for it allowed all the congregation to see and hear the service. In this compact and dramatic church, with its massive, square tower rising at the crossing, the short nave, the transepts, and the boldly curving apse gain equal prominence. As in other estate buildings, Hunt combined dark, rough pebbledash surfaces with rich red brick quoins and buttresses, while red tile dramatizes the flowing form of the conical apse roof and the peaks of the wings and tower. Considered by many the most beautiful church in the state when built, All Souls has been carefully maintained inside and out. Complementing the natural masonry walls and naturally finished wood furnishings are fine stained glass windows. Continuing as a parish church after Vanderbilt's

BN 74 *All Souls Episcopal Cathedral*

death, All Souls was designated the cathedral of the Western N.C. Episcopal Diocese in 1995.

BN 75 Samuel Harrison Reed House
1892; 119 Dodge St.; B&B

The big Queen Anne style house, once the center of a large estate, was built for Reed, whose father had developed the railroad village of Best. The family sold more than 1,000 acres to Vanderbilt for Biltmore, and Best was transformed into *Biltmore Village. Samuel prospered as a lawyer and hotel owner and built his fashionable residence on Reed Hill overlooking the estate village.

BN 76 Biltmore Forest
1920; Chauncey Beadle, landscape designer;
Donald Ross, golf course designer

Six years after George Vanderbilt's death in 1914, his widow, Edith, sold 1,500 acres of the estate to the Biltmore Estate Co. for the purpose of developing "a community where persons of moderate means could build homes that would embody on a smaller scale the same ideals that had actuated Mr. Vanderbilt." Prominent among the developers was Thomas Wadley Raoul, who sold his interest in the *Manor and Albemarle Park to focus on the new undertaking. The Biltmore Estate Co. promised that lots would be at least 2 acres, and as the local newspaper explained in 1920, "the idea is to throw restrictions around the property so that wealthy people from all sections of the country will be attracted here where they can purchase land and develop their own estates." The

area was promoted as "a sanctuary for the retired businessman and the active leaders of
the professions and of industry who wish to
escape in their homes from the tumult, un-
sightliness, and neurotic life of the modern
city."

Biltmore landscape architect Chauncey
Beadle, formerly associated with Olmsted
Brothers of Boston, assisted with the planning of the new community. Donald Ross,
the celebrated golf course designer best
known for his work at Pinehurst, designed
the central golf course. Baltimore architect
Edward L. Palmer Jr. designed the "quaint
chateau" style clubhouse. Picturesque French
Provincial style cottages by architect William Dodge formed a municipal and commercial cluster on Vanderbilt Rd. After her
daughter, Cornelia, married John Cecil and
moved into Biltmore, Edith Vanderbilt
moved into a "restrained Spanish" style house
called **The Frith** (1925; Bruce Kitchell [West
Palm Beach], architect; Frith Dr.).

Around the golf course, the original directors of the Biltmore Estate Co. built some
of the suburb's finest residences in Tudor
and French themes that subtly referred to
Biltmore. The **Judge Junius Adams House**
(1921; 11 Stuyvesant Rd.) is an especially fine,
half-timbered Tudor Revival residence, built
for a founder of the development company.
Another founder built the **William Knight
House** (1925–27; William Dodge, architect;
15 E. Forest Rd.), with a high hip roof and
circular tower in a French spirit. This was
among architect Dodge's first designs in a
romantic style that established his reputation as an architect as well as a talented silversmith. Many other Asheville business and
civic leaders also moved to Biltmore Forest
and built in a variety of styles.

Several notable Colonial Revival houses
date from the 1920s, including **Gunston
Hall** (1922–23; Waddy B. Wood [Washing-
ton, D.C], architect; 324 Vanderbilt Rd.),
modeled on the colonial house in Virginia
and built as a summer home for Dr. William
B. Mason, a descendant of George Mason,
builder of the original. There are later residences of similar style and scale. Biltmore
Forest continues to be one of Asheville's and
the state's most exclusive neighborhoods.

BN 77 The Spinning Wheel

*1939; William Waldo Dodge (Asheville),
architect; 1096 Hendersonville Rd.*

Built of logs reassembled from an earlier
house, the simple, 1-story building served as
the second location of the Spinning Wheel,
the weaving school and crafts shop established by Clementine Douglas, a leader in
the revival and promotion of mountain
handicrafts. Born in Florida, Miss Douglas
studied design at the Pratt Institute in New
York, then taught art and crafts in Massachusetts and New York schools. While
spending summers (1919–21) at a settlement
school at Smith, Ky., she grew interested in
the women's weaving traditions. After studying weaving and working briefly at Wilmer
Stone's studio in Saluda, N.C., she settled
with her mother at Beaver Lake near Asheville, where she opened a weaving studio
called the Spinning Wheel in 1925. For her
salesroom she reassembled a small log house
from another site. The use of the log cabin
image, decked with traditional implements
and crafts goods, was a favorite setting for
handicrafts sales. Employing and teaching
local women to weave a variety of patterns
and items on the looms, Douglas's Spinning
Wheel developed an extensive wholesale as
well as retail trade. It was featured in *Handicrafts of the Southern Highlands,* by her longtime friend Allen Eaton. Douglas was also a
founder of the Southern Highland Handicraft Guild and the first manager of the *Allanstand shop in Asheville under its auspices.

After weathering the Great Depression,
in 1939 Douglas moved the Spinning Wheel
to a prime location on the busy Hendersons-
ville Rd., acquiring another old log house to
reassemble as the salesroom, and built a residence behind it for herself and her mother.
William Waldo Dodge, Asheville architect
and silversmith, assisted in the project. After
closing the shop when trade dropped during
World War II, Douglas reopened the Spinning Wheel briefly after the war, then sold it
to Esther Bloxton, who operated it as a gift
and craft shop until 1970. (Nearby, at 1000
Hendersonville Rd., stands another rustic
shop made from a log house, the former
Biltmore Country Market, built by the

French Broad Garden Club in 1959, also supervised by W. W. Dodge.)

BN 78 Sayles-Biltmore Bleacheries

1925–27; Robert Fuller, architect;
Earle Sumner Draper, landscape designer;
S side NC 81 (Swannanoa River Rd.),
0.1 mi. E of S. Tunnel Rd., visible on
E side I-240 0.9 mi. N of exit 8

Located in a parklike setting beside the Swannanoa River, the industrial complex was built to bleach and dye fabric from southern textile plants. The complex comprises several massive reinforced concrete buildings with multilight windows. The towering brick smokestack is a landmark visible from I-240. A stuccoed bridge over the river is embossed with a ceramic tile name plaque. Frank Sayles, president of a group of fabric-finishing operations in New England, purchased the 200-acre site but died before construction began. The plant, which employed from 500 to 700 workers, closed in 1991.

BN 79 Sayles Village

1925–27; Robert Fuller, architect;
Earle Sumner Draper, landscape
designer; E side Wood Ave., S of
NC 81 (Swannanoa River Rd.)

The collection of some sixty modest frame bungalows and cottages was built as worker housing for the nearby *Sayles-Biltmore Bleacheries. Ranging up the steep riverside slopes, repeated examples of four small house types blend Bungalow and Colonial Revival motifs, and most have porches inset within the main roof. Described by the local newspaper as "one of the most attractive subdivisions of its kind to be found anywhere," the development was planned by Draper to have "tree-lined streets loop around a well-kept knoll overlooking the plant" and "wide paved streets wind over the hills with fine landscape effect which gives each one of the homes a distinctive setting." The "industrial community" originally comprised eighty 3- to 5-bedroom dwellings. Although construction of I-240 severed the village from the plant and led to the loss of many houses, the village remains a cohesive neighborhood.

BN 80 Foster Sondley House

1902, 1905; Richard Sharp Smith, architect;
N end SR 2032 (Haw Creek Rd.), Asheville
vic.; limited access

The large, informal house with capacious porches was designed by architect Smith and rendered in rough-textured, local granite-gneiss. Sondley purchased the property for his retirement because of its rural privacy and fine views and asked his friend Smith to design a house of stone to blend with the setting. Sondley was an attorney and local historian who wrote *A History of Buncombe County* and left his large collection of books to the Pack Library.

BN 81 West Asheville

Incorporated separately as West Asheville before it was consolidated with Asheville in 1917, the area along Haywood Rd. was linked to downtown by streetcar service ca. 1914. An extensive residential neighborhood comprises a range of early 20th-c. types, especially late Queen Anne style houses and bungalows. West Asheville's compact business district concentrates in the 400 and 500 blocks of Haywood Rd. A landmark is the vivid **West Asheville Fire Station** (1922; 421 Haywood Rd.), a stylized Flemish style brick building with tall, arched central opening and curvilinear front parapet, accented with exaggerated, white stone arches and roundels.

BN 82 Richmond Hill

1890; James G. Hill (Washington, D.C.),
architect; Richmond Hill Rd., Asheville vic.;
open as hotel

The large, 2-story frame Queen Anne style house was built for congressman and diplomat Richmond Pearson and designed by Hill, former supervising architect of the U.S. Treasury. The city's last grandiose late 19th-c. frame residence, it featured various woods from the region's forests in its luxuriously appointed interior. After suffering from neglect and fire, it was rescued, moved a short distance in 1984, and restored. It has been painstakingly refurbished for use as a restaurant and hotel. (See Introduction, Fig. 67.)

BN 83 Asheville School

1900 and later; John Milton Dyer (Cleveland), Anthony Lord (Asheville), architects; Chauncey Beadle, landscape design; Asheville School Rd. at jct. of US 19/23 and I-40

The preparatory school, featuring buildings in various English-inspired modes, was founded in 1900 by Newton Mitchell Anderson and Charles Andrews Mitchell from the University School in Cleveland, who wanted to establish a boarding school in a healthy, nonurban setting. The first building, **Anderson Hall** (1900; John Milton Dyer [Cleveland], architect), drapes Eastlake-like porches across a Tudoresque building of brick and applied half-timbering. Similar Tudor motifs appear in the massive **Mitchell Hall** (1903; probably John Milton Dyer) and other buildings. **Boyd Chapel** (1928; Thomas Hibben [Indianapolis], architect) is a stone structure with a Gothic theme rendered in an Art Deco manner.

Asheville designers also shaped the campus. At Boyd Chapel the stained glass windows and altar fittings were designed and executed by William Waldo Dodge, noted Asheville architect and silversmith and a founder of Six Associates; he had come to the *Oteen Center in 1918 to recover from war injuries, learned silversmithing there, and remained in Asheville to practice his craft as well as architecture.

Crawford Music House (1937) and **Memorial Hall** (1947; Anthony Lord, architect) continue the Tudor Gothic theme in brick with casement windows and decorated gables. Lord, another leading Asheville architect with an interest in handicrafts, also ran a blacksmith shop that produced ornamental ironwork reflecting his interest in arts and crafts. He was a founding member of the Southern Highland Handicraft Guild, and his ironwork appears in Asheville School buildings as well as at the National Cathedral in Washington, D.C., and several Asheville and *Biltmore Forest residences. In the 1930s Chauncey Beadle (landscape gardener at the *Biltmore Estate who had designed *Grove Park and *Biltmore Forest), whose stepsons were students at the school, donated his services to redesign the campus landscape with curving road and evergreen trees.

BN 84 Enka

1928 and later; Lockwood, Greene, engineers; William Waldo Dodge Jr., architect; Howard Brown Swope, landscape architect; US 19/23 at NC 112 at Enka

The company town was built as a model village for the nation's largest rayon-producing factory. In 1928 the Dutch-based American Enka Co. began construction of a rayon manufacturing plant on farmland west of Asheville. (In the early 20th c., production of rayon, a synthetic silk-like fabric made from chemically processed cotton or wood pulp cellulose, had increased with improved manufacturing and marketing.) The Asheville newspaper rejoiced over the proposed $10 million plant that promised to employ 3,500 workers, and local boosters likened its impact to the establishment of *Biltmore and the *Great Smoky Mountains National Park. Enka selected the site for its pure and abundant water from Hominy Creek, essential for rayon manufacture; its rail access; and its proximity to plentiful workers away from competing industrial employers or large cities.

The firm laid a railroad spur, dammed the creek to form Enka Lake, built a large factory, and began a planned residential village. In July 1929 local women and men trained by Dutch instructors produced the factory's first rayon. With round-the-clock production, by 1933 Enka's 10 million pounds of rayon a year made it the largest rayon-producing factory in the nation.

The community plan was a Dutch version of the garden city movement, a pleasant setting meant to boost employee morale and productivity. Enka employed landscape architect Harold Brown Swope of Asheville, trained under the Olmsted firm with experience at *Biltmore Estate. Like Chauncey Beadle, another Olmsted protégé in Asheville, Swope followed the Olmsted philosophy. He designed a curvilinear scheme with discrete sectors for various functions and classes of housing from upper managers to plant workers.

The managers' houses were designed by Asheville architect William Waldo Dodge (known for his residential work at *Biltmore Forest and elsewhere). Located chiefly on Lake Drive, these are large, stylish brick houses with tile roofs, rendered in a variety of Colonial Revival and Tudor Revival modes. Lockwood, Greene Engineers, a large firm specializing in textile industry work, planned the workers' houses, 1- and 2-story dwellings in both brick and frame, with a series of types being built repeatedly. The village also had a clubhouse, a filling station, a fire station, a commercial block, and a church, plus recreational facilities and parks.

By 1930 more than 100 workers' houses had been built, a fraction of the original scheme. Presumably the Great Depression and World War II prevented completion of the plan, though the factory continued in production. Although in 1958 American Enka sold the houses to individual owners and in 1985 the firm was purchased by Badische Corp., now BASF, much of Enka's original identity persists. (See Kathryn Anne Franks, "Enka, North Carolina: New Planning in an Early Twentieth Century Southern Mill Town" [M.A. thesis, University of Georgia, 1995].)

BN 85 Leicester

The linear roadside community, named for local resident Leicester Chapman, possesses several unusually well preserved and richly detailed Victorian houses. These include the **Dr. C. K. Hughes House** (ca. 1900; Mr. Parrish, carpenter; s side NC 63, O. 1 mi. w of SR 1378), an L-plan, 2-story Queen Anne style house with a bold, geometric "tree of life" gable ornament; the **J. M. Carver House** (ca. 1911; Frank Davis, carpenter; s side NC 63 at SR 1378), a lively Queen Anne composition set on a neatly terraced site, 1½ stories with an angled plan and sweeping porch; and the **John Davis House** (early 20th c.; s side NC 63, E of SR 1620), with

raised central gable, corner tower, and columned porch.

BN 86 Camp Academy
1897; N side NC 63, 1 mi. W of Leicester

A landmark along a busy road, the large, brick building has arched windows and pedimented entrance bay behind a wraparound porch. It was built as Camp Academy, a private academy founded by Alonzo C. Reynolds, a native of nearby Sandy Mush. He later became superintendent of the county's public schools and president of Biltmore College (now UNC-Asheville) and of present-day *Western Carolina University. After the academy closed, from the 1920s the building served as a hotel and apartment house.

BN 87 Adolphus A. Reynolds House
Late 19th c.; W side SR 1608,
0.3 mi. N of NC 63, Leicester vic.;
private, visible from road

A typical I-house with 2-story ell and brick end chimneys is expanded by the region's characteristic 2-tier, engaged front porch, plus a 2-tier shed porch along the ell. The whole is adorned with ornate sawnwork.

BN 88 The Brick Church
1876; E side NC 63, 0.3 mi. NW of
SR 1608, Leicester vic.

Standing on a knoll above the road, the simple, well-proportioned brick church was built to replace an antebellum log church. At the gable front a double door beneath a timber lintel opens into a sanctuary lighted by large 6/6 windows. An open belfry caps the gable roof. The name of the church recalls the rarity of rural brick construction in the 19th c. The large cemetery stretches up the slope. Among those buried there is Bascom Lamar Lunsford, longtime collector and performer of folk song and dance, who in later life resided near Leicester.

BN 89 Sandy Mush

A gently rolling and still-bucolic rural neighborhood occupies the valley that forms a broad bowl amid high mountains. Through it runs Sandy Mush Creek, a tributary of the French Broad River. Farming families raise row crops of corn and tobacco in the bottomlands along Sandy Mush Creek and its tributaries and graze their cattle in the pastures that cover the close-cropped rounded hills and reach up the lower mountainsides. Forested upper slopes form a verdant frame against the sky, with Sandy Mush Bald rising 5,152 feet at the northwest end. White farming families settled here as early as the 1820s. By the 1850s a number had farms of several hundred acres, and some owned slaves. The oldest surviving buildings date from the mid- and late 19th c., and many were built in the early 20th c.

The architecture of Sandy Mush illustrates the prosperity and up-to-date tastes of mountain valley farmers as well as the persistence of traditional log construction. White frame churches and the principal farmhouses stand near the creeks and roads in the center of the valley or on the pillows of land at the bases of the hills. Up the smaller roads and beyond them on private paths are numerous small log houses. Throughout the valley are frame and log barns of various types, some showing typical diagonal boarding and eave vents.

Beside the road that leads from NC 63, a

BN 89 *Will Waldrop Stores*

prominent landmark is the **Chrisley Wells House** (ca. 1880; s side SR 1389, 0.1 mi. w of NC 63) (**a**), a decorated Victorian farmhouse recently restored to its former glory, with kingpost and sunburst gable ornament and decorated porch. In a gentle valley beyond, the **Joseph S. Wells House and Barn** (ca. 1910; s and N sides SR 1389, 0.5 mi. E of SR 1401) (**b**) typify the Progressive-era farmstead. The capacious frame house takes an enlarged foursquare form and has a Colonial Revival porch and a shingled second story; the big gambrel-roofed barn built into the hillside is credited to carpenter Sid Albridge. The Wells family has long been numerous and prominent in the locale. On the road along N. Turkey Creek, the **James Adolphus Gillespie House** (ca. 1860; w side SR 1389, 2.0 mi. s of SR 1401) (**c**) is a locally rare, 2-story brick house, long vacant, which still maintains a strong presence; supposedly it was left unfinished because of the Civil War.

At the foot of a hill near the center of the community, **Paynes Chapel** (1889; Will Waldrop, carpenter; NE corner SR 1392 and 1401) (**d**) was built on land given by neighbor Malinda Payne. Its straightforward, gable-fronted form is beautifully proportioned and crisply detailed; strong lintels mark long 4/4 windows and the central entrance with transom, and gable returns and a delicate kingpost ornament rise beneath a simple belfry. The nearby **Malinda Payne House** (ca. 1878 and later; Will Waldrop, carpenter; w side SR 1394, 0.2 mi. N of SR 1401) (**e**) shows the rural carpenter's adoption of picturesque forms and decorative millwork. The 1½-story frame house was built in two sections: first the right-hand portion with cen-

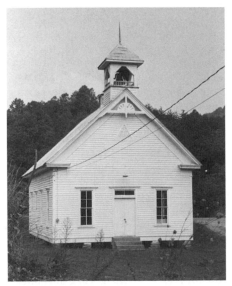

BN 89 *Paynes Chapel*

tral front roof gable, then the left-hand gabled ell with bay window. Both are enriched with lavish sawn and turned decoration.

The **Thomas Rogers House** (ca. 1912; N side SR 1392, at SR 1400) (**f**) is a 2-story frame house neatly finished with a turned porch. Builder Frank Davis is credited with this and the *J. M. Carver House in Leicester.

The ideal scene of the mountain country church is formed by the **Big Sandy Methodist Church** (1904; N side SR 1392, 0.2 mi. W of SR 1400) (**g**), standing on a hillside overlooking the bottomland. The gablefronted frame church is accentuated by a front steeple with belfry. The cemetery contains graves from as early as 1820, indicating the longevity of settlement in this area; the land for a church here was given by David Palmer in 1875. The previous frame church on the site had a brick basement where Sunday school was held, earning the name "the brick church," which some residents still apply to this building.

In the broad plain where Willow Creek joins Sandy Mush Creek, the **Will Waldrop Stores and House** (ca. 1895; E side SR 1395, just S of SR 1392) (**h**) recall the importance of country stores to rural communities. The two gable-fronted stores were built by Waldrop, a storekeeper as well as a carpenter. He built the southern, smaller one first and decorated the eaves with curving bargeboards. His house next door is a small, frame L-plan dwelling, altered over the years.

Beside Willow Creek the **John W. Wells House** (mid-19th c.; W side SR 1395, 1.1 mi. S of SR 1392) (**i**) was built for a farmer who owned 200 acres and two slaves in 1850. One of the finest antebellum houses in the county, it is a large, 2-story frame house with end chimneys, a center-passage plan, and the full-length, engaged porch often built in the region, probably due to South Carolina influences. On this and the other roads, frame and occasionally log houses, small churches, barns, silos, tobacco-curing racks, and other outbuildings of many eras define an agrarian landscape with a strong sense of community identity. A number of farmers are members of the Farmland Preservation Trust.

BN 90 Capt. William Bedent Smith House

Ca. 1870; N side SR 1756 at Madison Co. line; private, visible from road

The small but striking 1½-story farmhouse features bold Greek Revival detail and a steep-gabled central portico. It was built soon after the Civil War for Smith, who had served with his cousin Zebulon Vance in the Rough and Ready Guard.

BN 91 Log Cabin Motor Court

Ca. 1930; 330 Weaverville Hwy. (W side US 25, 1 mi. N of New Bridge exit from US 19/23/70), Weaverville vic.; open year-round

Clustered under tall trees, the collection of eighteen log cabin cottages perfectly captures the early years of auto-oriented tourism, with a rustic regional flair. When this highway was a main route from Chicago to Florida, the Foster family often allowed travelers to camp on their tree-shaded hillside by the road. About 1930 Mrs. Foster decided to build tourist cabins on the site, added a bathhouse to serve campers and cabin occupants, and within a few years shifted entirely to cabins. Informally arranged around an open courtyard, the cabins are built of round logs in the rustic style of the time. Gabled stoops over the doorways bear longtime cabin names such as "Mountain Dew" and "Hillbilly." There are single-room and one- and two-bedroom units, and some have kitchens. Bathrooms and fireplaces with stone chimneys were added later. The interiors are simply finished in natural wood. Preserved with care over the years, this is among the region's most intact and evocative motor courts. (See Introduction, Fig. 38.)

BN 92 Zebulon Baird House

1878; W side US 19/23 BUS, 0.2 mi. S of SR 1740, Weaverville vic.; private, visible from road

The big, stylish house presents a locally outstanding rendition of the picturesque cottage style. The 2-story, L-plan house retains its elaborate decorative scheme, including corbeled chimneys, bracketed bays, spiky window heads, bargeboards outlining the gables, and sawn and bracketed porch trim. Baird was listed in an 1883 Asheville directory as farming 300 acres.

BN 93 Weaverville

Called Pine Cabin in the 18th c. and later Dry Ridge, the town was eventually named Weaverville to honor the Reverend Montraville Weaver, who in 1873 gave money to build a local college; the Weaver family had been numerous in the area since the early 19th c. Along Main St. (US 19/23 BUS) and the flanking grid are commercial buildings, churches, and frame and brick houses principally from the late 19th and early 20th centuries. Beautifully preserved on Main St. is the **Weaverville Drug Company** (1920s; 26 Main St.), a tan brick building with a Spanish flavor in the bracketed tile roof, arched windows, and decorative brick panels; the drugstore has kept its pressed-metal ceiling and soda fountain. The former **West Service Station** (early 20th c.; 37 Main St.) across the street is from the same era, with decorative brickwork and a canopy on brick supports sheltering the gas pumps.

The **Weaverville Presbyterian Church** (1926; 30 N. Alabama St.) is one of the finest of the county's several notable early 20th-c. Gothic Revival churches rendered in rounded river rock, with a tall tower and especially skillful stonework. It was built during the pastorate of H. B. Dendy, also minister at *Dillingham Presbyterian Church. The town has a number of frame houses in

BN 93 *Weaverville Presbyterian Church*

Queen Anne, Bungalow, foursquare, and other styles. Scattered along a back street are several large brick buildings from the former **Weaver College** (1874–1920s; College St.) in simplified classical and Romanesque modes; the school closed during the Great Depression.

BN 94 Zebulon B. Vance Birthplace
Ca. 1795, 19th c., and mid-20th c. reconstruction; S side SR 1003, 0.6 mi. E of SR 2109, Reems Creek community; State Historic Site; open regular hours

The site commemorates the state's Civil War governor, Zebulon B. Vance, who was born in his father's log house on this site in 1830. A state legislator and U.S. congressman as a young man, he opposed secession until Union forces fired on Fort Sumter. He entered Confederate service promptly, raising a company of N.C. troops called the Rough and Ready Guard and serving as captain, then colonel. In 1862 Vance was elected governor on the Conservative ticket. He worked to keep N.C. troops adequately supplied and to alleviate wartime hardships suffered on the home front. Although he won election to the U.S. Senate in 1870, as an ex-Confederate he was unable to take his seat. In 1876 when the Democrats (former Conservatives) "redeemed" the state and ended Reconstruction, Vance was again elected governor. After two years he began a long service as U.S. senator. Vance was known for his concern for the common folk and for his often salty humor. After his death in 1894, he was lionized by the Democratic Party. A monument to him is the central feature of *Pack Square in Asheville. With fellow Democrat Charles B. Aycock, Vance is represented in Statuary Hall at the U.S. Capitol and on the state capitol grounds in Raleigh; Vance and Aycock are also the only two governors whose birthplaces are state historic sites.

Based on photographs and other evidence, the asymmetrical log house has been reconstructed using some original timbers, woodwork, and the chimney. The main, 2-story section has a hall-parlor plan; unusual is the placement of the 1-story, log

kitchen adjoining the house, rather than in a separate structure, and sharing a single massive brick chimney.

The 19th-c. outbuildings collected on the site display examples of local log construction. These include a smokehouse, a loom house, a corncrib, a springhouse, and a slave dwelling. Most are of half-dovetailed hewn log construction.

BN 95 Reems Creek Presbyterian Church

Early 20th c.; Richard Sharp Smith (Asheville), attributed architect; N side SR 1003, just E of SR 2109, Reems Creek community

The picturesque frame and pebbledash church with small belfry and spire is associated by local tradition with "the Biltmore House architect," and the style and pebbledash suggest Richard Sharp Smith. The congregation was organized ca. 1790 and is among the county's oldest.

BN 96 Barnardsville

Settled early in the 19th c., the village at the confluence of Big Ivy and Paint Creek gained a post office ca. 1872 and took its name from Job Barnard's store. The principal architecture dates from the turn of the century. Facing the main road (NC 197 at SR 1003) is a row of brick, frame, and deco-

rative concrete commercial buildings. The **Barnardsville High School** (1927) is a well-detailed, 2½-story brick consolidated school. The nearby **Agricultural Building** (1935), built during the Great Depression as a public works project to supplement the high school, is a 1-story stone building, with a massive chimney and fine stonework.

Recalling the long history of the community is the **Roberts-Maney House** (ca. 1800, ca. 1900; W side SR 1003, 0.3 mi. S of NC 197), a large dwelling built in several stages. It began as a 2-story log house, believed to have been built ca. 1800 and thus one of the oldest buildings in the county. The house has been expanded over the years, with a front ell added in the early 20th c. The farmstead includes a fine log smokehouse and corncrib, 20th-c. rock silos, a barn, and the Roberts and Maney family cemetery.

BN 97 Henry Stevens Carson House

Mid-19th c.; NE side SR 2173, 2.1 mi. SE of NC 197, Dillingham vic.; open limited hours

Located in the broad, picturesque valley along Dillingham Creek, the 1-story log house is one of only three in the county that follows a dogtrot plan. The house and the log kitchen are constructed with half-dovetailed corner notches and have stone chimneys (rebuilt). Henry Carson's mother, Margaret, was the daughter of local pioneer Absalom Dillingham; through her, Carson inherited the farm. The house was weatherboarded ca. 1899 and the passageway enclosed. The house has been moved across the road and restored by the Big Ivy Historical Society, with the logs and dogtrot passage exposed. Nearby is the frame, one-room **Big Ivy Schoolhouse** (early 20th c.), likewise preserved by the local society. Like other schools in the region, its large 6/6 windows light only the rear and one side of the building, reflecting an educational notion about the proper lighting for students at their desks.

BN 98 Dillingham

The rural community in the broad valley along Dillingham Creek, at the foot of high mountains along the Yancey Co. line, was settled in the 19th c. by members of the Dillingham family and others. The area was also known as Upper Ivy. A few 19th-c. log houses still stand in various states of repair.

The most striking aspect of the community is the extensive use of rounded rocks taken from the creek valley and used in construction. Chiefly these are 1½-story stone bungalows and cottages, usually seated on terraces or lower slopes overlooking the floodplain. There are several stone outbuildings, including at least one stone silo and some storage buildings set into the hillsides. Smooth, water-rounded stones abound along the creeks near the roads, and the hillsides are strewn with fieldstones. The Hensley brothers, local stonemasons, are credited with several of these buildings.

At the tidy settlement at the Dillingham crossroads (SR 2203 and SR 2178/2199) stands the chief assemblage. The **Dillingham Presbyterian Church** (1934; Anthony Lord [Asheville], architect; Charles Taylor, Alfred Dillingham, Will Jarrett, Stamey Carter, and the Hensley brothers, builders) is a strongly composed little church whose mass and simple forms emphasize the rough beauty of the river rock in a fashion that some have compared to medieval Saxon chapels. Steep, gable roofs rise from the low, weighty, buttressed walls, which are pierced by small rectangular windows and doorways. It was designed by Anthony Lord, a member of Six

Associates and one of Asheville's leading architects of the mid-20th c. and illustrates his ongoing interest in the arts and traditional craftsmanship. The church was built by local volunteers with donated materials. The minister, H. B. Dendy, was also pastor of the *Weaverville Presbyterian Church, built in similar fashion. Nearby stand two river rock **Bungalows** of the same era, as well as a garage, root cellar, and roadside pillars of the same distinctive stonework. The stone, there for the gathering, made an especially appealing construction material during the Great Depression. Of several dry-laid rock walls in the area, the most impressive is the long **Rock Wall** (19th c., S side SR 2173, 0.9 mi. E of SR 2165), which runs for 150–200 yards as a boundary marker.

BN 99 Carter-Swain House

Ca. 1826, mid- and late 19th c.; E side SR 2162, 0.8 mi. N of NC 197, Democrat vic.; private, visible from road

The house by the road embodies a long sequence of building. Tradition holds that the original 15-by-17-foot log section of the house was built by a Carter in 1826. Additions made throughout the 19th c. created the present central-passage I-house form with shed rooms, 1-story ell, and decorated 2-tier porch with upper porch room. "Uncle Johnny" Carter, who operated an inn here and a store, mill, and post office across the road during the mid-19th c., was such a "strong Democrat" that the place was known as Democrat until he moved his mill to Ivy Creek and established the present-day community of Democrat.

BN 99 *Carter-Swain House*

BN 100 Shadrack Guthrie House

Ca. 1825; W side SR 2160, 1.5 mi. S of NC 197, Democrat vic.; private, visible from road

Located beside the road that winds along the Sugar Creek valley, this unusual example of a 2-story log house is square in plan, 25 by 25 feet. The hewn logs are joined with half-dovetailed notches. The double-shouldered chimney of brick laid in mud has Flemish bond to the first shoulder. Originally the windows had only shutters, not glass. Tradition states it was built about 1825 for Shadrack Guthrie, who in that year owned about 300 acres on Sugar Creek. He and his wife had at least seven children. Very few early log houses stand so intact and so readily visible from the road.

BN 101 Peter Burrell House

1903; W side SR 2160, 1.7 mi. S of NC 197, Democrat vic.; private, visible from road

Located close to the *Shadrack Guthrie House, the Burrell House illustrates the longevity of log construction within a single neighborhood. It is a clear-cut example of a saddlebag-plan house, with two 17-foot-square pens of half-dovetailed logs flanking the stone chimney. Rear shed rooms and the shed porch across the front were built soon after.

BN 102 Oteen Veterans' Administration Hospital

Ca. 1924 and later; N side US 70 at jct. w/SR 2002, Oteen

In 1918 at Oteen the U.S. Army opened a hospital for soldiers training in the area for World War I. After the war it became a veterans' hospital specializing in tuberculosis and other respiratory diseases. The Asheville area was known as a center for those suffering from these ailments because of the benefits of the pure mountain air, the mild and often sunny winters, and the cool and pleasant summers. The initial buildings were simple frame structures. From 1924 to 1930 the Veterans' Bureau erected a series of handsome and substantial Georgian Revival buildings. The tiled and stuccoed structures

of the hospital itself and the two northernmost dormitory facilities all employ a consistent Georgian Revival vocabulary, including hip roofs, projecting central pavilions, rusticated quoins, and classical entrance surrounds and hoods. Many of the buildings featured large expanses of windows to provide maximum sunlight and fresh air. Frame staff residences west of Riceville Rd. were designed in a Neocolonial style to blend with the larger hospital structures. The modern Veterans' Administration Hospital occupies what was formerly the broad lawn, obscuring the originally generous site plan. The older structures are being put to a variety of uses.

BN 103 Warren Wilson College

1901 and later; SR 2416, 0.8 mi. N of US 70, Swannanoa vic.

Sited just north of the Swannanoa River in one of the most scenic and unspoiled sections of the valley, the school begun in 1894 as the Asheville Farm School continues as a small college where students still work on the school's farm in the broad valley below the wooded, hillside campus. (Nearby is one of the region's principal Native American archaeological sites.) The campus includes an assortment of informal 20th-c. buildings. The oldest, **Dodge House** (1901), is a Queen Anne-influenced frame dwelling. **Williams Museum** (1933–37) is a rustic pole log structure with gabled pavilions at each end, which initially housed the Farm School Presbyterian Church and served as the college auditorium.

BN 103 *Warren Wilson Presbyterian Church and College Chapel*

Buildings of the later 20th c., designed by leading Asheville firms, continue the use of natural materials and complement the wooded, hilly site. The **Kittredge Arts Center** (1977; Six Associates [Asheville]) is a well-detailed, reinforced concrete and glass structure with a fine auditorium and full working stage in its dominant wedge-shaped mass; several other campus buildings were also designed by Six Associates. The **Warren Wilson Presbyterian Church and College Chapel** (1961–64; Charles Sappenfield, J. Bertram King, Inc. [Asheville], architect) is a striking steep-gabled form with a chevron-patterned wood facade and natural stone walls, recognized by a NCAIA design award. The gneiss, quartzite, and feldspar came from nearby Bee Tree Valley, and much of the labor was donated by students, faculty, and others.

BN 104 Will Patton House

Ca. 1900; S side US 70, 0.1 mi. W of SR 2412, Swannanoa vic.; private, visible from road

This typical turn-of-the-century farmhouse is highly visible between I-40 and US 70. The I-house has exterior end chimneys, a shed porch, and a central raised gable accenting the facade. Its owner, dairyman Patton, was known as "the buttermilk king."

BN 105 Black Mountain College

1940–56; W side SR 2468, 1.8 mi. N of SR 2435, Black Mountain vic.; private camp (Camp Rockmont); no public access; Studies Building visible from road

Founded in 1933 and established on this campus beside Lake Eden in 1940, the experimental Black Mountain College was internationally known for its modernist innovations in American art and education. Among the faculty and students were leaders such as composer John Cage; choreographer Merce Cunningham; poet Charles Olson; artists Josef and Anni Albers, Willem and Elaine de Kooning, Robert Motherwell, and Franz Kline; and many others. The school was begun in 1933 by John Rice, its president, along with Theodore Dreier and other faculty and students formerly of Rollins

College in Florida. They leased buildings at the *Blue Ridge Assembly, a summer conference center, from Sept. through May. Seeking a permanent site, in 1937 the college purchased the Lake Eden camp developed by E. W. Grove and reused the existing stone and wooden lodges and other buildings.

New buildings were designed and built by faculty and students, most notably the large, lakeside **Studies Building** (1940–41; A. Lawrence Kocher, architect; visible from road) (see Introduction, Fig. 63). Important among the early faculty were former Bauhaus artist and professor Josef Albers and his wife Anni Albers. Through contact with Philip Johnson of the Museum of Modern Art, the Alberses found refuge from Nazi Germany at Black Mountain in 1933. In 1939, at Josef Albers's suggestion, architect Walter Gropius, another Bauhaus émigré teaching at Harvard, was invited to design a main building for Lake Eden. Gropius and his partner Marcel Breuer planned an ambitious complex to curve along the lake, and a model was exhibited at the Museum of Modern Art and published in the *New York Times* in 1940.

But the cost estimate far exceeded the college's means. John Rice approached architect A. Lawrence Kocher for a more economical design. Kocher was an accomplished teacher and architect, interested in low-cost building and known for his experimental Aluminaire House (with Albert Frey) and Plywood House (for the 1939–40 World's Fair). After consultation with Gropius, he planned a four-part facility that could be built in stages, with labor by students and faculty. Kocher came to Black Mountain to supervise construction and teach architecture (1940–43). Only the first section was ever built.

The Studies Building beside the lake is a long, rectangular block, 3 stories tall and 200 feet long. The upper 2 stories rest on steel and concrete pillars or pilotis, two of which are decorated with murals by artist Jean Charlot. At the west end a stone basement and stair tower anchor the structure visually to the hillside, while the rest of the building appears to hover on the pilotis. Continuous steel sash windows band the 2 main stories, which are sheathed in corrugated panels. Other buildings include several **Faculty Cottages** (early 1940s) created from available materials in a low-cost modernist mode, with at least one, the **Jalowetz Cottage**, designed by Kocher. Black Mountain College closed in 1956; much of the campus is now Camp Rockmont. (See Lawrence Wodehouse, "Kocher at Black Mountain," *Journal of the Society of Architectural Historians* 41, no. 4 [Dec. 1982].)

BN 106 Black Mountain

The salubrious and scenic location of the small town attracted several health and educational institutions, especially after the arrival of the railroad in 1880. The most famous was *Black Mountain College, whose unconventional faculty and students evoked more than the usual town-gown tensions with the local population. The small, railroad-supported **Central Business District** contains a typical assortment of corbeled brick turn-of-the-century stores. The **Black Mountain Depot** (early 20th c.; Sutton Ave. at Cherry St.) is a bracketed, hip-roofed frame structure. The premier residential avenues were **Vance Ave.** and **Montreat Rd.**, which are lined by pleasant, early 20th-c. dwellings.

BN 107 InTheOaks

1919–21, Frank Wallis & Son (New York), architect; 1922–23, Smith & Carrier; Chauncey Beadle, landscape designer; 510 Vance Ave., Black Mountain; private, limited public access

One of the region's informal but luxurious mountain estates centers on the residence designed by Frank Wallis & Son as an "authentic reproduction of a Tudor country manor." Wallis had previously worked in the office of architect Richard Morris Hunt and assisted in plans for *Biltmore Estate. Featured in *Architecture* magazine in 1921, "InTheOaks, Residence, Miss Lillian Emerson," was built for Emerson by her cousin and future husband, Franklin Terry, an industrialist who had pioneered in production of incandescent lighting. The couple married in 1923, having expanded the house with a recreational wing—ballroom, gymnasium, swimming pool, and bowling alley—designed by Smith & Carrier. The U-shaped house has the lower stories of rough-faced local granite ashlar, the upper ones shingled, and the roof rounded to simulate thatching. The landscape, with golf course, formal garden, and summerhouse, was designed by Chauncey Beadle of Biltmore Estate. It is now an Episcopal camp and conference center.

BN 108 Montreat

The most architecturally interesting of several religious educational centers in the region, Montreat's wooded campus has a series of impressive, naturalistic buildings rendered in local river rock and quarried stone. The Mountain Retreat Association, founded in 1877 by interdenominational ministers, established the religious retreat, which became a Presbyterian center by 1911. A few frame Queen Anne and shingled cottages remain, but the predominant architecture expresses the early 20th-c. penchant for romantic forms rendered in local stone. Key structures were designed by longtime association president Dr. Robert C. Anderson in association with local architects.

The **Gatehouse** (1922) at the entrance to Montreat is a picturesque composition in river rock, with "Montreat" spelled out in contrasting stones. For many years "gate boys" stationed here greeted guests and collected fees for entry to the complex. (See Introduction, Fig. 30.)

Overlooking Lake Susan, the center of the campus is dominated by the fortress-like **Assembly Inn** (1929; W. J. East, architect), a massive, river rock and quarried stone structure, with 3-story rounded pillars separating broad arched windows; the main lobby's stone walls and columns glitter with mica. Because the previous hotel had burned in 1922, Dr. Anderson emphasized fireproof construction, using wood only for the doors. The marble for the floors came from Tennessee; utilities were installed within the stone pillars in the lobby. During construction, one longtimer recalled, "when all the stones in the grounds seemed exhausted, the valves in the dam were opened, and the rushing water unearthed stone for a mile downstream. When more rock was needed, this procedure could be repeated indefinitely."

Also near the lake is the polygonal **Anderson Auditorium** (1922, Smith & Carrier; burned 1940; rebuilt 1941), with stone walls encompassing a 3,000-seat auditorium under an umbrella-like steel truss roof. Frame cottages scattered on the hillsides repeat the river rock in their foundations.

Across Lake Susan stand other stone buildings erected for **Montreat College,** founded in 1916 to make use of the retreat buildings during the winter: **Richardson Hall** (1932), with Craftsman motifs; **Gaither Hall** (1942), with arched entrance and a 600-seat chapel with Gothic woodwork of chestnut designed by Anderson; and **Howerton Hall** (1945–47), begun as a hotel but only partially completed before Anderson departed.

BN 109 Swannanoa Tunnel
1879; begins S side I-40, 0.3 mi. W of McDowell Co. line, Ridgecrest

The 1,800-foot tunnel was the last and longest of the tunnels necessary to bring the rails of the WNCRR over the Blue Ridge. Crews worked from both ends after a locomotive was hauled on temporary tracks over the gap. Maj. James Wilson, in charge of the project, telegrammed Zebulon Vance on Mar. 11, 1879: "Daylight entered Buncombe today through Swannanoa Tunnel. Grade and centers met exactly." Nearly 125 men, mostly convicts, died working on the Old-Fort-to-Ridgecrest section of the line. John

Ehle's novel, *The Road,* gives a vivid narrative of the perilous endeavor.

BN 110 Rafael Guastavino Estate (Rhododendron)
1895–1908; E side NC 9, 1.4 mi. S of I-40, Black Mountain vic.; on grounds of Christmount Christian Assembly, limited access

Now part of the campus of a religious retreat, the parklike 8-acre site retains ruins and landscape features dating from the occupancy of Guastavino, the important Spanish-born architectural engineer who came to Asheville to work at *Biltmore and established this small estate near Black Mountain as his private residence. The big frame house burned in the late 1940s, but surviving features include the house foundations, stone walls, a vaulted wine cellar, landscaped earthworks, and plantings. Of special interest are the ruins of a beehive kiln and its intact 60-foot chimney, where Guastavino manufactured ceramic tiles used in his patented "cohesive construction" technology.

BN 111 Blue Ridge Assembly
1912–30; Louis Jallade (New York), architect; David Getaz (Knoxville), contractor; S end of SR 2720, Black Mountain vic.

Grandly sited amid the mountains for which it is named, the YMCA conference center for the southeastern United States was established in 1912. The idea for a regional student conference and religious training center in the mountains was conceived by YMCA officer Willis D. Weatherford, who was also a founder of the Commission on Interracial Cooperation. He strove to make Blue Ridge "one of the forward-looking leaders of the entire south." The original core of large Colonial Revival structures includes the dominant original building, **Robert E. Lee Hall** (1912; Louis Jallade [New York], architect), an enormous, 3-story frame building with a heroic portico of 8 Doric type columns. Trained at the École des Beaux Arts, architect Jallade was active with the YMCA in New York and volunteered his services for the center. Contractor was David Getaz of

BN 111 *Robert E. Lee Hall, Blue Ridge Assembly*

Knoxville, whose son was supervising architect. Four smaller, 2-story buildings with porticoes define an informal courtyard, and to the rear are 19 frame cottages. *Black Mountain College was founded here in 1933 and used the buildings from Sept. to May until moving to the Lake Eden campus.

BN 112 B. K. Miller House

Ca. 1935; B. K. Miller, builder; E side US 74, 0.8 mi. SE of I-40, Asheville vic.; private, visible from road

The informal yet imposing 2-story pole log house is the county's finest example of this 20th-c. version of log construction. The symmetrical facade has twin 2-story stone and log porticoes with chevron-log gables, which flank a massive double-shouldered rubble stone chimney. Miller designed the house himself, it is said, and a Mr. Cordell, who had worked on the *Grove Park Inn, executed the stonework.

BN 112 *B. K. Miller House*

BN 113 John A. Lanning House

1839; E side SR 3128, 0.7 mi. S of US 74, Fairview vic.; private, visible from road

The unusually well-preserved log house was built for farmer John A. Lanning and his wife Susanna Gallimore and has continued in the family. The 1½-story saddlebag-plan dwelling has a central stone chimney and an asymmetrical plan with one pen 16 by 16 feet, the other 16 by 14. The upper half-story logs run the full length of the house. As at *Sherrill's Inn, the stair begins on the back porch with double runs that meet at a landing and ascend in a single run in the chimney space. Yellow pine logs are joined with fine full-dovetailed notches, and the gables project slightly—features unusual in the county. Walls are sheathed with boards inside and daubed on the exterior. Log farm buildings include a double corncrib and a barn. Lanning worked as a blacksmith and cobbler as well as a farmer. His property grew from about 300 acres in 1850 to nearly 1,200 acres by 1860, of which 70 were improved.

BN 114 S. J. Ashworth House

Ca. 1892; W side US 74, 1.1 mi. S of SR 3136, Fairview vic.; private, visible from road

Probably the most bookishly picturesque house in the county, the gabled cottage has a central-passage plan and bracketed porch, bay window, and fancy gable carpentry. After Ashworth's brother, a doctor, moved away and sold him his uncollected accounts, S. J. redeemed the bills in the form of work on his house.

BN 115 Sherrill's Inn

Ca. 1790s, ca. 1800, ca. 1834, and ca. 1922; W side US 74, 1.1 mi. N of Henderson Co. line, Fairview vic.; private, visible from road

One of the most evocative early landmarks in the county, this beautifully sited house embodies many eras of building and a long and lively history. Set on a gentle hill above the road and surrounded by immense boxwoods, the long, weatherboarded house encompasses two log sections. Built about 1806 by John Ashworth is the 2-story, saddlebag-plan house with a split-run stair that begins on the rear shed porch and rises in the chimney space. To the west is a smaller log structure, joined to the first house by a 20th-c. passage. Bedford Sherrill began operating an inn in the old house about 1840. Tradition maintains that a small, half-dovetailed meathouse on the property served as a frontier "fort" in the 1790s.

Sherrill's Inn served travelers throughout the 19th c., hosting many famous guests, including Zebulon Vance and Andrew Johnson. Charles Dudley Warner, as he reported in *On Horseback* (1889), dined at "Widow Sherrill's" on a visit to Hickory Nut Gap on his way to Judge Logan's (cf. *Pine Gables) across the mountain in Rutherford Co. He commended the "old, rambling, many-roomed" house with its "wide galleries on two sides" for its "good air and fair entertainment" as well as its "wide valley and mountain view." Apples were a principal crop, "sound and of good flavor." In 1916 the inn was bought by the McClure family, who restored it as a private residence and developed the landscape around it. It remains in the hands of the family, who continue the apple orchard and hold cider and apple sales that welcome visitors in autumn. (See Introduction, Fig. 18.)

BN 116 Newington
(Joseph B. Pyatt House; Blake House)

Ca. 1850; 150 Royal Pines Dr., Arden; B&B

In an unusual stone version of the picturesque cottage mode, the 2-story, double-pile house is built of random-coursed rough ashlar with limestone door and window labels of Italianate cast. A Gothic Revival touch appears in the distinctive front central peaked gable with bold curving bargeboards, complementing the bracketed porch and bay windows. This is one of several substantial houses in the picturesque mode that appeared along the Buncombe Turnpike in the antebellum era and is akin to *The Meadows and *Rugby Grange in neighboring Henderson Co.

BN 116 *Newington*

BN 117 Christ School

1906–present; E side SR 3196 at SR 3188, Arden vic.; private

The Episcopal boys' preparatory school was founded in 1900 by the Reverend Thomas Wetmore on the antebellum Alexander Robertson plantation. Local rough-cut brown mica schist is the primary building material; this distinctive stone, along with simple form and detail, recurs throughout the campus buildings. Notable among these are the 1906 Gothic Revival style **Chapel**, probably designed by founder Wetmore, and several Colonial Revival style structures designed by architect Erle G. Stillwell, including the **Dormitories** (1930, 1938, 1947) and the **School Building** (1941). The material continues in the recent cottage-like **Headmaster's House** (1968–69; Robert Daniels [Brevard], architect).

BN 118 Avery Creek Christian Church (former Union Church)

Ca. 1891; Merit Graham and Moses Cochrane, builders; W side NC 191, 0.2 mi. S of NC 146, Arden vic.

The simple frame gable-end church with modest carpentry decoration was executed by local builders. The original "Union" consisted of Baptists, Methodists, and Christians.

BN 119 Engadine

1885; S side US 19–23, 0.3 mi. E of Haywood Co. line; private, visible from road; B&B

The Queen Anne style house gains complexity from its inset porches, projecting tower, and varied shingled and sawnwork decoration. It boasted an early usage of central heat, running water, and electricity from its own generator.

Henderson County (HN)

Hendersonville (HN 1–10)

The county seat was laid out in 1841, three years after the formation of the county, when Judge Mitchell King of Charleston and Flat Rock settled a debate over its location by donating 50 acres "for the erection of the County Court House and public buildings." Two other county residents contributed additional acreage, and the town was born. Along with neighboring Flat Rock, antebellum Hendersonville hosted summer visitors from South Carolina and elsewhere. A stagecoach line was the only transportation until Independence Day 1879, when the first train rolled in on the Asheville & Spartanburg Railroad—more than a year before the iron horse arrived in Asheville. The town flourished anew as a tourist destination, with many boardinghouses and hotels catering to those seeking relief from the heat and ailments associated with the lowland South. In the 1920s Hendersonville attracted big band musicians and performers such as Cab Calloway, and it claimed to be the "dancingest little town in America."

Reflecting the growth era of the early 20th c., the downtown is one of western N.C.'s most impressive small-town commercial centers, with Neoclassical and Italianate buildings in brick and stone. Early 20th-c. neighborhoods, dotted by hotels and boardinghouses, flank the downtown, and suburban developments of the era rise on nearby

HN 1 *Henderson Co. Courthouse*

hills. Prominent in the town's architectural development was Erle Stillwell, an architect who had worked in Atlanta, then moved to Hendersonville to establish a practice in 1916—one of the few in the region outside Asheville. He was a leader in developing the profession in the state and, alone and as part of Six Associates, designed many buildings in Hendersonville and elsewhere in the region.

HN 1 Downtown Hendersonville

The commercial district focuses on Main St. from 1st Ave. to 6th Ave. The imposing **Henderson County Courthouse** (1905; Richard Sharp Smith [Asheville], architect; W. F. Edwards, builder; w side S. Main St. between 1st and 2nd Aves.) is the principal public edifice and one of several regional courthouses designed by Smith. A gold-domed cupola topped with a Blind Justice statue crowns the 3-story brick building. Corinthian porticoes mark the front entrance and the sides. A brick **Jail** (1926) adjoins the rear.

Near the courthouse are two rare commercial buildings from the mid-19th c., both 2 stories tall with hip roofs: the **Ripley Building** (ca. 1850; 101–5 S. Main St.) in stone construction and the **Ripley-Shepherd Building** (1847; 218 N. Main St.), said to have served as a Civil War commissary and later as the post office, a brick building with bracketed eaves.

Following the courthouse, Smith provided another Neoclassical design for the (former) **People's National Bank** (ca. 1910; Smith & Carrier [Asheville], architects; 225–31 N. Main St.), a 2-story building with a recessed entrance framed by Ionic columns beneath a stepped parapet. It was the town's first commercial building of reinforced concrete, a material Smith had used in Asheville's Central Bank (*Legal Building) in 1909. One of Main St.'s chief attractions is the **Justus Pharmacy** (ca. 1900; 303 N. Main St.), a 2-story stuccoed brick building.

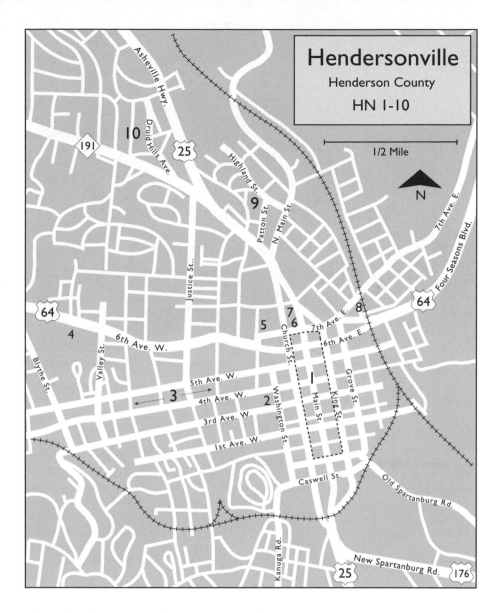

1/2 Mile

N

When the pharmacy installed a new soda fountain in 1907, the local *French Broad Hustler* marveled, "The latest appliances and cleanliness and quickness are incorporated in the big fountain, and the whole effect is most pleasing." The pharmacy still operates as a soda fountain and ice cream parlor, with a Coca-Cola mural on its side exterior wall.

A later facet of Neoclassicism appears in the **First Bank & Trust Company** (1923; Erle Stillwell, architect; 401 N. Main St.), a 3-story brick building with limestone pi-

lasters and terra-cotta ornament designed by resident architect Stillwell. The 2-story office building at **507–13 N. Main St.** (1909), which housed Clarke Hardware Co. and, later, Houston Furniture, was praised upon its completion in 1909 by the local *French Broad Hustler*: "substantial & built to last," "extremely handsome in appearance with its pressed brick front, enormous plate glass windows and large projecting balconies." A 1997 renovation revealed windows capped with keystones and a decorative cornice at

HN 1 *Maxwell Building, Main St.*

the first level. The 2-story **Maxwell Building** (ca. 1910; 529 N. Main St.) also re-emerged as an intact early 20th-c. commercial building when a restoration for the Mast Store uncovered the pressed-brick facade with ornate arched windows and cornice. The only hotel remaining on Main St. is the **Skyland Hotel** (1929; 534–44 N. Main St.), a 6-story tan brick building with cast-concrete details. Completed just months before the stock market crash, it survived the Great Depression and served as a hotel for several years. Just off Main St., the **Hendersonville City Hall** (1926–28; Erle Stillwell, architect; 145 5th Ave. E) is another Stillwell work, a Neoclassical brick building with a full-height portico and pedimented doorway.

HN 2 Hendersonville Inn (Aloah Hotel)

Ca. 1919; 201 3rd Ave. W

Originally called the Aloah, but known as the Hendersonville Inn since the 1930s, the small hotel just west of downtown is little changed from the town's early 20th-c. tourism heyday. Built by J. O. Bell (cf. Tuxedo), the 3-story brick building combines clean lines and restrained Colonial Revival details;

the interior with natural, dark-stained woodwork continues the simplicity of the exterior.

HN 3 4th and 5th Aves. W

The neighborhood west of Main St. developed primarily during the early 20th c. and displays many variations of the Colonial Revival, Dutch Colonial, and Craftsman bungalow modes. The **Clarke-Hobbs-Davidson House** (ca. 1907; 229 5th Ave. w), a 2½-story brick residence in a free Colonial Revival style, now serves as a Masonic meeting hall. A bungalow at **805 5th Ave. w** (ca. 1925) shows the Japanese influence on the Craftsman style. Two notable multifamily residences are the **Ambassador Apartments** and the **Maxwell Apartments** (1920s; 616 and 625 5th Ave. w), well-preserved red brick Colonial Revival apartment buildings adorned with urns, quoins, and pediments. An early rendition of the Colonial Revival style is **Westhaven** (ca. 1900; 1235 5th Ave. w; B&B), with its full-height Doric portico and a porte cochere. Local architect Stillwell's hand appears in several houses, including the large, Colonial Revival style **Charles**

Hobbs House (1924; Erle Stillwell, architect; 1230 5th Ave. w; B&B).

HN 4 Oakdale Cemetery
Est. 1882; N and S sides 6th Ave. W (US 64), between Valley and Blythe Sts.

The city cemetery begun in 1882 fills an open site west of downtown. Part of the cemetery originally used for the graves of African Americans lies on the north side of 6th Ave. w, while a Jewish section, created in 1938 and enclosed by a fieldstone wall and wrought iron fence, occupies the southern part of the burial yard. Oakdale is best known for the marble statue of an angel marking the graves of the Reverend H. F. Johnson, his wife, and son. It is described as one of the angel figures that stood at W. O.

Wolfe's shop in Asheville, an imported carving that stonecutter Wolfe admired but could never equal. Several angel markers are revered in the region's cemeteries; this one is generally thought to have inspired the title of *Look Homeward, Angel,* the novel by Wolfe's son Thomas. In 1975, after an overzealous Thomas Wolfe fan accidentally knocked the angel off its base, the city installed a 6-foot-high fence around the Johnson family graves.

HN 5 The Cedars
1914; 219 7th Ave. W

Jennie C. Bailey, whose husband J. W. Bailey was an official with Southern Railway, had the 3½-story brick Neoclassical hotel built to meet the growing demand for tourist accommodations. She opened the inn over her husband's objections and advertised in 1915, "No consumptives, open all year; Hot Water/Running Hot and Cold Water in Every Room, Apply to Mrs. J. W. Bailey, Prop. & Owner." With its capacious, Ionic-columned porches overlooking broad grounds, the hotel recalls the ambience of the early 20th c.

HN 6 Chewning House (Claddagh Inn)
Ca. 1906, 1912–22; 755 N. Main St.; B&B

The big frame house and its neighbor typify the many private dwellings remade as boardinghouses during the early 20th c. Standing just north of the commercial district, it was built around 1906 as a 2-story dwelling but was soon enlarged to 3 stories in Colonial Revival style, with 20 guest rooms.

HN 7 The Waverly
Ca. 1898; 783 N. Main St.; B&B

The oldest hotel in town, the 3-story frame house with Eastlake trim on its multi-tiered porch survived a 1910 fire and has served tourists since it opened as the Anderson Boarding House in the late 19th c.

HN 8 Hendersonville Depot
1902–4; SE corner of 7th Ave. E and Maple St.

HN 7 *The Waverly*

The unusually well preserved frame depot has a hip and gable roof with splayed eaves on curved brackets. The adjoining area developed as a railroad business district northeast of Main St. after the initial depot (1879) was built. Several 1- and 2-story brick buildings line 7th Ave. and flank the railroad tracks. Early 20th-c. brick street paving remains west of the depot. The former **Station Hotel** (1912–22; 729 Maple St.), a 2-story brick building with 2-tier porch, accommodated railroad passengers for several decades.

HN 9 Hyman Heights

Located on the eastern side of the Asheville highway, beginning at N. Main St., the suburb was platted in 1905 but took form in the early 1920s. It resulted from the subdivision of land surrounding **Killarney** (mid-19th c., early 20th c.; Richard Sharp Smith [Asheville], addition; NW corner Killarney and Patton Sts.), which began as a 1-story antebellum stone dwelling in a wooded setting. Smith designed an upper-story addition and porch that brought it to its English cottage appearance. Development of the suburb was encouraged by the construction of Hendersonville's first hospital, the 3-story brick **Patton Memorial Hospital** (1913; 1225 Highland St.), finished in simplified Colonial Revival style. By the mid-1920s the neighborhood had modest Colonial Revival, Tudor Revival, Craftsman, and foursquare houses occupying the sloping parcels.

HN 10 Druid Hills

In 1923 the Hendersonville Real Estate Co. and P. L. Wright began development of Druid Hills as a "suburban village." Restrictions required residents to submit plans to the company for approval, and houses were to be "maintained in good condition, and in general harmony with the surrounding property." Sandwiched between NC 191 and US 25 just north of downtown, the small suburb is laid out in a roughly circular fashion with a small triangular park as a focus. English named streets are lined with Colonial, Spanish, and especially Tudor Revival and English cottage style houses as well as several Craftsman bungalows, dating primarily from ca. 1923–26. A good selection appears on Druid Hills Ave., facing the park. Among these are a brick bungalow at 1629, a Mediterranean style brick house at 1609, a foursquare at 1523, and a stuccoed Tudor Revival cottage at 1519.

HN 11 Laurel Park

Hendersonville's first suburb and now a separate community, Laurel Park occupies Echo Mountain, whose peak towers over 1,000 feet above Hendersonville. In 1888 A. W. Smith, a lawyer from Georgia, and area native C. M. Pace purchased land on the mountain for a residential development. Laurel Park emerged as a popular recreational area, and several cottages were built at the base of the mountain. Until 1918 Smith and Pace operated a railroad along 5th Ave. from Hendersonville to Rainbow and Laurel Lakes (along Lake Dr.) and the picnic area at nearby Crystal Spring (Crystal Spring Rd.). Boardinghouses and hotels were built on the mountain.

In 1924 Florida and local investors organized Laurel Park Estates to develop the community. The next year ground was broken for the Fleetwood, a big hotel designed by architect Henry I. Gaines and Beacham & LeGrand (Asheville) for the top of the mountain at Jump Off Rock (w end Laurel Park Hwy.). But after the collapse of the Florida land boom in 1926, construction of the Fleetwood halted at the thirteenth floor.

The building was torn down in 1936, and its plumbing fixtures and other components were reused in the locale. Development languished in the late 1920s and did not pick up again until after World War II.

Diverse dwellings from the early development are tucked away on the curving mountainside roads. The whimsical **Gingerbread House** (1898, 1937; 2038 Laurel Park Hwy.) is part log cabin, part Tudor cottage, a rambling, rustic concoction with half-timbered front gables, rolled eaves, eyelid dormers, and log porch supports. **Suits Mama** (1914; sw corner of Crystal Spring Rd. and Davis Dr.), among the earlier houses, is a 2-story frame dwelling with 2-tier porches. The **Singletary-Robinson House** (early 20th c.; s side Robinson Lane, 0.1 mi. w of Briarcliff Dr.), a 2-story, round-pole log house with a massive stone chimney (said to survive from a 19th-c. house) is part of a complex with several log outbuildings.

HN 12 Kanuga Conference Center

1908–present; John Nolen, landscape architect; Richard Sharp Smith and J. Bertram King [Asheville], architects; W side SR 1283, 1.3 mi. SW of SR 1127, Hendersonville vic.; private, limited access

The parklike mountain retreat center began as the private Kanuga Lake Club, organized by Charlotte businessman George Stephens, later of Asheville. He planned a cooperative, unostentatious summer resort for some 200 "congenial" families who would join as members, "a happy village of rational people in a bracing climate, surrounded by picturesque scenery." To carry out his vision he employed nationally known city planner John Nolen (who planned Stephens's Charlotte suburb Myers Park in 1911 and produced a city plan for Asheville in 1922) and architect Richard Sharp Smith, formerly supervising architect for *Biltmore. As the *Charlotte Daily Observer* explained in 1908, "Mr. Nolen will furnish a general plan for the landscape treatment of the property and whatever is done will be by his advice. In the same way, the plans for all the houses, including the cottages of the club members, will either be drawn or approved by one architect so that jarring contradictions in design will not mar the beauty of the lake village."

Opened in 1909 with leading businessmen as members, the club flourished for several seasons but eventually failed, in part because the flood of 1916 washed out the Kanuga Lake dam. In 1928–29, at a time when several Protestant denominations were developing conference centers in western N.C., a corporation of Episcopal Church interests acquired Kanuga as a camp and conference center.

HN 12 *Cottages, Kanuga Conference Center*

Over time, new structures were added to accommodate the new purpose. The **Kanuga Lake Inn** (1967–68; J. Bertram King [Asheville], architect), a modernist U-shaped building in natural stone and wood, sits on a rise overlooking the lake. It replaced Smith's grand, shingled, Kanuga Lake Club House (1908–9).

An evocative survival from the early days are 6 rows of 39 carefully maintained, camp-style **Cottages** (1908–10; Richard Sharp Smith, architect), unpretentious, trimly finished rustic structures with screened porches and large windows. Built to accommodate various slopes, the wood-shingled and board-and-batten cottages are painted forest green with white trim and follow 5 basic plans from 3 to 7 rooms each.

West of the inn stands the **Chapel of the Transfiguration** (1939–40; S. Grant Alexander [Asheville], architect), a cross-plan, board-and-batten chapel designed by the architect who planned the rebuilding of *Calvary Episcopal Church, Fletcher. The outdoor **Chapel of St. Francis of Assisi** (1930s, 1941, 1963) stands in a wooded setting off the entrance road. A small stream flows between the simple wooden benches and the chancel and is spanned by bark-covered bridges that link worshipers with the stone altar.

Flat Rock (HN 13–27)

Flat Rock is a large, sylvan area that since the early 19th c. has been a summer community for wealthy Charlestonians and other South Carolinians escaping the heat of the low country. The summer colony, called "The Little Charleston of the Mountains," was known for its aristocratic way of life quite apart from the small farmers of the locale. Flat Rock's venerable history as a resort is reflected in summer country estates that represent a unique segment of elite southern social history. Several summer houses continue to be used for their original purpose. Only a few are visible from the road.

Named for a flat granite outcropping, the settlement developed in a high plateau (alt. 2,200 ft.) just north of the Saluda Mountains, the first range coming up from South Carolina. The spine of the community is

HN 26 *Argyle*

us 25, which follows much of the route of the Buncombe Turnpike; it is lined with old trees and punctuated by stone gates to the estates that lie back from the road. The typical estate has a major residence and a complement of outbuildings. Many houses provide summer comfort with deep porches and long windows—often French doors at the first story—but no specific Flat Rock architectural idiom prevails. The grounds are extensive and the houses far apart, for, as one local writer observed, "While society in the little community was rather closely knit, the nearness of their neighbors was not an element in their friendship."

The long procession of Charlestonians to the cool of Flat Rock began in the 1820s when Daniel Blake and Charles and Susan Baring sought relief from the miasmas of their rice plantations. While Blake took up a tract at *The Meadows at Fletcher, the Barings bought land at Flat Rock and built *Mountain Lodge; they were soon followed by Charleston's Judge Mitchell King, who established a summer home called *Argyle. With the construction of the Buncombe Turnpike in 1828, Flat Rock developed quickly as more South Carolinians found it convenient to make the journey, arriving by carriage with large families, many slaves, and wagonloads of luggage and provisions.

In the three decades before the Civil War, summer estates were established by owners who composed a veritable "Who's Who" of Charleston and the South. C. G. Memminger of Charleston (later secretary of the treasury of the Confederacy) built Rock Hill (now *Connemara) in 1838–39. Other estates were summer homes of prominent families such as the Rhetts, the Middletons,

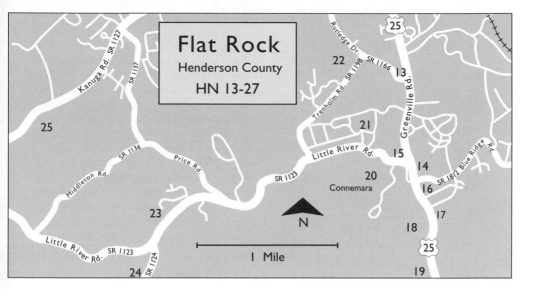

Flat Rock
Henderson County
HN 13-27

the Grimkés, the Trenholms, the Pinckneys, and the Pringles. Here, as a church history recalls, "a large section of southern aristocracy assembled regularly for the summer season . . . the women and children remaining from May until September, while the men went to and fro as their work dictated."

During the mid-19th c., Flat Rock residents indulged a shared taste for the picturesque style as promoted nationally by A. J. Downing. Adopting Downing's notion of the picturesque as suited to a romantic mountain setting, they built their "cottages" in the steep-gabled, Gothic style and in various Italianate modes with bracketed rooflines and decked them with latticed porches. These were among the earliest examples of picturesque fashions in the state, and part of a stream of such work that reached up the Buncombe Turnpike in the 1840s and 1850s. Twentieth-century remodelings, however, transformed all but a few houses, the *Woodfield Inn, and *St. John-in-the-Wilderness Episcopal Church.

During the Civil War, bushwhackers plagued the community, robbing houses and killing at least one prominent resident. But despite the effects of the war and Reconstruction and rapid turnover of many properties in Flat Rock, families continued their annual treks and enjoyed their old haunts

and old friends anew. The 1879 completion of the Asheville & Spartanburg Railroad across the Saluda grade—a project led by Flat Rock regular C. G. Memminger—eased the journey, and the community grew accordingly. In time, new infusions of money enabled old and new families to renovate and expand their summer houses in contemporary styles. One of the first was the Second Empire style aggrandizement of *Saluda Cottages. In the early 20th c., wealthy families enlarged and remade many of the houses in various Colonial Revival and Tudor Revival styles, with some of the latter designed by Asheville architect Richard Sharp Smith, best known for his work at *Biltmore.

In the late 20th c., Flat Rock, along with many of the most pleasant parts of the region, has experienced intensive development for retirees and families, and the old sense of quiet exclusivity has diminished. Historic Flat Rock, Inc., organized in 1968 and one of the state's oldest local preservation groups, has worked to maintain the character and architecture of the community. Even with changes, something of the unique quality of the community persists. Old and new families make their summer journeys to Flat Rock, where great trees and old houses stand beside the road, and gateways evoke private places beyond.

HN 13 St. John-in-the-Wilderness Episcopal Church

1833–34, 1852–54; Edward C. Jones (Charleston), architect; Ephraim Clayton, builder; NW corner US 25 and SR 1166

Erected by early Flat Rock residents Charles and Susan Baring as their private estate chapel in 1833 and conveyed to the Episcopal Church in 1836, the initial building took the form of an English rural chapel. In 1852 the church was "rebuilt," as noted on a marble tablet, when Charleston architect Edward C. Jones designed the transformation that expanded the church and added the tower.

Poised on a steep, wooded slope, St. John's evokes a Tuscan hill church with its sturdy corner tower and round-arched windows flanked by buttresses. Awning-type blinds bestow low-country shade at the windows along the sides. The round-arched motif continues within, where a round-arched, double hammer beam truss system rests on turned columns supported by bracket shelves. Some pews are marked with engraved plaques with family names; pew rents were discontinued in 1960.

The beautifully terraced and wooded churchyard holds fenced family plots with the graves and elaborate markers of parishioners, their family members, and others, including leading planter and merchant families, slaves, and freedpeople—Draytons, Grimkés, Middletons, Pinckneys, and many more. Old footpaths led from the church to nearby estates. Long used only during the summer season, the church began year-round services in 1958. (See Introduction, Fig. 22.)

HN 14 Old Flat Rock Post Office

1846; SE corner US 25 and SR 1123

A post office for Flat Rock was established in 1829. Believed to have been built ca. 1846 and adapted over the years, the 2-story, gable-fronted commercial type building served as the post office intermittently until 1965.

HN 15 Lowndes House and the Flat Rock

1884; NW corner US 25 and SR 1123

The T-plan frame house features a 1-story porch beneath a portico, with splayed eaves and latticed arches typical of 19th-c. Flat Rock; kingpost ornaments accent the steep gables. Richard I'On Lowndes built the house (which he called the Rock) near the large granite outcropping that was an ancient meeting place of the Cherokees and for which the community was named. Visible in the front yard of the house, the rock extends to the other side of the Greenville highway (US 25). The Vagabond School of Drama, N.C.'s first professional summer theater company, came to town in 1940 and acquired the house in 1956; it now serves the adjacent Flat Rock Playhouse summer theater.

HN 16 Peace's Store (The Wrinkled Egg)

Ca. 1900; SE corner US 25 and SR 1812

The frame service station and store recalls the importance of US 25 in the development of automobile tourism in Henderson Co. A longtime local gathering place, it was operated for decades by the Peace family as a general store and, later, also as a filling station that served motorists traveling from South Carolina to Flat Rock and beyond.

HN 17 Flat Rock Inn

1888; E side US 25, 0.3 mi. S of SR 1123; B&B

The 2-story, gable-fronted house was built as a relatively modest summer retreat for R. Withers Memminger, a minister from Charleston and the son of C. G. Memminger. Englishman Thomas Grimshawe and his wife, Elizabeth, bought it in 1911 and in 1930 passed it to their daughter, Greta Grimshawe King, and her husband, Campbell King, who made hot pepper sauce here.

HN 18 Woodfield Inn

1850–52; Edward C. Jones (Charleston), architect; Henry T. Farmer, builder; W side US 25, 0.3 mi. S of SR 1123; B&B and restaurant

To provide "a good commodious tavern" for summer visitors, Andrew Johnstone and Mitchell King built the 3-story frame hotel set back on a sweeping front lawn. Stock-holders' bills included $230 to E. C. Jones for plans—Edward C. Jones, architect for *St. John-in-the-Wilderness—and $7,000 to H. T. Farmer for building. The contractor and, later, the innkeeper was Henry Tudor Farmer, formerly a ward of the Baring family. He also built several other mid-19th-c. structures in the area. Recalling the 19th-c. popularity of the picturesque mode in Flat Rock, the 3-story, hip-roofed building retains scalloped cornices and a 2-tier porch with a diagonal latticed balustrade and lattice-framed arches. Variously known as the Farmer Hotel and the Flat Rock Hotel, the hostelry is claimed to be the oldest operating inn in the state.

HN 18 *Woodfield Inn*

HN 19 Tall Trees (Greenlawn)
Ca. 1840; W side US 25, 1 mi. S of SR 1123

The 2-story, hip-roofed house with bracketed eaves was built for Arthur Huger and Margaret King Huger, who received the land as a wedding gift from her father, Judge Mitchell King of *Argyle. The full-height portico with Doric columns was added in the 20th c.

HN 20 Connemara
Ca. 1839; S side SR 1123, 0.2 mi. W of US 25; National Historic Site; open regular hours

On land he bought from Charles Baring, Christopher Gustavus Memminger built a Greek Revival summer house, a symmetrical, 1½-story dwelling set high on a raised basement, as part of a farmstead that he called Rock Hill. Memminger, born in Ger-

many, was orphaned as a child in Charleston; was reared by Thomas Bennett, who became governor; and went on to become a legislator, secretary of the treasury for the Confederacy, and president of the Asheville & Spartanburg Railroad. In 1900 South Carolina textile industrialist Ellison A. Smyth bought the property; he changed the name to Connemara after his Irish ancestral homeland and constructed most of the farm buildings, the lake, and the stone walls to formalize it as his country estate.

HN 20 *Connemara*

The place is best known as the home (1945–67) of Carl Sandburg, the only American to receive Pulitzer prizes for both biography and poetry; he also produced works of history, children's stories, and fiction. His wife Paula raised goats on the farm, who nibbled away the formal layout created by Smyth. While at Connemara, Sandburg wrote his autobiography, *Always the Young Stranger*; a novel, *Remembrance Rock*; and several books of verse. The farm retains many of its outbuildings. After the writer's death in 1967, Connemara was developed as a National Historic Site by the National Park Service and maintained much as it was during the Sandburg years.

HN 21 Saluda Cottages
1836, 1887; N side SR 1123, 0.3 mi. W of US 25; private, visible from road

The towered mansion above its broad lawn was remade in 1887 from a simpler 2-story frame house. One of only a handful of towered Second Empire style houses in N.C., the stunning 2½-story house is dominated by a 3-story tower with a tiara of metal cresting and fronted by a Corinthian columned porte cochere. The original house was built for the Count Joseph Marie Gabriel St. Xavier de Choiseul, French consul to Charleston and Savannah; he named it Saluda Cottages because he also built 2 other frame houses nearby. After he moved to *Chanteloup, the place passed through several hands before Gen. Rudolph Seigling, former publisher of the *Charleston News and Courier*, expanded the house into its present form and called it Sans Souci.

HN 21 *Saluda Cottages*

HN 22 Mountain Lodge

1827–30, ca. 1940; SW side SR 1166, 0.1 mi. NW of SR 1198; visible from a distance

At their mountain lodge on a 3,000-acre estate, Charles and Susan Baring inaugurated Flat Rock's life as "The Little Charleston of the Mountains" and sold land to other summer colonists. Baring had come from England, married the rich widow Susan Heyward, and become a rice planter. To benefit her health the couple established a summer estate at Flat Rock, where they maintained an opulent way of life along English manorial lines. Built as an elaborate Federal style residence, the house gained a picturesque lattice porch and brackets during the mid-19th c., and in 1940 it was remodeled with an imposing full-height portico and a servants' wing.

HN 23 Teneriffe

Ca. 1855, ca. 1903; Richard Sharp Smith, architect; N side SR 1123, 0.1 mi. NE of SR 1124; private; B&B in season

The elaborate Tudor Revival house features half-timbering and pebbledash walls in the style popularized by architect Smith in *Biltmore Village and elsewhere in Asheville. It began as a picturesque frame cottage with sawnwork porch built for Dr. J. G. Schoolbred of Charleston. Under the ownership of New Orleans cotton broker Hugh Vincent (who had cornered the cotton market with Frank Hayne of *Beaumont), in 1903 the house was remodeled by Smith during an era of extensive local rebuilding.

HN 24 Camp Tonnawandah

1933–present; W side SR 1124, 0.35 mi. S of SR 1123

The complex of board-and-batten and log-sided buildings is representative of early 20th-c. summer camps in western N.C. Surrounding a swimming and boating lake are a large gym, dining hall, and a network of simple, wooden camper cabins. It was opened in 1933 by Grace Haynes, who bought an old fishing camp with its lodge built over the dam (still the dining hall) and transformed it into a girls' camp, which continues its traditional summer life.

HN 25 Beaumont

Mid-19th c., ca. 1915; Richard Sharp Smith, architect; Andrew Johnstone Dr., off Beaumont Dr., SW side SR 1127, 1 mi. SW of SR 1137

The hilltop and its surroundings were acquired in 1839 by rice planter Andrew Johnstone of Georgetown, S.C., who built a 1½-story summer house of locally quarried granite, with dormers and bargeboards in the Downing cottage mode. In 1864 Johnstone was murdered in his home by men posing as Confederate soldiers who had been "prowling about the pinery" while he dined with friends. About 1915, under the ownership of cotton broker Frank Hayne, architect Richard Sharp Smith expanded the house into a 2-story Tudor Revival residence surrounded

HN 25 *Beaumont*

by a 1-story, columned porch. He also designed a stable and servants' quarters. Beaumont now stands amidst a subdivision.

HN 26 Argyle
Early 19th c., mid-19th c., early 20th c.;
private, no public access or visibility

Judge Mitchell King, a distinguished Charlestonian and one of the founders of Flat Rock, is believed to have remodeled an existing ca. 1815 dwelling into a summer residence about 1830. The 2½-story frame house is enlarged by a deep, double-tier porch. Like other Flat Rock summer houses, Argyle gained lattice and bracketed trim in the mid-19th c., then was reworked in Neoclassical fashion in the

20th c. It is the only Flat Rock estate that remains in the original family.

HN 27 Chanteloup
1840–41, ca. 1870, ca. 1900;
Richard Sharp Smith [Asheville], architect;
private, no public access or visibility

The estate was begun by Count de Choiseul, who had built a house earlier at *Saluda Cottages. Around the turn of the century the house was remodeled by Asheville architect Richard Sharp Smith for the Norton sisters of Louisville, Ky. Built of uncoursed granite, the formally composed, 2-story, hip-roofed house with flanking wings and small classical portico stands on a hillside overlooking terraced gardens designed by the firm of Frederick Law Olmsted. After long neglect it is under restoration.

HN 28 High Bridge (Bridge #120)
1927–28; US 176, over the Green River,
between Saluda and East Flat Rock

In its day the highest bridge in the state at 138 feet above the river bed, the reinforced concrete bridge stretches 580 feet across the Green River gorge. There are four approach spans and three open-spandrel central arches—a spectacular sight from the riverside below. It was built by E. A. Woods &

HN 28 *High Bridge*

Co. of Andrews between May 1927 and April 1928. Because of deterioration, the bridge is slated for demolition.

HN 29 Tuxedo

The community around Lake Summit developed in the early 20th c. as a small industrial site and a resort attracting visitors from nearby Greenville, S.C., and environs. The **Green River Manufacturing Company** (1905–61; SE side US 25, opp. SR 1121) was begun in the early 20th c. as a yarn mill—later a cotton mill—and was the county's largest manufacturer for many years. J. O. Bell, with local builders, constructed the first sections of the multibuilding brick complex. He oversaw the plant's operation and became Tuxedo's founding father, postmaster, and magistrate. In the 1920s the Boys family began operating the plant under the name Green River Mills; it later became a J. P. Stevens facility. The original 1905 section has broad glass-block bays along one side. An early turnstile-type gate and gatehouse occupy the front yard.

Around **Lake Summit** are cottages from various eras, including several early 20th-c. bungalows and cottages with Craftsman detailing, some with rustic tree-branch stair railings and stone chimneys; many have early 20th-c. boathouses or party houses at the lake's edge. **Camp Mondamin** (early 20th c. to present; N side SR 1853 on Lake Summit; visible from S side of lake) is one of several summer camps established in the county during the first half of the 20th c. The complex includes board-and-batten and rustic structures informally arranged near the lake, such as a gambrel-roofed barn, outbuildings, and a pavilion. **Truss Bridge #63** (1921; Atlantic Bridge Co. [Charlotte]; SR 1852 at Lake Summit) is a Petit Camelback through-truss left in place when the adjacent concrete bridge was constructed.

HN 30 Davenport House

Ca. 1890; SE corner of jct. of SR 1218 and US 64, Horse Shoe vic.

The ornate little Queen Anne style house, unusually elaborate for a farmhouse, is cov-

ered in pebbledash stucco and features a prominent tower, metal-crested roof, and wraparound porch. Outbuildings include a barn with latticed vents.

HN 31 Shaws Creek Campground Church

1905; NE corner of jct. of SR 1309 and SR 1311, Yale vic.

Built for a Methodist congregation organized at a camp meeting ca. 1810, the small country church partakes of the Gothic Revival in its lancet windows and vestibule entrance, and brackets and sawnwork at the gable.

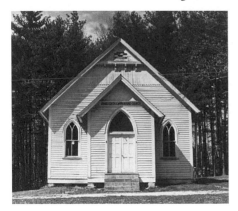

HN 31 *Shaws Creek Campground Church*

HN 32 Moss-Johnson Farm

1876–80, early 20th c.; Riley Barnett, builder; N side NC 191, between SR 1380 and SR 1463, Hendersonville vic.; open regular hours

The farm complex recalls the importance of both agriculture and tourism in the county's history. The centerpiece is a stylish, L-plan Italianate house built for Oliver Moss, who moved from South Carolina and operated a large farm, growing corn and engaging in the region's short-lived bright-leaf tobacco cultivation boom. Local builder Barnett constructed the 2-story house with bricks made from clay from the nearby banks of the French Broad River; the soft brick walls are covered in thin, red stucco with painted lines simulating mortar joints. Corbeled brickwork accentuates the arched windows, and a bracket cornice underlines the wide eaves. Rooms flanking a central passage are

HN 32 *Moss-Johnson Farm*

finished with crosseted door frames and fancy mantels. Outbuildings contemporary with the house include a board-and-batten **Granary** and a stuccoed brick **Smokehouse**.

In 1888 Moss sold the property to Robert and Mary Woodfin Liverett, whose widowed daughter, Sallie Liverett Johnson, later moved back home with her two young sons. After Robert's death in 1913, Sallie and her sons, Leander and Vernon, supported themselves by taking in summer boarders and made the place a favorite tourist mecca until after her death in 1958. To expand their tourist capacity, the Johnsons added a frame kitchen-dining ell to the house in 1915. Leander and Vernon built a comfortable but unheated **Boarding House** for summer boarders in 1923. They also built a large frame **Barn** with gambrel roof and vented eaves in 1923, and Vernon built a small house for himself in 1933. The brothers, longtime supporters of education, transferred the property to the local board of education. A new school was built on part of the land, and the farmstead is now operated as a museum by the county, with original furnishings and exhibits that quietly evoke farm life in the early to mid-20th c.

HN 33 Mills River Methodist Church
Ca. 1860–65; Americus Barnett, attributed builder; SE side SR 1328, 0.6 mi. NE of NC 280; Mills River vic.

The congregation traces its origins to the late 18th c., when James Brittain set aside part of his land for a camp meeting ground on this site. The first church was built in the 1820s. The present brick church, a simple, gable-fronted brick building with Greek Re-

vival detail, was begun around 1860 and completed at the close of the Civil War. The dominant portico is evidently a later 19th-c. alteration. A large cemetery contains many 19th-c. graves.

HN 34 Calvary Episcopal Church and Rectory
1859, tower; Edward C. Jones, architect; Ephraim Clayton, builder; rebuilt 1938; S. Grant Alexander [Asheville], architect; NE corner SR 1547 and US 25, Fletcher

The congregation was organized in 1857 at *The Meadows, the nearby home of Daniel Blake, who donated land for the church. In 1859 a Gothic Revival brick church was designed by Edward C. Jones of Charleston and built by Ephraim Clayton, who also built *St. John-in-the-Wilderness. After the church burned in 1934, a second Gothic Revival brick church replaced it, incorporating the surviving mid-19th-c. tower. The 2-story stone rectory (1885–86) stands across the road. The cemetery contains the grave of Edgar W. "Bill" Nye, journalist and humorist. Beginning in the 1920s the church allowed civic and patriotic groups to erect stones memorializing famous southerners, including Jefferson Davis, Francis Scott Key, Joel Chandler Harris, and Stephen Foster.

HN 35 The Meadows
Ca. 1860; S side SR 1547, 0.1 mi. W of SR 1545, Fletcher vic.

The large stone house is one of a number of imposing mid-19th-c. houses built along the Buncombe Turnpike in picturesque styles, and several in stone, such as *Rugby Grange and *Newington. The 2-story house of granite rubble is rendered in a simplified Italianate style with a bracket cornice beneath a hip roof. Daniel Blake was one of the first South Carolinians to establish a summer home in the area; he purchased land in 1827 near the new Buncombe Turnpike and soon built a residence. After that dwelling burned, Daniel's son Robert replaced it ca. 1860 with the present stone house. After several owners in the 20th c., the house is owned by a corporation.

HN 35 *The Meadows*

stone blocks quarried from nearby Burney Mountain is believed to have been erected by William Heyward of South Carolina before the Civil War, but it stood unfinished when it was acquired in 1868 by Gustaf Westfeldt, a retired, Swedish-born businessman who had lived in Mobile, New York, and England. Naming it for Rugby, the school in England, the Westfeldt family finished the house and added many other buildings over the years, as part of a large working farm that reached past the route of I-26.

HN 36 Rugby Grange

Ca. 1854–61, ca. 1868–70s; E. side I-26, 1.6 mi. S of NC 280, Fletcher vic.; private, no public access; visible in winter at a distance

Poised on its bluff, the big stone house is one of several mid-19th-c. essays in the picturesque mode that grew up along the Buncombe Turnpike (cf. *The Meadows at Fletcher and *Newington in Buncombe Co.). The massive, 2-story house is adorned in Italianate style with a bracket cornice, porch, and bay windows, plus a central cupola. The structure of uncoursed lime-

HN 37 Rockwood Inn

Ca. 1902; N side US 64/74A at Bat Cave; open regular hours

An unexpected sight on the old highway through Hickory Nut gap, the capacious Queen Anne style house features a peaked, cross-gabled corner tower and a wraparound porch. It was built for Adolph Hudgins and his wife as their home and a boardinghouse, then served as an inn from the 1920s into the 1960s. It is now a gift shop and residence.

Transylvania County (TV)

See Laura A. W. Phillips and Deborah Thompson, Transylvania: The Architectural History of a Mountain County *(1998).*

Brevard (TV 1–9)

The county seat and college town is best known as a center of summer camping and for its summer music festival. It was established as seat of newly formed Transylvania Co. in 1861, but completion of public buildings was delayed until after the Civil War. When the county was formed, it was peopled mainly by farmers who tended crops and orchards and raised livestock on the hillsides. White settlement had begun on the county's Davidson River and Cathy's Creek soon after the American Revolution. In the late 19th and early 20th centuries the county's forested slopes and beautiful waterfalls encouraged establishment of resort colonies, summer camps, and private and eventually national forest preserves at *Pisgah Forest. Industrial plants including lumber mills and tanneries also took advantage of the natural bounty.

Brevard grew slowly until the 1895 arrival of the Hendersonville & Brevard Railroad, which, with its successor the Transylvania Railroad Co., allowed the community to compete with neighboring towns already served by rail. The town grew from 350 people in 1898 to nearly 600 by 1900. Rail extensions in 1900 and 1903 to the formerly remote southwest part of the county stimulated growth of industry and tourism at Rosman and at Lake Toxaway, with its famed Toxaway Inn, and boosted Brevard's fortunes in the process.

The Brevard Board of Trade promoted tourism by touting the temperate winters as well as summers in the "Land of Waterfalls" amid "the Beautiful Sapphire Country." Several hotels and more than thirty family-run boardinghouses catered to the tourist trade. As the national summer camp movement developed, a national camping handbook identified Brevard as "the most important center for camps in the South."

A progressive spirit of improvement brought water and sewer lines, paved sidewalks, and other amenities by 1910. The *Cascade Power Co., built on the Little River in 1908 to power the Brevard Cotton Mill, provided electricity to the town as well. In addition to attracting wealthy tourists and industrialists, Brevard boasted a Methodist school, Epworth, which became Brevard Institute in 1909. The *Sylvan Valley News* (1907) exalted Brevard as "one of America's most beautiful towns," with beauty "both internal and external—internal because of its wide and well paved streets, lined on either side with shade trees," and residential sections "like great parks with beautiful homes with extensive, well kempt and shaded lawns; external because of the surrounding hills and mountains." "Brevard's stride has ever been forward; no falling off in population, a record of clean, steady growth and development."

Brevard's principal historic architecture dates from the 1890s–1930s era. Particularly distinctive is its varied stonework, including cut stone, rounded river rock, and jagged rocks. The best-known stonemasons were the Wright brothers—William Benjamin Franklin "Doc," James Robert, and Joseph Few Wright—who came from their native Hendersonville ca. 1919, having learned their trade from their father, James Robert Wright. Fred Mills, a black stonemason, learned his trade from the Wrights; he worked for them and also on his own and with another black stonemason, Avery Benjamin. These men in various combinations worked in the community from the 1920s into the 1950s, building churches, houses, walls, and other structures.

TV 1 Downtown Brevard

The **Transylvania County Courthouse** (1880–81; NE corner E. Main and N. Broad

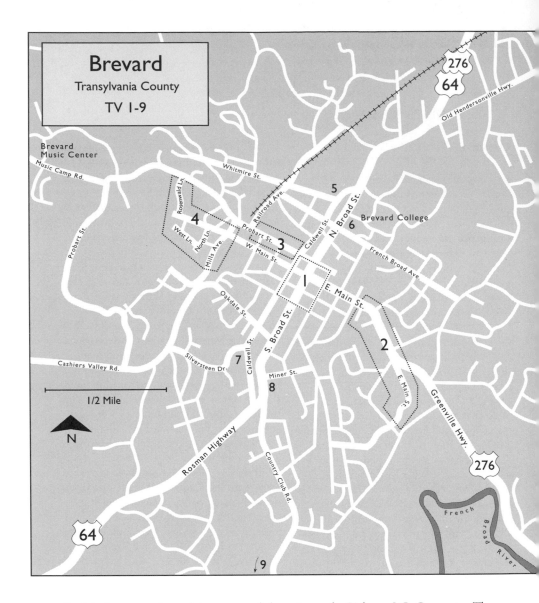

Brevard
Music Center

Music Camp Rd.

Whitmire St.

Brevard College

Rosenwald Ln.

West Ln.

North Ln.

Mills Ave.

Probart St.

Probart St.

Railroad Ave.

W. Main St.

Caldwell St.

N. Broad St.

French Broad Ave.

E. Main St.

Oakdale St.

S. Broad St.

Caldwell St.

Silversteen Dr.

Miner St.

E. Main St.

Greenville Hwy.

Cashiers Valley Rd.

Rosman Highway

Country Club Rd.

Old Hendersonville Hwy.

French Broad River

1/2 Mile

N

276

64

276

64

Sts.) is the centerpiece of the town and the oldest surviving courthouse in the mountain region. The T-plan, Italianate style brick building features segmental-arched windows and a 3-story entrance tower with mansard roof. Quoins emphasize the corners and the entrance. In a curious feature, the first-story facade has blind loopholes rather than windows.

Authorized in 1874, the brick building replaced the initial frame courthouse built in the 1860s. In traditional fashion the plans were drawn up after a visit to the courthouse in nearby Pickens, S.C. Contractor Thomas W. Davis's plans were approved in 1879, and construction was completed in 1881. The chain of influence continued when *Clay County Courthouse was designed after inspection of this building and that in Macon Co.

Radiating from the courthouse corner are brick commercial buildings of 1 to 3 stories. The earliest and most intact is the prominent corner building, the **McMinn Building** (1899; 2–6 W. Main St.), a 2-story brick block with corbeling and fine pressed-

TV 1 *Transylvania Co. Courthouse*

metal trim at street level, including free-standing metal columns fronting a recessed entrance at 6 W. Main—products of Mesker Bros. Front Builders, St. Louis, Mo. The first brick building in town after the courthouse, it was erected for leading merchant Nathan Van Buren McMinn and originally contained his Brevard Banking Co., a drugstore, and shops on the first floor, plus offices on the second; it remains in the family.

The big, 2-story **Aethelwold Hotel** (1903–4; R. P. Kilpatrick, contractor; SE corner S. Broad and E. Main Sts.), though decapitated of its third-story mansard roof, remains a strong presence with its corbeled brickwork and rusticated stone detailing recalling its former elegance. It was erected for Nathan McMinn's son John by Kilpatrick,

the town's leading builder at the turn of the century. The (former) **Brevard Banking Company** (1924; R. P. Kilpatrick, contractor; 73 W. Main St.), built for the bank founded by McMinn and originally housed in the McMinn Building, is a yellow brick building on a key corner, featuring an engaged portico of Tuscan columns typical of bankers' reassuring classicism of the 1910s and 1920s.

The former **U.S. Post Office** (Transylvania Co. Library; 1940; Louis Simon, supervising architect of the Treasury; 105 S. Broad St.) is a characteristic public works post office, a 1-story red brick building with limestone trim in simplified Georgian Revival style.

TV 2 East Main Street

The shaded residential avenue reaching east from downtown presents Brevard's prime collection of stylish residential architecture in a spectrum of early 20th-c. modes. Although many small towns once boasted such prestigious residential thoroughfares adjoining the commercial district, few have fared so well over the years.

St. Philip's Episcopal Church (1927; Louis H. Asbury [Charlotte], architect; Wright brothers and Fred Mills, stonemasons; 317 E. Main St.) anchors a key corner.

TV 1 *McMinn Building*

Home of a congregation that traces its origins to 1856, the Norman Revival church of stone was designed by Asbury, the noted Charlotte architect who worked in several western N.C. towns. It was among the first of Brevard's stone buildings executed by the Wright brothers and Fred Mills. The stone was donated by quarry owner William E. Breese. A number of houses in the neighborhood are credited to the same artisans. The workmen and stone supposedly from the same quarry created the **Charles E. Orr House** (1926; Wright brothers and Fred Mills, attributed stonemasons; 334 E. Main St.), a picturesque, 2-story English style stone house across the street, built for Brevard's postmaster.

The **William E. Breese Jr. House** (Inn at Brevard) (ca. 1901; 401 E. Main St.) is a big Southern Colonial style residence with 2-story Ionic portico; in a favored local practice the walls are covered with pebbledash (stucco textured with pebbles). It was built for Martha Woodbridge, who came from Richmond, Va., to establish a home for herself and her daughter Rebekah and son-in-law William E. Breese Jr., attorney and political figure, mayor, legislator, and district director of the Works Progress Administration (WPA). The house was opened as an inn and restaurant in 1955.

Brevard's most imposing residence is **Silvermont** (1916; French and Co. [New York], attributed architects; 455 E. Main St.; open limited hours). Standing in a parklike setting, the 33-room Georgian Revival residence is one of western N.C.'s most ambitious private houses beyond Asheville. Symmetrically composed and richly detailed, the brick house features a broad gambrel roof and a tall semicircular portico overlapping a wraparound porch. The interior retains its high-quality Georgian Revival millwork. The house was built for Joseph Silversteen, the Pennsylvania tanner who came to Transylvania Co. in 1902 and established tanning and timber businesses in Rosman and Brevard that made him the county's leading industrialist. At his death in 1958 Silversteen was described as the county's "wealthiest and most influential man." He and his wife Elizabeth Mount are said to have employed the New

York architectural firm of French and Co. to design their residence. Their daughter Dorothy Bjerg left the property to the county in 1972; the house (saved from demolition by a local preservation campaign) and its 8-acre grounds serve as the public recreation center.

TV 2 *Silvermont*

Beyond these opulent Colonial Revival statements, a more informal, often rustic mode prevails, with special strength in Craftsman-influenced forms. The **C. D. Chapman House** (1917; Mr. Norwood, builder; 458 E. Main St.) is a particularly intact shingled Craftsman style dwelling with river rock used in foundations, chimneys, porch piers, and retaining walls. Chapman was rector (1896–1917) of *St. Philip's Episcopal Church.

The earliest example of local stonework is the **Royal and Louise Morrow House** (1915; R. P. Kilpatrick, contractor; Mr. Norwood, carpenter; 563 E. Main St.), inspired by a "Craftsman Stone House" design published in Gustav Stickley's *The Craftsman* (June 1909) and described as evoking "picturesque cottages to be found in the north of England, the severity of line in the steeply sloping roof being broken by two long dormers." The stones came from the ruins of the 19th-c. Hume Hotel, the first stone building in the county, located on the Greenville highway. Royal Morrow, a civil engineer, designed several of the county's summer camps using rustic stonework and timber as well as working for the U.S. Forest Service; he also chaired the building committee for St. Philip's nearby.

Another face of local stonework appears in the **Max and Claire Brombacher House**

TV 2 *Royal and Louise Morrow House*

(ca. 1940; Wright brothers, stonemasons; 571 E. Main St.), a unique house with dark, jaggedly textured stone walls. Family tradition recalls that the masons first laid walls in their conventional stonework but that Mrs. Brombacher insisted they redo it, to make the house "look like it grew here," with no visible mortar or squared corners.

TV 3 Probart Street

The residential street near the business district contains representative houses mainly from the early 20th c. The street was named for W. Probart Poor, an early Brevard citizen who ran a store in the Red House; initially called Poor St., it was renamed at the behest of residents who found the name unsuitable. Several of the houses were built as speculative investments by local contractor R. P. Kilpatrick around 1910.

Among the oldest buildings in town is the **Red House** (19th c., 1912; 412 W. Probart St.), a 2-story stuccoed dwelling with a 2-tier porch. It was built on the site and may incorporate elements of a trading post built in 1851 for Leander Sams Gash. Showing mainly ca. 1890 architectural character, it has served as a boardinghouse ("the Red House"); the Epworth Institute school (founded 1895, predecessor of Brevard Institute); a dwelling; and a bed and breakfast.

The **Henry House** (1910s; Smith & Carrier [Asheville], architects; 300 W. Probart St.) is an elegant 1½-story residence with the first-story walls covered with pebbledash and the upper story shingled, complemented by the sophisticated blend of classical and Craftsman detailing characteristic of Asheville architect Richard Sharp Smith.

TV 4 Rosenwald School Neighborhood

The traditionally black neighborhood presents important work by leading local stonemasons. Long a vital community center, the **Rosenwald School** (1948; 400 Rosenwald Lane) was built after its predecessor burned in 1941; that 1923 school had been built with assistance from the Julius Rosenwald fund that aided construction of many southern schools for black students, and the new stone school retained the name. Like the contemporary *Pisgah Forest School, it is a 1-story schoolhouse built of local stone. Closed as a school in 1966, it houses offices of the board of education.

TV 4 *Fred Mills House*

Two nearby houses display the handiwork of leading local stonemasons on their own homes. The **Fred Mills House** (1916, 1930s; 303 West Lane) is a frame bungalow that was the home of the prolific and well-known stonemason Mills, a one-armed craftsman who learned his trade from the Wright brothers. He worked with the Wright brothers, on his own, and with Avery Benjamin, and he also worked at the Silversteen tannery. His wife, Ethel Kennedy Mills, was principal at the nearby *Rosenwald School. Fred Mills employed his skills and stone left over from his projects to enrich his home and present a sampler of his work: he stone veneered the house, built a porch with stone piers, and added walls, a walk, and other stone elements to the yard. The nearby **Avery Benjamin House** (1910, 1940s; 315 West Lane) began as a frame cottage, but

Benjamin, protégé of Mills, veneered it with stone and, over time, constructed stone porch posts, chimneys, foundations, walks, and retaining walls.

The **Jip Mills Store** (1920, 1927; 35 Mills Ave.) was built by Mills, a prominent citizen in Brevard's black community, and housed his grocery store and, later, his widow's beauty parlor; the brick building began as a 1-story structure but was expanded to 2 stories. It recalls the importance of small grocery stores in residential neighborhoods as well as the importance of black-owned businesses to the community.

TV 5 Transylvania Lodge
(William E. Breese Sr. House)
Ca. 1895; 500 N. Caldwell St.; private

The big frame house, covered with pebble-dash early in the 20th c., features a long, 2-tier porch well-used during its service as a summer boardinghouse. It was built for Asheville banker and Confederate veteran Breese, who retired here and named it Transylvania Lodge. (He had formerly built an elaborate residence, *Cedar Crest, in Asheville.) His daughters and a cousin ran the boardinghouse.

TV 6 Brevard College
Stone Walls and Gate
1936–37; Wright brothers, attributed stonemasons; NE corner N. Broad St. and French Broad Ave.

Brevard's prime display of local stonework appears in the walls and gate that border the college campus; a freestanding, arched gate at the corner is flanked by stone walls that extend more than 200 feet along each street. The Methodist-supported college opened in 1934 in the depths of the Great Depression as an economy merger of two Methodist schools (*Rutherford College and *Weaver College) on the campus of a third, Brevard Institute (est. 1895 as Epworth Institute), which had closed in 1933. The campus has seen several generations of simply detailed red brick buildings. Construction of the stone wall to define an athletic field at the southwest corner of the campus was a WPA project. Tradition reports that students helped the Wright brothers build the walls and gathered the rounded, multihued river rock from the Davidson River, a tributary of the French Broad River.

TV 7 John Duckworth House
1905; 408 S. Caldwell St.; private

Towered and turreted, the Queen Anne style house with its wraparound porch is the prime example of the late Victorian mode in Brevard. Located on a prominent lot, it was built for a real estate man.

TV 8 Godfrey-Barnette House
Ca. 1918; 411 S. Broad St.; private

The English cottage-style stone house with sweeping, clipped gables was among the first of Brevard's many stone residences. It was built for Jennie E. Godfrey, a popular high school teacher; students are said to have helped gather the stones.

TV 8 *Godfrey-Barnette House*

TV 9 Brevard Country Club
(Old Hickory Barbecue Restaurant)
Mid-1930s; 842 Country Club Rd.; open as restaurant

The rustic, rambling building displays the round logs and rough fieldstone in the Adirondack-inspired style frequently employed in the area's summer camps. Built as a public, municipal clubhouse with a 9-hole golf course, it was one of three WPA construction projects in Brevard.

TV 10 Montclove

1850s; private, no public access or visibility

Low-country South Carolinians built elaborate 19th-c. residences on mountain estates they established in the upper French Broad River valley. Only a few still stand, and those are remote from public view. Sited high above the river and built for Francis Withers Johnstone, Montclove is a picturesque L-shaped house with steep gabled roof and dormers, reflecting the Gothic Revival cottage style also popular in the summer colony at Flat Rock, where Johnstone's father had an estate (cf. *Beaumont). Captain Johnstone, active in forming Transylvania Co., led a company of county volunteers in the Civil War.

TV 11 Transylvania Tanning Company Smokestack

1916; SR 1344, Brevard vic.

Despite the importance of the industry to the county and the region, little remains from the big tanneries that once used tannin from the local chestnut and oak trees to tan skins into leather. The 180-foot-tall brick smokestack, tapered to a corbeled cap and with "T. T. Co." running down its length in contrasting brick, is the last structure standing of the Transylvania Tanning Co., established near Brevard by Joseph Silversteen, founder of a tannery and other factories at Rosman.

TV 12 Oak Grove Church

Late 19th c.; W side US 64/276,
just N of SR 1556, Brevard vic.

The simple frame church and its tidy cemetery form an oasis among the development along the highway. Graves in the churchyard are unusually old for the county, dating back to 1854. The congregation began in 1847 in association with a Methodist campground. The modest, 1-story, gable-fronted church has a gabled entrance vestibule and simple 6/6 sash windows. A large frame wing extends on one side. Long a Methodist church, it is now home to a Baptist congregation.

TV 13 Pisgah Forest School

1948; W side SR 1512, 0.2 mi. N of
SR 1504, Pisgah Forest

The long, 1-story school of native stone is said to have been constructed with WPA funds, though it was not completed until 1948. It is one of several stone schoolhouses built in the region by the program.

TV 14 Ecusta Paper Mill

1938 and later; SR 1512, Pisgah Forest vic.;
access restricted

Toward the end of the Great Depression, inventor Harry Straus of New York established the Ecusta Paper Co. on the Davidson River near Pisgah National Forest—a site that provided clean water and pure air plus proximity to the population and services of Brevard. The plant, which offered welcome employment opportunities to the depressed economy, provided amenities such as a cafeteria, an infirmary, and eventually a camp for employees' families. The factory employed an innovative process to make very fine paper, used as cigarette paper, from raw flax rather than linen rags, and when the onset of World War II cut access to European fine paper plants, Ecusta expanded production. The plant soon diversified to other products, including cellophane. Although enlarged and modernized over the years, the complex retains several original mill, warehouse, and other buildings. Especially distinctive is the **Cafeteria**, a 1½-story brick building with bracketed eaves, a front porch, and stone chimneys.

TV 15 Patton Houses

Late 19th c.; NW corner NC 280
and US 64/276, Pisgah Forest vic.;
private, visible from road

On the hillside overlooking the crossing of two important old roads—now a dense commercial intersection—stand two unusually ornate frame farmhouses, exemplifying late 19th-c. styles more characteristic of urban settings. The **Robert E. Patton House** (1880s) shows Gothic Revival, picturesque influence in its steep roof and its gables and dormers framing triangular-headed windows; it was built for a prosperous farmer who was the grandson of pioneer Elizur Patton. Just to the east the **Fitzgerald Patton House** (ca. 1895) displays the irregular massing and varied textures of the Queen Anne style, with half-timbering adorning the gables and a wraparound porch. After Robert Patton's first wife died, leaving an infant son, Fitzgerald, Robert built this house for his three maiden sisters and bachelor brother, providing for them to raise his son there.

TV 16 *Allison-Deaver House*

TV 15 *Robert E. Patton House*

TV 16 Allison-Deaver House

Early 19th c., mid-19th c.; NW side NC 280, 0.1 mi. NE of US 64/276, Pisgah Forest vic.; visible from road; open limited hours

One of the oldest frame dwellings in the state west of the Blue Ridge, the big house was built in stages and reached its present form by the mid-19th c. It began as a 2-story timber-framed house, with a 3-room plan and an exterior end chimney heating the larger room. This section evidently dates from the 1813–30 ownership of Benjamin Allison.

William Deaver bought the property in 1830, including "the house where said Allison now lives." A native of Buncombe Co., he married Margaret Patton of the Davidson River area in 1833. The family prospered, and by 1850 their 800-acre farm included 300 acres cultivated in corn and other grains. The Deavers, who had seven children, enlarged the house over the years. An expansion rendered in late Federal and Greek Revival style doubled the size of the house and reoriented it to accommodate a rerouting of the road. An additional large room on both floors produced an unusual central chimney arrangement, and unheated rooms enclosed the original front porch, which was now considered the rear of the house. Evidently in the 1850s the Deavers added the distinctive 2-tier engaged front porch, a feature seen elsewhere in western N.C. and often associated with the influence from coastal areas. The trim is similar to the *Woodfield Inn in Flat Rock. An exterior stair links the two tiers of the porch—another feature typical of the coastal region.

During the Civil War, William Deaver, aged seventy-one, is said to have been shot to death at his doorstep by Union bushwhackers in pursuit of his son James, a Confederate officer. The farm remained in family hands until the mid-20th c. and has been restored as a local project.

TV 17 Pisgah National Forest Bridges

Late 1930s; US 276, Pisgah National Forest

Along the winding route through the forest, a series of stone bridges carries the road across Looking Glass Creek. The **Gateway** to the National Forest is of heavy cut stone, with plaques honoring World War I dead. Four low stone bridges appear at approximately 1-mile intervals. Each has a central arched concrete span and concrete guardrails, with the end piers and retaining walls of beautifully laid cut stone topped by shaped concrete. These are described as the work of Italian stonemasons who later worked on the *Devil's Courthouse Tunnel on the Blue Ridge Parkway.

TV 18 Cradle of Forestry
(Biltmore Forest School)

1890s–1909; E side US 276, about 3.0 mi.
S of Blue Ridge Parkway; open regular hours

Located in Pisgah National Forest, the Cradle of Forestry complex commemorates the establishment here of the nation's first forestry school. When George W. Vanderbilt developed his vast *Biltmore Estate, his landscape architect Frederick Law Olmsted encouraged him to employ a forester to improve the eroded farm and forest lands he had acquired. A forestry program would enable Vanderbilt to profit from timber production and provide a national model at a time when America's timber industry was booming but the nation lacked any forestry management programs.

TV 18 *Black Forest Lodge*

At Olmsted's suggestion Vanderbilt hired forester Gifford Pinchot, a Pennsylvania native trained in France. Beginning in 1892 Pinchot developed a plan for the 7,000 acres at Biltmore to combine selective timbering with reforestation—the first application of long-term forestry principles in America. He also prepared an exhibit and pamphlet on "practical forestry" at Biltmore for the World's Columbian Exposition in 1893. In 1895, at Pinchot's recommendation, Vanderbilt purchased approximately 100,000 acres of forest around Mount Pisgah for a hunting preserve and timberland, which he called Pisgah Forest. (Additional land was bought and sold over the years.) Pinchot left Biltmore in 1895 and by 1898 was chief forester for the U.S. government.

The second Biltmore forester was Carl A. Schenck, a professionally trained young German. He began a systematic forestry program at Biltmore Forest and Pisgah Forest, and by 1898 had a working forestry plan for 120,000 acres—the first in the nation. Rangers stationed throughout the forest protected it against fire and deterred poachers. With Vanderbilt's support, Schenck founded the Biltmore Forest School, teaching practical forestry with headquarters at *Biltmore Village and a field school in Pisgah Forest. After Vanderbilt saw key investments fail, however, he considered selling Pisgah Forest in 1908, and in 1909 closed the forestry school. Schenck continued the school at other locations until 1913. In its short life the school trained more than 300 foresters and made a lasting mark on American forestry. In 1912 Vanderbilt sold timber rights in Pisgah Forest to the Carr Lumber Co., and in 1916 his widow sold 87,000 acres for the establishment of Pisgah National Forest, stipulating retention of the name.

At the Cradle of Forestry center are several restored and reconstructed structures from the Biltmore Forest School, including reconstructions of the schoolhouse, the commissary, a student dwelling, and Carl A. Schenck's office. Original to the site is the **Hiram King House** (1882), a 1-story, weatherboarded, chestnut-framed dwelling with stone chimneys and an engaged front porch. It was built for King and his wife Eliza on a 50-acre farm they bought in 1880. King, a carpenter and sawmill owner as well as a farmer, recalled Schenck, was considered "the rich man of the settlement," with the "largest and best house." With Vanderbilt's purchase of surrounding land, King's sawmill closed, and in 1901 he sold his land to Vanderbilt.

Of special interest are the two **Black Forest Lodges**, moved here from other sites in Pisgah Forest. Vanderbilt's forest rangers' houses, built ca. 1898–1904 at various spots in the forest, included several log "cabins" worth $50 to $100 each, as well as about a dozen of these "heavy timber houses," valued at $250 apiece. Designed by Schenck after models in the Black Forest where he had studied, they were built by local men, including Ulysses Reeves, who later recalled, "When we built the Black Forest Lodges, John Grant started building them. He was too religious, Dr. Schenck fired him, and Marion Whitaker took over the job. Webb Orr hewed the boards, John Watts built the chimneys." Chestnut and oak were used extensively, including the hand-rived roof shingles.

Only two survive: the **Rockhouse Creek Lodge (Black Forest Lodge)**, located on the interpretive trail and furnished for viewing by visitors, and the similar **Cantrell Creek Lodge**, near the visitors' center. The Rockhouse Creek Lodge is a wonderfully picturesque, timber-framed structure 1½ stories tall beneath a steep gable roof. Exposed heavy framing of chestnut features curved corner braces decorating the gables. In contrast to *fachwerk*, or half-timbering with masonry or plastered infill, here the spaces between timbers are filled with thick plank. (Photographs show other lodges had plaster infill.) The double sill sits on stone piers. Two main rooms flank a central stone chimney and open to an inset porch. These small Black Forest lodges add a unique Germanic motif to the region's rustic and romantic architectural repertoire inspired by the mountain setting.

See Harold T. Pinkett, *Gifford Pinchot, Private and Public Forester* (1970); Carl Alwin Schenck, *The Birth of Forestry in America: Biltmore Forest School, 1898–1913* (1974); and F. H. Tainter and B. M. Cool, *This Was Forestry in America: The Biltmore Forest School, 1898–1913* (n.d.).

TV 19 Devil's Courthouse Tunnel

1937; Blue Ridge Parkway,
1.1 mi. E of NC 215

Framed by circular-arched entrances of rough-cut native stone, the 720-foot-long tunnel runs through the rock formation known as Devil's Courthouse. It displays the excellent craftsmanship of the Blue Ridge Parkway's stonework; it is attributed to Italian stonemasons, but whether these were men from the Waldensian community around Valdese is not clear. Similar work appears in the stone retaining walls and guard

walls nearby. This was the last section of the parkway built in the county before the hiatus during World War II.

TV 20 Blythe-Whitmire Farm

Early 20th c.; N side SR 1504,
0.8 mi. W of SR 1528, Penrose vic.;
private, visible from road

In 1935 W. T. Whitmire, who worked at the nearby Penrose Quarry, bought the farm where Clyde Blythe had built a frame bungalow and a frame barn with gambrel roof, typical of Progressive era farmsteads. Whitmire soon began to apply his knowledge of stonework to his new property. He added a stone extension to Blythe's barn, then built a gambrel-roofed dairy barn with a frame loft atop a fieldstone base. About 1957 he began his masterpiece, which started as a stone, 2-car garage but evolved into a more creative and never-ending project. Whitmire and his children hauled rock from the Penrose Quarry and the French Broad River, and friends donated stones from other sources, as the stone structure beside the house developed into an unfinished composition akin to a small folly or romantic ruin, with open decks offering views of the nearby valley and mountains. Rock walls, minor outbuildings, and various ornamental features likewise display Whitmire's handiwork that continued until his death in 1984.

TV 21 Evan and Catherine Talley Farm

Ca. 1880 and later; N side US 64,
opp. SR 1528, Penrose vic.; private,
visible from road

This archetypal mountain valley farmstead lies beside a major highway. The 2-story frame dwelling takes an I-house form, with a hip-roofed porch, rear kitchen ell, and stone end chimneys. A breezeway links the ell to a smokehouse and springhouse. Shaded by big trees, the house and surrounding outbuildings fit among the gentle knolls and valleys. Local stone is used in retaining walls, chimneys, and foundations. The farm buildings include a large frame **Stock Barn** with a gable roof and central passage running the length of the barn; a concrete silo was added in the 1920s. Especially striking is the **Corn-crib**, a narrow frame building with slatted sides and a gable roof that reaches out to cover open sheds on both sides.

TV 22 Cascade Grocery

1908; Martin Luther Hamilton, builder; W side SR 1536, 0.1 mi. S of SR 1528, Little River vic.; private, visible from road

The country store and storekeeper's house often served as a social and economic landmark. Displaying the locally prevalent stonework, this 1-story store is built of ashlar stone blocks, with the storefront recessed in the gable end. Builder Hamilton is also said to have built the original *Cascade Powerhouse. The store was run by Charles Ashworth, who sold it to Volney McCrary in the 1930s; McCrary's 1-story frame house stands nearby.

TV 23 Cascade Power Company Dam and Powerhouse

1908–9, 1920s; E side SR 1536, 0.5 mi. S of SR 1534, Little River vic.; private, visible from road

The facility on the Little River was established and a dam built in 1908–9, when R. J. Pickleshimer and his sons formed the Cascade Power Co. to produce electric power for the family's Brevard Cotton Mill. Excess power was sufficient to establish the Brevard Light and Power Co. to serve the town as well. The initial dam was rebuilt, and the wooden powerhouse was replaced in the 1920s with a brick building that has the manager's domestic quarters on the second floor. The plant now provides electric power to the Duke Power Co.

TV 24 Cedar Mountain

US 276 at SR 1536 and 1560

Located near the state line, the community of Cedar Mountain developed after the Civil War when South Carolinians established a colony of summer cottages on the Greenville Rd., creating a successor to an antebellum summer colony at Dunns Rock. Set well back in the trees, most of the cottages are only glimpsed from the road, except in winter. They are generally unpretentious, informal frame dwellings dating from the 1880s onward. A community focal point is **Faith Memorial Chapel** (1938; W side SR 1100, 0.4 mi. S of US 276), an open-air chapel built by Episcopalians to serve as summer worship space, which welcomes all denominations. After a 19th-c. frame chapel fell into decay, nearby residents stored pews and other fittings in their homes, and these were restored to use in the new setting. In the stone and timber structure, the traditional pews beneath a steep-pitched, open truss ceiling suggest a conventional sanctuary, but the open sides and natural materials convey a sense of summer camp life.

TV 25 Carr's Hill Baptist Church

1903; E side SR 1538, 0.1 mi. S of SR 1537, E side US 276

Typical of the region, when the congregation was organized, members built the sanctuary on a prominent knoll terraced above the bottomlands. The simple frame church with gabled front vestibule and belfry gains presence from its site overlooking See Off Mountain Rd. The congregation descended from Dunn's Rock Baptist Church. Members planned and constructed the church and named it for the hill on which it stands, which was donated by member Carr Landreth.

TV 26 Federal Distillery

Mid-19th c.; W side US 276, 0.1 mi. N of SR 1103, Dunns Rock

The starkly plain, 3-story frame building once housed a federally licensed distillery, one of three such enterprises that once operated in the county. Federal licenses were issued to legal whiskey distilleries, hence the name Federal Distillery. Tradition claims this distillery ran from the 1850s until Prohibition. The heavy timber-framed building stands on a fieldstone basement; a water-wheel once powered the grinding of corn for mash. Distilling took place on the second floor. In recent years it has served as a pottery shop and camp headquarters for nearby

Camp Rockbrook. (Occupying much of a former summer estate, Rockbrook is one of several local summer camps featuring natural stonework and rustic timber buildings. Like the others, entrance to the camp is restricted to campers and their families and visitors.)

TV 27 Camp Illahee
Est. 1921; SW side SR 1114, 0.6 mi.
E of US 64; private, visible from road

Of the many summer camps established in the county between 1915 and 1930 for girls or boys, several still flourish, including Keystone (1916), Rockbrook (1921), and Gwynne Valley (1935). For generations, children have come from faraway towns and cities for several weeks, as a camp brochure explained, to learn skills in sports and woodcraft and to build "self-esteem, friendships, and true happiness" in a "rustic setting . . . specifically designed to allow the campers to come into close contact with nature." Typically the camps were built around an artificial lake, with Adirondack-style log and stone group facilities, and tents or cabins for age-grouped campers and their counselors. Continuing the sense that "nature and camp give us a much-needed respite from the busyness of civilization," these long-lived summer camps also place strong emphasis on campfire traditions that reach back through generations of young campers to the early 20th c.

Most of the camps occupy sites intentionally secluded from public highways. Camp Illahee may be glimpsed from the road. It was established in 1921 by Mr. and Mrs. Hinton McLeod as a camp for girls; the name is said to be Cherokee for "heavenly world." The earliest structures represent the forms favored by camp leaders in the early 20th c. Rustic stone and timber main buildings include **Tilley Lodge** (1921), the dining hall, a rambling, oft-expanded timber building with tree-trunk porch posts, and, by the original 1921 lake, **McLeod Lodge** (1924), which has bark-covered walls and a porch set on arches over the lake. These are complemented by traditional board-and-batten cabins with screened windows. More recent buildings continue the traditional character.

TV 27 *McLeod Lodge, Camp Illahee*

TV 28 Lance-Raines House
Late 19th–early 20th c.; N side SR 1108,
0.3 mi. W of SR 1103, East Fork vic.;
private, visible from road

The little house, now part of a Girl Scout facility, relates to the boxed houses once numerous in the region. When sawmills made planks cheap and available, such houses became a common successor to log building. In this variation, vertical boards are nailed to a minimal frame and exposed within. A beautiful dry-laid fieldstone chimney heats the single main room, and the rear shed is unheated. The earliest known resident was Joe Lance, who moved there in 1917, and it was later occupied by the Raines brothers, who applied the hand-split shingle roof and built the outbuildings.

TV 29 Flem Galloway House
1878; W side SR 1388, 2 mi. S of SR 1129,
Calvert; private, visible from road

Family tradition traces in detail the construction of this typical frame farmhouse, an I-house with stone end chimneys, a 2-story rear ell, and a 2-tier entrance porch sheltering double doors at both levels. The story goes that farmer John Flemming Galloway planned the house while serving in Virginia during the Civil War. After he returned home, he married Addie Siniard and employed local artisans to build a house like those he had seen in Virginia—contractor Joshua Orr, lumberman Bill Aiken, painter John Minor, stonemason Perry Wilson, and quarrymen and carters Hansel McCall, Sylvester Galloway, and Fillmore McCall. The outbuildings include a very large frame smokehouse with projecting front gable.

TV 30 Rosman

Located beside the upper French Broad River in a wide valley, Rosman retains a few vestiges of its early 20th-c. history as an industrial boomtown. Joseph Silversteen, a tanner from Pennsylvania, had visited the area for his health. He saw the industrial potential of the Toxaway area, with its proximity to large forests, the confluence of the branches of the French Broad River, and newly completed railroad (1900). He established the Toxaway Tanning Co. in 1901, soon followed by the Gloucester Lumber Co. and the Rosman Tanning Extract Co. He bought over 20,000 acres of forest from George Vanderbilt and ran logging railroads into the woods to carry logs to his factories near the main line. Known earlier as Jeptha, the settlement was called Toxaway until confusion arose with nearby Lake Toxaway resort; Silversteen dubbed it Rosman after two of his business associates, Joseph Rosenthal and Morris Osmansky.

Although Silversteen's factories have long since vanished, houses of the industrial era still stand. The **Silversteen House** (1902; w side SR 1371 at W. Main St.) is a 2-story frame house, a substantial but unpretentious residence built for Silversteen and his wife Elizabeth; it was soon outshone by their mansion *Silvermont in Brevard. A number of hip- or gable-roofed frame **Mill Houses** built for factory workers survive, with the chief concentrations on Church St., Chestnut St., and US 178. These include several house types built ca. 1910–15: 1-story, pyramidal-roofed houses with 4-room plans and hip-roofed porches, usually single-family dwellings; 1½-story, gable-roofed houses with porches, also single-family dwellings; and 2-story houses with hip roofs, 3 or 4 bays wide, with one or two doors for single-family or duplex living.

On the riverbank beside the bridge is the **Rosman Gaging Station** (1930s), one of several such stations built by the U.S. Geological Survey on county rivers beginning in the 1930s to measure river height and predict flooding in a land of high rainfall. This one is a plain, small, rectangular structure with a concrete base and small shingled room above, reached by a wooden walkway. There is another on the Davidson River near the entrance to Pisgah National Forest.

TV 31 Lake Toxaway Methodist Church
1912; N side SR 1301, 0.1 mi. NW of NC 281, Lake Toxaway

This characteristically simple mountain church was built for the Methodists of the old farming community of Toxaway on land donated by E. F. Jennings, second owner of Lake Toxaway. The weatherboarded, tin-roofed building has pointed arched windows along the sides and, at the gabled front, a gabled entrance tower with a louvered belfry. Tongue-and-groove beaded boarding sheathes the sanctuary walls. The church now serves residents of the Lake Toxaway development.

TV 32 Hillmont (Greystone Inn)
1915; Neel Reid (Hentz and Reid [Atlanta]); private drive at N side US 64, just W of Lake Toxaway; open as hotel

The picturesque house near Lake Toxaway is the lone survivor from what was once a grand resort complex that figured in the county's early 20th-c. resort boom. After the railroad reached the southwestern part of the county, mountain resort development intensified. Pennsylvania industrialist J. F. Hayes (who had come to the mountains for his health) began the Brevard Tanning

TV 32 *Hillmont*

Co. and the Carr Lumber Co. and also ventured into the growing tourist business. He founded the Toxaway Co., which built several lakes and deluxe inns, including the Franklin Hotel in Brevard and the Sapphire and Fairfield inns in Jackson Co. Among the grandest was Lake Toxaway, which he created by damming the Toxaway River in 1901. The celebrated and luxurious resort, promoted as "the Switzerland of America," claimed that 200 millionaires stayed there in its first year. In 1912 E. F. Jennings of Pittsburgh acquired the lake, inn, and more than 27,000 acres, then sold lots to create a resort colony around the lake.

Among the colonists was Lucy Camp Armstrong of Savannah. She commissioned Neel Reid, the Beaux Arts–trained Atlanta architect best known for his elegant Neoclassical and Georgian Revival designs, to plan her lake home, Hillmont. He designed an informal board-and-batten and weatherboarded residence with touches of Swiss mountain houses she had admired, with its levels stepping down the slope. In time she added a library in a Tudor mode, tennis courts, and other amenities. After the flood of 1916 tore away the dam, the lake dried up and the resort failed. Mrs. Armstrong was one of only four colony residents who remained. The once-elegant Toxaway Inn was razed in the 1940s. In 1961 the dam and lake were rebuilt with Hillmont as a clubhouse for a private resort community. Since 1985 it has been a luxury resort hotel.

Haywood County (HW)

See Betsy Farlow, Dan Lane, and Duane Oliver, Haywood Homes and History *(1993).*

Waynesville (HW 1–8)

Established as the seat of Haywood Co. when it was formed from Buncombe Co. in 1808, Waynesville was evidently named for Gen. Anthony Wayne, commanding officer of Robert Love, a prominent citizen who gave the land for the town. The community occupies a high mountain valley that until the 1880s was isolated and sparsely populated. The situation changed dramatically with the construction of the Murphy branch of the Western North Carolina Railroad (WNCRR), which reached Waynesville late in 1882. Reliable transportation opened the region to tourism and timber-related industries, which quickly became the mainstays of the county's economy. To cater to the visitors arriving to enjoy the local mineral springs and mountain air, citizens opened boardinghouses, and hotels sprang up in town and the surrounding countryside—including the celebrated Eagle's Nest high above Waynesville and the luxurious Sulphur Springs Hotel. Some were graced with spacious parklike grounds, ballroom pavilions, and other amenities. Timbering was the first major industry, with sawmills established at several points along the railroad, and tanning and furniture manufacturing at Hazelwood in the flat land south of Waynesville.

In this prosperous era, Waynesville's population grew from 225 in 1880 to 9,000 in 1930. Two business districts developed: the first near the railroad depot in a low-lying area called Frog Level and a later commercial focus along Main St.'s ridgeline. Depot St. ran up the hill and connected the two business districts. In the late 19th and early 20th centuries, residential neighborhoods grew up along the slopes east and west of Main St. Where simple, traditional architectural forms had been the norm prior to 1890, by the early 20th c. Waynesville had some of the most fashionable buildings in western N.C. outside Asheville.

Creation of the *Great Smoky Mountains National Park claimed 93 square miles of the northwest part of the county and forced the removal of many residents of the Cataloochee area. Waynesville promptly began to promote itself as the eastern entrance to the park to increase its share of tourists. Completion of the Blue Ridge Parkway through the county in 1966 and construction of I-40 through the Pigeon River gorge, authorized in 1955 and dedicated in 1968, brought new business to the town and county.

Many landmarks of the railroad boom years have vanished—the grand hotels, the railroad depot, and the sawmills and furniture factories. Nevertheless, the community retains a thriving Main St. commercial district and many residences from the late 19th and early 20th centuries, including notable renditions of Queen Anne and Colonial Revival styles.

HW 1 Downtown Waynesville

The Main St. commercial district owes its appearance to the early 20th-c. rebuilding associated with the advent of the automobile. At the turn of the century, nearly two decades after the railroad arrived, frame houses, churches, hotels, and stores still lined Main St. through town. Between 1900 and 1930 these 19th-c. structures were demolished to make way for the present 2-story brick commercial buildings. Typical of their era, these are generally simple in form and detail, some with arched windows and corbeled cornices.

The principal edifice is the **Haywood County Courthouse** (1932; Rogers & Rhodes, architects; Southeastern Construction Co., builders; w side N. Main St.), built early in the Great Depression. The county's fourth courthouse, the 3-story Neoclassical building is faced with smooth ashlar and

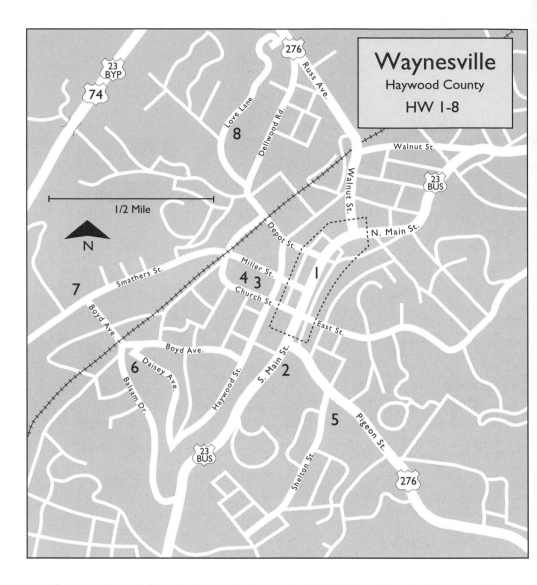

features a low relief portico formed by four 2-story Doric pilasters carrying a broad pediment. Tile floors and marble wainscoting enrich the interior, and the second-story courtroom is treated with Corinthian pilasters and classical bas-reliefs, including a Scales of Justice flanked by the Ten Commandments behind the judge's bench. (See Introduction, Fig. 66.)

North of the courthouse, **First Presbyterian Church** (1907; 462 N. Main St.), at the corner of Main and Walnut Sts., is a boldly massed design in tan brick with red tile roof and arched openings, a blend of Gothic Revival and Mission themes emphasized by a square entrance tower with peaked, tile roof on heavy brackets.

South of the courthouse, some individualized buildings punctuate the predominantly brick commercial rows. Especially striking is the former **Waynesville Library** (1912; 113 N. Main St.), a small building with a stepped parapet front of skillfully laid, round river rock, with radiating stones framing a large central arch and flanking smaller arches. Facing the courthouse is **Sherrill's Studio** (ca. 1940; 37 Depot St.), a locally unique example of the International style,

HW 1 *First Presbyterian Church*

with metal casement windows wrapping the corners at the third story and glass block flanking the entrance. George Sherrill was a leading photographer in the area for many years. His niece, Beulah Ensley, continued his business and tore down the existing building on the site to erect this novel structure, the work of a concrete building company of Miami; it is of reinforced concrete for two stories, brick at the third.

The former **Waynesville Post Office** (1917; James Wetmore, supervising architect of the Treasury; 16 S. Main St.) is a Neoclassical brick building featuring Doric pilasters with molded granite bases and caps beneath a full entablature; it is now the municipal building. Just off Main St. near the post office stands the former **Masonic Hall** (1927; William H. Peeps [Charlotte], architect; W. C. Phillips, builder; 37 Church St.), a 3-story brick structure designed by a noted Charlotte architect who was also a Mason. The facade treatment, rendered in concrete to resemble stone, displays a subtle progression of classical orders: engaged Doric columns and entablature frame the entrance, an unfluted Ionic order of freestanding columns and pilasters enriches the first level, and elongated, fluted Corinthian pilasters rise through the second and third stories.

HW 2 Dr. J. Howell Way House
1899; 145 S. Main St.

Built for a prominent physician, the 2½-story brick house near the business district blends the Queen Anne and Colonial Revival styles. Turned posts and balustrades adorn the wraparound porch, which extends to a

HW 1 *former Waynesville Library*

porte cochere. Attached at the corner is Dr. Way's 1-story, brick medical office.

HW 3 Boone-Withers House
Ca. 1883; Sam Liner, builder; 138 Church St.

Built early in the railroad era in a neighborhood west of the central business district, the 2-story Queen Anne style house displays characteristically lively massing, with a high hip roof broken by decorated peaked and clipped gable bays, curly bargeboards, and a wraparound porch with sawnwork trim. It was built for John Kader and Mary Kerr Boone; he was a teacher, owner of a lumberyard, longtime clerk of court, and chairman of the board of education.

HW 4 Thomas House
1896; 234 Church St.

The typical and somewhat altered Queen Anne style residence is notable as the home of James and Sarah Thomas. James was the son of William Holland Thomas, the adopted Cherokee chief, Confederate colonel, and legislator, whose grave is in Waynesville's Green Hill Cemetery.

HW 5 Shelton House

Ca. 1878, early 20th c.; 201 Shelton St.;
open as museum regular hours in season

An evocative survival from pre-railroad days in Waynesville, the large 2-story frame house displays a traditional form with a 2-tier, full-length recessed porch with chamfered posts. Floor-length windows open onto the porch. The interior has a center-passage plan and is neatly finished with wood-sheathed walls, paneled ceilings, and decorative wooden mantels; the 2-story rear ell was added in the early 20th c. The house was built for Stephen J. Shelton, a farmer, schoolteacher, Confederate officer, and county sheriff, and his wife Mahala Conley of Jackson Co. Complemented by a large early 20th-c. frame barn and a wooded setting recalling the farmstead, the house serves as the Museum of N.C. Handicrafts.

HW 5 *Shelton House*

HW 6 Smathers-Gautier House

Ca. 1895; 420 Daisey Ave.

The ebullient Queen Anne style house is among western N.C.'s most lavishly decorated Victorian-era dwellings, with sawn and turned millwork encrusting nearly every surface. Two 3-story octagonal towers adorned with stickwork spring from the mass of the house, and around it runs a wraparound porch filigreed with sawnwork and bracketed cornices. Located in an early suburb called Oak Park, it was built for George Smathers, attorney and judge, and his wife Daisey, for whom the street was named. From 1927 it was in the Gautier family.

HW 6 *Smathers-Gautier House*

HW 7 Frank Smathers House

1925–26; Richard deGarno (Miami),
architect; 724 Smathers St.

The picturesque residence is an unusual 1920s revival of Gothic Revival cottage form popularized by A. J. Downing, with a few Colonial Revival touches. The open H-plan house features steep gables with pinnacle pendants, a motif repeated in the trios of dormers and the arched entrance canopy. The house was designed by a Miami architect for Frank Smathers, a native of Waynesville who had become an attorney and judge in New Jersey, then practiced in Florida but kept the Waynesville property as a summer residence. His son George became a prominent congressman, and the family hosted presidents John F. Kennedy and Richard Nixon here.

HW 8 Clyde Ray Sr. House

1898–1900; Rhinehart Bros. (Pigeon Forge,
Tenn.), builders; 803H Love Lane; B&B

Crowning a hill overlooking the site of the railroad depot and old business core, the Queen Anne–Colonial Revival style house was built for Clyde Ray, a businessman who arrived soon after the railroad and became known as "the Merchant Prince" of Waynesville and its longtime mayor. With its broad, wraparound porch, it is one of several notable local examples of its style and retains original mantels, moldings, and ornate stair.

HW 9 Barber Orchard

Early 20th c.; S side SR 1243
(Old Balsam Rd.), 0.1 mi. SE of US 23/74,
Waynesville vic.; open in apple season

The stone buildings facing the road recall the countywide movement toward commercial apple growing in the early 20th c. Remnants of the orchard R. N. Barber established in 1903 stand at the base of slopes near Balsam Gap; his large orchard once blanketed the mountainsides near the Jackson Co. line. The business continues under the same name in the stone buildings built into the hillside. A rustic rock service station (ca. 1932), used as a retail outlet, has river rock pillars supporting the gabled service canopy. Stone apple houses and packhouses stand on the hill behind the store.

HW 10 Lake Junaluska Assembly

Opened in 1913 as a Methodist conference center, the complex of inns, cottages, and assembly facilities surrounds a 250-acre manmade lake. The cottages include some of the region's finest Craftsman bungalows, employing river rock and other rustic natural materials. Although Asheville architect Richard Sharp Smith was commissioned to design several cottages and other structures at the assembly, specific attributions have not been determined. R. R. Gaddis, a native of Waynesville, was among the men who executed the stonework at the *Lambuth Inn and subsequently built several river rock

HW 10 *Lakeshore Dr. Cottage*

houses and stone walls in the community, using stones selected from the Pigeon River; he also did extensive stonework in Canton.

Like *Montreat and other similar facilities, the center was planned to host religious conferences and retreats in a healthful location pleasant during the summer. It was named for the Cherokee leader Junaluska.

The main hotel is **Lambuth Inn** (1921, enlarged 1950s; Lambuth Dr.), a massive building dominated by a towering Ionic portico. The 3½-story frame structure rises from a first-story basement of river rock and is crowned by curved dormers and a central cupola. The inn, originally called Centenary Mission Building, was named for African missionary Walter Lambuth. At the opposite end of the lake is the **Colonial Hotel** (1922; E end N. Lakeshore Dr.), a

HW 10 *Lambuth Inn*

3-story frame building with double- and triple-tiered porches.

Centrally located beside the lake, **Stuart Auditorium** (1913; N. Lakeshore Dr.), a nearly circular structure with a metal truss roof, was originally open on all sides but has been enclosed with windows. **Memorial Chapel** (1946–51; N. Lakeshore Dr.), a Gothic Revival chapel of rough-coursed stone, has an open belltower and chancel end window with quatrefoil tracery.

A strong presence on the slope of the north lake shore are cottages built from 1913 through 1929 in many versions of the Colonial Revival, Craftsman, and rustic styles. **Sunset Inn** (ca. 1913; N. Lakeshore Dr. at Atkins Loop), one of the first cottages built, is a rambling Craftsman building converted to a hotel. The large bungalow called **Summer Daze** (ca. 1918; 415 N. Lakeshore Dr.) has a porch of river rock, and its walls are covered with board-and-batten and shingles; a stone garage is set into the hillside. Next door, at **Snug Harbor** (ca. 1914; 412 N. Lakeshore Dr.), a river rock porch fronts a rustic log bungalow. River rock also marks retaining walls and terraces, as at another river rock and frame bungalow, the **Dawson House** (ca. 1918; 917 N. Lakeshore Dr.).

Many other bungalows occupy wooded lots on secondary streets. Behind Lambuth Inn, the **Dobson House** (ca. 1925; 230 Atkins Loop) is a splendid wood-shingled bungalow with curving Oriental style rafters and purlins and a complex roof, along with a recessed porch, stairs, and stone posts. **Rainbow Cottage** (ca. 1914; 62 Old County Rd.), with an open balcony in the shed dormer, was built from a Sears, Roebuck kit. (See Introduction, Fig. 44.)

HW 11 Clyde

Farmers established settlements on the banks of the Pigeon River soon after the area was opened to whites in the 1780s, but not until the late 19th c. was a town formed and called Lower Pigeon. It was renamed Clyde for a railroad engineer after the WNCRR came through. Scattered buildings date from the late 19th and early 20th centuries. Several stand along Broad St. The **Clyde**

School (1941; Lindsey M. Gudger [Asheville], architect; W. Broad St.) is a building supported by the Works Progress Administration (WPA) and rendered in simplified moderne style, with chevron decorative motifs. Notable houses include a rustic log bungalow with stone chinking at 3063 W. Broad St. and a stone house at 3701 E. Broad St., with curved gable roof and casement windows lending an English cottage flavor.

Long predating the town, the **Shook House** (ca. 1800 and later; NW corner Morgan St. and Carolina Blvd.; private) incorporates one of the oldest houses west of the Blue Ridge. Part of the big frame house with double-gallery porch is a 2-story dwelling cited as the oldest timber-framed house in the county. Jacob Shook, a Revolutionary War veteran of German descent, came as an early settler ca. 1786 and built a house that burned in the 1970s. This house was evidently built for one of his sons, Peter or David. Methodist Bishop Francis Asbury visited in 1810 at the home of "Vater Shuck."

HW 12 Patton Farm

Ca. 1840, ca. 1880, 1912; N side SR 1523, 1.6 mi. W of US 19/23/74, Canton vic.; private, visible from road

The farm established around 1828 by James Patton beside the Pigeon River has continued in the family. Noted through the 19th c. as a place of hospitality for travelers, "Patton's" was marked on the 1833 McRae-Brazier map of N.C. There, as one traveler recalled, many a visitor enjoyed the company of "a good humored fine old gentleman as landlord, with his big country fireplaces and roaring hickory fires, a table groaning with all that was desirable to eat, good beds, and plenty of cheer, supper, lodging and breakfast, horse well fed and groomed, bill 50 cents, and this was uniform for 20 years." James Patton first built a log house near the river, then a larger house in the 1830s or 1840s. He owned extensive acreage and several slaves and raised fine horses and cattle.

Possibly including elements of the older house, the present farmhouse evidently dates from the post–Civil War period, during the tenure of James M. Patton, who continued his father's farming and stock-breeding pursuits. The 2-story brick dwelling shows touches of the Italianate style in its arched windows and corner pilasters; ca. 1912 grandson James S. Patton enlarged it with a large front gable and heavy porch. A 19th-c. gambrel-roofed barn and other outbuildings remain.

Canton (HW 13–17)

See Camille Wells, *Canton: The Architecture of Our Home Town* (1985).

Centered on the paper plant that is one of the region's principal industries, Canton is a distinctive early 20th-c. manufacturing town. The community began as Pigeon River, a small trading center and river ford, which had a post office by 1837 and was a stop on the Western Turnpike in the 1850s. When the WNCRR arrived in 1881 and halted at Pigeon River for nearly two years before construction proceeded west, the village emerged as a busy railhead. By the 1890s rails linked the town to points in every direction. In 1894 a new truss bridge spanned the river, and its nameplate—Wrought Iron Bridge Co., Builders, Canton, Ohio—inspired the name Canton.

The community was transformed after the Champion Coated Paper Co. located its subsidiary Champion Fibre Co. in Canton in 1906 to take advantage of the area's vast forest resources. Thereafter, the history of Canton and that of Champion were bound together. The town grew from 230 people in 1900 to 1,400 in 1910 and 5,000 in 1930—the largest town in N.C. west of Asheville. Some employees were managers and technical specialists who moved from distant locales, but most workers were regional natives who came to Canton to find jobs. In contrast to the timber companies who closed operations after depleting the woods, Champion stayed in the area and developed systematic forestry methods for sustained yield. From the beginning Champion was known for its high wages, and while many manufacturers closed or retrenched during the Great Depression, Champion continued and even thrived. Champion has continued

as a strong presence in the region and is the largest private employer in N.C. west of Asheville. In 1997 the company announced plans to sell the Canton facility.

The architecture of Canton reflects primarily the era from 1906 into the 1930s, and its substantial, often masonry houses, churches, and commercial buildings recall the prosperity of the company and its employees. Some residences were built by the company for employees, while others were constructed by individual families, including both company employees and the various professionals, merchants, and others drawn to the thriving town. The paper plant and downtown occupy the bottomland, and residential sectors wind up the hillsides.

HW 13 Champion Paper and Fibre Company

The paper plant is among the principal industrial sites in western N.C. and indeed the southern Appalachians. The extensive complex of brick and steel industrial buildings, kilns, smokestacks, and other structures spreads out in the floor of Pigeon River valley beside the large rail yard. The plant began operations in 1908 as the Champion Fibre Co. By 1916 it employed 1,000 workers and was worth $10 million, and by 1930 it had become the world's largest paper plant and one of the most powerful economic forces in western N.C.

Champion Fibre Co. was established by Peter G. Thomson as a subsidiary of his Champion Coated Paper Co. of Hamilton, Ohio, which he had founded in 1893 to produce high-quality coated paper suitable for halftone illustrations. Needing its own sup-

HW 13 *Champion Papers Office Building*

HW 13 *Champion Papers, 1932 Addition*

ply of spruce paper pulp, Champion acquired thousands of acres of N.C. forests,
including prime stands of old-growth spruce,
which grew only at high altitudes. Thomson
had discerned the potential of the area while
visiting his son at the *Asheville School and
soon purchased 40,000 acres of forest. The
company eventually acquired some 400,000
acres, a large part of which was eventually
sold for the *Great Smoky Mountains National Park.

Canton was selected for the pulp factory.
The site was advantageous because of its position on a level river plain, with a source of
abundant pure water, access to good railroad
connections, proximity to the forests, and a
supply of labor without local competition.
Construction of the huge plant, a $2 million
investment, began in 1906 but was slowed
by the panic of 1907 and unusually wet
weather. Brick construction on the massive
buildings was supervised by Englishman
Tommie Furness. Production at the plant
began in January 1908.

Thomson gave direction of the N.C. operation to his son-in-law Reuben Robertson.
He arrived initially to push forward construction but stayed for fifty years to become
"Mr. Champion." Under Robertson's leadership the factory expanded and diversified,
and the company developed as a large, carefully managed paternalistic system. The sul-
fite mill produced pulp from spruce. Another section of the plant used an innovative
method developed to extract from chestnut
timber both paper pulp and tannic acid, the
latter a profitable byproduct sold to the tanning industry.

In the early 1920s the factory began producing paper as well as pulp and soon be-

came the largest paper plant in the world as
well as the largest producer of tannic acid.
Average daily production in the mid-1920s
yielded 375 tons of pulp, 50 to 60 tons of
paper, and 500 barrels of tannic acid. Champion also developed a sulfate process for
making high-quality paper from the much
more abundant pine, an innovation that
transformed the industry.

After the firm's 1931 sale of 90,000 acres,
including prime spruce forest, to the national park, their use of pine increased, and
funds from the sale aided expansion and
modernization of the plant. The big 1932 addition, which included an immense (242-
inch), high-speed paper machine, greatly expanded paper production.

Located in the plain at the center of Canton, the plant dominates the valley, with
plumes from its smokestacks visible for
miles. Since the 1920s the plant has generated controversy over pollution to the Pigeon River, an interstate issue because the
river flows into Tennessee; various measures
have been taken to improve water quality
over the years, including a major modernization in the 1990s.

The plant comprises structures from various phases. Big, brick buildings of 3 to 7
stories, with towers and monitor roofs, were
built from 1906 through the 1910s. The **1932
Addition** is a long brick and concrete building with broad windows separated by pilasters. Other mills, warehouses, smokestacks,
and loading platforms take a variety of
forms. Contrasting with the utilitarian plant
is the formal public presence of the **Champion Papers Office Building** (1918; W. H.
Lord [Asheville], architect; Main St.), a symmetrical, 2-story brick building with Colonial Revival detailing. The Champion *Log*
reported that the brick came from Fletcher,
the granite from Mount Airy, and the wood
from Azalea, while the builders, including
resident engineer Charles Riddick, were all
Champion employees. (See Introduction,
Fig. 35.)

HW 14 Downtown Canton

The commercial area, with its curving
streets following the ridge rising from the

river, assumed much of its present form from 1910 into the 1930s. The former **U.S. Post Office** (1939; Louis A. Simon, architect; 32 Park St.), one of many WPA structures built in western N.C. during the 1930s, is a 1-story limestone building with classical details, a central cupola, and an arched entrance. Another facet of the classical theme appears in the **Colonial Theater** (1932; Benton & Benton [Wilson], architects; 55–57 Park St.), designed by the Wilson architectural firm in their red brick Colonial Revival style. Outfitted with the latest technology, and operating until 1970, the movie house was an early example of the elongated theater designed to accommodate a wide screen, balcony, and comfortable seats.

Main St. is lined by 2- and 3-story commercial buildings from the early 20th c., several of which were built by local architect-builder Joseph M. Wray. Among the best preserved is the **J. O. Plott Wholesale Grocery** (ca. 1910–20; Joseph M. Wray, architect/builder; 166–68 Main St.), a 2- and 3-story block with corbeled cornices. The 4-story **Canton Hotel** (ca. 1920; 21 Park St.), trapezoidal in plan to accommodate the streets and embellished with squares and bands of yellow brick, was constructed as an addition to the Imperial Hotel to serve business and pleasure travelers. The former **Haywood County Bank** (First Union National Bank; ca. 1930; 101 Main St.) is a brick and sandstone structure with pilasters and an entablature framing the entrance.

Southeast of the business district on Penland Ave., the **Canton High School** (1929–31; 70 Penland Ave.), now a middle school, exemplifies the large, handsomely finished public schools of the 1920s, built of brick with large windows and a decorative entrance bay at the diagonal corner. The nearby **Armory** (1936; 81 Penland Dr.) displays the blocky, fortress-like form used in many national guard armories of the era.

Residential Areas:
Champion's presence also defined the town's housing with a building boom that continued into the 1930s. Winding streets cover the hillsides, with densely placed houses large and small. There are substantial brick as well as frame dwellings, reflecting the prosperity of the community. Canton residents followed national trends in their houses, favoring revival styles, patternbook designs, and, especially, the bungalow in many forms. Local builders, including R. R. Gaddis, who had also worked at *Lake Junaluska, graced the community with fine stonework, most notably the smooth, rounded river rock, in foundations, porches, retaining walls, chimneys, and occasional buildings.

HW 15 Fibreville Hill

Some of the first houses built for Champion employees stand on and around Fibreville Hill, on the northwest side of town. As the elevation rose, so did the scale of houses and the status of residents. Among the earliest are those on Terrace Dr. The **Kerr-Fincher House** (ca. 1910; 1 Terrace Dr.) is a gabled bungalow built for an engineer, probably David J. Kerr. The **Furness House** (ca. 1903; 2 Terrace Dr.) was built as a dormered cottage for Tommie Furness, the English-born master mason at Champion. The **Damtoft-Mease House** (ca. 1920; 4 Terrace Dr.) is a 2-story stuccoed residence built for Walter Damtoft, who came as the company forester in 1920. Higher up, the substantial dwellings on **Skyland Dr.** were built for Champion supervisors, managers, technicians, and professionals in a variety of forms, including brick residences in Colonial Revival style. By contrast, Champion built the wood-shingled bungalows (ca. 1920) on **Thomson Ave.** to standard plans. On the lower-lying site of **Fibreville** along the west bank of the river, only a few remnants survive along **Fibreville St.** of the small gable-fronted bungalows and other modest dwellings built as workers' houses ca. 1906–10.

HW 16 Pennsylvania Ave.– Academy St. Neighborhood

On the hillsides south of the business district, residential lots were sold to individual owners. The houses include several large bungalows in frame, brick, and stone, and many were built for lawyers, doctors, dentists, and leading merchants, as well as top professionals at the mill; Champion's top management established homes in Asheville's prime suburbs. **Pennsylvania Ave.** has a notable selection of bungalows on a street advertised in 1916 as having "the Prettiest Views in Canton."

The most beautifully executed of the river rock buildings is **St. Andrews Episcopal Church** (1922; William Frank Bell, builder; 99 Academy St.), where subtly handled stonework complements the simple forms of the Early English Gothic Revival church. The crenellated bell tower finished with sandstone coping, buttresses, pointed-arch windows and doorways, and a tile roof are counterpoints to walls of smooth, round stones which the congregation gathered from the Pigeon River near Sunburst, and Champion hauled to town. Similar stonework forms the retaining wall. (See Introduction, Fig. 49.)

At **Locust Field Cemetery** (Academy St. at Locust St.), a ca. 1920 gateway of river rock and concrete defines the entrance at one of the oldest graveyards in the county, with markers dated as early as 1817. This was the site of the Locust Old Field Baptist Church, one of the first of its denomination in the region, begun in 1803 after missionary work by Baptist minister Humphrey Posey.

HW 17 Newfound St.

Extending through the residential area north of Main St., **Newfound St.** has notable houses of various types, especially bungalows, likewise with stone retaining walls. A contrast to the predominant single-family dwellings appears in the **Kirkpatrick (Camelot) Apartments** (1925; 3 Newfound St.), a 3-story brick apartment house with decorative concrete accents. The **Reese House** (1938; R. R. Gaddis, Deaver and Wallis Gaddis, builders; 10 Newfound St.) is a severely elegant stone house in an English vernacular revival mode, with steep-gabled wall dormers and casement windows. It was built for William C. Gaddis (a Champion employee) and his wife Mary Gaddis Reese from plans William had sketched. The builders, the town's principal stone masons, were Mary's father and brothers: "My brothers built this

house for me," she recalled. The **Wells House** (1930; R. R. Gaddis, builder; 44 Newfound St.) is a 1-story river rock house later modernized, and the nearby **Davis-Ramsey House** (ca. 1900, ca. 1930; 41 Newfound St.) is an early 20th-c. frame dwelling that Dr. Francis Davis encased in river rock ca. 1930.

HW 17 *75 Newfound St.*

HW 18 Mann House
Ca. 1858; SE side SR 1607, 0.25 mi. E of SR 1608, Newfound Gap vic.; private, visible from road

Representative of the county's many mid-19th-c. log dwellings, the 1-story log house has half-dovetailed notching and a stone end chimney. Shed porches shelter the front and back. The house was probably built for Isaac Mann, a minister.

HW 18 *Mann House*

HW 19 Kinsland House
1860s; E side NC 215, 0.75 mi. N of US 276, Woodrow vic.; private, visible from road

The large frame house, the county's most intact Greek Revival dwelling, takes a dramatic form, with the full-width, 2-tier porch inset deeply beneath the high, main gable roof—a treatment seen in coastal regions and occasionally in the west. Civil War veteran Joshua Kinsland built the house, which was later the home of his son, John T. "Dub" Kinsland.

HW 20 Blalock House
1890; E side SR 1105, opp. SR 1876, Woodrow; private, visible from road

One of several stylish late 19th-c. farmhouses in the county, the L-plan dwelling features a front-facing gable wing and a tower in the elbow of the facade behind a sawnwork-trimmed porch. It was built for Civil War veteran Capt. James A. Blalock, with a rear wing said to be the 1830s house of William Blalock.

HW 21 James Gwyn House
Ca. 1888; E side US 276, 5.2 mi. SE of NC 110, Cruso vic.; private, visible from road

Situated on a hillside with views of mountains and river valleys, the big, hip-roofed house is adorned with Italianate brackets and a broad, encircling sawnwork porch. The unusually stylish farmhouse expresses the background and wealth of its builder. Son of a leading Wilkes Co. family and a graduate in chemistry from the University of Virginia, in 1875 Gwyn established the farm with his wife Amelia Harper Foster of Greensboro, and here he carried out his agricultural philosophy of scientific self-sufficiency using organic techniques. During 1932–39 the farm served as the New College

HW 21 *James Gwyn House*

Community, offering a summer "hands-on" experience for students of Columbia University Teachers' College. The farm is now a golf course.

HW 22 Truss Bridge #79
1891; Phoenix Bridge Co., Philadelphia; SR 1112 over West Fork Pigeon River at SR 1111, 0.6 mi. S of US 276, Woodrow vic.

Fabricated in Pennsylvania and assembled on site, the 80-foot Pratt type through-truss bridge is the oldest highway bridge in N.C. still open to traffic.

HW 23 Pingree Priestly Plott House
Ca. 1870; W side SR 1111, 1.5 mi. S of US 276, Woodrow vic.; private, visible from road

The hillside farmhouse combines a traditional I-house form with the steep-gabled wing, bay windows, and triangular-headed windows of the picturesque cottage mode. It was built for Pingree Priestley Plott, mill owner and farmer of 1,300 acres, and Charity Osborne soon after their marriage in 1866. They established their farm on land inherited from his father, Jonathan Plott, who had settled in the area ca. 1830. (The Plott hound, a bear-hunting dog designated by the legislature as the "State Dog" in 1989, was bred in the 18th c. by another branch of the Haywood Co. Plott family.)

HW 24 Inman Chapel Universalist Church and Cemetery
Ca. 1900; SE side SR 1128, 0.05 mi. SW of NC 215, Sunburst vic.

Poised on a hillside not far from Cold Mountain, the simple frame church has a small, open-sided belfry above the front gable. It has an unusually rich history as one of the first Universalist congregations in the Southeast and the only one in the Southern Appalachians. The congregation, founded in 1868 by James A. Inman, a self-educated, progressive minister devoted to education and social issues, met for years in homes and a schoolhouse and sponsored a library, Sunday school, and schooling for black and white residents of nearby communities. In

HW 23 *Pingree Priestley Plott House*

1900 Inman gave the land for the chapel and cemetery, and the church was dedicated in 1903. The chapel closed after Inman's death in 1913, but in 1921 the Universalist convention reopened it under the Reverend Hannah Jewett Powell as a religious, educational, and health center serving an area transformed by logging. Since 1954 the chapel has been privately maintained.

HW 25 Mount Zion Methodist Church and Cemetery
1883; Abe and Joe Shank, builders; N side SR 1503, 2.1 mi. E of NC 209, Crabtree vic.

Standing in a beautiful, unspoiled mountain valley, Mount Zion is a rare example in western N.C. of a 19th-c. country church built of brick; it was called simply "The Brick Church." It repeats the familiar gable-fronted form; the central entrance replaced the original pair of doors. Mount Zion is one of the oldest congregations in a county where Methodism has a strong history. Organized ca. 1850, the congregation met for a time in a log building on land donated by member Joseph McCracken, then built this church on adjoining land given by his grandson of the same name. The cemetery

on a hill overlooking the church contains many 19th-c. graves, including memorials to Joseph and Sarah McCracken and other early settlers in the Crabtree Creek area.

HW 26 Cataloochee
Great Smoky Mountains National Park, NW of I-40 exit 20 at US 276; SR 1395 (partly unpaved) 6 mi. N of US 276 to park; follow signs to sites within park

Before the establishment of the *Great Smoky Mountains National Park, farmsteads, churches, and schools occupied the valleys of Big and Little Cataloochee creeks. Many of the families' ancestors had come to this section in the early 19th c. The Cataloochee Turnpike traversed the area in the 1840s. Most of the farms raised diverse crops and livestock, meeting their own needs and shipping produce to distant markets. At the turn of the century, Cataloochee township had 765 people and 137 households. When growing tourism brought regular visitors to the area, families opened their homes as boardinghouses, often adding rooms for the purpose, and some stocked trout streams for "fishers." Displaced in the 1930s when the Great Smoky Mountains National Park was

HW 26 *Palmer Chapel*

created, most Cataloochee families resettled elsewhere in the county, though some left the area.

In contrast to other parts of the park where only a few "pioneer" buildings were retained, at Cataloochee the National Park Service preserved a handful of buildings that recall a longer history that continues into the early 20th c. In 1938 Civilian Conserva-

tion Corps employees Charles S. Grossman and Hiram C. Wilburn conducted an inventory of the remaining buildings of the park, recording many in Cataloochee and fostering the preservation of these vestiges of the community that once flourished here. The area is divided into Big Cataloochee to the south and Little Cataloochee to the north.

In Big Cataloochee the **Palmer House** (ca. 1860, early 20th c.; information center, 0.5 mi. off Big Cataloochee Rd.) (**a**), built for George Lafayette "Fate" Palmer, began as a log house and took a dogtrot form. About 1901–5 Fate and his son Jarvis weatherboarded the structure and installed planed sheathing inside. Jarvis Palmer inherited the property in 1910, and about 1924 he added a kitchen and dining wing for boarders. The Palmers stocked trout streams for visiting fishers and boarded them during their visits. The outbuildings include a frame springhouse behind the dwelling and a large frame barn with ventilated eaves. (See Introduction, Fig. 56.)

At the ranger station on Big Cataloochee Rd., the **Hub and Marian Caldwell House** (1918–19) (**b**) is a frame Craftsman bungalow. The nearby **Messer Barn** (ca. 1900–1905) was moved from the Messer farm in

HW 26 *Caldwell House*

Little Cataloochee. It has a half-dovetailed log crib and a covered driveway beneath a frame loft. (Several other log outbuildings from Cataloochee were moved and rebuilt at the *Mountain Farm Museum in the park in Swain Co.)

Evocative of community life now vanished is **Palmer Chapel** (ca. 1900, 1920; Big Cataloochee Rd.) (**c**), a gable-fronted frame church with the central entrance recessed in a square tower. The simply finished sanctuary has typical wood-sheathed walls and plank pews. Circuit-riding preachers supplied by the Western N.C. Conference of the Methodist Episcopal Church visited about once a month to preach and lead the congregation in prayer and singing. The chapel is still the site of regular homecomings and reunions. **Beech Grove School** (1901; Big Cataloochee Rd.) (**d**) is a plain, 2-room schoolhouse with a single door at its front gable end and 4 windows on each side; like the church, the interior is finished with horizontal sheathing.

The **Caldwell Farm** (1903–6; Big Cataloochee Rd.) (**e**) was built on Ugly Creek for Hiram Caldwell and his family. The large frame house, which replaced a log dwelling, is an imposing structure with a tall, gable-on-hip roof, shingled gables, and a decorated wraparound porch; the tongue-and-groove interior sheathing was brought from Waynesville. Near the house is a small frame springhouse. Just across the road is an especially fine **Barn**, with four log cribs forming the core at the lower story, plus frame extensions on earthfast posts, all covered by a broad gable-roofed loft, which is aired by slatted vents.

Down the hiking trail the **Woody House** (ca. 1860, 1905; Rough Fork Rd.) (**f**) was built in two stages. Jonathan Woody erected the 1-room log house with loft about 1860, and his son Steve incorporated it into a T-shaped frame house with shingled dormers and a porch with turned posts.

Little Cataloochee (access limited), located across Noland Mountain from Big Cataloochee, was settled in the 1850s by families from the older community. About 1910 small-scale farming was supplemented by an extensive apple-growing business. Ac-

cess to this settlement is by unpaved road and a hiking trail. The restored **Hannah Cabin** (1864; Little Cataloochee Rd.) (**g**) was built for John Jackson and Martha Hannah, who moved here in 1857 and lived for a time in a cabin before building the half-dovetailed log dwelling. Poplar puncheons form the floor, boards cover the gaps between logs, and the chimney is of brick rather than the more usual stone. **Little Cataloochee Baptist Church** (1889; Little Cataloochee Rd.) (**h**) is a neatly crafted frame church of typical gable-fronted form, enriched by wave-patterned bargeboards and an open belfry with a cross-gabled roof and conical spire finished in fish-scale wood shingles. The church and its large graveyard are the scene of regular reunions that draw families from far and wide. Toward the end of the trail are remains of the former Messer and Cook farmsteads, including ruins of the Cook apple house, where fruit was graded and stored at the height of the orchard business.

HW 27 Walters Power Plant and Dam

1927–30; SR 1332 on Pigeon River, Waterville; visible from I-40 eastbound near state line; accessible from exit 451 in Tennessee

Deep in the Pigeon River ravine, the brick power plant is a landmark at the N.C.-Tennessee border. The plant is linked by a 6.2-mile concrete-lined tunnel to Waterville Lake, 12 miles upriver, formed by a concrete dam. (The dam is barely visible at the west end of Waterville Lake from I-40, between miles 11 and 12, eastbound; access restricted.) The dam plus the tunnel develop a head of 861 feet, which until World War II was the highest east of the Rockies.

The idea of a hydroelectric plant in this vicinity was explored by Benjamin Sloan, owner of Waynesville's Sulphur Spring Hotel. With others he organized the Haywood Electric Power Co. and the Great Smoky Mountain Power Co. and in 1905 built a dam and power plant on the Pigeon River that served Waynesville and Canton. After Sloan's death in 1922, Great Smoky's options on power sites were purchased by the Carolina Power and Light Co. (CP&L),

HW 27 *Walters Power Plant*

which announced plans for a major dam on the Pigeon River in 1926. Work began at the remote site in 1927 and was completed in 1930 by the Phoenix Electric Co., an affiliate of CP&L. Power from this plant has supported communities and industries through the region.

The project gained attention in trade journals because of the challenges presented by the remote location and difficult terrain. Getting equipment and materials to the sites was an immense problem, exacerbated by the lack of rail access past the power plant site. The contractors leased a narrow-gauge logging line, but it took a year to extend it 5 miles to the dam site. The project was further delayed by harsh weather and rock slides, a problem that continues to plague the gorge along the Pigeon River. Separate camps were set up for the crews working on the dam, the powerhouse, and the tunnel drilled through the mountain.

The magnificent concrete arch **Dam** is 180 feet high and about 900 feet long, with the spillway at the center of the arch. South-

west of the dam is the reinforced concrete intake gate to the tunnel. The 6.2-mile tunnel through the mountain carries the water down the slope of the terrain and divides into three penstocks before reaching the powerhouse. The **Powerhouse**, an imposing structure of brick, with tall windows alternating with pilasters above a concrete base, is set in solid rock. The facility is remarkably unchanged, with its original vertical reaction-type turbines and generators still at work.

To house workers at the remote site, CP&L built Waterville Village as a model community, with family houses, a boardinghouse, a school, a post office, and a clubhouse amid landscaped and terraced grounds. Of these, a few individual dwellings (simple frame bungalows), the 2-story clubhouse (now the plant manager's residence), and the small, frame schoolhouse still stand. In 1980 the site was designated the state's first Historic Civil Engineering Landmark by the N.C. Chapter of the American Society of Civil Engineers.

Jackson County (JK)

JK 1 Sylva

The finest vista of the town with its courthouse atop a hill, enframed by surrounding mountains, is from the north on US 19A/23. Settled in 1861 and incorporated in 1889, the town was named for local resident William Sylva. The arrival of the Western North Carolina Railroad (WNCRR) in 1883 boosted its fortunes and encouraged industries such as lumber mills and a tannery, which became a major paper mill. Although Webster had served as county seat since 1852, after the railroad bypassed the old town, Sylva business leaders—"Removalists"—campaigned to move the center of government. In 1913 local voters approved the move to Sylva, and the handsome courthouse was promptly erected. The principal architectural fabric dates from the railroad industrial era from the 1890s until the Great Depression.

Sylva's chief landmark is the **Jackson County Courthouse** (1914; Smith & Carrier [Asheville], architects; W. Main St.). With its hilltop position offering a dramatic Beaux Arts approach, this is one of the most spectacularly sited courthouses in the state. A cascade of steps rises to the Corinthian portico of the symmetrical, 2-story brick building with tall dome. Architects Smith & Carrier, the premier firm in the region, had used a similar design for the *Madison County Courthouse of 1907. (See Introduction, Fig. 41.)

The compact **Main St.** business district east of the courthouse contains notable turn-of-the-century commercial buildings. Storefronts have metal trim from the George L. Mesker and Co. Iron Works and the International Steel and Iron Construction Co., both of Evansville, Ind., and others. On the parallel, lower Mill St. the north ends of these buildings step down with the terrain.

The most imposing commercial building is the **C. J. Harris Building** (Sylva Supply Co.) (1898; 582 W. Main St.), a 2-story brick block with pressed-metal trim at the storefront, windows, and name parapet from the

Southern Foundry Co., Owensboro, Ky. It was erected for pioneer industrialist C. J. Harris, a native of Connecticut who came to Sylva from Denver in the 1890s and mined kaolin in Jackson, Mitchell, and other counties. Harris founded a tannery, a locust pin factory (pins used in electric insulators and for shipbuilding), a bank, and other enterprises and led the campaign to make Sylva county seat. The former **Tuckasegee Bank** (1928; 609 W. Main St.) across the street is an elegantly rendered little classical bank, fronted with white stone ashlar, where pilasters flank the tall arched windows and entrance and carry an entablature with date parapet.

JK 1 *C. J. Harris Building*

JK 1 *Tuckasegee Bank*

JK 2 Jackson Paper Manufacturing Plant (C. J. Harris Tannery; Sylva Paperboard Company)

1901 and later; E. Main St., East Sylva

Founded by C. J. Harris in 1901, the tannery on Scotts Creek near the railroad extracted tannin from chestnut trees to tan hides into leather. The plant was acquired in 1915 by the Armour Leather Co. and expanded for tannin production. In the 1920s plant manager Ernest Lyndon McKee learned that industrialist George H. Mead had developed a method for making cardboard from boiled wood chips—a byproduct of tanning. He saw the opportunity to sell chips to Mead, then arranged for Mead to purchase the factory. Mead's Sylva Paperboard Co. plant produced both tannin extract and paper for cardboard boxes until 1953, then focused on cardboard. With some 300 workers, the plant was the county's largest employer in the mid-20th c. but closed after facing pollution problems. Now a cardboard recycling plant, the large complex traces a story of repeated expansion and change, from the frame and brick tannery structures to the large masonry buildings of the paper mill.

JK 3 Dillsboro

The railroad town was founded by William Allen Dills, a Confederate veteran who in 1871 bought from his father a farm beside the Tuckasegee River. In 1882–83, when the long-awaited WNCRR came through the county, bypassing Webster but crossing Dills's farm, he promptly laid out the town of New Webster, or Webster Station, on his land; built a boardinghouse; and seeing it succeed, constructed the Mount Beulah Hotel (now the *Jarrett House), which he named for his youngest daughter. As the principal rail stop in Jackson Co., and an important embarkation point for Macon Co. and Franklin, the village thrived first as a commercial center and then as a summer resort. Residents took in guests, and stores were built beside the railroad. When automobile touring supplanted rail, Dillsboro accommodated the changes, but by the mid-20th c. its stature as a resort had sagged. In the late 20th c., however, the *Great Smoky Mountains Railway, headquartered here along with a railroad memorabilia museum, has renewed tourism.

Several small, gable-fronted frame stores on **Front St.** overlook the railroad beside the river. Among the best preserved is the former **Harris Clay Company Office** (ca. 1900), a 1-story gable-fronted building with broad shop windows flanking an inset entrance and an arched, louvered vent in the gable. It was built as the office of the clay— actually kaolin—mining company founded by C. J. Harris and his brothers, one of the first of many businesses he established in the region. Many 1- and 2-story frame residences decorated with millwork in simplified Queen Anne and Italianate styles line Webster, Church, and Depot Sts. and Haywood Rd. on the slope above.

The principal landmark is the **Jarrett House** (Mount Beulah Hotel) (1884, ca. 1910, and later; NE corner Haywood Rd. [US 19/23 BUS] and US 441; open seasonally). The 3-story frame hotel, built by W. A. Dills as the Mount Beulah Hotel, was acquired by Frank Jarrett in 1894 and flourished as Jarrett Springs Hotel, known for its country-style cooking. It takes the form of a big, 3-story, gable-roofed house, with center passage, rear ell, and porches at each story. About 1910 Jarrett added the west gabled wing. The mid-20th c. brought metal siding (1965) and porch posts (1975). But with its simple woodwork and beaded tongue-and-groove sheathing, the Jarrett House maintains its appeal as a resilient and nostalgic hostelry renowned for its cooking.

JK 3 *Jarrett House*

The **Greystone Building** (1938; Cardinus and Ernest Green, stonemasons; SW corner Haywood Rd. and Church St.) across the road is a 2-story commercial building, built as a restaurant and hotel by the county's leading stonemasons from local river rock that was usually restricted to chimneys and foundations. Several picturesquely detailed frame houses stand on the edges of town. On Haywood Rd. (SR 1514) above town near the railroad, the **J. J. Hooker House** (ca. 1890; S side SR 1514, 0.3 mi. W of US 23/441) is a locally rare example of a textbook Gothic cottage in board and batten, complete with a cross plan and steep gabled bays with sawnwork bargeboards. It was built for Hooker, an attorney, judge, and founder of a mica- and clay-mining firm. Nearby is the **John and Flora Watkins House** (ca. 1890; S side SR 1514, Haywood Rd., just W of US 23/441; B&B), a Queen Anne style house with angled towers, gables, and porches in unusually lively format. It was built for John C. Watkins, local merchant and magistrate, and his wife Flora Zachary. After John's death in 1899, Flora, like other local residents, took in boarders. On the opposite side of town, across the railroad, the **S. T. Early House** (ca. 1891; 373 Hemlock St.) is a large T-plan frame house with fine millwork at the eaves and on the porch. It was built for a sawmill owner on land he bought from W. A. Dills in 1890.

JK 4 Great Smoky Mountains Railway

Headquartered in Dillsboro, this tourist railway runs between Dillsboro and Andrews along part of the Asheville–Murphy Branch of the WNCRR. The railroad had various owners over the years, including Southern Railway Co., with which it merged in 1894, and after 1982 the Norfolk Southern Co., formed from the merger of Southern and Norfolk Western. In 1988, when Norfolk Southern sought to abandon the 67-mile portion of the route from Dillsboro westward, the state purchased it and first leased, then sold the route to the Great Smoky Mountains Railway (GSMR). The GSMR runs tourist excursions on vintage cars powered by diesel or steam locomotives.

GSMR excursions traverse routes that transformed the region, including many extremely steep grades and difficult construction segments. The **Cowee Tunnel** (1883–84) just west of Dillsboro is a ¼-mile tunnel hacked through the rock by convict laborers during eighteen months of back-breaking, sometimes fatal, work. The GSMR line appeared in movies made in western N.C. in the 1990s, including *My Fellow Americans* and *The Fugitive*, with the wreckage of the bus-train crash from the latter now an attraction on the route near Dillsboro. As of 1998, this is the only passenger service on the entire WNCRR that once brought tourism prosperity as well as industrial growth to western N.C. Current plans call for reinstating regular passenger service from Salisbury to Asheville.

JK 5 Old Field Church
1845; end of SR 1711, off SR 1449, 0.4 mi. S of US 19A/23

Set on a long hillside amid many gravestones and plots, the utterly plain frame church is the county's oldest. The simple, weatherboarded meetinghouse suggests the character of other mid-19th-c. rural churches now lost. The entrance is in the windowless gable end, with windows on the remaining sides. Benches face and flank the pulpit at the opposite gable end. The church was built to replace an earlier log structure.

JK 6 Balsam
SR 1701 at Norfolk Southern Railroad

The Murphy Branch of the WNCRR was completed to Waynesville in 1882 and to Dillsboro via Balsam Gap in 1883. Contrary to the original plan to tunnel through Balsam Mountain, the railroad was built up and down the steep Balsam grade. At 3,315 feet, Balsam was known as the highest depot east of the Rocky Mountains, served by the highest standard-gauge railroad in the East. Upon reaching the apex at Balsam, trains stop to reset brakes for the descent—1,160 feet in 6.8 curving miles on the west side.

At the railroad crossing stand essential community institutions: **Knight's Store**

JK 5 *Old Field Church*

(1902), a classic country store, 1 story tall with large display windows sheltered by an awning beneath a stepped false front, and the **Balsam School** (1940; S side SR 1700 at SR 1701), a small brick schoolhouse that was a modern facility when erected but closed when local schools were consolidated in 1951; it is now a community center. Nearby is the **John Knight House** (1904; E side SR 1701, 0.2 mi. S of SR 1700), the storekeeper's bracketed, Italianate dwelling with bracket cornice. Moved from trackside and used as a dwelling, the former **Balsam Depot** (1907; SR 1701, 0.1 mi. from railroad crossing) is a weatherboarded frame building with its distinctive flared hip roof and wide, bracketed eaves.

JK 7 Balsam Mountain Inn

1908; W side SR 1700 at SR 1701, Balsam; B&B

One of southwestern N.C.'s largest (over 100 rooms) and most popular inns, the Balsam Mountain Springs Hotel was built for businessmen Joseph Kenney and Walter Christy in 1908. Overlooking the WNCRR at its highest point, the inn attracted summer visitors who arrived by train to enjoy the

cool mountain air and the "spicy aroma of the balsam."

The capacious 2½-story frame inn features a full-width double porch usually lined with rocking chairs. Long colonnades of turned Tuscan columns at both levels of the porch embody a simplified Colonial Revival style, while the gambrel roof with dormers and corner towers echoes Queen Anne style massing. Built on a modified U-plan, the inn has broad, double-loaded corridors lined by guest rooms, all finished with narrow beadboard and simple Colonial Revival millwork. Through long years of use, the place has continued remarkably unchanged. A careful renovation in the 1990s gave it new life as a year-round inn, where visitors may sit on the porch and watch occasional trains labor up the steep grade, stop, and slowly descend.

JK 8 Webster

The pretty hilltop town near the Tuckasegee River was founded in 1852 as seat of Jackson Co. the year after it was formed from portions of Cherokee and Haywood counties. With the county named for Democrat Andrew Jackson, a concession to local Whigs

JK 7 *Balsam Mountain Inn*

named the seat for Whig leader Daniel Webster. Positioned near the junction of the Western Turnpike with the Tuckasegee River and the road south, Webster thrived as the county's main trading center throughout the 19th c.

Competition emerged in the 1880s when the WNCRR bypassed it to the north, stimulating growth in Dillsboro and Sylva. Asserting that "no town is more beautifully situated," Webster leaders strove to attract a school and draw new citizens. But growth was slow, and after long agitation by "Removalists," in 1913 Sylva became county seat. Webster remained a small community with tree-lined streets, picket fences, and late 19th- and early 20th-c. frame buildings retaining a village identity. From its hill in the Tuckasegee River valley, the community enjoys distant views of high mountain ranges on all sides.

The **Webster Methodist Church** (1881; Webster Rd.) is a striking example of Gothic Revival rural architecture, with elaborate carpentry work emphasizing the belfry, triangular-headed windows, and recessed front entrance. Next door is the **Webster School** (1937; Webster Rd.), one of several Works Progress Administration schools in the re-

gion built of native stone. Among the notable frame dwellings are the **Moore House** (1886; Webster Rd.), with its prominent front roof gable and decorated porch, and the **Hedden House** (1902; Buchanan Loop at Webster Rd.), a locally outstanding Queen Anne style house, built for lumberman Elisha Calor Hedden and boyhood home of Governor Dan K. Moore ("Dan, Dan, the Mountain Man" was his campaign jingle), who did much to aid the region's development in the mid-20th c. At the south edge of town by the river stands the **Webster Baptist Church** (1900; S side NC 116 opp. Webster Rd.), a simple frame church with open belfry and tall spire.

JK 9 Cullowhee

The community centers on **Western Carolina University**. Founded by Professor Robert Lee Madison in 1889, the school developed from the Cullowhee High School into a constituent of the University of North Carolina system. The hilly campus has several red brick buildings from the 1920s and 1930s onward. **Moore Hall** (1925) is the oldest, a Colonial Revival building with a long arcaded porch. During the Great Depres-

JK 8 *Webster Methodist Church*

sion, assistance from the Federal Works Agency, Public Works Administration, supported construction of 8 campus buildings. Best preserved of these is **Madison Dormitory** (1939; Ronald Greene and W. Stewart Rogers [Asheville]), a 3½-story brick building with simple Colonial Revival trim, a style that continues in other Public Works buildings. A contrast appears in the **Breese Physical Education Building** (1939), a rare use of rough-dressed local stone in a large building.

The oldest landmark in Cullowhee is **St. David's in the Valley Episcopal Church** (1883–87; S. Truman Jones, builder; E side SR 1002, opp. Whitmire Stadium), a Gothic Revival chapel of stuccoed brick, with lancet openings and a south side entrance porch in a traditional English plan. Accentuating the steep gables are stylized truss motifs, with that of the porch noted for casting a dovelike shadow. The simply finished sanctuary has a scissors truss roof. The mission was established in 1882 during efforts by Bishop T. B. Lyman and the Reverend David Hillhouse Buel of Asheville to expand the Episcopal Church in western N.C.; Buel's earlier familiarity with Gothic Revival churches in Maryland may have influenced the design of St. David's. The church closed in 1941, but in 1958 Rufus Morgan (cf. *Penland School, *St. John's Episcopal Church, Cartoogechaye) encouraged its renewal.

JK 10 Speedwell Baptist Church

1902; W side SR 1326, 0.4 mi. N of SR 1001, Speedwell vic.

Sited on its prominent knoll, the white frame church takes a distinctive form, with a polygonal entrance bay supporting a hexagonal shingled tower. It is named for the blue-flowered veronica that grows in the area.

JK 11 East Laport

Beside the roads and rivers that wind through the hills, churches and farmsteads accentuate the bucolic landscape of late 19th- and early 20th-c. farming communities. East Laport's name recalls its position at the site of an 18th-c. trading post where the French traded with the Cherokees.

In a characteristic placement, the **East Laport Church** (1922; E side SR 1735, O. 2 mi. from NC 107) stands high on a hilltop overlooking the bottomlands of the Tuckasegee River. Built for workers in the Blackwood Lumber Co. village then located here, it also housed a school, and for years it has served both Baptist and Methodist congregations. The gable-fronted frame church has round-arched windows and a side tower with open belfry.

Near the church a farming valley extends along the stream, and upon a knoll stands the **Davis Zachary House** (1911; W side SR 1735, 0.5 mi. N of NC 107, East Laport), a well-kept Queen Anne style farmhouse with front porch regarding the river; a large frame barn stands on the hillside below the meadow. The Zachary family moved here from Cashiers early in the 19th c. and raised cattle, sheep, and horses.

JK 12 Judaculla Rock

Ca. 3000–1000 B.C.; S side SR 1741, 0.5 mi. from jct. w/SR 1737, Caney Fork vic.; limited access

One of the most important petroglyphs in North America, Judaculla Rock is the largest and best-known example of prehistoric rock art in N.C. (No other petroglyphs in western N.C. are readily visible.) The soapstone boulder—measuring some 16½ by 11 feet—is densely covered with carvings. Variously made by incising, pecking, and smoothing, the designs appear to include human figures, a turtle, salamanders, and other forms. The carving is believed to date from the late Archaic period (ca. 3000–1000 B.C.), but its purpose and date remain unknown. Lying in Caney Fork Creek valley, about 4 miles from its confluence with the Tuckasegee River, Judaculla Rock is unique in its association with a larger Archaic period site, including a soapstone quarry. The rock is owned and preserved by Jackson Co.

JK 13 John R. Brinkley House
1929; NW side NC 107, 1.1 mi. N of SR 1172, East Laport vic.

River rock entrance walls emblazoned with the name "Dr. John R." "Brinkley" proclaim the original owner of the neat bungalow of river rock construction. During a spectacular career as a medical maverick, Brinkley maintained links with his native Jackson Co. and built this country retreat as well as erecting the **Aunt Sally Marker** (1937; 1 mile N

on NC 107) to the beloved aunt who raised him.

As a young man Brinkley left for the Midwest and took up medicine. In the 1920s he gained fame as the "Goat Gland King" and the "Kansas Ponce de Leon" for performing some 16,000 transplants of goat gonads to men hoping for rejuvenation. Rapidly becoming a millionaire, Brinkley built a hospital in Milford, Kans.; established KFKB ("Kansas First, Kansas Best") in 1923, one of the most powerful radio broadcasting stations in the country, from which he broadcast a profitable medical and prescription radio program; and ran three revolutionary political campaigns for the governorship of Kansas using radio, sound trucks, and airplane travel—almost beating Alf Landon in 1932.

After being investigated by the American Medical Association and losing his medical license in Kansas, Brinkley moved to Del Rio, Tex., where he built a new hospital and opened the powerful radio station XER across the border in Mexico in 1935. A popularizer of "border radio"—Mexico did not limit the power as the U.S. did—Brinkley shaped the country music industry by featuring such musicians as the Carter family and western N.C.'s Samantha Bungarner of Jackson Co. He was prosecuted for tax evasion, was sued by former patients, and had

JK 12 *Judaculla Rock*

JK 13 *John R. Brinkley House*

his station shut down by Mexican authorities. He declared bankruptcy, and he died suddenly in 1942.

JK 14 Tuckasegee Wesleyan Church

Ca. 1920; E side NC 107, access road just N of SR 1134, Tuckasegee

Perched on a hilltop high above the road, the small frame church exemplifies the common mountain practice of locating churches on hills and knolls. Above the tin-shingled gable roof, an open belfry is topped by a metal replica of an open Bible. The congregation was founded ca. 1920 as an outgrowth of the Glenville Wesleyan Church.

JK 15 Thorpe Power Plant (Glenville Power Plant)

1940–41; E side NC 107, 2.1 mi. N of SR 1131, Tuckasegee vic.

"A stately building in a rare setting of surrounding hills," as the local newspaper reported at its dedication, the brick powerhouse is a landmark beside the road, its mass dramatized by its emphatic Gothic Revival detailing. Contrasting with the modernism of contemporary Tennessee Valley Authority plants, pilasters rise to a terra-cotta roof coping and separate tall windows with pointed

arched transoms. The concrete base is banked into the steep slope. To the north, on the nearby hillside above NC 107, stand several associated **Workers Houses**, gable-fronted frame dwellings of simplified bungalow type.

Even before Franklin D. Roosevelt called in Dec. 1940 for America to swing into production for "the great arsenal of democracy," Nantahala Power and Light Co. accelerated plans for hydroelectric plants (cf. *Nantahala Complex) to support aluminum production for aircraft. Nantahala, formed in 1929 by the Aluminum Co. of America (Alcoa), had owned the power site on the Tuckasegee River at Glenville (formerly called Hamburg) for some time, but the prospect of wartime demand spurred its immediate development.

Work began in June 1940, and 1,500 men labored around the clock to build Glenville's dam, tunnels, and powerhouse. East Laport, with a rail link to Sylva, became a workyard. A massive rock and earth dam (150 feet high, 1,310 feet long, and 830 feet thick at the base) created the 1,470-acre reservoir. Three tunnels were drilled to carry steel pipes 3½ miles to deliver water from Glenville lake to the powerhouse. The drop of 1,200 feet maximizes the waterpower by creating an effective head of 1,169 feet—the highest east of

JK 15 *Thorpe Power Plant*

the Rocky Mountains. The powerhouse's twin-runner, horizontal impulse turbine, the largest of its kind in the nation, is still in operation. The dam was closed early in 1941, and at the dedication on Oct. 13, 1941, Governor Melville Broughton pushed the button to start operations. Glenville yielded enough power to make aluminum for two "Flying Fortress" bombers per day. The facility was renamed in 1951 for J. E. S. Thorpe, president of Nantahala Power and Light Co. from its founding in 1929. The firm was sold to Duke Power Co. in 1988.

JK 16 Norton School

1913; S side SR 1144, 0.2 mi.
E of SR 1143, Norton

Carefully preserved as a community center, the plain gable-fronted frame schoolhouse typifies many of its era. Such neatly finished, well-lighted, and well-heated one-room schoolhouses represented great strides for public education in rural communities where crude, dark, and drafty log and frame structures had often been the rule. Like *Whiteside School, behind the entrance vestibule the classroom has generous 9/9 sash windows on the left side, none on the

right, a measure said to prevent shadows from falling on the students' work. Located on a scenic road, the school is part of a quiet rural community along Grassy and Norton creeks below the towering Yellow Mountain.

JK 17 Alexander Gardens

1920s; N side US 64, 0.3 mi.
E of NC 107, Cashiers

Early in the development of tourist facilities along US 64, the scenic mountain route, local resident Warren Alexander (who also owned tourist cabins at Grimshawes) built a small roadside business complex—a barbershop, service station, and store, all with steep gable-roofed forms and covered with the novelty "log" sheathing then popular for its rustic effect.

JK 18 High Hampton Inn

1932; Erle Stillwell (Hendersonville),
architect; E side NC 107, 1.5 mi. S of
jct. w/US 64, Cashiers; resort hotel

Located in a spectacular valley with views of towering balds and cooled by its 3,500-foot elevation, High Hampton is one of the most evocative of the rustic inns of western N.C.

The grand old hotel captures the invigorating blend of natural materials and first-class but informal accommodations geared to healthful outdoor recreation, popular during the early 20th c. With Linville, High Hampton presents the region's prime collection of chestnut-bark-covered buildings.

More remote than the South Carolina summer colony at Flat Rock, by the 1840s the Cashiers Valley was the summer retreat and farm of South Carolina planter Wade Hampton II. His son, Wade Hampton III, Confederate general and political leader, continued the tradition, and in 1890 niece Caroline Hampton and her husband William Stewart Halsted purchased the place and called it High Hampton.

In the early 1920s High Hampton was purchased by Ernest Lyndon and Gertrude Dills McKee. Ernest was president of the Sylva Tanning Co. and Sylva Electric Co. Gertrude, daughter of Dillsboro founder W. A. Dills, was a leading N.C. clubwoman, reformer, and proponent of education, who in 1930 was elected N.C.'s first woman state senator. To develop a family resort, the McKees added a small inn for vacationers and converted existing buildings to summer cottages. They built an 11-hole golf course with sand greens designed by J. Victor East of Australia, golf pro at Biltmore Forest Country Club in Asheville (it was later expanded to 18 holes with grass greens), and they installed the clay tennis courts, croquet lawn, and walking trails.

After the inn burned in 1932, McKee commissioned architect Erle Stillwell to design a larger inn using the chestnut-bark-covered rustic style. Even as McKee's factory processed the chestnut chips for tannin, his retreat displayed the beauty of the thick and water-resistant bark. Stillwell's design uses simple rectangular forms, a dormered gable roof, and uncomplicated spaces to set off the bark-clad walls, bark-covered stickwork railings of porches and balcony, and stone and natural wood interiors.

Near the inn are cottages from various eras, some with chestnut-bark walls. **Lake Cottage** (1922) takes a chalet form; others are board and batten with rustic stonework. Some cottages are reworked outbuildings. Still in family ownership, High Hampton has been maintained as a mountain resort.

JK 19 Church of the Good Shepherd
1895; W side NC 107, 0.3 mi. S of SR 1118, Cashiers

Episcopalians' devotion to the Gothic Revival appears in a simple weatherboarded structure with lancet windows and a sanctuary with open truss roof. Episcopal missionary John A. Deal found natural support

JK 18 *High Hampton Inn*

among the Hampton family of South Carolina Episcopalians summering in Cashiers. The family aided in building the church in 1884 and rebuilding after it burned in 1892.

JK 20 Grimshawes (Whiteside Cove)

The rural community extends along Whiteside Cove Rd. (SR 1107) and others that curve through the valleys and hills beneath the towering cliffs of Whiteside Mountain. Two small structures recall community institutions when travel was more difficult.

The tiny **Grimshawes Post Office** (ca. 1903, 1975; W side SR 1107, 4.0 mi. S of NC 107) is a 5½-by-6-foot frame structure, with a gable-fronted porch and walls covered with vertical split logs. A post office was established at Whiteside Cove in 1878, and the little building was constructed ca. 1903 by postmaster Thomas Grimshawe, about the same time he built summer tourist cabins near his home. By the 1930s Warren Alexander ran the cabins and the post office. In 1947 the post office was hauled about a mile to the home of postmistress Mae Passmore, where it gained fame and a special postmark as the smallest post office in the nation: "Why, folks from all over the world wrote here to get letters posted with the Grimshawes postmark," remembered Mrs. Passmore. Closed by the U.S. Post Office in 1953, it was trucked up to Whiteside Mountain to serve as a concession stand. In 1975 local residents moved it to this spot on the Passmore property and restored it as a bicentennial project.

Whiteside School (ca. 1910; E side SR 1107, 4.7 mi. S of NC 107) in its narrow cove is an especially well preserved small schoolhouse. With its gable-end entrance and belfry, it resembles a church. There are few windows on the right-hand side, a feature thought to prevent shadows on the students' schoolwork.

JK 21 Jewel J. Revis Bridge (Truss Bridge #63)
Early 20th c.; Owego Bridge Co. of Wilmington, Ohio; S side US 74 at SR 1392 over Tuckasegee River

JK 20 *Whiteside School*

Stretching 160 feet and divided into 9 panels, this Camelback Truss bridge is one of the most prominent metal truss bridges in the N.C. mountains. This type of through-truss, with its polygonal top chord of exactly 5 slopes, was a late 19th- and early 20th-c. refinement of the polygonal-topped Parker Truss. It offered greater standardization and economy of construction as well as better stress distribution. The Parker in turn was an improvement of the popular 19th-c. Pratt Truss.

JK 22 Mac's Indian Village
1937; SR 1563 (Tee Pee Rd.) opp. US 441 BUS/BYP fork, Cherokee vic.

As motor tourism began to recover from the Great Depression and burgeoned at the *Great Smoky Mountains National Park and at Cherokee, several entrepreneurs de-

JK 21 *Jewel J. Revis Bridge*

JK 22 *Mac's Indian Village*

veloped motor courts with a variety of "Indian" motifs. Few survive from as early as the 1930s, and none rivals Mac's Indian Village for nostalgic roadside architecture appeal. In 1937 L. F. "Mac" McHaney constructed the complex beside Soco Creek. A central 2-story office building and residence is flanked on each side by 8 tepee-fronted tourist cabins. The cabins are small, conventional frame structures. At the front of each, McHaney built a tall, curved metal tepee facade, painted with stylized decorations and with its peak outlined in neon; tourists walk into the "tepee" front and open the paneled door into a tidy cabin.

JK 23 Cherokee Methodist Church and Keener House

Ca. 1847, early 20th c.; N side US 19 at SR 1427, Soco vic., Qualla Boundary

In 1847 the Holston Methodist Conference sent Horace Ulrich Keener to serve as the first resident missionary at the Echota Mission, Waynesville circuit. The mission was established near here on land given by William Holland Thomas, the merchant, legislator, and adopted Cherokee who helped the Indians to remain on their land during and after the Cherokee Removal of 1838. Keener also established a school for the Cherokees. The mission continued from 1840 to 1885. The small, half-dovetailed log dwelling, described as being built as Keener's home in 1847, was moved here from a nearby site and rebuilt in 1959 to commemorate Keener's work. The gable-fronted, stone **Cherokee Methodist Church** was built early in the 20th c. for the congregation that descends from the mission.

Macon County (MA)

MA 1 Franklin

The mountain county seat and tourist center lies on a high plateau above the Little Tennessee River, with circuitous streets following the hilly terrain. It occupies the site of *Nequassee, an important Cherokee town for centuries. White occupation of the site began in 1820 after the treaty of 1819 redefined Cherokee boundaries. The town, named for Governor Jesse Franklin, became the seat of Macon Co. when it was formed in 1829 and named for Nathaniel Macon, powerful congressman from Warren Co. The first courthouse was built in 1829 and served until the second was completed in 1882, a brick, Italianate edifice similar to those in Transylvania and Clay counties. It was razed in 1972. Its jaunty mansard-roofed belfry is the centerpiece of a small park across Main St. from the third courthouse, a massive masonry structure that fills the corner site.

Main St. is lined by brick commercial buildings from the late 19th through the mid 20th c. Among the oldest is the 2-story brick **Pendergrass Building** (1904; 6 W. Main St.). From this store near the courthouse, Florence and Jesse Pendergrass sold clothing, food, tobacco, household goods, hardware, and farm equipment to county residents. A strong local example of the International style appears in the **Nantahala Power and Light Company Building** (1952; 17 W. Main St.), designed by staff architects of Alcoa, the original owner of the regional power supplier. Horizontal bands of corrugated metal between continuous sash windows give a streamlined effect, and the clean brick walls rise to a flat, ledgeless roof. East of the courthouse the **Scott Griffin Hotel** (1926–27; 13 E. Main St.) was touted by the local paper on its completion as "easily one of the best commercial hotels west of Asheville." Named for the father of one of the builders, the 4-story brick building had offices and shops at ground level and 36 guest rooms above, "attractively furnished, with

hot and cold water in each room," while a heated roof garden hosted concerts, dances, and banquets year-round. The 2-story (former) **U.S. Post Office** (1935; Louis A. Simon, supervising architect of the Treasury; 38 E. Main St.) typifies the red brick, Colonial Revival architecture of many Works Progress Administration (WPA) post offices.

Behind the courthouse stands the **Franklin Presbyterian Church** (ca. 1856; 45 Church St.), one of the oldest church buildings in southwestern N.C. The red brick, Greek Revival temple-form church, erected for a congregation organized in 1833, has large rectangular windows on the sides and two double doors at the gable front. **St. Agnes Episcopal Church** (1888; William Gould Bulgin, builder; 27 Church St.), which served as mother church for the denomination in the area, was erected by the builder of the *Clay County Courthouse. The brick church has a steep gable roof and a gabled front entrance with brackets and stickwork.

MA 1 *Franklin Presbyterian Church*

MA 1 *Jesse Siler House*

Reflecting its relatively early settlement for the region, Franklin retains some notable 19th-c. houses. The **Jesse R. Siler House** (ca. 1810s, ca. 1820s, ca. 1900; 115 W. Main St.; private) contains one of the oldest houses in southwestern N.C. It began as a 2-story log dwelling probably built in the 1810s and described as "an improved Indian cabin." Since the land had been in Cherokee territory until 1819, it is unknown if the house was built for a Cherokee family or a white trader. Siler, a merchant and farmer, acquired the property in 1821 and expanded the log dwelling with frame additions, finished in late Georgian–early Federal character quite remarkable in western N.C. Another expansion ca. 1900 produced the present large house with monumental portico.

At the opposite end of Main St. stands the **Albert Swain Bryson House** (ca. 1875; Pine Lane at W. Main St.; private), a big, exuberantly eclectic brick house built for Bryson, a town magistrate, farmer, and building contractor. The 2-story house has a tall hip roof, a large gable on each side, bracketed eaves, and peaked window heads, plus a 1- and 2-tier porch. The **Franklin Terrace Hotel** (1888, early 20th c.; 67 Harrison Ave.; B&B) is another eclectic brick building, with a cupola and Italianate corbeling and window hoods. Built as a Methodist boarding school for women, it served as a public school (1902–10), then became a leading tourist hotel and gained its 2-tier porches.

MA 2 Nequassee (Nikwasi) Mound
*Date unknown; S side E. Main St.
(US 441 BUS), 0.1 mi. E of Depot St.*

The only visible evidence of Cherokee occupation in what is now Franklin is the large earthen mound covered in grass, upon which the townhouse stood. Franklin covers the site of Nequassee, a major settlement among the Cherokee towns of western N.C. The town of as much as 100 acres had about 100 dwellings and several hundred inhabitants. Native people had occupied Nequassee from ca. 750–200 B.C. In 1776 Gen. Griffith Rutherford razed the town, but evidently some families returned to the area.

Nequassee is best known as the location of a 1730 meeting between Sir Alexander Cuming and several Cherokee leaders, where the Cherokees first pledged their allegiance to the English. Today the mound, located in a riverside commercial section, is owned and protected by the town and accessible to view. (See Introduction, Fig. 9.)

MA 3 St. Cyprian's Episcopal Church
1890; James Kennedy, builder; E side SR 1166, N of US 64, Franklin vic.

One of the few black Episcopal churches in western N.C., St. Cyprian's originated as a mission in 1887, when James Kennedy, working with John A. Deal, the priest in charge of missionary work in southwestern N.C., began teaching in the Colored Episcopal Mission School in a tannery packinghouse near Franklin. The school emphasized manual training for men and boys and cooking and sewing instruction for girls. By 1888 the newly ordained Kennedy had become director of St. Cyprian's Mission, and in 1890 he and Deal built the original portion of St. Cyprian's Church. An accomplished carpenter, Kennedy crafted the altar, baptismal font, cross, and altar railing. He served the congregation for over twenty years. In 1920 he became archdeacon of the diocese, the highest position available to black churchmen at that time. The simple gable-fronted building with lancet windows was expanded in 1985 to create a long side-gabled structure with a central vestibule and belfry.

MA 3 *St. Cyprian's Episcopal Church*

MA 4 Franklin Power Company Hydroelectric Dam

Ca. 1929; end of SR 1327 on N shore of Lake Emory, 0.6 mi. NW of SR 1328

Franklin's power plant on Lake Emory delivered electricity to about 300 town residents before Nantahala Power and Light Co. purchased and upgraded the facility in 1933 to serve other parts of the county. The classically detailed brick structure features a cast-concrete cornice and tall, multipaned windows with arched transoms and keystones. The spillover dam is west of the powerhouse.

MA 5 Fish Weir

Date unknown; Little Tennessee River, view from parking area on W side NC 28 at SR 1338, Wests Mill vic.

The Cherokees were the earliest known users of this V-shaped stone fish weir. To supplement their diet of corn, squash, fruits, and small game, they trapped fish by placing a basket downstream at the smaller opening of the weir. Whites who settled in the Cowee Valley in the 19th c. continued to use and maintain these traps. This weir, which measures approximately 100 feet across, is visible from the riverbank when the water is low.

MA 6 Wests Mill (Cowee)

Late 19th–early 20th c.; SR 1350 and SR 1340, E of NC 28 at Cowee Creek

For centuries Native Americans lived and farmed at this site along Cowee Creek and in the broad valley near the Little Tennessee River. In his travels in 1775 naturalist William Bartram described the Cowee community as consisting of 100 dwellings dominated by a townhouse atop an earthen mound. **Cowee Mound** (w side NC 28, 0.6 mi. NW of Wests Mill; no public access) still stands in the valley and is barely visible from a distance across the river. In the 18th c. the place also attracted the attention of white settlers, who mined lead, silver, and gemstones and established the community of Wests Mill. The larger area is still known as Cowee.

The present village, overlooking the Little Tennessee valley, comprises a cluster of frame houses and stores along Cowee Creek. A highway historical marker (w side NC 28, opp. SR 1350) commemorates the tons of fine clay that Wedgewood Pottery extracted and shipped from a nearby pit in 1767. **Cowee School** (1943; E side SR 1340, just S of SR 1341), erected by the WPA on the site of a Civilian Conservation Corps (CCC) camp,

MA 6 *Clyde and Minnie West Store*

is a long, low building of native stone with an Art Deco motif at the north entrance.

The **Bryson-Rickman Store** (1895, 1924; E side SR 1341, just past SR 1340) is a characteristic 2-story frame store building that retains its storefront and many interior fittings. Tom Rickman bought the store in 1924 from Horace Bryson and added the side porch for his second-story residential quarters; he operated the store into the late 20th c. The **Morrison House** (ca. 1900; E side SR 1340, at SR 1350) is a 2-story weatherboarded dwelling with decorative porch. The **Vonnie West House** (ca. 1900; N side SR 1350, at SR 1340), a 2-story, front-gabled house, features decorative sawn porch brackets and an attached stone outbuilding. The former **Post Office** (ca. 1910; N side SR 1350, 0.05 mi. W of SR 1340) is a diminutive, 1-story frame building. The nearby **Clyde and Minnie West Store** (ca. 1900; N side SR 1350, at NC 28) is a 2-story front-gabled building with an intact storefront. According to local tradition, Methodists traded at the West Store, while Baptists preferred the Bryson-Rickman Store.

MA 7 Pleasant Hill A.M.E. Zion Church
Ca. 1900; NW side SR 1350, 0.6 mi. NE of SR 1340, Wests Mill vic.

The simple frame church stands as the chief reminder of the African American community once located in the Cowee Valley. A double-leaf door opens in the gable front, and sash windows mark the sides. Families maintain the old cemetery west of the church.

MA 8 Little Tennessee River Suspension Footbridges
Early to mid-20th c.; Little Tennessee River, W side NC 28 at SR 1358 and W side NC 28, 0.3 mi. S of SR 1355, between Wests Mill and Oak Grove

Steel cables provide strength and flexibility to these primarily wooden footbridges. The graceful structures were built across rivers to serve families living on the riverbank opposite the highway.

MA 9 Rose Creek Truss Bridge
Early 20th c.; SR 1456 at NC 28, Ruby Mine

The single-lane Pratt through-truss bridge spans the Little Tennessee River to connect the community of Ruby Mine with NC 28.

MA 10 William Morrison House
Ca. 1832, 1920; N side 1358, 0.25 mi. E of jct. w/SR 1359, Etna; private, visible from road

The 2-story log house exemplifies dwellings built by some of the county's most prosperous early white settlers. Morrison, a native of Burke Co., assembled property that reached from the present Macon-Swain border to the Cowee Valley. Weatherboards cover the log walls of the hall-parlor plan house; a 1-story front addition dates from the early 20th c.

MA 11 Tellico Valley

This long valley in northern Macon Co. shelters an unspoiled rural landscape. A narrow, mostly unpaved road parallels Tellico Creek as it winds through a valley where dense forests alternate with open pastures, then emerges at the lofty vista at Tellico Gap.

Samuel Ramsey founded a community in the valley in the late 19th c. An enterprising carpenter, Ramsey built a general store, gristmill, sawmill, flour mill, planing mill, blacksmith shop, and post office at Tellico. He also built many of the late 19th- and early 20th-c. frame farmhouses that line both sides of the road. The **Byrd House** (ca. 1890; S side SR 1365, 0.2 mi. W of SR 1364) is a neat, 2-story frame house with shingles. **Tellico Baptist Church** (1907–8; SE side SR 1365, 1 mi. W of SR 1364), a frame building erected for a congregation organized in 1884, stands amid a cemetery on a steep grassy clearing with the Big Ridge Mountains to the north. It has a hip roof, front belltower, and braced eaves. A picturesque **Barn** (ca. 1940; S side SR 1365, 2 mi. W of SR 1364), typical of the burley-tobacco barns of the area, stands in a broad pasture, its central gabled section flanked by sheds.

A series of 2-story frame houses and farmsteads built for the prosperous Ramsey family anchors the valley. Samuel Ramsey, the patriarch, built the **Laura Martha Ramsey House** (early 20th c.; s side SR 1365, 2.6 mi. W of SR 1364; private) for his seventh child and her family. It typifies the 1½-story saddlebag form with a central stone chimney and a truncated second-story gabled portico—a treatment seen throughout northern Macon Co. A frame corncrib, barn, privy, and smokehouse stand nearby.

The long stretch of low **Stone Walls** (20th c.; 0.5 mi. on SR 1365, 2.8–3.2 mi. W of SR 1364) was begun by Samuel Ramsey and extended by later owners. The walls flank the road near the **Samuel Ramsey House** (ca. 1880, ca. 1900; N side SR 1365, 3.0 mi. W of SR 1364; private), which was the center of the community Ramsey established. Ramsey built the original parlor and 3 bedrooms; his son, Robert, added a center passage and a third floor with a gable-on-hip roof. Fanciful heart-shaped spindled openings accent the front porch.

Farther up the road, Samuel Ramsey built the **Harley Ramsey House** (ca. 1900; s side SR 1365, 3.2 mi. W of SR 1364; private) for his sixth child. The 2-story dwelling has a central stone chimney and full 2-story

porch with decorative sawnwork in sunburst motifs. The **George Ramsey House** (ca. 1898; s side SR 1365, 3.5 mi. W of SR 1364; private), built for Samuel's fourth child, follows the same 2-story, single-pile form with central stone chimney, and similar decoration graces the 2-tier portico and 2-tier back porch. The valley narrows near the 1-story, board-and-batten **Lorna Cook House** (early 20th c.; s side SR 1365, 3.9 mi. W of SR 1364; private). The road begins a precipitous ascent to about 4,000 feet at Tellico Gap, where it is passable from late spring to early fall but is not maintained in the winter.

MA 12 Dean House

Ca. 1900; E side SR 1364, 0.3 mi. N of SR 1372, Burningtown vic.; private, visible from road

The highly visible, frame saddlebag dwelling exemplifies a curious house form characteristic of Macon Co. It stands 1½ stories high, without front windows at the upper level. The front gable of the taller, full-height porch intersects the central chimney as it pierces the roof's ridge; the truncated upper level of the porch is barely high enough to

MA 11 *Samuel Ramsey House*

accommodate a person and appears as a primarily decorative element. An early 20th-c. barn and corncrib stand directly across the road. The house was built for the Dean family and has remained in the family.

MA 12 *Dean House*

MA 13 Bill Slagle House

Ca. 1910–15; NW side SR 1392,
1.1 mi. W of SR 1372, Burningtown vic.;
private, visible from road

Typical of the many boxed houses built around the turn of the century, the structure of the house is made by nailing vertical boards to light sills and plates, and the exterior appearance resembles board and batten. Constructed by local carpenters, it stands on high piers and has a front porch. Such houses often succeeded log dwellings after sawmills became accessible.

MA 14 Holly Springs School

1916; B. J. Hurst, builder; W side SR 1513,
opp. SR 1521, Holly Springs community

The typical frame, T-plan school has large sash windows and transomed double doors in the front gable; it was built for the county by B. J. Hurst for $745.

MA 15 Bell-Bryson Farm

1890s, ca. 1900; W side SR 1674, 0.3 mi.
S of SR 1672; private, visible from road

Surrounded by barns, a mill, and other early 20th-c. outbuildings, the house by Nickajack Creek is the centerpiece of a mountain farmstead. In a characteristic sequence,

MA 14 *Holly Springs School*

Samuel Bell, a furniture maker, built the small 1½-story portion, and farmer William Bryson added the large 2-story section and converted the original house to a kitchen.

MA 16 US 64

1928; from Gneiss to Highlands

US 64 through the majestic Cullasaja Gorge remains one of the region's most memorable scenic highways. Hairpin curves, steep overlooks, and spectacular views of Cullasaja and Dry Falls offer an uncommon motoring experience.

The construction of US 64 through the precipitous Cullasaja Gorge presented a monumental challenge to engineers and workers during the infancy of mountain highway building. In 1923–24 Dave "Straight Line" Gibson, a highway commission site engineer, conducted a survey between Gneiss and Highlands. He sent his field notes to the commission's headquarters in Raleigh, where the design office drafted plans for the highway. The construction department, after reviewing the plans, deemed the road unbuildable and abandoned the project. But soon the highway commission's newly formed district office in Asheville revived the plan to build the impossible. In 1925 John Smith, the project engineer, and T. Brewster, the superintendent, mobilized air compressors, wagon drills, a steam shovel, converted farm wagons for hauling, 14 mules, and 2 horses along with about 20 black prison laborers. The workers set up a series of camps along the way as the highway was built. The final camp, on the east side of Highlands, served the crew while they completed the road into Jackson Co.

MA 17 Cliffside Lake Recreation Area

1930s; CCC; entrance at N side US 64 at SR 1620

CCC workers constructed Cliffside Lake and most of the surrounding rustic-style **Picnic Shelters**. These structures of stone and timber possess a straightforward and powerful architectural character that derives from the overscaled, massive round logs used as the defining design element. Evocative of the rustic style executed in the Adirondack Mountains and in the great national parks of the West, they were based on standardized plans for such recreational structures.

MA 18 Highlands

Located on a high plateau, the town lies in an area long famed for its diversity of plant and animal species, including rare plants identified by André Michaux in the 18th c. The resort town owes its existence to two midwestern developers who recognized its potential. In the mid-1870s Samuel T. Kelsey, who later developed Linville, and Clinton C. Hutchinson, who had founded two towns in Kansas, purchased over 800 acres in Blue Ridge township and laid out a 1½-square-mile town. They originally called it "Kelsey's Plateau" but soon changed the name to Highlands and published and distributed nationwide a pamphlet exalting its pure water and air and agreeable climate. Highlands quickly became a summer resort town attracting families from South Carolina, Georgia, New Orleans, and elsewhere. In 1879 Charleston businessman S. Prioleau Ravenel built the first 2-story house, which was also the first summer dwelling in town. By 1883 Highlands boasted a post office, two hotels, a newspaper, a gristmill, a lumber mill, and retail stores. The early 20th-c. saw continued development and clinched the town's reputation as a resort for prosperous tourists and summer residents.

Early 20th-c. Highlands supported a remarkable collection of informal, rustic-style architecture. Characterized locally by rounded logs set in horizontal, diagonal, and vertical patterns; chestnut-bark siding; and balustrades and porch railings of rhododendron branches, the form flourished from the 1920s onward. Joe Webb, a local contractor who did the most to propagate the rustic mode, translated its use of natural logs and

MA 17 *Cliffside Lake Picnic Shelters*

branches into a building form that proved popular and livable. Webb's houses attracted the favor of summer and full-time residents, and his work remained in high demand from the 1920s into the 1940s.

Many of the finest 19th- and early 20th-c. houses in Highlands are secluded behind thick hedges—mostly rhododendron—that protect the privacy of residents. Among the areas with distinctive architecture away from public view, the Satulah Mountain neighborhood has an extensive collection of Queen Anne, Craftsman, and rustic houses of the early 20th c.; at the Highlands Country Club the private 18-hole golf course designed by Donald Ross is surrounded by architecturally notable guest cottages and vacation houses; and in Webbmont on the side of Flat Mountain, Joe Webb built a collection of his signature round-pole log houses.

Downtown Highlands comprises a few blocks of 1- and 2-story commercial buildings lining Main St. Although Kelsey and Hutchinson laid out Main St. in 1875, most of the buildings date from the 20th c., and the earliest ones have undergone renovation. Two important early hotels stand at the principal crossroads. The **Highlands Inn** (1879; NE corner E. Main and N. 4th Sts.) (see Introduction, Fig. 29) is a 3-story frame building with a full-width, 2-story porch overlooking Main St. The **Edwards Hotel** (ca. 1880, 1934–35; SE corner S. Main and E. 4th Sts.) has a 2½-story frame section with a double-tier porch, plus a 3-story brick and stone addition by Wilton Cobb, local builder and hardware store owner.

Farther down Main St. stand two frame churches from the early years of Highlands. **First Presbyterian Church** (1885; Marion Wright, builder; 471 Main St.) is a picturesque Italianate church on a hillside surrounded by hemlocks, rhododendron, and an original mortise-and-tenon picket fence. Margaretta Ravenel and her sister, Clarissa Burt, funded construction by local carpenter Wright. The steep gable roof is softened by clipped gables; a square belfry carries a pyramidal roof with finial. The **Episcopal Church of the Incarnation** (1896; 111 N. 5th St.), on a corner at the end of Main St., is a small, Gothic Revival church with a steep

gable roof and an octagonal shingled belfry atop a corner tower, finished inside with poplar sheathing and an exposed scissor truss. James Kennedy, a black deacon in charge of Franklin's *St. Cyprian's Episcopal Church, crafted the poplar pews with carved end panels.

MA 18 *Highland Hiker*

At the east end of the business district is the **Dr. E. E. Reinke House (Highland Hiker)** (1932; 100 E. Main St.), the most readily visible of the rustic log houses by local contractor Joe Webb. The T-plan house of saddle-notched logs features Webb's trademarks, including vertically placed logs adorning the gables and branches in decorative patterns. It was built for Dr. Reinke, a Vanderbilt University professor who was the first director of the *Highlands Biological Station, for his residence during the summer stays at Highlands.

Near the southeast edge of town is the **Highlands Biological Station** (265 6th St.), founded in 1927 near Lake Ravenel as the Highlands Museum and Biological Laboratory to study the diverse flora and fauna of the area. The **Weyman Memorial Laboratory** (1930–31, 1958; Oskar Stonorov [Philadelphia] and McKendree Tucker and Albert Howell [Atlanta], architects) was among the first buildings. The small wooden structure—a notable early example of the International style, with smooth matchboarded walls, a flat roof, and ribbons of windows—was published in Henry-Russell Hitchcock and Philip Johnson's influential book *The International Style* (1932). But the flat-roofed building proved unsuited to the damp locale with its extremely high rainfall (80–120 inches a year) and heavy snows. In 1958 the

MA 18 *First Presbyterian Church*

institution regretfully remodeled it with a pitched roof and asbestos shingles. (See Ernest Wood, "A Look at an Early Modernist Building in North Carolina," *North Carolina Architect*, Jan./Feb. 1978.)

MA 19 Godfrey-England-Doggett House

1932; Joe Webb, builder; E side Cullasaja Dr., 0.15 mi. N of US 64, Highlands; private, visible from road

Characteristic of Joe Webb's work, the picturesque 1½-story round-pole log dwelling features shed dormers and vertically placed logs in the gables. A rhododendron railing embellishes the north porch. Webb built the house for W. E. Godfrey and his sisters, Anne England and Mary Doggett. W. E. Godfrey taught physics at Clemson College (now University). Cullasaja Rd. was originally called Clemson Rd. after the many professors who had summer homes there.

MA 22 *Brabson House*

MA 20 Horse Cove
SR 1603, SE of Highlands

Horse Cove attracted white settlers as early as the mid-19th c., including Highlands's first mayor, Stanhope Walker Hill, who settled in this valley in 1837. Rolling hills and dense, fragrant forests of spruce and pine bordered by massive mountain faces characterize the cove, named for the livestock Cherokees ranged here. Blackrock Branch, Edwards Creek, and Bull Pen Creek ramble through the valley, while sheer-faced Blackrock Mountain rises to the northeast, and Fodderstack, Rich, and Chestnut Mountains rise on the southwest. The road through Horse Cove continues southeast through Forest Service land and eventually crosses the Chattooga River at the Jackson Co. line. Small seasonal frame cottages from the 1920s through the 1940s stand along the road through the community, and more substantial year-round residences reflect architectural styles seen in Highlands.

Residents of the community built the **Church in the Wildwood** (1938; s side sR 1603, 0.75 mi. w of sR 1608) as a nonde-

nominational summer chapel, with some of the material for the simple frame building coming from a former CCC camp nearby. Large windows light the dark wood interior, and unhewn logs support the front gable porch. The adjoining Horse Cove cemetery has graves predating the church.

The **Frank Hill House** (1880–93; jct. of sR 1603 and sR 1608; private) is a 2-story, cross-plan dwelling adorned with decorative shingles in the gables and multicolored glass around the ornate doors. The rear ell served as a post office and store in the late 19th c. when the surrounding community was called Victoria. Hill, a carpenter and son of Stanhope Walker Hill, began its construction in 1880.

MA 21 Otto School
1941; W side US 23/441,
0.35 mi. S of SR 1114, Otto

One of several stone schools built by the wpA, the Otto School opened in 1941 as the first consolidated school in the county. The elongated building features a pedimented front and side entrances and parapeted end walls. Classrooms and offices flank the long corridors that extend from the central auditorium. The school stands on a hill overlooking the former railroad village of Otto, which was spawned by the Tallulah Falls Railroad, which ran north to Franklin in 1907. But the line—which came to be called the "Total Failure"—shut down in 1961 after years of financial loss, spelling the demise of Otto.

MA 22 Brabson House
1884, early 20th c.; W side SR 1118,
0.6 mi. S of SR 1115, Otto vic.

Located in a gently sloping pasture, with forested mountains beyond, the frame farmhouse was built for Alexander C. Brabson, a country doctor who served this section of the county from ca. 1870 until his death in 1917. A native of Tennessee, after soldiering in the Civil War he graduated from the University of Nashville School of Medicine and moved to Macon Co., where he boarded with Dr. George Rush and in 1881 married his daughter, Cora Rush. Dr. Brabson was known for his treatment of "milk sickness," an ailment prevalent before pasteurization and attributed to cows' consumption of toxic plants. Like many country doctors, he traveled by horseback to his far-flung patients and supplemented a largely in-kind income with farming, beginning with 38 acres and expanding to more than 200 acres. The Brabsons' 2-story frame house has a somewhat unusual plan, with a center chimney flanked by two main rooms that open into a central lobby entrance. The rear kitchen ell was connected to the house ca. 1906. Outbuildings include a corncrib, storage sheds, and a ca. 1920 concrete silo.

MA 23 Gillespie Chapel
1880s; Zeb Conley, builder; N side SR 1128,
0.2 mi. E of SR 1131, Upper Cartoogechaye

Local builder Zeb Conley constructed the picturesque hillside building, which served for its first five years as a school. In 1886 Methodists acquired the property and soon added a 3-level, bell-roofed octagonal tower. The interior is simply finished and contains plain wooden pews. A cemetery spreads out on a precipitous hill rising behind the church.

MA 23 *Gillespie Chapel*

MA 24 St. John's Episcopal Church

1945; N side SR 1308, 0.1 mi. W of SR 1307, Cartoogechaye

Macon Co. native Rev. Rufus Morgan built this little board-and-batten Gothic Revival church to replace an 1888 church torn down in 1925. The site had remained empty, and many of the churchyard graves were moved to Franklin, where most of the old St. John's congregation worshiped. Morgan (whose sister, Lucy, founded the *Penland School of Crafts) served numerous churches throughout the region. His love for his native mountains and the outdoors shaped the chapel's rustic design and its log belltower. In addition to the graves of Rufus and Lucy Morgan, the adjoining cemetery contains the graves of Cherokee Indian Chuttahsotee and his wife, Cunstagih, who were interred here in 1878.

MA 25 Wilson Lick Ranger Station

1916, 1969; W side Forest Service Rd., 1.1 mi. N of SR 1310, Wayah Gap

The U.S. Forest Service built this simple, shingle-covered cottage in 1916, the year of the establishment of the Nantahala National Forest. The station, the oldest Forest Service ranger outpost in the state, was used until 1931. The men who stayed here kept a lookout for forest fires and also built and maintained trails. Later, wildlife protectors used it as a base. In 1969 the Forest Service replaced the chestnut-bark siding with shingles.

MA 26 John B. Byrne Fire Tower

1935–37; CCC; end of Forest Service Rd., 4.2 mi. N of SR 1310, Wayah Gap

In 1935 the CCC began construction of the fire tower on Wayah Bald, one of more than fifty such structures the CCC built in western N.C. It was named in memory of the supervisor of Nantahala National Forest. Originally the tower stood 60 feet tall and had three floors. The second level allowed the public to enjoy spectacular mountain views in all directions, while the third was reserved for two forest rangers on the lookout for fires. In 1947 the Forest Service dismantled the top floor of the tower, which had fallen into disrepair, and built an exterior stair to the public observation deck; a roof on hemlock posts was added later.

MA 27 Nantahala Power and Light Company Complex

1942; SW corner US 19 and SR 1310, Beechertown

Built to meet the power needs of World War II, the Nantahala plant at Beechertown lies near the Nantahala River, but the water that powers it comes from the dam forming Nantahala (Aquone) Lake far upstream and is carried 5 miles through tunnels to the powerhouse. The plant initially supplied power chiefly for Alcoa's wartime aluminum productions in Tennessee. The complex includes a concrete, 3-story powerhouse. At Beechertown the company also built a small village with several frame bungalows, a community building, and a suspension footbridge over the Nantahala River.

Swain County (sw)

The mountainous county, which encompasses some of the highest peaks of the Appalachians, is drained by the Little Tennessee, Tuckasegee (Tuckaseigee), Oconaluftee, and Nantahala rivers. The county has an especially complex history as the heartland of the Eastern Band of the Cherokee Indians, center of a late 19th-c. lumber boom, and the site of major 20th-c. federal projects that redefined its landscape.

*Kituwah (near present-day Bryson City) was the considered the ancient "mother town" of the Cherokees. It lay along the river called Tuckasegee, from the Cherokee name meaning "crawling terrapin." Part of the Middle Towns of the Cherokees, the relatively remote settlements here were also called Out Towns.

White settlement began along the Oconaluftee River, a tributary of the Tuckasegee, in the early 19th c. A number of Cherokees remained in the area, and several registered tracts near Quallatown (in present-day Jackson Co.) on the Oconaluftee River after the treaty of 1819 constricted the Cherokee Nation to lands west of here. During and after the forced removal of the Cherokees from the Cherokee Nation tract in 1838, these Quallatown Indians were able to remain on their lands. The Qualla Boundary, now encompassing some 56,000 acres, is the largest tract of several held in trust for the Eastern Band of the Cherokees.

For much of the 19th c., white and Indian residents engaged in small-scale farming and lumbering, but as elsewhere the coming of the Western North Carolina Railroad (WNCRR) in the 1880s and many smaller logging railroads revolutionized the local economy. Big logging firms, including the Ritter Lumber Co. and the Champion Fibre Co., built sawmills for the timber they cut at astonishing rates from the ancient forests—the county's 1920 timber production was valued at $2 million—and sawmill villages and towns grew up along the creeks and railroads.

In the early and mid-20th c., the county underwent another drastic change with the creation of Nantahala National Forest (1911), the *Great Smoky Mountains National Park (1926–30s), and Fontana Lake (1942–44), which provided many construction jobs, essentially depopulated much of the county, and introduced large-scale tourism. After the national park was authorized in 1926, land was acquired over several years from the timber companies and many individual farm families. The park now covers two-thirds of the county. *Fontana Lake began to fill in 1944 and soon covered 10,000 acres, including several villages as well as farms. For the remainder of the century, former residents who crossed the lake by boat to visit hillside graveyards pointed out the sites of their former homeplaces as the boat cruised over them.

SW 1 Bryson City

After Swain Co. was formed from Jackson and Macon counties in 1871 and named for Governor David Swain, the county seat was established beside the Tuckasegee River. It was called Charleston until 1889, when it was renamed for a local resident to avoid confusion with Charleston, S.C.

After the WNCRR's Murphy branch arrived in 1884, the ensuing lumber boom transformed Bryson City from a small riverside trading center for white and Cherokee farmers into a busy mercantile town. Timber prosperity supported construction of a new courthouse, several churches, stores, and residences. Growth was slowed, however, by the Great Depression and the departure of the large lumber companies, many of whom sold their depleted timberlands to the *Great Smoky Mountains National Park.

Several local citizens led in the creation of the park. One of the best known was Horace Kephart, whose study, *Our Southern Highlanders* (1913), was based on his work among Swain Co. people; his grave, marked by a boulder, is in the Bryson City cemetery. Today Bryson City is a small mountain valley town seasonally enlivened by the tourists visiting the national park, the national forest, Fontana Lake, and Cherokee.

The centerpiece is the **Swain County Courthouse** (1908; Frank Pierce Milburn [Washington, D.C.] and Richard Sharp Smith [Asheville], architects; Falls City Construction Co. [Louisville, Ky.]; Fry and Main Sts.), a small version of the popular Neoclassical courthouse, strongly rendered with an octagonal cupola and Ionic portico. County records suggest the design was a joint project of Milburn and Smith; the latter, who had formed an important regional practice, was the former supervising architect at *Biltmore. The nature of the collaboration is not known.

Near the courthouse, the business district on Main and Everett Sts. spans the river and contains a cluster of early 20th-c. brick commercial buildings. Beside the courthouse, the former **Bryson City Bank** (1908; Main and Everett Sts.; Chamber of Commerce) is a stout, handsomely detailed brick building with large arched openings and a broad roof overhang carried on brackets.

The former **Clampitt Hardware Store** (1911; Main St.) is a classic example of its type, with corbeled brickwork, arched windows at the second story, and glass display windows at street level showing the full range of goods within. The former **Bennett's Drugstore** (1905; Everett St.), a simple, 2-story brick structure, is of historical interest. The drugstore was established by Dr. A. M. Bennett, a country doctor, whose son Dr. Kelly Bennett became a leading pharmacist, promoter and photographer of the region, state legislator, and local and regional civic leader. In the early 20th c. he and his friend Horace Kephart led efforts to create the Great Smoky Mountains National Park. In a rented office above the drugstore Kephart wrote much of *Our Southern Highlanders*.

The **Bryson City Depot** (1894–95; J. D. Elliot [Hickory], builder; Everett St. at railroad track) was built for the Southern Railway, successor to the WNCRR, on the route from Asheville to Murphy that was completed in 1891. In Nov. 1894 the *Manufacturer's Record* announced that Southern had contracted with J. D. Elliot of Hickory to build a depot in Bryson City. The 1-story frame building is neatly finished with German siding, decorative window and door frames, and fancy vertical sawnwork beneath the broad, bracketed eaves. Among

SW 1 *Swain Co. Courthouse and former Bryson City Bank*

sw 1 *Bryson City Depot*

the only active depots in the region, it serves as a stop on the *Great Smoky Mountain Railway. Crossing the Tuckasegee River at Bryson City in Swain Co. is the **Nantahala #2 Truss Bridge** (1899; Phoenix Bridge Co.), a 169-foot, pin-connected through-truss bridge that was relocated here from the Nantahala River in 1944 when the railroad was rerouted for the construction of *Fontana Dam and Lake.

The **Bryson City Presbyterian Church** (1891; Bryson and Everett Sts.) is a tall, frame building with Gothic Revival windows and unusually steep-gabled facade and tower. It was built for a congregation established in 1881.

SW 2 Frye-Randolph House and Fryemont Inn

1895, 1921–23; Fryemont Rd.,
Bryson City; private; B&B

The neighboring house and inn overlook the town and the river from a prominent hilltop. Both were built for Amos Frye and Lillian Rowe Frye, attorneys and early advocates for the establishment of the *Great Smoky Mountains National Park. In 1895, the year the couple married, Amos Frye built on the hillside a small 1½-story frame dwelling with ornate millwork trim; early in the 20th c. the Fryes expanded it to create an L-plan house with multiple gables and a stone-pillared porch. Responding to the growth of mountain tourism, in the early 1920s the couple built the rustic inn, employing the rough stonework, board and batten, and poplar-bark-shingled walls characteristic of the region, complemented on the interior by natural wood and stonework. Lillian Frye continued to practice law and operate the inn until shortly before her death in 1957. The two buildings are now in separate ownership as B&B inns; the Frye-Randolph House remains in the family.

SW 3 Estes-Clark House

Ca. 1876; W side SR 1337, 0.1 mi.
N of SR 1340, Deep Creek vic.;
private, visible from road

Described as the county's oldest house still in family use, the 1½-story log dwelling exemplifies the dogtrot plan, with two 18-foot square rooms linked by an 8-foot open passage covered by a common gable roof. Both sections have typical half-dovetailed notching. Foundation piers are of stone, but the end chimney—one of two originally—is of brick. The house was built for William and Jane Hoyle Estes, who farmed a 300-acre tract on Deep Creek.

SW 4 Kituwah Mound

15th–18th c.; E side US 19, 1.4 mi. S of
SR 1168, Ela vic.; private, barely visible

at a distance from road and railroad,
between Ferguson Field airstrip and river

The Cherokee town site was occupied throughout most of the 18th c. and had been occupied intermittently since at least the 15th c. Located beside the Tuckasegee River just below the confluence with the Oconaluftee River, in an area known as Governor's Island and Ferguson Fields, the town is believed to have covered some 30 to 40 acres. It includes remnants of an earthen platform about 6 feet high and 200 feet in diameter. Traditionally Kituwah is regarded as the "mother town" of the Cherokees. Kituwah was burned by British troops during the French and Indian War. Near here was the home of Yonaguska (Drowning Bear), the 19th-c. Cherokee chief who adopted William Holland Thomas. The Kituwah site was acquired by the Eastern Band in 1996.

SW 5 Thomas Chapel

Ca. 1891; W side SR 1351,
1.1 mi. N of US 19, Ela vic.

Occupying a sloping site with its informal graveyard above it, the simple gable-fronted frame church has tall, narrow 4/4 windows flanking the central entrance and marking the sides. A slim belfry tops the gable, which is accented by small brackets. The neatly finished church was built on Galbraith Creek on land acquired from Laura and James Thomas.

SW 6 Hyatt House

1880; Thad Buchanan and Manus Welch,
builders; E side SR 1168, 0.5 mi. N of US 74,
Ela vic.; private, visible from road

The farmstead on the bank of the Tuckasegee River occupies a prominent site created in a fashion typical of farmers who built along floodplains. Through cutting and filling, workmen formed a broad shelf in the hillside, providing a platform overlooking the riverbottom. The symmetrical, simply detailed 2-story brick house has a latticed, central entrance porch, and a rear kitchen–dining room wing. Frame outbuildings (ca. 1900) include a board-and-batten meat-

house and a barn of frame and rock-faced concrete block, with the lower story banked into the hillside. Soon after the formation of Swain Co., Abel and Sarah Moody Hyatt sold their farm in neighboring Jackson Co. and moved here with their four children. After living for a time in an existing house, they erected this substantial brick house, a rarity for its era. The 1880 census showed the family operating a farm with 70 acres improved and 100 unimproved, where they raised livestock, corn, and wheat. In the 1880s collector Edward Valentine of Richmond boarded with the Hyatts while investigating the nearby *Kituwah Mound and other Native American sites.

SW 7 Floyd Farm and Mill

Late 19th–early 20th c.; SE side
SR 1355 at SR 1362, 0.7 mi. N of US 19;
private, visible from road

Set in a broad valley in the curve of the road, the farmstead and gristmill epitomize the agrarian mountain valley landscape of the turn of the century. The 1½-story, L-shaped frame house encloses an older log house. Nearby stand a frame barn, a half-dovetailed log corncrib, and a log smokehouse. Across the road, the tall frame gristmill recalls the diversified enterprises of many farmers who offered milling services to their neighborhoods. This farmstead was the home of John and Cally Cooper Floyd, who built the mill on Coopers Creek. John was a member of the Floyd family that originally settled on the Oconaluftee River and farmed the land known as Floyd Bottoms, site of the present-day *Oconaluftee Visitor Center in the *Great Smoky Mountains National Park.

Cherokee (SW 8–14)

The town near the confluence of the Oconaluftee and Tuckasegee rivers is the principal urban center of Qualla Boundary. The Eastern Band of Cherokee Indians holds here some 56,000 acres known as the Qualla Boundary (the largest Indian reservation east of the Mississippi), plus several smaller tracts in this and other southwestern N.C. counties.

sw 6 *Hyatt House*

This area lay east of the borders of the Cherokee Nation lands defined in the treaty of 1819 (see Introduction, Fig. 10). Soon after 1819 several Cherokee families acquired tracts in this vicinity, separate from the Cherokee Nation. William Holland Thomas, a white merchant who became the adopted son of the chief, Drowning Bear (Yona-guska), and who later became a chief himself, worked from 1831 onward to help the Cherokees acquire and retain their land here. When the Cherokee Nation was forced from their tribal lands during the 1838 removal, with Thomas's aid the Qualla Cherokees remained on their land; others who eluded removal soon joined them. By the end of 1838 some 700 Cherokees resided in and near Quallatown, and another 400 lived along the Cheoah, Valley, and Hiwassee rivers. In 1845 Thomas helped the Qualla Cherokees organize as a company holding the land. They eventually became known as the Eastern Band of Cherokee Indians.

Faced with uncertain relationships with the state and federal governments, over the years the Eastern Band struggled to maintain their legal status and their traditional culture, often against tremendous pressures. In 1924 the Cherokees became U.S. citizens, and their land was placed in trust with the U.S. government, with the result that it was removed from the county tax rolls in Swain, Jackson, Cherokee, and Graham counties. The land may not be sold to non-Cherokees, though it can be sold among the Cherokees and leased to others for limited periods. There are now more than 11,000 Cherokees in the Eastern Band, most of whom reside in this area.

The establishment of the *Great Smoky Mountains National Park in the 1930s, along with the construction of the *Blue Ridge

Parkway, which terminates here, had lasting effects on the culture and economy of the Eastern Band, chiefly in the introduction of tourism. Cherokee occupies a strategic position at the eastern entrance to the park on US 441, which crosses the park to Gatlinburg and Pigeon Forge, Tenn. During the immediate post–World War II period, after the war's hiatus in tourism, the Eastern Band focused on economic development aimed at the rapidly expanding tourist trade. The Eastern Band worked in cooperation with the Southern Highland Craft Guild and the Western North Carolina Associated Communities (WNCAC), the latter of which established the Cherokee Historical Association (CHA), an organization central in the development of Cherokee tourism. In the 1990s establishment of big gambling facilities at Cherokee injected new money and new challenges into the community. The 1980s and 1990s have also seen revitalization of cultural traditions, including Cherokee dances, music, and language, and since 1984, annual gatherings of the Eastern and Western Bands.

For the Eastern Band, as historian John Finger explains, the "tourist bonanza" had paradoxical effects on their culture. Tourism "gave the Cherokees a vested interest in resisting complete assimilation into the larger American society," and paradoxically it has "heightened Cherokee self-awareness but has also necessitated a public display of 'Indianness' far removed from historical or contemporary Cherokee culture."

The town of Cherokee offers the principal public, tourist-oriented presentation of the Eastern Band's history and traditions. The popular image of Cherokee evokes the roadside stores along US 19 and US 441, with their displays of Indian goods of many types, including traditional Cherokee crafts as well as products of the market-driven imagery of the plains Indians, such as tepees and feather war bonnets. Beyond the tourist strip, the CHA offers a different presentation of the heritage of the Eastern Band. Contemporaneously with other 20th-c. American recreations of the past, the CHA and the Eastern Band undertook the production of an outdoor historical drama, *Unto These Hills*,

at the *Mountainside Theater; creation of *Oconaluftee Indian Village as a historic village with representative buildings; and establishment of the *Museum of the Cherokee Indian.

SW 8 Central Cherokee

19th c., early 20th c.; W side US 441N, just N of US 19S jct., between Sequoyah Trail and Drama Rd.

Near the main street in the heart of Cherokee are several key community sites. Behind a frame concession shelter lies a level, open area with bleachers, the **Ceremonial Ground** of the Eastern Band. Here are held traditional dances, ball games, the annual fair, and other tribal events. Just south of the ceremonial ground stand several Eastern Band administrative buildings. The **Cherokee Council House** is a 1½-story frame structure, built in the early 20th c. and moved here in the mid-20th c. and modernized over the years. It continues its role as the center of tribal government, with its principal chamber for meetings of the Tribal Council. The 12-person council includes members elected from the 6 townships of the reservation; the principal chief and vice-chief are elected from the reservation at large. Near the Council House is a small streetside park, the **Veterans Memorial**, commemorating Eastern Band members who served and died in the Armed Forces.

The **Bureau of Indian Affairs** (BIA) complex comprises several simply detailed, 1- and 2-story masonry buildings from the mid-20th c.

At the junction of US 19 and US 441 is the **Cherokee Baptist Church**, a substantial, gable-fronted stone building erected for a congregation that traces back to early 19th-c. missionary work.

SW 9 Museum of the Cherokee Indian

1976; Six Associates, Inc. [Asheville], architects; W side US 441N, 0.5 mi. N of US 19S, Cherokee

Winner of a 1977 Honor Award from the N.C. American Institute of Architects, the museum was praised as a building that "rises out of the ground with great force and dignity and relates well to the mountains as a backdrop." A series of simple, powerful triangular forms steps back in orderly sequence; their configuration at once reiterates the slopes of the mountains beyond and clearly expresses the spaces within. Natural wood sheathing of narrow vertical boards covers the wall surfaces without interruption from top to bottom. Designed to house exhibits illustrating the history and culture of the Cherokees, the museum was "intended to illustrate by its design the sense of scale and care for materials that has been characteristic of this people." In 1952 the CHA purchased the Museum of the Cherokee Indian, the private museum collection of some 50,000 artifacts of Mr. and Mrs. Samuel Beck. Subsequently the Eastern Band and the CHA commissioned the Asheville architectural firm to design this facility. (See Introduction, Fig. 68.)

SW 10 Mountainside Theater

1949–50; Albert Bell, designer; W side
US 441N, access road 0.6 mi. N of US 19S

A landmark in the development of tourism in the region, the grand amphitheater was built for the outdoor drama *Unto These Hills*. The powerful saga of origins and escape traces the story of the Eastern Band, including the Cherokee Removal and the heroic legends associated with those who resisted removal. In 1935 and 1937 a historical pageant called *The Spirit of the Smokies* was staged, but not until after World War II did efforts begin on production of an ongoing Cherokee drama to appeal to tourists' interest in Indian history. Aware of the success of the *Lost Colony* outdoor drama on Roanoke Island, in 1947 the WNCAC—representing eleven counties—agreed to sponsor the drama and formed the CHA, a largely white organization, to manage the project. The undertaking was a cooperative venture among the WNCAC, the CHA, the BIA, the Carolina Playmakers of the University of North Carolina, and the Eastern Band. UNC dramatist Kermit Hunter wrote the script, based generally on the 1930s pageants.

Although originally a flat theater site was planned, Samuel Selden, director of Carolina Playmakers at UNC and of the *Lost Colony* drama held at the 1937 Waterside Theater in Manteo, fell in love with the mountain setting and insisted on creating a dramatic Mountainside Theater. It was de-

SW 10 *Mountainside Theater*

signed by Albert Bell, who also designed the Waterside Theater. Local businessman and engineer Ross Caldwell volunteered his time to transform the site. Cherokee stonemasons and other workers constructed the facility, a tiered theater of some 2,900 seats with three stages. Pole log shelters and stone and brick seating tiers complement the natural setting. The first production was held on July 1, 1950, attracting immediate acclaim and success, and it continues as an immensely popular summer attraction; it has played to more than 5 million people since its opening.

SW 11 Oconaluftee Indian Village

Est. 1952; W side US 441, access road 0.6 mi. N of US 19S, Cherokee; open regular hours mid-May–late October

Soon after opening the *Unto These Hills* drama, the CHA began with state assistance the creation of the adjoining village as an outdoor presentation of Cherokee cultural traditions, including agriculture, crafts, and architecture. Consciously emulating Williamsburg, reconstruction of buildings representing several eras took place in the early 1950s, based on research, notes, and sketches prepared by Dr. John Witthoft, Pennsylvania State Museum, and Dr. T. M. N. Lewis and Professor Madeline Kneberg, Department of Anthropology, University of Tennessee. Construction was accomplished by Cherokee workers under the superintendence of P. A. Willett, engineering technician with the BIA. (See Introduction, Fig. 11.)

Set within a palisade, the village illustrates traditional planning elements, including an open **Square Ground**, described as a restricted, sacred site for meetings, seasonal dances, and other rituals. The arrangement of reconstructed buildings within the village leads the visitor back through time. The **1800 Cabin** illustrates the simply built log dwellings of the 19th c., reflecting continuing contact with white settlers and the needs of expedient building—a 1-room house built with logs left round and joined with saddle notches, daubed with clay and straw, and heated by a stick and clay chimney on a stone base. The **1750 Cabin** of hewn logs represents the log houses built by the Cherokees after limited contact with white settlers, examples of which were noted by naturalist William Bartram and others in the 1770s. Log construction may have been introduced to the Cherokees by traders who came from coastal Carolina towns and settled among the Indians in the mid-18th c.

Two other buildings illustrate traditions established before white contact. The **1540 Home** represents the Cherokee houses seen by DeSoto and other early travelers. The windowless rectangular structure is built with large poles set in the ground, with walls woven of saplings and covered with mats, which were covered with clay. Sheltered by a thatched roof, it has an earthen floor. The large **Council House** has seven sides rising to a high pole roof, above the central fireplace. Seven banks of seats around the fire accommodated meetings of the village population, who sat according to the seven Cherokee clans.

Located on the nearby Nature Trail is the **Toineeta Cabin**, described as an actual 19th-c. Cherokee dwelling moved from another site in the Qualla Boundary. The small house is built of hewn, half-dovetailed logs. In contrast to most surviving examples where the gable is framed and weatherboarded, in this house logs form the gable as well, and pole rafters support the wood-shingled roof. This method was sometimes called a cabin roof. The dwelling is said to have been built from trees cut by John Dobson and erected by Loney Toineeta for his father, "Old Man" Toineeta. The elder Toineeta, a widower, lived in the house with his daughter until his death in 1902, after which Loney Toineeta

sw 11 *1800 Cabin, Oconaluftee Indian Village*

sw 11 *Council House, Oconaluftee Indian Village*

and his family occupied the dwelling. He died in 1928, leaving the house to his wife Sallie Swimmer; she was the daughter of the great Cherokee storyteller, "Swimmer," whose sharing of his knowledge of tribal traditions with ethnologist James Mooney was reflected in Mooney's *Myths of the Cherokee* (1900). Sallie Swimmer occupied the cabin with her grandchildren until she died in 1948. The cabin was moved here in the late 1950s and restored.

SW 12 Boundary Tree Lodge and Tourist Motor Court

Late 1940s; W side US 441N, 2 mi. N of US 19, at N edge of Cherokee

The complex of substantial stone buildings, at the edge of the town near the *Great Smoky Mountains National Park entrance, reflects the Eastern Band's important investment in tourism in the immediate post–World War II era. As early as the 1930s, Cherokee leaders sought to improve opportunities for tribal tourism enterprises by acquiring from the National Park Service the land known as the Boundary Tree Tract,

strategically located near the park highway and named for an ancient poplar that had marked an old boundary line.

After acquiring the property in 1946 the tribe began to develop the site. With assistance from the BIA, the Cherokees constructed key buildings for tourist-oriented businesses. Primarily Cherokee workers erected the buildings of native stone. In 1948 they completed the gas station, which was leased to the Standard Oil Co., and by the next year had finished the lodge and 18 motel units. The latter, typical of motor courts of the era, are 1-story double units with motel rooms flanking open carports. This was the first of many tourist facilities in Cherokee; several others are owned by Cherokee families with landholdings in advantageous roadside locations.

SW 13 Big Cove School

Early to mid-20th c.; Big Cove Rd., Qualla Boundary

The 2-story frame school, now used as a day-care center, was probably built in the 1940s to replace an earlier log school erected by Quaker teachers. It is located beside the road that follows the creekbed through a rugged landscape. Through the mid-20th c. there were many log and boxed houses within Qualla Boundary, but nearly all of these have been replaced by modern dwellings. Big Cove was one of the most conservative sections of Qualla Boundary, where traditional dances, fluency in the Cherokee language, and other traditions remained strong. For many years Cherokee children were discouraged in school from speaking the Cherokee language, but today it is taught in school.

SW 14 Nununyi Mound

15th–18th c.; E side Oconaluftee River, W side SR 1368, 1.4 mi. N of US 19, Cherokee; private, barely visible at a distance

The Cherokee town site appears to cover at least 20 acres on the east bank of the river. The remains of the earthen townhouse mound are about 10–12 feet high and 150 feet in diameter. Archaeological investigations indicate that this site, like *Kituwah Mound, was occupied from as early as the 15th c. The town was burned in 1776 by the troops of American Capt. William Moore in his campaign to destroy the Cherokees' Middle Towns during the American Revolution.

Great Smoky Mountains National Park (SW 15–18)

Covering most of Swain Co. and large portions of Haywood Co., the Great Smoky Mountains National Park has transformed the region's history and economy as well as the landscape. The park comprises more than 520,000 acres in N.C. and Tennessee, of which over half lies in N.C. — 216,000 in Swain Co. alone. The name given this area is intensely descriptive of the blue mist that clings to the mountains and drifts into the valleys, making each distant view a series of ever paler blue waves as far as the eye can see. The Cherokees, it is said, called these mountains Shaconage, "Place of Blue Smoke."

The idea for a great national park in the eastern U.S. originated as early as 1880. Through the efforts of leaders from N.C.

and Tennessee, the movement to reclaim a landscape under siege from lumbering gained strength in the early 20th c. With the formation of the National Park Service in 1916 and persistent campaigning by local advocates, the Great Smoky Mountains National Park was authorized by Congress in 1926.

The millions of dollars for acquisition came from state contributions, the federal government, and a crucial $5 million matching gift in 1928 from the Laura Spelman Rockefeller Memorial, donated by John D. Rockefeller Jr. Development of the park began early in the 1930s. The park was formally established in 1934 and dedicated by President Franklin D. Roosevelt in 1940.

Land acquisition proceeded slowly. In contrast to the great national wilderness parks of the American West, where much of the land was already in government hands, the land designated for the park was privately held, and much of it had long supported farms and villages. About 75 percent of the N.C. territory was held by thirteen corporations, mainly large timber companies. Within the authorized boundaries in N.C. and Tennessee, the Champion Fibre Co. held until 1931 about 93,000 acres, including prime old-growth spruce, which the company sold after lengthy negotiations.

Substantial acreage was owned by individual farming families. Although some sold willingly, others resisted being removed from their land, especially amid hard times. As many as a thousand landowners lost their land during park removal.

Although most of the park was acquired by the mid-1930s, a thickly settled section along the north shore of the Little Tennessee River remained in private hands. When the urgent energy demands of World War II pushed forward the creation of *Fontana Dam and its lake, the north shore section was taken through an arrangement among the Tennessee Valley Authority, the state, and the National Park Service. The north shore was a long-settled area of towns, railroads, roads, and farms.

Especially well known is the Hazel Creek area along a tributary of the Little Tennessee River now celebrated for its fishing. In the early 20th c. it was the site of railroads, copper mines, the W. M. Ritter Co.'s huge lumbering operation—over 200 million board feet of lumber came from the area—and the lumber mill town of Proctor and other settlements. Today hikers see remnants of farming and lumbering days. Some of the land was inundated by the lake, while other areas were incorporated into the park. A large section was rendered inaccessible once the lake covered the road. Despite promises made to build a road to the old north shore homeplaces and graveyards cut off by the lake, the route was only partially completed. It stops abruptly and is known locally as the "Road to No-where."

In developing the park, the general policy was to eliminate standing buildings and to return the landscape to natural forests. A few old buildings were saved to illustrate the traditional way of life in the region. Typically those preserved were the "pioneer" log buildings, while the more elaborate and modern houses, farm buildings, and stores were destroyed, thus intensifying the popular image of the Appalachians as a primitive rural culture.

Much of the initial work was accomplished by the Civilian Conservation Corps (CCC) during the 1930s. At its peak in the mid-1930s the CCC had more than 4,300 young men at work in the park, building roads, trails, campgrounds, and structures, and thus transforming old timberlands and farms into a national park. In most of the park, reforestation has been so complete that it is startling to see the old photographs of mountain farmsteads, lumber mills and logging camps, railroads, and towns that existed here at the beginning of the 20th c. (See Ed Trout and Margaret Lynn Brown, *Historic Buildings of the Smokies* [1995], and Michael Ann Williams, *Great Smoky Mountains Folklife* [1995].)

SW 15 Oconaluftee Visitor Center

1940–41; CCC; E side US 441N, 0.8 mi. N of Blue Ridge Pkwy., Great Smoky Mountains National Park; open regular hours

The simple, gable-roofed stone building with an exposed truss roof and stone-paved floor was one of the many CCC construction projects in the *Great Smoky Mountains National Park. It was built as offices for the N.C. portion of the park.

SW 16 Mountain Farm Museum

Late 19th–early 20th c.; 1952–53; E side US 441, 0.8 mi. N of Blue Ridge Pkwy., Great Smoky Mountains National Park; open regular hours

The idea for a mountain farm outdoor museum in the Great Smoky Mountains National Park originated in the 1930s. In the late 1930s and early 1940s CCC employees Charles Grossman, a landscape architect, and Hiram C. Wilburn made a photographic record of the surviving buildings in the park as part of the cultural landscape, as well as collecting artifacts and historical information. The men urged preservation of more buildings than were actually saved. But their work formed the basis for the retention and interpretation of a few buildings here and at Cataloochee, where some later structures survive.

The assemblage here was created in 1952–53. Originally called the Pioneer Farmstead, it was intended to illustrate white farmers' life in the region before the establishment of the park. Located beside the Oconaluftee River in one of the first areas of the county settled by whites, the level riverside tract was the site of the extensive Enloe family farm, which included a big 2-story frame house and frame as well as log outbuildings. The house was removed, but the large log and frame barn was kept. Other buildings, including a log dwelling, were moved here from more remote upland farmsteads in the park territory, creating an ensemble quite different from that which had developed on this prime site beside the road. Nevertheless, the outdoor museum offers public access to several traditional building forms and construction techniques representative of the Appalachian region.

The **Davis House** (ca. 1900; moved from the Indian Creek–Thomas Divide area, Swain Co.) was built by farmer John E. Davis and his family and neighbors, using hand-hewn chestnut logs—some as wide as

sw 16 *Mountain Farm Museum*

18 to 22 inches—joined with half-dovetailed notches and with narrow interstices covered with split boards. The roof is covered with wooden shingles. The house contains 1 main room with a loft above, plus a front porch and a 1-story rear kitchen ell with a side porch. Stone chimneys have been rebuilt. (See Introduction, Fig. 58.)

As noted in the National Park Service interpretation, much of a farm family's time was spent in the farmyard and in the various outbuildings. The **Meathouse** (moved from Little Cataloochee in Haywood Co.), a windowless, half-dovetailed log structure, was built for the salting, smoking, and storage of meat, chiefly pork. The **Apple House** (from Little Cataloochee) was originally set into a hillside to insulate the lower portion. The **Chicken House** is a square-notched log structure on fieldstones. The **Corncrib** (from Thomas Divide) is a half-dovetailed log structure evidently originally associated with the dwelling; it had a hinged section of roof for loading in corn, as well as a front door for removing corn. Another **Corncrib and Gear Shed** (from Indian Creek), of round, V-notched logs, was arranged asymmetrically to allow a wagon to be driven under the shed portion and the corn tossed into the crib section. The **Blacksmith Shop** (from Cades Cove, Tenn.), of notched, hewn logs widely spaced, sheltered the farmer's forge and shop; this simple structure has logs filling the gable and a pole roof,

in contrast to the more finished method of framing and weatherboarding the gable. The **Springhouse** (from Cataloochee), of half-dovetailed logs, was built near a cool spring and protected perishable foods such as eggs, milk, and butter, which were set in a log trough of cool water channeled from the spring.

The **Barn** (original to the site, moved about 200 yards) is a large and impressive structure of half-dovetailed hewn logs, arranged with a central drive-through flanked by stalls. Its broad gable roof covers the high loft and reaches beyond the walls to form a shelter for work and equipment, creating an overall measurement of 59 by 60 feet. In a typical western N.C. usage, the wall just beneath the eaves is vented to provide air to the hayloft. (See Introduction, Fig. 61.)

The farm museum also interprets agricultural practices, including the family garden and swept yard, as well as the diverse crops mountain farmers produced and the reliance on livestock, especially hogs, which were marked and allowed to forage in the forests. Range laws requiring the penning of animals came later to mountain counties than to more thickly settled sections of the state. Also important is the replication of the split-rail and paling fences. Essential to keep grazing livestock out of gardens and crops, fences needed to be "horse-high, hog-tight, and bull-strong."

SW 17 Mingus Mill

*Late 19th c.; Sion Thomas Early, builder;
1930s, CCC; W side US 441, 1 mi. N of
jct. w/Blue Ridge Pkwy., Great Smoky
Mountains National Park*

The plain, functional, 3-story frame gristmill recalls the importance of waterpowered
gristmills to the rural economy and social
life. Especially interesting is the waterpower
delivery system: a flume raised on tall log
cribs carries water from the millrace (a short
distance upstream), then drops the water
down a squared wooden penstock, from
which the water is channeled to power the
turbine. The turbine powered two sets of
grinding stones—one for corn, one for
wheat—and a system of grain elevators.

The mill on Mingus Creek is thought to
have been built for John Mingus, whose father, Jacob, was a settler of German descent.
John's son-in-law Rufus Floyd and his sons
and other members of the Floyd family operated the mill and farmed in the area. The
mill ran until the 1920s, was restored by the
CCC in 1937, and reopened briefly in the
early 1940s. It was reconditioned and reopened in 1968 by the National Park Service,
which has rebuilt the millrace, flume, crib-
bing, penstock, and turbine. The mill operates seasonally each year.

sw 17 *Mingus Mill*

SW 18 Smokemont (Oconaluftee) Baptist Church

*1912; E side US 441N, at entrance to
Smokemont Campground, 3.2 mi. N of
Oconaluftee Visitor Center, Great Smoky
Mountains National Park*

The simple, gable-fronted frame church,
with a central entrance tower topped by a
belfry, typifies many churches built when
the proliferation of sawmills made frame
construction easier than ever before. This
Baptist congregation, long known as Oconaluftee (or Ocona Luftee, or simply Lufty),
was organized in 1836; like other rural
churches it served as a social as well as religious center. The name of the community
and the church changed in the early 20th c.
when the Champion Fibre Co. established a
sawmill and company town on the Ocona-

luftee River and called it Smokemont; a
standard-gauge railroad led to Smokemont,
and a narrow-gauge continued above it.

Smokemont was part of the land taken
into the *Great Smoky Mountains National
Park in the 1930s. The National Park Service
campground here was one of many CCC
projects. It includes the **Smokemont Campground Restroom Building** (1930s; CCC), a
craggy little stone building with the hall-
mark CCC hefty woodwork and rough stone
walls.

SW 19 Brush Creek Baptist Church

*Ca. 1900; N side SR 1129, 0.6 mi. NW of
NC 28, Needmore vic.*

Home to a very early congregation in the
area, the beautifully simple, well-preserved
white frame church is unusually large for a
country church of its era. It stands 2 stories
tall, with tall 4/4 sash windows lighting the
sanctuary, and it has an apse at the rear.

Brush or Brushy Creek Baptist Church was organized in 1832 with the pioneer Baptist minister Humphrey Posey as its first pastor. The oldest church in the Tennessee River Association, it is mother church to many congregations. The original church stood near the road downstream on the Little Tennessee River. After the present church was built on a higher site early in the 20th c., the county bought the old church for a schoolhouse.

Graham County (GH)

GH 1 Robbinsville

When Graham Co. was formed from Cherokee Co. in 1872 and named for former governor William A. Graham, the county seat was authorized and named for a local family. The community remains small, the center of a mountainous county largely occupied by national forests and Fontana Lake. The Snowbird Cherokees are an important presence in the western part of the county and are among the most traditionalist of the eastern Cherokees.

Robbinsville's unpretentious early 20th-c. architecture is notable chiefly for the local stone of vibrant and varied orange hues. Several 1- and 2-story houses and commercial buildings along Main St. are faced with this colorful stone. Some of the commercial buildings on the eastern side of the street are actually frame structures perched on tall piers on the hillside that drops precipitously from the ridge.

The **Graham County Courthouse** (1941–42; Barber & McMurry, architects; Main St. at Old US 129) is a T-plan building of the native stone, with a central portico of heavy square piers. The county's third courthouse, it was built by the Federal Works Agency, Works Projects Administration of North Carolina. The 1894–95 courthouse it replaced was reportedly the last frame courthouse built in N.C. The courthouse is described as being nearer to the capitals of six other states than to its own.

GH 2 Junaluska's Grave

D. 1850; monument 1910; SE side SR 1127, 0.5 mi. S of Main St., Robbinsville

In 1910, in an era of growing attention to local Cherokee heritage, the Gen. Joseph Winston Chapter of the Daughters of the American Revolution dedicated the monument at the grave of the Cherokee leader Junaluska. The boulder, dragged by oxen to the site, carries a plaque commemorating Junaluska and his wife Nicie. The unveiling

ceremony included presentations by Cherokee as well as white speakers and choruses.

Junaluska, a native of the area and a proponent of peaceful coexistence between Cherokees and whites, led Cherokee volunteers who fought with Andrew Jackson against the Creeks and the British during the War of 1812. He played a heroic role in Jackson's 1814 victory at Horseshoe Bend, and some accounts credit him with saving the future president's life. After the war Junaluska obtained several hundred acres in southwestern N.C. and continued to farm there. In 1838 Junaluska and his family were deported to Oklahoma. Tradition states that his wife and children died from the journey and that Junaluska rued his aid to Jackson, proponent of removal. In 1843 he walked back to N.C., where in 1847, in recognition of his service at Horseshoe Bend, the legislature returned to him a portion of his land; part of the farm where he spent his last years is the site of Robbinsville.

GH 3 Bemis Hardwood Lumber Company Plant

Ca. 1927; W side SR 1127, on Long Creek, opp. jct. w/SR 1110, Milltown vic.

During the western N.C. lumber boom, the Bemis Hardwood Lumber Co. was one of many big milling operations established to process local timber. Most of these enterprises disappeared with the depletion of the forests and the creation of the *Great Smoky Mountains National Park; Bemis and Champion were among the few that continued operation into the late 20th c. In 1924 H. C. Bemis, a West Virginia sawmill owner, purchased timberlands in the region and established a band mill beside Long Creek. He shipped much of the equipment from his mill (est. 1905) at Bemis, W.V. In 1925 Bemis completed the Graham Co. Railroad, begun in 1912 by the Whiting Manufacturing Co. The Bemis firm continued as a major local employer and civic presence, specializing in quality hardwood lumber. Most of the 1920s mill buildings burned in 1967. Although a new mill was erected on the site, the 1920s boiler room and the fuel house remain, large brick buildings with stepped gables, rare survivors of a once-powerful industry in the region.

GH 4 Stecoah

Early 20th c.; SR 1228 and 1226, S side NC 28

Taking the name of an 18th-c. Cherokee village, this community was settled by whites in the 1830s and by 1849 had a church that also served as a school. There are several late 19th- and early 20th-c. frame dwellings. Stecoah's most distinctive buildings are those constructed of local stone. The **Stecoah Grocery** (1918; SE corner SR 1226 and SR 1228) was built of stone from the Nantahala Gorge by Dee Jenkins, justice of the peace, who is said to have held court sessions in the store; it served as a post office as well as a store and is still a community gathering place. The **Stecoah School** (1930; E end SR 1228) is a large 1-story facility with gymnasium and other buildings; built after a 1930 fire destroyed the 1926 consolidated school, it is now a community center. Similar stonework appears in the **Stecoah Baptist Church** (ca. 1933), which features a tall entrance tower with arched base. Likewise replacing an earlier building that burned, it was erected as a communal endeavor.

In this vicinity along NC 28 there are many farmsteads with frame houses of various eras and typical frame mountain barns with gambrel and gable roofs featuring diagonal boarding and vents beneath the eaves.

GH 5 Bear Creek Smoky Mountain Railroad Depot

1966; E side SR 1201, at jct. w/US 129, Bear Creek; private, visible from road

Looking for all the world like a ca. 1900 railroad depot, with its shaped brackets carrying a broad overhanging roof, this is a replica built for tourists on the Graham Co. Railroad (GCR). The GCR was chartered in 1905 and partly built by the Whiting Manufacturing Co. in 1912, but not until 1925 did the *Bemis Hardwood Lumber Co. complete

the difficult 15-mile stretch from Topton to Robbinsville. Hauling freight until 1970, the GCR became famous as the last steam freight line in the nation. In 1966 the Bear Junction site was developed, featuring a "Scenic Steam Train" with a Shay engine running from Bear Creek to Nantahala Gorge. The carefully detailed little depot was erected by Government Services, Inc., which operated *Fontana Dam Village, and the *Bemis Hardwood Lumber Co. The train no longer comes here, and the depot is now part of a small residential development.

GH 6 Fontana Dam and Powerhouse

1942–44, 1946–47; TVA architectural staff (with Mario Biancolli); SR 1245, 1 mi. NE of NC 28; buildings open to public May–Oct.

The magnificent dam forming Fontana Lake is the largest dam in the Tennessee Valley Authority (TVA) system, and at 480 feet high by 2,365 feet wide and 375 feet thick, it is the tallest dam east of the Rocky Mountains. Positioned at one of the few sites in eastern North America suitable for such a high dam, Fontana's powerful form is dramatized by its setting. The huge concrete slope reaches from mountainside to mountainside across the Little Tennessee River, and steep mountain slopes stretch out in the distance beyond Fontana Lake. (See Introduction, Fig. 64.)

In contrast to arched dams such as *Cheoah, in which curved forms hold back the water, Fontana is a straight gravity structure based on sheer mass. The dam is built so that water does not spill over the top. A spillway gate on the eastern extension funnels into two 34-foot-diameter tunnels through the east abutment—tunnels that diverted the river during construction—to carry overflow into the river downstream. At the foot of the tunnels, a deflector shoots the rushing water 150 feet into the air for 400 feet downstream, diffusing its power and preventing it from eroding the foundation rock below the dam.

Built during World War II to supply power to plants manufacturing aluminum for aircraft and processing uranium in secret operations at Oak Ridge, Tenn., Fontana Dam was planned and constructed with im-

GH 6 *Fontana Dam*

GH 6 *Fontana Dam Powerhouse*

GH 6 *Fontana Dam Visitors' Building*

pressive speed to meet wartime demands and to cope with shortages of workers and materials. The Aluminum Co. of America (Alcoa) had previously begun acquisition of this and other power sites along the Little Tennessee River. Alcoa had initially planned two dams of about 225 feet, but with advancing technology decided on a single dam of 450 feet. In the mid-1930s the TVA and Alcoa had discussed a transfer of the Fontana property. After the outbreak of war in Europe, the TVA and Alcoa reached an agreement in 1941 that transferred Alcoa's Fontana holdings to the TVA. Congress authorized the Fontana project on Dec. 12, 1941; construction started on Jan. 1, 1942, less than a month after the attack on Pearl Harbor; the dam was closed on Nov. 7, 1944; and power generation began on Jan. 20, 1945.

As *The Fontana Project* report (1950) relates in detail, the $70 million project was one of astonishing scale and complexity, made more challenging by the remote location. Crews of as many as 5,000 men worked in three shifts around the clock, six days a week. Fourteen people were killed during construction. Stone used for aggregate in the

concrete was quarried nearby (site visible at the Swain Co. end of the bridge below the dam). For the dam, 2.8 million cubic yards of concrete were poured in place from different levels simultaneously, supplied by trains that ran back and forth to the site. To prevent the concrete from cracking as it set—a major problem with such a huge mass—the dam was divided into monoliths with transverse and longitudinal contraction joints, each cooled by steel tubing circulating cool water. When the concrete had set and cooled, the joints were grouted to form a single mass.

After closure of the dam in 1944, Fontana Lake covered 10,000 acres, flooding the sites of farms and towns in Graham and Swain counties. When the water level in the lake is dropped at 5-year intervals to allow inspection and maintenance of the dam, remains of railroads and other structures may be seen in the lake bed.

Like *Hiwassee Dam in Cherokee Co., Fontana Dam embodies the integration of all design elements to create a powerful public presence for the TVA—from the planning of the site to the simple grandeur of the dam and powerhouse to the signage and hardware. It was the work of the TVA architectural staff, though Mario Biancolli is credited with a leading role in the design. The **Powerhouse** at the base of the dam, built of reinforced concrete, is an imposing structure in itself, but it appears tiny in comparison with the dam that looms above it. The interior of the powerhouse is a splendidly austere and cavernous space, with tall window bays formed by great concrete piers that carry arches across the chamber. The concrete surfaces are subtly textured by the impression of the narrow board forms. On the front wall stretches the classic motto, "1942 Built for the People of the United States 1945."

In keeping with the emphasis on public pride in the TVA system, Fontana—the TVA's most visited dam—has a strong educational component. The **Visitors' Building** (1946–48) near the top of the dam is a beautiful little moderne structure completed at the end of the project. A low building designed to blend into the site, it is finished outside with Indiana limestone and inside with marble walls, terrazzo floors, and aluminum fittings. A semicircular window wall gives a spectacular view of the dam and its setting. The curve is repeated in the railed platform that extends beyond the building and leads to the top of the dam. A funicular tram runs down to the powerhouse, which welcomes visitors in season.

GH 7 Fontana Village
1942–44; SR 1246, 0.2 mi. S of NC 28; open to public

Built by the TVA as the construction village for *Fontana Dam, the village near the southern edge of the *Great Smoky Mountains National Park has become a mountain resort. Although several buildings have been removed and most have been updated, the complex retains a number of the community facilities and houses built by the TVA in the early 1940s. These structures have attracted scholarly attention for their importance in the history of manufactured housing.

As early as the 1933 construction of the Norris Dam in Tennessee, the TVA built movable and prefabricated housing for the hundreds or thousands of workers needed at the often remote sites of its huge construction projects. At Fontana the need for rapidly built housing was especially intense because of the scale of the project and the isolation of the site. There had been previous lumber and copper mine workers' villages named Fontana in the vicinity. Located on high ground in Welch Cove, the TVA's Fontana Village went up speedily, with dwellings for families and dormitories for single workers, cafeterias, a hospital, a school, a shopping center, and recreational facilities. Typical of the time and place, there were separate housing and recreation facilities for

GH 7 *Fontana Village Housing: A-6's, 1943*

black, Cherokee, and white workers. Once the dam was completed, and the war was won, the purpose of the village shifted to tourism.

Surviving 1940s buildings exemplify a variety of TVA forms and plans and methods of construction. Most of the houses that still stand are those designated "permanent" and "temporary." These are used as rental cottages called "Laurel" and "Dogwood."

The most substantial were **Permanent Houses**, such as the cottages #424 and #427. Built for top personnel, these were conventional frame dwellings stick-built on site; they were set on concrete block foundations and had gable roofs, screen porches, double-hung sash, and hardwood floors. The 25 permanent houses exemplified several 2- and 3-bedroom plans, some repeating forms used by the TVA at Kentucky Dam Village and other sites.

Also of conventional frame construction were the **Temporary Houses**, set on wood posts, with double-hung windows and gable roofs and often with entrances in the gable ends. Among the 155 built were 2-bedroom, 3-bedroom, and duplex models, some exhibiting designs used previously at *Hiwassee.

Few remain of the less conventional "Demountable" and "Trailer" or prefabricated houses. At Fontana, 100 **Demountable Houses** were brought from Hiwassee. Built at Sheffield, Ala., in 1941, they had seen one or two previous uses before arriving at Fontana. These were 2-cell and 4-cell demountable frame structures with flat roofs; each cell measured 7½ by 22 feet. Each of the 68 2-cell houses (15 by 22 feet) had a living room, a kitchen recess, a bedroom, and a bathroom. The 32 4-cell houses (30 by 22 feet) had 3 bedrooms.

The **Trailer Houses**, as they were initially called, were prefabricated houses delivered to the site on trailers. Made to TVA plans and specifications, they were manufactured complete with plumbing, electrical work, fixtures, built-in and movable furniture, appliances, screens, and linoleum floors. Similar in layout to the 2-cell Hiwassee demountable houses, they were composed of 2 sections, each 7 feet 9 inches by 24 feet by 8 feet, made of stressed-skin plywood con-

struction. Fontana received 104, of which 4 were experimental and 100 were TVA prefabricated house type A-6. The **A-6** model—one of several TVA designs—had a living-dining room, a kitchen, a bedroom, and a bathroom. Sections were rolled off trucks on tracks to wood post foundations and joined together. Steps were added, plumbing and electric systems were connected, and within two hours of delivery the unit could be ready for occupancy. The story is told that workers waited at the prepared house site with their suitcases until the house was delivered and assembled, then moved in.

The rectilinear prefabricated houses with shallow roof and ribbon windows exemplified modernist design ideals of the era. The A-6 design reflects the involvement of TVA chief architect Roland Wank in the TVA's housing design program. As of 1998 only 6 of the demountable and trailer houses (A-6s) were still standing at Fontana, including cottages #915–#920. Many others have been moved away and reused on sites scattered around the region.

Some of the present frame buildings were group facilities in the construction village. The **Hospital** is now the administration building; the **Temporary School** is now the registration center; the **Permanent School** is a recreation center; the **Grocery Store and Dry Goods Store** is now the cafeteria, and so on. Most have been extensively remodeled.

Surviving from an earlier era is the **Gunter House** (ca. 1875), a 2-room log house of half-dovetailed construction with gable-end stone chimneys; the finished interior includes flooring of wide split boards (4 by

GH 7 *Gunter House*

1½–2 feet). The house was built ca. 1875 for Jesse and Nancy Catherine Gunter and has been retained as a museum in the resort complex.

See Marian Moffett, "Looking to the Future: The Architecture of Roland Wank," *Arris* 1 (1989): 5–17, and "Manufactured Housing: The TVA Experience," *Arris* 5 (1994): 31–39; Roland Wank, "The Trailer House," *Architectural Record*, Feb. 1943; United States Tennessee Valley Authority, *The Fontana Project*, Technical Report no. 12 (1950).

GH 8 Santeetlah (Rhymer's Ferry) Powerhouse

1926–28; S bank Little Tennessee River, at end of SR 1246, visible from NC 28 in Swain Co., 4.6 mi. E of US 129

The handsome brick powerhouse beside the Little Tennessee, built by Alcoa, stands 4 stories tall, with pilasters separating large windows. Its waterpower comes not from the Little Tennessee but from Santeetlah Dam 5 miles south on the Cheoah River. Pipeline and tunnels carry water from the dam to the surge tank, then down through 947-foot penstocks to the powerhouse. The water then flows into the Little Tennessee and adds to the waterpower at *Cheoah Dam downstream.

GH 8 *Santeetlah Powerhouse*

GH 9 Cheoah Dam and Powerhouse

1916–19; E side US 129 at the Little Tennessee River, Tapoco

This first dam built on the Little Tennessee River stands 225 feet high and was described at the time of its construction as the highest overflow dam in the world. As early as 1910, Alcoa explored the watershed of the Little Tennessee River for power sites for aluminum production. During the next few years the company acquired land and hydroelectric power rights from several owners in western N.C. and eastern Tennessee. The N.C. holdings were combined under the name of one of the companies acquired, the Tallassee Power Co. (est. 1905). In 1915, faced with escalating demand for aluminum caused by the war in Europe, Alcoa pro-

ceeded to develop the Cheoah site. Rail lines were extended to the site by 1916, the first concrete for the dam was poured in March 1917, and the dam was closed on Dec. 8, 1918. Beside the curved concrete dam stands the handsome masonry powerhouse, which features a long, graceful arcade of tall windows overlooking the river. Cheoah Dam was featured in the 1993 movie *The Fugitive*. (See Introduction, Fig. 32.)

GH 10 Tapoco Lodge

1930; W side US 129, Tapoco, confluence of Cheoah and Little Tennessee rivers; private, open seasonally as lodge

The 2½-story brick lodge beside the tumbling Cheoah River was built for Alcoa as a company facility in association with development of nearby *Cheoah Dam. The community, which began as a survey camp and construction village called Cheoah, was renamed Tapoco (Ta-PO-ca) in 1916, with the name coined from Tallassee Power Co., a subsidiary of Alcoa. Initially accessible chiefly by rail, the site became a tourist destination after the completion of NC 108 (later US 129) in 1931.

GH 10 *Tapoco Lodge*

The brick lodge, composed of a line of linked units, is finished in restrained Colonial Revival style and has changed little. Much of the furniture is original. The buildings show Alcoa's concern for fire-resistant construction and extensive use of aluminum—the gleaming aluminum roof, plus railings, signs, and other fittings. The complex, located along a stream in a picturesque cove, also includes several tourist cottages. Up the cove is the old **Theater** (1940s?), a large metal quonset hut that gained a curved aluminum front with ticket office and projection booth.

GH 11 Snowbird Mountain Lodge

1940–41; Ronald Greene [Asheville], architect; Bill Moore [Andrews], contractor; W side SR 1127, approx. 6 mi. NW of Robbinsville; open seasonally as lodge

The latest of the rustic mountain lodges built before World War II, Snowbird Moun-

tain Lodge stands on a mountaintop site surrounded by the Snowbird Cherokee lands and the Nantahala National Forest. During the 1930s, as national interest in Appalachian tourism mounted, Chicago travel agent Arthur Wolfe operated regular train and bus tours that included stops in Gatlinburg, Bryson City, Asheville, and *Tapoco Lodge. After Tapoco stopped hosting tour

GH 11 *Snowbird Mountain Lodge*

groups, Wolfe decided to build his own lodge. With some difficulty he found an available and suitably picturesque mountain site near the Joyce Kilmer National Forest, a section of old-growth forest dedicated in 1936 and named for the author of the poem "Trees," who died in World War I.

Wolfe commissioned Asheville architect Ronald Greene (cf. *Jackson Building, Asheville) to design a rustic "Swiss Chalet" lodge of local materials. It was constructed by local workmen supervised by contractor Bill Moore of Andrews. The lodge is built of native stone, saddle-notched chestnut logs, and frame construction. The interior has walls sheathed in local chestnut, silver bell, basswood, pine, maple, and wild cherry, and rooms were named accordingly. The open T-plan has a large, rustic lounge on the south, which opens to a terrace with a spectacular view of the Snowbird Mountains stretching for miles into the hazy distance.

Clay County (CY)

CY 1 Hayesville

The seat of a spectacularly beautiful mountain county of steep, forested slopes, small hillside farms, and glorious views, Hayesville was named for George W. Hayes, the legislator instrumental in forming Clay Co. (named for Henry Clay) from Cherokee Co.

in 1861. With much of the county covered by national forests, the population remains small, and the principal businesses are lumbering and recreation.

Hayesville's chief landmark is the **Clay County Courthouse** (1887–89; William Gould Bulgin, architect; Main St.) on its square in the center of town. The small but

CY 1 *Clay Co. Courthouse*

splendid Italianate brick courthouse, one of the oldest in the N.C. mountains, still serves its original purpose. It retains its original exterior character, with bracketed eaves, segmental-arched windows, and a central entrance tower that rises to a cross-gabled belfry. The second story, which contains the courtroom with its large windows, is accentuated by a sawtooth belt course.

The building's construction is unusually well documented. After the county's first courthouse burned in 1870, county representatives employed a traditional approach to design. After visiting nearby courthouses as potential models, they requested plans, specifications, and costs from those in Transylvania and Macon counties. W. G. Bulgin was paid $15 for plans and specifications. In Sept. 1887, J. S. Anderson contracted to erect the building for $7,240; he completed the job by Nov. 4, 1889, and was awarded $559.50 for extra costs.

The courthouse on its central square continues as a focus of community pride. In recent years local merchants have enhanced the storefronts framing the courthouse square with porches whose turned posts and distinctive wooden brackets echo the details of the courthouse.

South of the courthouse, on a hill overlooking the downtown, stands the former **Clay County Jail** (1912; George Love and Thomas Lovin, contractors; Paul Jail Building Co., St. Louis; Main St.; open limited hours), built to replace a log jail. The neatly finished 2-story brick structure resembles a substantial dwelling, with arches over the barred sash windows and a dormer on the hip roof. In a typical arrangement, local men built it, and the cells were manufactured by an urban jail furnishing specialist. It is now a local history and arts museum.

CY 2 Spikebuck Town
16th–18th c.; N side SR 1140, 0.9 mi. W of US 64, Veterans Recreation Park, Hayesville vic.; private, visible from a distance

The Cherokee town was occupied intermittently from the 16th to the 18th c., with several hundred people evidently living in a town that covered at least 40 acres. The

community included a large townhouse mound, marked today by an earthen mound 16 feet tall and about 180 feet in diameter. The mound is on private property but is visible across the creek from the Veterans Recreation Park.

CY 3 Bill Moore Farm
Ca. 1860 and later 19th c.; N side SR 1307, 0.8 mi. W of SR 1330, Tusquitee vic.; private, visible from road

As settlers took up land in the narrow valleys between the mountain slopes, several families established farmsteads along Tusquitee Creek. They grew crops on the arable land and set their herds of livestock to range in the meadows and forests. Their farmhouses back up against the mountainside and overlook the streams and meadows below. Of several 19th- and early 20th-c. farmsteads along this winding creekside country road, the Moore house and outbuildings are among the best preserved. Known as one of the county's oldest houses, the 2-story frame house with stone chimneys is believed to have been built for Capt. Bill P. "Irish Bill" Moore just before the Civil War. The 2-tier gabled entrance porch with ornate sawn balustrade typifies late 19th-c. work in the area. There are several outbuildings, including a 1-story gable-fronted frame store, chicken houses beside the road, and a barn.

CY 4 Chatuge Dam
1941–42; end of SR 1146, SE of US 64 via SR 1140

Authorized by Congress in July 1941, construction of this TVA dam on the Hiwassee River began immediately and was completed sufficiently to close the dam by the following February, in time to meet wartime power demands. Less spectacular than *Fontana and *Hiwassee dams, the main dam is an impervious rolled earthfill embankment, 2,850 feet long and 144 feet high. It is the only TVA-built dam entirely of rolled earth. The most striking feature is the spillway at the east end of the main dam, a concrete chute with curved weir and a "ski-jump" end sill.

Cherokee County (CE)

Murphy (CE 1–8)

Located at the confluence of the Hiwassee and the Valley rivers, the county seat of the westernmost county in N.C. nestles among the surrounding mountain slopes. The compact downtown centers on one of the state's finest Beaux Arts classical courthouses.

Murphy is one of a long series of settlements at the joining of the rivers. This was an old site of Cherokee habitation when A. R. S. Hunter opened a trading post in the 1820s. Here the U.S. government established Fort Butler, headquarters of the Eastern District, where the army assembled the Cherokee in 1838 before leaving for Oklahoma on the "Trail of Tears." When Cherokee Co. was established in 1838 with the county seat located across the Hiwassee from the fort, the General Assembly authorized the county court to use the buildings "put up by the Army at Fort Butler" until a courthouse and jail were built. Although some proposed naming the county seat for the Cherokee leader Junaluska (cf. *Junaluska's Grave), the town was named for Archibald DeBow Murphey, early 19th-c. advocate of internal improvements in N.C. A brick courthouse was built on the central square in 1848, and the town was incorporated in 1851.

A quiet country town for fifty years, Murphy was the center of a county of contrasts. The broad, fertile river bottomlands provided a hospitable setting for farmers with substantial holdings in land and slaves; farther up in the coves, smaller subsistence farms and hunting predominated. A number of Cherokee families remained after eluding the removal of 1838.

Late in the 19th c. Murphy faced the transformation wrought by the railroad. The Marietta & North Georgia Railroad (later the Louisville & Nashville) came from the south in 1888, and the Murphy Branch of the Western North Carolina Railroad (WNCRR) was completed from the east in 1891, linking Murphy to the broader world of trade. "More than half a century has passed like a dream, and we are living in the fast age," marveled the local *Cherokee Scout* in 1893. Ambitious businessmen built stylish houses, especially along Valley River Ave.; a towered Romanesque Revival brick courthouse was built on a new site a block from the old courthouse square, then rebuilt after a fire; and wooden stores gave way to brick ones.

Further growth came in the early 20th c., particularly during the 1920s, as local business expanded along with lumbering and quarrying industries. Brick commercial blocks were erected, banks and a public library opened, citizens erected monuments to local history, electric lights and a waterworks were installed, and yet another courthouse was built after a fire. The central business blocks on Peachtree, Tennessee, and Hiwassee Sts. and Valley River Ave. contain several notable early 20th-c. 2- and 3-story brick commercial buildings mainly from the 1920s.

The Great Depression, coupled with depletion of timberlands, ended an era of growth. After the national forest program was authorized by the Weeks Act in 1911, timber companies sold extensive acreage to the U.S. government for the national forest. During the same era, the Tennessee Valley Authority (TVA) acquired a large tract near the center of the county for *Hiwassee Dam and lake, and much of that land also became national forest. Roughly a third of the county is part of the Nantahala National Forest. In the late 20th c. much of the broad and beautiful Valley River valley—also known as the Konnaheeta Valley—has been consumed by the flatland-hungry highway US 19/129. After losing population in the mid-20th c., the county has reversed that trend, and Murphy has seen renewed vitality in its business and institutions.

CE 1 Cherokee County Courthouse

1926–27; James J. Baldwin (Asheville), architect; NE corner Peachtree and Central Sts.

The architectural glory of Murphy, its tall dome silhouetted against the distant mountains, gives unexpected drama to the town skyline. One of the finest Beaux Arts classical courthouses from the state's early 20th-c. courthouse construction era, the building's sophisticated design and opulent execution contrast with the prevalent simplicity of the county's architecture.

Architect James Baldwin, a 1905 graduate of the University of South Carolina, worked for Milburn, Heister & Co. in Columbia and in Washington, D.C., and for Reuben H. Hunt in Chattanooga. He returned to South Carolina to practice with partner C. Gadsden Sayre (1909–15). After a decade on his own, Baldwin opened an office in Asheville, about the same time he gained the commission for this courthouse.

In a departure from the symmetry usual in Neoclassical courthouses, Baldwin took dramatic advantage of the corner site—that of the preceding 1890s courthouse lost to fire—by orienting the composition with its heroic Corinthian portico diagonally toward the corner. He stepped back the facade and bent the side elevations to fill the lot. The unusual plan is surprisingly shallow, with offices along corridors in two unequal wings that angle from the ceremonial entrance and

rotunda. The second-floor courtroom occupies the end of the longer, left-hand wing.

In a spectacular display of local stone, Baldwin faced the building with the beautiful Regal blue marble quarried along the Valley River between Murphy and Andrews. The interior features local marbles in the inlaid floor of the brightly lit rotunda and in the courtroom tablets engraved with the Ten Commandments. When the $256,000 courthouse was dedicated on Nov. 12, 1927, it was lauded by the orator as an advertisement of the county and its marble: "I understand, already, that people are contemplating buying your marble for building in this state and other states."

CE 2 Cherokee County Historical Museum
1922; NE corner Central and Peachtree Sts.

Built as a Carnegie Library, the simply finished, 2-story brick structure was erected after a long library campaign by women of the community. It now contains a local history collection, the core of which constituted Palmer's Museum at Marble, an assemblage of some 2,000 prehistoric and historic artifacts collected by Arthur Palmer over more than 70 years; the collection was

CE 1 *Cherokee Co. Courthouse*

purchased and made available to the county by legislator Herman H. West of Murphy.

CE 3 Church of the Messiah
1896; corner of Central and Peachtree Sts.

The picturesque little Carpenter Gothic church displays the characteristic steep gable roof, an open belfry, and peaked porch trimmed with sawnwork. Interior fittings include heart pine paneling and fine stained glass. The congregation traces its origins to the 1853 efforts of Dr. Jarvis Buxton of *Trinity Episcopal Church, Asheville, to encourage an Episcopal mission, but only with the arrival of the railroad and of Alfred and Fannie Morgan, devoted Episcopalians from Macon Co., was there sufficient support to erect a church. The Morgans' children were Lucy Morgan (cf. *Penland School) and Rufus Morgan (cf. *St. John's Episcopal Church, Cartoogechaye). The church is said to have been designed by the Reverend F. W. Wey and built for $1,800, with construction supervised by James Fletcher and supported largely by the Beal and Morgan families.

CE 4 Harshaw Chapel
Dedicated 1869; corner of
Central and Church Sts.

The hilltop brick church is the principal vestige of prerailroad days in Murphy. With its pedimented gable end and large 9/9 sash windows, the simple Greek Revival church resembles other mid-19th-c. churches in southwestern N.C., including *Franklin Presbyterian Church and *Mills River Methodist Church; the shingled steeple is probably later. Now preserved by the Daughters of the American Revolution, the church was evidently built during the 1860s for the town's first Methodist congregation. The land was donated in 1844 by Joshua Harshaw, a leading local farmer who acquired the property in the Indian land sales. A marble plaque over the door states, "I Joshua Harshaw do make a free will gift of this house to the Methodist Episcopal Church at Murphy N.C. this May 1, 1869."

The surrounding cemetery, which predates the building, includes graves of several

CE 4 *Harshaw Chapel*

early settlers, among them Abram Enloe, best known as a onetime employer of Nancy Hanks, who moved to Kentucky and later became the mother of Abraham Lincoln.

CE 5 Murphy United Methodist Church
1922; Valley River Ave.

Presiding over Valley River Ave. from the sharp curve in the road, the imposing brick church shows the domed Neoclassical Revival form characteristic of many Methodist churches of the early 20th c. It was erected during the prosperous 1920s after local Methodists outgrew *Harshaw Chapel. The interior, which features fine stained glass, has an auditorium-plan sanctuary with curving pews and additional seating in recesses beneath the balconies.

CE 6 Robert Akin House
1870s; 121 Valley River Ave.; private

Believed to be the oldest house in Murphy, the I-house with brick end chimneys was the home of Confederate veteran and schoolteacher Akin; it has remained with descendants and survived commercial developments all around it.

CE 7 Robert Lafayette Cooper House
1890–91; 109 Campbell St., just off Valley River Ave.; private

Railroad money and sawmills supported construction of several ornately decorated local residences. Among the most vivid is this frame house built for railroad lawyer Robert Lafayette Cooper soon after the railroad arrived; Cooper became a banker, sawmill industrialist, and mayor of Murphy. Displaying the irregular plan typical of the Queen Anne style, it has bays projecting from a central mass focused on a large entry hall, a polygonal corner tower, and a wraparound porch that blossoms into a corner pavilion, both with matching bellcast roofs.

CE 7 *Robert Lafayette Cooper House*

CE 8 Murphy L&N Depot
1913; N side US 19/129 BUS at Railroad St.

The bracketed, frame depot was built for the branch of the Louisville & Nashville Railroad that began as the Marietta & North Georgia in 1888. The WNCRR depot in Murphy no longer stands.

CE 9 Harshaw House
1880–82; private, no public visibility or access

Three Harshaw brothers, sons of Abram Harshaw who came from France to Burke Co. in 1778, were among the first whites to establish themselves as large farmers in the Hiwassee River plain. John, Joshua, and Abram Harshaw bought prime farmland during the sale of Indian lands and by the 1850s were among the wealthiest men in the county and the largest slaveholders. The family prosperity continued after the Civil War, supporting construction of one of the county's grandest farmhouses. About 1880 banker and farmer Abram McD. Harshaw and his wife Florence, who had been living in a log house on the farm of his father,

Abram, erected on the bluff overlooking the river a 10-room brick house, built on an L-plan and decorated with ornate sawnwork. The farmstead also comprises several outbuildings, including a V-notched log barn.

CE 9 *Harshaw House*

CE 10 George W. Hayes Farm
Ca. 1850–early 20th c.; Mr. Harden, J. S. Allen, builders; NW corner of SR 1426 and SR 1373, Tomotla; private, visible from road

Exemplary of river valley farmsteads, the Hayes farm developed over the years. The 2-story house, which was built in the mid-19th c. and may include a log section, has a broad two-tier porch and brick chimneys at the gable ends. The house originally faced north toward the old road and eventually the railroad. In the 1920s it was reoriented with a bungalow-type porch to face the new highway on the south. Around the house is an especially fine collection of typical outbuildings, including a springhouse, a chicken house, and a drive-through corncrib of half-dovetailed logs.

The house was built for George W. Hayes, who is described as having served as interpreter during the Cherokee Removal and received for his services 700 acres on the Valley River at Tomotla. After the death of his wife Nancy, he married Elizabeth Stewart in 1842, and here they raised a large family. Family tradition records that a Mr. Harden built the house in 1850 and J. S. Allen erected the chimneys. The post office for Tomotla was here, and George Hayes, his son Jefferson, and his granddaughter Leila served intermittently as postmaster or postmistress until 1948. During service in the General Assembly (1843–61), Hayes introduced the bill to create Clay Co. from Cherokee Co., and its seat was named Hayesville in his honor.

CE 11 Marble

Now nearly a ghost town, the railroad village of Marble possesses a cluster of frame buildings from its early 20th-c. prime. First called Marble Springs, it was best known for its proximity to a rich vein of marble, but its residents also profited from local gold, iron, and talc mining, as well as from timbering. One lumber company built a long flume from Snowbird Gap that carried timber into Marble.

Best approached from the south on SR 1519, Marble's unpretentious 1- and 2-story frame houses and commercial buildings overlook the railroad tracks from both sides along SR 1428 (old US 19). South of the tracks stand the **Abernathy Store** (ca. 1920; SE corner SR 1519 and SR 1428), a 1-story, gable-fronted general store with large windows flanking a recessed entrance beneath a pent roof, and the **N. W. Abernathy House**, the storekeeper's 2-story house with hip roof. Across the tracks are the Queen Anne style **Bob Anderson House**; a series of 1-story **Stores**; and the **Masonic Hall**, a gable-fronted, 2-story structure with recessed entrance, said to have been constructed as a schoolhouse.

CE 12 Andrews

The broad Valley River valley has nurtured settlements for centuries. Until it was destroyed in 1975, the Andrews Mound beside the river near Andrews was among the best-preserved townhouse mounds in N.C. When the Murphy branch of the WNCRR was routed through the bottomlands of the Valley River in 1890, an influential landowner caused its path to bypass the old community of Valley Town in favor of an undeveloped tract that was soon platted to create

a new town—named for WNCRR vice-president A. B. Andrews. With access to rails and timber, the town grew quickly during the 1890s. J. Q. Barker established the Kanawha Hardwood Co. in 1897 and soon built the Snowbird Valley Railway to Graham Co. forests, and in 1899 Franklin Pierce Cover and his sons chose Andrews for their tannery. Schools and churches were begun, and the town was incorporated in 1905. With streets named Cherry, Chestnut, Locust, etc., Andrews thrived as a forest-based manufacturing center until the 1930s, when the Great Depression coincided with the depletion of the forests.

Standing beside the railroad that gave the town life, the most striking reminder of the ambitious founding era is the **Franklin Pierce Cover House** (1900; Wilson St., 0.2 mi. N of Second Ave.; private), which is unique in the town and county for its scale, its brick construction, and its elaborate detail. Dominated by a powerful 3-story polygonal corner tower, it is enriched with corbeled cornices and segmental-arched windows. The house was built for Franklin Pierce Cover, who founded the F. P. Cover and Sons Tannery. Son of a Maryland tanner, Cover and his brothers had operated tanneries in Virginia. In 1899 he and his son Samuel scouted western N.C. for fresh tanbark sources and selected Andrews for its railroad and proximity to forests. They opened the tannery in 1900 and moved into the brick mansion they had built in the raw new railroad village. After Franklin Cover died at age forty-nine in 1903, his sons Samuel and Giles continued the business, which eventually held some 20,000 acres of timberlands. During the 1930s the tannery closed. Its factory buildings and workers' housing are gone; 17,000 acres of its holdings were sold to the U.S. government and became part of the Nantahala National Forest. The house remained in the family until the late 20th c.

Next door stands the simpler foursquare residence built for the next generation, the **Giles Cover House** (ca. 1910; 34 Wilson St.; B&B). It was the home of Giles Cover and his wife Lillian Brittain Cover, a member of the Brittain family of Peachtree. A pioneer

CE 12 *Franklin Pierce Cover House*

political figure in the 20th c., she worked for woman suffrage in the 1920s and served three terms in the state legislature and in several appointed positions in the 1940s and 1950s.

Stewart Road Rural Loop Drive:
North of Andrews, a stretch of rural landscape evokes the pastoral character of the Valley River bottomlands before the advent of the super-highway that now bisects it. This was considered part of the old Valley Town community. Valley Town was the site of an early 19th-c. Indian trading post as well as earlier Cherokee settlements along the river.

Several farmsteads along Stewart Rd. (SR 1389) and nearby roads survive in a quiet section, where farmland backs up to the forested Snowbird Mountains and reaches down to the pastures beside the river. The *Great Smoky Mountains Railway along the WNCRR route traverses the valley. Broad and gentle river valleys such as this were the setting for western N.C.'s principal agricultural settlements; their

easy terrain has also attracted the most intense highway and commercial development in recent decades. Extending north from SR 1391, a steep National Forest road called the Tatham Gap Road crosses the mountain to Robbins-ville; local tradition relates that this road served as the route from Fort Montgomery (at present-day Robbinsville) south to Fort Butler (at present-day Murphy) during the Cherokee Removal.

CE 13 George Walker House
Ca. 1914; Mr. Stratton, contractor; E side SR 1388, 0.1 mi. S of SR 1389, Andrews vic.; private, visible from road

Framed by its shade trees, the unusually large and stylish Queen Anne farmhouse is a 2½-story frame dwelling with tall hip roof, irregular plan, and wraparound porch. It was built for George B. Walker and his wife Martha Barker. The son of settlers William and Margaret Walker of the nearby *Walker's Inn, in 1874 George moved as a young man to newly established Robbinsville, where he bought a trading post and became first post-master, first representative to the General Assembly, and a prominent business figure. In 1911 he returned to his native section, established a cattle farm, and continued political and business activities. He reportedly employed a Robbinsville contractor to model this house after his residence there.

CE 14 Piercy-Adams Farm
Late 19th–early 20th c.; N side SR 1389, 0.2 mi. E of SR 1388, Andrews vic.; private, visible from road

The prominently sited farmstead presents a remarkably complete ensemble from the diverse agriculture of the late 19th and early 20th centuries. The straightforward 2-story frame house has brick and stone chimneys and a 2-tier front porch typical of the region. Behind the house are a frame washhouse with brick chimney, a stone canning house, a crib barn, and agricultural sheds. Across the road stand a large gambrel-roofed barn and a silo. The place has been owned by the Piercy and Adams families; the Adamses moved here in 1921, renovated the house, and erected some of the outbuildings.

CE 15 Samuel Stewart House
Ca. 1906; N side SR 1389, 0.3 mi. E of SR 1391, Andrews vic.; private, visible from road

Exemplifying a treatment often used in western N.C., the symmetrical 2-story frame farmhouse features a decorative two-tier, full-width porch. The farm was purchased in 1846 by James Stewart, who with his wife Harriet occupied an old Indian house until they built in 1847 "the first framed house in Cherokee County." In 1852 Stewart established a tannery that was one of the county's first industries, but it closed soon after he died in 1863. After Harriet Stewart died in 1895, their son Hugh Samuel Stewart and his wife Cynthia settled on the family farm; they lived in the old house for a few years, but when it became too crowded, they replaced it with this larger one ca. 1906. The Stewarts' diversified farm included livestock, orchards, and vineyards.

CE 16 Valleytown Cemetery Chapel
1904; E side US 19 BUS at SR 1505, Andrews

Sited on a knoll with spectacular views of the surrounding mountains, the frame chapel takes a somewhat unusual form, with the entrance in the long side rather than the more usual gable-end placement. It formerly had a more elaborate porch and entrance. Its simplicity, batten shutters, and brick piers represent the unpretentious wooden churches once prevalent in the region. The small building is now used for services for the adjoining cemetery, which contains graves of many early citizens.

CE 17 Walker's Inn
Ca. 1844; NE corner of SR 1505 and SR 1393, Andrews vic.; private, visible from road; B&B

One of the most prominent and evocative vestiges of early white settlement in Cherokee Co., the house is part of the old Valley Town community east of Andrews, a village that was the site of one of William Holland Thomas's trading posts before the Cherokee Removal. The dwelling began as a log house—the southeastern half of the present structure—and was enlarged into a weatherboarded, 2-story building with a center-passage plan, an engaged 2-tier porch, plus rear shed additions and an ell for kitchen and dining room. A log outbuilding with half-dovetailed notching stands behind the dwelling. (See Introduction, Fig. 20.)

Family tradition recalls that William Walker and his wife Margaret Scott moved into the log house when they married in the early 1840s, though evidently Walker did not formally acquire the land until 1852 or 1853. The house was either an existing Cherokee dwelling or newly built for the couple. The Walkers were among the first settlers in the Valley Town area after the county was opened for white settlement. Walker had come to the area as a young man with William Waugh, a pioneer merchant in the area. Walker attained local prominence as a judge and, in 1846, first postmaster of Valley Town. As their family grew, the Walkers expanded their house to essentially its present size.

Strategically located on the State Rd., which had been built with funds from the sale of Cherokee lands, the Walkers' house like many roadside dwellings came into use as an inn. It was an important stopping place on the road between Franklin and Murphy by the time Frederick Law Olmsted toured the region in 1857. Describing his journey in his book *The Slave States*, he reported that he had spent the night of July 6 at "an unusually comfortable house, known throughout all the country as 'Walker's,'" at which "the wealthy planters from the low country make a halting station on their journey to certain sulphur springs farther north and east." Olmsted found the food at the inn "abundant and various" but too greasy for his taste.

During the Civil War, William Walker served in the Commissary Department of the Confederate army; in 1864 he was captured at his home by Union soldiers and never returned. His widow, Margaret, continued to operate the inn. After her death in 1899, it became a private residence. In the mid-20th c. the house was restored by their granddaughter, Margaret Walker Freel, who collected local lore, wrote a history of the county, and narrated her family's story in *Unto the Hills* (1976). In the 1980s the old inn was reopened to travelers as a bed and breakfast establishment.

CE 18 Mosteller House

Late 19th c.; N side SR 1505, 1 mi.
E of SR 1502, Junaluska Creek vic.;
private, visible from road

The quintessential mountain log house was built for James Madison Mosteller and his wife Eliza Kitchen Mosteller, who came to the Junaluska or Valley Town area of the county about 1880. In typical fashion, the 1-story house is built with half-dovetailed notch construction and has a fine stone chimney at the gable end. A shed porch shelters the front, while a kitchen and dining room ell extends to the rear. Long identified as the family homeplace, the dwelling has been popularly depicted in paintings and photographs as an evocative mountain homestead.

CE 18 *Mosteller House*

CE 19 Brittain House and Store

Late 19th c.; S side SR 1535, 0.3 mi. E of
NC 141, Peachtree; private, visible from road

The cluster of frame buildings at Peachtree evokes the era of the country store and its farmer-storekeeper. The 1½-story frame house with gabled dormers and the nearby 2-story, gable-fronted frame store were built for Marcus Brittain or his son William. Descendant of early settlers in Guilford and Buncombe counties, Marcus Brittain worked as a local contractor, built railroad bridges in Oklahoma, operated a foundry on Hanging Dog Creek and a store in Murphy, and had a farm and store in the Peachtree community. William P. Brittain, who carried on the mercantile business in Peachtree, probably remodeled the dwelling about 1892. The store (with a plaque that states, "Store of William P. Brittain opened June 13, 1884") is probably "the Store House" deeded from father to son in 1888. It also served as the Peachtree post office and social center.

CE 20 John C. Campbell Folk School

1925 to present; E and W sides SR 1564 at
Clay Co. line, Brasstown

Interweaving American and European traditions, the architecture of this important folk school campus, founded in 1925 by Olive Dame Campbell and Marguerite Butler, recalls a complex chapter in the educational and cultural history of the Southern Appalachians. From their marriage in 1907 until his death in 1919, John C. and Olive Dame Campbell devoted themselves to the study of rural life in the Southern Appalachians.

With assistance from the Russell Sage Foundation, they sought to record and preserve the region's traditional culture while improving economic and cultural opportunities for the people. As shown in David Whisnant's *All That Is Native and Fine*, the Campbells were part of a larger, often paradoxical movement that focused missionary attention on the "primitive" Appalachian region.

Early in her travels in the mountains, Olive Campbell gathered many folk songs. She persuaded English folk musicologist Cecil Sharp to visit the area and accompanied him during his 1916 journey to collect songs in the "Laurel Country" of Madison Co. and elsewhere. Their work resulted in *English Folk Songs from the Southern Appalachians* (1917).

The Campbells also planned to establish an Appalachian folk school modeled on the Scandinavian folk school movement, begun in Denmark in the 1840s to educate rural people. But this dream was delayed when World War I canceled John's study trip to Scandinavia, and in 1919 he died at age fifty-one. Olive completed and published in his name *The Southern Highlander and His Homeland* (1921), a work of lasting influence in the study of the region.

Olive Campbell then enlisted the aid of Marguerite Butler (a teacher at the Pine Mountain Settlement School in Harlan Co., Ky.), and the two set off to study folk schools in Scandinavia. In 1925 they chose Brasstown, N.C., as the site for the school, partly because of local support in funds and labor. Named for John Campbell and aided by the Russell Sage Foundation and the Carnegie Foundation, their "Folk School on the order of the Danish Folk Schools" included a model farm and offered courses in agriculture, handicrafts, health, and cultural activities drawn from local traditions as well as Danish songs and dances.

The women began the school in an existing dwelling, now called **Farm House**, which stands at the center of the gently rolling 366-acre campus. They soon built **Keith House** (1926–28), a 2-story frame building designed by Olive Campbell's niece Dorothy Bacon as the administration build-

ing. They also acquired the **Log House Museum** (late 19th c., 1926), a dogtrot log house composed of two cabins moved from nearby sites in 1926 and restored as an example of local building traditions, with help from neighboring families—probably the state's first preservation project to save rural vernacular structures. Both sections have half-dovetailed notching; one section is heated by a stone end chimney, the other by a reconstructed wooden chimney of V-notched logs. The puncheon floor is a typical cabin feature, now seldom surviving.

CE 20 *Log House Museum*

Other buildings reflect the influence of two European staff members who arrived in 1926. George Bidstrup, a young Danish farmer who had taught in Danish folk schools, directed the demonstration farm, taught Danish gymnastics to local residents, and eventually married Marguerite Butler and became director of the school in 1952. Leon Deschamps, a Belgian forester, surveyor, and engineer, came from the Pine Mountain Settlement School in Kentucky to teach forestry and supervise construction. Under Bidstrup and Deschamps, the school gained barns, houses, a mill, and other structures with European folk architecture elements, including half-timbering, stonework, and carved leaf and flower motifs. The **Mill House** (1928) is a picturesque composition with arcaded stonework at the first story and half-timbering at the second. The **Milking Barn** (ca. 1930), now a blacksmith shop, is a half-timbered barn with oak leaf designs carved in the timbers.

By 1930 the folk school offered several programs, including a demonstration farm under Bidstrup's leadership; cooperative as-

CE 20 *Mill House*

sociations, including the long-lasting Brass-town Carvers Guild, to encourage local crafts and farm production; and other educational and recreational activities. With Frances Goodrich of *Allanstand and others, Olive Campbell helped found the Southern Highland Handicraft Guild. Today the school operates primarily as a craft and folk arts center.

CE 21 Cobb Farm
1860s–1940s; S side US 19/129,
2.5 mi. S of US 64/19/129, Bellview vic.;
private, visible from road

The typical mountain farmstead, nestled into a hillside terrace beside Cobb Creek, is best known for its association with the childhood of baseball great Ty Cobb. The center of the farm is the much expanded log house begun for John Franklin and Sarah Waldrop Cobb about the time of their marriage in 1863. The original section was a 1-room dwelling of large logs joined with half-dovetailed notches; it retains its field-stone chimney, exposed ceiling joists, and enclosed stair to the sleeping attic. Over the

years the Cobb family added a frame kitchen ell (1870s) toward the road and other rooms to the east from ca. 1901 to the 1940s.

The Cobbs owned a farm of 150–220 acres, cultivating 18 to 35 acres of corn, wheat, and orchards. Among the outbuildings near the house are a 19th-c. log smoke-house, a root cellar set into the hillside, a frame washhouse, and a sheltered spring-house with stonework from 1941, including a plaque reading "Ty Cobb / Senior Grand-son / World's Baseball Champion."

Although Tyrus Raymond "Ty" Cobb grew up in neighboring Georgia and was called the "Georgia Peach," he spent a cru-

CE 21 *Cobb Farm*

cial part of his youth on this farm with his grandparents. His father, a schoolteacher who hoped Ty would become a doctor or a lawyer, discouraged his interest in baseball. But when as a teenager Ty made summer visits (1897–1903) with Grandpa and Grandma Cobb, he was allowed to pursue the sport, and his aunt Nora Cobb often drove him by buggy to Murphy or Andrews to play baseball. Of these times, he later recalled, "A decision I'd have to make before long—between college and a career no other Cobb had elected—began to take shape here." After a minor league tryout in 1904, Cobb joined the major league Detroit Tigers in 1905, thus beginning his unparalleled career as batter and fielder. Despite his controversial sportsmanship, Cobb was leading vote-getter in the initial Baseball Hall of Fame in 1936. The present owner informally welcomes visitors interested in the "World's Greatest Baseball Player" and accommodates vacationers in Cobb Creek Cabins.

CE 22 Mull-Shields House

Late 19th c.; W side SR 1120, 1.0 mi.
N of SR 1123, Culberson vic.; private,
visible from road

Of the small log houses once numerous in the county, few survive intact and within view of public thoroughfares. Although little is known of its history, this house beside the road exemplifies a characteristic type in straightforward fashion. It is a single-pen, half-dovetailed structure with a partition creating two rooms, each with a doorway. The sturdy end chimney is built of stone, and a rear frame shed and ell extend the living space. For most of the 20th c. the house has been occupied by the Shields family, part of a large local family. It stands near the former railroad village of Culberson, where a handful of late 19th-c. frame dwellings clusters around the crossroads.

CE 23 Young Barn

20th c.; NW corner of US 64 and SR 1130,
Hothouse vic.; private, visible from road

Beside the highway stands one of western N.C.'s many early and mid-20th-c. barns

featuring diagonally applied siding, evidently a structural as well as decorative feature. This barn is especially eye-catching because of its well-preserved advertisement painted on the roof, "See Beautiful / Rock City / atop Lookout Mt." Many such signs promoting the Tennessee attraction still appear on barns throughout the region. The nearby 1½-story frame farmhouse with stone chimneys was probably built ca. 1904 by Wes Young, who purchased the land in 1885.

CE 23 *Young Barn*

CE 24 Hickey House

Ca. 1880, 1920s; W side NC 294, 0.3 mi. N of
SR 1130, Suit vic.; private, visible from road

Dramatically sited on a knoll rising from the broad valley below Pack Mountain, the farmstead is positioned, like many in western N.C., on a terrace set into the hillside. The site emphasizes the unusual form of the farmhouse, with a hip-roofed main block encircled by 2-tier porches that command splendid views. The house began as a smaller one built for James and Ruth Hickey about 1880. Their son Decatur and his wife Sarah expanded the residence to its present form, evidently in the 1920s. Decatur Hickey was a leading farmer in the Suit community, a county commissioner, and operator of a general store. For a time the Letitia post office was located in the house, which has remained in the family. Among the outbuildings is a gambrel-roofed barn with slatted walls, a building type locally popular in the early 20th c.

CE 25 Mason-McNabb House

1840s; W side SR 1312, 0.2 mi. N of NC 294, Suit vic.; private, visible from road

Tucked into a valley, this picturesque farmstead centers on a small, weatherboarded log dwelling. The house is one of the few in the county that follows a dogtrot plan, with two log pens separated by an open passage. In a typical pattern, the dogtrot passage has been enclosed, and an engaged porch and rear shed additions added. The house is believed to have been built by the Mason brothers in the 1840s and sold to William and Celia McNabb in 1883. The McNabbs farmed here for many years; their compact farmstead reflects changing agricultural uses, with a gambrel-roofed barn with slatted sides, a chicken house, and a log crib built into the hillside.

CE 26 Joe Wolf House

Late 19th c.; private, no public access or visibility

The remote log farmhouse is among the county's few 19th-c. structures associated with the continued tenure of Cherokee farmers on Hanging Dog Creek and other sections after the Cherokee Removal. Some evaded capture; others made their way back

east. The dwelling began as a 1½-story, half-dovetailed log house; it was expanded over the years with frame extensions. Owned by Floyd Arms during much of the 20th c., the house had as its earliest remembered occupant Joe Wolf, a Cherokee preacher who is buried nearby. Deeds indicate that Wolf owned the property from 1872 to 1892 and bought it from another Cherokee, John Axe. Young Wolf and The Axe were listed as heads of household on Hanging Dog Creek in the 1835 Cherokee census.

CE 27 Fields of the Wood

N side NC 294, 0.2 mi. S of SR 1157; open to public

The unique religious theme park memorializes the origins (1896–1903) of the Church of God of Prophecy. The 216-acre complex takes its name from Psalm 132:6, "We found it in the fields of the wood." The most famous feature, occupying the slope of Ten Commandments Mountain, is described as the world's largest Ten Commandments—300 feet wide with white concrete numerals 12 feet tall and letters 5 feet tall, flanking 321 steps ascending to a large New Testament.

The park began in 1941 with efforts of leaders of the pentecostal Church of God of

CE 27 *Fields of the Wood*

Prophecy to memorialize their heritage. As one marker relates, this was the site of the cabin of W. F. Bryant Jr., who belonged to a Baptist church "instrumental in the holiness/pentecostal revival that swept this area beginning in 1896." Early leaders in the church, first known as the Holiness Church of Camp Creek, included Bryant, Richard Spurling, and A. J. Tomlinson, the latter joining in 1903 and becoming a dynamic evangelist. Within 20 years the church had grown to more than 20,000 members in several states and countries; today it has more than a million members.

Over the years, church leaders have expanded the park and added features funded by churches in different states. The earliest elements date from 1940–50 and include the entrance gates, the baptismal pool, and the Arise Shine marker, which like the Ten Commandments are fashioned of white-painted concrete. More recently the park has built memorials depicting the life of Christ, including replicas of Golgotha and Joseph's Tomb. Ascending the mountain opposite the Ten Commandments is a staircase explaining the Protestant tradition and the beliefs and heritage of the Church of God of Prophecy. The park also includes a gift shop, a snack bar, and picnic facilities. Long preceding the flashier religious theme parks of the later 20th c., Fields of the Wood is advertised on billboards throughout the region and welcomes thousands of visitors annually.

CE 28 Hiwassee Dam, Powerhouse, and Unit 2 Pump-Turbine

1936–40; TVA architectural staff (Roland Wank, chief); Pump-Turbine, 1954–56, Allis Chambers Co. and TVA; SR 1314 at Hiwassee River; open to public regular hours

The massive dam, used for flood control and power generation on the Hiwassee River, is one of 5 major dams on tributaries of the Tennessee River and one of 54 dams in the TVA system. Authorized by Congress in 1935, construction of Hiwassee Dam transformed the county's economy and much of its landscape, introducing electricity and other signals of progress, while flooding acres of old farmland. During World War II, Apalachia [*sic*] Dam was built a short distance downstream; that dam (no visitor facilities) is in N.C., but the powerhouse is in Tennessee.

Designed by the TVA architectural staff under the leadership of Roland Wank, the Hungarian-born engineer who became the first chief architect (1933–44) for the TVA, Hiwassee displays the characteristic integration of every element to compose a powerful design with great public presence. As surviving drawings illustrate, Wank's TVA architectural team paid careful attention to the proportions and detail of every element, from the overall site plan to the massive and simple forms of the dam, powerhouse, and great gantry crane to the art deco lettering and aluminum hardware fittings. Hiwassee Dam is considered one of the finest in the TVA system in terms of design.

The concrete dam is 307 feet high and 1,376 feet long, with the road running across the top. When completed in 1940, it was described as the highest overspill-type dam in the world. The powerhouse, set into the dam at the lower road level, is a sleek structure with art deco lettering HIWASSEE inscribed above the entrance, and in the reception lobby, the TVA motto "1937 Built for the People of the United States 1940." In the platform in front of the powerhouse are two massive turbines, above which looms a huge, streamlined 275-ton steel traveling gantry crane on tall legs, which runs on tracks and lifts the turbines for repairs.

Important in engineering history, in 1954–56 the Hiwassee Dam gained the first integrated pump-turbine used in a power plant in the nation. Designed by the TVA and the Allis Chalmers Co. and built by Allis Chambers, its Unit 2 pump-turbine was described as the largest pump in the world, with 102,000 horsepower and the capacity to pump 1.75 million gallons per minute. The Hiwassee #2 Reversible Pump-Turbine was named a National Historic Mechanical Engineering Landmark by the American Society of Mechanical Engineers in 1981: "This integration of pump and turbine was the first of many to be installed in power plant systems in the U.S.," explains a plaque. "As a 'pump storage' unit in the Ten-

CE 28 *Hiwassee Dam and Powerhouse*

nessee Valley Authority's system it offered significant economies in the generation of electrical energy."

The point of the pump-turbine is that not only does the turbine generate hydroelectric power from water coming down through the dam, but in periods of low energy demand in the larger TVA system the pump-turbine can be put on "reverse" to pump water from the lower Apalachia Lake back up into Hiwassee Lake to be reused for

generating power during peak demand. The pump-storage system pioneered at Hiwassee has been used elsewhere in the TVA system; the Raccoon Mountain plant (1970–77) in Tennessee is solely a pumped storage facility with a mountaintop reservoir.

To house Hiwassee's construction workforce of as many as 1,200 men, a nearby **Village** with housing, a cafeteria, a school, a hospital, and recreation facilities was created; the village is now the location of the

Bear Paw private residential development (access limited). Although the community buildings are gone, approximately 30 of the small frame dwellings still stand along the curving roads up the hillsides overlooking Hiwassee Lake. Typically they are covered in vertical boarding and have inset porches, often screened; many display local stonework in their prominent chimneys, founda-tions, steps, retaining walls, and various landscape features. A number of the Hiwassee demountable houses were moved to *Fontana when the TVA began that huge undertaking. See Marian Moffett and Lawrence Wodehouse, *Built for the People of the United States: Fifty Years of TVA Architecture* (1983).

Glossary

This glossary has been adapted from lists of architectural terms that have appeared in survey publications on historic architecture in N.C., including especially Dru Gatewood Haley and Raymond A. Winslow, *The Historic Architecture of Perquimans County, North Carolina* (1982); Davyd Foard Hood, *The Architecture of Rowan County, North Carolina* (1983); Peter B. Sandbeck, *The Historic Architecture of New Bern and Craven County, North Carolina* (1988); and Kelly A. Lally, *The Historic Architecture of Wake County, North Carolina* (1994). See also Carl R. Lounsbury, *An Illustrated Glossary of Early Southern Architecture and Landscape* (1994), and Ed Trout and Margaret Lynn Brown, *Historic Buildings of the Smokies* (1995).

Adam or Adamesque: See *Federal style.*

Akron plan: A design for Sunday schools developed by an Akron businessman and Sunday school teacher in the 19th c. for maximum efficiency in use of space. A central room for general teaching was surrounded by smaller rooms, opening from it, for smaller class groups. Often an Akron-plan Sunday school was attached to a church with an *auditorium plan*, and in some examples the two could be combined by opening a partition, to provide a larger auditorium for large services.

anta, antae (in antis): *Pilasters* or piers at the corners of a building. Typically these are used at the ends of a colonnade (pair or row of columns) as part of a *portico* set into (rather than projecting from) the building, so that the antae flank the colonnade. This is described as a portico "in antis." Usually the antae are simpler than the columns they flank.

apse: A semicircular or polygonal portion of a building, such as a church or a courthouse.

arcade: A row of arches supported on piers or columns, attached to or detached from a wall.

architrave: The lowest part of a 3-part classical *entablature* (architrave, frieze, cornice). Often used by itself as a casing for a window, door, etc. A single architrave consists of an inner *bead*, a broad band, and an outer raised molding; a double architrave has two bands separated by a molding.

Art Deco: A style of decorative arts and architecture popular in the 1920s and 1930s, characterized by geometric forms and exotic motifs. So called by later era historians from the popularization of the style at the Exposition Internationale des Arts Décoratifs et Industriels Modern, held in 1925 in Paris.

Arts and Crafts: An approach to decorative arts and architecture in late 19th- and early 20th-c. Britain and America that emphasized handicrafts and direct expression of materials and construction. One of many movements that developed in reaction to the Industrial Revolution, it took its name from the Arts and Crafts Exhibition Society (est. 1888). In N.C. exponents of the Arts and Crafts movement had a strong influence in shaping the revival of pottery, weaving, and other traditional crafts and techniques. The movement's influence on architecture included emphasis on natural (often native) materials, including rough stonework, pebbledash, chestnut bark, and rustic timbers as well as handcrafted metalwork. See also the related *Craftsman* style.

ashlar: Stonework consisting of individual stones that are shaped and tooled to have even faces and square edges.

auditorium plan: A plan employed in late 19th- and early 20th-c. church architecture, in which the *sanctuary* is treated like the auditorium of a theater, to maximize good sight and hearing of the word preached from the pulpit. Often the floor is slanted down toward the pulpit, which may be in front or in a corner, and pews may be arranged in curved or angled fashion concentrically from the pulpit. Sometimes confused with the *Akron plan*, which was a Sunday school plan often built in conjunction with an auditorium plan sanctuary.

balustrade (baluster): A series of regularly spaced uprights (balusters) topped by a railing to provide an ornamental and protective barrier along the edge of a stair, roof, balcony, porch, etc. Balusters (and railings) were typically heavy and *turned* in the 18th c. as part of the *Georgian style*, became simpler and slenderer—often extremely delicate—in the *Federal style* of the late 18th and early 19th centuries, grew heavier again in the mid-19th c. with the *Greek Revival* and *Italianate* styles, and gained heft and ornateness with the *eclecticism* of the late 19th c.

bargeboard: A board attached to and covering the sloping edge of a *gable roof* or *dormer*. Often sawn in a decorative, curvilinear design when used in the picturesque styles of the mid-19th c., especially the *Gothic Revival*. Also called vergeboard.

bartizan: A small, overhanging turret projecting from a tower, often rounded, sometimes polygonal; a feature of chateauesque, *Gothic Revival*, and *Romanesque Revival* styles, especially on church towers.

bay: (1) An opening or division along a face of a building; for example, a wall with a door flanked by two windows is three bays wide. (2) The space between principal structural members, as in a timber frame, the space between posts. (3) A projection from the *facade* of a building, in particular a polygonal or semicircular projection with windows, called a bay window.

bead: A rounded molding semicircular in section, often used to finish an edge or corner of a wooden element, such as a *weatherboard* or *flush sheathing* board. A bead provides a neat appearance and protects against splitting and wear.

Beaux Arts: A style or school of design characterized by the academic and *eclectic* use of historical—typically *classical*—architectural elements, usually on a monumental scale, as promulgated by the École des Beaux Arts in Paris in the 19th c. The Beaux Arts style attained great popularity in American architecture from the 1890s through the 1920s, especially in public architecture, banks, and mansions. Beaux Arts design stressed rational and hierarchical planning in form, layout, and detail. Beaux Arts classicism produced monumental architecture—epitomized and popularized by the

World's Columbian Exposition of 1893 in Chicago—that employed Roman and Renaissance *orders* and forms on a grand scale, with imposing formality and dignity. Through commissions to nationally and regionally active architects, and through the federal government's supervising architect of the Treasury, a number of N.C. towns gained public buildings, especially post offices, in Beaux Arts influenced styles in the early 20th c.

belt course: A projecting horizontal course of brick, stone, or wood used on exterior walls, usually to delineate the line between stories, also called a *string course*.

board and batten: A method of covering a wall using vertical boards, with narrow strips of wood (battens) covering the joints between the boards. Popularized in the mid-19th c. as a suitable covering for modest wooden buildings in the picturesque movement, especially cottages and Gothic churches. The *Carpenter Gothic* style typically employs board-and-batten walls and decorative *bargeboards*.

bond: The pattern in which masonry, particularly brickwork, is laid to tie together the thickness of the wall; specifically, the pattern of the *headers* and *stretchers* seen on the outer face of the masonry. A header is a brick laid through the wall so that only its short end is visible. A stretcher is a brick laid along the wall so that its long side is visible. The principal bonds used in N.C. were *English bond*, *Flemish bond*, and *common bond*.

In English bond, a row of headers alternates with a row of stretchers, creating a very strong wall. English bond was used from the 17th c. well into the 18th c. but became rare by the end of the 18th c.

In Flemish bond, stretchers and headers alternate in each row and are staggered vertically, with each header centered over the stretcher below, creating a decorative checkerboard effect. Especially in the 18th c. the use of all *glazed headers* emphasized this pattern. (Glazed headers attained a vitrified, dark, shiny surface during firing because they were placed toward the heat in the brick kiln.) Flemish bond was used from the 17th c. into the early 19th c. and occasionally into the mid-19th c. It was the predominant bond in the 18th c. Often 18th-c. brick buildings displayed English bond up to the water table and Flemish bond above it.

Common bond (also called American bond) has 1 row of headers to 3, 5, or 7 rows of stretchers. Until the late 18th c., 1:3 bond predominated; 1:5 and 1:7 ratios grew more frequent in the 19th c. Common bond was more economical than Flemish bond, and in some early and mid-19th-c. buildings the principal *facades* were of Flemish bond; the others, of common bond. In the mid-19th c., stretcher or all-stretcher bond came into use, with the outer banks bonded to interior ones with concealed diagonal bricks. Flemish bond, as either a solid wall or a veneer, saw renewed use in *Colonial Revival* architecture.

boxed: A method of construction using vertical planks without a frame, to form a wooden box. Sometimes also referred to as plank construction. The structure consists of *sills* to which planks were nailed at the corners to form corner posts, which then supported a headboard. More vertical planks were nailed to the upper and lower bands to form the walls. A *common-rafter roof* completed the structure. Window and door openings were sawn out. The vertical planks are thus structural and visible inside as well as out. Sometimes battens are nailed over the interstices between the planks. Some boxed houses were subsequently *weatherboarded*. In western N.C. boxed construction was widely employed in the late 19th and early 20th centuries, once sawmills were established, and in some areas into the mid-20th c. Boxed houses were common in lumber villages and other industrial communities; but they were also built as farmhouses, and they often succeeded traditional log construction as a building method. From the exterior, boxed construction is easily mistaken for *board and batten*, which has vertical boards applied to a frame. Early 20th-c. photographs show the frequency of boxed construction for the region's houses, for both white and Cherokee residents. Although the method was not considered as durable as frame construction, numerous examples still stand.

bracket: A device—ornamental, structural, or both—set under an overhanging element, such as the *eave* of a building. Brackets are especially characteristic of the *Italianate* style. Also, the decorative element attached to the ends of steps in a staircase.

bungalow: A house type and architectural style popular in the early 20th c. Typically defined as a relatively modest, 1½-story dwelling of informal character, the bungalow traced its origins to British colonial dwellings in India, as well as to the *Arts and Crafts* movement of the 19th c. Popularized through magazines and plan books, the bungalow was promoted as a wholesome, natural, inexpensive, modern, and convenient house. It saw its greatest development in California, which lent sunny associations of an ideal home. Its basic characteristics include a low-slung silhouette with a dominant roof form, usually a *gable* or *clipped gable* roof; 1½-story height even in larger examples; deep overhanging *eaves*; broad porches—*engaged* or attached—with square, squat brick piers supporting wood posts, which are often tapered; and informal plans emphasizing open spaces and deemphasizing *passages*. Decorative elements, particularly in bungalows rendered in the characteristic *Craftsman* style, stressed straightforward expression of construction elements, such as exposed *rafter* ends, triangular *brackets* beneath the roof, and natural shingles. Some bungalows incorporated Japanese and other Oriental motifs; a few featured Tudor or Spanish motifs; and in N.C. simplified *Colonial Revival* detailing was also popular. In N.C. bungalows began to appear in the mid-1910s, became wildly popular in the 1920s, persisted through the 1930s, but were seldom built after World War II, when the ranch house dominated the market for unpretentious, modern, convenient houses. The Aladdin Company, which had a factory in Wilmington, N.C., produced thousands of prefab bungalows, many of which were erected in N.C.

buttress: A vertical mass of masonry projecting from or built against a wall to give additional strength at the point of maximum stress. Sometimes wooden buttresses are added to frame *Gothic Revival* style buildings as decorative features.

capital: The topmost member, usually decorated or molded, of a column or *pilaster*. Each classical *order—Doric, Ionic, Corinthian, Composite,* etc.—has its characteristic capital.

Carpenter Gothic: A popular term referring to the mid-19th-c. adaptation of the *Gothic Revival* style to wooden buildings produced by carpenters, typified by *board-and-batten* walls and decorative *bargeboards* and porch trim.

castellated: Featuring elements associated with castles, such as *crenellation* and turrets.

center-passage plan (center-hall plan): A plan in which the hall or passage extends through the center of a house and is flanked by one or more pairs of rooms. A center-passage plan two rooms deep—with four main rooms divided by the passage—became especially popular among large houses in the Georgian period and is sometimes referred to as a Georgian plan (also as a *double-pile* plan). This plan continued in widespread use long past the Georgian period, especially from the mid-19th c. onward.

chair rail: A horizontal board or molding fixed on a wall at or about the height of the top of a chair; often the topmost member or cap of *wainscoting*. Until the mid-19th c. this feature was called a chair board.

chamfer: A traditional method of finishing a post, beam, *joist*, or other element, in which the square corners are beveled (cut away at an oblique angle). Often the chamfer ends in a decorative terminus or chamfer stop, the most common in N.C. being the curved lamb's tongue chamfer stop.

chancel: The end of a church containing the altar and often set apart for the use of clergy by a railing or screen. A chancel may be extended as a distinct architectural unit projecting from the main body of the church.

classical: Embodying or based on the principles and forms of ancient Greek and Roman architecture.

Classical Revival: A general term referring to styles that reuse the principles and forms of ancient Greek and Roman architecture. See *Greek Revival, Beaux Arts, Colonial Revival, Neoclassical.*

clipped gable: A gable where the peak is truncated for decorative effect; often seen in *bungalows.*

coastal cottage, coastal plain cottage: A recent, general term for 1½-story dwellings characterized by *engaged* or inset porches, so called because of their predominance in the coastal plain and tidewater areas of N.C. Not a standard architectural term, but useful locally as a shorthand word for a common form.

Colonial Revival: A late 19th- and early 20th-c. American architectural style that drew freely on architectural motifs associated with the American past, including not only elements of the Colonial period but also those of the early national era and even the *Greek Revival* and a host of *classical* designs. The *Southern Colonial Revival* and the *Georgian Revival* were developments of the broader Colonial Revival movement. The popularity of the Colonial Revival, chiefly in residential architecture, paralleled the closely kin *Beaux Arts* classicism in public and institutional architecture. In N.C. the Colonial Revival saw occasional use as early as the 1880s, grew in popularity in the mid- and late 1890s—often mixed with the late *Queen Anne* style—and became a dominant residential style in the early 20th c. It has maintained its popularity in various guises throughout the 20th c.

colonnette: A small column, generally employed as a decorative element on mantels, overmantels, and *porticoes.*

common bond: A method of laying brick wherein one course of *headers* is laid for every 3, 5, or 7 courses of *stretchers.* Also called American bond. See *bond.*

common rafter, common-rafter roof: One of a series of rafters of uniform size, spaced evenly along a roof. In a common-rafter roof, the roof is made entirely of pairs of common rafters, which may join at the apex in a ridgepole or be joined in opposing pairs by a lapped joint without a ridgepole. This type of roof was extremely common in N.C. from the earliest buildings on. See also *principal rafter.*

Composite order: A classical order characterized by a column whose *capital* combines *Ionic* volutes and *Corinthian* acanthus leaves.

corbel: A projecting brick or stone, used for supporting or decorative purposes in masonry construction. In a corbeled *cornice*, each row projects farther out than those below it.

Corinthian order: One of the five classical architectural orders, developed in the 5th c. B.C. The most ornate of the orders, its column is characterized by a *capital* with acanthus leaves and curled ferns.

corncrib: A building, usually small, for storing shelled corn or ears of corn. Usually a separate structure, sometimes attached to a barn; sometimes built with solid walls, sometimes with spaces between logs or slats for ventilation. A common outbuilding on N.C. farms from the 17th c. into the mid-20th c.

cornerblock: A square element, either plain or decorated with a circular or other design, usually marking the upper corner of a window or door *surround.* Typical of the *Greek Revival* style during the mid-19th c.; also widely employed ca. 1890–1910.

cornerboard: A vertical board applied to an external corner of a frame building to finish the *facades* and cover the ends of the *weatherboards.* Often treated with a *capital* and base to form a corner *pilaster.*

cornice: The uppermost part of a 3-part classical *entablature* (architrave, frieze, cornice); also, a horizontal molded element used to crown the wall of a building, *portico,* or doorway. The term is loosely applied to almost any horizontal molding forming a main decorative feature, such as a molding (nowadays often called a crown molding) at the junction of walls and ceiling in a room. When enriched with *dentils* or *modillions,* it is called a dentil cornice or a modillion cornice. A raking cornice extends along a slanting (raking) side of a *gable* or *pediment.* A boxed cornice is a simple treatment with a vertical fascia board and a horizontal soffit board enclosing the ends of the ceiling *joists* where they project at the *eaves.*

Craftsman: A style of furniture and architectural design promoted by Gustav Stickley's magazine *The Craftsman* as an American interpretation of the *Arts and Crafts* movement. The style emphasized informal plans and forms, natural materials, and direct expression (or suggestion) of construction. Stickley's magazine and those influenced by it promoted a variety of house forms, including revivals of English cottage forms. Most popular, however, was the *bungalow.* Typical Craftsman details include heavy, tapered porch posts on heavy bases or plinths; exposed *rafter* and purlin ends beneath broad *eaves;* and exaggerated angular eave *brackets* and other carpentry features. Interior Craftsman elements often include simple, naturally finished woodwork and built-in cabinetry.

crenellation, crenellated: Alternating indentations and raised sections (embrasures and merlons) of a *parapet,* creating a toothlike profile sometimes known as a battlement. In the medieval period these were defensive features of castles. Crenellated rooflines, especially on towers, are most often used in the *Gothic Revival* style.

cresting: Ornamental ironwork used to embellish the ridge of a *gable roof* or the curb or upper *cornice* of a mansard roof.

crib: A corncrib; also, a log structural unit of a barn or other farm building, making up double-crib barns and other forms.

crossette: A lateral projection of the head of the molded frame (architrave) of a door, window, mantel, or *panel;* also known as an "ear." The motif is characteristically used in *Georgian style* architecture in the mid- to late 18th c. and recurs in *Greek Revival* and *Italianate* work in the mid-19th c. and in *Colonial Revival* work (esp. *Georgian Revival*) in the early 20th c.

cupola: A small structure, usually polygonal, built on top of a roof or tower, mostly for ornamental purposes, sometimes as an observation point.

dentils: Small, closely placed blocks set in a horizontal row (like little teeth, dim. of *dens:* dentil), used as an ornamental element of a classical *cornice.* Distinguished from *modillions,* which are spaced farther apart. Cornices might have courses of both dentils and modillions.

distyle: Having two columns, typically in a portico *in antis*.

dogtrot: A plan seen principally in log houses in which two *pens* (log-walled units) are separated by an open *passage*. Relatively rare in N.C. today.

Doric order: A classical order characterized by heavy columns with simple, unadorned *capitals* supporting a *frieze* of vertically grooved tablets or triglyphs set at intervals. Renaissance architectural authorities classified the order into the Greek Doric order, in which the column has no base, and the Roman Doric, in which the column stands on a base. The Doric order, often greatly simplified, was popularly used in N.C., especially in *Greek Revival* buildings during the antebellum period.

dormer, dormer window: An upright window, set in a sloping roof, with vertical sides and front, usually with a gable, shed, or *hip roof*. Used to light rooms in a half-story.

double-pen: A plan used in log houses in which two pens, each with its own end chimney, are placed side by side. See *pen*.

double-pile: A plan two rooms deep, most often used to refer to a *center-passage plan* house that is two rooms deep on either side of the passage.

double-shouldered chimney: An exterior chimney the sides of which angle inward to form shoulders twice as it ascends from the base to the cap, accommodating a fireplace in each of two stories. Typically in N.C. double-shouldered chimneys were employed through the 18th c. and into the 19th c. but were gradually supplanted by single-shouldered chimneys in the early 19th c. See *shoulder*.

dovetail: A joint in woodworking, commonly used in furniture and in plank or log building, wherein a piece of timber is cut (like a dove's tail) with two outward flaring sides meant to fit into correspondingly shaped spaces in adjoining members. A half-dovetail has only one edge flared; the other is straight. Various framing members might be dovetailed together. The most frequently noted usage is in construction of hewn or sawn plank (and sometimes log) structures with full- or half-dovetailed corner notches. In much of N.C. this method continued to be used in small outbuildings, from the 18th c. through much of the 19th c.

eave: The edge of a roof, usually above a *cornice*, often overhanging to shed water beyond the face of the wall. Eaves were often flush with the wall at the *gable* ends of 18th- and early 19th-c. buildings. Mid- and late 19th-c. eaves normally extended beyond the walls.

eclectic, eclecticism: An approach to design, including architecture, in which elements are selected from a variety of sources—historical, stylistic—and combined. Often applied to mid- and, especially, late 19th-c. architecture such as the *Queen Anne* style.

ell: A wing or extension of a building, often a rear addition, positioned at right angles to the principal mass.

engaged porch: A porch whose roof is continuous structurally with that of the main roof of the building. Typically in eastern N.C., a double-slope roof shelters an engaged porch. Partial *rafters* are attached to the main rafters of a *gable-roofed* house at a point partway down the gable slope, so that the roof breaks to a gentler slope within the block of the house and continues outward over the porch. *Shed rooms* to the rear may be treated in the same fashion. In an inset porch, the porch is set entirely within the block of the house, under a gable roof composed of a single set of rafters.

English bond: A method of laying brick wherein one course is laid with *stretchers* and the next with *headers*, thus bonding the thickness of brick together and forming a high-strength bond of alternating courses of stretchers and headers. See *bond*.

entablature: The upper horizontal part of a classical *order* of architecture, usually positioned above columns or *pilasters*. It consists of three parts: the lowest molded portion is the *architrave*; the middle band (plain or decorated) is the *frieze*; the uppermost molded element is the *cornice*. Variously adapted and simplified entablatures are incorporated into doorways, windows, mantels, and the like.

exposed face chimney: In a frame house, an *interior end chimney* built so that the outside face or "back" of the chimney is exposed rather than covered with *weatherboards*. It may be exposed as far up as the *eave* line or only in the first story. This feature appears in N.C. in New Bern and its environs. It also occurs in other areas along the Atlantic seaboard.

exterior end chimney: A chimney located outside the wall of a building, usually rising at the *gable* end.

facade: The face or front of a building.

fanlight: A semicircular window, usually above a door or window, with radiating *muntins* suggesting a fan.

Federal style: A style of *Neoclassical* architecture popular in America in the late 18th and early 19th centuries, reflecting the influence of the *Adam* style, the Roman-inspired mode of Scots architects Robert and James Adam, which emphasized delicate, linear forms, attenuated proportions, and curved forms and spaces. In N.C. the Federal style began to appear along with the continuing *Georgian style* about 1800, and many buildings into the 1810s and even the 1820s show elements of both styles. The Federal style became widely popular in the 1810s and 1820s and continued into the 1830s and, in some areas, the 1840s, despite the growing influence of the *Greek Revival* style. The style is characterized by the use of delicate Neoclassical ornament such as fans, garlands, and sunbursts and by attenuation of such elements as *balusters*, window *muntins*, columns, and *pilasters*. Popularized by English and American builders' guides, it lent itself to individualized interpretation, particularly in lavish *reeding* and gougework, by local artisans.

fenestration: The arrangement of windows on a building.

finial: A vertical ornament placed on the apex of an architectural feature such as a *gable*, turret, or *pediment*.

Flemish bond: A method of laying brick wherein *headers* and *stretchers* alternate in each course and, vertically, headers are placed over stretchers to form a bond and give a distinctive checkerboard pattern. See *bond*.

flume: A channel or chute to carry water. At waterpowered mills flumes carried water

from an impoundment to the mill, and in the lumbering industry huge flumes carried water that floated logs sometimes several miles downgrade from the forest to the sawmill or other processing facility.

flush sheathing: A wall treatment consisting of closely fitted boards with tight joints, all laid in the same plane to give a uniform, flat appearance. Boards may be finished with a *bead* on one edge. Used in N.C. in interior finishes but also on the portion of an exterior wall sheltered by a porch, where it gives a smoother, more interior-like character than would lapped *weatherboards*.

flutes, fluted, fluting: Shallow, concave grooves running vertically on the shaft of a column, *pilaster*, or other surface.

foursquare, American foursquare: A popular house form 2 stories tall with a *hip roof*, taking a straightforwardly square shape and generally without elaborate decoration. The type was quite popular in the late 19th and especially the early 20th centuries, amid the Progressive era's emphasis on simplicity and practicality, but the terms "foursquare" or "American foursquare" are recent coinages, not period names.

frieze: The middle portion of a classical *entablature*, located above the *architrave* and below the *cornice*. It may be plain or ornamented. By extension, the term is often used to describe the flat, vertical board used beneath a cornice and above the *weatherboards* of a frame building, and also for the flat board between the *pilasters* and shelf (cornice) of a mantel.

gable: The triangular portion of a wall formed or defined by the two sloping sides of a ridged roof.

gable roof: A roof formed with two opposing planes sloping to a common ridge, forming triangular *gables* at the ends. Sometimes called a pitched roof or A-roof. Gable roofs were the most common roof form in N.C. buildings.

gambrel roof: A roof with two pitches rising to a ridge, the upper slope being markedly flatter than the lower one. In eastern N.C., gambrel-roofed houses were built in the 18th c. and continuing into the early 19th c. The form was revived and sometimes called

"Dutch" or "Dutch colonial" in the early 20th-c. *Colonial Revival* era.

Georgian plan: See *center-passage plan*.

Georgian Revival: A revival of Georgian architectural forms, both in England and America, and as part of the larger *Colonial Revival* style in America. In N.C. the style became especially popular after about 1910 and often took the form of symmetrical, restrained designs with rich *classical* detail, quite frequently in a Virginia vocabulary. The Georgian Revival was particularly popular for public buildings, churches, and residences, often executed in red brick with contrasting white.

Georgian style: The prevailing architectural style of the 18th c. in Great Britain and the North American colonies. Popularly called Georgian style (not a term at the time) after the monarchs who reigned during its heyday, George I, George II, and George III. It is derived from *classical* Renaissance and Baroque forms and was shaped in Britain by architects such as Christopher Wren and James Gibbs. Builders' guides published in England, such as those of Batty Langley, Abraham Swan, James Gibbs, William Salmon, William Pain, and others, made the elements of the style available to craftsmen and clients. As expressed in relatively simple form in N.C., the Georgian style is characterized by symmetrical forms and plans, relatively heavy *classical* moldings, *raised panels*, robust classically derived ornament, and such motifs as *pediments*, *modillion cornices, turned balustrades*, and *crossetted surrounds* on doorways, windows, and mantels. Georgian motifs appeared in a few N.C. buildings in the 1750s, but fully realized examples of the style came only in the late 1760s and thereafter. Use of the Georgian style continued into the early 19th c., often in transitional combinations with the *Federal style*.

glazed header: A brick having a glossy dark surface, ranging in color from gray green to almost black, formed through direct exposure to flame and intense heat during the firing process. In *Flemish-bond* brickwork this glazed surface is often used for decorative effect; the brick is laid so that the glazed ends of headers emphasize the checkerboard pattern in the wall or, in some cases, delineate letters, numerals, or other designs. Such work appeared in the mid-18th c. in northeastern N.C. and in the late 18th and early 19th centuries in the western piedmont.

Gothic Revival: The revival of the forms and ornament of medieval Gothic architecture, characterized by the use of the pointed arch, *buttresses*, pinnacles, and other Gothic details. Begun in Europe in the late 18th c., the Gothic Revival came into N.C. use in the mid-19th c. (though there were a few early gestures in the style in the 1810s and 1820s, chiefly in work by architect William Nichols). The Gothic Revival style appeared occasionally in residential architecture in picturesque cottages (a few in the 1850s, more in the post–Civil War era) influenced by the publications of Andrew Jackson Downing, but it was vastly more popular in religious architecture. Introduced in the state by the Episcopal Church in the 1830s and 1840s, the Gothic Revival flourished from the 1850s onward as a predominant religious style and has continued in use in church architecture through the 20th c.

graining: A decorative painted treatment on wood, usually used to simulate exotic or costly woods, sometimes stylized to the point of abstraction.

Greek Revival: The mid-19th-c. revival of the forms and ornamentation of the architecture of ancient Greece. The Greek Revival, often much simplified, was the most popular style in N.C. from the 1830s until the Civil War. A few early motifs appear in the 1810s and 1820s in work by architect William Nichols, and in some areas elements of the style persist into the 1870s. Builders' guides by Asher Benjamin and Minard Lafever were widely used sources. The Greek Revival dominated fashionable architecture and was translated by local carpenters into greatly simplified versions. It is characterized by broad, rectilinear, usually symmetrical forms; wide *friezes* and *pilasters*; flat surfaces; doors and window frames marked by *cornerblocks*; and heavy mantels featuring columns and *entablature*, or a plain pilaster and frieze format. Porches are often treated as *porticoes*, with the *Doric order* frequently employed—and simplifications thereof often with squared *pillars*. Courthouses and churches were often rendered as gable-fronted temple forms with projecting or recessed porticoes, but this treatment was rare in residential architecture.

half-timber, half-timbering: Timber-framed construction with the framing members exposed and usually infilled with brick or plastered wattle and daub. In the late 19th and early 20th centuries, simulated half-timbering was a popular decorative element in *Queen Anne, Tudor Revival,* and various other styles, where it carried romantic English associations.

hall-parlor plan: A traditional plan consisting of two principal rooms: a larger "hall," often nearly square, and an adjoining smaller "parlor." In most instances the hall was entered directly from the outside and had a fireplace centered on the end wall. It was the room where most domestic activities took place and from which doors led to other rooms and to the stairs. The smaller parlor was usually for sleeping. This plan was used from the late 17th c. through the 18th c. in top-quality houses in N.C. and continued into the mid-19th c. in middling and small houses.

header: A brick placed in a wall so that the short end faces outward. Used with *stretcher* bricks to form a *bond* in the wall.

hexastyle: Having six columns, usually referring to a *portico*.

hip roof: A roof that slopes back equally from each side (usually four) of a building. A hip roof may have a pyramidal form or have a slight ridge. A hip roof on a porch usually has three slopes, the center one being widest.

I-house: A term coined by geographer Fred Kniffen to describe a certain house type commonly seen in states beginning with the letter *I*, but also seen frequently elsewhere, including N.C. Kniffen applied the term to 2-story houses one room deep and two rooms or more wide. The tall, thin profile also suited the term "I-house." The term is employed as a convenient shorthand for a common form but has no basis in traditional architectural language.

inset porch: See *engaged porch.*

interior end chimney: A chimney positioned inside the end wall of a house.

International style: A term first used by Henry-Russell Hitchcock and Philip Johnson in 1932 to describe the nontraditional architecture that had begun in the 1920s in Europe and was appearing in the United States. Simplified, abstracted forms, rejection of historical allusions, and direct expression of volume and materials were among its characteristics. Before World War II the style was most popular in advanced urban settings and among especially progressive clients. It became more generally used after World War II and continued into the 1970s. The Bauhaus and Miesian styles are related developments.

Ionic order: One of the five orders of classical architecture, which was associated with the Ionian Greeks and was used by the Greeks and the Romans. The order is characterized by a column whose *capital* features large volutes (spirals), sometimes enriched with other decoration. The Ionic order was considered to be between the plain *Doric* and the elaborate *Corinthian.*

Italianate: A revival of elements of Italian Renaissance architecture popular during the mid- and late 19th c., influenced by both villas and palazzos. Characterized by the presence of deep overhanging *eaves* and *cornices* supported by ornate *brackets*, arched windows often with heavy hoodmolds, and, less often, square towers placed centrally or asymmetrically. In antebellum N.C., where examples appeared by the 1840s and 1850s, the style was restricted to large towns and progressive rural areas and found favor among elite, relatively cosmopolitan clients. Later in the 19th c. the style found widespread use in commercial and industrial as well as residential architecture.

joist: One of a series of parallel timbers or beams, usually set on edge, that span a room from wall to wall to support a floor or ceiling; a beam to which floorboards, ceiling boards, or plaster laths are nailed. In the 18th c., ceiling joists meant to be left exposed in a neatly finished house were often finished with a *bead* or *chamfer.*

keystone: The central, wedge-shaped stone at the crown of an arch or in the center of a *lintel*.

kitchen: A room or building used for cooking and sometimes eating. In the 17th, 18th, and much of the 19th c., common practice in N.C., especially in the countryside but also in towns, was the use of a freestanding kitchen as one of the domestic outbuildings. This was regarded as a specifically southern practice, variously attributed to keeping the heat, smells, and threat of fire separated from the dwelling house. Kitchens commonly had large chimneys with cooking fireplaces until the late 19th c. Some had one room, some two, with a separate dining room, and many had upper chambers for servants. In the late 19th and early 20th centuries kitchens became more frequently attached to the main house by a breezeway or *passage*, and in more and more cases were incorporated into the main block of the house as cooking technology changed from open fireplaces to cookstoves.

lintel: A horizontal element of wood or stone that spans an opening. In masonry construction it frequently supports the masonry above the opening.

marbling: Painted treatment on wood simulating the color and texture of marble. Now often called marbleizing, but the 18th- and 19th-c. term was "marbling."

medallion: A large, typically circular or oval ornament that adorns the center of a ceiling.

meetinghouse: A place of worship or public gathering, often preferred by dissenting denominations and sects over the word "church" when describing a building. Meetinghouses were typically plain rather than elaborated. They were planned to focus on the word, with emphasis on the pulpit rather than the altar. In a meetinghouse plan, typically benches or pews were arranged around the pulpit, which was often on the long side (often the north) rather than in the *gable* end. In many cases the main entrance was on the long side opposite the pulpit, and secondary entrances opened on the two gable ends.

Moderne: A general architectural term applied to designs from the 1920s through the 1940s and sometimes the 1950s, defined by stylized forms, often streamlined with smooth curves and flat planes.

modillion: A horizontal *bracket*, often in the form of a plain block, supporting the underside of a *cornice*. Undercut modillions, with an S-curved bottom outline, were used in classically detailed buildings.

mortise and tenon: A joint made by one member having its end cut as a projecting tongue (tenon) that fits exactly into a groove or hole (mortise) in the other member. Once joined in this fashion, the two pieces are often secured by a peg. In traditional framed buildings, many elements are so joined.

muntin: The strip of wood separating the panes of a window *sash*, often molded.

Neoclassical: A general term for an approach to design drawing inspiration from ancient Greek and Roman precedents. It is often used in reference to the revival of Roman, then Greek classical forms in the late 18th and early 19th centuries (the *Federal* and *Greek Revival* styles), and also to the renewed interest in classicism around the turn of the 20th c., though the latter is frequently called Neoclassical Revival or *Beaux Arts* classicism.

newel, newel post: The principal post used to terminate the railing or *balustrade* of a flight of stairs.

order: In *classical* and *Neoclassical* architecture, the basic unit of design, composed of a column with base, shaft, *capital*, and *entablature*, proportioned and detailed according to certain rules codified in the Renaissance and based on observation of ancient Roman examples. Each order—Tuscan, *Doric*, *Ionic*, *Corinthian*—had its own distinctive features and proportions. In N.C. some architects and builders used British, then American, books that explained these rules and illustrated both the elements and how to work out the proportions. Often the motifs of the orders were freely adapted in actual use.

Palladian: An approach to design associated with the buildings and books of the 16th-c. Italian architect Andrea Palladio and popularized by British architectural books of the 18th c. The term is often used to describe buildings with a symmetrical three- or five-part composition, usually consisting of a large central block flanked by (usually smaller) wings. It is also applied to buildings with a central pedimented *pavilion* projecting from the *facade*.

Palladian window: A window design featuring a symmetrical, three-part arrangement with a central arched opening flanked by lower, square-headed openings and separated from them by columns, *pilasters*, piers, or narrow vertical *panels*. Inspired by the work of Renaissance architect Andrea Palladio, who like many of his contemporaries, often used this motif. The period term was "Venetian window."

panel: A portion of flat surface set off by molding or some other decorative device. Generally, *raised panels* were used as well as flat panels in the 18th and early 19th centuries as part of the *Georgian style*. Flat panels became popular with the *Federal style* in the early 19th c. and continued in use throughout most of the century, though slightly raised panels came back into use late in the 19th c. and were reiterated in the *Georgian Revival* style.

parapet: A low wall along a roof or terrace, used as decoration or protection.

passage: An enclosed space leading between rooms, today usually called a "hall" or "hallway." In the 17th, 18th, and much of the 19th c. the term "passage" was employed, and "hall" more often referred to a principal major room.

paved shoulder: In a brick chimney, the treatment of the sloped transition from the wider base to the narrower shaft by a smooth diagonal surface topped with bricks laid flat like pavers on the slope. This treatment was generally used in the 18th c. but was superseded in the early 19th c. by the *stepped shoulder*.

pavilion: A portion of a building's *facade* that projects forward slightly to give architectural emphasis, sometimes accentuated by a *pediment* or other feature.

pebbledash: The regional term popularly used for a method of finishing a mortared surface in which pebbles are incorporated as an aggregate to give a rough texture. The thick mixture of mortar (cement) and pebbles is thrown against the wall. (In the architecture of the Arts and Crafts movement in England, architect C. F. A. Voysey and others employed pebbledash for its natural appearance, often combined with shingles, rough stone, and other elements. Technically "pebbledash" referred to mortar with pebbles thrown against the final coat, while *roughcast* referred to a mortar incorporating a stone aggregate.) This method was employed at *Biltmore Estate and *Biltmore Village in the 1890s and soon entered the popular regional building vocabulary. Although in their drawings and specifications, architects Richard Morris Hunt and Richard Sharp Smith used the term "roughcast" for this finishing method, "pebbledash" was in local use by the late 1890s and continues to the present for mortar with pebbles mixed in.

pediment: A crowning element of *porticoes*, *pavilions*, doorways, and other architectural features, usually of low triangular form, with a *cornice* extending across its base and carried up the raking sides. Sometimes broken in the center as if to accommodate an ornament; sometimes open at the bottom; sometimes of segmental, elliptical, or serpentine form.

pen: A rectangular or square structural unit. The term is usually used when referring to log buildings and specifies a structure enclosed by log walls. Most single-pen log houses had only one room in the space enclosed by the logs, but within a single pen there may be partitions dividing the space into smaller rooms, such as a *hall-parlor plan*. Many dwellings in N.C. were single-pen structures. Often these were expanded into two-pen houses following the *double-pen, saddlebag*, or *dogtrot* plans.

penstock: Pipe or other conduit to carry water to a turbine or waterwheel; a sluice to control the flow of water.

pent: A single-sloped lean-to or *shed*, typically small, attached to a building, or, such a roof.

piano nobile: The principal story in a building;

the term is usually employed when the main story is above the ground story and is taller and more elaborately treated than the story beneath. Characteristic of Renaissance palaces, the treatment appears in N.C. chiefly in public buildings such as courthouses where the courtroom is in the second story.

piazza: An Italian term for a plaza. Used in the 18th, 19th, and 20th centuries in N.C. for a covered porch, pronounced with a short *a*, and usually for a porch large enough to accommodate seating.

pilaster: A shallow pier or rectangular column projecting only slightly from or attached to a wall. Pilasters are usually decorated like columns with a base, shaft, and *capital*.

pillar: A general term for a vertical supporting member, often used interchangeably with "pier," "post," and "column." Commonly used for fairly massive examples, often square in section, as opposed to columns that take a particular *order* and are circular in section.

porte cochere: A projecting porch that provides protection for vehicles and passengers. A common feature of the *Queen Anne, Colonial Revival,* and *bungalow* houses of the late 19th and early 20th centuries. Predecessor of the carport.

portico: A roofed space, open or partly enclosed, often with columns and a *pediment*, usually employed as centerpiece of the *facade* of a building and to shelter the main entrance. Typically treated in *classical* fashion.

principal rafter, principal-rafter roof: A member of a pair of large, diagonal framing members composing a truss roof. In a principal-rafter roof, the large principal rafters carry horizontal purlins, upon which rest secondary *common rafters*. This roof type was unusual in N.C. except in especially large or heavily built structures and in Germanic framed buildings in the piedmont.

puncheon: A slab of wood used for flooring; often, half of a split log, with the upper side smoothed flat and the lower side left round. Puncheon floors were used frequently in log houses, but relatively few examples are known to survive. They were often replaced when sawmills became numerous and convenient.

Queen Anne: A popular late 19th-c. revival of early 18th-c. English architecture, characterized by irregularity of plan and massing and a variety of textures. In N.C. the style was frequently rendered in wood in residential architecture, with asymmetrical plans, high *hip roofs* with projecting *gables* and *dormers*, and abundant mass-produced, *eclectic* ornament. The style continued into the early 20th c. and was frequently executed with *Colonial Revival,* classically inspired detail.

quoins: Ornamental blocks of wood, stone, brick, or stucco placed at the corners of a building and projecting slightly.

rafter: A structural timber rising from the plate at the top of a wall to the ridge of the roof and supporting the roof covering.

raised panel: A portion of a flat surface, as in the panel of a door or *wainscot*, that is set off from the surrounding area by a molding or other device and is raised above the surrounding area. Raised panels were especially typical of *Georgian* architecture and appeared in N.C. from the 18th c. into the early 19th c.

reed, reeding: Decoration consisting of parallel convex moldings, often vertically applied to a column or *pilaster*, derived from a bundle of reeds.

return: A horizontal portion of a *cornice* that extends part of the way across the *gable* end of a structure at *eave* level.

Romanesque Revival: A 19th-c. revival of pre-Gothic medieval architecture, characterized by round-headed arches, often with heavy stone-faced stone or brick walls, sometimes with foliated *terra-cotta* ornament.

rosehead nail: A handmade, wrought-iron nail having a broad, conical head. Often the heads of such nails have four or five faces or facets formed by the hand hammering process.

roughcast: A method of finishing a mortared or stuccoed surface in which the outer coat contains a stone aggregate to roughen the texture. Long employed in English building, roughcast was also used in colonial America, but the term was generally replaced by "stucco" by the mid-19th c. At *Biltmore Estate and *Biltmore Village, architects Richard Morris Hunt and Richard Sharp Smith specified "Rough Cast" surfaces, and Smith continued the practice into the early 20th c. The Truck Farmer's cottage at Biltmore was specified to have "roughcast work to be composed of good clean pebbles and Lafarge cement, on expanded metal laths." The resulting finishes have pebbles incorporated as the aggregate in the mortar, a type of finish that is regionally called *pebbledash*.

saddlebag: A plan in which two single-pen rooms are joined together, separated by a single interior chimney. Especially common in log houses but also applied to small frame houses with two rooms flanking a center chimney.

sanctuary: (1) A term used generally for a church, a holy place, or the main worship space within a church. (2) The portion of the church containing the principal altar, within the *chancel* and east of the choir.

sash: The frame, usually of wood, that holds the pane(s) of glass in a window. It may be movable or fixed. It may slide in a vertical plane or may pivot. Windows with double-hung sash are sometimes described by the number of panes in the upper and lower sash, such as 9/9 (9 over 9), 9/6 (9 over 6), etc. In period documents, however, they were not described in that way, but by the total number of panes (lights), thus, for example, 15 lights of sash.

Second Empire: An *eclectic* style derived from the grandiose architecture of the French Second Empire of Napoleon III, popularly used in America from the 1860s to the 1880s, especially for public buildings, and characterized by heavy ornament and high mansard roofs with *dormers*. At the time it was frequently called the "French" style. In N.C. the Second Empire style was relatively rare and mainly urban, appearing in residences and a few public and commercial buildings associated with the recovery of wealth after the Civil War.

segmental arch: An arch formed on a segment of a circle or an ellipse.

shed, shed room: (1) A 1-story appendage to a larger structure, covered by a single-slope roof that "leans" (as in "lean-to") against the principal building mass. A shed porch is one with such a single-slope roof. Often a rear shed or shed rooms may be built as a rear, balancing pendant to a front porch of similar form, or as a pendant to an *engaged porch*, in which case the double-slope roof form is usually repeated. (2) A simple, general-purpose outbuilding, often used for storage.

shotgun: A house or house plan one room wide and two or more rooms deep, with the narrow, usually gable-fronted, end toward the street. The entrance opens directly into the front room, and doors lead directly into each successive room proceeding to the rear. This narrow house form was built most often in African American neighborhoods, though not exclusively so, and some writers argue that it had its origins in New Orleans, the West Indies, and ultimately African precedents. In N.C. the form was built most in the rapid urbanization of the early 20th c.

shoulder: The sloping shelf or ledge created on the side of a masonry chimney where the width of the chimney changes. Sometimes called "weathering."

sidelight: A framed area of fixed glass of one or more panes located to either side of a door or window opening.

side-passage, side-hall plan: A plan with an unheated (no chimney) passage along one side and one or (usually) two heated rooms on the other, with the main entrances at the front and rear of the passage. Side-passage plans were especially common in late 18th- and early 19th-c. townhouses, but the plan was also used in rural dwellings. In the late 19th and early 20th centuries, many towns saw construction of hundreds of side-passage plan houses 2 stories tall with *gable* fronts, especially as working- and middle-class dwellings on narrow lots.

sill: A heavy horizontal timber, positioned at the bottom of the frame of a wood structure, that rests on top of the foundation; also, the horizontal bottom member of a door or window frame.

smokehouse: A small building where meat (mainly pork) is cured by smoking, and subsequently stored, usually hanging from *joists* or *rafters*. A common outbuilding type in N.C., typically built of frame or log without windows and of tight construction.

Southern Colonial Revival: A primarily residential style within the broader *Colonial Revival*, which drew upon themes popularly associated with the antebellum plantation house but included under the broader term "colonial." The typical "Southern Colonial" residence featured a massive, full-height *portico* that overlapped a 1-story porch or terrace that extended across the front *facade* and in some cases around the side(s) of the house. Houses of this style were typically fairly symmetrical, with broad center *passages*, and some examples retained vestiges of *Queen Anne* massing. The style was quite popular from the 1890s to the 1910s in N.C. and appeared in designs by many local and regional architects.

Spanish Colonial Revival, Spanish Revival, Spanish Mission Revival: The revival of designs associated with the Spanish colonial missions in the American Southwest and in Mexico and translated loosely in popular architecture into stuccoed buildings with red tile roofs and a variety of motifs such as arched openings, exposed timbers, and towers. The style was relatively rare in N.C. but did appear in a few towns in the 1910s and 1920s, particularly in railroad buildings and residences.

spindle frieze: A row of lathe-turned members (spindles), usually as a decorative feature of a porch below the *cornice*.

stepped shoulder: On a brick chimney, a sloping ledge formed by the successively stepped course of bricks to make the transition from the lower, wider base to the narrower stack. Generally in N.C. stepped shoulders appear in the early 19th c., superseding the *paved shoulders* typical of the 18th c.

stretcher: The long face of a brick when laid horizontally.

string course: A projecting course of bricks or other material forming a narrow horizontal strip across the wall of a building, usually to delineate the line between stories; also called a *belt course*.

surround: The border or casing of a window or door opening, sometimes molded.

terra-cotta: A ceramic material, molded decoratively and often glazed, used for facings for buildings or as inset ornament. Tobacco farmers experimented with terra-cotta blocks for their curing barns in the 1920s and 1930s.

tobacco barn: A building in which tobacco is cured. Typically in eastern and piedmont N.C. these are flue-cure tobacco barns, built specifically for curing bright-leaf tobacco through a carefully regulated process of heating the barn full of tobacco. In some portions of western N.C., burley tobacco is grown and is air cured by hanging it in well-ventilated barns, which may be purpose-built or general-purpose barns. See the Introduction for a discussion of tobacco barn types and usage.

Tower of the Winds: The Horologium of Andronikos Cyrrhestes in Athens, which has columns showing a distinctive variation of the *Corinthian order*, with the *capitals* lacking volutes and having a row of palmlike leaves. The motif was used occasionally in the antebellum era—in N.C. especially in Wilmington—and again in the early 20th c.

transom: A horizontal window unit above a door.

tripartite: Having three parts. Often applied to symmetrical buildings with a principal central feature or block and subsidiary flanking elements.

triple-A: A locally used, nonstandard colloquialism for the roof form especially popular after the Civil War, where a center front *gable* (often a cross-gable, sometimes simply a gabled wall *dormer*) rises from the *facade* roofline. Coined in the mid-1970s by Franklin County health inspector Thilbert Pearce during an architectural survey of Franklin County conducted with the authors of this guidebook, the term is now widely used as a shorthand reference to a common form.

Tudor Revival: A popular style, primarily residential, in the early 20th c., characterized by motifs associated with Tudor and Jacobean English architecture, particularly *half-timbered* walls (often applied rather than structural), diamond-paned casement windows, steep *gables*, irregular plans, and chimneys with multiple stacks or chimney pots. Rather rarely used in N.C., except among expensive houses, typically interspersed among the more popular *Colonial Revival*, especially *Georgian Revival* styles.

turned: Fashioned on a lathe, as in a *baluster*, *newel*, or porch post.

Venetian window: See *Palladian window*.

Victorian: A general term for a period, the reign of Queen Victoria (1837–1901), and often used broadly to describe the wide variety of *eclectic* revival styles that were intro-duced in British and American architecture during that era.

wainscot: A decorative or protective facing applied to the lower portion of an interior wall or partition.

weatherboards, weatherboarding: Wood siding consisting of overlapping horizontal boards usually thicker at one edge than the other. More commonly used in N.C. than the term "clapboard." The usual method of covering a frame building in N.C.

Bibliography and Sources of Information

SELECTED BIBLIOGRAPHY

Arthur, John Preston. *Western North Carolina: A History from 1730 to 1913*. Raleigh: Edwards & Broughton, 1914.

Asbury, Francis. *Francis Asbury in North Carolina: The North Carolina Portions of the Journal of Francis Asbury*. With notes by Grady L. E. Carroll. Nashville: Parthenon Press, 1964.

Ashe County Heritage Book Committee. *The Heritage of Ashe County, North Carolina*. Winston-Salem: Hunter Publishing, 1984.

Avery County Bicentennial Commission and Avery County Historical Society. *Avery County Heritage*. Banner Elk: Puddingstone Press, 1976.

Badger, Anthony J. *North Carolina and the New Deal*. Raleigh: Archives and History, 1981.

Bartram, William. *Travels and Other Writings*. New York: Library of America, 1996.

Becker, Jane S. *Selling Tradition: Appalachia and the Construction of an American Folk, 1930–1940*. Chapel Hill: University of North Carolina Press, 1998.

Bell, John L., Jr. *Hard Times: Beginnings of the Great Depression in North Carolina, 1929–1933*. Raleigh: Archives and History, 1982.

Bishir, Catherine W. *North Carolina Architecture*. Photographs by Tim Buchman. Chapel Hill: University of North Carolina Press, 1990.

Bishir, Catherine W., Charlotte V. Brown, Carl R. Lounsbury, and Ernest H. Wood III. *Architects and Builders in North Carolina: A History of the Practice of Building*. Chapel Hill: University of North Carolina Press, 1990.

Black, David R. *Historic Resources of Downtown Asheville, North Carolina*. Asheville: City of Asheville and Division of Archives and History, 1979.

Blackmun, Ora. *Western North Carolina: Its Mountains and Its People to 1880*. Boone: Appalachian Consortium Press, 1977.

Boyden, Lucile Kirby. *The Village of Five Lives: The Fontana of the Great Smoky Mountains*. Fontana Dam, N.C.: Government Services, 1964.

Brunk, Robert S., ed., *May We All Remember Well: A Journal of the History and Cultures of Western North Carolina*. Vol. 1. Asheville: Robert S. Brunk Auction Services, 1997.

Bryan, John M. *G. W. Vanderbilt's Biltmore Estate: The Most Distinguished Private Place*. New York: Rizzoli and the American Architectural Foundation, 1994.

Burke County Historical Society. *The Heritage of Burke County*. Winston-Salem: Hunter Publishing, 1981.

Buxton, Barry M. *A Village Tapestry: The History of Blowing Rock*. Boone: Appalachian Consortium Press, 1989.

Caldwell County Heritage Book Committee. *The Heritage of Caldwell County, North Carolina*. Winston-Salem: Hunter Publishing, 1983.

Campbell, Carlos C. *Birth of a National Park in the Great Smoky Mountains*. Knoxville: University of Tennessee Press, 1960.

Cherokee County Historical Museum. *The Heritage of Cherokee County, North Carolina*. Edited by Alice D. White. Winston-Salem: Hunter Publishing, 1987.

Cooke, Edward S. "Talking or Working: The Conundrum of Moral Aesthetics in Boston's Arts and Crafts Movement" and "The Aesthetics of Craftsmanship and the Prestige of the Past: Boston Furniture-Making and Wood-Carving." In *Inspiring Reform: Boston's Arts and Crafts Movement*. Wellesley: Davis Museum and Cultural Center, 1997.

Cooper, Patricia Irvin. "Cabins and Deerskins: Log Building and the Charles Town Indian Trade." *Tennessee Historical Quarterly* 52, no. 4 (Winter 1994): 272–79.

Cotton, J. Randall, Suzanne Pickens Wylie, and Millie M. Barbee. *Historic Burke: An Architectural Inventory of Burke County, North Carolina*. Morganton: Historic Burke Foundation, 1987.

Dickens, Roy S., Jr. *Cherokee Prehistory: The*

Pisgah Phase in the Appalachian Summit Region. Knoxville: University of Tennessee Press, 1976.

Duls, Louisa DeSaussure. *The Story of Little Switzerland.* Richmond: privately published, 1982.

Dykeman, Wilma. *The French Broad.* New York: Rinehart, 1955.

Eller, Ronald D. *Miners, Millhands, and Mountaineers: Industrialization of the Appalachian South, 1880–1930.* Knoxville: University of Tennessee Press, 1982.

Farlow, Betsy, Dan Lane, and Duane Oliver. *Haywood Homes and History.* Hazelwood: Oliver Scriptorium, 1993.

Federal Writers' Project, WPA of North Carolina. *North Carolina: A Guide to the Old North State.* Chapel Hill: University of North Carolina Press, 1939.

Finger, John R. *Cherokee Americans: The Eastern Band of Cherokees in the Twentieth Century.* Lincoln: University of Nebraska Press, 1991.

———. *The Eastern Band of Cherokees, 1819–1900.* Knoxville: University of Tennessee Press, 1984.

Frome, Michael. *Strangers in High Places: The Story of the Great Smoky Mountains.* Garden City: Doubleday, 1966.

George, Michael. *Southern Railway's Murphy Branch.* Collegedale, Tenn.: College Press, 1996.

Graham County Centennial. *Graham County Centennial, 1872–1972.* Robbinsville: privately published, 1972.

Henderson County Genealogical and Historical Society. *The Heritage of Henderson County, North Carolina.* Winston-Salem: Hunter Publishing, 1985.

Hill, Michael. *Guide to North Carolina Highway Historical Markers.* 5th ed. Raleigh: Division of Archives and History, 1990.

Hill, Sarah H. *Weaving New Worlds: Southeastern Cherokee Women and Their Basketry.* Chapel Hill: University of North Carolina Press, 1997.

Inscoe, John C. *Mountain Masters, Slavery, and the Sectional Crisis in Western North Carolina.* Knoxville: University of Tennessee Press, 1989.

Jenkins, Hazel C. *The Heritage of Swain County, North Carolina.* Winston-Salem: Hunter Publishing, 1988.

Jolley, Harley C. *The Blue Ridge Parkway.* Knoxville: University of Tennessee Press, 1969, 1977.

Jones, George Alexander, ed. *The Heritage of Henderson County, North Carolina.* Vols. 1 and 2. Winston-Salem: Hunter Publishing, 1985, 1988.

Jordan, James C., III, and Jane Ellen Starnes, eds. *Southern Arts and Crafts, 1890–1940.* Charlotte: Mint Museum of Art, 1996.

Kephart, Horace. *Our Southern Highlanders.* 1913. Reprint. Knoxville: University of Tennessee Press, 1976, 1984.

Lea, Diane E., and Claudia Roberts (Brown). *An Architectural and Historical Survey of Tryon, North Carolina.* Raleigh: Cultural Resources, 1979.

Macon County Historical Society. *The Heritage of Macon County, North Carolina.* Edited by Jessie Sutton. Winston-Salem: Hunter Publishing, 1987.

Mathews, Jane Gianvito, and Richard Mathews. *The Manor and Cottages, Albemarle Park, Asheville, N.C.* Asheville: privately published, 1991.

Moffett, Marian, and Lawrence Wodehouse. *Built for the People of the United States: Fifty Years of TVA Architecture.* Knoxville: University of Tennessee Press, 1983.

Morley, Margaret W. *The Carolina Mountains.* Boston: Houghton Mifflin, 1913.

Noblitt, Philip T. *A Mansion in the Mountains.* Boone: Parkway Publishers, 1996.

Pantas, Lee James. *The Ultimate Guide to Asheville and Hendersonville.* Alexander, N.C.: Ralph Roberts, WorldComm, 1998.

Phillips, Laura A. W. *Simple Treasures: The Architectural Legacy of Surry County.* Mount Airy: Surry County Historical Society, 1987.

Phillips, Laura A. W., and Deborah Thompson. *Transylvania: The Architectural History of a Mountain County.* Brevard: Transylvania County Joint Historic Preservation Commission, 1998.

Poole, Cary Franklin. *A History of Railroading in Western North Carolina.* Johnson City: privately published, 1995.

Powell, William S. *Dictionary of North Carolina Biography.* 6 vols. Chapel Hill:

University of North Carolina Press, 1979–96.

Reid, Christian. *"The Land of the Sky;" or, Adventures in Mountain By-Ways.* New York: Appleton, 1876.

Sakowski, Carolyn. *Touring the Western North Carolina Backroads.* 2d ed. Winston-Salem: John F. Blair, 1995.

Sandhausen, Hildegard, and Barbara McRae. *Little Journeys: A Photo Tour Guide through Historic Macon County.* Franklin: Terasita Press, 1996.

Schenck, Carl Alwin. *The Birth of Forestry in America: Biltmore Forest School, 1898–1913.* Santa Cruz: Forest History Society and the Appalachian Consortium, 1974.

Shapiro, Henry D. *Appalachia on Our Mind: The Southern Mountains and Mountaineers in the American Consciousness, 1870–1920.* Chapel Hill: University of North Carolina Press, 1978.

Sheppard, Muriel Earley, with illustrations by Bayard Wootten. *Cabins in the Laurel.* Chapel Hill: University of North Carolina Press, 1935.

Sizemore, Jean. *Alleghany Architecture: A Pictorial Survey, Alleghany County, North Carolina.* Sparta: Alleghany County Historical Properties Commission, 1983.

Swaim, Douglas. *Cabins and Castles: The History and Architecture of Buncombe County, North Carolina.* With essays by Talmage Powell and John Ager. Asheville: City of Asheville, County of Buncombe, and Division of Archives and History, 1981.

———, ed. *Carolina Dwelling.* Raleigh: North Carolina State University School of Design Student Publication, 1978.

Trout, Ed, and Margaret Lynn Brown. *Historic Buildings of the Smokies.* Gatlinburg, Tenn.: Great Smoky Mountains Natural History Association, 1995.

Van Noppen, Ina Woestemeyer, and John J. Van Noppen. *Western North Carolina since the Civil War.* Boone: Appalachian Consortium Press, 1973.

Warner, Charles Dudley. *On Horseback: A Tour in Virginia, North Carolina, and Tennessee.* Boston: Houghton, Mifflin, 1889.

Wells, Camille. *Canton: The Architecture of Our Home Town.* Canton, N.C.: Canton Historical Commission, 1985.

Wells, John E., and Robert E. Dalton. *The South Carolina Architects, 1885–1935: A Biographical Dictionary.* Richmond: New South Architectural Press, 1992.

Whisnant, David E. *All That Is Native and Fine: The Politics of Culture in an American Region.* Chapel Hill: University of North Carolina Press, 1983.

Williams, Michael Ann. *Great Smoky Mountains Folklife.* Jackson: University Press of Mississippi, 1995.

———. *Homeplace: The Social Use and Meaning of the Folk Dwelling in Southwestern North Carolina.* Athens: University of Georgia Press, 1991.

———. *Marble and Log: The History and Architecture of Cherokee County, North Carolina.* Murphy: Cherokee County Historical Museum, 1984.

———. "Pride and Prejudice: The Appalachian Boxed House in South-western North Carolina." *Winterthur Portfolio* 25, no. 4 (Winter 1990): 217–30.

SOURCES OF INFORMATION

Division of Travel and Tourism
N.C. Department of Commerce
430 N. Salisbury St., Raleigh, NC 27611
919-733-4171, or 1-800-VISIT NC
(1-800-847-4862)

Map Section
N.C. Department of Transportation
P.O. Box 25201, Raleigh, NC 27611
919-733-7600

Division of Parks and Recreation
N.C. Department of Environment,
  Health and Natural Resources
512 N. Salisbury St., Raleigh, NC 27611
919-733-4181

Archaeology and Historic Preservation
  Section
Division of Archives and History

N.C. Department of Cultural Resources
109 E. Jones St., Raleigh, NC 27601-2807
919-733-4763

State Historic Sites
Division of Archives and History
N.C. Department of Cultural Resources
532 N. Wilmington St., Raleigh, NC
  27604-1147
919-733-7862

Preservation North Carolina
P.O. Box 27644, Raleigh, NC 27611-7644
919-832-3652

Western Office, Archives and History
1 Village Lane, Biltmore Village, Suite 3
Asheville, NC 28803-2677
828-274-6789

Great Smoky Mountains Railway
P.O. Box 397, Dillsboro, NC 28725-03397
1-800-872-4681

Great Smoky Mountains National Park
423-436-1200

Blue Ridge Parkway
828-298-0398

Photography Credits

Most of the photographs used in this volume are from the North Carolina Division of Archives and History. The following photographs from other sources are used with permission and acknowledged with thanks.

Asheville–Buncombe Co. Historic Resources Commission, Richard Sharp Smith Collection: Annie West House (Fig. 47).

Ewart M. Ball Collection, Ramsey Library, University of North Carolina at Asheville: Biltmore Estate (Fig. 4); Sherrill's Inn (Fig. 18); Grove Park Inn (Fig. 48); S&W Cafeteria (BN 23); Public Service Building (BN 24); Battery Park Hotel and Grove Arcade (BN 33–34); Weaverville Presbyterian Church (BN 93); High Hampton Inn (JK 18); Swain Co. Courthouse and former Bryson City Bank (SW 1).

Biltmore Estate, Asheville: Biltmore House, western view (BN 72), Truck Farmer's Cottage (BN 72).

Cherokee Historical Association, Cherokee: 1750 Cabin (Fig. 11); 1800 Cabin (SW 11).

Division of Travel and Tourism, North Carolina Department of Commerce, Raleigh: Mountain view—Hugh Morton photograph (Fig. 2); Linn Cove Viaduct (Fig. 65); Clogging Dance Team, Haywood Co. Courthouse (Fig. 66); Fort Defiance (CW 16); Black Forest Lodge (TV 177); Whiteside School (JK 20); Council House (SW 11).

Duke University Rare Book, Manuscript, and Special Collections Library, Durham: Biltmore House (BN 72); Lambuth Inn (HW 10).

George and Roberta Gardner Assoc., Hillsdale, N.Y., and Balsam Mountain Inn: Balsam Mountain Inn (JK 7).

Great Smoky Mountains National Park Library, Gatlinburg, Tenn.: Corncrib, Cataloochee (Fig. 55); Davis Log House (Fig. 58); Enloe Barn (Fig. 61).

Dick Mauldin, private: Museum of the Cherokee Indian (Fig. 68).

Robert Merritt, private: Pilot Mountain (p. 107).

North Carolina Collection, Pack Memorial Library, Asheville: Asheville (p. i); Pisgah and the Rat from West Loggia, Biltmore (Fig. 1); Grove Park Inn terrace (Fig. 6); Patton's Hotel (Fig. 19); Cutover farmland (Fig. 36); Pack Square, ca. 1900 (Fig. 45); Pack Square, ca. 1929 (Fig. 46); Nu-Wray Inn (YC 1); The English Inn (ML 5); Downtown Asheville, aerial view (BN 1); High Bridge (HN 28); Fontana Dam (GH 6).

North Carolina Collection, Wilson Library, University of North Carolina, Chapel Hill: Nequassee Mound (Fig. 9); St. John-in-the-Wilderness (Fig. 22); Western N.C. Railroad and Fountain (Fig. 24); Highlands Inn (Fig. 29); Gatehouse, Montreat (Fig. 30); Granite Capital, Mount Airy (Fig. 31); Boxed House (on Buck Creek) (Fig. 59); Sparger Brothers Tobacco Co. (SY 6); Chatham Manufacturing Co. (SY 25); Federal Building (WK 10); Wade Hampton Harris Memorial Bridge (WK 24); Arrowhead Monument (MC 9); Lake Lure Inn (RF 21); Graystone Inn (AL 12); Gragg House (WT 9); Weaving Cabin (ML 3); Marshall (p. 195); Flatiron Building (BN 28); Citizen-Times Building (BN 35); Grove Park Inn (BN 53); Asheville High School (BN 64); Assembly Inn (BN 103); Robert E. Lee Hall (BN 111); Judaculla Rock (JK 12).

Penland School of Crafts: Worlds Fair Cabin, 1933 (ML 3).

Sarah Pope Postcard Collection, private: Creekside (Fig. 21); Battery Park Hotel (Fig. 42); Trade St. (Fig. 42); Caldwell Co. Courthouse (CW 1); N.C. School for the

Deaf (BK 14); McDowell Co. Courthouse (MC 1); First Baptist Church (MC 1); Church of the Transfiguration (PL 21); Biltmore (BN 72); Cherokee Co. Courthouse (CE 1).

Gordon H. Schenck Jr., Charlotte: Warren Wilson College Chapel (BN 103).

Southern Appalachian Photographic Archives, Mars Hill College, Mars Hill, N.C.: Montague Building (MD 5).

Tennessee Valley Authority, Norris, Tenn.: Fontana Dam Powerhouse (GH 6); Fontana Village (GH 7); Hiwassee Dam and Powerhouse (CE 28).

Western Carolina University Special Collections, Hunter Library, Cullowhee: Micaville School (Fig. 62).

Index

Page numbers in **boldface** represent the main entry for a subject; *italic* page numbers represent illustrations.

Abbott, Stanley W. (landscape architect), 86–88

Abbuehl, Edward H. (landscape architect), 88

Abernethy Memorial Church (Rutherford College), **160**

Academies. *See* Schools and academies

Adams, Judge Junius, House (Asheville), **294**

Addams, Clifford (muralist), 265

Adirondack style, 59, 60, 72, 330, 372

Aerie, The (Glen Alpine), **162**

Aethelwold Hotel (Brevard), **327**

African Americans, 20, 31, 32, 80

—architectural sites: Billy Cundiff House (Surry Co.), 117; Lincoln Heights Rosenwald School (Wilkesboro), 129; North Wilkesboro Graded School and High School, 131; Gaston Chapel A.M.E. Church (Morganton), 151; Jonesboro Neighborhood (Morganton), 152; Philo G. Harbison House (Morganton), 153; St. John's A.M.E. Zion Church (Rutherfordton), 175; Joshua D. Jones House (Polk Co.), 187; Stony Knoll (Polk Co.), 187; Stony Knoll Library (Polk Co.), 187; Church of the Good Shepherd (Tryon), 190; Stony Crest (Tryon), 190; Eagle Street Commercial District (Asheville), 268; Mount Zion Missionary Baptist Church (Asheville), 268; YMI Building (Asheville), 268; Hopkins Chapel A.M.E. Zion Church (Asheville), 276; St. Matthias Episcopal Church (Asheville), 276; Fred Mills House (Brevard), 329; Rosenwald School (Brevard), 329; Avery Benjamin House (Brevard), 329–30; Jip Mills Store (Brevard), 330; St. Cyprian's Episcopal Church (Macon Co.), 368; Pleasant Hill A.M.E. Zion Church (Macon Co.), 370

Agricultural Building (Buncombe Co.), **301**

Agriculture, 10, 20–21, 60, 63, 81, 82

Akin, Robert, House (Murphy), **405**

Akzona-Biltmore Building (Asheville), 264, **267**

Albemarle Inn. *See* Reynolds, Carl V., House

Alcoa (Aluminum Company of America), 44, 76, 367, 396, 399–400

Alexander, S. Grant (architect), 316, 323

Alexander County, 93 (map), 136–38

Alexander County Jail (Taylorsville), **136**

Alexander Gardens (Cashiers), **362**

Allanstand Complex (Madison Co.), 71, 72, **253–54**

Alleghany County, 96 (map), 197–201

Alleghany County Courthouse (Sparta), **197**, *197*

Allen-McElroy House (Marshall), **248**

Allis Chambers Co. (engineers), 415

Allison-Deaver House (Transylvania Co.), 25, **332**, *332*

Allison-Stepp House (Old Fort), **169**, *169*

All Saints Episcopal Church (Linville), 52, **224–25**

All Souls Episcopal Cathedral (Asheville), **293**, *293*

Aloah Hotel. *See* Hendersonville Inn

Aluminum Company of America. *See* Alcoa

Alva Theater (Morganton), **150**

Ambassador Apartments (Hendersonville), **312**

American Legion Post 29 (Lenoir), **141**, *141*

Anderson, Robert C. (designer), 305–6

Anderson, Nelson, Farm (Madison Co.), **251**

Andrews (Cherokee Co.), **407–8**

Andrews Geyser (McDowell Co.), *36*, **170**

Andrews Mill Complex (Rutherford Co.), **185**

Andrews Mound (Cherokee Co., destroyed), 13

Antioch Baptist Church (Rutherford Co.), **183**, *183*

Antioch Methodist Church (Alleghany Co.), **201**

Apalachia Dam, 415

Appalachia, image of, 4, 69–71, 74, 79, 389

Appalachian Hall (Asheville), **285**. *See also* Kenilworth Inn

Appalachian Heritage Museum (Watauga Co.), **214**

Appalachian State University (Boone), 51, **212–13**, 214

Apple growing and sales, 63, 82, 138, 202, 343, 352

Architectural practice, 55–56, 58, 263–64, 310

Argyle (Flat Rock), 316, *316*, **321**

Arney, Marshall, House (Burke Co.), **157**

Arney, William J., House (Burke Co.), **157**

Arney's Chapel (Burke Co.), **157**

Arrowhead Monument (Old Fort), **168**, *168*

Art Deco style, 58, 419

—selected examples: Avery Avenue School (Morganton), 151; City Building (Asheville), 265–66; First Baptist Church (Asheville), 269; Kress Building (Asheville), 270; S&W Cafeteria (Asheville), 270, *271*; Shell Station (Asheville), 271; U.S. Post Office and Courthouse (Asheville), 271; Merrimon Ave. Fire Station (Asheville), 283; Asheville High School, 285

Arts and Crafts movement, 55, 60, 72, 419

—selected examples: in Linville, 52, 223–25; Grove Park Inn (Asheville), 282–83; Biltmore Village (Asheville), 292–93; High Hampton (Cashiers), 362–63; Snowbird Mountain Lodge (Graham Co.), 400. *See also* Craftsman style; Crafts revivals; Crafts schools and workshops

Asbury, Louis H. (architect), 55, 152, 171, 173, 178, 327

Ashby, Thomas Benton, House (Mount Airy), **115**

Ashe County, 96 (map), 202–10

Ashe County Arts Center (West Jefferson), **203**

Ashe County Cheese Co. (West Jefferson), **203**

Ashe County Courthouse (Jefferson), 53, **202**, *203*

Asheville (Buncombe Co.), 56–59, *56, 57*, **259–96**, 260–61 (maps); City Building, *57*, **265**, *266*; Art Museum, **266–67**; Cotton Mills, 286; High School, **285**, *285*

Asheville & Spartanburg Railroad, 33, 34, 188, 191–92, 310, 317

Asheville-Biltmore Hotel, **269**

Asheville School, **296**

Ashworth, S. J., House (Buncombe Co.), **307–8**

Assembly Inn (Montreat), **305–6**, *306*

Atkinson, Samuel J., House (Surry Co.), **119–20**

Atlantic Bridge Co., 322

Auchmuty Hall (Valle Crucis), **220**

Auditorium plan: in churches, 67, 419

—selected examples of: Grassy Creek Methodist Church (Ashe Co.), 67, 207; First Baptist Church (Asheville), 269; Central Methodist Church (Asheville), 274; Murphy United Methodist Church, 405

Aunt Sally Marker (Jackson Co.), 361

Austin, William B., Law Office (Jefferson), **202–3**

Avery, Isaac, House. *See* Swan Ponds

Avery Avenue School (Morganton), **151**, *151*

Avery County, 97 (map), 223–31

Avery County Courthouse (Newland), 53, **223**, *223*

Avery County Jail, former (Newland), **223**

Avery Creek Christian Church (Buncombe Co.), **309**

Avery House (Morganton), **153**

Avondale Methodist Church (Rutherford Co.), **177**

B and B Motor Company Building (Asheville), **276**

Bacon, Henry (architect), 52, 223–25

Baird, Zebulon, House (Buncombe Co.), **299–300**

Baird Farm (Valle Crucis), *65*, **219**

Bakersville (Mitchell Co.), **232–33**

Bald Creek Valley (Yancey Co.), 244; School, **244**

Baldwin, James J. (architect), 264, 403–4

Baldwin Locomotive Works, 213

Ballew, Mr. (brickmason), 167

Ballew Arcade (Lenoir), **141**

Ballou House (Ashe Co.), **208**

Balsam (Jackson Co.), **356–57**; Depot, 357

Balsam Mountain Inn (Jackson Co.), **357**, *358*

Bank of Mount Airy (Surry Co.), **113**, *113*

Bank of North Wilkesboro, first and second former (Wilkes Co.), **130**, *130*

Bank of Pilot Mountain (Surry Co.), **116**

Bank of Tryon (Polk Co.), **188**

Banks, 53

—selected examples: First National Bank (Mount Airy), 112–13; Bank of Mount Airy,

Church of the Transfiguration (Saluda), **193**, *193*

Citizens Bank Building (Burnsville), **240**

Citizen-Times Building (Asheville), 264, **274**, *274*

City Building (Asheville), *57*, **265**, *266*

Civilian Conservation Corps (CCC), 75–76, 88, 182, 369, 373, 389, 391

Civil War, 28–32, 143, 317, 332, 410

Claddagh Inn. *See* Chewning House

Clampitt Hardware Store (Bryson City), **380**

Clarke-Hobbs-Davidson House (Hendersonville), **312**

Claxton School (Asheville), **283**

Clay County, 105 (map), 401–2

Clay County Courthouse (Hayesville), 367, **401–2**, *402*

Clay County Jail (Hayesville), **402**

Claymont Hill (Wilkes Co.), **134**

Clayton, Ephraim (builder), 30, 186, 240, 261, 275, 318, 323

Clearmont School (Yancey Co.), **246**

Cleghorn (Rutherford Co.), **179**, *179*

Cleghorn Mill (Rutherfordton), *175–76*

Clemmer, Robert (architect), 142

Cleveland, Robert, House (Wilkesboro), *22*, **126**, 133

Cliffside (Rutherford Co.), **178–79**; Baptist Church, **178**; Methodist Church, **178**; School, **178**; Mill, **178**, *179*

Cliffside Lake Recreation Area (Macon Co.), 76, **373**, *373*

Clinchfield Manufacturing Co. Mill and Village (Marion), **166**

Clinchfield Railroad, 33–35, 34 (map), 163, 171, 234–35, 236–38

Clover Hill (Caldwell Co.), **143**, *143*

Clyde (Haywood Co.), **344**; School, **344**

Coal mining, 10, 41

Cobb, Henry Ives (architect), 60, 282

Cobb, Tyrus Raymond "Ty," 412–13

Cobb Farm (Cherokee Co.), **412**, *412*

Cochrane, Moses (builder), 309

Cocroft, Rex (engineer), 226

Coffey, Clarence (architect), 141, 221

Coffey House (Boone), **213**

Coffey's General Store (Caldwell Co.), **147**

Colleges and universities, 51, 79

—selected examples: Black Mountain College (Buncombe Co.), *77*, 304–5; Davenport College (Lenoir), 139; Rutherford College (Burke Co.), 160; Appalachian State University (Boone), 212–13; Lees-McRae College (Banner Elk), 229–30; Mars Hill College (Madison Co.), 250; University of North Carolina at Asheville, 264–65; Asheville-Biltmore College (Asheville), 277; Weaver College (Weaverville), 300; Warren Wilson College (Buncombe Co.), 303; Montreat College (Buncombe Co.), 306; Brevard College (Brevard), 330; Western Carolina University (Cullowhee), 358–59

Colonial Apartments (Asheville), **278**

Colonial Revival style, 55, 58, 75

—selected examples: R. N. Marion House (Surry Co.), 120; Federal Building (Wilkesboro), 128; Franklin Pierce Tate House (Morganton), 152; James D. Ledbetter House (Rutherford Co.), 176; Graystone Inn (Roaring Gap), 201; Flat Top Manor (Watauga Co.), 215–17; Westglow (Watauga Co.), 217; Albemarle Inn (Asheville), 281; Robert E. Lee Hall (Buncombe Co.), 307; Silvermont (Brevard), 328; William E. Breese House (Brevard), 328

Columbus (Polk Co.), **186**; School, **186**

Commerce Building (Asheville), **266**, *267*

Cone, Moses H., Memorial Park, **215–17**, *216*

Conference centers. *See* Religious retreats and conference centers

Congregational Church of Christ (Tryon), **189–90**

Conley, Zeb (builder), 377

Connelly Springs (Burke Co.), **160**

Connemara (Flat Rock), 316, **319**, *319*

Consbeer Motors Building (Asheville), **276**

Cook, Lorna, House (Macon Co.), **371**

Cook, Will (stonemason), 229

Cooper, Robert Lafayette, House (Murphy), **405–6**, *406*

Copeland, Isaac and Staney, House (Surry Co.), **110**

Copper mining, 10, 202

Cordell, Mr. (stonemason), 307

Corncribs, 65, 111. *See also* Farm complexes; Outbuildings

Corpening, John E., House (Caldwell Co.), **143**, *143*

Corpening House (Caldwell Co.), **142**

Cottage style. *See* Picturesque style

Country stores, 66

—selected examples: Marion Brothers Store (Surry Co.), 119; in Rockford (Surry Co.),